ZEALOTRY AND ACADEMIC FREEDOM

Neil *Hamilton*

ZEALOTRY AND ACADEMIC FREEDOM

a legal and historical perspective

Transaction Publishers
New Brunswick (U.S.A.) and London (U.K.)

Library of Congress Catalog Number: 95-819
ISBN: 1-56000-205-0
Printed in the United States of America

Library of Congress Cataloging-in-Publication Data

Hamilton, Neil W.
    Zealotry and academic freedom : a legal and historical perspective / Neil Hamilton.
        p. cm.
    Includes bibliographical references and index.
    ISBN 1-56000-205-0 (acid-free paper)
    1. Academic freedom—United States—History—19th century. 2. Academic freedom—United States—History—20th century. 3. Radicalism—United States—History—19th century. 4. Radicalism—United States—History—20th century. 5. College teachers—Legal status, laws, etc.—United States—History. 6. College teachers—United States—Political activity—History. I. Title.
LC72.2.H36   1995
378.1'21—dc20   95-819
                                                                                        CIP

Dedication

For Bob Oliphant, my colleague, and all professors who publicly defend freedom.

Contents

Preface

The reader should understand the genesis of this book to gain perspective on my interest in writing it and the book's organization and framework. The book takes my scholarship in a new direction. From 1973 through 1987, my study, teaching, and research focused on regulated industries, government ownership, administrative law, and antitrust. I spent a great deal of time on my teaching and by the mid-1980s was one of the highest rated teachers on my faculty. After publishing a book on government enterprise in 1981, I published a number of law review articles over the next six years. William Mitchell College of Law awarded me a chair in regulatory policy in 1982. On issues of admissions, hiring, retention, promotion, and tenure within the faculty, I have always been one of the most outspoken, if not the most outspoken, advocates for high standards of academic quality and achievement. Of course strong advocacy of high standards sometimes creates collegial disharmony in a peer review system that requires faculty members to evaluate the performance of colleagues with whom they have worked. Differences of opinion on personnel decisions sometimes led to incidents of rudeness and incivility, but this was unusual. Normally differences of opinion in the evaluation of a colleague's academic quality were handled in a professional manner.

All of this changed in the late 1980s. Personnel decisions often became occasions for an inquisition. Beginning in February, 1987, I experienced sixty-six months of accusations of moral turpitude and ten investigations because of strong support for academic quality in admissions and personnel decisions. All of the accusations were unsupported. Nine investigations were dismissed; one was withdrawn. None even reached a probable cause determination.

I was the subject of five internal investigations of academic speech in the period February, 1987, through October, 1991. The first was for alleged "blatant racist action" in attempting to turn one faculty member of color against the complainant, another faculty member of color; the second, for alleged "racist behavior" in using the classroom to bias students against the complainant; the third, for alleged "abuse of academic office" in casting an unfavorable light on the complainant; the fourth, for an alleged breach of confidentiality occurring thirty-three months earlier that offended a student complainant, a supporter of the faculty complainant in the earlier matters; and the fifth, for alleged discrimination under the college's discrimination policy in sending a confidential memorandum to the faculty and a Board of Trustees Committee containing group data from 1985–90 indicating problems of academic performance and bar passage as a result of one of the most aggressive group preferences admissions policies among the 168 ABA accredited law schools, thus offending five students of color who obtained the confidential memorandum. Investigators found either no factual or no legal basis for any of the accusations. However, the faculty member investigating the fifth complaint also found that the confidential memorandum was insensitive to the feelings of minority students and that I should make a public apology and resign from an elected faculty position. I did neither. The students filing the fifth complaint also filed a complaint against me with the American Association of Law Schools, an accrediting authority for the law school. Although the Association places such complaints in its accrediting files, it has no procedures for investigating student grievances.

I was also the subject of five external investigations; the first three were race-discrimination lawsuits, filed by the faculty complainant mentioned above in June, 1987, July, 1988, and August, 1989, naming me individually as a colleague and alleging a conspiracy with the administration to deprive the complainant's civil rights. I was dismissed out of all three lawsuits as there were no material facts in dispute and the complainant was unable to produce evidence to support the claims. After the dismissals of the three lawsuits, the Minnesota Department of Human Rights investigated another complaint against me. The Commissioner of Human Rights took no action on the complaint against me during the one-year period authorized by the Human Rights statute. After the tolling of the statute, the charges were withdrawn when the college settled the complaint against it. This matter is subject to a confidentiality agreement.

Over fourteen months after the statute tolled on the complaint filed at the Minnesota Department of Human Rights, a complaint filed with the Office of Lawyers Professional Responsibility charged me with three counts of perjury for alleged inconsistencies in sworn statements occurring during earlier investigations. Two months later a second complaint alleged that my response to the first complaint was perjury. The Director of the Board found no probable cause to support the accusations. This was appealed. In July, 1992, the Board of Professional Responsibility also found no probable cause to warrant a disciplinary proceeding.

Not a single charge against me reached even a probable cause determination, let alone a determination on the merits. Yet, five and one-half years of investigations directed at my academic speech supporting academic quality had a devastating impact. The inquisition ran my life. The defense of these compounded unsupported charges required nearly all available energy beyond just meeting classes. Defense required over 4,500 hours of my time.

Research and writing stopped. Public service stopped. Teaching suffered, morale plummeted. The drumbeat of accusations seriously damaged good name and reputation. Future career opportunities closed. Spouse and children bore constant stress and fear of loss of livelihood.

My initial reaction as the accusations of bigotry, the lawsuits, and the investigations cascaded over me was shock and confusion. What is happening? Why me? How could I be assaulted from the left? I had been socialized to believe that the threat to academics was from the right. I was a moderate Democrat, a supporter of aggressive affirmative action who had chaired an appointments committee that in 1984 and 1985 had made four offers to African-American candidates, the last one successful. I was stunned by accusations that were so antithetical to my aspirations that they fundamentally undermined self-concept. It was like being swept off my feet and tumbled by a series of large waves.

Another source of substantial confusion was the absence of significant public collegial support. Why did so few of my colleagues publicly protect my right to advocate academic quality? Didn't academic freedom protect me from unfounded accusations of moral turpitude against and compounded investigations of my ideas? Many colleagues sought either to appease my accusers to buy peace or to avoid controversy by shielding themselves from an awareness of what was happening. Some advanced their political agenda by facilitating the inquisition. Collegial silence regarding the coercive tactics that totally dominated my life led to feelings of isolation and despair.

In 1987 and 1988, I thought the initial accusations, investigations, and lawsuits would be resolved and the inquisition would go away like a bad dream. I was terribly naive. The bad dream turned into a nightmare. As soon as one investigation neared dismissal and closure, another investigation followed. The cumulative burden was grinding me down; physical exhaustion and emotional numbness threatened my health and ability to work.

By accident in 1989 I ran across Ellen Schrecker's book, *No Ivory Tower: McCarthyism and the Universities*. The impact of McCarthyism's tactics on its targets paralleled my experience. The book also referred to several earlier periods of suppression of academic speech. I decided to educate myself about what had occurred during earlier periods of suppression of academic speech and what was happening currently. As I did more reading, I discovered that periods of suppression had occurred frequently in higher education and that I had much in common with academics who had been assaulted many years in the past. Even though I had few public allies and experienced isolation now, this discovery dramatically reduced my confusion and substantially increased my peace of mind and inner strength.

This book is the product of my self-education. The process of researching and writing the book was one of discovery. I did not start with specific hypotheses to test. I discovered a continuing history of waves of zealotry in higher education, an evolving history over the past century and a quarter since the emergence of the modern university where the professoriat repeatedly encountered suppression that undermined the professoriat's efforts to create an autonomous space for academic speech within the university free from interference. This history is explored in chapter 1.

Chapter 2 outlines my inquiry into the current period of suppression. As chapter 2 describes in detail, I came to understand how admissions and personnel decisions became one of the critical battlegrounds for a new ideological zealotry. A fundamentalist academic left in some humanities and social science faculties opposes alleged hidden structures of oppression in our Eurocentric culture. Standards of academic quality and merit-based performance evaluations are examples of masks for oppression and bigotry. A faculty member's vocal support for academic quality thus may become a basis for accusations of bigotry and investigations.

These inquiries into the history of suppression of academic speech also led me to investigate the meaning of academic freedom. Even after teaching for over a decade in higher education, I knew pathetically little about academic freedom. When the inquisition started in 1987, I had not even read the American Association of University Professors 1940 Statement of Principles on Academic Freedom and Tenure, incorporated by reference into my faculty's tenure code. Neither of the law faculties on which I served had a widespread remembered tradition among the faculty concerning academic freedom.

I had naively assumed that academic freedom meant that the university was an environment substantially free of coercion of competent academic speech. My inquiry revealed that the lust to censor is much stronger than I thought, and that it flares up frequently in periods of serious repression of academic speech. I found, to my chagrin, that the professoriat's tendency to condone coercion by silent acquiescence is also much stronger than I assumed, and that many faculties have done rather poorly in defending academic freedom. Academic freedom's ability to protect alleged heretics during a wave of suppression is in fact quite tenuous. The degree to which it provides any defense for heretical speech greatly depends upon whether colleagues have the courage to step forward publicly to defend the accused's right to speak.

Clearly chapter 2's inquiry into the current wave of suppression will generate controversy. The critique will dispute the accuracy of my description and analysis of the current wave of zealotry from the fundamentalist academic left. There are several likely variations on the theme that chapter 2 is inaccurate. One variation of this challenge to accuracy is that the chapter is just another example of the kind of reductive, partisan, and primarily anecdotal argument that is so prevalent in the debate over "political correctness." The claim will be that the chapter grossly exaggerates any suppression by using the same tired horror stories endlessly recycled for political purposes. The reader will in fact find a much broader and more exhaustive body of evidence here than has appeared in other research on the topic. Much of the evidence is anecdotal, but short narratives are the type of evidence generally available for all periods of suppression, including McCarthyism. Implicit in the criticism of anecdotal evidence is the premise that other evidence would be more objective and legitimate; of course many scholars writing about perceived oppression today use narrative and story as the best method to understand the experience of oppression. In any event, I agree that better evidence would be helpful and strongly recommend a survey of the most likely targets in any period of zealotry to determine the degree of suppression. In this period, since the zealotry is from the fundamentalist academic left, the most likely targets are dissenting centrist and conservative faculty members and those faculty members publicly advocating standards of academic quality.

A second variation of a challenge to the accuracy of chapter 2's description of the current zealotry is that I am biased because of my personal experience. I have put this experience up front so that the reader can assess for him or herself the impact of first-hand experience on credibility. Earlier narratives by targets of zealotry are taken as legitimate evidence of what happened. For example, Professor Owen Lattimore of Johns Hopkins University, a Mongolian specialist, was a target of McCarthyism in the 1950s. Lattimore's most important purpose in his book, *Ordeal by Slander*, was "to give a clear and consecutive account of what happened, because I believe that the story shows clearly the danger to which we are all exposed. It might have happened to you.... And of one thing I am convinced: it is important for as many people as possible to learn soon that 'it can happen here.'"[1] Like Lattimore, I experienced five and one-half years of compounded investigations followed by perjury charges. In both cases, even though none of the accusations were true, the inquisition ran our lives. Like Lattimore, I have tried to give a clear and accurate account of what is happening.

The effort to provide a much broader and more exhaustive body of evidence to rebut the denials that there is any problem of suppression currently may lead to criticism that the stories in chapter 2 are repetitious. To address this concern, I moved many stories into the endnotes. There may also be criticism that I give too much attention to Owen Lattimore's story when many other academics were also the objects of McCarthyism's inquisition. While there were many other academic targets, Lattimore was arguably the most notorious. Lattimore was a paradigmatic case where McCarthy used all the coercive tactics at his command to spread fear in higher education by making Lattimore a symbolic target. We have a much fuller account of what happened in this case than in others because of Lattimore's autobiographical book, *Ordeal by Slander*, Robert Newman's biography, *Owen Lattimore and the "Loss" of China* (1992), and Lionel Lewis' *The Cold War and Academic Governance: The Lattimore Case at Johns Hopkins* (1993).

In closing, I urge the reader to reflect on the danger of the lust to suppress others' speech to which academics are particularly exposed. Lattimore was accused, without warrant or warning, of being "the top Russian espionage agent in this country." I felt blindsided by accusations that strong advocacy of academic quality was bigotry. History instructs that "it can happen here." Our tradition of academic freedom responds to this simple historical reality. The tradition of academic freedom offers protection against the lust to suppress only insofar as each new generation of academics remembers and has the courage publicly to defend it.

Note

1. Owen Lattimore, ORDEAL BY SLANDER vii–viii (1951).

Acknowledgments

This book was possible only because of the support of many people. I owe them the deepest debt of gratitude. My colleague, Bob Oliphant, gave me steadfast and strong public and private support during the entire five and one-half years of investigations and tribunals. Without him, I could not have kept my job. Professors Marcia Gelpe and Dan Kleinberger, Dean James Hogg, and former Associate Dean Matthew Downs also gave substantial public and private support. My counsel, Richard Ihrig, defended me through each set of accusations and investigations with practical wisdom, warm friendship, and exceptional advocacy skills. My wife, Uve, and my children, Shaan, Maya, and Kyra, gave me a safe place to share the fears and exhaustion that could not show at work. Their love and devotion sustained me. My friends, Marcia Murphy, Walt Bachman, and Shirley Schoffelman also provided wise counsel and unwavering emotional support.

My research assistants, Allison Baskfield, Linda Thrasher, Andrew Pugh, Rhett Berry, Robin Blackledge Blair, Christine Kucera, and Daniel McGarry, put in many arduous hours on basic research for and development of the manuscript. Cheri Fenstermaker handled the seemingly endless revisions of the manuscript on the word processor with great skill and good cheer.

And very special thanks go to the reference librarians at William Mitchell College of Law, Anna Cherry, Pat Dolan, and especially Betty Karweick, who provided me with outstanding and tireless support in tracking down countless unusual requests. Librarian Paddy Satzer also deserves much credit for her excellent index to the book.

The views expressed in this book are my own and not necessarily those of any of the persons who assisted me in producing it. I do not speak for my employer.

I gratefully acknowledge the following publishers and publications for permission to use previously published material:

A.W. Astin, W.S. Korn & E.L. Dey, (1991), *The American College Teacher: National Norms for the 1989–90 HERI Faculty Survey*. Reprinted with permission of the Higher Education Research Institute, UCLA.

The Commission on Academic Tenure in Higher Education, *Faculty Tenure: A Report and Recommendations by the Commission on Academic Tenure in Higher Education*, pp. 44–45. Copyright © 1973 by The American Association of University Professors, The Association of American Colleges, and Jossey-Bass, Inc., Publishers. Reprinted with permission.

Introduction

Bound up inextricably with freedom of academic thought and speech are the great cultural movements and ideas that humankind lives by, particularly the strong ideologies or world views that matter so much that people are willing to fight and even to die for them. These strong ideologies are in incessant conflict with freedom of speech. Reflecting on a career spent protecting free speech, columnist Nat Hentoff concludes that censorship of opposing views remains the strongest drive in human nature. Throughout history, one group or another has been labeled too dangerous to be heard. "In that respect, men and women, white and of color, liberals and Jesse Helms, are brothers and sisters under the skin."[1] The lust to interfere with the "wrong" thoughts and speech of others can come from any direction. In the United States it is often camouflaged by an unbounded hypocrisy concerning free speech.[2] The censor extols the virtues of free speech while carving out an exception in the name of a higher morality. In education, people usually tolerate opposing views on ideas they do not regard as important, but then rationalize intolerance into necessity when disagreement involves a strong ideology vital to them.[3] The direction from which the intolerance comes shifts over time as cultural movements and ideologies wax and wane in strength. For example, historian Howard Beale, writing in 1941, noted that many Americans viewed the religious intolerance of the seventeenth century as a relic of the Dark Ages because they had ceased to care seriously about religion, but in 1941 they were ready to suppress educators who questioned capitalism or nationalistic patriotism. Thus, Beale concludes, teachers in each century and locality have been allowed freedom to discuss ideas that did not seem to matter and denied freedom on issues about which people did seriously care.[4]

This has clearly been true during some periods in American higher education over the past century and a quarter since the emergence of the modern university after the Civil War. In these 125 years, universities in the United States experienced seven waves of zealotry aimed at suppressing freedom of academic thought and speech. Freedom of academic thought and speech has been assaulted by the religious fundamentalism of trustees and administrators in the late nineteenth century, the unfettered capitalism of trustees at the turn of the century, patriotism in World War I, anticommunism prior to World War II, McCarthyism in the early 1950s, student activism in the mid to late 1960s,

1

and the fundamentalism of the radical academic left in the late 1980s and early 1990s.

This history strongly supports Hentoff's theme that the lust to interfere with the "wrong" thoughts and speech of others sometimes wears an academic, sometimes a political, sometimes a moral or religious garb. Waves of zealotry come and go, often one in each generation. At bottom the problem of freedom of academic thought and speech in higher education is essentially the same no matter which strong ideology is the justification for the repression.

The common characteristics of these recurrent waves of zealotry aimed at suppressing freedom of academic thought and speech are evident. Each has been rooted in an ideology—that is, a comprehensive set of beliefs about the world and the principles that ought to guide it. Strong ideology as used here implies some degree of dogmatism and closure. Each ideology has claimed that society is either deeply sick or severely threatened, and that this particular ideological movement has special knowledge of what to do about it. Inherent in some of these ideologies is permission or encouragement for the coercion of others' thought and speech.

While dogmatically held beliefs about society's problems and proper remedies may limit the scope of the ideologue's academic inquiry, they do not necessarily result in the coercion of others' academic inquiry. Not every lust, even that of interfering with the "wrong" speech of others, is acted upon. A strongly ideological social scientist, for example, may decide to play by the rules of the liberal intellectual system and not seek to suppress others from checking ideological claims.

Suppression of others results when extreme proponents of an ideology embrace zealotry to impose and enforce the ideology. Zealotry enforcing an ideology within the university has common features:

1. belief unshakable in its correctness substituted for thorough gathering of the relevant evidence, accuracy in its recording and use, careful and impartial consideration of the weight of the evidence, analytical reasoning from the evidence to the proposition, and internal consistency (whereas a strong ideology implies dogmatism and closure, zealotry insists on them);[5]
2. rejection of the notion that "you might be wrong" and refusal to subject beliefs to the normal checking process of academic inquiry to rectify error;
3. conviction that the ideology occupies moral ground higher than free speech and the liberal intellectual system and that heretics must be prevented from harming the higher morality;
4. belief that dissent is not merely wrong but is lying by denying the evident truth and thus deserves punishment;
5. tactics of harassment and intimidation to suppress and eliminate the immoral heretical thought and speech, particularly the labeling of disagreement as an act of moral turpitude; and
6. tactics of manipulative persuasion substituted for responsible assertion,[6] reasoned debate, and fairness and balance in argument and controversy.[7]

In a liberal intellectual system, the primacy of evidence, reason, and fa, argument in pursuing knowledge and free speech in rectifying error is widely accepted. Practically speaking, in a liberal intellectual system, the university is the one community whose mission is specifically the seeking, making, and disseminating of knowledge through the use of evidence, reason, and unrestricted professional criticism. It is the principal center of thoroughness in the gathering of evidence, accuracy in its recording and use, care and impartiality in its consideration, analytical reasoning from the evidence to the proposition, and internal consistency and fair representation of opposing views.[8] These skills are the heart of the checking process that produces knowledge. The principal purpose of the university is to use these skills in research and teaching to discover and disseminate knowledge.

The preamble to the American Association of University Professors' (AAUP) 1940 statement points out that "institutions of higher education are conducted for the common good and not to further the interest of either the individual teacher or the institution as a whole. The common good depends upon the free search for truth and its free exposition."[9]

Ideological zealotry attacks this search for knowledge and its free exposition at the university. Experience tells us that it doesn't matter if the ideology is of the left or the right, or has religious, social, or cultural roots; the search for knowledge and the combination of strong ideology and zealotry don't mix. Almost all widely accepted knowledge was once considered heretical and insensitive to an existing ideology or world view. Creating new knowledge will always be painful to believers in existing ideologies.

The old principle of the Inquisition is revived in each wave of zealotry from whatever direction. Academics who hold wrong and hurtful opinions should be punished for the good of society. The offended have a right both to an apology and redress. Jonathan Rauch observes in *Kindly Inquisitors*, "If [those causing pain] cannot be put in jail, then they should lose their jobs, be subjected to organized campaigns of vilification, be made to apologize, be pressed to recant. If government cannot do the punishing, then private institutions and pressure groups...should do it."[10]

To protect freedom of thought and speech in pursuit of knowledge from zealotry, the professoriat in the United States developed the concept of "professional academic freedom" over the last seventy-five years. The development of the concept of professional academic freedom in the United States in turn built upon several centuries of effort in European universities. European scholars initially had to institutionalize the pursuit of knowledge in the university. They then sought to create an autonomous space for intellectual inquiry within the university free from external interference. Building upon this European tradition, professional academic freedom in the United States grants professors the right to be free of interference by university employers in research, teaching, and intramural and extramural utterance. It also imposes on

rs correlative duties of competence and ethical conduct.
legial body has correlative duties to defend academic free-
ε individual duties. It is this tradition of faculty self-gover-
ew of professional competence and ethics that makes
nic freedom unique, not the tenure system, which has many
parallels in other settings. Over the last thirty-five years, the courts have developed the concept of "constitutional academic freedom," which is a constitutional doctrine that insulates the core academic affairs of higher education from interference by the state.

While the concept of professional academic freedom is widely extolled; reality is another matter. There have been numerous individual instances where a professor's academic freedom has been violated because of a unique dispute with the administration and governing board. The American Association of University Professors (AAUP) receives approximately a thousand such complaints a year and investigates the worst of them. The individual professor who does not receive adequate procedural due process may be vindicated by AAUP intervention. Academic freedom has also been assaulted repeatedly by waves of zealotry, and repeatedly the defense of academic freedom has fallen short in these periods. Academic freedom will never be finally won. It exists in the face of zealotry only for as long as the professoriat publicly defends it.

Many academics do not seem aware of our continuing struggles for the principles of academic freedom. Many seem oblivious to the fact that a period of zealotry has occurred roughly every fifteen to twenty years; and, if history repeats itself, an academic may experience at least two waves in a forty-year career. Moreover, the principles of academic freedom, particularly the correlative duties of professional academic freedom, often seem unappreciated, misunderstood, and sometimes misguided in application. For example, a recent study of the professional values of graduate students and professors in departments of chemistry, civil engineering, microbiology, and sociology at major research universities found significant research misconduct. The study found that a great need exists for "serious and continuing attention to the content and transmission of professional values and ethical practices from faculty members to students and among faculty colleagues."[11] Thus, with every generation of academics it is necessary to educate ourselves and to educate others both within and without the academy about academic freedom and its importance.[12] Given the history that a period of zealotry from without or within the university has occurred approximately every fifteen to twenty years for the last 125 years, it is also critical that each generation of academics prepare itself to defend academic freedom. It is the legacy handed from generation to generation of university teachers. We hold it in trust and are under a duty to defend it publicly. The purpose of this book is to educate the professoriat and the public first, about the danger of the lust to censor to which academics are particularly exposed, second, on the tradition of academic freedom as it has developed over the past seventy-five years, and third, on measures to buttress the defense of academic freedom.

The first three chapters document the seven waves of ideological zealotry that have threatened freedom of thought and speech in American higher education since the emergence of the modern university after the Civil War. These periods of zealotry to enforce strong ideologies in higher education originated in a variety of sources: the general public; national, state, and local government; the governing boards of regents or trustees; the administration, the faculty, or the students. During any wave, it was difficult to predict the ideological direction from which the next zealotry would come. In each period, zealots labelled disagreement as heresy, demonstrating the moral turpitude of the heretic and justifying a variety of coercive tactics to harass and to eliminate heretical academic thought and speech. A favored tactic has been to subject alleged heretics to investigation and tribunal. The general faculty response of silent acquiescence in coercive tactics has been the ballast of the ideological zealotry in each wave.

Chapters 4 through 8 then examine closely the development of protection for freedom of academic thought and speech over the past seventy-five years. They proceed by analyzing the meaning of academic freedom and related First Amendment doctrines in the order that they developed historically. Chapter 4 examines how the professoriat, without protection for academic speech during the late 1800s as the modern university emerged, created a safe harbor termed here *professional academic freedom*. The principal protection for freedom of expression for the individual scholar employed in higher education is the rights granted by professional academic freedom. Academic employment contracts, academic professional organizations, particularly the American Association of University Professors, and accrediting authorities in higher education define and protect professional academic freedom. Chapter 4 also explores the much-neglected correlative duties of professional academic freedom. The tradition of professional academic freedom grants rights to individual professors conditioned on the performance of correlative duties of competence and ethical conduct. The faculty as a collegial body has correlative duties to defend academic freedom and enforce the individual duties.

Chapters 5 through 7 analyze how the courts have protected freedom of academic thought and speech. Chapter 5 explores how the First Amendment doctrine of constitutional academic freedom protects the university and individual scholars from interference by federal, state, and local government. Chapter 6 analyzes how the First Amendment protects the freedom of speech of professors employed by public universities. Chapter 7 focuses on the prudential doctrine of academic abstention in judicial review of academic decisions, the thrust of which is to protect academic decisions from undue interference by the courts themselves. Chapter 8 explores where the theory of academic freedom fails in practice.

Chapters 9 through 11 focus on how to buttress the defense of academic freedom. In chapter 9, the essay focuses on the reasons why faculties and administrations generally fail to defend professional academic freedom in the face of zealotry. The chapter also explores why the fundamentalism of the radical academic left poses a unique threat to undermine professional academic freedom. The chapter proposes a number of remedial measures, particularly education of the professoriat concerning our tradition of professional academic freedom, its importance to our work, and our duty to defend the tradition publicly.

Chapter 10 analyzes the application of the correlative duties of professional academic freedom to the ideological zealotry of the moment, a fundamentalism advocated by some faculty and student zealots that is being enforced through harassing and abusive conduct. As a remedy the essay proposes some principles of faculty conduct that the faculty and governing board can use to rein in the worst excesses of the faculty zealot.

Finally, chapter 11 deals with effective responses by the targets to the coercive tactics of the zealots in any period of zealotry. The chapter also explores the unique problems of the target in dealing with the current fundamentalism originating in the faculty.

Notes

1. Nat Hentoff, FREE SPEECH FOR ME—BUT NOT FOR THEE 5, 17 (1992).
2. *See id.* at 1.
3. Howard K. Beale, A HISTORY OF FREEDOM IN TEACHING IN AMERICAN SCHOOLS, xii (1941).
4. *Id.* at xiii.
5. Ideas can be held and expressed with passion and intensity. However, excessive zeal tends to ignore constraints of professional competence in the development and expression of ideas.
6. An academic takes personal responsibility for the professional competence of her assertion.
7. Balance requires an academic to set forth justly the divergent facts and views of others.
8. *See* Benno Schmidt, *Universities Must Defend Free Speech*, WALL STREET JOURNAL (May 6, 1991): A16.
9. *See* American Association of University Professors (AAUP), *1940 Statement of Principles on Academic Freedom and Tenure, reprinted in* AAUP, POLICY DOCUMENTS AND REPORTS 3 (1990).
10. Jonathan Rauch, KINDLY INQUISITORS 6 (1993).
11. Judith Swazey, Karen Louis, and Melissa Anderson, *The Ethical Training of Graduate Students Requires Serious and Continuing Attention*, CHRONICLE OF HIGHER EDUCATION (March 9, 1994): B1, B2.
12. *See* Paul H. L. Walters, *Presidential Address to the 72nd Annual Meeting of the American Association of University Professors, reprinted in* 72 ACADEME (1986): 1a.

Part I

Zealotry in American Higher Education

1

Six Waves of Zealotry from 1870–1970

This history of zealotry in higher education begins with the emergence of the university in the United States after the Civil War. Richard Hofstadter and Walter Metzger, in their book *The Development of Academic Freedom in the United States,* find that prior to the Civil War, "[t]he university as it exists today, or as it then existed in Germany, had not yet appeared except in a very few places, and even in those on a very small scale."[1] The American college prior to the Civil War was centered in tradition. It looked to the classics of antiquity for the tools of thought, to Christianity for the bylaws of living, and to stringent rules and discipline to control the immaturity and contumacy of youth.[2]

The emergence of the university in the period from 1865–1890 was an educational revolution in the United States. New academic goals only debated in the years before the war became reality. "To criticize and augment as well as to disseminate the tradition-at-hand became an established function—a great departure for a system that had aimed primarily at cultural conservation."[3] Research became a major function along with teaching. Beyond research and teaching, the university aspired to serve the whole community in its vast variety of needs.[4] In addition, "the academic profession took on, for the first time in a full measure, the character, aspirations, and standards of a learned profession. Within the university, the growth of resources, the proliferation of activities, the assemblage of large faculties gave impetus to bureaucratization."[5] Finally the methods and concepts of the scientific method began to displace the authority of religion.[6]

These new, revolutionary goals and ideas prevailed only gradually in the decades immediately following the Civil War; even by the early 1880s, many older Eastern colleges had still not become universities.[7] During this period, the major threat to academics pushing for reform was religious sectarianism and zealotry.

Religious Fundamentalism of Administrators and Faculty in the Nineteenth Century

During the post-Civil War period, pious educators suppressed heretics who sought to transform the university curriculum to include science, modern lan-

9

guages, social science, and an elective system.[8] These traditional educators supported the ideology of higher education known as "mental discipline."[9] "Mental discipline" held that the mission of higher education was the disciplining of the mental and moral capabilities and potential talents that God had given to the students.[10] This mission reflected a traditional Protestant orthodoxy that saw the development of the will, or discipline, to push mental and moral capabilities to their limits as the principal goal of life.[11]

This educational orthodoxy demanded an acceptance of Biblical authority, including the account of miracles.[12] Yale president Noah Porter stated in 1880 that "I must assume, first of all, that Christianity is true as history...that it is of supreme importance to every individual man and the human race."[13] Even as late as 1891, an Iowa educator insisted that religion must dominate the atmosphere of a college.

> No voice against Christ should ever be raised within...recitation rooms...or commencement platforms. Freedom of thought or speech cannot be stretched to warrant such license, nor can common respect for Christian founders or gratitude for privileges enjoyed, or benefits received allow it. Principles on which a college stands are not to be assailed from within.[14]

This orthodoxy was widely shared by both administrators and senior faculty during this period. Many of them were in fact trained as clergy.[15] When administration and faculty widely share a common orthodoxy, disagreements may be minimal, and issues of freedom of academic speech rarely arise. For example, at Columbia University G. Stanley Hall remarked in 1879 that "a great many men who taught philosophy in American colleges felt no need of a larger and freer intellectual atmosphere."[16]

This kind of Christianity permitted and encouraged intolerance for new ideas or criticism of the existing orthodoxies. The college was to set standards with respect to these truths. "Error was to be energetically eliminated."[17]

A number of tactics were used to suppress heresy. Faculty applicants were expected to lay bare their religious convictions as a normal part of their credentials, and pious academics rejected candidates not committed to traditional ideology. For example, Yale, Princeton, Rochester, Wesleyan, Amhearst, Brown, and Oberlin all looked at the religious qualifications of candidates in the 1870s and 1880s.[18] Synods made determined efforts to warn trustees, and trustees in turn to instruct presidents to reject the applications of Darwinists during this period.[19]

Administrators in this period also rated instructors largely on their moral character, which in turn was seen to depend closely upon religious belief.[20] Disciplines like the sciences that challenged the traditional ideology were sometimes given a starvation budget and ignored. If administrative efforts to hold the line on orthodoxy by exclusion or suggestion failed, threat and tirade followed.[21] Academics disagreeing with the traditional ideology were also sometimes verbally assaulted in the press and from pulpits as godless and immoral.[22]

Although dismissal was relatively uncommon, it did happen. In 1873, a large gift from Commodore Vanderbilt to Central University in Nashville, Tennessee, converted the school from a school for the training of clergy to a university. Methodist bishops comprised the Board of Supervisors. The administration hired a conservative evolutionist, Alexander Winchell, to teach. In 1878 Winchell published research that suggested the origin of man predated the biblical Adam. Religious journals accused Winchell of attempting to destroy the truths that were given in the Gospel. The President dismissed Winchell.[23] In 1877, Cornell refused to reappoint the philosopher Felix Adler because Adler's lectures suggested that some of the central doctrines of Christianity were discoverable in other religions as well and Adler allegedly was developing "strongly rationalistic views" in his students.[24] In 1881, again fearing that the faculty was irreligious, the Cornell board considered asking for the resignation of the entire faculty, but settled for the forced resignation of one professor.[25] In 1880, a survey of the presidents of Yale, the University of Rochester, Princeton, Lafayette, Amhearst, Union, Williams, Hamilton, and Brown reported that the presidents did not allow it to be taught that "man, at least so far as his physical structure is concerned, was evolved from irrational animals."[26]

Students were subject to extremely close supervision for moral and religious purposes.[27] Yale, for example, imposed penalties on students for active disbelief in the authenticity of the Bible.[28] At Princeton, mere rumors that a student was a corrupting influence were sufficient to show guilt. A student then had the burden to vindicate himself.[29]

The result of these coercive tactics was considerable suppression of academic thought and speech. The ideological zealotry created a significant prohibited zone from which many professors would steer clear. Even so, Hofstadter and Metzger found in their study of academic freedom that "in a situation where the margin of safe divergence is obscure, the pale of orthodoxy undiscernible, the penalties of heresy unpredictable, the cautious man will blunder and the man of moderation will be martyred. One of the consistent and significant features of these academic freedom cases was that the participants were temperate evolutionists who, in the course of events, were trapped into conflict with authority and were surprised into suffering for the cause."[30] These coercive tactics to protect traditional ideology and to stave off educational reform were ultimately unsuccessful. They gave way to the competitive pressures of students' demands for more intellectual stimulation and more exposure to current developments in science and other new fields.[31]

Unfettered Capitalism of Trustees and Regents at the End of the Nineteenth Century

About a decade after the struggle between freedom of academic inquiry and speech and religious fundamentalism died down, a new period of zealotry started over freedom in the social sciences. The late 1880s and 1890s saw a revolution in college and university finances as successful businessmen gave large gifts to higher education and in return took control of the governing boards.[32] The ideology of many industrialists early in the Industrial Revolution was unfettered capitalism. In the late 1800s, as the social sciences developed, a number of social scientists, particularly economists, began a critical analysis of the economic order. They challenged unfettered capitalism by advocating social and political reforms like low tariffs, the inflation of the currency, recognition of labor unions, government regulation of business, and public ownership of basic industries.[33]

This criticism directly challenged the ideology of the benefactors of many universities. It was immoral for those receiving beneficence to criticize the benefactor. Through positions as trustees and regents of some universities, industrialists attempted to coerce and eliminate this heretical academic thought and speech. For example, during the crisis that followed the Haymarket riots between labor and police in 1886, when Professor Henry Carter Adams gave a lecture at Cornell denouncing the behavior of industrialists, the Cornell Board of Trustees decided not to reappoint him.[34] There were many more examples in the 1890s. In 1894, a member of University of Wisconsin's Board of Regents charged that Professor Richard Ely's research supported strikes and boycotts. A special committee of the Board of Regents summoned Professor Ely to justify his views. Rather than attacking lay interference with his ideas, Ely chose to defend by demonstrating the conservatism of his thought.[35] In 1895, the trustees and administration of the University of Chicago dismissed Professor Edward Bemis for his outspoken advocacy of public ownership of railroads and utilities.[36] In 1897, political scientist James Allen Smith was dismissed from Marietta College for "anti-monopoly" teaching.[37]

In the 1890s the controversy was heated between the proponents of the free coinage of silver that inflated the currency and favored debtors and supporters of the gold standard that suppressed inflation. Industrialists on governing boards generally supported the gold standard. In 1897 the governing board at Brown University gave President E. Benjamin Andrews the choice between resigning or accepting the trustees' views against free silver. He eventually resigned.[38] Much of the press sided with the trustees. "'When a professor attempts to teach free-silverism in a gold-bug college,' asked the *Minneapolis Times*, 'why should he not be turned out if he lacks the grace voluntarily to resign?'" *The Philadelphia Commonwealth* declared, "The trustees had indeed a right to expect him to shape his teachings in economics to meet their views." *The New York Mail and Express* announced, "This was not a blow at free speech, but a recognition of the absurdity of a free-silver champion drawing a salary from a sound-money corporation for teaching the students that which the supporters of the university condemned as pernicious and dangerous."[39]

There were several other cases. In 1899 after a Republican victory in statewide elections, Frank Parsons and Edward Bemis were removed from the faculty at Kansas State Agricultural College because of their "positions on economic questions."[40] Hofstadter and Metzger point out that during this period victorious politicians saw academic posts at Kansas State Agricultural College as political spoils. Parsons and Bemis had been hired in 1896 when Democrats and Populists had won statewide elections and had then dismissed some conservative economists.[41] Columbia and the University of Pennsylvania also dismissed radical professors in this period.[42]

The most well-known case of trustee coercion of heretical academic speech was the dismissal of Professor Edward Ross from Stanford University in 1900. Ross was a member of a group of economists who challenged laissez faire capitalism and sought to influence public policy. Ross had campaigned vigorously for free silver, a ban on Asian immigration of low-cost labor, municipal ownership of utilities, and public scrutiny of railroads. Jane Lathrop Stanford, widow of a California rail baron and sole trustee of Stanford, thought that these views compromised the university. She sought to have Ross dismissed. The president of the university, David Starr Jordan, ultimately forced Ross to resign.

Ross gave his side of the story to the press. In response, Jordan indicated that Ross had been forced to resign because of his "slangy and scurrilous" way of speaking and not for the substance of what he said, and that Ross had worse but unmentionable faults that the administration could no longer bear. Jordan asked the faculty to pledge loyalty to the president or risk reprisals. One faculty member was dismissed for defending Ross, and seven others resigned. In December of 1900, the American Economic Association voted to conduct an investigation of the dismissal of Ross. To the community of social scientists recently organized by specialty, an ideological dismissal did far more than just injure a disciplinary colleague; such dismissals also announced that the specialty was a branch of lay morality rather than a full-fledged science, and it also cast doubt on the honesty and independence of those who gave the trustees no offense. The board of inquiry's report documented that the charges against Ross had no foundation, while his charges against the university were plausible.[43] A large number of newspapers and journals this time took the side of the dismissed professor and condemned the Stanford authorities.[44]

Many of these cases were well known in higher education. These cases made it clear that the governing boards at some universities were going to suppress the advocacy of controversial social or political reforms of capitalism. Professors who voiced criticism found themselves subjected to many threats, from subtle discomforts to the possibility of dismissal.[45]

A number of faculty members gave strong support to those under attack and were very concerned about academic freedom.[46] The Ross case in particular had a significant impact influencing leading academics to create the American Association of University Professors (AAUP). Two of the most influential founders of the AAUP were personally involved in the Ross case and were much influenced by their experience. Arthur Lovejoy was an associate professor at Stanford when Ross was dismissed. Lovejoy resigned in protest against the action. He carried away the conviction that "modern professors faced a subtle peril—attacks on academic freedom that were officially disguised as something else." The target of a pretextual dismissal could not get vindication. Lovejoy believed that "the academic right to dissent could not be safeguarded in this country while curtailments of it masqueraded under other names." Several years after being called to Johns Hopkins University as a full professor, Lovejoy in 1913 drafted a letter to colleagues at nine other leading universities signed by seventeen full professors at Johns Hopkins. The letter urged them to join in the formation of a new national association of professors to undertake the "gradual formulation of general principles respecting the tenure of the professional office and the legitimate ground for the dismissal of professors."[47] Professor E. R. A. Seligman at Columbia, another major proponent of the formation of the AAUP, had been the chief investigator and reporter for the American Economic Association in the Ross case at Stanford.[48]

The fear of monied trustees and their zealotry to enforce capitalist ideology appears in the AAUP's "General Declaration of Principles of Academic Freedom," published in 1915.

> In the early period of university development in America the chief menace to academic freedom was ecclesiastical, and the disciplines chiefly affected were philosophy and the natural sciences. In more recent times the danger zone has been shifted to the political and social sciences....

The political and social sciences may challenge capitalism, and,

> as the governing body of a university is naturally made up of men who through their standing and ability are personally interested in great private enterprises, the points of possible conflict are numberless. When to this is added the consideration that benefactors, as well as most of the parents who send their children to privately endowed institutions, themselves belong to the more prosperous and therefore usually to the more conservative classes, it is apparent that...pressure from vested interests may...be brought to bear upon academic authorities.[49]

Patriotism of World War I

During World War I, the dominant ideology in the country was patriotic support for the war. Trustees, administrators, and faculty colleagues were willing to penalize antiwar views or activity.[50] Hofstadter and Metzger found that, "all over the nation, patriotic zealots on boards of trustees, in the community, and on the faculties themselves, harassed those college teachers whose passion for fighting the war was somewhat less flaming than their own."[51] The zealots were not content to look for overt forms of disloyalty; they sought to penalize subtle traces of disloyalty in ideas. Any belief that raised doubts in a zealot's mind became evidence of disloyalty.[52]

Columbia University was one of the worst examples where in March, 1917, the board of trustees and the president instituted a general program of investigation in order to ascertain whether any faculty member taught or disseminated doctrines "which are subversive of, or tend to the violation or disregard of, the Constitution or laws of the United States...or which tend to encourage a spirit of disloyalty to the government of the United States, or the principles upon which it is founded."[53] The trustees appointed a committee of nine, consisting of five deans and four faculty members, to assist the inquiry into the tendency of teaching in the university.[54]

Columbia President Nicholas Murray Butler withdrew the privilege of academic freedom for the duration of the war. In his June, 1917 commencement address, President Butler warned, "What had been tolerated before becomes intolerable now. What had been wrongheadedness was now sedition. What had been folly was now treason.... There is and will be no place in Columbia University...for any person who opposes or counsels opposition to the effective enforcement of the laws of the United States or who acts, speaks, or writes treason."[55]

After Professor J. McKeen Cattrell sent a letter to three Congressional representatives in August, 1917, urging them not to approve a bill authorizing the use of American conscripts in Europe, the Columbia trustees dismissed him for disloyalty. The trustees also dismissed both Professor Henry Dana for encouraging student agitation against the Conscription Act while it was pending, and Dr. Leon Fraser for critical remarks made a year earlier about a military camp in New York. In the fall of 1917, after a newspaper accused Professor Charles Beard of condoning a speaker who was alleged to have said, "To hell with the flag," the trustees initiated an investigation and a tribunal against Beard. Beard carried the burden to convince the board that he had never condoned the statement. Although finding that Beard did not condone the statement, the board ordered him to warn his colleagues that teachings "likely to inculcate disrespect for American institutions" would not be tolerated.[56] Beard resigned after the trustees dismissed Cattrell and Dana. Two other professors resigned a month later.

In 1917 and 1918, many professors around the nation were the subject of loyalty investigations and at least twenty were dismissed upon charges of disloyalty.[57] For example, in September, 1917, after an anonymous complaint of disloyalty against Professor William Schafer for having said that the Hohenzollerns should not be wiped out root and branch, the Board of Regents of the University of Minnesota investigated Professor Schafer, giving him fifteen minutes' notice of a two-hour questioning session, subsequent to which the Regents fired him. The Board stated that "his attitude of mind...and his expressed unwillingness to aid the United States in the present war, render him unfit and unable rightly to discharge the duties of his position."[58] In the fall of 1917, the University of Virginia charged Professor Leon Whipple with disloyalty for a speech in which he stated that "we can win the war only by freeing the spirit of democracy in the Germans by good-will," and that "war does not remove the menace of autocracy, [nor] make the world safe for democracy." After a tribunal before the Board of Visitors, the Board dismissed Whipple.[59] In 1918, the Nebraska State Council of Defense accused twelve University of Nebraska professors of assuming "an attitude calculated to encourage among those who come under their influence, within and without the university, a spirit of inactivity, indifference, and opposition towards this war and an undesirable view with respect to the several fundamental questions inseparable from the war."[60] The board of regents investigated the twelve. After the investigation, the university charged three professors variously for not believing in internationalism, impeding the sale of liberty bonds, and criticizing patriotic colleagues. After a tribunal, the board dismissed all three professors.[61]

At the end of the war, superpatriots continued the zealotry by attacking liberals, labor unions, and college professors as "Reds" who were undermining the American way of life.[62] In this atmosphere of spying and suspicion, a professor's remark taken out of a classroom lecture might bring headlines and alumni uproar.[63] In 1919, a faculty committee appointed at the University of Minnesota to investigate the problem of restraints upon faculty speech listed four factors that limited academic freedom, "a post-bellum intolerance and its concomitant fear; a certain readiness (by university officials) to receive criticism of faculty members whose long service should act as a presumption in their favor; an aggressive and impudent willingness of men representing forces outside the university to spy on teachers and to exert pressure on the authorities; and a tendency in the university to succumb to the idea that a university's function is an institution for the indoctrination of opinion."[64] The instructor most active in preparing the committee report was dropped and the report never came before the faculty.[65]

There were instances where administrations or faculty defended academic freedom. The Faculty of Political Science at Columbia and a number of the senior professors protested the board's violation of the principles of academic freedom.[66] Harvard President Abbott Lowell took a strong stand supporting academic freedom in wartime in his 1917 annual report. In response to alumni threats to withdraw funding because of an openly pro-German professor, the Harvard Corporation stated officially that the "University cannot tolerate any suggestion that it would be willing to accept money to abridge free speech."[67]

Even the fledgling American Association of University Professors conceded in 1917 that there should be some restrictions on the freedom of speech of professors during wartime. The AAUP struggled to draw a line justifying limitations of academic freedom while limiting the restrictions so that no permanent injury would be done to the intellectual independence of scholars throughout the country. The AAUP was aware that in times when popular feeling has been deeply stirred, "the charge of 'treason' may pass as virtually equivalent to the proof of it."[68]

Zealous patriotism led to the conclusion that any treasonable utterances or attitudes by teachers could be considered a threat to national security and were therefore punishable. In its report, the AAUP listed grounds for dismissal of a faculty member based on the faculty member's attitudes and conduct in relation to World War I. Professors convicted of disobedience to any statute or lawful executive order relating to the war could be dismissed. Teachers were forbidden to engage in propaganda designed to cause others to resist or evade military service or military authorities. For example, if teachers praised desertion or labeled war as immoral, they could be dismissed. Teachers were also to avoid dissuading others from rendering voluntary assistance to the war effort. Foreign professors were required to refrain from any act tending to promote the military advantage of the enemy. Foreign professors were to take care not to give any reasonable ground that they contemplate such acts or were conspiring with disloyal persons.[69]

In the Second World War, there were apparently no cases reported to the AAUP where academics were disciplined or dismissed over the issues of pacifism, subversive expression, or subversive action. Committee A of the AAUP, formed to investigate abuses of professional academic freedom, reported in 1943 that the United States' involvement in the war "has not yet aroused the unjustifiable passions and baseless suspicion characteristic of so much campus hysteria twenty-five years ago."[70]

Anticommunism Prior to World War II

In the mid-to-late 1930s, anticommunism again became a mainstream concern.[71] Central to this ideology of anticommunism was the image of the Communist party. In this ideology, the party was not a regular political party, but rather a conspiracy, dominated by and in the interests of the Soviet Union, to overthrow the American government. The methods whereby the party pursued this objective were: (1) the rejection of private and professional ethics; (2) totally secret operations; (3) the use of scurrilous and abusive language in attacks on opponents; (4) the coercion of intellectual independence to the party line; and (5) the indoctrination of students.[72]

There were few respectable voices within the academic community or outside of it who questioned these assumptions. Over the course of several years, the ideology of anticommunism met with almost universal acceptance in all constituencies of the academic community.[73]

The conclusion that followed from the acceptance of these assumptions about the Communist party's purpose and methods was that party members pursued aims and methods that were alien and incompatible with academic life. The secretive nature of the communists' activities and conspiracies meant that their subversive intentions would rarely be evident in overt speech or conduct, but rather, must be inferred from patterns of association. Merely belonging to such an organization or associating with known communists made a faculty member unfit for continued service.[74]

This condemnation of mere association was a development different from earlier periods of zealotry in American higher education. The academics who lost their jobs in earlier waves of zealotry were individual dissenters. It was their specific public speech and activity that led to discipline or termination of employment. In the late 1930s, administrators and colleagues began for the first time to exclude academics for their associations as well as their activities.[75] Accusation based on suspicion was justified in fighting secretive subversive intentions and activity. Thorough investigation was a critical tool to ferret out secretive associations.

The initial investigations and terminations occurred at the initiative of both administrators and faculty.[76] Several untenured professors were not renewed because of radical political activity in 1935 and 1936.[77] In 1936 Professor Morris Schappes at City College of New York (CCNY) was the first tenured professor dismissed for radical political activity; he was later reinstated.[78]

The first university to explicitly bar members of the Communist party from faculty service was the University of California. In 1939–1940, Kenneth May was a mathematics teaching assistant whose communist political activities caused the department chair to recommend termination of employment on the grounds that party membership conflicted with academic responsibilities. The Regents agreed in October, 1940, and found that "membership in the Communist Party is incompatible with membership in the faculty of a State University."[79]

At the same time, in 1940, the state legislature of New York sought to expose academics who were party members by thorough investigation, collecting names and information, and subpoenaing suspects to testify. In the midst of legislative hearings revealing names of alleged communists at CCNY, the New York Board of Higher Education issued a resolution stating that it would not "retain as members of the collegiate staffs members of any Communist, Fascist or Nazi group."[80] The Board then suspended all teachers named publicly as communists by legislative witnesses, and dismissed or did not reappoint untenured faculty who were named. The Board then brought quasijudicial tribunals against tenured faculty members for conduct unbecoming a teacher.[81] Participation in the publication of CCNY's bargaining unit's shop paper, the *Teacher-Worker,* was an additional charge against some faculty members. Tribunal committees found the paper "indecent, vicious, and coarse."[82] Ultimately these in-house quasijudicial proceedings resulted in the dismissal of twenty people; eleven more resigned while their cases were pending.[83]

With America's entry into the war on the side of the Soviet Union, the elimination of domestic communists was no longer an urgent matter. However, zealotry in the service of anticommunist ideology proved highly successful prior to World War II. The tactics of labeling of disagreement as an act of moral turpitude and utilizing public accusations, investigations, threats, and dismissals sent a clear message: heretical academic inquiry and association with heretics would be suppressed.

McCarthyism in the Late 1940s and Early 1950s

Ideology

The eradication of communism from American life became an official ideology of the federal government on March 22, 1947, when President Truman signed executive order 9835. That order created a loyalty security program and authorized economic sanctions against communists, suspected communists, and sympathizers associated with the communists. Other institutions across the country, including the universities, followed suit over the next six years, ultimately building up to the Congressional hearings in 1953.[84] "McCarthyism" draws its name from the most vociferous anticommunist politician during this period, Senator Joseph McCarthy from Wisconsin.

Once again the alleged secretive nature of communist activities meant that communist subversive intentions would rarely be evident in overt speech or conduct, but must be inferred from patterns of association. Given the scope of the threat to national security, accusation based on suspicion alone seemed justified in fighting secretive subversive intention and activity. Investigation and tribunal were critical tools to ferret out these secretive associations and conspiracies.

Coercion of Competent Academic Inquiry by Tactics of Public Accusation, Social Ostracism, Investigation, and Threats to Employment

In its application to academic thought and speech, the objective of the ideology was to eliminate actual communists from higher education and to suppress thought and speech about communism. Suppression and coercion of academic thought and speech are not readily or meaningfully quantifiable. Yale professor C. Vann Woodward observed that "one might more relevantly inquire how many public executions it takes to quell resistance in an occupied city, or how many lynchings to terrify a race."[85] It is clear, however, that McCarthyism in its application to academic thought and speech was effective on some campuses. It produced one of the most severe episodes of repression in the universities that the United States experienced in this century.[86]

It helps to view McCarthyism as it played out in universities as a two-stage process, where both government and the university carried responsibility rather than as a single movement carried out by government alone. National and state government initiated the ideology to eliminate communism from American life.[87] Through investigations and hearings, government also administered the first stage of identifying objectionable groups and individuals. The press, the public, university trustees and administrators, and faculty colleagues administered the second stage of punishment by making additional accusations and by inflicting personal and professional penalties on the accused.[88]

Government investigations and hearings. As early as 1949, state legislatures initiated investigations and hearings and imposed loyalty oaths to expose communists in education. Ultimately, nearly all the states conducted some type of investigation or tried to enact some kind of law to eliminate communist teachers.[89]

At the federal level, approximately 20 percent of the witnesses called before the various governmental investigating committees were academics.[90] Many more academics were subjected to an investigation, but were never called to testify formally. Nonetheless, members of congressional committees or staff would sometimes make public charges against them and then drop the matter.[91] FBI and other government investigators routinely leaked dossiers to right-wing legislators and friendly journalists.[92] Since investigations and legislative hearings were not judicial proceedings, politicians could use witnesses whose testimony would not stand up in court.[93] The FBI considered even anonymous accusations as evidence.[94] These committee hearings and public statements very effectively created headlines for political purposes.[95] Many targets of such tactics were unable to obtain any fair due process inquiry into the facts. In other cases targets suffered long delays of several years before obtaining any due process.[96]

The use of repeated false accusations followed by investigations and tribunals to create the "big lie" was the most successful tactic of McCarthyism. The story of Professor Owen Lattimore, an expert on Mongolia at Johns Hopkins University, is a model of how these tactics worked.

Lattimore wrote in *Ordeal by Slander* that McCarthyism used well-tried propaganda methods in its efforts to influence public opinion and control thought. First, Lattimore observed that extreme groups flourish in dissension and turmoil. To keep themselves in the news, and to suppress other's speech, they need a never-ending supply of symbolic targets that they can use to incite public passion. In order to stop a well-qualified expert from expressing opinions, the tactic of McCarthyism was to accuse the person of moral turpitude:

Accuse him of being an espionage agent. Bring in a witness to accuse him, not on the grounds of what the expert has written, but on the ominous suggestion that he "organized" other writers. Accuse him of being the "architect of Far Eastern Policy." Throw a bomb which emits clouds of nauseous smoke and then turn in a false fire alarm. The next step is to use the simple propaganda device of insisting over and over again, even weeks after complete evidence has disclosed the false alarm, that where there is so much smoke there must be some fire.[97]

Lattimore knew that he was a symbolic target. If he could be intimidated, or if people could be frightened into not associating with him, "it would be a long step toward successful intimidation of all university research and teaching.... [This attack] was going to be an all-out effort to knock me out of circulation and to terrorize others."[98]

Wisconsin Senator Joe McCarthy initiated the terrorist campaign against Lattimore in March of 1950, alleging that Lattimore was the top Soviet espionage agent in the United States, the center of the communist conspiracy. This triggered sixty-four months of accusations of moral turpitude, investigations, and hearings. Almost no charge was too tenuous or farfetched for the FBI to investigate.[99] McCarthy's principal tactic was vilification through both the repetitive lie about Lattimore's communist activities, renewing an accusation after it had been disproved, and the alternative lie, switching from one unsupported charge to another.[100]

McCarthy was also skilled in using accusation by headline to exploit the repetitive lie, thus winning the battle for public opinion regardless of the facts.[101] The public is influenced by the assumption that where there is so much smoke there must be some fire. For example, McCarthy used the trick of guilt by association over and over. He would allege repeatedly that Lattimore's connections to known communist organizations were subversive. Lattimore found that the tracking down and full documentation of each lie was very time consuming and expensive. "And when, finally, we had straightened out the record, the fact was not quoted anywhere to show that I had proved a charge against me to be false. It just wasn't important enough to be news. Nor did it have the slightest effect on the smears."[102]

The investigations and congressional hearings had no procedural protections to provide Lattimore with notice of who accused him of what or of the documents on which the accusations were based. There were no protections to screen out hearsay or to subject false accusations to cross-examination.[103] Questions were not asked to obtain information, but to try to lay a trap for Lattimore. His accusers, armed with documents detailing events occurring ten to fifteen years earlier, asked exhaustive questions of Lattimore about those events, hoping that his answers from memory would provide a contradiction on which they could base a perjury charge.[104]

Ultimately, when all the accusations in investigations and hearings came up unsupported, McCarthy supporters seized on inconsistencies in several years of sworn statements to bring perjury charges against Lattimore. A grand jury indicted him on seven counts in December, 1952. After the courts dismissed two of the counts, the Justice Department issued a new indictment with two additional counts of perjury. Finally, in June of 1955, after the courts also dismissed these counts, the Justice Department ended its prosecution.[105]

Lattimore discovered that the university professor stands in an exposed salient when the winds of zealotry are blowing. "Frequently, even if no charge has been proved against him, he needs only to be successfully smeared to lose his position under conditions which make it difficult for him to find other academic employment."[106]

Even though no charge was ever proven, the costs of sixty-four months of accusations and investigations to Lattimore and his family were staggering. During this period, the inquisition destroyed his life. Lattimore wrote to his lawyers, "Until a decision is reached my life as a teacher, a writer, a lecturer, and in many instances as a friend, is at a standstill, and my seriously damaged reputation can not only not be repaired but will continue to deteriorate as [the zealots] continue to blacken my name and the picture of me as a subversive character hardens in the public minds, and there is nothing I can do to change it."[107] In *Ordeal by Slander,* he also wrote, "Perhaps the greatest costs [of these attacks on the target] are to his work, his career, or his health, but the actual financial expenses to himself and to the friends who come to his assistance, are enormous.... However, while it isn't easy for a man of my age to see his savings disappear it is even more distressing to find himself in a position where he has to accept financial help."[108]

McCarthyism's principal tactic of repetitive lies ground down Lattimore's spiritual and emotional energy, leading to exhaustion. Charge after charge was dismissed yet replaced with a new accusation that had to be tracked down and answered.[109] Each day of questioning left Lattimore feeling beaten to a pulp.[110]

There were almost no social invitations in Baltimore since people were afraid to be seen with him. Lecture invitations dried up from 100 in 1949 to 3 in 1951.[111] Most of the academic world avoided him like the plague.[112]

Johns Hopkins, his own university, treated Lattimore with ambivalence. Many trustees felt that Lattimore should be disciplined,[113] but many individual faculty members publicly supported Lattimore's academic freedom.[114] A faculty committee investigating Lattimore in 1952 found that the university should maintain a neutral stance with regard to Lattimore until there was a resolution of the matters before the civil authorities. The faculty committee recommended an investigation at some future date if the administration became convinced that the evidence produced in civil or criminal proceedings indicated Lattimore's incompetence.[115] The Board of Trustees was convinced that if Lattimore were punished, there was a risk some faculty would resign.[116]

After Lattimore was indicted in December, 1952, Johns Hopkins suspended him indefinitely with pay until a federal court ruled on the charges.[117] Some faculty colleagues supported Lattimore through a defense fund. Many ignored the appeal for assistance. Over time, an increasing number of faculty became concerned about reputational damage to the university.[118] Several months after the indictment, the president reorganized the university to abolish the school that Lattimore directed. While Lattimore continued as a faculty member, this eliminated his administrative position.[119] Thirty-seven leading Asian scholars in the United States and Europe wrote letters of support. Every single one of these Asian scholars was investigated by the FBI.[120] One untenured supporter of Lattimore's at Johns Hopkins, John Defrancis, lost his job when the Page school was abolished. He was unable to teach in his specialty for ten years until the stigma of association with Lattimore subsided.[121]

Adverse publicity and the reaction of the universities. Subsequent to a public accusation of communist activity or association, the second punishment stage of McCarthyism was initially administered by the press and public opinion. The charges themselves, whether ultimately proven true or false, had a shattering effect on lives and careers.[122] Academics were assumed guilty and had either to prove that they were not or to make some kind of political confession.[123] Personal lives suffered heavily by social ostracism, desertion by friends and colleagues, and threats by fanatics.[124] Very few of the accused had at some time been connected to the Communist party in some way. The vast majority were not; the accusations and investigations were simply a means to vent accumulated resentments against liberal intellectuals.[125] However, people who were accused who had no connection to the party seemed to suffer the most. "These innocent liberals were unprepared for their Kafkaesque ordeal and had trouble understanding, let alone accepting, what their government was doing to them."[126] They began to absorb the values of their accusers and questioning themselves.[127]

Some universities also administered official punishment to professors subject to a government investigation or an accusation of communist activities or sympathies. If a faculty member appeared before a legislative investigating committee, the university almost always launched its own investigation to determine if the professor was fit to hold an academic position. Some administrations would also initiate an investigation upon receipt of accusations from anonymous sources.[128]

To explore the ramifications of McCarthyism for the professoriate, Paul Lazarsfeld and Wagner Thielen, Jr., interviewed 2,451 social scientists at 165 randomly selected four-year undergraduate colleges in the spring of 1955.[129] The respondents reported 798 incidents where a professor had been the target of accusations in the several years preceding the interview. Twenty-nine percent or 231 of the incidents involved charges of political extremism and disloyalty, such as communism, subversion, or un-American activity. The cases in which there was at least some specification of the nature of the communist association or belief constituted less than one-half of those in which the issue of communism was raised. In the majority of cases, all the respondents said simply that the accused professor had been called "communist."[130] Lazarsfeld and Thielens posit that there appeared to have been a considerable enlargement in the kinds of thoughts and acts that revealed a professor's hidden communism to include unconventional and left-of-center political views or even mere criticism of the current order of things.[131]

Thirteen percent, or 103 incidents did involve straightforward accusations of left-of-center political views. Right-of-center political accusations accounted for 2 percent of the reported incidents. Miscellaneous political charges the authors were unable to classify accounted for 8 percent, or sixty-four incidents. Accusations on "specific nonpolitical issues" like "religion, segregation, economics and others" accounted for 19 percent, or 152 incidents.[132]

The data did not clearly identify the originator of the accusation in 25 percent of the incidents. Of the remaining 75 percent, roughly half of the accusations originated from groups outside the university, such as the legislature or conservative community organizations, and one-half originated from persons or groups connected with the university, such as trustees, alumni, administrators, students, or faculty. Lazarsfeld and Thielens found that when the university administration took a professor to task politically, in most cases it was not with accusations of communism and subversion, but more often with accusations of unacceptable radicalism on other issues like religion or segregation.[133]

If a university specified formal charges against a target, the universities often used pretextual accusations of incompetence and insubordination against the target; seldom did the charges refer directly to political beliefs or activities. *Cold War on Campus,* Lionel Lewis's study of 126 cases involving professors whose appointments were threatened because of alleged radical political beliefs, notes that, "Looking at the charges alone, one often would hardly know that the cases were about politics. It would, of course, create unnecessary problems for administrators to acknowledge publicly that they were attempting to monitor the thinking of faculty or that they might be abridging someone's civil rights."[134]

Once public accusations of communism arose against a professor, normal rules of evidence and the normal presumption of innocence did not apply. The allegations themselves seemed to serve as evidence.[135] "Universities did not have to prove that the professors in question were communists; the professors had to prove that they were not.... [P]rofessors who claimed to have left the party had to prove that they had done so sincerely."[136] Once accused, the target essentially had to prove a negative regarding his or her state of mind. They had to demonstrate that they had no covert disloyalty. One method was to take a public oath of loyalty.

Whether or not the university imposed formal discipline on the accused, the ordeal of repeated internal investigations took an enormous toll on the target. A typical case is that of Philip Morrison, a tenured associate professor of physics at Cornell University, who endured five years of accusations and investigations. After a report by the House Committee on Un-American Activity accused Morrison of communist influence on April 1, 1951, the university president called him in to describe pressures from alumni and trustees and to advise him to curtail his controversial activities. Twenty months later, after the *New York Times* reported that testimony to the Senate Internal Security Committee revealed that Morrison had an incriminating procommunist record, the president formed a faculty committee to investigate whether there were grounds for dismissal. The committee found that Morrison was open to severe censure for his methods and association, but that he was not guilty of offenses making him unfit to teach.

A few months later, in the spring of 1953, the Senate Internal Security Subcommittee subpoenaed Morrison to testify. The adverse publicity led to more threats from alumni. In the fall of 1953, the president wrote Morrison, asking him "to show cause in writing to me why I should not institute proceedings for your dismissal from the university." Morrison responded that he would make greater efforts to cooperate with the university to minimize discomfort.

In 1955 the president refused to recommend Morrison's promotion from associate to full professor. In 1956 the president did make such a recommendation. The Board of Trustees ordered an investigation and hearing on Morrison's activities. Finally approving the promotion, the Board adopted a report that criticized Morrison's judgment and requested him to "take special care in the future to avoid such participations as may embarrass the university."[137]

Cold War on Campus catalogues twelve other cases similar to Morrison's where a faculty member experienced accusations of moral turpitude and extended investigations, but no ultimate adverse employment consequence. Frequently once the university initiated an investigation, this spawned more charges and investigations.[138] In writing *Cold War on Campus,* Lewis studied 126 cases at fifty-eight institutions of higher education in which the appointment of one or more faculty was threatened because of alleged radical political beliefs.[139] Based on his research, Lewis believes that the fifty-eight institutions included in his study presumably are a significant proportion of the national total where such cases occurred.[140]

While Lewis' book does not provide a comprehensive list of the fifty-eight institutions and the 126 individual cases, the book discusses by name thirty-seven of the institutions that account for ninety-five of the individual cases. Of these ninety-five individual cases, sixty-nine involved dismissal, a substantial proportion of which were nonrenewals of untenured faculty members. Thirty-one of the sixty-nine dismissal cases occurred at the University of California in 1949–1950 for refusal to sign a loyalty oath.[141] In eighteen of the ninety-five individual cases, the institution imposed an investigation, a tribunal, and, in some cases, a paid suspension on the accused, but then ultimately resolved the matter by retaining the accused. In seven of the ninety-five individual cases, the institution censured the accused or put the accused on probation, but did not terminate employment. In one case, the institution withdrew tenure, but retained the accused on a year-to-year contract.

While Lewis discusses in some detail sixty-nine cases resulting in dismissal, other writers have estimated that as many as 100 professors lost their jobs.[142] Although evidence is sketchy, it appears that a significant number of quiet dismissals of embarrassing untenured targets also occurred.[143] Even a quiet dismissal had serious career consequences beyond the loss of present employment. Because of an academic blacklist maintained through personal channels of communication, academics who lost their position as a result of accusations and investigations had trouble finding a new one.[144]

Simply having controversial ideas was a problem. Universities were reluctant to hire, and donor organizations were reluctant to give grants to, controversial teachers. The prevailing viewpoint was, why ask for trouble?[145] It was far easier to block the initial employment of a professor who had controversial ideas than to terminate a professor from employment.[146]

Results

These tactics of public accusations of moral turpitude, media headlines, social ostracism, investigations, tribunals, and—in from approximately ninety to one-hundred cases—dismissal, were effective on some campuses in suppressing heretical thought from the left, and independent thought generally in controversial areas. Owen Lattimore wrote in *Ordeal by Slander* that the attacks of McCarthyism had the effect of intimidating scholars, inhibiting the freedom with which they stated their facts and conclusions on controversial issues, and harming the quality of their work. This was a particular calamity in the area of Far East studies, where knowledge was already pitifully inadequate.[147]

Lazarsfeld and Thielens, interviewing 2,451 social scientists in 1955, found that 28 percent reported that a colleague's academic freedom had been threatened and 20 percent felt that their own academic freedom had been threatened.[148] Roughly 30 percent of the respondents were or had been members of political groups that advocated a program or cause that had become unpopular or controversial. Approximately 14 percent reported that someone had criticized them for belonging to this political group, but only 1.8 percent thought that belonging to the political group had adversely affected the respondent's academic career.[149] Another .5 percent reported that even though nothing had happened so far, they were very worried that a membership in a group may some day have an adverse impact, and an additional 4.3 percent were somewhat worried about an adverse effect.[150]

A higher percentage of the respondents worried about possibilities of harm resulting from something they said. Forty percent worried about the possibility that a student might inadvertently pass on a warped version of what the respondent had said that would lead to false ideas about the respondent's political views; 27 percent wondered if some political opinion they expressed might affect job security or promotion at the college.[151]

In terms of actual changes in conduct, 9 percent of the respondents said they had toned down their writings; 12 percent reported increased care in assigning potentially controversial works to their classes.[152] A higher percentage of respondents thought colleagues avoided controversy in publications and speeches (17 percent) and exercised increased care in assigning potentially controversial material to their classes (19 percent).[153]

Taken together, these data indicate that the majority of professors felt no curtailment of their own academic freedom or that of colleagues. Roughly one-fifth of all responding social scientists felt that their academic freedom was directly threatened. Conservative professors reported only one-half the level of concern or direct threat than did liberal professors.[154] Since roughly 70 percent of the respondents voted Democratic in 1948 and 1952,[155] this means that roughly 12 percent of the professors to the right of center felt threatened compared to 24 percent of those to the left of center. Roughly one-tenth of all 2,451 respondents (one-half of those threatened) adjusted their speech and conduct to reduce their exposure. Less than 2 percent of the 2,451 respondents felt their career had been adversely affected (one-tenth of the group who felt threatened).

These data support a conclusion that although the majority of professors were unaffected, the tactics of McCarthyism did have a substantial impact. It seems reasonable to assume that these aggregate data mask an underlying reality of very dramatic impacts on some campuses and very little impact on others. Lionel Lewis' study of 126 cases at fifty-eight institutions of higher education in which a professor's appointment was threatened because of alleged radical political beliefs supports a thesis that the worst excesses of McCarthyism were limited to a relatively small number of campuses. For example, during the decade 1947-1956, Lewis reports only fifty-eight institutions of higher education (out of the 1900 existing at the time)[156] where evidence meeting his criteria establishes that a professor's appointment was threatened. Of the sixty-nine terminations that Lewis reports occurred during the period 1947-1956, thirty-one occurred between 1949 and 1950 at the University of California. The remaining thirty-eight occurred over the other nine years. While few in number, these terminations were presumably widely known and highly symbolic. Lewis concludes that the "chilling effect [of the 126 cases he studied] on the expression of all ideas by both faculty and students was significant, although in fact there is no way to measure adequately their full impact."[157]

Faculty and Administrative Response

While national and state governments struck a serious blow to the freedom of academic thought and speech in the first stage of McCarthyism, groups within some universities implemented the second stage of punishment. The trustees responded to outside pressure and were directly responsible for what happened, yet the trustees were essentially outsiders. Though legally in control, they rarely involved themselves on a day-to-day basis with individual cases or the development of academic policy. Many administrators and faculty members exercised considerable power and supported punishment. They could have, had they wanted, prevented much of what happened. Administrators could have refused to investigate accusations that clearly undermined academic freedom. While many did, many did not. Many seemed oblivious to the power of an investigation to chill academic speech. One university president ordered, "We welcome any investigation. We will make our facilities available, and we delight at this opportunity."[158] Faculty members could have publicly condemned the assault on academic freedom. Some did. Many did not.[159]

Lionel Lewis, in his study of 126 cases in which the appointment of a faculty member was threatened, places the responsibility principally at the door of administrators. It was fear of adverse publicity and the consequent loss of prestige, reputation, and financial support that pushed administrators to take action against faculty members. Administrators who moved against accused faculty members did so in the belief that they had a special duty to eliminate a condition that could be harmful to the university's image.[160]

Administrators in later years commonly defended their actions by claiming that in the frenzied years of McCarthyism, they were virtually under siege by the government, the public, the media, alumni, and trustees, and that complete capitulation was necessary to ensure institutional survival. Lewis emphasizes that some administrators did successfully defend targets against a succession of charges; this puts the lie to this defense. He cites in particular the administrations at Illinois Institute of Technology, MIT, Antioch College, the University of Rochester, the University of Connecticut, Yale University, and the University of Chicago.[161] These examples of the possibility of standing firm "left open to all academic administrators the opportunity to evaluate competence and integrity— which are the essence of an effective tenure system, the mainstay of academic freedom—before imposing sanctions." Lewis concludes that "the failure of so many academic administrators to protect their institutions was a failure in courage that created a great deal of human wreckage."[162]

The Lazarsfeld and Thielens study of 2,451 social scientists in 1955 casts some further light on the administrative response to McCarthyism. Overall, 46 percent of the respondents reported that some group or person had accused a faculty member of being subversive or engaging in un-American activities in the past few years; however, 28 percent stated that someone's academic freedom was actually threatened.[163] Lazarsfeld and Thielens broke this data out further to determine whether the reputational quality of the college affected the proportion of accusations and threats (see table 1.1).[164]

The data make two important points. First, the higher the reputational quality of the college, the higher the proportion of accusations and actual threats to academic freedom. The impact of McCarthyism was heaviest at the elite

TABLE 1.1

Reputational Quality of the College	Proportion of respondents reporting accusations	Proportion of respondents stating that someone's academic freedom was threatened
Low	19%	16%
Medium Low	24%	18%
Medium High	50%	33%
High	63%	35%

schools. Second, the difference between the proportion of respondents reporting accusations and the proportion perceiving an actual threat is a rough indicator of how often administrators absorbed the attack and protected the professor from accusations.[165] While accusations and actual threats to academic freedom were much more common at the high-quality colleges, the administrations at the more elite colleges converted a smaller proportion of accusations into actual difficulties for the faculty member. Lazarsfeld and Thielens credit administrations for this absorption and protection. In support of this conclusion, they also find that out of the 46 percent of the respondents who reported an accusation against faculty member of subversion or un-American activity, almost two-thirds reported that the administration protected the faculty member from attack.[166]

The same data from which Lazarsfeld and Thielens draw a somewhat heartening message of administrative courage also support Lewis's conclusions drawn from a study of 126 cases where the faculty member's employment was threatened. Lazarsfeld and Thielens find that at one-third of the medium-high and high reputation colleges, and at one-fifth of the low or medium-low reputation schools, someone's academic freedom was threatened. In other words, a significant proportion of campuses witnessed threats to academic freedom at their institution, and Lewis selected his case studies where a professor's employment was directly threatened from among these campuses.

Lewis believes the faculty at most institutions were observers. "Aside from those who served on a hearing committee, most were silent witnesses."[167] Faculty who sat on hearing committees were generally sympathetic to accused colleagues, but Lewis notes that faculty on the committees accepted without question the assumption that investigations into the politics of colleagues were necessary and that the target had an obligation to account to institutional authorities for his or her political beliefs and activities.[168]

The Lazarsfeld and Thielens statistics show that 66 percent of the social scientists responding believed that most of their colleagues would back them up if they were accused of being leftist, 28 percent expected less than complete support, and 6 percent were uncertain. Lazarsfeld and Thielens recount that while many professors targeted by accusations and threats were backed by their colleagues, other respondents recall not a single gesture of collegial support because of either fear or indifference.[169] In the great majority of such incidents there is little evidence of self-recrimination for not having supported a colleague under fire.[170]

Lazarsfeld and Thielens suggest that "one reason that colleagues are infrequently backed is that many teachers are willing to join a support movement, but few to initiate it.... Underlying this reluctance to lead a support movement may be the sense that heading such a protest renders an individual particularly vulnerable, for it is the conspicuous leadership which is often singled out for punishment."[171] For another group of faculty, association with suspected persons was thought to bring stigmatization and danger. A third group's reluctance to back accused colleagues resulted from a collegial inclination to follow the middle of the road along with the crowd and to disapprove of unconventionality. Both of these latter groups withdrew from colleagues who became controversial after public accusations occurred.[172]

An interesting aspect of the academy's response to McCarthyism is that while many academics were essentially left of center with 70 percent voting Democratic in 1948 and 1952,[173] Schrecker finds that from the perspective of the targeted professor, almost all colleagues failed to speak publicly to try to prevent what happened when they could have done so.[174]

> As they dig into their memories, the protagonists of the academic freedom battles of the 1940s and 1950s almost uniformly reserve their bitterest condemnation for those of their colleagues who failed to support them.... It was the behavior of their fellow academics, especially the self-professed liberals among them, that really rankled. In most cases it was not so much what these people did that upset the blacklisted professors, as it was what they did not do. They did not organize; they did not protest; they did not do anything to reverse the tide of dismissals.[175]

Schrecker also finds that at no point did the vast majority of the trustees, administrators, and faculty who punished suspected communists admit that they were suppressing dissent. On the contrary, they often claimed that they were defending free speech and academic freedom.[176] Lewis also reports that as a matter of course, administrators "ardently denied that acts of free expression, such as a contentious talk widely reported in the press, were controlling factors and put faculty at risk."[177] It is critical, therefore, to go beyond the rhetoric of the period to examine what trustees, administrators, and faculty were doing rather than what they were saying. Many academics faltered. They were participating in or condoning punishment of ideas by their silence.

Why such a weak defense? Why not even limited public protests against this assault on academic freedom? Why did so many old friends, former fellow students in graduate school, and colleagues flee to the hills and behave like a bunch of frightened rabbits?[178]

Were academics as a profession less courageous than any other comparable group of middle-class Americans at the time? The blacklisted professors perceived members of their own profession as being particularly timid.[179] In their reminiscences, the blacklisted men and women kept returning to the theme of the collective guilt of their colleagues. Most colleagues may have been privately sympathetic, but with few exceptions they did not make their positions public.[180] Chapter 9 explores possible reasons for this faculty response.

Student Activism in the Mid- to Late 1960s

Ideology

During the 1960s, many student groups were actively seeking radical political and social change. Among the major groups were Students for a Democratic Society (SDS), Student Non-Violent Coordinating Committee (SNCC), Peace and Freedom Party, Congress for Racial Equality (CORE), National Student Association, the Progressive Labor Movement, and a half dozen organizations that developed around one or another phase of the Vietnam War.[181] These were generally called the "New Left."

These student groups differed among themselves—sometimes fiercely— on ideological issues, but the leaders of these groups shared strong beliefs at a fundamental ideological level. They also differed on tactics. Some remained principally pacifist in nature, adopting the tactics of community organizing and nondisruptive protest. Some ultimately embraced zealotry to coerce and intimidate academic thought and speech.

Left institutional theories take as their starting point societal contradictions and the way contradictions engender and exacerbate inequality and exploitation.[182] The leaders in New Left student groups believed that the current structures of social organization in the United States were oppressive. Through them, elite members of society (the establishment) were able to exploit and manipulate the masses in the United States and the Third World.[183] The New Left's purpose, therefore, was to liberate these exploited classes of people. Todd Gitlin, president of SDS in 1963, stated that the major guiding theme of early New Left politics was that "power must be shared among those affected, and resources guaranteed to make this possible."[184]

These beliefs about the oppressive and illegitimate nature of the existing social structure led student leaders to oppose social authority in general.[185] The students had "an impatient mistrust of all central authority, regardless of its source or form."[186]

The university itself was a power elite and, like the state, had no legitimate power.[187] For the New Left, all universities were representative of the society in which they existed. This was why they were assaulted. For the revolutionary young, their schools were the most immediate symbol of the hated social authority.[188] Thus, for example, during the student uprising at Columbia University in the spring of 1968, the radical white students wanted acknowledgment that the university administration had no legitimate right to exercise authority of any sort, and the radical African-American students wanted an acknowledgment that the authority of the white administration was racist and, thus, illegitimate.[189]

Ultimately, by pushing the population into extreme polarization the student leadership hoped to fundamentally restructure society.[190] The immediate objective of New Left student groups was to help radicalize the American student body by directly linking campus issues to the great social and political issues of the time.[191] So, for example, the specific immediate grounds of the Columbia uprising in 1968 were both Columbia's membership in a consortium of universities doing defense research and allegations of insensitivity surrounding the university's plan to build a gymnasium in Harlem. However, the declared intention of the student leadership of the uprising was much larger—the connection of these campus events to oppressive structures in society generally and the destruction of those structures.[192] In an open letter to the president of Columbia on April 22, 1968, Mark Rudd, an SDS leader, wrote, "We will destroy your world, your corporation, your University."[193] Authority in any form, but particularly at the university, was to be treated with contempt and defiance. Business as usual in institutions of authority was to be impeded and stopped.[194] Inherent in this ideology was permission and encouragement of extreme measures to coerce and intimidate others.

It is critical to understand that for the student leadership of the New Left, the Vietnam War was often not the principal cause of the worst excesses of zealotry unleashed on the campuses. For example it was merely a subordinate charge in the indictment of social authority in the student uprising at Columbia.[195] From the standpoint of organized New Left student groups, the war provided a basis for single issue operations like the Vietnam Summer in 1967, but it was only one social issue to use in radicalizing students to see that the country was ruled by an illegitimate oligarchy devoted to the power and privileges of a few.[196] The SDS took up one cause after another in service of this ideology: civil rights, straight-line Vietnam protest, draft resistance, poverty and homelessness, the police state in northern slums, and various campus issues.[197]

A good example of this search for issues to expose the university's oppression is SDS leader Mark Rudd's comment subsequent to the Columbia uprising. "Let me tell you. We manufactured the issues. The Institute for Defense Analysis is nothing at Columbia. Just three professors. And the gym issue is bull. It doesn't mean anything to anybody."[198] A critical objective for the New Left leadership was to find symbolic incidents of oppression around which to incite passion and mobilize broader social forces.

Leadership of some of the New Left student groups sharing this fundamental ideology embraced zealotry to coerce and intimidate academic thought and speech. SDS, consisting principally of white students in the north, east, and west, was one of those that did embrace zealotry.[199] As the principal group shaping the tone and spirit of the New Left during the mid-1960s, its particular ideological development bears some study in order to understand why SDS adopted tactics of coercion.

The ideas that were the motive force behind the SDS went through three phases: from 1962 to 1964, 1965 to 1967, and 1968 to 1969. These divisions are not rigid; many themes of earlier periods lasted into later periods.[200] The first phase, from 1962–64, was essentially nonideological. By pointing out how things were so desperately wrong with American society, the movement hoped to trigger a deep personal moral response and personal outrage. From personal moral response and outrage would flow involvement and action. The future would unfold spontaneously in the course of taking action.[201] The word "existential" was used to describe both SDS's early improvisational character and its appeal to discover personal meaning in the release of outrage and anger toward society.[202]

Even though there was no clearly defined set of programmatic answers, the SDS constitution did set forth an overall concept of a participatory democracy. The vision was of "a democratic society, where at all levels the people have control of the decisions which affect them and the resources on which they are dependent."[203] The linking of freedom and democracy was repeated in the 1962 Port Huron Statement and in other documents.[204] "Freedom" in this context meant not just plurality of choice, but power. It was viewed as the right to live under conditions that one had helped to set. To be free, students needed to exercise power in their universities, workers in the factories, and the poor in their communities.[205] True democracy meant that levels of participation by the people had to be raised greatly.[206] For the SDS leaders, a free society would democratize all institutions.[207]

This initial phase of the ideas motivating the SDS ended by 1965 because SDS was unable to clearly affect war, housing, or employment policies despite massive community organizing efforts to change public opinion. Out of disillusionment, the SDS engaged in a concerted search for an ideology to provide a stronger intellectual framework for activism.[208] "There was a growing sense that without revolutionary theory there can be no revolutionary practice."[209] Moreover, growing support for student protest against the war revealed a latent radicalism among *students*. The SDS needed an ideology to explain the society that was playing such a despicable role in the war.[210]

At the same time as the search for ideology commenced in earnest, there was a dramatic rise in the rhetoric of revolution, and because of the disappointments of earlier efforts, a decline in the popularity of the slogan "participatory democracy."[211] Todd Gitlin, an early president of SDS, observed that

nothing substantial in the country can change without a revolution, by which I mean a tumultuous and total change in the power relations of the society.

And...without such a change, without an underplowing of the society...nothing that we might propose will take root. So what we really want, it turns out, is the dismantling of the entire institutional apparatus of the society.[212]

The major difficulty confronting the SDS and the student New Left in the effort to develop a revolutionary ideology was the question of agency, that is, who would make the revolution?[213] Two elements must coincide in any realistic revolutionary theory. The first element is a group of people who would make the revolution, and the second is some concrete source of deepest discontent sufficient to radicalize that group of people.[214] Tom Hayden, writing in the mid-1960s, acknowledged that "there simply is no active agency of radical change—no race, class, or nation—in which radicals can invest high hopes as they have in previous times."[215] SDS had to find an agent capable of making an American revolution.

By far the most popular view among the SDS during the 1965-67 period was that they themselves, the young intelligentsia, would serve as agents of the new revolution. They themselves were the most alienated segment of the population with the greatest interest in revolution.[216]

This commitment to the students and young intellectuals as the agent of revolution was at the same time a weakness of the student New Left. The revolution was now placed in the hands of an elite, unrepresentative segment of the populace. Not only did New Left ideology remain limited primarily to the academic world, but its greatest success among students was to be found at elite universities. Moreover, the new theory inevitably subordinated economics, since this suggested agent of revolution suffered no material deprivation.[217]

In the late 1960s the SDS moved into a third distinct phase. Ideological formulas and revolutionary rhetoric that grew in the 1965-67 period now gained ascendancy and spokespersons competed for the most strident tone and hardest line.[218] The SDS needed a revolutionary ideology; Marxism-Leninism was the only credible developed body of revolutionary ideology available.[219]

By 1968 Marxism came to occupy a central position in the theoretical development of the SDS. At the SDS 1969 convention all major factions agreed they were Marxist-Leninist and pro-Maoist communists.[220] However, sects of the organization interpreted Marxist-Leninist thought differently, causing substantial disunity within the SDS and among the New Left organizations.[221]

In 1968, the SDS passed a resolution that called for the transformation of the SDS from a protesting student movement into a revolutionary youth movement.[222] By 1969, the Port Huron Statement's concepts of participatory democracy had been "assigned to the junk-heap of history."[223]

From 1965 onward, the SDS moved from community organizing, teaching, public speeches, rallies, demonstrations, and political campaigns toward more coercive—and ultimately revolutionary—tactics. Its major thrust of 1968 and 1969 was to wrest control of the educational process in universities from the administrative bureaucracy.[224]

Coercion of Competent Academic Inquiry by Tactics of Confrontation

The tactics of the student New Left from 1962–64, and continuing to a significant degree into 1965 and 1966, were aimed at the reform of society in keeping with the concept of participatory democracy.[225] Protests were largely through "conventional channels" typified by hundreds of SDS sponsored "teach-ins" against the Vietnam War and also by community action programs that attempted to organize poor and minority groups for political action.[226] To achieve freedom in the sense of power sharing, student leaders envisioned a coalition of grassroots organizations under indigenous leaders.[227]

Disillusionment with the lack of success of participation in the normal democratic process in affecting policy led to a concerted search for a revolutionary ideology to support a more aggressive activism. This phase saw a radicalization of tactics relying less on changing public opinion through traditional means and more on forcing issues to the front by all means necessary.[228]

Over the period 1965–67 there was a dramatic rise in rhetoric of revolution. This was accompanied by increasing emphasis on tactics of resistance and confrontation to achieve ideological objectives.[229] Borrowing from the successful tactics of the Berkeley free-speech movement in taking over buildings, the New Left introduced a new form of coercion: the campus confrontation.[230] For example, in 1966 students at Harvard and Brown attempted to physically prevent government officials from expressing viewpoints with which the students were in disagreement.[231] Over the following months, there were a number of instances where students hounded, harassed, and blocked speakers from delivering messages in opposition to the students' ideology.[232]

By early 1968, revolutionary rhetoric had gained ascendancy, and activist radical students turned to more extreme measures both to promote their ideology and to eliminate heretical thought and speech.[233] In 1968 and early 1969, the tactics used during two uprisings at Columbia and at New York University were parallelled at a number of universities throughout the country.[234] The Columbia uprising in April, 1968 started with the occupation of both the administration building and the major building for classrooms and faculty offices. A dean and two assistants were held captive for more than twenty-four hours.[235] The week-long occupation triggered other student conduct: faculty research and class notes ransacked and destroyed, administration correspondence and files destroyed, spitting on and punching faculty members, and violent and abusive language sustained throughout. A strike following the occupation closed down the university for a month.[236]

In December, 1968, an organized group of SDS members at New York University disrupted the campus speech of the ambassador to the United Nations from South Vietnam. They threatened him physically, poured water on him, and prevented the ambassador from speaking. Shortly thereafter, the SDS disrupted the speech of columnist James Reston and organized a rally calling for "open admission to the university of black, Hispanic and white working-class high school seniors regardless of their qualifications."[237] For the next several days large groups of students moved in noisy demonstrations from study halls to classrooms. From January though April, administrative offices, classroom buildings, and the student center were seized, occupied, and in some cases, vandalized. Students forced their way into a faculty meeting using threats of violence. During May, 1969, an administrative building, the building housing the Institute of Mathematical Sciences, and the student center were again forcibly occupied. Radical students then demanded that the university pay $100,000 to the Black Panther Defense Committee on the threat of destruction of the computer in the Institute of Mathematical Sciences. The administration offered to try to raise $10,000 to $15,000. This was rejected. Subsequent to the deadline given by the strikers, they lit the fuse to a bomb device in the computer center and cleared the building. Two professors rushed into the building to douse the fuse just before the bombs were ignited. Eight days later, the students left the student center under threat of eviction by police; fifteen days later they left the administration building under the same threat. The damage to university property from vandalism exceeded $125,000.[238] These events were duplicated at many other universities.[239] In the spring of 1969 campus radicals sought to replicate many "Columbias."[240]

One survey, based on study of 232 institutions over the first six months of 1969, discovered 292 protests and demonstrations. Twenty-four percent involved either violence or destruction of property (more than $8 million) or both. There were at least eighty-four bombing or arson incidents on U.S. campuses in these months. In one, at Santa Barbara, a university employee was killed when a bomb he picked up exploded. At least two students were shot to death by police in other, separate incidents. Three thousand, six hundred fifty-two students were arrested; 956 were either suspended or expelled. The major demand in most of these actions (59 percent) had to do with race: instituting of black studies programs; increasing the numbers of black students and faculty; better facilities. The memorable photo of that spring, reproduced by countless media, showed the black students who had seized Willard Straight Hall on the Cornell campus brandishing rifles and (empty) ammunition bandoliers. Student power was the second major issue (42 percent). In only 1 percent of the demonstrations was the draft a factor. Other war-related issues—ROTC, military-industrial on-campus recruitment, university research or investment in tools of war—accounted for 25 percent. As a single issue Vietnam was almost never mentioned.[241]

The American Council on Education commissioned a Special Committee on Campus Tensions whose 1970 report emphasized that the crisis in higher education was by no means uniform across the range of colleges and universities. During the 1968-69 academic year, the council found that 524 out of about 2300 colleges and universities in the United States (23 percent) experienced at least one incident of violent or disruptive protest.[242] Of the 524 institutions, an estimated 145 experienced violent protest and an estimated 379 experienced nonviolent, but disruptive protest.[243] Major protest incidents were about twice as likely to occur at private universities as at public universities. More than one in three of the private universities experienced violent protest during 1968–69, while one in eight of the public universities experienced incidents of comparable severity. In general, the larger the institution, the more likely it was to have experienced violent or disruptive protest. Finally, the more selective a university, the more likely it was to have experienced a violent or disruptive protest. About 85 percent of the most selective universities had disruptive incidents, while universities in the lowest category of selectivity experienced no such incidents.[244]

The Special Committee on Campus Tensions also found that in 1968–69, student power was an issue in roughly three-quarters of the institutions experiencing violence or disruption. United States military policy was a reported issue in 38 percent of the institutions experiencing violence and disruption. Including other issues such as ROTC programs or military research on campus meant that military issues were raised on roughly half the campuses that experienced violence or disruption.[245]

In 1970, the President's Commission on Campus Unrest made similar findings as to the causes of campus protest. A central demand was the unfulfilled promise of full justice and dignity for blacks and other minorities. A second focus of students was opposition to the Indochina war. The third target was the shortcomings of a modern university in terms of goals, curriculum, and power relationships.[246]

Following the Cambodia incursion and student deaths at Kent State and Jackson State, the spring of 1970 saw an even greater number of disruptive protests and demonstrations, this time linked more closely to antiwar sentiment. In May and June of 1970, close to half of the undergraduate campus population was involved in the first national student strike of long duration. Students succeeded in closing down or impairing the operations of approximately 425 colleges and universities.[247] By the fall of 1970, this activity dropped dramatically and there were few major demonstrations.[248]

From early 1968 through June of 1970, student zealots wielded an extensive array of tactics of confrontation and disruption on many campuses. The tactics of confrontation included the shouting down of speakers and the use of ridicule, rudeness, obscenity, and other uncivil forms of speech and behavior to embarrass and defy faculty and administration.[249] New York University professor Sidney Hook believed that the deliberate use of violent language to degrade and silence those who could not be refuted by evidence and logic was a serious threat to reasoned discourse. Hook observed that there had been nothing like this assaultive rhetoric in the history of American education.[250] Those who tried to uphold standards risked being denounced as reactionary, insensitive, or racist.[251] Disagreements with students of color could lead to charges of bigotry.[252] The tactics of confrontation included subjecting faculty committees to struggle meeting tactics of insults and jeers from the audience.[253] Struggle meetings are public meetings where zealots can surround the target and make false accusations to generate passion and anger against the target. Some professors who challenged the zealots' ideology experienced systematic campaigns of harassment.[254] They also risked class disruption,[255] public humiliation through struggle meeting tactics of surrounding and confronting the accused professor, and physical threats.[256]

The tactics of disruption were substantially more coercive than those of confrontation. The Columbia uprising was an important model because it built upon the disruptive tactics used in the Berkeley free-speech movement four years earlier: occupation, faculty and administration confusion, police intervention and student injuries, indignation of moderate students and faculty, a major strike, and, finally, endless consideration of reforms in administration, governance, and disciplinary procedures.[257] At a number of universities, student zealots organized large groups of students to disrupt or prevent normal operations of the university.[258] A favorite tactic was forced occupation of office and classroom buildings.[259] A principal objective of major incidents on the campus was to provoke confrontation with the administration, faculty, and civil authorities.[260] A fundamental ideological proposition of the student New Left was that the university was a bastion of an oppressive society. By provoking the university, the student leaders hoped that it would respond in excess of the measures appropriate to remedy the provocation. Any disproportionate response would make plausible to the student body the radicals' fundamental ideology that society and the university were oppressive and brutal.[261] For example, the brutality of the police in response to the student uprising at Columbia had precisely this effect.[262]

In addition, student activists used major incidents, such as forced occupations, to present lengthy lists of non-negotiable demands. Since a major purpose was not to reform but to demonstrate the oppressiveness of the university and the society by forcing the university into confrontation, any concession or reform by the university would stimulate new demands to force the confrontation. Demands escalated as concessions were made.[263]

Results

There is no comprehensive study of the impact of student zealotry in the mid- to late 1960s on university governance, curricular change, methods of teaching, the climate of scholarship, and the freedom of academic thought and speech.[264] Some universities suffered much more than others, with the large, elite universities having the highest probability of violent or disruptive protest. The coercion that occurred on a significant proportion of the campuses was unprecedented in the history of American education.[265] In his study of the 1960s, Professor Seymour Martin Lipset concluded that "clearly higher education has been affected more severely than at any previous time."[266] The conventions of freedom of academic thought and speech and rational discourse were substantially damaged.[267] The faculty and the administration at many universities yielded to coercion out of fear.[268]

Faculty, administration, and students learned that a small number of radicals can bring a university to its knees.[269] They learned the extreme susceptibility of universities to symbolic incidents around which radicals can incite passion and mobilize extremists and the general student body. Radicals learned that faculties were frequently unwilling to defend academic freedom.

The extreme tactics of the zealots successfully influenced large numbers of nonradical students and faculty. The President's Commission on Campus Unrest found that "as extremist tactics became more extreme and violent, moderate tactics became less moderate and began to include strikes and disruptions.... The overall trend of the past decade has clearly been toward more widespread and more violent protest.... Tactics once considered outrageous and immoral by almost all students were justified and encouraged by some and tolerated by many more."[270]

Without a thorough study of the victims of the coercion, faculty, administrators, and the nonrevolutionary students, it is impossible to quantify the lingering results of the repression of the 1960s. During and immediately after the disturbances, some faculty suffered emotional breakdowns.[271] Many faculty suffered exhaustion. There was substantial destruction of collegial respect. For years afterward, colleagues wouldn't speak to others who had crossed picket lines.[272] A professor at San Francisco State commented in 1989 that "perhaps we're beginning to grow out of the strike division between those of us who crossed the picket line and those who did not, but campus politics is still divided on that basis, and the old memories haven't yet faded."[273] Former Yale University President Benno Schmidt recently commented that ever since the 1960s

> universities have lived with the threat of disruption whenever anyone comes to campus with a controversial message. The first victims of such suppression are the students and faculty who do not have their own convictions tempered by exposure to other points of view, even if ultimately unpersuasive. But the more serious loss is suffered by the university, because these acts of suppression tend to contribute to a pall of conformity.[274]

Faculty and Administrative Response

Administrators employed a number of approaches in dealing with student disturbances. Some vigorously protected academic freedom. The approach taken by Notre Dame University called for the following:

> that any student who substitutes force for rational persuasion will be given fifteen minutes to meditate. If their meditation has not changed their behavior, they will

be asked for their ID cards and suspended on the spot. Those who do not turn in their cards will be legally charged with trespassing."[275]

The hard-line approach espoused by San Francisco State President S. I. Hayakawa called for clearly stated warnings to disrupters and the liberal use of police force to quell disorder.[276] Disciplinary or police action occurred in 39 percent of the 292 protests in 1969 studied by the Urban Research Institute.[277] More common were approaches calling for "appeals to reason" to keep communication open, "the diplomatic tactic" of well-timed concessions or compromises, and "genuine negotiations" involving joint student-faculty-administration-trustee committees in negotiations.[278] While there were some exceptions, in general these latter approaches amounted to capitulation to the demands of the students.[279] The longer the disruption or seizure, the more likely one or more student demands were granted. The administration granted at least one demand in 56 percent of the disruptions lasting two to five days and 67 percent of the disruptions lasting seven to fourteen days.[280]

Much depended on whether violence occurred. The administration and faculty response was much stronger against violent protest than against disruptive protest.

> Some major civil or institutional action (arrest, indictment, dismissal or suspension) was taken against individuals at three-fourths of the institutions where there were violent protests. Similarly punitive measures were taken by 22 percent of the institutions that had nonviolent disruptive protests. Sixty-two percent of the institutions report that administration or faculty negotiated issues with demonstrators when the protest was violent, but 83 percent negotiated when the protest was nonviolent.[281]

In general, the reaction of many faculties to student disruption was initially complacency, then compromise, and finally appeasement.[282] At many universities, students encountered little formal deterrence because university administrators and faculties often failed to punish illegal acts.[283] Some professors gave direct assistance to student radicals. An analysis of demonstrations occurring in 1967-68 found that faculty were involved in the planning of over half of the student protests. In close to two-thirds of them, faculty bodies passed resolutions approving the protests.[284]

The number of faculty who protested violations of academic freedom was small.[285] The tendency was for the faculty to make scapegoats out of the administrators for the faculty's own lack of courage.[286] Many faculty members lost all courage to stand up for academic freedom and face people who had primal passion. Yale history professor and former dean Donald Kagan wrote that freedom of speech at the university is vital, but it is not free; it has a high price.

> Here at Yale we have not been willing to pay the price. The fault is general: in our administration because they have failed to lead the defense of freedom; in our

faculty because we have not protested that failure and demanded a more vigorous defense; and in our students because they have too easily been led astray.[287]

University of Pennsylvania professor Alan Kors believes that there was a very large group of faculty that was intellectually very skeptical of the claims being made by the activists, but who

> were quite literally bullied by the intensity of other people's convictions. The liberals on American college campuses were the key group and they absolutely caved in. All they wanted to do was buy peace, to buy calm, or to assuage their own guilt.... Thus, they went along, pushed by the strongest winds out of lack of character, lack of backbone, lack of conviction, and lack of ethics.[288]

Harvard professor Nathan Glazer emphasizes that liberal faculty members liked to make the distinction that they approved of the radicals' aims and disagreed only as to means.[289] This response, however, gave credence to the radicals' argument that the university reacts only to disruption and violence. Radical students were able to establish that their issues were important, and thus in the minds of many students, the radical tactics of disruption were justified.[290]

During the Berkeley free-speech movement, the 1964 campus confrontation on which the 1968 Columbia uprising was modeled, one professor observed that faculty and administrators behaved like buffalo being shot, "looking on with interest when another of their number goes down, without seriously thinking, that they may be next."[291] This same response continued in the late 1960s. The President's Commission on Campus Unrest found that faculties and administrations often responded to student disruption with confusion.[292] Kenyon Professor Fred Baumann's chief memory is that everything he thought faculty believed in—the openness of the university to all forms of rational discourse, the unacceptability of violence, the sacredness of academic standards, and academic freedom—turned out to have been only lip service. Professors were unwilling to stand up in public for what they claimed in private.[293] For Professor Sidney Hook, the decisive event of the 1960s was the collapse of moral courage in higher education and the collegial silence that condoned intimidation and allowed it to become respectable.[294]

Kagan, Kors, Baumann, and Hook fail to give sufficient weight to the general tendency of professors not to support the academic freedom of views for which they hold no sympathy. In analyzing data obtained from more than 60,000 professors who responded to the Carnegie Commission's survey of faculty opinion in 1969 and by making a supplementary telephone interview of 472 academics in 1972,[295] Professors Everett Ladd, Jr. and Seymour Martin Lipset concluded that the general ideological predisposition that faculty brought to political issues was a major determinant of the way they responded to the coercive tactics of the student radicals.[296] The more liberal to left a professor was on wider political social issues, the more likely he or she was to give at

TABLE 1.2
Political Posture of Academics and the General Public in the United States,
1969–70 (in percentages)[301]

Political posture	Faculty	U.S. public
Left	5	4
Liberal	41	16
Middle-of-the-road	27	38
Moderately conservative	25	32
Strongly conservative	3	10

least tacit—and sometimes active—support to student radicals.[297] Ladd and Lipset found that the association between a left-of-center posture in politics and relatively high support for the student protests of the late 1960s was extremely close.[298] Liberal professors often concluded that protestors had a good point and that the university ought to negotiate and compromise. They found it difficult to uphold strong action against the demonstrators.[299]

Ladd and Lipset's finding of an extremely close association between a left-of-center posture in politics and relatively high support for the student protests is combined with a finding that the politics of American academics has been disproportionately on the left for almost all of this century.[300] This was true during the late 1960s, as indicated by table 1.2.

Ladd and Lipset concluded further that the skew to the left is much more pronounced at the elite, research-oriented universities.[302] They also observed that aggregate data at the university level tended to understate the degree to which the left dominated individual fields. Ladd and Lipset expected some field-related variation on political attitude, but discovered that

> the degree of this differentiation is really quite extraordinary. For example, 81 percent of clinical psychologists described their politics as "left" or "liberal" in the Carnegie survey, as compared with 61 percent of professors of English, 39% of chemists, 25 percent of mechanical engineers, and just 17 percent of faculty in colleges of agriculture.[303]

In the social sciences, 64 percent of the faculty reported themselves as left or liberal.[304]

Ladd and Lipset concluded that discipline differentiates faculty to such a high degree that there was not a politics of academia, there was the politics of each discipline.[305] This discipline differentiation they attributed to several factors: (1) a given discipline selectively recruits people with views consistent with those of the dominant political orientation; (2) activist students will be attracted to discipline dominated by the left, like social science; and (3) discipline socialization causes those with conflicting views to leave voluntarily.[306] Faculty backing for the student protests of the 1960s varied greatly by field.[307]

Paradoxically, Ladd and Lipset found that faculty members on the left criticized their disciplines for being fundamentally conservative. For example, while sociology was one of the most liberal disciplines in academia, the literature by left-oriented scholars alleged that "sociology has been the 'handmaiden' of the Establishment."[308] The critics on the left within the social sciences attacked their profession for being "fundamentally conservative."[309]

There were islands of faculty courage putting to the lie the argument that the tide of student unrest and disruption overwhelmed all defense of academic freedom. For example, one hundred Columbia University faculty members signed the following public statement on March 10, 1969:

> The tradition of the university as a sanctuary of academic freedom and center of informed discussion is an honored one, to be guarded vigilantly. The basic significance of that sanctuary lies in the protection of intellectual freedoms: the rights of professors to teach, of scholars to engage in the advancement of knowledge, of students to learn and to express their views, free from external pressures or interference. These freedoms can flourish only in an atmosphere of mutual respect, civility and trust among teachers and students, only when members of the university community are willing to accept self-restraint and reciprocity as the condition upon which they share in its intellectual autonomy.
>
> Academic freedom and the sanctuary of the university campus extend to all who share these aims and responsibilities. They cannot be invoked by those who would subordinate intellectual freedom to political ends, or who violate the norms of conduct established to protect that freedom. Against such offenders the university has the right, and indeed the obligation, to defend itself. Nor does the sanctuary of the university protect acts violating civil or criminal law, which are illegal whether committed on or off the campus.[310]

In 1973, a joint commission of the Association of American Colleges and the American Association of University Professors found that the social turmoil of the safe 1960s resulted in acute problems of professional misconduct on campuses. "[M]ost ominously, assaults upon academic freedom from within the institution by or with the toleration of members of the faculties themselves have gone unpunished."[311] One legacy of the faculty response to the tactics of the 1960s was tolerance and condonation of abusive and coercive conduct in clear violation of professional standards. Another legacy of the 1960s is the long-term ideological bent of some disciplines. Ladd and Lipset noted in 1975 that "the ideological bent of a discipline subculture...possesses 'staying power.' The array of fields, in terms of the political outlook of their members, described here appears as a persistent feature of academic life."[312]

Notes

1. Richard Hofstadter & Walter Metzger, THE DEVELOPMENT OF ACADEMIC FREEDOM IN THE UNITED STATES 262 (1955).
2. *See id.* at 278-79.

3. *Id.* at 277.
4. *Id.*
5. *Id.* at xii.
6. *Id.* at xii; *see also id.* at 261–62.
7. *Id.* at 338–39.
8. *See* Laurence R. Veysey, THE EMERGENCE OF THE AMERICAN UNIVERSITY 21, 36–38, 40 (1965).
9. *Id.* at 21.
10. *Id.* at 22–23.
11. *See id.* at 24–25.
12. *Id.* at 24–25; *see also* Hofstadter & Metzger, *supra* note 1, at 279.
13. Veysey, *supra* note 8, at 42; *see also* 46.
14. *Id.* at 46.
15. *Id.* at 39. One estimate is that prior to the Civil War, 90 percent of the college presidents were ministers, and 35 percent of the professors were clergymen. Hofstadter & Metzger, *supra* note 1, at 297. Harvard appointed its first lay president in 1869, Yale in 1899, and Princeton, Amhearst, and Dartmouth in the twentieth century. *Id.* at 352.
16. Veysey, *supra* note 8, at 47; *see also* Hofstadter and Metzger, *supra* note 1, at 292, 297.
17. Veysey, *supra* note 8, at 43.
18. Vesey, *supra* note 8, at 47–49; see also Hofstadter & Metzger, *supra* note 1, at 287.
19. Hofstadter & Metzger, *supra* note 1, at 326.
20. Veysey, *supra* note 8, at 45.
21. See Hofstadter & Metzger, *supra* note 1, at 326.
22. Veysey, *supra* note 8, at 49.
23. Hofstadter & Metzger, *supra* note 1, at 330–31.
24. *Id.* at 340.
25. Walter Metzger, *Academic Tenure in America: A Historical Essay, reprinted in* FACULTY TENURE 93, 123 (1973).
26. Hofstadter & Metzger, *supra* note 1, at 334.
27. Veysey, *supra* note 8, at 33.
28. *Id.* at 33–34.
29. *Id.* at 34.
30. Hofstadter & Metzger, *supra* note 1, at 327.
31. Veysey, *supra* note 8, at 49, 55.
32. Ernest Earnest, ACADEMIC PROFESSION: AN INFORMAL HISTORY OF THE AMERICAN COLLEGE 1636 TO 1953 240–41 (1953).
33. *See* Ellen W. Schrecker, NO IVORY TOWER: MCCARTHYISM & THE UNIVERSITIES 14 (1986).
34. *Id.* at 15.
35. *Id.* at 15–16. For a different view of the Ely matter, see Hofstadter & Metzger, *supra* note 1, at 426–34. They argue that Wisconsin did protect Ely's academic freedom. However, Ely did plead that he had never acted on any of his sympathies, but if he had so acted, he acknowledged he would be unfit to teach.
36. Schrecker, *supra* note 33, at 16.
37. Hofstadter & Metzger, *supra* note 1, at 421.
38. *See id.* at 421.
39. Howard K. Beale, A HISTORY OF FREEDOM OF TEACHING IN AMERICAN SCHOOLS 229 (1941).
40. Hofstadter & Metzger, *supra* note 1, at 421.

41. *Id.* at 424–25.
42. Jerry Frug, *McCarthyism and Critical Legal Studies*, 22 HARV. C.R.-C.L. L. REV 665, 668 (1987) (reviewing Ellen W. Schrecker, NO IVORY TOWER: MCCARTHYISM & THE UNIVERSITIES (1986)).
43. Walter Metzger, *Academic Tenure in America: A Historical Essay*, *reprinted in* FACULTY TENURE 93, 137–41 (1973).
44. Hofstadter & Metzger, *supra* note 1, at 440.
45. *See* Beale, *supra* note 39, at 228. Hofstadter & Metzger argue that dismissals in the 1890s are attributable to a variety of factors. The ideology of industrialists on the governing board was only one factor, and many boards did protect academic freedom. The personal animosity or support of the university president towards the accused was also a significant factor. Hofstadter & Metzger, *supra* note 1, at 450–51.
46. *See* Hofstadter & Metzger, *supra* note 1, at 440.
47. Metzger, *supra* note 43, at 135–36.
48. *Id.* at 148.
49. AAUP, *The 1915 General Declaration of Principles of Academic Freedom* (1915), *reprinted in* ACADEMIC FREEDOM & TENURE app. A at 155, 165–167 (Louis Joughlin ed. 1969).
50. *See* AAUP, *1917 Report of Committee on Academic Freedom in Wartime*, 4 AAUP BULL. 35–42 (1918) [hereinafter 1917 Report].
51. Hofstadter & Metzger, *supra* note 1, at 495–96.
52. *Id.* at 496.
53. *Id.* at 498.
54. *Id.*
55. Schrecker, *supra* note 33, at 20.
56. Hofstadter & Metzger, *supra* note 1, at 501–02.
57. *See* Schrecker, *supra* note 33, at 20.
58. *Id.* at 21–22; *see* Hofstadter & Metzger, *supra* note 1, at 497.
59. Hofstadter & Metzger, *supra* note 1, at 497.
60. *Id.*
61. *Id.*
62. Ernest Earnest, *supra* note 32 at 259.
63. *Id.* at 261.
64. *Id.* at 261–62.
65. *Id.* at 262.
66. Hofstadter & Metzger, *supra* note 1, at 498.
67. *Id.* at 502. Administrators at Princeton, the University of Wisconsin, and Wellesley also held their ground in the face of public and alumni threats targeting heretical professors. Ernest Earnest, *supra* note 32, at 262–63.
68. *See* 1917 Report, *supra* note 50, at 31.
69. *See* 1917 Report, *supra* note 50, at 34–41.
70. AAUP, Academic Freedom and Tenure, Report of Committee A for 1942, 29 AAUP BULL. 65–67 (1943); *see also* AAUP, Academic Freedom and Tenure, Report of Committee A for 1943, 30 AAUP BULL. 19 (1945).
71. *See* Schrecker, *supra* note 33, at 72–73.
72. *Id.* at 74.
73. *Id.* at 73–74.
74. *Id.* at 74.
75. *Id.* at 24.
76. *See id.* at 68.
77. *Id.* at 63–65.

78. *Id.* at 66–67.
79. *Id.* at 75.
80. *Id.* at 79–80.
81. *Id.* at 81.
82. *Id* at 82.
83. *Id.*
84. *Id.* at 4–5.
85. C. Vann Woodward, *The Siege*, N.Y. REV., Sept. 25, 1986, at 3 (reviewing Ellen W. Schrecker, NO IVORY TOWER: MCCARTHYISM & THE UNIVERSITIES (1986)).
86. Schrecker, *supra* note 33, at 9.
87. *See id.* at 9, 340.
88. *Id.*
89. Woodward, *supra* note 85, at 6.
90. *Id.* at 3.
91. Schrecker, *supra* note 33, at 140.
92. *Id.* at 257; *see also id.* at 276.
93. *Id.* at 7.
94. *See id.* at 5.
95. *Id.* at 7.
96. *See id.* at 303; Woodward, *supra* note 85, at 6, 8.
97. Owen Lattimore, ORDEAL BY SLANDER 222–23 (1950).
98. *Id.* at 17.
99. Lionel Lewis, THE COLD WAR AND ACADEMIC GOVERNANCE: THE LATTIMORE CASE AT JOHNS HOPKINS 51 (1993) [hereinafter ACADEMIC GOVERNANCE].
100. Lattimore, *supra* note 97 at 208–09; *see also id.* at 7. As soon as one accusation was dismissed, Lattimore was confronted with the same thing all over again. *Id.* at 462.
101. *See id.* at 130; *see also* Robert P. Newman, OWEN LATTIMORE AND THE LOSS OF CHINA 392 (1992).
102. Lattimore, *supra* note 97, at 210.
103. *See id.* at 124–25; Newman, *supra* note 101, at 326.
104. Newman, *supra* note 101, at 373–74.
105. *See id.* at 413–16; ACADEMIC GOVERNANCE, *supra* note 99, at 33–38.
106. Lattimore, *supra* note 97, at 205.
107. Newman, *supra* note 101, at 443.
108. Lattimore, *supra* note 97, at 213–15.
109. *Id.* at 132–33, 208–09; *see also* Newman, *supra* note 101, at 462.
110. Lattimore, *supra* note 97, at 197.
111. Newman, *supra* note 101, at 354.
112. *Id.* at 441.
113. ACADEMIC GOVERNANCE, *supra* note 99 at 129 and 132.
114. *Id.* at 130–35.
115. *Id.* at 132; Newman, *supra* note 101, at 381, 438–39.
116. ACADEMIC GOVERNANCE, *supra* note 99, at 134.
117. *Id.* at 147.
118. *Id.* at 150–55.
119. Newman, *supra* note 101, at 437, 443.
120. *Id.* at 438–39.
121. *Id.* at 440.
122. Woodward, *supra* note 85, at 6. Lionel Lewis found that "the notice brought by a political controversy had an immediate effect on undoing reputations.... In an

instant, new and unfavorable social identities were given to many who had been known as individuals of unblemished character—some for over a long period of time." Lionel Lewis, COLD WAR ON CAMPUS 206 (1988).

123. Schrecker, *supra* note 33, at 233.
124. *See id.* at 299, 302-03.
125. *See* Lewis, *supra* note 122, at 269. "Anything or anyone displeasing was labeled communistic." *Id.* at 8. "[A]ny political activity to the left of New Deal liberalism that resulted in unfavorable attention to an institution was seen as something to be avoided [such as]...furthering the rights of racial minorities...activity in the Progressive Party...or backing Henry Wallace." *Id.* at 208.
126. Schrecker, *supra* note 33, at 303.
127. *Id.* at 303-04.
128. Lewis, *supra* note 122, at 253-54.
129. Paul Lazarsfeld & Wagner Thielens, Jr., THE ACADEMIC MIND: SOCIAL SCIENTISTS IN A TIME OF CRISIS 3-7 (1958).
130. *See id.* at 50, 54.
131. *Id.* at 55-57.
132. *Id.* at 50. Fifty of these "nonpolitical" charges centered on religious matters, principally in denominational schools. Thirty involved complaints about a professor's controversial position on economic or business issues, usually critical of a group in the local community. Twenty-five incidents dealt with race and segregation issues, usually involving colleges in the border states or further south and complaints about a professor's involvement with a civil rights group. *Id.* at 62-65.
133. *Id* at 68-69.
134. Lewis, *supra* note 122, at 97-101, 109-11, 250-51.
135. *Id.* at 123-24; *see* Schrecker, *supra* note 33, at 232-33.
136. Schrecker, *supra* note 33, at 233; *see* Lewis, *supra* note 122, at 152. Lewis observes that those who went through the "ordeal of campus hearings" were assumed to be guilty of something. Unlike a court trial, committee proceedings did not require that a case be made against the accused. The accused had to establish his or her innocence.
137. Lewis, *supra* note 122, at 210-22.
138. *Id.* at 81-82, 86-89, 91-95, 110-11, 131-33, 138-44, 222-26, and 226-32.
139. *Id.* at 279.
140. *Id.*
141. *Id.* at 197-200.
142. Woodward, *supra* note 85, at 3.
143. *See* Schrecker, *supra* note 33, at 241-64.
144. *See id.* at 263.
145. *Id.* at 267; *see id.* at 146.
146. *Id.* at 280; *see* Lewis, *supra* note 122, at 23.
147. Lattimore, *supra* note 97, at 173-74.
148. Lazarsfeld & Thielens, *supra* note 129, at 171, 378.
149. *See id.* at 384.
150. *Id.* at 384-85.
151. *Id.* at 76.
152. *Id.* at 192.
153. *Id.* at 194; *see also id.* at 102, 204, 212-218.
154. *Id.* at 154.
155. *Id.* at 28.
156. *See* Lewis, *supra* note 122, at 12.
157. *Id.* at 279.

158. *Id.* at 94-95.
159. Schrecker, *supra* note 33, at 10-11.
160. Lewis, *supra* note 122, at 208, 268-69. On the other hand, the faculty's public support for a target's academic freedom could influence a board of trustees not to punish the target. ACADEMIC GOVERNANCE, *supra* note 99, at 130-35 and 208-09.
161. *See id.* at 24, 222, 266.
162. *Id.* at 266-67.
163. Lazarsfeld & Thielens, *supra* note 129, at 171.
164. *See id.* at 173.
165. *See id.* at 171-74.
166. *Id.* at 174.
167. Lewis, *supra* note 122, at 264-65.
168. *Id.* at 150-53.
169. Lazarsfeld & Thielens, *supra* note 129, at 232.
170. *Id.* at 233.
171. *Id.* at 233-34.
172. *Id.* at 233-34, 104.
173. *See id.* at 28. Some departments were substantially further to the left than others. For example, sociology professors self identified as more liberal than economics professors. *Id.* at Table 23.
174. Schrecker, *supra* note 33, at 10-11, 311-12. Seymour M. Lipset, REBELLION IN THE UNIVERSITY 188-89 (1976).
175. Schrecker, *supra* note 33, at 308.
176. *Id.* at 10.
177. Lewis, *supra* note 122, at 49.
178. Schrecker, *supra* note 33, at 299.
179. *Id.* at 300.
180. *Id.*
181. Sidney Hook, ACADEMIC FREEDOM AND ACADEMIC ANARCHY 7-8 (1970) [hereinafter Hook, ACADEMIC FREEDOM].
182. David L. Westby, THE CLOUDED VISION: THE STUDENT MOVEMENT IN THE UNITED STATES IN THE 1960s 220 (1976).
183. Cyril Levitt, CHILDREN OF PRIVILEGE: STUDENT REVOLT IN THE SIXTIES 147 (1984).
184. Edward E. Ericson, Jr., RADICALS IN THE UNIVERSITY 2 (1975).
185. *See* Diana Trilling, *On the Steps of Low Library: Liberalism & the Revolution of the Young*, COMMENTARY, Nov. 1968, at 29, 38; *see generally* Hook, ACADEMIC FREEDOM, *supra* note 181.
186. James W. Tuttleton, ACAD. QUESTIONS, Spring 1990, at 80, 81 (reviewing Jacques Barzun, THE CULTURE WE DESERVE (1989)).
187. *See* Trilling, *supra* note 185, at 29-30, 36, 38.
188. *Id.* at 30.
189. *See id.* at 38, 44, 45. "By 1968, radicals were almost unanimous in viewing the university not as a center of teaching and scholarship but rather as an institution guilty of 'complicity' with a 'system' charged with being immoral, unresponsive and repressive." President's Commission on Campus Unrest, REPORT OF THE PRESIDENT'S COMMISSION ON CAMPUS UNREST 34 (1970).
190. *See* Trilling, *supra* note 185, at 49.
191. Hook, ACADEMIC FREEDOM, *supra* note 181, at 7-9.
192. These extreme intentions certainly did not motivate everyone who participated in the uprising. The focus here is on the ideology of the student leadership.

193. Trilling, *supra* note 185, at 29, 39.
194. *See* Raymond Aron, THE ELUSIVE REVOLUTION: ANATOMY OF A STU-
      DENT REVOLUTION 63 (1969).
195. *See* Trilling, *supra* note 185, at 29, 49–50.
196. Julian Foster & Durward Long, PROTEST! STUDENT ACTIVISM IN
      AMERICA 198 (1970).
197. Nancy Zaroulis & Gerald Sullivan, WHO SPOKE UP? AMERICAN PROTEST
      AGAINST THE WAR IN VIETNAM 1963–1975 238 (1984).
198. Maryl Levine & John Naisbitt, RIGHT ON 70 (1970). The IDA and the gymna-
      sium issues at Columbia were tactical issues for the SDS activists. "One demon-
      strated the cardinal point in SDS ideology that the university is subverted by the
      inhuman ends of an imperialist government; the other demonstrated that the con-
      scienceless power structure deprives the poor and the black of parkland and fa-
      cilities." The principal cause which these tactics served was the "ceaseless search
      of the SDS to find means of attacking the basic character of a society and gov-
      ernment they wished to transform, 'by any means possible.... '" Nathan Glazer,
      REMEMBERING THE ANSWERS 295–96 (1970).
199. *See* Foster & Long, *supra* note 196, at 185–86.
200. Ericson, *supra* note 184, at 1.
201. *See id.* at 1–3, 24, 26; Levitt, *supra* note 183, at 139.
202. *See* Trilling, *supra* note 185, at 29–30.
203. Foster & Long, *supra* note 196, at 190.
204. *Id.*
205. *Id.* at 191.
206. *Id.*
207. *Id.* at 192.
208. The Student Nonviolent Coordinating Committee (SNCC) also went through a
      transition in this period. Because of the lack of success of community action in
      achieving fundamental social changes in the early 1960s, the SNCC staff de-
      bated whether SNCC could achieve these goals while remaining tied to the rhetoric
      of interracialism and nonviolent direct action. By May, 1966, the new SNCC
      Chairman, Stokely Carmichael, articulated a need for black power and black
      consciousness by separating themselves from white people and by building black
      controlled institutions. *See* Clayborne Carson, IN STRUGGLE: SNCC AND THE
      BLACK AWAKENING OF THE 1960's 1–3 (1981); *see also* August Meier &
      Elliott Rudwick, BLACK PROTEST IN THE SIXTIES 19–21 (1970).
          The emphasis of black power was on self help, racial unity, and among the
      most militant, retaliatory violence. Arguments for retaliatory violence ranged
      from advocacy of the legal right of self defense to attempts to justify riots and
      guerilla warfare. *See* Meier & Rudwick, *supra*, at 20. One of SNCC's major
      goals in 1967 was to build support on southern black campuses. At Texas South-
      ern University, SNCC supporters forcibly occupied a university building; and at
      South Carolina State College, SNCC helped organize a student boycott of classes.
      In response to police intervention and a failure to meet students' demands, stu-
      dents pelted cars with rocks and engaged in some vandalism. At both Texas South-
      ern and South Carolina State, police ultimately retaliated with extensive gunfire,
      injuring one at Texas Southern and thirty three at South Carolina State. *See* Carson,
      supra, at 244–50.
209. *See* Ericson, *supra* note 184, at 24.
210. *See id.* at 25.
211. *Id.* at 27.
212. *Id.*

213. *See id.* at 31.
214. *See id.* at 33; *see* Westby, *supra* note 182, at 222-23.
215. Ericson, *supra* note 184, at 31.
216. *Id.* at 32.
217. *Id.* at 33; *see* Westby, *supra* note 182, at 222-23.
218. Ericson, *supra* note 184, at 40.
219. *See id.* at 30; Levitt, *supra* note 183, at 177.
220. Ericson, *supra* note 184, at 41.
221. *Id.* at 41-42; *see* Westby, *supra* note 182, at 178.
222. Ericson, *supra* note 184, at 43.
223. Zaroulis & Sullivan, *supra* note 197, at 237.
224. *Id.; see also* Foster & Long, *supra* note 196, at 190.
225. Donald E. Phillips, STUDENT PROTEST, 1960-1969: AN ANALYSIS OF THE ISSUES AND SPEECHES 57 (1980); *see generally* Westby, *supra* note 182, at 178.
226. Phillips, *supra* note 225, at 57.
227. *See* Foster & Long, *supra* note 196, at 187, 196.
228. *See id.* at 196-98.
229. Phillips, *supra* note 225, at 67.
230. John Patrick Diggins, THE RISE AND FALL OF THE AMERICAN LEFT 248-49 (1992).
231. William W. Brickman & Stanley Lehrer, CONFLICT AND CHANGE ON THE CAMPUS: THE RESPONSE TO STUDENT HYPERACTIVISM 19-20 (1970).
232. Benno Schmidt, *Universities Must Defend Free Speech*, WALL ST. J., May 6, 1991, at A16; *see generally* Hook, ACADEMIC FREEDOM, *supra* note 181, at 80-87.
233. The President's Commission on Campus Unrest found that after 1967, perhaps influenced by the terrible riots in Detroit and Newark in the summer of that year, the political views of the radical students became more extreme and they began to employ new tactics designed to shock the American people into a radical perspective on American society. THE REPORT OF THE PRESIDENT'S COMMISSION ON CAMPUS UNREST 42 (1970).
234. *See* Sidney Hook, OUT OF STEP: AN UNQUIET LIFE IN THE 20TH CENTURY 547 (1987) [hereinafter Hook, OUT OF STEP].
235. *See* Trilling, *supra* note 185, at 29. Ultimately students occupied at least three other buildings. James Kunen, THE STRAWBERRY STATEMENT: NOTES OF A COLLEGE REVOLUTIONARY 20-32 (1968).
236. *Id.* at 43.
237. Hook, OUT OF STEP, *supra* note 234, at 552-53.
238. *See id.* at 552-60.
239. *See id.* at 549, 563.
240. *See* Zaroulis & Sullivan, *supra* note 197, at 238.
241. *Id.* Twenty-four percent of the 292 incidents involved disruptions of classes or administrative functions and twenty-six percent involved the seizure or obstruction of a building. Urban Research Corp., STUDENT PROTESTS 1969 SUMMARY 21 (1970).
242. American Council on Education, CAMPUS TENSIONS: ANALYSIS AND RECOMMENDATIONS 9-10 (1970).
243. *Id.* at 7.
244. *Id.* at 9-10.
245. *Id.* at 11.
246. THE REPORT OF THE PRESIDENT'S COMMISSION ON CAMPUS UNREST 3-4 (1970).

247. *See* Seymour M. Lipset, REBELLION IN THE UNIVERSITY 5 (1976); Richard Flacks, MAKING HISTORY: THE RADICAL TRADITION IN AMERICAN LIFE 167 (1988); John Patrick Diggins, THE RISE AND FALL OF THE AMERICAN LEFT 261 (1992).
248. Lipset, *supra* note 247, at 5.
249. *See* Phillips, *supra* note 225, at 67; Dorothy Rabinowitz, *Power in the Academy: A Reminiscence & A Parable*, COMMENTARY, June 1969, at 42, 45.
250. *See* Hook, ACADEMIC FREEDOM, *supra* note 181, at 85-86.
251. *See* Hook, OUT OF STEP, *supra* note 234, at 550; Hook, ACADEMIC FREEDOM, *supra* note 181, at 82; Tuttleton, *supra* note 186, at 81-82.
252. *See* Hook, ACADEMIC FREEDOM, *supra* note 181, at 101; Rabinowitz, *supra* note 249, at 45.
253. Hook, ACADEMIC FREEDOM, *supra* note 181, at 87.
254. *See id.* at 80-83.
255. *See* Hook, OUT OF STEP, *supra* note 234, at 591.
256. *See* Peter Shaw, THE WAR AGAINST THE INTELLECT: EPISODES IN THE DECLINE OF DISCOURSE at XIV (1989); Hook, ACADEMIC FREEDOM, *supra* note 181, at 43, 80-85.
257. President's Commission on Campus Unrest, REPORT OF THE PRESIDENT'S COMMISSION ON CAMPUS UNREST 36 (1970).
258. Phillips, *supra* note 225, at 67.
259. *See* Hook, ACADEMIC FREEDOM, *supra* note 181, at 6; Trilling, *supra* note 185, at 29.
260. *See* Hook, ACADEMIC FREEDOM, *supra* note 181, at 8-9.
261. *See* Trilling, *supra* note 185, at 38-40; Glazer, *supra* note 198, at 291, 295-301.
262. *Id.*
263. *See* Trilling, *supra* note 185, at 41; Brickman & Lehrer, *supra* note 231, at 19-20, 273.
264. Hook, OUT OF STEP, *supra* note 234, at 590; Woodward, *supra* note 85, at 10.
265. The President's Commission on Campus Unrest found that "The crisis on American campuses has no parallel in the history of the nation." REPORT OF THE PRESIDENT'S COMMISSION ON CAMPUS UNREST 1 (1970). *See* Hook, ACADEMIC FREEDOM, *supra* note 181, at 80. There was little student political activism prior to 1900 except campus specific protests against dormitory food, specific professors or other local issues. A political American student movement first developed in the period 1900-1930. A variety of student organizations—political, fraternal, religious, national coordinating groups—developed in this period but they had virtually no impact on American society and very little within the university. A significant student antiwar movement developed in the 1930s with the participation of a range of student groups from the communists and socialists to religious groups like the YMCA and pacificists like the Fellowship of Reconciliation. In 1934, 1935 and 1936, the student antiwar movement organized national peace rallies; an estimated 500,000 students demonstrated nationally in 1936. By 1939, discord among radical student groups and shifts in public opinion regarding rearmament limited the impact of the antiwar student groups. The main thrust of the student antiwar in the 1930s was foreign policy and a general sense of a social system in crisis. Student unrest was not aimed at the university itself. Philip G. Altbach, STUDENT POLITICS IN AMERICA: A HISTORICAL ANALYSIS 13, 52-53, 66-69, 102-05 (1974). The 1960s was the first period where widespread student agitation was aimed at the university itself. *Id.* at 5, 229. In the 1960s, "students saw the universities as examples of much that was wrong in society and turned on it because it was a relatively defenseless institution in a society which was increasingly repressive."

Id. at 230. The 1960s marked the height of student activism in the United States. Id. at 227. The level of student discontent was unprecedented and the universities were disrupted and damaged in an unprecedented manner. *Id.* at 211 and 225.

266. Lipset, *supra* note 247, at 194.
267. Hook, OUT OF STEP, *supra* note 234, at 551, 563, 590-91.
268. *Id.* at 550, 563.
269. THE REPORT OF THE PRESIDENT'S COMMISSION ON CAMPUS UNREST 43 (1970). The physical environment of a campus makes it relatively easy for radicals to mobilize students with common sentiments and with a common predisposition to take direct political action. *Id.* at 82.
270. *Id.* at 46-47.
271. *See* Trilling, *supra* note 185, at 51.
272. Carol Iannone, *Paradise Lost at San Francisco State*, ACAD. QUESTIONS, Spring 1989, at 48, 56.
273. *Id.* at 60.
274. Schmidt, *supra* note 232.
275. Phillips, *supra* note 225, at 82.
276. *Id.*
277. Urban Research Corp., *supra* note 241, at 27.
278. Phillips, *supra* note 225, at 83-84.
279. *See* Hook, OUT OF STEP, *supra* note 234, at 590; Alan C. Kors, Interviewed by Carol Iannone, *Thought Reform and Education: A View from the University of Pennsylvania*, ACAD. QUESTIONS, Fall 1988, at 75, 78.
280. Urban Research Corp., *supra* note 241, at 33.
281. American Council on Education, CAMPUS TENSIONS: ANALYSIS AND RECOMMENDATIONS 11 (1970).
282. *See* Hook, OUT OF STEP, *supra* note 234, at 549-51, 563-64; Rabinowitz, *supra* note 249, at 42-43.
283. THE REPORT OF THE PRESIDENT'S COMMISSION ON CAMPUS UNREST 81 (1970).
284. Lipset, *supra* note 247, at 201, 198. Trustees were concerned because of "the high proportion of campus disruptions in which members of the teaching staff (mostly the younger and lower ranked members) took part." American Council on Education, CAMPUS TENSIONS: ANALYSIS AND RECOMMENDATIONS 33 (1970).
285. Hook, OUT OF STEP, *supra* note 234, at 549-50; *see* Rabinowitz, *supra* note 249, at 47.
286. Hook, ACADEMIC FREEDOM, *supra* note 181, at 90.
287. Nat Hentoff, FREE SPEECH FOR ME BUT NOT FOR THEE 114 (1992). The Woodward Report on freedom of expression at Yale (named for the committee chairman, C. Vann Woodward) describes varying degrees of faculty defense of academic freedom. In a 1963 incident involving the withdrawal of an invitation to speak to Alabama Governor George Wallace, many faculty publicly defended Wallace's right to speak. Faculty public defense of academic freedom was not nearly so vocal when threats of disruption forced General Westmoreland to cancel a speech in 1972, and in 1974, few faculty spoke when disruption prevented Professor William Shockley from speaking. The Woodward Report issued in 1975 reaffirmed Yale's commitment to defend freedom of expression. *Report of The Committee on Freedom of Expression at Yale*, 4 HUMAN RIGHTS 357, 363, 365, 371 (1975).
288. Kors, *supra* note 279, at 82.

289. Glazer, *supra* note 198, at 302, 304.
290. *Id.* at 305.
291. Hook, ACADEMIC FREEDOM, *supra* note 181, at 236.
292. REPORT OF THE PRESIDENT'S COMMISSION ON CAMPUS UNREST 36-37 (1970).
293. Fred Baumann, *Excerpts of Remarks*, 2 ACADEMIC CONCERNS 1 (Spring 1991).
294. Charles J. Sykes, THE HOLLOW MEN: POLITICS AND CORRUPTION IN HIGHER EDUCATION 17 (1990) (quoting Sidney Hook).
295. Everett C. Ladd, Jr. & Seymour M. Lipset, THE DIVIDED ACADEMY: PROFESSORS AND POLITICS xi and 4-5 (1975).
296. *Id.* at 210.
297. Lipset, *supra* note 247 at 201, 198.
298. Ladd & Lipset, *supra* note 295, at 43-44.
299. *Id.* at 208. Many professors distinguished between approval of the cause of the student radicals but disapproval of extreme tactics. *Id.* at 35 and 204. The shared goals made faculty reaction to student protest ambivalent. *Id.* at 212.
300. *Id.* at 14-15, 55. *See also id.* at 17 (for 1913-14) and 19-20 (for 1930s).
301. *Id.* at 26.
302. *Id.* at 91-92, 142-48, 198-99, 85.
303. *Id.* at 56, 368-69.
304. *Id.* at 60.
305. Id. at 92.
306. *Id.* at 69-70, 106.
307. *Id.* at 65.
308. *Id.* at 111.
309. *Id.* at 121.
310. Brickman & Lehrer, *supra* note 231, at 410-11.
311. Commission on Academic Tenure in Higher Education, FACULTY TENURE 42-43 (1973).
312. Ladd & Lipset, *supra* note 295, at 92.

2

Fundamentalism of the Radical Academic Left in the Late 1980s and Early 1990s

Zealotry hostile to freedom of academic thought and speech has historically originated in a variety of sources: lay boards of trustees and administrators, the lay public, government, and, in the 1960s, students. The newest threat is from the group that academic freedom was designed to protect: the professoriat itself. As Professor Paul Walters observed in his 1986 presidential address to the AAUP:

> The most dangerous threat to academic freedom... is that which comes from within the professoriate itself. For we bring to the academy our own deeply held political, religious, economic, and social convictions, convictions which make some of us rise in anger against colleagues whom we see as leftist, rightist, racist, sexist, atheistic, or anti-semitic. But insofar as we, educators and scholars, deny academic freedom to others, just as far do we sanction others who would deny it to us.[1]

In their 1975 book, *The Divided Academy,* Professors Everett C. Ladd, Jr. and Seymour Martin Lipset also sounded a warning concerning faculty members' ideology. Based on their study of professors and politics in the 1960s, Ladd and Lipset concluded that "the political thinking of academics is exceptionally ideological." They are particularly susceptible to ideological division and conflict.[2] "The ideological character of professorial thinking," Ladd and Lipset found, "is of considerable conceptual importance to understand academic political life, particularly the bitterness expressed against those of differing orientation."[3]

This essay avoids the use of the vague and general term *political correctness* or *PC* to describe the current zealotry. The term is used inconsistently and imprecisely in the popular media, usually to refer to the use of coercive tactics to suppress insensitive speech, but sometimes also to refer to issues of ideology and policy. Sensitivity concerning speech issues are only the tip of the iceberg of the underlying ideology.

A substitute phrase that captures all of the issues is difficult to formulate. The best of the available choices is the fundamentalism of the radical academic left. Fundamentalism has recently been understood to mean the militantly conservative movement in American Protestantism in opposition to modernist tendencies. More generally, fundamentalism is not just about religion, but about the inability to seriously entertain the possibility that one might be wrong.[4] The ideology and tactics of faculty zealots currently fit within the description of a militantly radical left movement in American higher education in opposition to alleged hidden structures of oppression in our Eurocentric culture, including the classical liberal tradition of rationality and the checking of beliefs through empiricism and free speech.[5] The movement is hostile to dissent. There is some dispute whether the movement is appropriately placed on the extreme left. Yale professor David Bromwich points out that it is only recently that commentators have put a left-wing gloss on the thought of postmodern scholars like Paul de Man or Jacques Derrida.[6] Radical left historically has implied a Marxist bent, but many regard the positivism of Marxism as the antithesis of postmodernism generally and deconstruction in particular. However, the tradition of the left is to encourage powerless groups to intervene in history.[7] Essentially the postmodern radical left has shifted from the traditional radical left's Marxist focus on economic relations as the source of oppression and class struggle to cultural hierarchy as the source of oppression.[8] In any event, radical left seems an appropriate description insofar as liberals perceive extremists in the postmodern schools and diversity movement to their left.

Ideology

Since the late 1980s, some academics have been attempting to impose their deeply held political, social, and moral convictions in ways that threaten and deny the freedom of academic thought and speech of their colleagues. Of course the presence of political, social, and moral concerns in academic inquiry is appropriate. That such concerns are held as an ideology and expressed passionately does not in itself threaten the freedom of academic thought and speech of others. Danger to freedom of academic thought and speech arises when zealotry is unleashed to enforce an ideology.

Some faculty members holding extreme views in two general movements in education today combine ideology and zealotry in ways similar to past waves of zealotry that suppressed freedom of academic thought and speech. Academics with extreme views in either the numerous postmodern schools or the movement for diversity based on race, gender, or other status claim that society is deeply sick, that their movement has special knowledge, and that alternative views should be suppressed.

Ideology of the Postmodern Schools

Consider first the ideology of faculty members holding extreme views in the numerous postmodern schools.[9] While there is no central body of doctrine among the postmodern schools, their central focus is the inherent instability and cloudiness of language and the indeterminacy of meaning. Postmodern schools of literary criticism have, in varying degrees, undermined belief in stable, discernible textual meaning and some, like deconstruction, not only deny that language can mean anything unambiguously, but assert that language inevitably subverts whatever it means to say. Professors Paul Gross and Norman Levitt explain deconstruction to mean that, "The verbal means by which we seek to represent the world are incapable, it is said, of doing any such thing. Strings of words, whether on the page or in our heads, have at best a shadowy and unstable relation to reality." These strings of words or texts are "unstable, inherently self-contradictory, and self-canceling."[10] Following from this premise of the instability of language and the indeterminacy of meaning, the critical legal studies movement posits the complete indeterminacy of legal rules.

The central belief of these postmodern schools is that accurate representation of reality and objective knowledge are myths. There is no knowledge: there are merely stories or "narratives" devised to satisfy the human need to make some sense of the world.[11] Each picture of reality is a product of social or personal factors. All concepts of the good and human potential are artificial and relative. Thus, existing systems are built on assumptions that are either indeterminate or biased.

A postmodern perspective desires freedom from "the particular little iron cage that the rationalistic discourse, at that moment, is constructing around us."[12] The postmodern program consists of "shattering congealed forms of life by showing that they have no particular integrity."[13]

It is important to understand that extreme proponents in the postmodern schools do not support the idea of contingent knowledge subject to constant testing in an effort to move continually toward the ideal of knowledge or human good. They reject the idea that there is any ideal of knowledge or human good toward which to move. They deny the possibility that reason may lead even to some slight degree of enduring wisdom.

Thus, if movement toward objective knowledge or value is impossible, the social, political, and economic arrangements of society cannot be justified by a claim that any particular arrangement is objectively superior to any other. Each arrangement is solely the expression of differences in power among classes and status groups.[14] All "knowledge" and "values" are the product of these power differentials. Some voices have the cultural power to define good and bad, true and false, or excellence and inadequacy, while others must live inside those definitions because they are relatively voiceless.[15]

The world, thus, is permeated by hidden, impersonal structures that oppress the powerless. Rationality, objectivity, standards of excellence, and merit are slogans designed to convince the downtrodden that subordination is justice.[16]

The postmodern teacher and scholar must probe all aspects of modern life to uncover these hidden and unseen modes of oppression and "to demystify the mechanisms that rule people's lives under the guise of accepted necessities."[17] He or she must attack the legitimacy of the most powerful, those who have silently structured the agenda and terms of debate. Intellectual life, teaching, and scholarship itself, thus, are forms of political struggle among classes and status groups.

In his book, *Doing What Comes Naturally*, Duke English professor Stanley Fish asks whether might makes right in this political struggle. He answers that, "in a sense, the answer I must give is yes, since in the absence of a perspective independent of interpretation, some interpretative perspective will always rule by virtue of having won out over its competitors."[18]

The question is, where does this ideology lead in terms of an action agenda? Having repudiated objectivity and any nonrelative concept of human good or knowledge, and having established that current interpretations of reality—including current social arrangements—are simply the outcome of hierarchical power, extreme proponents in the postmodern schools do not necessarily put forward any specific programs to replace the shattered current forms of reality.[19] Critical skepticism of this sort tends strongly toward nihilism.[20] Nevertheless, many postmodern scholars and teachers actively pursue a political agenda. The tradition of the American left in which they are rooted has been to help the oppressed to participate in history.[21] The tradition of the left is constituted by the interaction between leftist intellectuals and the masses of oppressed persons. Leftist intellectuals search for means to implement in history their values and visions on behalf of the oppressed.[22] Many of these leftist intellectuals realize that intellectual work per se has been insufficient as a means to influence history. The intellectual work has to be linked to practical action to convince the oppressed to claim power.[23]

A number of postmodern scholars and teachers acting in this tradition seek to give voice and power to the oppressed.[24] Through a postmodern critique pointing out that the current rules and forms of society lack any legitimacy and are simply the result of the power of the groups currently at the top of the hierarchy, these academics seek to destabilize the existing hegemonic structures, making resistance possible. As subordinated persons become aware of the vast hidden structures of oppression and their own oppressed status, they will adopt resistance. The ideology will transform subordinate relations.[25] The ultimate goal is a radically egalitarian democracy in which public spaces proliferate where the oppressed become increasingly capable of self-management.[26] This radically egalitarian democracy or "critical democracy" should produce an ethical conversion to the priority of labor over capital and the elimination of all economic and social injustices.[27]

The activist postmodern intellectual must socialize the oppressed to achieve this ultimate goal of a radically egalitarian democracy. The objective is to develop the oppressed individual's capacity for criticism of the established culture, transcendence of role conformity created by that culture, and action.[28] The oppressed must become aware of and offended by the structures of oppression at work in both institutional and everyday life. Once the oppressed are socialized, structural change can occur through politics, strategic mobilization, mass action, and public conflict.[29]

This socialization can occur if activist postmodern intellectuals capture the meaning giving bodies in society, principally education, to promote the ideology.[30] Miami University [Ohio] education professors Henry Giroux and Peter McLaren explain how critical educators must take the ideological and political initiative in education:

> Within the last decade, a group of critical educational theorists has emerged.... In this work, schooling is viewed as a form of cultural politics, one which focuses on the centrality of power and struggle in defining both the nature and purpose of what it means to be educated.

They write that the core of critical educational discourse has been a two-fold task.

> First as a language of protest, critical educational theory has attempted to develop a counterlogic to those relations of power and ideologies in American society that mask a totalitarian ethics.... Second, this perspective has attempted to develop a critical theory of education as part of a radical theory of ethics aimed at constructing a new vision of the future. In this view, American schooling becomes a vital sphere for extending civil rights, fighting for cultural justice, and developing new forms of democratic public life within a life-affirming public culture.[31]

Stanford education professor Martin Carnoy argues that schools should serve as sites dedicated to counterhegemonic struggle and resistance to weaken the grasp of dominant hidden business class values and norms. The struggle is for control of the schools.[32] Professor Giroux concurs that schools are a form of cultural politics and that schools should be sites for counterhegemonic struggle and ideological contestation and conflict.[33] Educators must challenge those oppressive social forces that sustain themselves by spurious appeal to objectivity, science, knowledge, and universality.[34]

The university is thus a major battleground for the activist postmodern professor. Educational institutions should be converted into "agencies for reconstructing and transforming the dominant status quo culture."[35] Law teaching, for example, should be a process of political sensitization and indoctrination.[36] In an article in the *Harvard Educational Review,* University of Wisconsin professor Elizabeth Ellsworth rejects the attempt to hide this political agenda. In her teaching and scholarship, she writes:

> [I] wanted to avoid colluding with many academic writers in the widespread use of code words such as "critical," which hide the actual political agendas I assume such writers share with me—namely, anti-racism, anti-sexism, anti-elitism, anti-heterosexism, anti-ableism, anticlassism, and anti-neoconservatism.

> Further, when educational researchers advocating critical pedagogy fail to provide a clear statement of their political agendas, the effect is to hide the fact that as

critical pedagogues, they are in fact seeking to appropriate public resources (class-rooms, school supplies, teacher/professor salaries, academic requirements and de-grees) to further various "progressive" political agendas that they believe to be for the public good.... But however good the reasons for choosing the strategy of subverting repressive school structures from within, it has necessitated the use of code words such as "critical," "social change," and "revitalized public sphere," and a posture of invisibility."[37]

These efforts have met with considerable success. Philosopher Richard Rorty observes that "the power base of the left in America is now in the universities since the trade unions have largely been killed off.... The universities have done a lot of good work by setting up, for example, African-American studies programs. They have created power bases for these movements."[38] The "new American cultural left," Rorty comments, "has come into being made of deconstructionists, new historicists, people in gender studies, ethnic studies, media studies, a few left over Marxists, and so on. This left would like to use the English, French, and Comparative Literature Departments of the universi-ties as staging areas for political action."[39]

Ideology of Extreme Advocates of Diversity

The ideology of extreme faculty advocates of diversity (or its rhetorical equivalent, multiculturalism) also maintains that American society is deeply sick. The ideology's principal beliefs are: (1) racism, sexism, homophobia, and related other prejudices are endemic and culturally sanctioned; (2) big-oted attitudes, whether held privately or publicly, consciously or unconsciously, must be eliminated; (3) inequities based on racial, gender, or other oppressed status must be rectified; (4) the cultural, political, social, and economic power of those in an oppressed status must be dramatically advanced by fundamen-tal restructuring of American society, including the university; (5) the world view of each individual is largely determined by race or other status differ-ences; (6) African, Native, Asian, and Latino/Puerto Rican Americans are vic-tims of intellectual oppression because current values like intellectual quality and structures like meritocracy are merely the expression of the majority's Eurocentric culture; (7) Eurocentric history, science, literature, philosophy, music, and art should not be "privileged" in any way over that of non-Euro-pean civilizations, since all judgments of value are relative and hegemonic; and (8) the experiences associated with a particular oppressed status create a distinctive voice in conceptualizing and addressing intellectual issues.[40]

Extreme advocates of diversity have had a strong political agenda. They use a number of devices for putting these beliefs into operation in education. First is preferential admissions and faculty hiring systems focused on achiev-ing representation for each oppressed group (and its views) according to its proportion in society as a whole. A second device is major curricular reform that mandates sensitivity training, multicultural courses, the study of oppression, and de-emphasis of Eurocentric culture and values. The curriculum should abandon the idea of a cultural center. The curriculum should give full expression to the intellectual and moral equality of diverse cultures. Authors are representative of these cultures and the curriculum should be representative with authors from all cultures. A third device is monitoring and controlling permissible speech regarding diversity to ensure sensitivity as defined by the oppressed status groups.[41]

While diversity (or multiculturalism) was born of the good intentions of the civil rights movement and derives from principles that many faculty members hold dear, it is important to distinguish the ideology of extreme faculty advocates of diversity from that of traditional civil rights supporters. If a puritan is defined as someone who exaggerates a virtue until it becomes a vice, the analogy is appropriate here. Richard Bernstein in *Dictatorship of Virtue* explains that diversity or multiculturalism "represent, at least in theory, a sensibility of openness to the enormous cultural difference that has always existed in American life, but whose fullness has been suppressed by the might of the dominant European culture.... Multiculturalism in this sense would seem to be the logical extension of the civil rights movement of the 1960s."[42] Yet Bernstein finds that extreme advocates of diversity have slid toward ideological excess, dogmatism and political ambition for power.[43]

Common Ideological Ground

Extreme advocates in the postmodern schools and the diversity movement share common ideological ground and convoy frequently together. They agree that the current rules and forms of American society lack inherent legitimacy and are in place simply because of the oppressive power of the status groups currently at the top of the hierarchy, principally Eurocentric white males. This hierarchy of power and social privilege based on status must be reversed, and the oppressed must be enfranchised. Extremists in both movements agree that they must control the institutions that produce and legitimatize culture, particularly education, to socialize the oppressed. In education, concepts of objectivity, rationality, academic merit, the search for knowledge, or other Eurocentric constructs like individual equality, democracy, or the free market, have no intrinsic value or better justification than beliefs and perceptions held by oppressed persons. Indeed, academic quality and meritocracy, for example, are simply a mask for oppression. Education and intellectual life must be politicized to give power and voice to the concepts and ideas of oppressed groups.

The *Chronicle of Higher Education* reports in October, 1993, that a new age of "post-theory" signals a more overtly cultural focus for postmodern theorists and a turn to political content. This creates greater common ground with diversity advocates.

"The new faces on the block are the new historicism, cultural studies, post-colonialism, and gender studies," says W. J. T. Mitchell, professor of English at the University of Chicago and editor of the journal *Critical Inquiry.*

Those approaches to literary criticism are concerned less with philosophical questions about meaning and language and more with culture. "Literary studies today are interested in how people define themselves—through categories such as race, class, gender, or ethnicity," says Michael Denning, Chairman of American Studies at Yale University.[44]

This newer direction is more overtly political. Professor Frederick Crews, Chairman of the English Department at the University of California at Berkeley, observes that "in the 1980's, post-structuralism formed a green-card marriage with the American left. It latched onto a political content and lingo." New York University English professor Denis Donoghue explains that "literary critics have become district attorneys" in this new turn to politics.[45]

All ideological zealotry threatens freedom of academic thought and speech. The threat is more severe from ideologies like the postmodern schools or the diversity movement where either encouragement or permission for coercion of others is inherent in the ideology. For example, extremists in the postmodern schools essentially argue that we are living under an oppression based on lies, and that with proper analysis the hidden vast structure of oppression, including the university itself, will be revealed. Implicit, and sometimes explicit, is the assumption that if the reformers can only get control of the schools, the curriculum, and the dominant language structures, they can reveal the oppression, convince the oppressed to see the world as totally politicized, empower the oppressed to engage in politics, and correct the oppression.[46] This supports a high degree of—if not total—politicization of the university, and condones the use of coercive tactics to achieve that politicization. Extreme advocates in the postmodern schools may not accept as legitimate any criticism of the coercion used in the struggle because such criticism is based on hegemonic, Eurocentric concepts of fairness. To take another example, the ideology of the diversity movement demands the elimination of bigoted attitudes, whether held privately or publicly, consciously or unconsciously. A standard device of the ideology is monitoring and controlling speech regarding diversity to ensure sensitivity as defined by oppressed status groups. For example, mere disagreement with a person of color may be labeled racially insensitive or oppressive. The more extreme advocates of diversity see the world as divided into essentially two groups: those who have suffered and those who cause suffering. They may not accept as legitimate any criticism of coercion used by those who have suffered to right the wrongs of the past.[47] Oppressors cannot respond without charges of retaliation.[48] Ideologies that divide the world into the oppressors and the oppressed condone coercion of those categorized as oppressors. For example, Michael Lerner, author of *The Socialism of Fools: Anti-Semitism on the Left,* writes that in this construct,

Jews are said to have power.[49] Lerner believes the reality is that Jews are only given the appearance of power by the ruling elite so that they can serve as the focus of anger that might otherwise be directed at the elite.[50] Because of the perception that Jews have power, they become the subversive "other" who is oppressing "us," the people.[51] The resentment of oppression among the left and among the oppressed generally is then directed at the Jews as a recognizable agent of the oppressors.[52] This perception, Lerner writes, leads the left to steadfastly refuse to acknowledge that anti-Semitism deserves attention.[53] Some African-Americans also see Jews as oppressors; this accounts for the growing anti-Semitism among African-Americans.[54]

Coercion of Competent Academic Inquiry by Tactics of Public Accusation, Social Ostracism, Investigation, Tribunals, Threats to Employment, and Disruption of Speeches, Classes, and Administrative Functions

With the permission or encouragement of these ideologies, some faculty members and students holding extreme views in the postmodern schools and the diversity movement have combined ideology with a zealotry that has suppressed the competent academic thought and speech of others. The group of faculty who combine postmodern and diversity ideology with zealotry will be identified as the fundamentalist academic left. In contrast to the zealotry of the 1960s student activism, the zealotry of the late 1980s and early 1990s is led primarily by faculty who find the opinions of one of their colleagues offensive.[55] These faculty members encourage and support the zealotry of students in suppressing the views of professors they oppose.[56] Some administrators are sympathetic to and supportive of this zealotry. Former Yale dean Donald Kagan has described the situation as "a revolution from the top down."[57]

Former Yale president Benno Schmidt believes that "the most serious problems of freedom of expression in the U.S. today exist on our campuses." The assumption of a number of professors is that the purpose of higher education is to induce a correct opinion rather than to search for wisdom and to liberate the mind. On many campuses, perhaps most, Schmidt believes there is little resistance to growing pressure to suppress, and to punish, rather than to answer, dissenting views.[58]

In a May, 1994 commencement speech, historian Arthur M. Schlesinger, Jr., condemned "the agitation for censorship" that currently finds "a special location in our universities."[59] "In the good old days," Schlesinger recalls, "conservatives and hyperpatriots were the militant advocates of repression and censorship. But in a bizarre twist of roles, attacks on the First Amendment and the demand to suppress the thought we hate come these days from the left. Even more ironically, that demand is centered in our universities—exactly the place above all others where unlimited freedom of expression had previously been deemed sacred. And those who lead the assault...do so in the name of the multicultural society."[60] "The celebration of diversity" also ironically "concludes in a demand for conformity."[61]

Former Harvard president Derek Bok concurs:

> In recent years, the threat of orthodoxy has come primarily from within rather than outside the university.... [Z]ealous proponents have sometimes gone further to assemble a daunting list of ideas...that one can utter only at the risk of being labeled racist, sexist, hegemonic, homophobic, patriarchal, gynophobic, or worse. While such tactics are clearly within the bounds of free speech, they are nonetheless regrettable when they utilize ridicule or intimidation to make their point.

> Much worse are deliberate attempts to harass professors, censor students, or disrupt speeches by visitors believed to hold unacceptable views on race, gender, foreign policy, or other controversial subjects.... Regrettably, however, incidents of this kind seem to have occurred with some frequency around the country.[62]

President Bok distinguishes between suppression of competent academic inquiry and speech through public accusations of bigotry and social ostracism on one hand and suppression as a consequence of deliberate attempts to harass professors and disrupt speech on the other. While not precisely clear, Bok seems to include investigations, threats to employment, and disruption of speeches, classes, and administrative functions in the second category. Bok recommends that the university use education to discourage the former, but penalties to prohibit the latter. This chapter follows the same general analytical structure, addressing first suppression of competent academic inquiry and speech through public accusations of bigotry. The chapter then turns to deliberate attempts both to harass professors through investigations and to disrupt academic speech.

At this point there is no exhaustive interview survey outlining the stories of the targets of the current period of zealotry similar to Ellen Schrecker's survey of the universities' treatment of the targets of McCarthyism. However, the popular media have picked up and reported the stories of some of the targets in this wave. There are also a number of articles in scholarly journals recounting stories of coercion. These stories are the principal evidence analyzed in this essay.

The evidence bears careful consideration for several reasons. First, it is common for newspaper reports to have factual errors. Second, to the extent that the victim's account of an incident is the only source of evidence, the degree of suppression is probably overstated. There is another side to the story. On the other hand, there are three reasons why the degree of suppression is probably understated by the evidence used here. First, free speech advocate Nat Hentoff asserts that only a small percentage of the assaults on free speech are covered by the press for it has only so much space.[63] The stories in the popular media are therefore the tip of the iceberg. Second, if the story is complicated, the popular press tends not to report it because the public cannot follow it. Stories involving the ideology and tactics of the fundamentalist academic left tend to be complicated. For example, the use of pretextual charges of bigotry and investigations to suppress advocates of academic quality in admissions and personnel decisions is often a complex story. Under the rubric, "political correctness," the popular press is printing only the simplest stories of suppression. Third, many stories of suppression are not told out of fear. Because an accusation of bigotry substantially damages the target and the university, the accused usually tries to avoid media attention. The target may simply concede and the suppression remains hidden. For example, Professor David Bryden who, for the past eight years has been editor of the journal *Constitutional Commentary,* reports numerous instances where scholars refused to publish articles or to write book reviews on topics relating to race or gender because of fears of hate mail, reputational harm, and career damage.[64] As to the claim that ancient Egypt was a black nation, essayist John Leo reported that he "phoned seven Egyptologists at random around the country, and all seven said it was completely untrue, then asked that their names not be used."[65]

The evidence outlining the coercive tactics used in this current wave of zealotry is more detailed than the discussion of tactics in the earlier six waves. The reason for the lengthy compilation of evidence is the extensive public denial that there is any significant coercion of academic speech today. The general theme of the denial is that the same tired horror stories are endlessly recycled for political purposes. The effort to provide a much broader body of evidence to rebut this denial may lead to criticism that the stories in chapter 2 are repetitious. To address this criticism, a number of the stories appear in the endnotes.

Suppression of Competent Academic Inquiry and
Speech Through Public Accusations of Bigotry

Public accusations of bigotry and social ostracism of faculty and students. The zealot's chief weapon against those professors or students who disagree with the orthodoxies of the postmodern schools or the diversity movement is public humiliation through accusations of bigotry. Since the mission of the fundamentalist academic left is to expose the hidden structures of oppression in the culture, it is a small and natural step for the zealot to expose hidden motives of oppression and bigotry rather than to address the content of ideas. Disagreement is reduced to some putative underlying political or psychological motive. Professional conflict either over issues involving ideology, such as group preferences based upon status in admissions or hiring, or with individuals from a status group on any issue they may perceive as sensitive, frequently results in public accusations of bigotry toward oppressed status groups.[66] Dean Colin Diver of the University of Pennsylvania Law School observes that "if someone argues vociferously that affirmative action is unconstitutional or immoral, that person is certain to be called racist."[67] Dean Geoffrey Stone at the University of Chicago Law School concurs that "anyone who disagrees or raises doubts runs into the risk of being thought of as a racist, sexist or homophobic."[68] Professor Stephen Carter of Yale also observes the common use of accusations of racism against those who defend traditional standards.[69] He further comments that "still, the ungentle truth remains: that black intellectuals who dissent from the orthodoxy are all too often silenced by ad hominem criticism from many leaders of the black community, as well as from other intellectuals, who ought to know better."[70] Competent statements of fact or analysis are often turned into a question of base motive.[71]

False accusations of bigotry to suppress dissenting views are occurring in higher education. For example, when Harvard professor Harvey Mansfield wrote an article linking grade inflation and aggressive affirmative action, fifty minority students protested at parents' weekend in March, 1993, calling for an official investigation into "institutional racism."[72] When the Ohio State English Department was considering a remedial writing program for graduate students in 1988, Professor Phoebe Spinred argued that if students couldn't write at this point in their career, they shouldn't be in graduate school. The colleague making the proposal immediately accused her of racism.[73] After the 1992 publication of Arthur Schlesinger, Jr.'s book, *The Disuniting of America: Reflections on a Multicultural Society*, a novelist and english instructor at Berkeley denounced him as a follower of the neo-Nazi, David Duke.[74] Commenting on the same book, Duke professor Stanley Fish concludes that Schlesinger's arguments have the effect of perpetuating racial stereotypes and make him a "shoo-in" as a racist.[75]

Accusations of bigotry by association are also occurring. Several professors and members of the Black Law Students Association of the District of Columbia School of Law attacked Professors Thomas Mack and Robert Katz from the school for representing a Georgetown University Law Center student who wrote an article criticizing Georgetown's affirmative action program. Suggesting that the representation was harmful to blacks, the fundamentalists demanded that Mack and Katz withdraw from the case or take a leave of absence until the case was over.[76]

The strategic use of accusations of prejudice to exploit the stigmatization of racial bigotry bears careful analysis. The tactic is used in several forms. One variation is that facts are themselves a form of hegemonic oppression and are irrelevant. The charge of bigotry is based simply on whether the feelings of an oppressed person are hurt.

Another variation rests on facts, but the accusation of bigotry may not have factual or analytical support meeting any standard of academic competence and fairness. The standard used is frequently similar to that of the advocate. There is a gulf between the advocate's partisanship and manipulative persuasion and the scholar's standards of thoroughness, accuracy, impartiality, and consistency. The advocate strains the limits of attorneys' professional conventions to present only argument and evidence favorable to a client's interests. Regarding facts, half-truth by omission is encouraged and in many cases mandated; the advocate has an obligation not to present confidential facts known to be adverse to the client except to correct evidence submitted earlier known to be false. Such conduct violates a scholar's duties of professionally competent research and teaching.

President Bok notes that

> campus debates on such subjects...suffer from a kind of double standard. In writing papers, taking examinations, or publishing articles, students and faculty try hard to be objective, to recognize opposing arguments, to marshall evidence with care. When political issues are at stake, however, discussions quickly become partisan, demagogic, and filled with inaccuracies and exaggerations. Such debates...are [not] worthy of the university's commitment to thoughtful, dispassionate analysis.[77]

The key point is that this variation adopts the advocate's tactics of manipulative persuasion. Accusations may be based on conjecture, gossip, hearsay, the twisting of any ambiguity, half-truth by omission, exaggeration, or even beyond the advocate's morality, misrepresentation.[78] Misinformation may be constantly repeated to create adverse perceptions of the accused.[79]

Regardless of the variation used, in education today a public accusation of bigotry made against competent academic inquiry or speech has a devastating impact on the accused. In teaching, a charge of bigotry is similar to a criminal indictment in terms of moral turpitude. Such charges carry substantial stigmatization.

For some, the accusation itself is treated as a conclusion of fact. The accusation alone is thought sufficient to warrant punishment. Yale professor Stephen Carter observes that "Russell Baker...has proposed that racism has become in the 1990s what communism was in the 1950s, and I very much fear he is right. We have reached a point where the accusation of racism is treated as a conclusion of fact; and the fact is thought sufficient to warrant punishment, perhaps even dismissal."[80]

For many others, the accused educator is assumed guilty until proven innocent. Even charges by unnamed informers carry great weight.[81] It is difficult, if not impossible, for the accused to prove the negative that she or he harbors no prejudice.[82] Offering testimony on behalf of the accused also may be an oppressive act.[83] An accusation that someone in an oppressed group perceives the accused as oppressive or insensitive is essentially unanswerable. Failure to confess insensitivity and apologize may be characterized as additional evidence of bigotry.[84]

For faculty members, public accusations of bigotry made against competent academic inquiry or speech are highly damaging for four reasons. First, it is lacerating for an academic to be accused of what she has detested her entire adult life. This is debilitating at a deeply personal level.[85] Second, academics have a pervasive fear of being labeled with charges of moral turpitude because of injury to reputation and career opportunity.[86] Once a false accusation of moral turpitude occurs, the truth never catches up. A subset of people always believes it. Third, fighting back against a false accusation of bigotry involves a great sacrifice of time and energy and considerable loss to teaching and scholarship.

Fourth, public accusations of bigotry against competent work lead to hostility and ostracism from many colleagues and students. For example, when Professor Alan Gribben cast the sole dissenting vote opposing the creation of an M.A. concentration in Ethnic and Third World Literature at the University of Texas English Department, rumors were spread throughout the campus and off-campus communities alleging he was a racist.[87] Colleagues refused to speak to him or sit near him at department meetings.[88] He was not invited to faculty functions, and the department newsletter failed to mention his awards and publications. Hate notes appeared in his mailbox. Students were urged not to enroll in his courses.[89] A colleague called to express sympathy about what was happening, "[b]ut I have a family I have to think about and so I have to ask a favor. Please don't stand in my doorway and talk to me when other people are watching."[90] Based on an extended interview study of thirty women involved with women's studies programs, Professors Daphne Patai and Nuretta Koertge report that many respondents experienced hostility, antagonism, and accusations of moral turpitude if they articulated views that were not politically pure.[91]

Yale professor Stephen Carter writes that for African-American scholars, the response to dissenters who do not talk correctly about racial preferences is

> often painfully straightforward: the dissenters face ostracism, expulsion, official death. We purge them.... Purges are never pretty. They are not meant to be. The more ruthless and complete the campaign in which one's opponents are eliminated, the more emphatic the warning sent to those who might dissent in the future: Beware, the message reads. See how we deal with those who deny the official word. Don't get on the wrong side, or you could be next. A purge is, in its essence, a denial of the right to think.[92]

Although we generally think of purges as a strategy of totalitarian governments, Carter observes that purges occur in the West also, and few "are more disheartening, and more threatening to freedom, than the disdainful treatment of intellectuals who dare to challenge fashionable academic orthodoxy. And a particularly tragic example of this treatment is the isolation of intellectual dissenters who happen to be black."[93]

When Julius Lester, an African-American professor at the University of Massachusetts-Amhearst, criticized the remarks of some black leaders as anti-Semitic, colleagues in his department stopped speaking to him. He observed, "The experience of shunning is a very profound one...I can't describe what it's like to come onto the floor where your department is and to walk down a hallway and people lower their voices or they stop talking or they close the doors as you walk by—just to walk through that atmosphere of hostility, week in, week out."[94]

Ostracism and abusive conduct may be combined. Professor Cynthia Griffin Wolff holds a chair in humanities at MIT and has been a distinguished lecturer in women's and cultural studies. She opposed the promotion of two candidates for tenure in the literature section based on her evaluation of their scholarly work. Some colleagues saw the candidates' work as politically important in the framework of postmodern and diversity ideology. In the spring of 1988, they excoriated Professor Wolff for her academic views. They embarked on an unrelenting campaign of verbal abuse and isolation toward her. They stopped speaking to her and initiated false rumors alleging that Professor Wolff had engaged in professional misconduct. She brought litigation against MIT seeking damages and a declaratory judgment resulting from the Institute's wrongful acquiescence in a persistent and continuing pattern of professional, political, and sexual harassment. The litigation was settled favorably for Professor Wolff. She transferred to the Writing Program to escape harassment.[95]

Competent student inquiry and speech in the classroom also suffer from tactics of hostility and ridicule. For example, a recent survey conducted by the Section of General Practice of the American Bar Association finds that many law students fear reprisals if they disagree with professors' political views. Sixty percent responded that there were professors who were intolerant of political beliefs that differed from their own. Of those students, 48 percent saw evidence of intolerance frequently or very frequently. Fifty-one percent of the law student respondents don't always feel free to express disagreement with the professors' political perspectives in class, in papers, and on exams.[96] The specific tactics used to suppress students' classroom speech are chastising students with ad hominem attack and lowering grades.[97]

Yale professor of English David Bromwich writes in *Politics by Other Means,* "As near as I can estimate, fifteen students, over the past six years, talked to me of their sense of an unspoken limit on allowable opinions in class. It does not suggest a panic—but a teacher who claims never to have heard such a confidence is living under a stone.... With graduate students the matter was more serious: they had relevant anecdotes from the job market."[98]

The written comments to the ABA survey indicate that law students do not perceive law faculties as politically diverse. Law faculty tend to fall on the left side of the political spectrum, ranging from moderate left to radical left.[99] Jane Bahls, writing in the *Student Lawyer* about the survey, comments that the phenomenon of using the classroom as a forum to advance political beliefs is limited almost exclusively to professors on the radical left.[100] University of Minnesota professor David Bryden notes that leading law schools have "hardly any" orthodox political conservatives and only a couple professors who have "publicly dissented from any tenet of liberal orthodoxy."[101]

Students also fear being publicly labeled with accusations of bigotry and publicly humiliated by other students. Whether the principal cause of student fears is coercion by faculty, by other students, or both, does not seem critical. The bottom line is that significant numbers of students at many universities, whether at Stanford, New York University, Harvard Divinity School, or Brown are censoring themselves on the critical issues of the day.[102] "It's not what you want at a University", said Russell Ellis, vice-chancellor at the University California-Berkeley. Ellis acknowledged that many students suffer from what he termed "expressive fears."[103] "[I]n many interviews, students talked about being afraid to talk about concerns or ideas that could not remotely be regarded as blatantly racist or sexist. Rather, they are afraid to say anything about a controversial topic that they feel could be misconstrued."[104]

Struggle meetings. Public accusations of bigotry may also be accompanied by "struggle-meeting" tactics. Chinese dissident Nien Cheng describes struggle meetings as public meetings where zealots surround the target and make accusations consisting of misrepresentation and exaggeration to generate passion and anger against the accused, who is forced to make a confession.[105] Faculty and student zealots sometimes seek to create public settings where they can in concert surround and confront the accused individual with charges of bigotry. This public humiliation and group intimidation are highly debilitating and may lead to coerced self-criticism.[106]

Sensitivity training sessions are public settings where struggle meeting tactics can be used effectively. For example, in 1990 the dean of the University College of the University of Cincinnati organized sensitivity training for faculty. The trainer for the session asked all the women to stand. The trainer asked each to declare the institution granting her undergraduate degree. Those with degrees from prestigious universities were required to remain standing. This procedure was followed for the men, and then again for both women and men with respect to graduate degrees. One woman instructor was left standing. This woman, the trainer claimed, "is a member of the privileged white elite." With her blonde hair, blue eyes, and white skin, "she is the most likely person to succeed." When the group returned for a second session, the trainer announced that they would vote on the most beautiful woman in the room, but no contest was really necessary, they all knew the winner would be the young instructor identified earlier. She was asked to stand again, but was so distraught she did not do so. The struggle meeting technique of isolating and humiliating those with "illegitimate" entitlements was successful.[107]

Media attention. Public accusations of bigotry may be followed by press attention and headlines in both campus and general circulation media.[108] Zealotry feeds on symbolic incidents around which to incite passion and anger. Zealots try to make the target into a highly visible media symbol of bigotry. University of Michigan President James Duberstadt observed that "we have very capable student activists, just like in the sixties, when Tom Hayden was here. They know how to create media events better than we do. When we don't listen to them, the press treats the University as a hotbed of racism."[109] Faculty activists may also be skilled at using the press. Professor Paul Lauter of Trinity College distributed packets of material at a 1992 workshop for community organizers in academia. The materials outlined how to generate publicity and manipulate the media.[110]

A press campaign to vilify a professor can be highly effective. For example, following the university provost's apology for initiating an improper investigation against him, Professor Allan Mandelstamm at Virginia Tech was the target of a two-month newspaper letter-writing campaign.[111] Similarly, Harvard professor Stephan Thernstrom was the target of nine weeks of press headlines in the Harvard Crimson concerning his alleged racial insensitivity.[112]

Public accusations of bigotry and public humiliation impose enormous costs on competent academic inquiry and speech. Academic reputations are extremely vulnerable to media charges of moral turpitude. Once such charges are published, a subset of the community always harbors suspicion. In addition to the emotional toll on the accused, damage to the accused's reputation and career opportunity, and ostracism from colleagues and students,[113] fighting back involves enormous sacrifices of time to respond orally and in writing. The fight may continue on a long-term basis. The targets and potential targets of accusations must spend exceptional energy avoiding any ambiguity that could be twisted into accusations.[114] To lay persons, such accusations may sometimes seem petty and frivolous; the reality is that they exhaust the strongest of spirits.[115]

The accused's hope for procedural due process in many instances may be futile. Procedural due process demands fundamental fairness in the sense that individuals are not penalized unless a decision-making process involving some sort of hearing first takes pains with the facts and the application of the appropriate rules to the facts. Public accusations of bigotry and media coverage substantially damage an academic before there is any fair process to determine the truth or falsity of the accusations. If no formal charges are filed, the accusations may never be the object of a fair investigation and hearing.[116] It may be in the zealot's advantage to have innuendo played out in forums where there is no chance that pains will be taken with the facts.

President Bok distinguished between suppression of competent academic inquiry and speech through public accusations of bigotry and suppression as a consequence of deliberate attempts to harass professors and to disrupt speech. We turn now to these latter strategies.

Suppression of Competent Academic Inquiry and Speech Through Deliberate Attempts to Harass Professors and Disrupt Speech

The impact of investigation and the threat of investigation on competent academic inquiry and speech. While public accusations of moral turpitude significantly chill competent academic inquiry and speech, more chilling is an internal or external investigation of the accusations for two reasons. First, any investigation imposes substantial additional reputational and psychological costs on the accused. If an investigation goes forward, the investigation gives a greater appearance of validity to the charges.[117] This further damages the accused's community standing and professional opportunity. During the period of the investigation, the accused is under a cloud within the community and also suffers psychological exhaustion from uncertainty and the threat of grave harm. During the investigation the accused is left roaming through the fields of limbo where dwelt what Dante called "the praiseless and the blameless dead."[118] When the investigation leads to a tribunal or hearing, the damage to the accused is magnified. The existence of the tribunal gives more legitimacy to the accusations.

Even after a target of an investigation is vindicated, the scars remain. Research indicates that physicians, accused of negligence but vindicated by court trial, are more constrained, cautious, and uncertain with patients. Vindication cannot totally restore the trust between physician and patient that is essential. The physician knows it might happen again.[119] Even after an investigation results in vindication, the same is true of targeted professors in their relationships with colleagues and students.

Second, an internal or external investigation imposes a substantial drain on the target's time, energy, and financial resources. Once an investigation is initiated, the accused can no longer choose to be left alone. He or she must respond or suffer the risk of having the charges taken as admitted with the threat of sanctions ranging from grave damage to professional reputation at a minimum, to possible suspension, expulsion, or termination. A competent response to an investigation of accusations of bigotry requires both substantial time and energy to accumulate and review evidence and draft responses, and financial resources. Appearing before a tribunal is physically and emotionally exhausting.

The financial costs of an investigation include retention of counsel. In any investigation involving serious charges with potentially devastating consequences, the accused should not appear *pro se*. The adage that "a lawyer who represents himself has a fool for a client" is the product of years of experience by seasoned litigators.[120] Disciplinary matters present the model situation where a person should not represent him or herself. Emotional responses to charges of professional misconduct seem to be the norm; there is so much at stake that the accused *pro se* cannot help but lose objectivity. The danger is especially great during the critical investigatory stages, where credibility judgments are made and facts are initially found.[121] An internal tribunal with ambiguous rules on discovery, evidence, cross examination, and other procedures demands exceptionally competent counsel.

An external investigation occurring when competent academic inquiry or speech of a student or a professor is subject to an adjudicative tribunal outside the university is even more chilling than an internal investigation. In adjudicative proceedings outside the university, the accused is forced to respond in an even more formal and alien procedural setting and must have counsel. The possible consequences include money damages as well as harm to reputation and employment. External adjudicative tribunals grind the accused emotionally and financially. As Judge Learned Hand stated, "[A]s a litigant I should dread a lawsuit beyond almost anything else short of sickness and death."[122]

Investigations of competent faculty or student inquiry or speech based upon public accusations of bigotry are occurring. For example, Al Gini, a professor who won three teacher-of-the-year awards at Loyola University in Chicago, was branded a racist after he told a class that the term "nigger" is no longer socially acceptable. He was questioned by four university offices and the U.S. Department of Education Civil Rights Office. Gini was cleared following an eight month investigation.[123] Fifty demonstrators at Berkeley marched into anthropology professor Vincent Sarich's class to disrupt it after he expressed his opinion in the alumni magazine that the university's affirmative action program discriminated against Asian and white applicants. Responding to the demonstrators' list of demands, the anthropology department formed two committees to investigate the charges: one as a forum for student complaints about Sarich, and the second to examine Sarich's published lecture notes.[124]

Professor Michael Levin at City University of New York (CCNY) published controversial ideas about race. There was no evidence either that Professor Levin misbehaved in the classroom or that Levin's writings were harmful to students inside the classroom.[125] The university did not question the professional competence of the published ideas. Nevertheless, CCNY President Bernard Harleston created a seven-member faculty committee to investigate whether Professor Levin had engaged in conduct unbecoming a member of the faculty or some other form of misconduct.[126] The court found that the threat of disciplinary charges implicit in the investigation did have a chilling effect on Professor Levin's First Amendment rights.[127]

Because the fundamentalist academic left believes that standards of academic quality and merit-based performance evaluations are masks for oppression and bigotry, a faculty member's public support for academic quality can lead to both vilification and investigation. Judith Kleinfeld, professor in the education department at the University of Alaska-Fairbanks, devoted twenty-three years of her academic career to the improvement of educational opportunities for Native American students. In September, 1991, after a speech on Native American education, she responded to a question from the audience stating that university professors were under "equity pressure" to graduate Native American students who were sometimes inadequately prepared for teaching careers. She spoke in opposition to simply passing some students through the system. Native American leaders denounced Kleinfeld as racist and demanded that the university discipline her. Kleinfeld became the object of public protests on the campus. The administration transferred her out of the education department; she now teaches psychology courses. After receiving a complaint about Kleinfeld's September, 1991 speech, the U.S. Department of Education's Office of Civil Rights (OCR) initiated an investigation of Kleinfeld for failure to comply with Title VI of the Civil Rights Act of 1964. In the course of a four-month investigation OCR invited Kleinfeld's colleagues to submit examples of her racist thought or speech. OCR also reviewed her writings and research. Ultimately, OCR ruled that Kleinfeld's remarks had not violated the rights of students and had simply been her views about practices that she believed should be reviewed.[128]

The recent wave of campus anti-hate speech policies and vague harassment and discrimination policies raise the specter of further investigations against competent student and faculty inquiry and speech. The number of institutions of higher education that investigate and punish speech pursuant either to specific codes or as part of their overall rules of conduct is a matter of some debate. Nat Hentoff estimates that over 300 universities and colleges investigate speech in this manner.[129] A recent study gives more accurate data on these developments. In 1993–94, the Freedom Forum First Amendment Center at Vanderbilt University surveyed the 533 public colleges and universities that offer at least a bachelor's degree. Student handbooks or other materials were received from 384 schools.[130] Slightly more than 60 percent of the schools surveyed (231) prohibited harassment, which implicitly and often explicitly includes verbal harassment. Rules in this category banned all verbal abuse or verbal harassment and made no content distinctions.[131] If a similar proportion of the 149 schools that did not respond have similar rules, approximately 320 public colleges and universities would have rules banning verbal abuse and harassment. If the same proportion were true for the 1,269 private colleges and universities offering at least a bachelor's degree,[132] approximately 1,081 public and private universities would have rules forbidding verbal abuse and harassment.

Under these broad harassment and discrimination policies, complaints against pure speech will trigger an investigation. To enforce these codes and policies, the universities have created a bureaucracy to investigate and prosecute accusations against heretical speech. The combination of the speech codes and vague harassment and discrimination policies and a bureaucracy to enforce them threatens the freedom of academic inquiry and speech on major issues of the day for two reasons. First, the area of proscribed speech is not clearly defined. An accusation under the codes or policies may occur simply because an oppressed person is offended by written or spoken comment. When professors must guess at what conduct threatens serious sanctions, faculty will necessarily steer far wider of the prohibited zone. Any anti-hate speech rule inescapably entails some elastic terms, due to the inherent imprecision of key words and concepts common to all such rules. For example, the rules commonly employ one or more of the following terms: "demeaning," "disparaging," "harassing," "insulting," "intimidating," and "stigmatizing."[133] The reach of such vague terms is anything but clear, and it is inevitable that competent academic inquiry and speech will suffer accusations and investigations under these policies.[134]

The second reason that these speech policies threaten freedom of academic inquiry and speech is that once an accusation of bigotry is made, the bureaucracy goes forward and the accused is also subjected to an investigation and often a tribunal. Many of these university bureaucracies appear to be influenced by fundamentalist academic left ideology.[135] The tribunals often do not observe procedures of fundamental due process fairness. The accused may not have the right to face and question the accuser. There may be short notice of the charges and tribunal, and the investigation and tribunal proceedings are secret.[136] The tribunals often do not consist solely of peers. Ironically, the accused's attempts to let sunshine into the process may subject the accused to further charges of retaliation.[137] Since many students and faculty wish to avoid the embarrassment and toll of an accusation of bigotry, *and* an investigation, *and* a tribunal, they will steer wide through self-censorship, and competent academic discourse will suffer.[138] The threat of investigation and tribunal by zealous prosecutors under vague standards creates a vast penumbra of proscribed speech on major issues of the day.

Former Yale President Benno Schmidt points out that these speech policies empower groups of faculty and students with roving commissions to punish expression they consider offensive. Indeed, at Mankato State University the idea of a roving commission was literally true; members of the Women's Studies Department deployed a group of student informants to monitor sexist, racist, or homophobic language in classroom discussion.[139] Schmidt points out that speech policies enforced by faculty and students unleash a vague and unpredictable engine of suppression. Vague formulas, even in the hands of disciplined judges, are a disaster for free expression. "What can we expect of such formulations in the hands of students and faculty, however well-meaning?"[140]

These speech codes and harassment and discrimination policies have been used to suppress heretical views. In striking down the University of Michigan's speech code, the federal court found that the university had failed to consider the impact of a formal complaint, investigation, and possible hearing on speech protected by the First Amendment. The court cited several instances where the university applied the policy forcing a student through an investigation and hearing for allegedly harassing statements made in the course of academic discussion or research. For example, in December of 1988 a graduate student in social work was charged with harassment based on sexual orientation for classroom comments that he believed homosexuality was a disease and that he intended to develop a counseling plan for changing gay clients to straight. Following an investigation, the speech policy administrator found probable cause for a formal hearing. While the formal hearing panel unanimously found the student not guilty of harassment based on sexual orientation, the court saw a First Amendment problem in subjecting protected speech to an investigation and tribunal.[141]

The speech subject to accusation and investigation under these speech policies ranged from academic and journalistic comment to rude and offensive slurs. The universities greatly underestimated both the difficulty of administration of speech policies and the opportunity they create for investigation to suppress and chill competent speech. Administrators and faculty forgot that the most successful tactic of McCarthyism was the creation of a formal apparatus to subject academic speech to accusations of moral turpitude, investigations, and tribunals. A good example of the problem of overbreadth of speech codes and the use of investigation to suppress dissent and enforce fundamentalist ideology occurred recently at the University of Pennsylvania. George Pavlik, a student columnist for the college paper, wrote articles criticizing civil rights legislation, Martin Luther King Day (because Dr. King was an alleged plagiarist), and the multicultural attack on Eurocentric culture. In March of 1993, a judicial inquiry officer informed Pavlik that thirty-one charges of racial harassment had been filed against him and were under investigation. When Pavlik asked for a copy of the exact charges, the judicial inquiry officer responded, "You need to ask?" The officer offered to dismiss the charges if Pavlik were to meet with thirty-one of his accusers for a "discussion." Pavlik rejected the settlement. Eventually Pavlik's faculty adviser convinced the president and the judicial inquiry office to dismiss the charges.[142]

These policies are also used to suppress heretical speech by professors. In 1994 the American Association of University Professors heard from about three professors per week who believed they had been unfairly accused of sex harassment.[143] Ann Franke, counsel for the AAUP, observes that universities have seen a sharp increase in the number of sexual harassment charges that focus on the content of classroom lectures or reading material. Sexual issues are becoming more difficult to discuss in the classroom, she believes. "The dividing line between what is sexual harassment and legitimate academic discourse is not well-established right now...and the concern is that a kind of self-censorship takes place and gets in the way of legitimate subjects of academic inquiry."[144] If these standards are allowed to stand, she warns, "Lectures will need to be so bland so that no one has a negative reaction to them."[145] The AAUP condemns sexual harassment, adds AAUP Associate General Secretary Jordan Kurland, but, "[o]ver the past two years, sexual harassment has been singled out as a very special sort of offense that requires a different kind of due process. We've always been opposed to that." On some campuses, the officials investigating these complaints act as "judge, jury and coach."[146]

The institutionalized apparatus of prosecutors not only investigates complaints and empanels tribunals, but may also monitor classroom speech. For example, in fall semester, 1993, the Office of Equal Opportunity and Affirmative Action and the Women's Center at the University of Minnesota created a program of Classroom Climate Advisors. If a student feels uncomfortable about a race or gender classroom- or course-related issue, the student can request the appointment of a classroom climate advisor who will help both to develop a strategy to deal with the problem and to implement it. The advisor will also accompany the student to see the instructor. If this is unsuccessful, the student can file a formal complaint.[147]

The threat of investigation and tribunal is chilling. The creation of an institutionalized apparatus of zealous prosecutors within the university itself to monitor speech, to conduct investigations of speech under vague standards, and to support tribunals sends an unmistakable and threatening message to faculty and students: Steer clear of the possibility of offending any oppressed person or group or risk accusation, investigation, and tribunal.

Another variation on the same theme is the threat of investigation by professional organizations. For example, the American Historical Association has adopted a Statement on Standards of Professional Conduct that defines sexual harassment to "include all behavior that prevents or impairs an individual's full enjoyment of educational or workplace rights, benefits, environment or opportunities, such as generalized sexist remarks or behavior."[148] The Executive Director is authorized to investigate complaints by requesting the accused to respond in writing within ninety days. The written record is then reviewed by members of the Professional Division, which may make findings and recommend public disclosure of the individual case.[149]

In his 1994 book, *Hate Speech: The History of an American Controversy,* University of Nebraska professor Samuel Walker provides the first comprehensive account of the history of hate speech controversies and the punishment of offensive speech in the United States. He finds that, "the proliferation of restrictive campus speech codes was wholly unprecedented: never had there been such strong support for punishing offensive speech."[150] With support of a well organized set of campus advocates, the campus speech code movement has been the most successful effort in American history to restrict offensive speech.[151] The Education Department's March, 1994 guidance on racial harassment for its civil rights investigators further facilitates the investigation of speech under vague standards by a prosecutorial bureaucracy. The guidance "defines 'racial harassment' to include creation of a 'racially hostile environment' through any 'verbal statements' that are 'sufficiently severe that [they] would have adversely affected the enjoyment of some aspect of the [institution's] educational program by a reasonable person, of the same age and race as the victim.'"[152]

Investigations of "diversity" policies and "diversity" perceptions by accrediting agencies also may suppress competent student and faculty academic inquiry and speech. Any possible threat to accreditation will trigger substantial faculty and student fear because unaccredited schools lose government funds, resulting in a strong tendency to concede whatever is necessary to accommodate the accrediting agency.

For example, Middle States Association of Colleges and Schools adopted diversity standards in 1988. Under the standards, review teams evaluate both the "diversity" content of the college's curriculum and the college's recruitment and retention of minority students, faculty, and trustees. In submissions to the Department of Education, Middle States stated that the diversity issue was discussed in 221 accrediting cases. In one case, Baruch College of the City University of New York, Middle States delayed accreditation because of a lack of minority faculty members; and in another, Westminster Theological Seminary, Middle States held up accreditation because of the absence of women on the governing board. An Education Department report said that of twenty cases examined by the Department, Middle States diversity standards were causing problems and prompting the use of quotas in seven. An Education Department advisory committee member said that in response to Middle States diversity standards, it had become part of university administrative culture to force professors to adopt various policies or change their courses to promote diversity.[153] Under pressure by the Department of Education, Middle States voted in late 1991 that the diversity standards would not be a mandatory condition of institutional accreditation.[154]

Threats to employment. Former Johns Hopkins professor Fritz Machlup observed over twenty-five years ago that there are many ways of intimidating a scholar other than termination of employment. Among these are threats to reasonable teaching and committee assignments, access to research funds and materials, promotions, salary increases, and reasonable working conditions. Intimidation also occurs through harassment and vilification and hostile investigations that are expensive of money, time, and emotional and physical energy.[155] In addition, threats to initial appointment at any faculty, opportunities for prestigious public service, or appointments at other faculties are other means of intimidating a scholar.

Many of these threats to employment may follow from public accusations of bigotry directed against competent academic inquiry and speech. Such accusations damage a faculty member's reputation, and a scarred reputation has a negative impact on many academic employment decisions. Investigations and tribunals compound the reputational damage and the negative impacts.

For example, threats to teaching assignments and to research funds are occurring. Harvard professor Harvey Mansfield describes "the plight of conservative or nonfeminist faculty members [in the humanities] whose courses are not accepted, who get 'the short end of the stick' on assignments, and who are intellectually 'under siege' among their colleagues. Faculty lives have been made miserable, and as a result, some have taken early retirement."[156]

Public accusations of bigotry can clearly affect a professor's grants. The Pioneer Fund supports the study of genetic, environmental, and demographic influences on conformity, intelligence, altruism (and other traits), and their effects on human populations. Some of the research involves heredity, some race, but little concerns both. The fund has supported projects such as Professor Thomas Bouchard's major study of identical twins at the University of Minnesota. The fund also supported education Professor Linda Gottfredson at the University of Delaware in her research on the implications of ability differences for educational and employment policy. The research in part investigates whether variations in the distribution of aptitudes can explain some differences in educational and vocational achievement among racial or ethnic groups. The grant flowed through the university.

In 1990 fundamentalist faculty members questioned the propriety of the University's ongoing relationship with the Pioneer Fund in light of the University's stated commitment to diversity. One faculty member alleged that the Pioneer Fund was "an organization with a long history of supporting racism, anti-semitism, and other discriminatory practices." After an investigation, a faculty committee found that a preponderant portion of the activities supported by the Fund either seek to demonstrate or start from the assumption that there are fundamental heredity differences among people of different racial and cultural backgrounds. This was found to be incompatible with the University's goal of diversity. The university decided that it could not accept funding from the Fund to support Professor Gottfredson's research. An arbitrator found that the university violated Gottfredson's contractual rights of full academic freedom in research and the publication of results. Public perceptions do not overcome this right.[157] A different faculty committee found that Professor Gottfredson was not recommended for promotion on ideological grounds, specifically, her disagreement with the university's policy on affirmative action.[158]

Research scholar and former legal aid lawyer David Wasserman at the University of Maryland's Institute for Philosophy and Public Policy was not so fortunate. On May 1, 1993, after full review by a peer review panel, the National Institutes of Health approved a $78,000 grant to fund a conference entitled "Genetic Factors in Crime: Findings, Uses, and Implications." The conference was designed to subject research on genetics and crime to close scrutiny, and included some of the foremost critics of that research, as well as leading researchers.

Black and mental-health activists attacked the conference for allegedly endorsing genetic explanations of crime and lending support to a "racial program of social control." The National Institutes of Health responded by freezing and then declining to release the grant money. The activists celebrated the cancellation and said that many similar research initiatives by the federal government still need to be halted.[159]

A scarred reputation could also have a negative impact on salary increases and promotions within an institution. The administration may go so far as to reprimand a professor, causing further damage to opportunities for promotions and salary increases. For example, during an alumni day panel on diversity and pluralism at Harvard Divinity School in June of 1990, Professor Jon Levenson argued that diversity must include diversity of ideas. "To bring the engagement of ideas about, we shall have to attend to those factors that impede its emergence. These include not only insensitivity, but hypersensitivity, not only a lack of caring, but also a lack of candor, a refusal to speak the truth as one is given to see it because of fear of offending." Levenson, mentioning no names, commented that proponents of Harvard Divinity School's dominant viewpoint were doing all they could to stifle the expression of opposing views. After several faculty protested Levenson's right to express that opinion, the acting dean reprimanded Levenson.[160]

A scarred reputation means more difficulties in securing appointments at other faculties or prestigious public service and speaking opportunities.[161] For example, University of Wisconsin art history professor Richard Long was accused by two white male graduate students of being racist, sexist, and homophobic. He was summoned before a faculty investigating committee, but no formal charges were ever made. The accusation and the appearance of an investigation stood for four months until the matter was dropped. "'Rumors circulated for six months, and I never had my day in court,' said Long, who feels that his opportunities for grants and appointments are now dead."[162]

Finally, the social ostracism that follows accusations of bigotry poses a more subtle but serious threat to reasonable working conditions that both support and provide opportunity for professional growth. Ostracism seriously reduces opportunities for collegial interaction necessary for professional growth. Such ostracism is particularly damaging to the professional advancement of untenured faculty and candidates seeking appointment.

In a variation of the ostracism theme, faculty and student zealots may seek to encourage students not to register for courses taught by the accused. Low student enrollments make the accused vulnerable to adverse employment consequences. At San Francisco State University, Robert C. Smith, a distinguished African-American scholar, began the fall 1990 semester teaching "Black Politics" with an enrollment of forty-five students, thirty-five of whom were African-American. Some students, claiming Professor Smith's course in the political science department was an attack on the Black Studies Department, called Smith a racist. They disrupted the class and attempted to get students to drop the class. Several faculty members in Ethnic Studies supported the boycott. At the end of the semester, only five students remained in the class.[163] At Ohio State College of Law several students protested Professor Louis Jacobs's selection of an evidence text in the spring of 1992. The text was allegedly sexist because one case file involves the rape of a woman. The course was elective and the students organized a boycott.[164]

A more formal variation on the same theme is administrative action to deter students from enrolling in the courses of the accused. Professor Michael

Levin published controversial views about race. Even though the CCNY administration acknowledged that Professor Michael Levin's teaching was highly competent, professional, and fair to all students, the administration in the fall of 1988 requested Professor Levin to withdraw from teaching a required introductory course in mid-semester because of fear of demonstrations and fear that some students might feel uncomfortable being taught by a professor holding controversial views on diversity issues.[165] For the latter reason, in the spring, 1990 and fall, 1990 semesters, the administration created shadow sections for Professor Levin's classes, and wrote to all students registered in Professor Levin's classes stating that Professor Levin had "expressed controversial views" and informing them of the availability of a shadow section to be taught by another instructor. Enrollment in Professor Levin's classes fell significantly.[166] The trial court found that this pressure on students to abandon Professor Levin's classes injured Professor Levin in his standing and tenure as a member of the faculty in order to suppress his expression of ideas.[167]

Another variation on the same theme occurs when faculty zealots seek to have the accused removed from responsibilities for faculty governance. Elizabeth Fox-Genovese, Eleanore Raoul Professor of the Humanities at Emory University, served as director of Emory's Women's Studies Program from 1986–1992. She insisted that the program be ideologically open.[168] As the graduate program in women's studies grew and gained national visibility, a group of faculty and graduate students with a much more radical view of women's studies organized to take control of the women's studies program.[169] Beginning in 1990, they made a series of complaints against Professor Fox-Genovese to the dean of the Institute of Liberal Arts, including an accusation that Fox-Genovese interfered with teaching when she insisted that teaching assistants in the department's 101 course work with the instructor of record to prepare a common exam and grading standard. Other complaints dealt with organization of the department and power issues. Without giving notice of the specific complaints to Fox-Genovese, the dean took the position that he had to respond to the organizational complaints of those who had a political agenda.[170] Feeling betrayed by the administration and without support for an ideologically open program, Fox-Genovese resigned her position in women's studies and transferred to teach in the history department.[171] Subsequently, the former associate director of the women's studies program sued Fox-Genovese for sexual harassment and sex discrimination, seeking two million dollars in damages.[172]

The cumulative effect of public accusations of bigotry, investigations, ostracism, and threats to employment may be sufficient to force a tenured professor out of his or her department. For example, Professor Julius Lester was purged from the Afro-American Studies Department at the University of Massachusetts at Amhearst when he wrote critically of the anti-Semitic remarks of black novelist James Baldwin. All fifteen of Lester's colleagues vilified him and his work as having "a vicious attitude towards blacks and black organizations." They collaborated on a report demanding that Lester leave the department. Lester was forced to transfer to the Judaic and Near Eastern Studies Department.[173] Professors Cynthia Griffin Wolff at MIT, Judith Kleinfeld at the University of Alaska-Fairbanks, and Elizabeth Fox-Genovese at Emory University were also forced to transfer to new departments or programs. In an extended interview study of faculty in Women's Studies Programs, Professors Daphne Patai and Noretta Koertge encountered three tenured women's studies faculty members who had resigned from their programs and transferred to traditional departments because of long-term hostility and antagonism toward dissent. A number of others had quietly withdrawn from activity within the program.[174] Professor Alan Gribben was forced out of the University of Texas and took a position at Auburn University.[175] Professor Allan Mandelstamm at Virginia Tech resigned his tenured position after repeated investigations.[176] Harvard professor Harvey Mansfield reports instances of early retirements because of coercive tactics.[177]

While there have been investigations and discipline under harassment and discrimination codes and policies, there appear to be no instances where universities have instituted formal proceedings under a tenure code to penalize a tenured professor for competent academic inquiry or speech that opposes fundamentalist academic left ideology. This may be a difference without a distinction since findings and recommendations from a proceeding under a harassment or discrimination policy preempt tenure code protections. For example, University of New Hampshire English professor Donald Silva, a thirty-year veteran teacher, was severely disciplined for classroom speech alleged to have violated a harassment policy. When students in a spring semester, 1992 technical writing course were having trouble understanding the concept of focus in their writing, Silva explained, "Focus is like sex. You seek a target. You zero in on your subject. You move from side to side. You close in on the subject. You bracket the subject and center on it. Focus connects experience and language. You and the subject become one." A few days later Silva gave an example of a simile that he originally saw twenty years earlier in a brochure on belly dancing. "Belly dancing," he said, "is like Jello on a plate with a vibrator under the plate."

Several women students complained about these classroom comments. The university's Sexual Harassment and Rape Prevention Program conducted an investigation. The director of Silva's school created shadow sections so that any of Silva's students who wished to do so could transfer out, and later formally reprimanded Silva, finding that his sexual remarks had "created an intimidating, hostile, and offensive academic environment." The director's proposed punishment was that Silva make a public apology, attend weekly counseling with a psychotherapist, and reimburse the university $2,000 to cover the cost of setting up an alternative section of his course to accommodate students who could no longer study with him. Silva rejected this offer of settlement because even if his remarks did not reflect good judgment, they had not created an "offensive learning environment" and should have been protected by academic freedom.

Silva appeared at a formal hearing in early 1993, before a panel of two students, two faculty, and a staff person, all chosen and trained by the university. The panel found Silva's comments and his behavior to be offensive, intimidating, and contributing to a hostile academic environment. A few weeks later, an appeals panel, consisting of three faculty and two students selected and trained by the university, also found that Silva had created a hostile and intimidating environment. The administration adopted the recommendation of the appeals panel that Silva be suspended without pay for one year and that as a condition of returning to work, he undergo therapy at his own expense with a counselor selected by the university.[178]

In October, 1993 Silva brought a lawsuit against the university claiming violation of his First Amendment rights. In September of 1994, the federal court found that Silva's classroom statements "advanced his valid educational objective" and "were made in a professionally appropriate manner as part of a college class lecture." The judge further found that the application of the university's sexual harassment policy to Silva's classroom statements violated the First Amendment. The judge ordered the university to reinstate Silva pending a determination on the merits of his constitutional claims.[179] An AAUP investigating committee found that the University of New Hampshire had effectively placed Silva on indefinite suspension since he could not return until a university-selected counselor certified that Silva was "ready to return to the classroom." The committee found that this was tantamount to a dismissal. The committee further determined that the university had engaged in "numerous serious departures from standards of academic due process" in Silva's case.[180] In December, 1994, the university settled the lawsuit by reinstating Silva, agreeing to pay him $170,000 in legal fees and $60,000 in back pay, and removing all references to allegations of sexual harassment from his file.[181]

Untenured professors, serving without the protection of academic due process, are more vulnerable. For example, Frederick Spiegel, an emeritus professor at the University of Missouri, Columbia, made a critical remark about an opinion by Justice Thurgood Marshall. An African-American student demanded to know why the professor did not, in the same breath, criticize white justices who had issued opinions unfavorable (in the student's perception) to civil rights? After class Spiegel expressed his opinion that racism is not an exclusively white phenomenon, and that "if the minority/majority roles were reversed, it is quite possible that blacks might treat whites just as badly." The student filed a formal complaint with the vice-provost for minority affairs who, without having heard Professor Spiegel's side of the incident, notified Professor Spiegel that his services would no longer be required.[182]

Another example of the vulnerability of the untenured occurred at Dallas Baptist University. Assistant professor of Sociology David Ayers was fired because of an article titled "The Inevitability of Failure: The Assumptions and Implementations of Modern Feminism," published in 1990. The article made him a target of coercive tactics and pretextual accusations. In 1991–92 the administration scheduled him to speak on the article at a faculty colloquium. Feminists in the faculty urged the administration to cancel the colloquium. They organized a boycott of Ayers's speech. Students told Ayers that other faculty were attacking him by name in their classrooms. Subsequently, Ayers distributed to his class his article and a copy of a colleague's rebuttal paper distributed at a second faculty colloquium. Ayers's class was "The Study of the Family." The rebuttal paper accused Ayers of intellectual dishonesty and abuse of evidence. Ayers joked that the rebuttal paper was the "razor-sharp edge of the assassin's sword."

The administration charged Ayers with unauthorized distribution of a colleague's paper, discussion of the subject matter of faculty colloquia during class time, and making harsh references in class about a colleague. The administration formed an ad hoc committee to investigate the charges. The dean of the College of Humanities and Social Sciences, John Jeffrey, wrote to all deans at Dallas Baptist, pointing out that the ad hoc committee and its investigation were contrary to the procedures called for in the faculty handbook. The vice-president for academic affairs canceled the committee and ordered Dean Jeffrey to investigate the charges against Ayers. The vice-president wrote, "As far as the outcome of this inquiry is concerned, I believe an apology...from Professor Ayers is in order." Dean Jeffrey responded in a memorandum to all deans and refused to investigate charges which, even if true, would not represent any perceivable wrongdoing in light of the faculty handbook and AAUP guidelines.

The administration delivered notices of termination to Ayers and Jeffrey the next week. They were administratively suspended in the 1991–92 academic year and paid for the remainder of their three-year contracts. They were given one day to vacate their offices.[183]

After his dismissal, Ayers applied for a position at another Southern Baptist school, Mississippi College. The interviews went well, and the school's dean told Ayers he was the best qualified candidate for the job. After a feminist in the sociology department at Mississippi College objected to Ayers's views on feminism, the chair of the sociology department told Ayers that the department couldn't possibly hire him.[184]

Assessment of the full extent to which threats to employment are occurring in this wave of zealotry is difficult because many adverse employment decisions like rejection of application for employment, the nonrenewal of contracts for untenured faculty, or sanctions under a speech or harassment policy are done quietly or are done ostensibly for other reasons. City University of

New York professor Louis Menand writes that for some professors merely the absence of a political intention or a multicultural focus in another professor's work constitutes *prima facie* disqualification for professional advancement.[185] It is clear from the evidence available that threats to employment are occurring. A survey of the most likely targets, professors who are publicly dissenting from any of the tenets of fundamentalist ideology and professors to the right of center in the humanities and social sciences, would clarify the severity of threats to employment.

Disruption of speeches, classes, and administrative functions. The most direct method of suppressing competent academic inquiry and speech with which zealots disagree is to prevent it from occurring through disruption. Such incidents have occurred when heretics attempt to speak on campus. For example, when Jeanne Kirkpatrick, former United Nations Ambassador in the Reagan Administration, has attempted to present her views of politics and foreign affairs on campuses—whether Berkeley, or the University of Minnesota, or elsewhere—she has been shouted off the podium.[186]

The threat of disruption exists whenever a speaker delivers a message unpopular to zealots. For example, in 1989 Professor Alan Dershowitz at Harvard was shouted down by the members of the Black Law Students Association when he asked C. Vernon Mason, an activist lawyer who defended fraudulent rape victim Tawana Brawley, for some proof, any proof, of the accusations that Mr. Mason made on her behalf.[187] On March 14, 1991, 200 students at the State University of New York at Binghamton organized a protest based on a rumor that a member of the Ku Klux Klan was speaking at a National Association of Scholars meeting. They verbally abused and menaced Professor Richard Hofferbert, speaking to the meeting on "Letters from Berlin 1990: Fall of the Wall." Some participants brandished sticks. One, holding a cane, paced behind the speaker as he attempted to give his lecture. A student threw one of the speaker's framed photographs across the room, blew his nose into a tissue and conspicuously stuck the tissue into the speaker's drinking glass, and threw a wad of gum at one of the lecturer's colleagues. A student admitting that he attended the lecture to hear the speech was knocked to the ground.[188] On October 28, 1991, campus Republicans and other organizations staged a pro-America rally at the University of Wisconsin in Milwaukee. They invited Mark Belling, a local conservative talk show host, as one of the speakers. Protesters armed with whistles drowned out the speakers. They also threw candles and coins, hitting some of the speakers. Belling left before being called to the podium.[189]

Another direct method of suppressing competent speech is to disrupt classes of professors with whom zealots disagree. For example, in April, 1987, a group of students demonstrated loudly outside Professor Levin's class, disrupting the class, blocking entry and exit, pushing security personnel, and making threats of harm. In March of 1989, about twenty students burst into Professor

Levin's class, chanting and shouting, blocking exits, and causing the class not to continue. In March of 1990, thirty-five students entered Professor Levin's classroom, chanting and shouting and breaking up the class.[190]

Students may suffer similar treatment for voicing an unpopular view. Professor Nadine Strossen at New York University relates an incident in which a male in one of her classes suggested that the father of an unborn child should have equal say with the mother in the question of abortion. "He was immediately descended upon by students who were screaming," Strossen says. "Any student in that class would immediately say, 'forget it, I would never express that position.'"[191]

In addition to the disruption of speeches and classes, zealots may disrupt administrative functions by using blockades and forced occupations of buildings to suppress academic speech or decisions with which they disagree. For example, in the spring of 1987, minority students and their supporters occupied the office of Stanford University President Donald Kennedy to protest that the required course in Western Civilization was too Eurocentric.[192] In the fall of 1990, fifteen students occupied the dean's office at the University of California at Berkeley School of Law for four hours and refused to leave. They demanded that the next five faculty hires must be females, minorities, gays, disabled persons, or scholars in critical legal studies.[193] In the spring of 1991, about twenty-four minority students at the University of Vermont barricaded themselves in the president's office for four days after the president declined to recommit the administration to a 1988 agreement outlining minority hiring and recruitment goals for the university. The 1988 agreement was negotiated by the preceding president after a similar student occupation in 1988. The students also picketed the home of the chairperson of the Board of Trustees.[194]

In May of 1992, 250 students occupied the chancellor's office at the University of Massachusetts-Amhearst to protest minority hiring issues. Some 200 protesters also broke into the offices of the campus newspaper, trashing the office, smashing a window, damaging equipment and personal property, and threatening staff members to demand more minority control of the paper.[195] A few days later, to protest lack of progress in meeting demands, forty demonstrators again vandalized the newspaper office, shoving staff members to the floor and locking two staff members in a closet.[196] In the spring of 1993, one hundred students forced the closing of the administrative offices at Pomona College for two days to demand more minority hiring.[197] In November of 1993, about seventy Cornell University students occupied the administration building for four days to protest the defacement of part of an outdoor art exhibit by Hispanic artists. Although the graffiti did not contain racial slurs, the protesters charged that they were racially motivated and that the university president had not denounced the defacement.[198] In April of 1994, about seventy-five students from the "Multi-Ethnic Empowerment Initiative" at Bates College occupied the admissions office for about eight hours, calling for the recruitment of more minority students.[199]

Newer strategies include vandalism, arson, or the threat of fire to cause disruption. Demanding the elevation of the Chicano Studies program to become a department in the spring of 1993, hundreds of Hispanic students smashed large plate glass windows and damaged furniture to occupy the faculty center at UCLA. They did between $35,000–$50,000 of damage to the building.[200] In the fall of 1993, an underground student group at Cornell University called Tupak Amaru III threatened violence until Cornell hired more Hispanic professors. The group vandalized two campus buildings in the spring of 1993 and set a fire in a dormitory mail room in September of 1993 that police found to be arson.[201]

Another new tactic to silence heretical speech is the theft and destruction of copies of student newspapers that run stories critical of fundamentalist ideology. This is book burning. For example, on November 1, 1993, thieves took 10,000 copies of a student newspaper at the University of Maryland, replacing them with notes accusing the paper of being racist. Campus criticism centered on three items: the newspaper's coverage of the university's decision to suspend a black fraternity for five years after the filing of criminal charges against twenty-four members alleging severe hazing of pledges; a fashion supplement published October 20 in which critics alleged all eight models were white but where the editors claim seven models were white and one black;[202] and mistakes in articles about Frederick Douglass and W. E. B. Dubois. An officer of the Black Student Union commented that "it's nonviolent, and whoever did it got their point across."[203]

Organization and tenacity of zealots in suppressing speech. Zealots in the fundamentalist academic left cut across faculty and student lines. They are willing to do what faculty liberals, centrists, and conservatives almost never have been willing to do—play political hardball within the faculty itself. To suppress the competent speech of dissenters, some extremists are willing to make public accusations of bigotry using manipulative persuasion, to demand investigations, to engage in media campaigns, to threaten employment, and to organize students to disrupt speeches, classes, and administrative operations.[204]

In researching his book *Signs of the Times,* David Lehman heard the same analogy, or variants of it, from so many professors at different universities that it was hard to escape a sense of ubiquity. "As in an inquisition, you are measured by your allegiance—you're found religious or you're burned." The deconstructionists, Lehman writes, have a reputation for being absolutely ruthless behind the scenes in pursuit of their agenda.[205]

The behind-the-scenes community organizing tactics of the fundamentalist academic left bear examination. Two new groups of professors, the Union of Democratic Intellectuals (UDI) and Teachers for a Democratic Culture (TDC), held their first meeting titled, "Culture Wars: Reconstructing Higher

Education," at Hunter College in April, 1992. These groups, numbering 1500 members, formed to defend multiculturalism, radical feminism, and other postmodern scholarly approaches from conservative attacks. Professor Paul Lauter of Trinity College, Connecticut, distributed packets of material to the UDI/TDC organizers' workshop. Many of the items were community organizing materials from the 1960s outlining how to generate publicity and manipulate the press.

The materials also outline how to organize a faculty. The organizer must focus on the most disgruntled faculty, articulate their discontent, and identify the main culprit. The objective is to build the largest coalition possible against the main culprit. Tactics must be directed at this "specific target." Issues must be personalized and polarized around the target. For each target, ask what tactics the target fears most: actions, confrontations, public hearings, strikes, law suits, or picketing. The organization must concentrate all its efforts at the target's weakest point, for example, a conflict of interest charge against a single individual. The materials outline the advantages of selecting rooms for meetings, actions, or demonstrations where the target will perceive that the room is filled with adversaries. The materials also suggest using the "principle of encirclement." Encirclement means the more tactics used against a target at once, the better. For example, if a law suit is in progress, bring in a regulatory agency to investigate while at the same time exposing the target's nonpayment of taxes and picketing the target. If the target can be overloaded, victory is more likely.[206]

The fundamentalist academic left also has the tenacity to subject targets to vilification for extended periods. Professor Ian MacNeil notes that "if political activists are not satisfied, they will continue to hector the accused for an indefinite period, years if necessary."[207] This certainly was also true for Professor Alan Gribben, and Professor Allan Mandelstamm. This long-term hectoring may seem petty, even frivolous, to lay persons; but it does exhaust the strongest of spirits.

The university community is highly vulnerable to any group of faculty that is well organized and is willing to utilize coercive tactics. There seems to be a critical mass of radical faculty in some faculties. A 1989–90 UCLA study of faculty members at 392 colleges and universities found that 6.5–8.2 percent of professors at universities report themselves to be far left.[208] At universities with 500 faculty for example, approximately thirty-five to forty faculty members on the average would be on the far left. Professors on the far left are concentrated in humanities and social science faculties. If only some of these adopt the tactics of zealotry to enforce their ideology, academic freedom is at risk in those faculties.

Results

There is not yet an in-depth survey or interview study of targeted professors at a broad cross section of colleges and universities to explore the tactics and results of this wave of zealotry. Such a survey would focus on the experience of faculty members publicly dissenting from some element of fundamentalist ideology.[209] The limited survey data available indicate that a significant number of faculty members see problems of academic freedom in higher education today. A 1993 survey of historians by the *Journal of American History* found that 20.3 percent of the respondents in the United States cited "political correctness" (in the sense of political constraints on speech or conduct) as a problem.[210] A 1992 survey by the Carnegie Foundation for the Advancement of Teaching found that 19 percent of faculty respondents in the United States disagreed that academic freedom is strongly protected in the United States, 37 percent were either neutral or disagreed that their administration supports academic freedom, and 34 percent disagreed with the statement that, "In this country there are no political or ideological restrictions on what a scholar may publish."[211]

It is clear that instances of suppression of competent academic inquiry and speech are occurring in some liberal arts colleges and in humanities, social science, and law faculties at some universities. At a minimum, there is widespread use of public accusations of bigotry and social ostracism to suppress ideas dissenting from fundamentalist academic left ideology. Investigations and tribunals through an institutionalized structure of speech codes, discrimination, and harassment policies, and the diversity bureaucracy are a major weapon to threaten heretics on many campuses. In some faculties, threats to employment, and disruption of speeches, classes, and administrative functions are utilized as tactics to more effectively suppress dissenting speech.

Do these tactics work? It is very difficult to quantify the suppression of inquiry and speech. As Yale professor C. Vann Woodward has commented, one might more easily inquire into how many public executions it takes to quell resistance in an occupied city. The critical fact is that public accusations of bigotry will generate fear in an academic community. Investigations, tribunals, threats to employment or student standing, and disruption will compound this fear.

Such tactics will have the greatest impact in suppressing the speech of the most vulnerable people in the academic community. The best place to start in assessing results is to ask for whom is the toll from public accusations, public humiliation, and social ostracism the greatest?

Students will fear these tactics and consequences the most. As the Bahls study points out, students fear low grades and the hostility of their professors.[212] These consequences will damage their opportunities for professional advancement. Younger students are also generally at a stage of life where they are more vulnerable to peer and hierarchical pressure and the fear of embarrassment and social ostracism. The experience of Stanford Law School Dean Paul Brest is that students are highly vulnerable to orthodoxy. "[T]he students who suffer the most are not the outspoken ones with strongly held views on the right or left. Rather, they are the majority who do not have set convictions about various controversial issues of morality, politics, and law. College, and even law school, is a time to explore those ideas through discourse."[213]

Candidates for faculty appointment, untenured professors, and administrative staff are also highly vulnerable to tactics of public humiliation and ostracism. Any allegation of bigotry will severely harm chances for appointment or promotion.[214] They know that if any subset of the tenured faculty actively opposes their candidacy or promotion, the chances for professional opportunity and advancement are greatly reduced. They may also be denied the collegial support and interaction necessary for their professional development. An investigation will drain away even more energy from scholarship, teaching, and public service, making the accused's retention vulnerable to pretextual veto. Staff are also without the protection of academic freedom and are highly vulnerable to faculty assault.

Tenured professors are less vulnerable to loss of employment; but all know that public accusations of bigotry will impair the possibility of grants, further academic advancement, salary and benefit determinations, mobility in the profession, and public service opportunities, and may diminish student enrollment in the accused's classes. Everyone in the community knows that an investigation and tribunal carries substantial financial and emotional costs and the risk of adverse employment consequences.

Deans and presidents are also vulnerable to tactics of public accusation of moral turpitude, public humiliation, ostracism, investigations, and disruption. A major part of their job is to foster public confidence in the institution in order to attract students and faculty, place graduates in employment or further education, and raise government and private funds to supplement tuition revenues. Presidents and deans are especially vulnerable to adverse media attention and the public perception created by such attention, regardless of the facts. Public accusations of moral turpitude and adverse media attention threaten their employment security and opportunity for advancement or mobility as an administrator.

The toll of public accusations of bigotry and public humiliation is especially high for any professor who has devoted time and energy to address race and gender issues. It is lacerating to a faculty member's self concept to be charged with the very conduct against which the faculty member has fought.

Ostracism is also most effective against those who fear exclusion from a group with whom they identify and wish to belong. A substantial number of liberal arts, humanities, social sciences, and law faculties seem to be dominated by faculty members holding political views that are left of center. For example, at most law schools, there are hardly any serious orthodox conservative law faculty and at most a few faculty members who are publicly dissenting from any tenet of left-of-center political orthodoxy.[215] Thus, the targets of these public accusations are typically not professors with extreme views or ideologies. On the contrary, as Professor Reynolds Farley of Michigan commented, "Most of us are moderate to liberal Democrats; and the issues we raise are the basic social dilemmas our society faces."[216]

With respect to students, *Village Voice* reporter Nat Hentoff comments that:

> By and large, those most intimidated—not so much by the speech codes themselves but by the Madame Defarge-like spirit behind them—are liberal students and those who can be called politically moderate.

> I've talked to many of them, and they no longer get involved in class discussions where their views would go against the grain of...righteousness. Many, for instance, have questions about certain kinds of affirmative action.... Others have a question about abortion.[217]

The coercive tactics employed by zealots pose the most substantial threat of adverse consequences to the most vulnerable groups in the academic community, students, candidates for academic employment, and untenured professors. These tactics also have posed a significant threat to tenured professors, deans, and presidents.

Given the existence of these adverse consequences, normal human behavior is fear and avoidance of the possibility of such consequences.[218] It does not take too many stories to generate such fear and avoidance of possible controversy. Once such fear is abroad, the mere threat of coercive tactics will provide substantial leverage. It has become commonplace during the late 1980s and early 1990s to hear and read stories where competent academic inquiry and speech result in public accusations of bigotry, investigation, tribunal, threats to employment, and disruption. Every faculty member and administrator knows such stories. It is reasonable that a large proportion of the students also are aware of such stories.[219]

It is clearly not the case that no student or untenured faculty member will publicly dissent from fundamentalist ideology. It clearly is the case that the greater the vulnerability of the group, the greater will be the risks of public dissent for individuals within that group. The greater the risks, the smaller the subset of individuals in that group who will have the courage to take the risk.

For the large majority in the academic community, the most common result of these tactics is self-censorship.[220] Former Yale President Benno Schmidt notes that the greatest danger of these tactics is not just to those punished, but to the vastly greater number of speakers who will steer clear of possible punishment.[221] Many students and faculty have learned to keep their mouths shut to avoid accusations.[222] For example, law professors report an enormous unwillingness of students to argue even hypothetically on the "wrong" side of fundamentalist ideology because of fear of being accused of bigotry.[223]

Professors may adopt extraordinary measures to attempt to foster open debate. For example, Professor Nadine Strossen at N.Y.U. School of Law and President of the ACLU has resorted to allowing students to make their views known on topics like affirmative action through anonymous notes to be read in class.[224]

Some professors take preventive measures or censor their teaching to avoid false accusations and investigations. For example, some professors tape their lectures,[225] or attempt to have witnesses present when dealing with students.[226] Some alter their teaching to use a lecture, rather than class discussion, on controversial subjects.[227] Some drop controversial topics from their courses;[228] and a few stop teaching controversial courses altogether.[229] Similarly, administrators will fear potential disruption from bringing in any speaker who dissents from fundamentalist movement ideology.

The results of these tactics on scholarship are more difficult to assess, although equally worrisome. As Former Harvard President Bok notes,

> Professors are no more courageous than anyone else. If they believe that expressing certain views or investigating certain subjects may expose them to student harassment or cost them a promotion or other advancement in their career, they may well seek other questions to explore. In this way, efforts to intimate or impose orthodoxy can limit the scope of scholarly debate on important issues of race, gender, foreign policy, and other controversial subjects and thus retard the growth of knowledge and understanding.[230]

The tactics of public accusation, social ostracism, investigation, tribunals, threats to employment, and disruption of speeches, classes, and administrative functions have been effective in suppressing competent academic inquiry and speech in some faculties. A number of faculties have been thoroughly politicized by this ideological zealotry, and both students and faculty protect themselves through self-censorship to avoid having a reputation scarred by accusations of bigotry. In combination, the ideology of the fundamentalist academic left and these tactics also may create a general sense of paranoia and cynicism that permeates academic life. The ideological mission to reveal hidden structures of oppression in society has led naturally to a mission to reveal the hidden bigoted motives of colleagues and the hidden conspiracies spawned by these hidden motives. This paranoia destroys the bonds of trust between colleagues and students and teachers that are necessary for robust intellectual life.[231] The notion that it all comes down to power and how to grab a share of it leads to cynicism. The notion of shared high purpose in community becomes more and more elusive, if not impossible to imagine.[232]

The most important consequence of all of this is silence. The threat of accusation and then investigation and tribunal by zealous prosecutors under vague standards creates a vast penumbra of proscribed speech. As many students and dissenting faculty retreat into their own private cocoon, the fundamentalist position goes almost undisputed in some faculties and the university is left empty as a place for real exchange of diverse ideas on the critical issues of the day.[233]

The students, the faculty, and the public pay a severe cost when they do not hear and debate a full range of views in the university.[234] Students and faculty cannot test their beliefs against contradictory forces to discover their worth. Traditional academic skills of accuracy and thoroughness in the collection and use of evidence, reasonable assertion, impartiality in the determination of the weight of the evidence, careful analytical reasoning, and fairness in argument or controversy are lost. These are the basic skills needed in order to disagree on topics involving intense passion. Zealotry builds intolerance and lack of mutual respect.

Students and the public also pay a significant price in terms of the opportunity cost of faculty time and energy devoted to zealotry or the defense against zealotry. Through their tuition, taxes, and contributions, students and the public pay both for the time that faculty zealots commit to coercive tactics, and for the time that accused faculty must commit to defense. This is a tragic waste of resources that should go to teaching and other productive work benefitting the students and the public.

The loss of diversity of opinion and debate also means that the university loses its intellectual integrity and its principal reason for existence in a democratic society.[235] The university in the grip of any partisan political agenda is not a university at all.[236] It cannot fulfill its mission to advance and disseminate knowledge because the normal checking process of a liberal intellectual system is disrupted. The politicization of the university by faculty also invites politicization of the university by external forces, thus undermining several centuries of effort to preserve the university's intellectual autonomy.

Former Yale President Benno Schmidt observed at the 1991 Yale commencement that "the essential academic values that ought to govern the universities are not being vigorously articulated and defended, and the result is a growing public sense that universities have lost their way.... The skepticism and suspicion with which universities are now greeted and treated even by friends of learning exceed anything I can recall."[237]

Faculty and Administrative Response

The Subgroups within the Faculty

This is the first wave of zealotry in the history of higher education in the United States involving populist intimidation from inside the university led principally by faculty. Because a subset of the faculty itself is utilizing tactics of public accusation, ostracism, investigation, tribunals, and threats to employment to suppress competent dissent, faculty response to the zealotry tends to be confused, and faculty public support for the target, muted.

This pattern of faculty response seems typical to former Yale President Benno Schmidt. "On many campuses, perhaps most, there is little resistance to growing pressure to suppress and to punish, rather than to answer, speech" expressing dissenting views that offend someone's sensitivity.[238] University of Minnesota professor Norman Fruman agrees that while many professors are unhappy with what is going on, they will not resist the tactics of zealotry.[239] Harvard professor Harvey Mansfield claims that "it's impossible to underestimate the timidity of professors." Too many are studiously avoiding the hot topics of the day.[240]

In his experience with public accusations of bigotry at Harvard, Professor Ian MacNeil found that a number of faculty and students made private supportive gestures. No professor or administrator at the law school or the university recognized publicly the dangers to academic freedom posed by false accusations of bigotry. "The most common response on American campuses in general, and Harvard University in particular, to those who would destroy academic freedom is, at best, apathy and avoidance, and, at worst, cowering appeasement."[241]

Professor Alan Gribben at Texas found that some colleagues were willing to give private support when he was falsely accused of bigotry; but they were unwilling to offend the activist faction and risk charges of bigotry. The majority went in fear of the zealots, avoiding even the appearance of disagreement.[242] Similarly, when University of Massachusetts professor Daphne Patai was called a racist for her decision not to fund an elective course on indigenous women proposed by two Native American graduate students, "Not one of my colleagues who clearly believed that the charges were absurd (and told me so privately) was willing to say so publicly."[243]

When Professor Henry Bauer at Virginia Tech sent an open letter to his dean and department heads in 1991 explaining why he would not serve on search committees under the new diversity guidelines, several dozen people thanked him privately. A television interviewer told him several professors agreed with his stand, but would not do so publicly. After the publication of his article defending a colleague accused of bigotry, he received a supporting letter from a senior tenured professor who asked that his response be kept confidential.[244]

Free speech advocate Nat Hentoff consistently finds that many faculty are fearful of public dissent on any issue of fundamentalist ideology. For example, a number of University of Michigan faculty would tell him only privately of their objections to the new "Interim Policy on Discriminatory Harassment by Faculty and Staff in the University Environment." This policy was promulgated after the federal district court struck down the Michigan speech code for students. Subject to investigation and disciplinary tribunal is any faculty or staff language that "has the purpose or effect of creating an intimidating, hostile, or offensive environment for academic pursuits, employment, housing, or participation in a University activity." As the president of another college told Hentoff recently, "Courage to speak out in dissent against such proposals is in limited supply these days among professors, including those who are tenured."[245] Hentoff found the same phenomenon at the University of Buffalo.

"At the University of Buffalo Law School, which has a code restricting speech, I could find just one faculty member who was against it. A liberal, he spoke only on condition that I not use his name. He did not want to be categorized as a racist."[246]

An assessment of faculty response to the current zealotry must go beyond rhetoric and to look at what faculty members and students do, not what they say. Columnist Nat Hentoff has consistently found that the lust to interfere in the "wrong" thoughts of others is camouflaged by an unbounded hypocrisy concerning free speech. The censor extols the virtues of free speech while carving out an exception in the name of a higher morality. This is particularly true in the current zealotry. Ideological zealots and faculty allies who are punishing colleagues for their ideas and positions must deny that they are suppressing academic inquiry and speech. Acknowledgment of the use of coercion against others tends to undermine both the moral and political power accruing to status as a victim, and the construct of an ideology based on the dichotomy between oppressors and the oppressed. The denial takes several forms. First, the zealots may claim standing as the "oppressed," and deny any legitimacy to the fears and claims of injustice of "oppressors." As Professor Daphne Patai experienced, "[S]ome memos actually did state that it was absurd for a white, tenured professor to claim she was being unjustly accused. By virtue of having a certain identity (white) and occupying a certain position (tenured), an individual would necessarily be guilty of whatever accusations a woman of color (or an untenured individual) might make against her."[247]

A second form of denial occurs when the concerns of targets are dismissed as unjustified or exaggerated.[248] At Carleton College, professors stopped teaching certain courses because of warnings and threats that the use of certain books would reveal the professor's racism. One of the professors who had canceled a course commented that "we don't have academic freedom here anymore." The response by some colleagues was that no one in the administration was preventing the professor from giving the course, and that if the frightened professor had stood firm, he or she would show the students what academic freedom is.[249] In general, faculty members who desire the quiet life and who seek to shield themselves from controversy may minimize the existence of zealotry and coercion to avoid responsibility.[250] Some commentators and professors pooh-pooh the idea that investigations and tribunals are coercive. Michael Kinsley of *The New Republic* saw no reason for a fuss over the investigation and tribunal that the University of Pennsylvania imposed on the student who called others "water buffalo." Similarly, Harvard professor Alan Dershowitz thought colleagues sounded just like Joe McCarthy when they essentially argued, "What's wrong with an inquiry [of a Harvard Law Review parody]? What's wrong with finding out the facts? What's wrong with issuing some subpoenas? What's wrong with having some hearings?"[251] Administrators in both the University of Michigan and the University of Wisconsin speech code cases denied that the codes had any chilling effect on the discussion of controversial issues or protected speech.[252] A stronger variation of the same theme finds any claim that the fundamentalist academic left is suppressing others' speech to be grossly exaggerated. For example, Duke English professor Cathy Davison wrote in *Academe* that the same half-dozen horror stories are endlessly recycled.[253] These are alleged to be isolated events blown totally out of proportion in the media.[254]

A third form of denial is to go beyond minimization of the threat and to make countercharges that those complaining about coercion are themselves making "false claims" and waging a "campaign of harassment and intimidation."[255] Concern about violations of academic freedom are alleged to be right-wing attacks on new trends in scholarship and pedagogy that have been manufactured by a conspiracy of conservative corporations, institutions, and individuals.[256] A stronger variation of this theme is to deny any coercion and to assert that those raising the issue of coercion are simply masking their hidden motives of bigotry. The American Association of University Professors' "Statement on Political Correctness" determined that criticisms of political correctness are actually based on "an only partly concealed animosity toward equal opportunity" for "women and racial and cultural minorities on campus."[257] The 1993 report of The National Council for Research on Women, *To Reclaim a Legacy of Diversity,* finds that accusations that advocates of change represent a new intolerance or a new McCarthyism are the most visible form of resistance to the civil rights movement and access to diverse populations.[258]

The lack of collegial support for the academic freedom of competent inquiry and speech and for the target personally weighs heavily on the accused. For Harvard professor Stephan Thernstrom, "Being the target of a witch hunt by one's students, with precious few sympathetic and encouraging words from one's colleagues, was...painful."[259] Collegial silence regarding the coercive tactics that totally dominate the life of the accused leads also to feelings of isolation and betrayal. Despair is common.[260] The accused withdraws further because of the absence of public support.

Occasionally, a faculty responds publicly to defend the accused and academic freedom. Subsequent to the invasion of Professor Vincent Sarich's classroom described earlier, the faculty senate at Berkeley made a public statement condemning the disruptive protest: "The attempt to silence opinions by the disruption of a class is a clear violation of the freedom of a teacher to teach and of students to learn."[261] When eight faculty members publicly denounced Professor William Simons at State University of New York-Oneonta for intimidation and coercion of women at a father's rights program where he introduced the speakers, a number of professors, including many in his department, gave him public support. They published supporting letters in the college newspaper demonstrating that the accusations were false.[262]

In those faculties where coercive tactics to suppress heretics are evident, faculty response has clearly not been monolithic. The faculty seems to be divided into a number of groups whose roles with respect to the zealotry differ dramatically.

1. *Zealots.* The group of ideological zealots who engage directly in activities to suppress heretical speech may be small in actual numbers.
2. *Target(s).* In order to suppress dissent, the zealots need to tack the hide of at least one heretic on the wall. Zealots need only a few symbolic examples to generate fear.
3. *Public support.* A small subset of faculty gives public (and private) support to the accused.
4. *Private support.* A small subset of the faculty will make private, but not public, supportive gestures to the accused.
5. *Avoidance and Apathy.* A significant number of faculty desire the quiet life, and do not want to risk vilification and unpopularity. They retreat into a private cocoon, shielding themselves from awareness of what is happening and censoring themselves.
6. *Appeasement.* A significant number of faculty will seek to negotiate and propitiate about almost any controversy including compounded, unsupported accusations of bigotry, investigations, or disruption of classes and speeches. They attempt to appease the zealots and buy peace. All principles are sacrificed to the principle of splitting the difference. Those falsely accused are characterized as "extremists on the other side."
7. *Facilitation.* Some faculty whose ideology and political objectives are advanced by the suppression of competent opposing ideas will not themselves throw bombs, but will actively both facilitate the zealots in doing so, and protect the zealots from any limits on or consequences for the use of coercive tactics.

The most difficult question to answer is why faculty defense for academic freedom is so weak. Why do so few faculty members publicly support the academic freedom of a target? Chapter 9 addresses this question more fully for all periods of zealotry, but some explanatory factors are unique to this current fundamentalism from the radical academic left.

University of Pennsylvania professor Alan Kors explains that the professors on the fundamentalist academic left who have a primal passion are remarkably few, but exercise extraordinary power.

> Then there was this very large group that was intellectually very skeptical of the claims being made on the Left, but who were quite literally bullied by the intensity of other people's convictions. The liberals on American college campuses were the key group and they absolutely caved in. All they wanted to do was to buy peace, to buy calm, or to assuage their own guilt. And they were afraid of not "seeming" pluralistic. Thus, they went along, pushed by the strongest winds out of lack of character, lack of backbone, lack of conviction, and lack of ethics.[263]

Yale professor Stephen Carter concurs that many black professionals mute what they are willing to say publicly because of an "ideology of solidarity;" and "many white intellectuals are likely to follow fashion, to remain silent, and to join in the ostracism...of dissenters."[264]

Professors Kors and Carter put forward an explanation for the failure of many faculty members to protect academic freedom in this wave of zealotry. The principal theme is that while the liberal faculty members who dominate many faculties may disagree privately with the ideological zealotry of the fundamentalist academic left, they remain silent out of an ideology of solidarity. The two premises of this explanation are that liberals adopt an ideology of solidarity with the fundamentalist left and that liberals dominate many faculties. Are these premises true?

The first premise is that liberal faculty members adopt an ideology of solidarity with the fundamentalist academic left that inhibits them from criticizing the fundamentalist left's coercive tactics in suppressing dissent. As a general proposition, the reality of human nature makes an ideology of solidarity with those of similar mind probable. Censorship of opposing views is one of the strongest drives in human nature. We have a natural tendency to interfere with the "wrong" thoughts and speech of others. A major premise of the doctrine of academic freedom is that this natural tendency to censor can be checked by an opposing duty to defend the competent speech of colleagues against zealotry. The historical record suggests that for many academics the natural tendency to censor opposing views prevails over the correlative duty to protect the academic speech of colleagues against zealotry. A faculty bystander's self-interest is served by permitting zealots to harass and intimidate views that the bystander opposes. There is also a strong tendency in human nature to rationalize actions that contradict known duties or principles in order to claim legitimacy for what is clearly a breach of duty. Thus, a typical faculty bystander may comment that the zealot's coercive tactics are for a good cause, and the bystander will not oppose them, even though the bystander does not fully approve of the tactics.

There are three reasons why liberal faculty members may be of similar mind with the causes of the fundamentalist academic left. First, liberal faculty members fall on a spectrum to the left of center politically. The fundamentalist left's espoused end of social justice through the empowerment of the oppressed has historically been a major cause of those to the left of center and has great moral appeal to them. Second, white persons to the left of center tend to have high degrees of guilt about the oppression that some groups in society have suffered. They find it easy to identify with the oppressed's expressions of anger and passion. They thus tend to give legitimacy to expressions of anger even when the expression crosses the line of coercion of others' speech. This guilt also leads to high levels of fear about appearing to be or actually being called reactionary or racist.[265] Third, liberals strongly reject prejudice and bias and endorse a duty of tolerance. Rooted in the virtue of caring deeply about others, the duty to be tolerant has expanded toward an affirmative duty to be sensitive toward the oppressed and, more recently, toward an affirmative duty not to hurt the oppressed with words. This recent shift from a duty to be tolerant toward a duty to be sensitive and a duty not to hurt the oppressed with words contradicts a historic principle of the liberal intellectual system and professional academic freedom—that in the pursuit of knowledge there is nothing wrong with offending others. Indeed almost all current knowledge was at one time considered heretical and greatly insensitive toward others' feelings. Many liberal faculty members have not yet resolved this contradiction.[266] On the other hand, the fundamentalist academic left knows how to take advantage of liberal guilt and liberal fear of hurting the feelings of the oppressed. Paula Goldsmid, former dean at Oberlin College, observed that "there is a great reluctance to say or do anything that goes against the liberal and 'progressive' Oberlin stance. Oberlin's liberal values can be turned to our advantage."[267]

The second premise of Professor Kors's explanation for the failure of many faculty members to protect academic freedom in this wave of zealotry is that liberal professors dominate many faculties. There is considerable evidence supporting the premise that many faculties consist almost entirely of individuals who are to the left of center politically.

A comparison of data from a UCLA survey of faculty members at 392 colleges and universities in 1989-90 with a survey of the general public in 1990 indicates that the political views of faculty members are skewed substantially to the left of the general public.[268] For example, at private universities 56.2 percent of the professors report themselves to be far left or liberal, whereas only 21 percent of the general public hold that political orientation. (See table 2.1.)

The data indicate also that the skew to the left becomes more pronounced at more elite, private universities and at universities offering more advanced study programs. The 1989 Carnegie study of professors' attitudes (see table 2.2) supports this conclusion.[269]

TABLE 2.1

Political Orientation:	Faculty at universities		Faculty at 4-yr colleges		General Public
	Private	Public	Private	Public	
Far Left	8.2%	6.5%	5.3	4.3	2
Liberal	48.0	42.1	37.0	35.7	19
Moderate	30.8	37.9	39.2	42.1	42
Conservative	12.5	13.1	18.3	17.5	28
Far Right	0.5	0.3	0.2	0.4	2

TABLE 2.2

Carnegie Classification	Liberal	Moderately Liberal	Middle-of the-road	Moderately Conservative	Conservative
Research university	34	33	16	14	3
Doctorate university	24	33	15	21	7
Comprehensive	26	33	14	20	7
Liberal Arts	24	35	14	21	6
Two-year	19	29	18	26	9

The UCLA data and the Carnegie data have similar findings. At private universities and at research universities, liberals, outnumbering conservatives by a ratio of approximately 4 to 1, dominate the institution.

Aggregate information at a university level tends to understate the degree to which the left dominates individual faculties. The Carnegie study (see table 2.3) indicates that faculties in the humanities and social sciences tend to be substantially more skewed to the left than faculties in business or engineering.[270] With 70 percent majorities in the humanities and social sciences, the left has commanding domination.

The Carnegie data aggregate information about departments from all institutions of higher education. A reasonable hypothesis is that humanities and social science departments at public universities offering more advanced study and at elite private universities will be more skewed to the left than the Carnegie aggregated data indicate. The data available support this hypothesis.

In the spring of 1987, the Colorado Review of the University of Colorado published a survey of the political affiliation of the faculty. Of 602 professors in the College of Arts and Sciences, less than 7 percent were Republicans. No Republican had been hired in the previous decade. Of the thirty-three departments in the College of Arts and Sciences, only one is chaired by a Republican; eleven departments, including the fifty-seven-member English

TABLE 2.3

Department	Liberal	Moderately Liberal	Middle-of the-road	Moderately Conservative	Conservative
Humanities	36	34	11	13	5
Social Sciences	34	36	16	12	3
Education	23	37	15	22	2
Business/ Communication	15	28	17	30	9
Engineering	13	28	24	29	7

TABLE 2.4

Stanford School or Department	No. of Profs registered to vote	% registered as:		
		Democrat	Independent	Republican
English	29	93.0%	3.4%	3.4%
Sociology	17	88.0%	12.0%	0.0%
Anthropology	15	86.7%	6.7%	6.7%
History	26	84.6%	11.5%	3.8%
Political Science	26	84.6%	7.7%	7.7%
Education	35	77.1%	14.3%	8.6%
Philosophy	13	76.9%	7.7%	15.4%
Economics	21	71.4%	4.8%	23.8%
Law	36	63.9%	13.9%	22.2%

Department, had no Republicans.[271] A 1987 survey of the political registration of Stanford University professors (see table 2.4) found that humanities and social sciences faculties were more skewed to the left than the Carnegie aggregate data indicated.[272]

The data available indicate that the left so totally dominates departments of humanities and social sciences at elite universities that moderate and conservative faculty have almost no presence. It seems a reasonable hypothesis that the left has at least majority control in humanities and social science faculties in a far wider band of institutions of higher education.

Dominance by the left does not by itself threaten academic freedom; ideological zealots from the extremes threaten academic freedom. There are virtually no faculty members from the far right at universities or four-year colleges, so there exists no threat to academic freedom from the far right within the faculty itself. However, the UCLA survey reported between 5 and 8 percent of the faculty at universities and four-year colleges have a political orientation on the far left. This percentage from the far left should be substantially higher in departments of humanities and social sciences at public universities offering advanced study and at elite private universities.

The current zealotry is based in this group on the far left. A number of the far left are willing to suppress the academic inquiry and speech of others to enforce their higher morality. These constitute the fundamentalist academic left. The liberals who dominate many humanities and social science faculties are sympathetic with the zealot's goals. Out of an ideology of solidarity, they generally silently acquiesce in and condone the suppression.

The liberals who dominate many faculties are not the only group of professors who fail to protect academic freedom of dissenters out of an ideology of solidarity with the fundamentalist academic left. Less productive faculty members who are threatened by high standards of intellectual quality and merit-based performance evaluation may also be attracted to the fundamentalist's ideology that academic standards and merit are masks for oppression. If drawing distinctions among people and behaviors, rewarding excellence, and punishing incompetence are illegitimate political acts of oppression, then the less productive faculty should not be on the bottom of the power hierarchy.[273] They are entitled to at least equal rewards, if not greater as compensation for past injustice. These faculty members may support the fundamentalist academic left's tactics.

The failure of many faculty members to defend academic freedom in the current period of zealotry is at least partially explained by the existence of numbers of faculty who fail to speak publicly out of an ideology of solidarity with the fundamentalist academic left. Out of self-interest, liberals, and the less productive may tend not to defend academic freedom from attack by the fundamentalist left. Chapter 9 returns to this topic to explore additional explanations for the faculty's general failure to defend academic freedom in periods of zealotry.

The Administration

Former Yale President Benno Schmidt observes that radicals are exploiting "a style of academic leadership that tends to be highly risk-averse, queasy about defending academic values, and inclined to negotiate and propitiate about almost anything."[274] The overriding risk that a large number of university administrators wish to avoid is public embarrassment of the university. Fundamentalists know that many administrators will bend to whatever wind is blowing the strongest and accommodate political pressure rather than exercise the courage publicly to condemn coercive tactics that suppress speech. First Amendment advocate Nat Hentoff concurs. "The college presidents and administrators I've met around the country are absolutely without any integrity or courage at all—most of them. There are a few exceptions. And that's why they are corroding the education of the people they are supposed to be educating."[275] Thus, when a faculty member is subject to public accusations of bigotry for competent academic inquiry and speech, some administrators give no public support in order to avoid any adverse media attention on the university.[276] Indeed, the administration may expect that the accused should accept guilt and apologize in order to spare the university any embarrassment.[277]

Administrative response on some campuses to the current variation of book burning, the theft and destruction of campus newspapers, also indicates a general unwillingness to protect freedom of speech. The most notable example occurred at the University of Pennsylvania in the spring and fall semesters of 1993. On April 15, the Black Student League seized and destroyed almost all

14,000 copies of the campus newspaper, the *Daily Pennsylvanian*. The Black Student League proclaimed that the newspaper was "insensitive to their issues," because a conservative student columnist had written articles critical of diversity ideology. President Sheldon Hackney responded initially that "two important university values, diversity and open expression, seem to be in conflict." A few days later, Hackney commented, "Taking newspapers is wrong, [but] I recognize that the concerns of members of Penn's minority community that gave rise to last week's protests are serious and legitimate."[278]

Sixteen faculty members from the University's law school wrote an open letter to President Hackney stating that "the important University values of diversity and open expression were not in conflict here. The offensive columns in no way prevented the University from carrying out its policy of diversity and its many programs to promote understanding. Removal of the newspapers struck at the heart of the most fundamental diversity which the University should foster—diversity of thought, views and expression."[279]

The university initiated two investigations of the incident. The university appointed an inquiry board of four administrators, a member of the university's police department, and a chief of police at another university to look at how campus police responded to the theft of the newspapers. The university also appointed a "judicial officer" to look into whether disciplinary action should be taken against the students who stole and destroyed the newspapers.

In April, before the inquiry board started its work, the chairperson for the inquiry board and the vice-provost for university life, Kim M. Morrison, stated that the committee would take into account the fact that the "students did not see their protest in the context of its being an infringement on free speech." She said it was inappropriate for the police to have intervened in a protest act, although the police could not have known that students were protesting when they grabbed the newspapers and ran.[280] The final report of the inquiry board, issued in August, 1993, adopted this same logic, finding that the theft of the newspapers was not a criminal act but a protest, protected by the university's "Open Expression Guidelines." Therefore, the campus police should have called administrators, who would then have sent "Open Expression Monitors" to mediate and attempt to resolve any further conflicts that resulted from the removal of the newspaper. Several police officers were publicly censured, one was suspended, and all were ordered into sensitivity training on working with people from diverse backgrounds.[281]

The "judicial officer," Professor Howard Arnold, recommended in September, 1993 that no disciplinary action be taken against those students responsible for the seizure. Professor Arnold found that "[m]istakes by students must be seen more as opportunities for education than as occasions for punishment."[282] The interim president and provost of Penn issued a statement suggesting that the protesters may have been unaware that their night theft was wrong, since there was nothing in the student handbook that said that taking newspapers was prohibited. "We will respond vigorously to any future violations of these principles [free speech and freedom of the press]."[283]

There are other similar examples of administrative inaction in the face of book burning. In the spring semester of 1993 at Dartmouth, the Black Freshmen Forum confiscated most of the 3,500 copies of the conservative student paper, the *Dartmouth Review*, for three weeks. Dean of Students Lee Pelton took no action, saying that the problem was "a distribution issue, not a free-speech issue.... There's no rule that says how many copies you can pick up."[284]

Fear of demonstrations that would disrupt speeches, classes, or administrative functions also paralyzes some administrators, rendering them incapable of defending academic freedom. For example, administrators at CCNY did nothing about disruption of Professor Levin's classes because they believed that enforcement of disciplinary rules would have invited chaos on the campus.[285] Similarly the president of Bowdoin took no disciplinary action against students blocking entrances to the administration building and the library, choosing instead to appease them by agreeing to bring their list of demands to the faculty.[286] After students occupied an administration building for two days in November, 1992, to protest an alleged incident of racism, the Georgia State University administration granted five of eleven student demands, including the reassignment of two deans and the padlocking of two fraternities before any investigation of allegations against the fraternities was undertaken.[287] In May, 1993, UCLA Hispanic students took over the faculty club, breaking windows, wrecking furniture, and carving graffiti into walls, to protest the administration's decision not to turn the Chicano-studies program into a department. The strife ended when the administration agreed to strengthen the Chicano-studies program by hiring more professors and protecting all ethnic studies programs from budget cuts.[288]

In contrast, there are examples of administrative courage in defending academic freedom. Dean John Jeffrey at Dallas Baptist University responded courageously to the request of the vice-president of academic affairs to investigate the academic speech of Professor David Ayers. Dean Jeffrey sent a memorandum to all deans, stating:

> I cannot investigate charges in which the actions of the faculty member are well within the parameters of the Faculty Handbook and the AAUP guidelines. For me to investigate charges in which there is no hint of impropriety would in itself constitute a violation of academic freedom and AAUP guidelines.

This response cost Dean Jeffrey his job. He was summarily terminated.[289]

Some administrators have taken strong steps to control disruption and protect academic freedom. Dean Jesse Choper at Berkeley refused to discuss student demands while they were occupying his office and interfering with the business of the law school. Fifteen students were arrested after occupying the office for four hours and refusing to leave.[290] In 1990, Dean Robert Clark at Harvard Law School had photos taken of students occupying his office, and warned them that if they did not leave, they would be in violation of university rules and would be disciplined.[291] In 1992, after nine students again occupied the hallway outside the dean's office at Harvard Law School, the students were found guilty of violating school rules and warnings went into their files.[292]

Escalation of Demands and the Difficulty of Appeasement

Concessions have not been very effective in buying peace with zealots from the fundamentalist academic left for three reasons. First, in the context of the university, the zealot's purpose is to expose the reality of the oppression within the university by forcing the university into confrontation and oppressive actions. The construct of fundamentalist ideology is that social reality consists of oppression by the powerful against the powerless. It assumes that oppression based on status is so endemic in American society that it has become invisible, even to some victims. Increasing tension based on race, ethnicity, gender, or other status difference is a necessity to expose this reality. Concessions or reforms within the university must therefore be met with new demands that ultimately force the confrontation.[293]

Second, in modern society, claims of unjust suffering and sacrifice are major keys to conscience and to politics.[294] Knowing that political power depends upon claims of unjust suffering and sacrifice, zealots must escalate their claims in the face of concessions. They cannot be appeased or they lose their status as victims and their political power.[295]

Third, zealots from the fundamentalist left realize political advantages by making extreme proposals and labeling opponents as extremists on the other side. Harvard law professor Duncan Kennedy advocates the tactical advantages of extreme proposals and taunting. "Things previously unthinkable become the extreme, and the center has to move."[296] If by vilification, zealots can make people believe that moderates are actually the extreme right, then people come to believe also that the left is the center.

An example may clarify this tactic. Fundamentalists from the academic left publicly advocate proportional representation of oppressed groups in admissions, grade distribution, graduation, and bar examination results. Advocates of academic quality and standards who argue against these proposals may be labeled reactionaries and vilified as bigots. If by labeling and vilification, zealots can make undecided people believe that opponents are reactionary bigots on the extreme right, the undecided tend to define desirable "middle ground" between the two extremes further to the left than would otherwise be true. The undecided also then tend to blame opposition as the cause of the ideological unpleasantness.

Summary

Universities are not overrun by zealots. The fundamentalist academic left appears to be a small proportion of many faculties, concentrated particularly in some humanities and the social sciences departments; yet fundamentalists often wield significant power in suppressing dissenting views in these faculties. Ideological zealots have discovered that extreme tactics, such as false public accusations of bigotry, investigations, and tribunals can be undertaken against heretics in many faculties without censure or comment by colleagues. The number of academics who publicly protest violations of academic freedom is very small. The silent acquiescence of the majority of the faculty to coercive tactics operates to isolate and ostracize the accused, and to empower the zealots.

The faculty's usual public behavior of silent submission to the fundamentalists' tactics is the ballast of this ideological zealotry. It allows intimidation to become respectable, and leaves the accused without remedy. This silence condoning coercive tactics stands itself as a phenomenon of equal interest to the tactics and their results; this essay returns to explore the reasons for this silence in chapter 9.

Notes

1. Paul H. L. Walters, Presidential Address to the 72nd Annual Meeting of the AAUP, *reprinted in* ACADEME, Sept.-Oct. 1986, at 1a.
2. Everett C. Ladd, Jr., and Seymour Martin Lipset, THE DIVIDED ACADEMY: PROFESSORS AND POLITICS 199 (1975).
3. *Id.* at 51.
4. Jonathan Rauch, KINDLY INQUISITORS 28 (1993).
5. Professor David Bromwich coined the phrase "the new fundamentalists" in his book, POLITICS BY OTHER MEANS 44–46 (1992).
6. *Id.*
7. Richard Flacks, MAKING HISTORY: THE RADICAL TRADITION IN AMERICAN LIFE 7 (1988).
8. Henry Giroux observes that in the last fifteen years, the relationship between culture and power has become a central concern of radical social theory. Moving beyond the Marxist position in which culture is viewed merely as a reflex of the economy, "leftist" theorists are constructing a view of social theory that links culture with all forms of power, including economic power. Henry Giroux, *Schooling as a Form of Cultural Politics: Toward a Pedagogy of Difference*, *reprinted in* CRITICAL PEDAGOGY, THE STATE AND CULTURAL STRUGGLE 125 (Henry Giroux & Peter McLaren eds., 1989). Adherents of the critical legal studies define themselves as a "left intelligentsia" committed to a radical political position. Peter Goodrich, *Sleeping with the Enemy: An Essay on the Politics of Critical Legal Studies in America*, 68 N.Y.U. L.REV. 389 (1993).
9. There is no one commonly accepted term that adequately captures all the ideological variations. The various choices that seem to be used as synonyms for postmodernism are poststructuralism, critical theory, theory, and 1968 philosophy.

10. Paul Gross & Norman Levitt, HIGHER SUPERSTITION: THE ACADEMIC LEFT AND ITS QUARRELS WITH SCIENCE 76 (1994). *See id.* at 5, 10, 38; Dinesh D'Souza, *Illiberal Education*, ATLANTIC MONTHLY, Mar. 1991, at 73-74.

11. Gross & Levitt, *supra* note 10, at 72. *See also* Hunter L. Prillamen, *"Critical" Law School Faculty: A Practice Perspective*, 14 J. LEGAL PROF. ANN. 3-5 (1989).

12. Robert W. Gordon, *Critical Legal Studies*, 10 LEGAL STUD. F. 335, 339 (1986).

13. Mark Tushnet, *Critical Legal Studies: An Introduction to Its Origins and Underpinnings*, 36 J. LEGAL EDUC. 505, 517 (1986).

14. Status is used as a shorthand for race, gender, affectional preference, disability, age, and religion.

15. Barry W. Sarchett, *What's All the Fuss About This Postmodernist Stuff?*, COLO. C. BULL., Feb. 1992, at 10, 15.

16. DEBATING P.C.: THE CONTROVERSY OVER POLITICAL CORRECTNESS ON COLLEGE CAMPUSES 6-7 (Paul Berman ed., 1992) [hereinafter "DEBATING P.C."]. Duke Professor Stanley Fish finds merit and fairness to be political prizes claimed when one political agenda dominates and defines what is normative. Reason is also a political entity that is claimed by the party that has managed to get the arguments that flow from its agenda identified with reason. Reason, fairness, and merit come only in partisan shapes. Stanley Fish, THERE'S NO SUCH THING AS FREE SPEECH AND ITS A GOOD THING TOO 4, 16, 20 (1994).

17. John Patrick Diggins, THE RISE AND FALL OF THE AMERICAN LEFT 347 (1992).

18. Stanley Fish, DOING WHAT COMES NATURALLY: CHANGE, RHETORIC AND THE PRACTICE OF THEORY IN LITERACY AND LEGAL STUDIES 10-11 (1989).

19. *See* Dinesh D'Souza, ILLIBERAL EDUCATION: THE POLITICS OF RACE AND SEX ON CAMPUS 175 (1991); Prillamen, *supra* note 11, at 3-5.

20. Professor Mark Tushnet states that "[t]he politics of the dominant position [of the critical legal studies movement] is the politics of decentering, disrupting whatever understandings happen to be settled, criticizing the existing order whatever that order is." Mark Tushnet, *Critical Legal Studies: An Introduction to Its Origins and Underpinnings*, 36 J. LEGAL EDUC. 505, 515 (1986). It is a program of "interminable critique." *Id.* at 516.

21. Richard Flacks, MAKING HISTORY: THE RADICAL TRADITION IN AMERICAN LIFE 7 (1988).

22. *Id.* at 108.

23. *Id.*

24. *See* D'Souza, *supra* note 19, at 175, 182-83.

25. Joel Handler, *Postmodernism, Protest, and the New Social Movements*, 36 L. & SOC'Y REV. 697, 701 (1992).

26. *Id.* at 698, 701.

27. Henry Giroux & Peter McLaren, *Schooling, Cultural Politics, and the Struggle for Democracy, reprinted in* CRITICAL PEDAGOGY, THE STATE AND CULTURAL STRUGGLE at xi, xxii, xxiv (Henry Giroux and Peter McLaren eds., 1989).

28. Flacks, *supra* note 7, at 226-27.

29. *Id.* at 247.

30. *See* Mark Kelman, *Emerging Centrist Liberalism*, 43 FLA. L. REV. 417, 428, 444 (1991). In an essay written while serving as a visiting professor at Cardozo

law school, Professor Peter Goodrich observed that teaching is the site of a new politics, and "the educational institution is a fundamental element in the future of radicalism." Peter Goodrich, *Sleeping With the Enemy: An Essay on the Politics of Critical Legal Studies in America*, 68 N.Y.U. L.REV. 389, 424 (1993).

31. Henry Giroux & Peter McLaren, *Schooling, Cultural Politics, and the Struggle for Democracy, reprinted in* CRITICAL PEDAGOGY, THE STATE AND CULTURAL STRUGGLE at xxi (Henry Giroux and Peter McLaren eds., 1989).

32. *See id.* at xxviii; Martin Carnoy, *Education, State and Culture in American Society, reprinted in* CRITICAL PEDAGOGY, THE STATE AND CULTURAL STRUGGLE 21-22 (Henry Giroux and Peter McLaren eds., 1989).

33. *See* Giroux, *supra* note 8, at 130, 141.

34. *Id.* at 147.

35. Giroux & McClaren, *supra* note 27, at xxxi, xxi, xxiii, xxvii.

36. *See* Richard Devlin, *Legal Education as Political Consciousness—Raising or Paving the Road to Hell*, 39 J. LEGAL EDUC. 213, 223 (1989); David Fraser, *If I Had a Rocket Launcher: Critical Legal Studies as Moral Terrorism*, 41 HASTINGS L.J. 777, 802 (1990).

37. Elizabeth Ellsworth, *Why Doesn't This Feel Empowering? Working Through the Repressive Myths of Critical Pedagogy*, HARV. EDUC. REV., August 1989, at 297, 300-301, 319.

38. *Justifying the Existence of Heterodoxy*, HETERODOXY, Nov. 1992, at 6. Rorty recently commented that most Americans still identify with and take pride in our country, despite its failings, but "many of the exceptions to this rule are found in the colleges and universities, in the academic departments that have become sanctuaries for left-wing political views." Richard Rorty, *The Unpatriotic Academy*, N.Y. TIMES, Feb. 13, 1994, Sec. 4, at 15.

39. Sidney Hook, *Civilization and Its Malcontents*, NAT'L REV., Oct. 13, 1989, at 30, 33.

40. *See generally* Peter M. Shane, *Why Are So Many People Unhappy? Habits of Thought and Resistance to Diversity in Legal Education*, 75 IOWA L. REV. 1033, 1037 (1990); David Bromwich, POLITICS BY OTHER MEANS: HIGHER EDUCATION AND GROUP THINKING 18-19 (1992); John Bunzel, RACE RELATIONS ON CAMPUS 112, 126-129 (1992); James Traub, *Back to Basic: P.C. vs. English*, NEW REPUBLIC, Feb. 8, 1993, at 18-19; Richard Huber, HOW PROFESSORS PLAY THE CAT GUARDING THE CREAM: WHY WE'RE PAYING MORE AND GETTING LESS IN HIGHER EDUCATION 47-48 (1992).

41. *See generally* Office of The President, Stanford University, FINAL REPORT OF THE UNIVERSITY COMMITTEE ON MINORITY ISSUES (1989); Office of the Vice President for Academic Affairs and Provost, Ohio State University, OHIO STATE UNIVERSITY ACTION PLAN (1987); Office of the Chancellor, University of Wisconsin at Madison, THE MADISON PLAN (1988); Office of the President, University of Michigan, THE MICHIGAN MANDATE: A STRATEGIC LINKING OF ACADEMIC EXCELLENCE AND SOCIAL DIVERSITY (1990).

42. Richard Bernstein, DICTATORSHIP OF VIRTUE 5 (1994).

43. *Id.* at 6-9, 73-74.

44. Karen Winkler, *Scholars Mark the Beginning of the Age of 'Post-Theory'*, CHRON. HIGHER EDUC., Oct. 13, 1993, at A9.

45. *Id.* at A17.

46. *See* DEBATING P.C., *supra* note 16, at 23.

47. *See* Joseph A. Amato, VICTIMS AND VALUES: A HISTORY AND A THEORY OF SUFFERING 211-12 (1990).
48. *See* D'Souza, *supra* note 10, at 10, 134.
49. *See* Michael Lerner, THE SOCIALISM OF FOOLS: ANTI-SEMITISM ON THE LEFT 58, 61 (1992).
50. *Id.* at 64.
51. *Id.* at 65, 67.
52. *Id.*
53. *Id.* at 62.
54. *Id.* at 122-23. Arch Puddington observes that the campus speeches of Khalid Abdul Muhammed indicate growing virulent black anti-Semitism on many campuses. Arch Puddington, *Black Anti-Semitism and How It Grows*, COMMENTARY, April 1994, at 19, 21-22.
55. John Silber, STRAIGHT SHOOTING: WHAT'S WRONG WITH AMERICA AND HOW TO FIX IT 85 (1989); Benno Schmidt, *Universities Must Defend Free Speech*, WALL STREET J. (May 26, 1991), at A16; *see* Derek Bok, THE PRESIDENT'S REPORT 1989-1990 HARVARD UNIVERSITY 11-14 (1991).
56. *See* D'Souza, *supra* note 19, at 98-100, 151-52; Silber, *supra* note 55, at 82-83.
57. D'Souza, *supra* note 19, at 15.
58. Schmidt, *supra* note 55.
59. Arthur Schlesinger, Jr., *Annual Doctoral Commencement, City University of New York* (May 26, 1994), at 5.
60. *Id.* at 3-4.
61. *Id.* at 8.
62. Derek Bok, *Universities: Their Temptation and Tensions*, 18 J.C. & U.L. 1, 7 (1991).
63. Nat Hentoff, FREE SPEECH FOR ME BUT NOT FOR THEE 9 (1992).
64. *See* David Bryden, *Scholarship About Scholarship*, 63 U. COLO. L. REV. 641, 648-49 (1992). Many cases involving charges under speech and harassment policies go unreported because of the secrecy of the investigation process and the professor's willingness to accept a plea-bargained sanction rather than risk public embarrassment and hostility from the employer. Courtney Leatherman, *Fighting Back*, CHRON. HIGHER EDUC., March 16, 1994, at A17, A18. The experience of Michael Greve, director of the Center for Individual Rights in Washington, D.C., is that many untenured professors take charges of bigotry lying down. "They try and settle them behind closed doors because they are humiliating." Brian Jackson, *Bible Scholar Sues to Fight Taint of Sexual Harassment*, CHICAGO SUN-TIMES, March 25, 1994, at News p. 5. Michael McDonald, president of the Center, agrees that "for every professor who fights these things, there are literally hundreds who are having their speech chilled." Edward Walsh, *Sexual Ethics in the Seminary*, WASH. POST, May 13, 1994 at D1. In 1994, an AAUP investigating committee at the University of New Hampshire "was informed that many faculty members—the actual number is unclear— have been confronted by administrative officers with complaints of sexual harassment and have signed statements apologizing for perceived misconduct." These files are confidential, so the investigating committee could not verify this. *Academic Freedom and Tenure: The University of New Hampshire*, ACADEME, Nov.-Dec. 1994, at 79.
65. Jonathan Rauch, KINDLY INQUISITORS 11 (1993). After several *Harvard Law Review* editors published a parody of work by a murdered feminist scholar, NPR reporter David Wright sought comment from students and faculty. He discov-

ered, "In this most verbal community, many students declined to be interviewed on tape lest their comments offend one group or another. Even the stars of the faculty...all asked that some of their comments not be included in this report because their metaphors might offend." *Harvard Law Review Article Sparks Debate*, NPR Morning Edition, May 4, 1992.

66. *See* D'Souza, *supra* note 19, at 129, 172, 246; *see* Stephan Thernstrom, *Introduction*, ACAD. QUESTIONS, Winter 1990-91, at 14. For example, Professor Daphne Patai notes:

> In my own women's-studies program at the University of Massachusetts, I found myself called a racist because, as acting director, I had been unable to come up with extra money for an elective course on indigenous women that had been proposed by two Native-American graduate students. Simultaneously, I had used the last bit of money in our budget to finance a required course on the intellectual foundations of feminism, to be taught by a teaching assistant who happened to be white.... I tried to explain that "racism" had nothing to do with the events in question. This simple denial brought a storm down upon my head. I was told by a young black colleague that when a woman of color says she has experienced racism, she is the authority on that experience and cannot be challenged.

Daphne Patai, *The Struggle for Feminist Purity Threatens the Goals of Feminism*, CHRON. HIGHER EDUC., Feb. 5, 1992, at B1-B2. Wellesley Africana Studies Professor Anthony Martin, in his new book, *The Jewish Onslaught: Dispatches from the Wellesley Front*, dismisses the arguments of anyone who has criticized his work on African influence on ancient Greece on the ground that critics have racist motives. Mary Lefkowitz, *Combating False Theories in the Classroom*, CHRON. HIGHER EDUC., Jan. 19, 1994 at B1.

Jeremy Zwelling, a Wesleyan professor, published an open letter to the president telling of false accusations of bigotry by students. In one course, members of his own faith accused him of assigning anti-Semitic readings from the Old Testament. In a second, women students sabotaged a seminar with charges of emotional rape and lethal misogyny. A third course almost collapsed under abusive protests that he was a racist and an elitist. C. Vann Woodward, *Freedom & the Universities*, N.Y. REV., July 18, 1991, at 32, 37 (reviewing Dinesh D'Souza, ILLIBERAL EDUCATION: THE POLITICS OF RACE AND SEX ON CAMPUS (1991)).

67. Jane Easter Bahls, *Dissenting Opinions*, STUDENT L., Sept. 1991, at 12, 15.

68. Arlynn L. Presser, *The Politically Correct Law School*, ABA JOURNAL, Sept. 1991, at 52-53.

69. *See* Stephen L. Carter, REFLECTIONS OF AN AFFIRMATIVE ACTION BABY 26-27, 169 (1991).

70. *Id.* at 113.

71. For example, when Professor Julius Lester at the University of Massachusetts, Amhearst questioned whether some of James Baldwin's remarks were anti-Semitic, his colleagues lambasted him publicly as "self-serving and devious," having "a vicious attitude towards blacks and black organizations," and not being able to avoid "stereotypical attacks on the black community." *Id.* at 110. Duke English Professor Stanley Fish finds "a straight line between contemporary hostility to black studies, ethnic studies, gay and lesbian studies, and the...frankly racist writings of the late nineteenth and early twentieth century." Stanley Fish, THERE IS NO SUCH THING AS FREE SPEECH, AND IT'S A GOOD THING TOO 12 (1994).

72. Notebook, CHRON. HIGHER EDUC. March 31, 1993, at A27.
73. Peter Collier, *War Stories*, HETERODOXY, December 1992, at 7.
74. Heather MacDonald, *Toward Yugoslavia?*, COMMENTARY, June, 1992, at 61. Harvard Law Professor Randall Kennedy observes that the strategic use of accusations of prejudice to exploit the stigmatization of racial bigotry has received little scholarly attention. "[F]or illumination, one must turn to essayists, journalists, and novelists. This stratagem, however, is real; those who employ it occasionally reap considerable benefits." The immediate response to this article by Professor Kennedy was a whispering campaign, an effort to discredit him, a suggestion that he had done something wrong. Randall L. Kennedy, *Racial Critiques of Legal Academia*, 102 HARV. L. REV. 1745, 1809-10 (1989). Carter, *supra* note 60, at 109.
75. Stanley Fish, THERE'S NO SUCH THING AS FREE SPEECH, AND IT'S A GOOD THING TOO 86 (1993).
76. Anne Kornhauser, *More Fallout Over 'Admissions Apartheid'; Advocates for Georgetown Law Student Draw Fire*, LEGAL TIMES, May 20, 1991, at 10. In December of 1988, Professor Ernest Goodman at State University of New York at Oneonta made a public defense of the importance of selecting literature in education based on the quality of writing rather than race or gender of the author. Eight faculty members responded to Goodman in the student newspaper charging that they were being intimidated by those on campus who shared Professor Goodman's views. They claimed that there had been intimidation of students and professors associated with Black Studies, Women's Studies, and Ethnic Studies on numerous college campuses. "Here, at our college last week...a program [on Father's Rights] sponsored by the Pre-Law Society and Dr. William Simons, brought without notice to our campus a speaker from one of the leading anti-feminist organizations in the United States.... At the very end of this program, community women report that they were physically surrounded by hostile members of the audience and felt intimidated." A second letter charged Professor Simons was responsible for the atmosphere—rude and aggressive with mutterings of "dyke" and "bitch" when women challenged the speakers.
A videotape showed all these charges to be totally false. Moreover, Simon, an advisor to the Young Democrats, did not share the views of Goodman, an advisor to the Young Republicans. The fundamentalists used falsehood and character assassination to attack Professor Simon and guilt by association to discredit Professor Goodman. William Simons, *Intimidation as Academic Debate*, ACAD. QUESTIONS, Spring 1993, at 63–69.
77. Bok, *supra* note 55, at 8. For example, after two visiting professors popular with students were not hired for tenure-track positions, a group of students and professors charged through e-mail and protests that there was a conspiracy to "purge" lesbians from Pomona. They provided no evidence. Courtney Leatherman, *Pomona College Rejects Charges That It is Purging Lesbians*, CHRON. HIGHER EDUC., Feb. 16, 1994, at A24.
78. *See* D'Souza, *supra* note 19, at 196, 199; Ian R. MacNeil, *Harvard Law School*, COMMENTARY, Mar. 1990, at 10–11. For example, after anonymous complaints against Professor Allan Mandelstamm, the highest rated teacher by students, the Virginia Tech administrators refused to look at class videotapes or student class evaluations. Allan Mandelstamm, *McCarthy's Ghost: Reminiscences of a Politically Incorrect Professor*, 9 CRISES 14, 16–18 (1991). An example of the use of misrepresentation to create a struggle meeting was the false announcement to students and the press that the first formal meeting of the National Association of Scholars on the campus of SUNY-Binghamton was a meeting of a white su-

premacist group that had invited KKK members to the lecture. *See* Aldo Bernardo, *Portrait of an Initial NAS Meeting*, MEASURE, May 1991, at 2, 3. In 1992, fundamentalist students at the University of California, San Diego, circulated fliers falsely characterizing Professor George Reisman's speech on western civilization as "open racism—the equivalent of the Rodney King beating." This created a struggle meeting. Anita Susan Grossman and Thomas wood, *Free Speech Under Fire: Barbarism at UC San Diego*, CALIF. SCHOLAR, Winter, 1992-93 at 12.

79. *See* Silber, *supra* note 55, at 96; *see* MacNeil, *supra* note 78; Mandelstamm, *supra* note 78, at 16-18.

80. Carter, *supra* note 69, at 187.

81. *See generally* MacNeil, *supra* note 78, at 10; Mandelstamm, *supra* note 78, at 16-18.

82. *See* D'Souza, *supra* note 19, at 6, 201, 203, 275.

83. *See id.* at 150.

84. *See generally* Mandelstamm, *supra* note 78, at 16; Patai, *supra* note 66, at B1.

85. *See* D'Souza, *supra* note 19, at 6, 194-95. Professor Stephan Thernstrom, for example, has been a teacher and scholar of ethnic history at Harvard University. He has also been editor of the Harvard Encyclopedia of American Ethnic Groups. For nine weeks in 1988, Thernstrom was the target of a variety of news stories in the *Harvard Crimson* accusing him of "racial insensitivity" in teaching his course, The Peopling of America. Randall Kennedy, *The Political Correctness Scare*, 37 LOYOLA L.REV. 231, 238 (1991) (Professor Kennedy believes that Thernstrom egregiously overreacted to the stigma and that there was no issue of academic freedom). *Id.* at 241-43.

86. For example, Professor Laraine Fergerson at Bronx Community College sought faculty support for a resolution recognizing Professor Leonard Jeffries' First Amendment rights to speak on campus in May, 1992, but protesting Jeffries' bigoted remarks. She was able to generate barely a whisper of protest because many faculty members felt "particularly vulnerable" to charges of insensitivity, and feared charges of racism and student volatility. Laraine Fergerson, *"The Politics of Fear" on a CUNY Campus*, MIDSTREAM, May 1994, at 27-28.

87. Professor Gribben supported the concentration at the Ph.D. level, believing that graduate students should first ground themselves in the classic texts of English and American literature. *See* Joseph Salemi, *Lone Star Academic Politics: Persecution in the University of Texas at Austin*, MEASURE, August 1990, at 4. *See also* MacNeil, *supra* note 68 (similar story of social and professional ostracism from faculty and students after students charged MacNeil with "repeated instances of sexism"). *But see* Mark Tushnet, *Political Correctness, the Law and the Legal Academy*, 4 YALE J. LAW & HUMAN. 127, 133 (1992) (MacNeil's claim that he was not sexist was unpersuasive).

88. Salemi, *supra* note 87, at 5.

89. *Id.*

90. Peter Collier, *Incorrect English*, HETERODOXY, May 1992, at 8, 9.

91. Daphne Patai & Noretta Koertge, PROFESSING FEMINISM 13-20, 184, 217 (1994).

92. Carter, *supra* note 69, at 102.

93. *Id.* at 103.

94. Thomas Short, *How Politicized Studies Enforce Conformity: Interviews with Julius Lester and Elizabeth Fox-Genovese*, ACAD. QUESTIONS, Summer 1992, at 48, 52. Students also experience ostracism. After a student senator at Wellesley

publicly opposed a lecture invitation to Al Sharpton because of his anti-semitism, she was subjected to a steady stream of personal attacks. She was falsely accused of perpetuating racial slurs. Rumors spread that she was the leader of an underground neo-Nazi group. Eventually no one would talk to her. Alyson Todd, *Growing Up Absurd at Wellesley*, HETERODOXY, March, 1993 at 18. After Princeton senior Harold Wenglinsky publicly criticized organizers of a Take Back the Night March for preventing students with other points of view from expressing themselves, he was intimidated into silence by social ostracism, public and private accusations of being an "evangelist of the rape culture" and a "rapist," and two death threats. Jonathan Rockoff, *Villified for View at Princeton*, PHILADELPHIA INQUIRER, May 29, 1991, at 6-BJ.

95. Complaint, *Wolff v. Massachusetts Instit. of Tech.* (Commonwealth of Mass.-Middlesex County No. 92-2430, 1992). Another tactic is simply abusive conduct in the form of insulting words toward colleagues. Professor Kenny Williams observes that at Duke University:

> The new group is in control precisely because the foremost thing for them is not scholarship and collegial relationships but power. If scholarship were the real concern, the department would function through dialogue.... [I]t seems that the new group's primary tactic is to be, not simply impolite, but rude and often crude.

Kenny J. Williams, *Caste and Class in a University Setting*, ACAD. QUESTIONS, Spring 1991, at 41, 58.

96. Steven C. Bahls, *Political Correctness and the American Law School*, 69 WASH. U. L.Q. 1041, 1044 (1991).

97. *Id.* at 1048, 1050. For another story of faculty hostility and ridicule of competent student speech in the classroom, *see* Mona Walsh Holland, *Inside the Politicized Classroom: A Student's Account of a Seminar on Indian Treaty Rights*, ACAD. QUESTIONS, Winter 1991-92, at 44.

98. David Bromwich, POLITICS BY OTHER MEANS 239 n.14 (1992).

99. *See* Bahls, *supra* note 96, at 1055 n.58.

100. *See* Bahls, *supra* note 67, at 17.

101. David Bryden, *It Ain't What They Teach, It's The Way They Teach It*, PUB. INTEREST, Spring 1991, at 51, 52, *reprinted in* David Bryden, *The Role of the Respectable Left*, MEASURE, July 1991, at 7.

102. *See* DEBATING P.C.: THE CONTROVERSY OVER POLITICAL CORRECTNESS ON COLLEGE CAMPUSES 218 (Paul Berman ed., 1992) (students at N.Y.U. and Brown state that they censor themselves in class on issues of race, gender, or sexual preference); John Bunzel, RACE RELATIONS ON CAMPUS 68, 123 (1992) (Stanford students are fearful of being accused as racist, and have to be careful all the time); John Hinton, *Ivy League Theology*, ACAD. QUESTIONS, Spring 1993, at 37, 42-43 (Harvard Divinity School students who are pro-life will speak only anonymously out of fear of social ostracism. The sole male student in class on feminist theology who complained class was failing to deal with professed subject was informed by the instructor that he was sexist and merited therapy); Arlynn Presser, *The Politically Correct Law School*, A.B.A. J., Sept. 1991, at 52-53 (To get honest discussion, Professor Nadine Strossen at N.Y.U. allows students to submit anonymous notes to be read in Constitutional Law). *See generally* Nat Hentoff, FREE SPEECH FOR ME BUT NOT FOR THEE 153-59 (1992).

103. Louis Freedberg, *College Controversy: A Campus Fear of Speaking Freely*, S.F. CHRON., Oct. 30, 1991, at A1.

104. *Id.*

104. *See* Nien Cheng, LIFE AND DEATH IN SHANGHAI 150–55 (1987).
106. *See* Jeanne J. Kirkpatrick, *My Experience with Academic Intolerance*, ACAD. QUESTIONS, Fall 1989, at 21, 22–23; Louis Jacobs, *A Report: Political or Pedagogical Correctness?*, ACAD. QUESTIONS, Spring 1993, at 59, 61; Dan Wetzel, *Is Mob Rule Any Way to Fight Racism*, BOSTON GLOBE, May 17, 1992, at 86 (describing negotiations in front of 200 activists who participated by hissing, shouting, and threatening Wetzel).
107. Nino Langiulli, *When it Came to "That" at the University of Cincinnati*, MEASURE, March 1993, at 1–3; Walter Williams, *UC 'Sensitivity' Session Did Involve Nazi Tactics*, MEASURE, June 1993, at 8; Abraham Miller, *Inside the Sensitivity Session*, INTERCOLLEGIATE REV., Fall 1992, at 39, 41–42.
108. *See* D'Souza, *supra* note 19, at 101, 140, 149, 199.
109. *Id.* at 140.
110. Paul Lauter, Materials for Participants in UDI/TDC Organizer's Workshop, April 9, 1992.
111. Mandelstamm, *supra* note 78, at 17.
112. Stephan Thernstrom, *Who's Right about the Student Left?*, HARPERS, Feb. 1992, at 4–5.
113. *See generally id.* at 8–9.
114. *See* MacNeil, *supra* note 78.
115. *Id.*
116. *See* Dinesh D'Souza, *In the Name of Academic Freedom, Colleges Should Back Professors Against Students' Demands for 'Correct' Views*, CHRON. HIGHER EDUC., Apr. 24, 1991, at B1, B3 [hereinafter D'Souza, *Students' Demands*].
117. As Justice Scalia noted in *Morrison v. Olson*, 487 U.S. 654, 713 (1988), "Nothing is so politically effective as the ability to charge that one's opponents are not merely wrongheaded, naive, and ineffective, but, in all probability 'crooks.' And nothing so effectively gives appearance of validity to such charges as a Justice Department investigation."
118. *See Florida Bar v. Randolph*, 238 So.2d 635, 638-39 (Fla. 1970).
119. Sara C. Charles & Eugene Kennedy, DEFENDANT: A PSYCHIATRIST ON TRIAL FOR MEDICAL MALPRACTICE 218–22 (1986).
120. *Kay v. Ehrler*, 111 S. Ct. 1435, 1438 (1991).
121. Charles E. Lundberg, *A Fool for a Client*, BENCH & BAR, Dec. 1991, at 22.
122. Learned Hand, *The Deficiencies of Trials to Reach the Heart of the Matter*, 3 ASSOC. BAR CITY N.Y., LECTURES ON LEGAL TOPICS 89, 105 (1926).
123. Tony Blass, *Careful What You Say*, MINN.'S J.L. & POLITICS, July 1991, at 10, 15; Rauch, *supra* note 4, at 148. Professor Allan Mandelstamm, rated outstanding teacher in the university at four different universities, was subjected to two investigations at Virginia Tech based on anonymous complaints of an alleged sexist remark in class. He was not provided fundamental due process in terms of a decision making process that both gives adequate notice of the charge and a hearing that takes pains with the facts. The decision maker refused to examine either student evaluations or videotapes of the alleged incidents. Mandelstamm, *supra* note 78, at 16–18. Four women students brought sexual harassment charges against all six members of the University of Minnesota's Department of Scandinavian Studies, including a female professor, for conduct such as disagreeing with a student about the role of a female character in a story, and about the rewriting of a paper, disagreeing with a student about the significance of rape in a story, and greeting a student in a nonsupportive way. After an eight-month investigation, the University's female affirmative action officer dismissed as

groundless all the student charges. The accused faculty members were profoundly shaken, both personally and professionally. They described the investigation as "terrifying" and "totally demoralizing." *See* Katherine Kersten, *Effort to Protect Women at 'U' Has a Stifling Effect*, STAR TRIB., May 14, 1990, at A11.

George Mason University law professor Michael Krauss used two examples in a 1993 Torts class to explore whether recent behavior might constitute the tort of assault. The first involved a Nazi party demonstration in front of a Holocaust survivor's home where uninformed demonstrators advocated implementation of Hitler's "Final Solution." The second example was a Ku Klux Klan demonstration on a street in a previously all-white neighborhood, in front of a house into which a black family just moved: the hooded Klansmen burned a cross and screamed "Kill the niggers." A faculty colleague, later joined by three others, filed a complaint with the dean and the university's Board of Visitors. Twenty students, none of whom had attended the class, both petitioned the dean to require the professor's written apology and contacted the media. Although defense required hundreds of hours of Professor Krauss' time, the dean defended his academic freedom. An African American student in the class subsequently protested that she had been chilled from preparing for class by Professor Krauss' use of the "N-word," and that therefore her grade reflected "discrimination on the basis of race." A faculty committee investigated and dismissed the complaint. On appeal, the university president appointed a second committee that investigated and dismissed the complaint. The student appealed to the Civil Rights division of the U.S. Department of Education. Without allowing Professor Krauss to examine the complaint, the Department of Education conducted an extensive investigation. The Department found no evidence of racial discrimination. The hours spent on responding to two years of complaints and investigations and the drain this imposed on two academic years "can be imagined by the reader." Michael Krauss, *When You Face the PC Inquisition*, WASH. TIMES, Jan. 27, 1995, at A21.

Students experience coercive investigations lacking fundamental due process. In October, 1993, a Vassar student charged junior Max Fraad-Wolff with making a homophobic phone call, which was recorded on the accusing student's answering machine. The harassment bureaucracy arranged for the tape to be played in student dormitories and residence halls and urged students to come forward to report the names of other students. Forty names were gathered. The harassment administrator scheduled Fraad-Wolff's hearing five days from the notice of the complaint. At the hearing, the harassment official in charge of the hearing denied Fraad-Wolff both the assistance of counsel, a tape recording of the hearing, and handwritten contemporaneous notes of the hearing. A second harassment official provided hearsay evidence in place of two students who were allegedly afraid of confronting Fraad-Wolff. The harassment official hearing the case rejected both evidence of an earlier false accusation by the accusing student and a voice print test that would clear Fraad-Wolff. The harassment official hearing the case found Fraad-Wolff not guilty but informed him that a further hearing would be convened any time the accusing student brought new evidence. Fraad-Wolff withdrew from Vassar on November 15, 1993. Richard Wolff, *Repression in the Guise of Sensitivity: The Vassar Example*, DEMOCRATIC CULTURE, Spring, 1994, at 4–6.

In the spring of 1993, Oberlin's campus humor magazine, *Below the Belt*, published a parody of an article that appeared in another journal edited by minority students. The authors of the parody turned the line, "Dirt, dirt, dirt. That's what too many East Asians in this country have been eating," into "Dirt, dirt, dirt. That's what those stir fry chicken strips are." The minority students brought racial harassment charges against two editors of the humor magazine claiming that the publication of the parody before the final exam period created a hostile educational environment for minority students. A tribunal cleared the accused students but the tribunal was a bewildering experience. "We didn't know what the burden of proof was," one explained. "We didn't really know how to prove ourselves innocent." Christopher Shea, *The Limits of Speech*, CHRON. HIGHER EDUC., Dec. 1, 1993 at A38.

124. Anita Susan Grossman, *Political Correctness at Berkeley: The Case of Vincent Sarich*, CALIF. SCHOLAR, Spring 1991, at 9. *See* Jerry Adler, et al., *Taking Offense*, NEWSWEEK, Dec. 24, 1990, at 50; *Campus Life: Berkeley; Campus is Split Over Statements by a Professor*, N.Y. TIMES, Dec. 23, 1990, Sec. 1, Pt. 2, at 28 [hereinafter *Berkeley*]; *Professor Claims Berkeley Puts Diversity Above Excellence*, WASH. TIMES, Nov. 26, 1990, at A3. In a law and economics case, law professor Robert Heidt regularly used a classic example of a public good involving four coolies who hire a wagon driver to make sure that no one free rides on the pulling of his other three teammates. After a student complaint, the acting law dean at the University of Indiana, Bloomington, investigated the complaint, and after obtaining the professor's explanation, asked the Academic Regulations Committee to investigate further (which they refused) and then referred it to the Dean of Faculties. Professor Heidt found the investigation onerous and felt his salary had been adversely affected because of it. *See* Robert Heidt, Memorandum to William Hanson, Associate Dean of Faculties, September 10, 1991. In 1993, political science professor John Shockley informed his department chair at Western Illinois University that his officemate was skipping classes, returning papers with grades but without actually reading them, failing to keep office hours, and spending his time locked in the office with a female graduate student with whom the officemate might be having a romantic liaison. The female graduate student brought campus sexual harassment charges against Shockley for spreading stories. In December 1993, a tribunal ruled in favor of Shockley. The student also filed a complaint with the Illinois Department of Human Rights. Shockley filed suit in March of 1994 to enjoin the state agency from harassing him by forcing him to hire a lawyer and respond to the sexual harassment accusations. Elaine Hopkins, *Professor Accused of Harassment Sues*, PEORIA JOURNAL, March 5, 1994, at 6. Santa Rosa Junior College Journalism Professor Roger Karraker set up single-sex computer bulletin boards at student request. In 1993, some students posted crude remarks about several women students on the male-only bulletin board. Professor Karraker shut the bulletin boards down within minutes after receiving a complaint about the remarks. Several students complained to the U.S. Education Department's Office of Civil Rights and Professor Karraker spent several months out of the classroom on "administrative leave" during the Civil Rights Office investigation. Karraker found the investigation to be Kafka-esque. John Schwartz, *Some On-Line Guidelines Are Out of Line with Free Speech Rights*, WASH. POST, Oct. 3, 1993, at F25.

125. *See Levin v. Harleston*, 770 F. Supp. 895, 912-13, 920, 923-24 (S.D.N.Y. 1991), *aff'd in part & vacated in part*, 966 F.2d 85 (2d Cir. 1992).

126. *See id.* at 911.

127. *Levin v. Harleston*, 966 F.2d 85, 89 (2d Cir. 1992). A white male's aggressive teaching style can lead to charges of racism or sexism and investigations. At Virginia Tech, in addition to the Mandelstamm situation, two students complained that another white male faculty member's aggressive strident teaching style was

racist. After investigation, the equal opportunity office found no clear evidence of racism but the professor did commit acts that might be characterized as insensitive. The office recommended that the professor should write apologies to the two students, the professor should be reassigned to a different class, and that the professor should attend sensitivity training. Henry Bauer, *Affirmative Action at Virginia Tech: The Tail That Wagged the Dog*, ACAD. QUESTIONS, Winter 1992–93, at 72, 80–81. The threat of investigation is also chilling. Several female students recently threatened Harvard Professor Alan Dershowitz with sexual harassment charges for creating an atmosphere hostile to women during two days of classroom work on the situation of men falsely accused of rape. Charles Radin, *An Ivory Cower; Some Say 'PC Cops' Making Professors Cringe*, BOSTON GLOBE, Jan. 20, 1993, National/Foreign, at 1.

128. Michael Greve & Joseph Shea, *When the Feds Weigh in on P.C.*, LEGAL TIMES, January 25, 1993, at 38; *Professor Exonerated on Discrimination Charge*, CHRON. HIGHER EDUC., Sept. 23, 1992, at A-5. The author's experience described in the Preface is very similar to that of Professor Kleinfeld.

129. Hentoff, *supra* note 63, at 390–91. Another estimate is that 350 campuses have speech codes. Carol Innerst, *Senate Silence Expected on Proposal Defending Free Speech on Campus*, WASH. TIMES, Sept. 11, 1992, at A-10.

130. Arati Korwar, WAR OF WORDS: SPEECH CODES AT PUBLIC COLLEGES AND UNIVERSITIES 21 (Freedom Forum First Amendment Center 1994).

131. *Id.* at 24–25 (Almost 36 percent of the schools surveyed have rules punishing verbal abuse based on membership in a specific group). A survey of the 20 public universities with the largest student enrollment found that 10 of the universities had adopted policies that specifically address "hateful or harassing speech or conduct." Richard Page & Kay Hunnicutt, *Freedom for the Thought Fact We Hate*, 21 J. COLLEGE & UNIV. L. 1, 4 (1994).

132. U.S. Dept. of Education, National Center for Educ. Statistics, DIGEST OF EDUCATION STATISTICS 269 (1993).

133. Nadine Strossen, *Regulating Racist Speech on Campus: A Modest Proposal?*, 1990 DUKE L. J. 484, 529.

134. *See id.* at 528 n.211, 529 n.217.

135. Christopher Shea, *Eye on the Judicial Process*, CHRON. HIGHER EDUC., Feb. 9, 1994, at A37.

136. *Id.*

137. If a professor accused under a speech policy informs other faculty members that the allegations are unfair, this may lead to additional charges of retaliation and reprisal. When Mesabi Community College Professor Richard Osborne publicly objected to an all-female counseling staff, the counselors filed a sexual harassment complaint against him with the Minnesota Community College System. Osborne sent a memo to members of the faculty association about the complaint and read a summary of the complaint at the faculty association meeting. After an investigation, the college's investigator found none of the allegations constituted sexual harassment, but that telling faculty members about the complaint was an act of retaliation and reprisal. The president put a letter of reprimand in Professor Osborne's file. *Mesabi Professor Sues Over Free Speech Rights*, STAR TRIBUNE, April 9, 1994 at 2B. In behalf of Professor Osborne, the Minnesota ACLU and the Center for Individual Rights filed suit in federal court alleging that the letter of reprimand abridged Osborne's academic freedom. As part of a settlement reached in October, 1994, the college agreed to rescind the letter of reprimand, to remove it from Osborne's file, and to transfer all documents relating to the sexual harassment case to the Office of the

Attorney General. *Free Speech Wins*, 198 CIVIL LIBERTIES NEWS, Dec. 1994, at 1.
138. *See* Strossen, *supra* note 133, at 528-29.
139. Blass, *supra* note 123, at 15.
140. Benno Schmidt, *Universities Must Defend Free Speech*, WALL ST. J. May 6, 1991, at A16.
141. *Doe v. Univ. of Mich.*, 721 F. Supp. 852, 865-66 (E.D. Mich. 1989). Another incident cited by the Michigan court involved the first class of a second-year dentistry course regarded as one of the most difficult in the curriculum. To allay fears, the instructor divided the students up into small sections to discuss anticipated problems. One student stated that "he had heard that minorities had a difficult time in the course and that he had heard that they were not treated fairly." The minority professor teaching the class filed a complaint on the grounds that the comment was unfair. Following investigation, the student agreed to apologize. *Id.* Another federal court in Michigan, citing a pattern of alleged speech policy violations being followed by investigation and enforcement, struck down the Central Michigan University speech code for similar reasons. *Dambrot v. Central Mich. Univ.*, 839 F.Supp. 477, 482 (E.D. Mich. 1993).
Before a federal court struck down the University of Wisconsin's speech code, one of the code administrators on just one Wisconsin campus had investigated ten formal complaints and found no violations of the code. Several complaints were directed at critical cartoons in the student newspaper; another complaint was for calling several students "primitive dinosaurs," and so on. Across the University of Wisconsin system, nine students drew disciplinary sanctions after investigations. For example, a student was placed on probation and ordered into sensitivity training for calling another student "Shakazulu." Shaka was the founder of the Zulu empire in the nineteenth century. The accused student insisted that the term was not intended to be offensive, but the campus director of student life decided that the term was perceived by the listening student as rude and therefore found a violation of the speech code. The same administration failed to apply the rule after a student called another a "redneck," which is defined as a disparaging name for an uneducated white farm laborer. *See* Barry Siegel, *Fighting Words: It Seemed Like a Noble Idea—Regulating Hateful Language*, L.A. TIMES, March 28, 1993, at 14; *UWM, Inc. v. Board of Regents of Univ. of Wis. System*, 774 F.Supp. 1163, 1167, 1179 (E.D. Wis. 1991).
142. Samuel Francis, *Penned in by PC Ethnic Cleansing*, WASH. TIMES, May 4, 1993, at F1; Richard Bernstein, *Play Penn*, NEW REPUBLIC, Aug. 2, 1993, at 16-17. A second recent example of the use of a speech code investigation at Penn to enforce fundamentalist ideology occurred in January, 1993. Around midnight on January 13, five African-American women were loudly celebrating outside of a high-rise dormitory. Eden Jacobowitz, a freshman coming to Penn from a yeshiva, was trying to write an English paper. He yelled out his window, "shut up you water buffalo," a translation of the Hebrew word, *behameh*. This is a common insult meaning foolish or rude person, used by one Hebrew-speaking Jew to another. It has no known racial connotation. Water buffalo are domesticated oxen used in Asia.
The police investigated a complaint of racial harassment. The judicial inquiry officer reviewed the police reports, interviewed Jacobowitz four times, and concluded that Jacobowitz had intended a racial slur because his accusers interpreted water buffalo to mean large black animals that live in Africa. She decided Jacobowitz was guilty of racial harassment. He could take her decision to hearing or take her offer of a settlement. The charges would be dropped if he would

write a letter of apology and present a proposal for a sensitivity training program for himself. Notice of his violation of the racial harassment policy would stay in his file. Jacobowitz refused. The case was scheduled for hearing on April 26. After the national press focused on the story, the hearing was delayed several times. A panel of faculty and students eventually heard only Jacobowitz's motion to dismiss on May 14. It denied the motion. A full hearing was scheduled for September 9. On May 25, the five women requested that the charges be dropped. Jacobowitz lived with the accusations of moral turpitude, investigations, tribunals, and the threat of serious sanctions for four months. Professor Alan Charles Kors, who represented Jacobowitz, commented that on most campuses, many people are intimidated. University of Pennsylvania physics professor Michael Cohen, who has taught for thirty-five years at Penn, believes that, "The racial harassment policy on campus is a general form of intimidation.... I was around during the McCarthy era and this is much worse, there has been nothing like this." Bernstein, *supra*, at 17; Michael Hinds, *Blacks at Penn Drop a Charge of Harassment*, N.Y. TIMES, May 25, 1993, at A-10; Christopher Shea, *Resolution of Racial-Harassment Case at U. of Penn. Leaves Everyone Dissatisfied*, CHRON. HIGHER EDUC., June 2, 1993, at A24-A25; Nancy Roman, *Penn's Delay of Trial for 'Slur' Called Political, But Not Correct*, WASH. TIMES, April 27, 1993, at A-1; Robert Leiter, *'Water Buffalo' a Racial Slur? Penn. and Student Disagree*, ETHNIC NEWSWATCH, April 30, 1993, at 24; Laurence Stans, *Speech Impediments*, ROLLING STONE, August 5, 1993, at 45-49.

The university's board of inquiry to look into the procedural aspects of the case concluded that the judicial procedure failed the five women who had requested that the charges be withdrawn. The causes of the denied justice were efforts by outside organizations such as the American Civil Liberties Union and the press and the adverse publicity the case generated. The harassment code contained flaws which could not withstand the stress of intense publicity. *Editorial, The Penn File: An Update*, W.S.J., April 4, 1994, at A14.

In another case in April of 1994, a Kent State University senior displayed a sign at the student center urging homosexuals to "think straight." After several students complained to the administration, the senior took the sign down because he did not want to face a possible disciplinary hearing for what the student conduct code calls,"behavior deemed detrimental to the university community." Debra Dennis, *Student Alleges KSU Code Stifles Free Speech*, PLAIN DEALER, May 4, 1994, at 1B.

143. Courtney Leatherman, *Fighting Back*, CHRON. HIGHER EDUC., March 16, 1994, at A17, A18. The media have picked up some of these cases. For example, a male student in Professor Lawrence Jorgensen's class in the American political system at Los Angeles Valley College asked about the availability of extra credit. Jorgensen replied that, "No, I can't accept credit cards because I don't have a machine, I won't accept checks because of the economy, and I don't accept sexual favors because of AIDS. So you will all have to do the assigned work." A female student brought harassment charges. Professor Farrel Broslewsky, "designated representative" for Professor Jorgensen, wrote to the sexual harassment compliance officer that "[f]irst your office encourages the filing of malicious complaints of sexual harassment so that your office can open secret files on the accused instructor. You deny the instructor the opportunity to confront the accuser, you refuse access to the files, you obstruct efforts of the falsely accused instructor to be exonerated." Alexander Cockburn, *Beat the Devil*, THE NATION, April 11, 1994 at 475, 476. At Wayne State University, a member of the Tlingit Indian

tribe filed a complaint against a white professor who she said had used deroga-
tory terms like "squaw" in a course on American Indians. Campus officials investigated the charge and said last summer [1993] that they had found no evidence
of racism on the professor's part. At Iowa State, four students filed grievances
complaining that a white teacher of African American history courses behaved
curtly, cut off classroom discussion, and faced the "white" side of the classroom
too much. The history department conducted an investigation which cleared the
professor. Denise Magner, *When Whites Teach Black Studies*, CHRON. HIGHER
EDUC., Dec. 1, 1993, at A19, A20. Responding to an argument that sexuality
was socially learned, sociology professor Stephen Sanderson at Indiana University of Pennsylvania commented that while he was making no judgment on homosexuality, it was "a kind of biological abnormality." The student filed a
complaint and an investigation followed. Sanderson believes that it is chilling to
investigate complaints for stating views in the classroom. Courtney Leatherman,
Fighting Back, CHRON. HIGHER EDUC., March 16, 1994, at A17, A18. *See
Liberal Harassment*, DEMOCRATIC CULTURE, Spring, 1994, at 27–28 for two
similar stories. At the University of Wisconsin, Milwaukee, two women graduate students filed sexual harassment complaints against feminist theory Professor Jane Gallop in late 1992. They claimed that while Gallop pretended to be a
feminist, in reality, she did not take these women seriously as students. After a
lengthy investigation, the university's Office of Affirmative Action found no
harassment but chastised Professor Gallop for something of which there had
been no complaint: a too intense, too personal, too volatile *pedagogical* relationship with one student. Jane Gallop, *Feminism and Harassment Policy*, ACA-
DEME, Sept.-Oct. 1994, at 16–18. A number of similar stories appear in Paul
Trout, *Second Thoughts on Sexual Harassment*, MONTANA PROFESSOR,
Spring, 1994, at 9–11.

In response to student demands that only a Native American should teach
Native American Studies at Chico State University, History Professor Joseph
Conlin wrote a letter to the editor of the local newspaper arguing that such demands were unrealistic because few Native Americans had Ph.D.'s in history
and those that did took jobs at prestigious universities with higher salaries. "By
the time you get to the level of Chico State University—speaking generally
again—little more is required of Affirmative Action faculty than that they show
evidence of a majority of vital life signs." In March, 1993, the American Indian
Club filed complaints under the university's racial harassment policy. In May,
the university's investigator found that Professor Conlin's written behavior was
responsible for "creating a demeaning learning and working environment" in
violation of the harassment policy and advised the president of possible sanctions, including suspension without pay, demotion, or dismissal. Five months
later, the president wrote that while he deplored Conlin's disruptive, insensitive,
inaccurate, and hurtful comments, he would not take disciplinary action in light
of Conlin's First Amendment rights. A few weeks later, Chico State scrapped its
racial harassment policy because of its unconstitutionality. Joseph Conlin, *How
the Rudest Man in Chico Fought the Law — And Won*, SACRAMENTO BEE,
January 16, 1994, at F1; Richard Ek, *College Drops Harassment Ban*, S.F.
CHRON., Dec. 4, 1993, at A18.

144. Dirk Johnson, *'Word Cops' Monitor a Classroom*, STAR TRIB., May 13, 1994,
at 4A.

145. Brian Jackson, *Bible Scholar Sues to Fight Taint of Sexual Harassment*, CHI-
CAGO SUN TIMES, March 25, 1994, at News, p. 5.

146. *Fighting Back, supra* note 143, at 18.

147. Memorandum to faculty from Patricia Mullen, Director of the Office of Equal Opportunity and Affirmative Action and Betty Kroll, Director of the Minnesota Women's Center (August 30, 1993).

148. American Historical Association, STATEMENT ON STANDARDS OF PROFESSIONAL CONDUCT (1993) at 5.

149. *Id.* at 9–11.

150. Samuel Walker, HATE SPEECH: THE HISTORY OF AN AMERICAN CONTROVERSY 127 (1994).

151. *Id.* at 133.

152. Stuart Taylor, Jr., *A Clintonite Threat to Free Speech*, LEGAL TIMES, May 9, 1994 at 27. The broad definition of harassment in the guidance together with the department's investigatory power are chilling. In fiscal 1993, the department issued thirty-five rulings in cases alleging racial harassment at colleges. It found violations in six. Scott Jaschik, *U.S. Issues Policy on Racial Harassment*, CHRON. HIGHER EDUC., March 23, 1994, at A22.

153. Scott Jaschik & Robert R. Schmidt, Jr., *College Accreditors Spur Use of Quotas, Federal Officials Say*, CHRON. HIGHER EDUC., Dec. 4, 1991, at A37, A43.

154. Scott Jaschik, *Middle States Moves to Compromise on Diversity Rules*, CHRON. HIGHER EDUC., Dec. 18, 1991, at A25, A29. In February of 1994, the Western Association of Schools and Colleges adopted diversity guidelines that were criticized as overly prescriptive and regulatory. Courtney Leatherman, *All Quiet on Western Front—For Now*, CHRON. HIGHER EDUC., March 2, 1994, at A17. Stanford President Gerhard Casper, with the unanimous support of Stanford's Faculty Senate, objected to Western's overstepping accreditation's traditional bounds. "WASC is seeking to become the arbiter of social and educational standards on every campus it accredits." *'In' Box*, CHRON. HIGHER EDUC., February 16, 1994, at A23.

155. *See* Fritz Machlup, *On Some Misconceptions Concerning Academic Freedom*, reprinted in AAUP, ACADEMIC FREEDOM AND TENURE 177, 184–85 (Louis Joughin ed. 1969).

156. Craig Lambert, *The Radical Conservative: Harvey Mansfield*, HARV. MAG., Jan.-Feb. 1993, at 52, 54.

157. Craig Anderson, *Political Correctness on College Campuses: Freedom of Speech v. Doing the Politically Correct Thing*, 46 SMU L. REV. 171, 221–22 (1992); *See* Jan H. Blits, *The Silenced Partner: Linda Gottfredson and the Univ. of Del.*, ACAD. QUESTIONS, Summer 1991, at 41–42.

158. Nino Langiulli, *Dispatches From the War Zone*, MEASURE, March 1992, at 5, 6. Smith College also attempted to block grants from the Pioneer Fund to Professor Seymour Itzkoff for a series of books on the evolution of human intelligence. Smith backed off after warnings that the College violated Professor Itzkoff's academic freedom. Blits, *supra* note 157, at 44.

159. David Wheeler, *Meeting on Possible Links Between Genes and Crime Canceled After Bitter Exchange*, CHRON. HIGHER EDUC., Sept. 16, 1992, at A-7, A-8; David Wasserman, *In Defense of a Conference on Genetics and Crime: Assessing the Social Impact of a Public Debate*, CHRON. HIGHER EDUC., Sept. 23, 1992, at A-44.

160. John Hinton, *Ivy League Theology*, ACAD. QUESTIONS., Spring 1993, at 37, 43–44. A more recent similar case involves bible scholar and former academic dean, Professor Graydon Snyder, at Chicago Theological Seminary. In March, 1992, "[In] a discussion of the role of intent in sin, Professor Snyder recited a story from the Talmud, the writings that make up Jewish civil and religious law, about a man who falls off a roof, lands on a woman and accidentally has inter-

course with her. The Talmud says he is innocent of sin, since the act was unintentional. A woman in the class was offended, not by the sexual theme, but because she believed the story justified brutality toward women. She filed a complaint against Professor Snyder." Dirk Johnson, *A Sexual Harassment Case to Test Academic Freedom*, N.Y. TIMES, May 11, 1994, Education at 2.

The Sexual Harassment Task Force investigated and held hearings on the complaint. Snyder asserts that while he was questioned twice by the task force, he never received formal notice of the charges and was not permitted to hear or cross examine adverse witnesses. After a year, the Task Force found that Snyder had "engaged in verbal conduct of a sexual nature" that had the purpose or effect of, "unreasonably interfering with an individual's work or academic performance or [of] creating an intimidating, hostile or offensive working or academic environment." Edward Walsh, *Sexual Ethics in the Seminary*, WASH. POST, May 13, 1994, at D1. The Task Force issued a public formal reprimand of Professor Snyder, placed him on probation, directed that he seek psychological therapy and attend sexual harassment workshops, and ordered the taping of his classes by school officials. In February, 1994, Snyder filed a lawsuit claiming defamation and denial of due process of law against the seminary. See, Johnson, *supra*; Walsh, *supra*; Adrienne Drell, *Bible Scholar Sues to Fight Taint of Sex Harassment*, CHICAGO SUN-TIMES, March 25, 1994, at News p. 5.

161. For example, the student activists in the MacNeil situation sought to prevent Harvard from considering Professor MacNeil for a tenured position. *See* Macneil, *supra* note 78, at 10. When a friend of Professor Stephan Thernstrom sought to put together a prestigious advisory panel to bring about more effective teaching of history in the secondary schools, she found that mentioning Professor Thernstrom as a potential panelist caused potential appointees to note that Professor Thernstrom had been involved in a racial incident at Harvard and was controversial. Thernstrom, *supra* note 66, at 15-16. In an attempt to silence opposing views, a feminist philosopher urged a journal not to print writings of Professor Christine Sommers critical of feminist scholarship. Scott Jaschik, *Row Over an Unpublished Article Illustrates the Enmity in the Political Correctness War*, CHRON. HIGHER EDUC., Jan 15, 1992, at A16. For some professors involved in the interviewing process, African American candidates for teaching positions who dissent from the view of the diversity movement are not considered as acceptable. *See* Bahls, *supra* note 67, at 15-16; Ian Haney-Lopez, *Community Ties, Race, and Faculty Hiring: The Case for Professors Who Don't Think White*, 3 RECONSTRUCTION 46, 48 (1991).

162. Rogers Worthington, *Wisconsin Debates 'Correct' Viewpoint*, CHIC. TRIB., June 16, 1991, at 19.

163. *See Hard-Won Acceptance Spawns New Conflicts Around Ethnic Studies*, N.Y. TIMES, Jan. 2, 1991, at B-8; Anita Susan Grossman, *Turmoil at S.F. State Over Black Students*, CALIF. SCHOLAR, Spring, 1991, at 10. This occurred also in the Gribben case, where colleagues urged students not to take courses from the accused, and not to use the accused as a thesis advisor. *See* Salemi, *supra* note 87, at 5. French Professor Robert Cohn at Stanford published a criticism of militant feminism in the campus paper. After discovering that graduate students were boycotting his courses because of his views, he took early retirement in 1992. Langiulli, *supra* note 158, at 7-8; Robert G. Cohn, Letter to Editor, COMMENTARY, June 1992, at 18; *see also* Lambert, *supra* note 156, at 54, where Harvard Professor Harvey Mansfield states that he knows of early retirements because of harassment. In July of 1989, anonymous members of the "Student Coalition Against Mitchell's Madness" publicly circulated a memorandum at the author's

college directing students not to register in the classes of nine faculty members who had advocated academic standards and excellence. A word-of-mouth campaign continued through 1992–93 encouraging students not to register in the courses of professors alleged to be hostile to the diversity movement's ideology.

164. Louis Jacobs, *A Report: Political or Pedagogical Correctness*, ACAD. QUESTIONS, Spring 1993, at 59, 61.

165. *Levin v. Harleston*, 770 F. Supp. 895, 907 (S.D.N.Y. 1991), *aff'd in part & vacated in part*, 966 F.2d 85 (2d Cir. 1992).

166. *Id.* at 907–08.

167. *Id.* at 917–18. In the fall semester of 1992, University of Michigan sociology professor David Goldberg, an authority in statistical analysis, taught Sociology 510, called Social Statistics. The course is required for graduate students in Sociology. In March, 1993, a group of unnamed graduate students, via a widely distributed letter signed by seven student organizations, accused Goldberg of racial and sexual harassment and professional incompetence in his teaching of social statistics. The letter called for a public investigation and Goldberg's dismissal from teaching required courses. The students claimed that Goldberg's statistical analyses were race and gender biased. The department chair met with a group of graduate students. Without a hearing or opportunity for Goldberg's rebuttal, the chair assured the students that Goldberg would be removed from teaching Sociology 510 and no longer assigned to teaching required courses. After a number of faculty informed the department chair that they did not support Goldberg's removal from Sociology 510, the chair reassigned Goldberg to teach Sociology 510 but scheduled a new section to be taught by another professor for those students who wanted to avoid Goldberg. *PC Gone Wild: The Goldberg Case*, MICHIGAN SCHOLAR, September, 1993 at 2–3.

168. Professor Fox-Genovese published an award-winning book on Southern women's history; her new book, *Feminism Without Illusions: A Critique of Individualism*, both criticizes feminists for considering the rights of the individual over what is best for the community and defends the idea of a literary canon. *See* Scott Heller, *Emory U.'s Director of Women's Studies Quits, Describing Complaints as 'Political Power Play'*, CHRON. HIGHER EDUC., Feb. 12, 1992, at A-13, A-18; Carol Iannone, *Professor Elizabeth Fox-Genovese*, ACAD. QUESTIONS, Summer 1992, at 56.

169. Iannone, *supra* note 168, at 59–60.

170. *Id.* at 62–64. Similarly, in the fall of 1990, Professor Stanley Fish, chairperson of the English Department at Duke, wrote the provost claiming that professors joining the National Association of Scholars were racist, sexist, and homophobic and therefore should no longer have the right to participate in tenure and curriculum decisions. Carolyn Mooney, *Academic Group Fighting the 'Politically Correct Movement' Gains Momentum*, CHRON. HIGHER EDUC., Dec. 12, 1990, at A-13, A-16; Michael Neth, *Johnny One-Note*, 60 AM. SCHOLAR 608, 612–13 (Autumn 1991).

171. Iannone, *supra* note 168, at 62–64; Heller, *supra* note 168, at A-13.

172. Courtney Leatherman, *Colleague Sues Ex-Director of Women's Studies at Emory U. for Sexual Harassment and Bias*, CHRON. HIGHER EDUC., March 3, 1993, at A15.

173. Carter, *supra* note 69, at 109–10.

174. Patai & Koertge, *supra* note 91, at 11–12.

175. Professor Gribben lost his position as chairperson of Graduate Studies at the University of Texas because of his dissenting views. After two years of vilification, Professor Gribben began to apply for positions elsewhere in the country. A

number of English departments that initially scheduled interviews abruptly broke off negotiations. Friends informed him that individual faculty members at Texas were in contact with these schools telling them not to hire Gribben because he was a racist and a sexist. Professor Gribben finally secured a position at a branch of Auburn University. *See* Salemi, *supra* note 87, at 5–6.

176. Professor Mandelstamm at Virginia Tech was also forced out of his tenured position through repeated investigations based on anonymous complaints where administrators failed to give adequate notice of the charges and failed to take minimal pains with the facts by looking at evidence. He resigned, and believes that no university would hire a sixty-two-year-old professor alleged to be a racist and sexist, regardless of a distinguished teaching record. Mandelstamm, *supra* note 78, at 18.

177. Lambert, *supra* note 156. *See* Kay S. House, *Letter to the Editor*, KEY REPORTER, Winter 1993/94, at 11; Robert Cohn, *Letter to the Editor*, COMMENTARY, June 1992, at 18.

178. Richard Bernstein, *Guilty if Charged*, N.Y. REV. OF BOOKS, Jan. 13, 1994, at 11–14; Courtney Leatherman, *U. of New Hampshire Wrestles With Issue of Sexual Harassment in Wake of Professor's Suspension*, CHRON. HIGHER EDUC., January 12, 1994, at A18.

179. *Silva v. University of New Hampshire*, 1994 WL 504417 at 16, 17.

180. *Academic Freedom and Tenure: University of New Hampshire*, ACADEME, Nov.-Dec. 1994, at 78, 80.

181. *'In' Box*, CHRON. HIGHER ED., Dec. 14, 1994, at A19.

182. NEWSDAY, Dec. 3, 1990, at 86. Frederick Spiegel, *Endangered Theses*, COLUMBIA DAILY TRIBUNE, Oct. 16, 1990, at 7. When Murray Dolfman, a lecturer at the University of Pennsylvania, found no one in his legal studies class who could identify where the term "involuntary servitude" could be found in the American Constitution, Dolfman expressed surprise that while he, as a Jew and a former slave, celebrated Passover, the black students, whom he likewise called "ex slaves," did not celebrate the passage of the Thirteenth Amendment. After class, several minority students accused Dolfman of racial insensitivity. Dolfman met with the students and apologized if they had taken offense. He thought the students accepted his apology. A few months later during Black History Month, this incident was raised repeatedly to illustrate how bad things are at Penn. President Sheldon Hackney reprimanded Dolfman and called for an investigation. Meanwhile approximately 200 students disrupted a large lecture class Dolfman was teaching. When he tried to move to a different room, the students disrupted that class. Hackney then asked for and received a formal apology from Dolfman. About 200 students occupied Hackney's office seeking Dolfman's dismissal. Hackney suspended Dolfman for a semester, and ordered him both to participate in sensitivity training and to be monitored by the Legal Studies Department. *See* D'Souza, *supra* note 19, at 201–02; Bernstein, *supra* note 142, at 17–19. In 1992, the Wharton School, citing budgetary reasons, did not renew Dolfman's contract. Richard Bernstein, DICTATORSHIP OF VIRTUE 115 (1994). Assistant Professor Jeff Wallen, who taught European literature at Hampshire College in Massachusetts, was not rehired when he failed to "present an adequate Third World perspective." When Wallen protested that the works of Richard Wright and Jorge Luis Borges were part of his curriculum, a colleague wrote, "I seriously question his understanding of the Third World Expectation." Wallen attributed the loss of his position to a failure on his part "to teach that the story of Western Civilization is the history of imperialism, racism, and oppression." BOSTON GLOBE, Dec. 20, 1990, at 97; NEWSDAY, *supra*.

During fall semester, 1993, Communications Professor Gerald Gee at Florida A&M University tried to shake his public relations class out of their apathy by paraphrasing the term, "slave mentality," from Jerry Farber's 1967 book, *The Student as Nigger*. Gee told his class that "Sitting around and waiting for opportunities or not taking advantage of the opportunities that there are is kind of what some would call a nigger mentality.... It's the sort of thing that can keep people in the back of the bus forever." Several students filed a complaint. The university president informed Gee that his contract would not be renewed because of violations of the university's harassment and discrimination policy. The Board of Regents did not endorse the action because the university had not followed its own disciplinary procedures. The university ultimately imposed a two-week suspension without pay. Sabrina Miller, *Strong Words had Wrong Impact*, ST. PETERSBURG TIMES, Dec. 19, 1994, at 1A.

183. Joseph Salemi, *Political Correctness at Dallas Baptist University: The Firing of David Ayers and John Jeffrey*, MEASURE, Aug-Sept. 1992, at 1-13. Professor Louis Menand disagrees with Salemi's "unsubstantiated claims about the influence of radical feminists at Dallas Baptist." Menand concludes, based on unspecified evidence, that it seems most likely the dismissals "were prompted by the conviction that a refusal to apologize under the circumstances was un-Christian." Louis Menand, *The Culture Wars*, N.Y. REV., Oct. 6, 1994, at 21.

184. *Id.* at 12.

185. Louis Menand, *What Are Universities For? The Real Crisis on Campus is One of Identity*, HARPER'S, Dec. 1991, at 47, 52.

186. Dinesh D'Souza, *Cap and Goon; Facing up to the New Intolerance on Campus*, WASH. POST, Apr. 7, 1991, at D1; Tom Sontag, *Neo-McCarthyism*, STAR TRIB., July 13, 1991, at A13. After Brandeis University announced its intention to bestow an honorary degree on former ambassador Kirkpatrick in the spring of 1994, a group of professors and students protested. The university administration called Kirkpatrick and in effect asked her to withdraw. Editorial, *Disgrace at Brandeis*, JERUSALEM POST, May 15, 1994, at 6.

187. Eric Felten, *Freedom to Think at Harvard Law*, WASH. TIMES, July 17, 1991, at E1.

188. Herbert London, *In the Bunkers of Binghamton*, ACAD. QUESTIONS, Fall 1991, at 15, 16. David Beers writes that this incident was much less ominous because: (1) it involved a simple disrupter, not an entire audience; (2) the disruption lasted four minutes; and (3) the sticks supposedly brandished consisted of one walking stick, used as such, and a handful of pledge canes, carried as symbols of fraternity membership. David Beers, *What Happened at SUNY*, in BEYOND P.C. 107, 108 (Patricia Aufderheide ed. 1992). On May 13, 1992, fundamentalist students and faculty at the University of California-San Diego used tactics very similar to those at SUNY-Binghamton to disrupt a speech. A conservative student group had arranged for Professor George Reismann to speak on a published paper defending the openness of western civilization. The protesters circulated a flyer denouncing the "academic racists" who were engaging in "open racism" that must not go unchallenged. About a third of the 250 in attendance at the speech consisted of protesters who shouted down Professor Reisman, interrupting him with taunts, obscenities, and epithets. A faculty member told Professor Reisman, "[Y]ou have no right to speak here," and advised him to "get off the campus as soon as you can." Anita Grossman and Thomas Wood, *Free Speech Under Fire: Barbarism at UC San Diego*, CALIF. SCHOLAR, Winter 1992-93, at 12-13. A speech may also be disrupted to protest university policy. In March of 1989, 100 students charged the stage during Howard University's convocation ceremony

to protest the appointment of a conservative to the Board of Trustees. Bill Cosby was prevented from speaking. *See* D'Souza, *supra* note 19, at 98.

189. Hugh Murray, Letter to the Editor, *Liberals' Behavior Reveals Their Hypocrisy*, CHRON. HIGHER EDUC., Nov. 27, 1991, at B4. University of Wisconsin News Release Regarding Union Concourse Incident, October 28, 1991. In 1991 protesters at Yale University shouted down Louis Sullivan, Health and Human Services Secretary in the Bush Administration, and effectively prevented him from making himself heard to a group that had invited him to speak. *See* Schmidt, *supra* note 140, at A16. When Pennsylvania Democratic governor, Bill Casey, attempted to speak at Cooper Union in October, 1992, on the topic, "Can a Liberal be Pro-life?", he was driven out by jeers and shouts from 100 pro-choice protesters. At Cornell University in the same month, about 150 demonstrators disrupted a pro-life conference attended by about 100 people from higher education. Kyle Hughes, *Free Speech Takes a Beating in N.Y.*, GANNETT NEWS SERVICE, Nov. 3, 1992. At Portland State in the fall of 1992, twenty protesters from the Bi-Sexual Gay and Lesbian Alliance positioned themselves in the front row and disrupted Peter Colliers' speech on homosexuality and political correctness. The protesters repeatedly raised and lowered signs saying PIG, LIES, and BIGOT throughout the speech. David Horowitz, memorandum titled Oregon Betrayal, November 2, 1992 (on file at the National Association of Scholars). The threat of disruption may cause a university to withdraw lecture engagements. After Khalid Abdul Muhammed gave anti-Semitic speeches at Howard University which met enthusiastic support among some radical students, Howard's administration ultimately decided to cancel a campus lecture on slavery by Yale Professor David Davis, who converted to Judaism in 1988. The atmosphere was too volatile. Mary Cage, *A Life Spent Interpreting the History of Slavery*, CHRON. HIGHER EDUC., May 4, 1994, at A6.

190. *Levin v. Harleston*, 770 F. Supp. 895, 903–05 (S.D. N.Y. 1991), *aff'd in part & vacated in part*, 966 F.2d 85 (2d Cir. 1992). After publication of his article questioning affirmative action in the alumni magazine in November, 1990, seventy-five students marched into Anthropology Professor Vincent Sarich's class at Berkeley, shouting, "bullshit" and "racist" and drowning out the lecture. *See Taking Offense, supra* note 124; *Berkeley, supra* note 124. Similarly, at San Francisco State, to protest the offering of a course on black subjects outside the Black Studies Department, fifty to sixty shouting demonstrators interrupted Professor Robert Smith's first class in "Black Politics" in the fall of 1990. Two of Smith's later classes were similarly disrupted. Protesters also shouted down the President and other speakers at a university-wide convocation in early September. Anita Susan Grossman, *Turmoil at S.F. State Over Black Studies*, CALIF. SCHOLAR, Spring, 1991, at 11. The first two fall 1990 classes of two University of Denver faculty members with views on social and economic equality critical of the left were disrupted by protest rallies. *Professor Claims Berkeley Puts Diversity Above Excellence, supra* note 124. After Professor Murrey Dolfman was accused of racially insensitive remarks, approximately 200 students occupied his class at the University of Pennsylvania in the fall of 1988 to prevent him from teaching. *See* D'Souza, *supra* note 19, at 201–02. In fall semester, 1993, a student in Professor Christie Farnham Pope's black history course at Iowa State asked, "Why was a white woman teaching this course?" After that the student constantly disrupted the class. In a remark made outside of class, the student threatened a jihad, or holy war, against the professor. The department chair then barred the student from the course, although he was later allowed to return. Members of the university's Black Student Alliance began holding sit-ins in Professor

Pope's classroom. The Alliance predicted that, "the campus is about to explode." Four students in the course filed grievances complaining about Professor Pope's teaching and accusing her of cutting off classroom discussion. The history department conducted an investigation, but found no wrongdoing. Denise Magner, *When Whites Teach Black Studies*, CHRON. HIGHER EDUC., Dec. 1, 1993, at A19-A20; Christie Farnham Pope, *The Challenges Posed by Radical Afrocentrism*, CHRON. HIGHER EDUC., March 30, 1994 at B1, B2.

191. Kenneth R. Clark, *Must Freedom Offend? 'Safe Speech' Forum Makes Weapons of Words in a War Over Discourse*, CHICAGO TRIB., June 5, 1991, at C7. After Princeton senior Harold Wenglinsky criticized a Take Back the Night March for excluding other points of view, he was intimidated into silence by public accusations that he was a murderer and rapist, ostracism, and two death threats. Jonathan Rockoff, *Vilified for Views at Princeton*, PHILADELPHIA INQUIRER, May 29, 1991, at 6-BJ.

192. *See* C. Vann Woodward, *Freedom and the Universities*, N.Y. REV., July 18, 1991, at 32, 33 (reviewing Dinesh D'Souza, ILLIBERAL EDUCATION: THE POLITICS OF RACE AND SEX ON CAMPUS (1991). In the spring of 1989, students took over the administration building at Howard University for three days, submitting a list of demands including an Afrocentric curriculum and removal of a conservative trustee. As individual demands were met by the administration, the protesters kept adding new ones including student review and approval of all new trustees and no liability for the destruction of university property. *See* D' Souza, *supra* note 19 at 100-102. In the spring of 1990, a contingent of law students at Columbia University protesting school policy on diversity issues occupied the dean's office and sent telegrams to alumni pleading for pressure on the administration. *See* Bahls, *supra* note 67, at 15. Also in the spring of 1990, students protesting the presence of Professor Michael Levin on the faculty forcibly occupied part of the college administration building at CCNY. *Levin v. Harleston*, 770 F. Supp. 895, 911 (S.D. N.Y. 1991), *aff'd* in part & vacated in part, 966, F.2d 85 (2d Cir. 1992).

193. *Berkeley Students Occupy Office in Growing Fight Over Diversity*, NAT'L L.J., Nov. 12, 1990, at 4 [hereinafter *Berkeley Students*]. Students protesting the absence of black women professors at Harvard Law School blocked the dean's office lobby twice in the fall of 1990. Felton, *supra* note 187. That fall, minority students at Cleveland State University occupied portions of the administration building protesting the departure of a top African-American administrator over a pay controversy. Courtney Leatherman, *Turmoil at Cleveland State Over Black Administrator's Departure Focuses Attention on Issues Facing Minority Affairs Officials*, CHRON. HIGHER EDUC., Sept. 12, 1990 at A17, A20. In the same semester, 250 students at SUNY-Binghamton occupied a dean's office and made a number of demands relating to diversity issues. *See* Bernardo, *supra* note 78, at 4; George Basler, *Sit-in at SUNY*, BINGHAMTON PRESS, Nov. 3, 1990 at 1A. Similarly, forty to fifty students at Bowdoin College for several hours blockaded the entrances to the library and the administrative building in the fall of 1990. They demanded that the president sign a list of demands to increase the number of minority professors and create a faculty position on gay and lesbian studies. Gary Crosby Brasor, *An Alumnus Learns How Might Makes Right at Bowdoin*, ACAD. QUESTIONS, Winter 1991-92 at 49, 52-53. Students also occupied the chancellor's office of the University of Illinois-Chicago to protest administrative response to racial tension. Kim Cobb, *Colleges Teach Tolerance, Some in Intolerant Fashion*, HOUSTON CHRON., Nov. 26, 1991, at A1.

194. *Angry Vermont Students Seize President's Office*, CHRON. HIGHER EDUC., Aug. 1, 1991, at A2; Anthony Flint, *University of Vermont Protest Needs Support to Succeed*, BOSTON GLOBE, May 5, 1991, at 78.

195. Mary Cage, *On Campuses Across the Country, Outrage and Disgust Greet Acquittals of Police Officers in Los Angeles*, CHRON. HIGHER EDUC., May 13, 1992, at A-33, A-36. A group of students also took over the Amhearst administrative building to protest a number of minority issues. *Id.* A number of other occupations and blockades occurred during 1992. In April of 1992, nine students occupied the hallway in the Harvard Law School dean's office for twenty-four hours to protest minority hiring. Ken Myers, *Two Controversial Incidents Said to Spotlight Harvard Woes*, NAT'L L.J., May 25, 1992, at 4. In the same month, police arrested 253 demonstrators who occupied the administration building at Brown University to protest an admissions policy that considers ability to pay as a factor. *253 Students Arrested in a Sit-In at Brown U.*, CHRON. HIGHER EDUC., April 29, 1992, at A-5. In May, 100 students occupied the administration building at the University of Illinois protesting for more Hispanic professors and students. *University of Illinois Defends Action in Sit-ins*, CHICAGO TRIB., Oct. 15, 1992, at C-9. During the fall of 1992, seven protestors disrupted a regents' meeting at the University of Minnesota to force the university to ban ROTC. Gregor Pinney, *7 Students Arrested Protesting ROTC Policy at 'U' Regents Meeting*, STAR TRIB., Oct. 10, 1992, at B-1. Similarly, 300 students occupied the administration building at the University of Rhode Island to protest racism, and to make demands including majors in African American families and Indian studies and a course that compares the writings of Thomas Jefferson and Malcolm X. *Rhode Island Students Protest Racism*, UPI, Nov. 11, 1992. Eighty students closed down the administration building at Georgia State to protest alleged racial discrimination. Marlene Karas, *Racial Incidents Draw Protests*, ATLANTA J. & CONST., Nov. 9, 1992, at A-1. Five protestors obstructed operations at Columbia University's administration building to protest the demolition of the building where Malcolm X was assassinated. Tristin Adie, *Suppressing the Spirit of '68*, NEWSDAY, March 3, 1993, at 84.

196. Dan Wetzel, *Is Mob Rule Any Way to Fight Racism?* BOSTON GLOBE, May 17, 1992, at 86–87.

197. *Students Protest Over Minority Hiring*, CHRON. HIGHER EDUC., Feb. 10, 1993, at A-4. In the spring of 1993, seventeen students were arrested for disorderly conduct in occupying the chancellor's office at the University of North Carolina-Chapel Hill. They demanded immediate action on the construction of a black cultural center. Notebook, CHRON. HIGHER EDUC., April 21, 1993, at A-37. One hundred and fifty students occupied the administration building and blocked entrances at the University of California-Berkeley to demand that the administration elevate the status of the ethnic studies program. *46 Students Arrested in Berkeley Protest*, CHRON. HIGHER EDUC., April 14, 1993, at A-4.

198. *Hispanic Students at Cornell University Protest Defacement of Artwork*, CHRON. HIGHER EDUC., Dec. 1, 1993, at A4.

199. *Bates College Students Protest Lack of Minorities*, CHRON. HIGHER EDUC., April 13, 1994, at A4; *see also Black Students Protest Blame for Assault*, CHRON. HIGHER EDUC., March 23, 1994, at A4 (Fifty students held an overnight sit-in at LeMoyne College's administration building); Aldo Bernardo, *Balkanization of Culture at Binghamton's Harpur College*, MEASURE, May/June 1994, at 3, 5 (In November of 1993, demonstrators broke up a meeting of the college council to discuss a diversity requirement. In May of 1994, demonstrators occupied the office of the provost for thirty-six hours over the same issue.).

200. Jack McCurdy, *UCLA's 'No' on Chicano Studies Dept. Brings Violent Protest*, CHRON. HIGHER EDUC., May 19, 1993, at A-16.
201. *Student Group Says It Set Fires at Cornell U.*, CHRON. HIGHER EDUC., Sept. 22, 1993, at A6. Also in September, several hooded protesters ran through two campus buildings at Berkeley, pulling fire alarms to protest the anti-illegal immigration policy of some California politicians. Christopher Shea, *Hispanic Students, Frustrated Over Pace of Reforms on Campuses, Raise the Ante*, CHRON. HIGHER EDUC., Oct. 13, 1993, at A40.
202. Mensah Dean, *Half-run of UMd. Paper Stolen; Racism Cited in Notes on Racks*, WASH. TIMES, Nov. 2, 1993, at C5.
203. *Newspaper Copies Vanish After Accusations of Racism*, NEW YORK TIMES, Nov. 3, 1993, at B-15. Similar theft and destruction of student newspapers occurred at other campuses. At Pennsylvania State University, a trustee of the university woke in the middle of the night on April 22, 1993, to a large pile of student newspapers burning in his front yard to protest editorials critical of the women's studies program. Jeff Muir, *Universities Ignore Violence and Vandalism Against Conservative Student Publications*, CHRON. HIGHER EDUC., June 2, 1993, at B-2. In mid-April 1993, 14,000 copies of the University of Pennsylvania's student newspaper were stolen by a group of black and Latino students to protest racism, particularly the column of Gregory Pavlik, a conservative student who wrote provocatively about race. Howard Goodman, *Penn Paper is Trashed*, PHILADELPHIA INQUIRER, April 16, 1993, at A-1. Similar events occurred during spring and fall semesters, 1993, and spring semester, 1994, at the College of Holy Cross, North Carolina State University, the University of Wisconsin, Johns Hopkins University, Dartmouth, Duke, and Franklin and Marshall College. *See* Muir, *supra*; Howard Kurtz, *A Trash Course in Free Speech: College Newspapers Pitched in Protest*, WASH. POST, July 29, 1993, at C1; Notebook, CHRON. HIGHER EDUC., Oct. 13, 1993, at A40; Notebook, CHRON. HIGHER EDUC., April 20, 1994, at A33; David Folkenflik, *Duke Flares Over Paper Protest*, DURHAM HERALD-SUN, Sept. 28, 1993 at 1A.
204. Alan Kors, Interviewed by Carol Iannone, *Thought Reform and Education: A View from the University of Pennsylvania*, ACAD. QUESTIONS, Fall 1988, at 75, 83.
205. David Lehman, SIGNS OF THE TIMES: DECONSTRUCTION AND THE FALL OF PAUL DE MAN 72, 77 (1991).
206. Paul Lauter, Materials for Participants in UDI/TDC Organizer's Workshop, April 9, 1992.
207. Macneil, *supra* note 78, at 10. In the author's situation described in the Preface, the fundamentalist academic left supported five internal investigations, three lawsuits, a Human Rights Department investigation, and a Lawyers Board of Professional Responsibility investigation over a five-and-one-half-year period.
208. *The Nation: Faculty Attitudes and Activities, 1989–90*, CHRON. HIGHER EDUC., April 24, 1991, at A32.
209. Harvard Professor Randall Kennedy writes that the strategic use of accusations of prejudice to exploit the stigmatization of racial bigotry has received little scholarly attention. The strategy is real. Randall Kennedy, *Racial Critiques of Legal Academia*, 102 HARV. L. REV. 1745, 1809–10 (1989).
210. Karen Winkler, *Survey Finds Historians Worried About Profession*, CHRON. HIGHER EDUC., Jan. 20, 1995, at A18.
211. Earnest Boyer, Philip Altbach, Mary Jean Whitelaw, THE ACADEMIC PROFESSION 98–101 (1994).
212. *See* Bahls, *supra* note 96, at 1048, 1050.

213. Paul Brest, *The Disorderly University: A Reply to Tushnet*, 4 YALE J. L. & HU-MAN. 381, 383 (1992). Harvard Law Professor Alan Dershowitz agrees. "As a teacher, I can feel a palpable reluctance on the part of many students, particularly those with views in neither extreme and those anxious for peer acceptance, to experiment with unorthodox ideas...to challenge politically correct views, and to disagree with minority feminist or gay perspectives." Alan Dershowitz, CONTRARY TO POPULAR OPINION 112 (1992).

214. In his criminal law class at Harvard, Professor Alan Dershowitz teaches the law of rape as an example of a cutting-edge subject that poses a sharp conflict between the rights of defendants and their accusers. Dershowitz takes a "devil's advocate" position on these issues in class discussion. A group of students complained about Dershowitz's teaching of the rape issues. A student threatened that he would be "savaged" in the student evaluations, and a small group of students gave him very poor evaluations. "When the evaluations arrived," Dershowitz recounts, "I realized how dangerous it would be for an untenured professor to incur the wrath of the political correctness patrol.... Are there other, less established, teachers being coerced into changing their teaching by the fear of negative evaluations, which can be fatal to tenure? You bet they are, and it poses a real danger to academic freedom." Alan Dershowitz, CONTRARY TO PUBLIC OPINION 117-18 (1992).

215. David P. Bryden, *It Ain't What They Teach, It's The Way They Teach It*, PUB. INTEREST, Spring 1991, *reprinted in* David Bryden, *The Role of the Respectable Left*, MEASURE, July 1991, at 6. At the author's faculty, a professor viewed as the in-house radical on the left while in private practice is now labeled a reactionary because of public disagreement with some elements of fundamentalist ideology.

216. *See* D'Souza, *Students' Demands, supra* note 116, at B3.

217. Nat Hentoff, *"Speech Codes" On the Campus and Problems of Free Speech*, DISSENT, Fall 1991, *reprinted in* DEBATING P.C.: THE CONTROVERSY OVER POLITICAL CORRECTNESS ON COLLEGE CAMPUSES 215, 217-18 (Paul Berman ed., 1992) [hereinafter Hentoff, *"Speech Codes"*]; *see* Nat Hentoff, *Politically Correct at N.Y.U. Law*, WASH. POST, Nov. 3, 1990, at A23.

218. Russell Jacoby points out that fear of a humiliation leads to a withdrawal. A study of racism at Stanford found that many white students fear inadvertently insulting black students. "I'm scared to be called a racist. You've got to be careful all the time." Russell Jacoby, DOGMATIC WISDOM: HOW THE CULTURE WARS DIVERT EDUCATION AND DISTRACT AMERICA 81-82 (1994). For example, after Northeastern University Engineering Professor Peter Furth wrote an article urging the university to tolerate homosexuality but not to promote it through aggressive recruitment of gay faculty and staff members, he was called a bigot. Professor Furth said that forty people on the campus have indicated private support for his position but are afraid to speak up for fear of being attacked. *'In' Box*, CHRON. HIGHER EDUC., March 9, 1994, at A16.

219. Many of the faculty members at the University of New Hampshire who met with an AAUP investigating committee is 1994 "voiced acute concern about conditions for academic freedom at the University of New Hampshire. Their concern is based in large measure or upon the course of action followed in Professor Silva's case. These faculty members saw the administration as enforcing the university's sexual harassment policy without taking principles of academic freedom into adequate account. The investigating committee shares this view." *Academic Freedom and Tenure: The University of New Hampshire*, ACADEME, Nov.-Dec. 1994, at 79.

220. *See* Hentoff, *"Speech Codes"*, *supra* note 217, at 218.

221. *See* Schmidt, *supra* note 140.

222. *See* Bahls, *supra* note 67, at 15-16; Bryden *supra* note 64, at 648; Rauch, *supra* note 4, at 11. Barbara Epstein observes that, "I frequently find myself in discussions that seem to be dominated by a collective fear of saying something wrong: fear of betraying a racist, sexist or homophobic attitude, or criticizing a movement made up of women, people of color, or homosexuals. I find this atmosphere of self-intimidation among students, among faculty, and in progressive circles outside the university." Barbara Epstein, *Political Correctness and Identity Politics*, BEYOND P.C., 148, 149 (Patricia Aufderheide ed. 1992). Professor Laraine Fergerson at Bronx Committee College describes pervasive fear among faculty that they would be called racists if they publicly criticized Leonard Jeffries' bigoted remarks. Laraine Fergerson, *"The Policy of Fear"* on a CUMY Campus, MIDSTREAM, May, 1994, at 27-28.

223. Arlynn Lieber Presser, *The Politically Correct Law School*, A.B.A. J., Sept. 1991, at 52, 53; *see* Bahls, *supra* note 96, at 1047-48.

224. Presser, *supra* note 223, at 53.

225. Nat Hentoff, *Whitewashing Political Correctness*, WASH. POST, Sept. 21, 1991, at A23. Harvard Law Professor Alan Dershowitz will not teach the subject of rape without having a recording. Alan Dershowitz, *Interview with Alan Dershowitz*, THE DEFENDER, March, 1994, at 6.

226. Barry Gross, *Salem in Minnesota*, ACAD. QUESTIONS, Spring 1992, at 2, 6.

227. Bahls, *supra* note 67, at 16; Gross, *supra* note 226.

228. *See* Bryden, *supra* note 215, at 8; Hentoff, *supra* note 225; Rogers Worthington, *Wisconsin Debates 'Correct' Viewpoint*, CHICAGO TRIB., June 16, 1991, at C19; *Interview with Dershowitz*, *supra* note 225, at 6-7. "Those faculty members who voiced concern for academic freedom went on to express their belief that numerous professors are engaging in self-censorship by avoiding controversial materials in the classroom...." *Academic Freedom and Tenure: The University of New Hampshire*, ACADEME, Nov.-Dec. 1994, at 79.

229. *See* D'Souza, *supra* note 19, at 150, 197, 248; Thernstrom, *supra* note 112, at 5; Nat Hentoff, *The Uphill Battle of The First Amendment*, WASH. POST, Sept. 1, 1990, at A31.; *Interview with Dershowitz*, *supra* note 185 at 6-7; Denise Magner, *When Whites Teach Black Studies*, CHRON. HIGHER EDUC., Dec. 1, 1993, at A20.

230. Bok, *supra* note 62, at 8; *see also* Bryden, *supra* note 215, at 8.

231. For example, John Bunzel did in-depth interviews with fifty-four undergraduates at Stanford in 1988 and 1989. Twenty-four respondents were black. At a campus leading the nation in efforts to promote diversity ideology and among a student body substantially more liberal than the public as a whole, Bunzel found that students perceived more, not less racial tension over the years of their study. The black students viewed discrimination on campus as "covert," "invisible," and "elusive." The number who could give specific examples of racist behavior they had experienced or observed was very low, yet the substantial majority of black students felt estranged and suspicious because of their belief in the fundamentalist ideology of oppression. John Bunzel, RACE RELATIONS ON CAMPUS: STANFORD STUDENTS SPEAK OUT 23, 75, 116-17, 133-34 (1992).

232. Jean Elshtain, *Education Beyond Politics*, PARTISAN REVIEW, Summer 1992, at 343, 406-07.

233. Interview with Leon Botstein, President, Bard College, *Nightline: "Political Correctness" on U.S. Campuses* (ABC television broadcast, May 13, 1991). *See* David Bryden, *Scholarship About Scholarship*, 63 COLO. L. REV. 641, 648-49

(1992); Russell Jacoby, DOGMATIC WISDOM: HOW THE CULTURE WARS DIVERT EDUCATION AND DISTRACT AMERICA 82 (1994).

234. See Bok, supra note 62, at 8.
Benno Schmidt notes:

> The first victims of such suppression are the students and faculty who do not have their own convictions tempered by exposure to other points of view, even if ultimately unpersuasive. But the more serious loss is suffered by the university, because there acts of suppression tend to contribute to a pall of conformity.

Schmidt, supra note 140.

235. Bahls, supra note 96, at 1048.

236. Benno Schmidt Jr., Yale Baccalaureate Address (May 26, 1991).

237. Id.

238. Schmidt, supra note 140.

239. Norman Fruman, Book Review, ACAD. QUESTIONS, Winter 1990-91, at 82, 85 (reviewing Roger Kimball, TENURED RADICALS: HOW POLITICS HAS CORRUPTED OUR HIGHER EDUCATION (1989)).

240. Anthony Flint, Mansfield's Leaving Would Be Harvard's Loss, BOSTON GLOBE, June 6, 1993, at 41.

241. MacNeil, supra note 78, at 11.

242. See Salemi, supra note 87 at 5-6. During the period when the Black Student Alliance at Iowa State University organized sit-ins in Professor Christie Pope's class and her department investigated formal grievances against her, "Most black faculty members were reluctant to support a white woman against black students. White faculty members did not wish to appear to be racists, and in any case, had no personal knowledge of how I conducted my class. White students in class felt intimidated by black students. Black students—members of my class and nonmembers—were under intense pressure to present a united front." Christie Farnham Pope, The Challenges Posed by Radical Afrocentrism, CHRON. HIGHER EDUC., March 30, 1994, at B2.

243. Patai, supra note 66, at B2.

244. Henry Bauer, Affirmative Action at Virginia Tech: The Tail That Wagged the Dog, ACAD. QUESTIONS, Winter 1992-93, at 72, 82.

245. Nat Hentoff, Pusillanimous Professors, WASH. POST, April 17, 1993, at A-23.

246. Hentoff, supra note 217, at 217.

247. Patai, supra note 66, at B2.

248. In a 1994 article in Academe, University of Buffalo Professors Lionel Lewis and Philip Altbach report that they interviewed 210 faculty on seven campuses last year about the impact of political correctness and other kindred matters in their lives. The special issue of political correctness had "relatively little salience among our respondents," but two out of three were alarmed by budget cuts. Lionel S. Lewis and Philip G. Altbach, The True Crisis on Campus, ACADEME, Jan.-Feb. 1994, at 24. The article does not indicate the methodology used to select the sample, particularly the campuses or the faculties selected. As in both McCarthyism and the student activism of the 1960s, problems of coercion in the current zealotry are evident only on some campuses and in some faculties. In addition, there may be few professors who are publicly dissenting from tenets of the current orthodoxy and who would be suppressed. Many faculties in the humanities and social sciences are skewed substantially to the left of the political spectrum, and dissent may be unlikely.

249. Nat Hentoff, *The Uphill Battle For the First Amendment*, WASH. POST, Sept. 1, 1990, at A-31.

250. Peter Shaw, THE WAR AGAINST THE INTELLECT: EPISODES IN THE DECLINE OF DISCOURSE at xix (1989).

251. *Crossfire*, Transcript #834 Cable Network News, May 17, 1993; *Harvard Law Review Article Sparks Debate*, National Public Radio Morning Edition Show, May 4, 1992.

252. *Doe v. Univ. of Mich.*, 721 F.Supp. 852, 865 (E.D. Mich. 1989); *University Wis.-Madison Post v. Board of Regents of Univ. of Wis.*, 774 F.Supp. 1163 (E.D. Wis. 1991).

253. Cathy Davidson, *"PH" Stands for Political Hypocrisy*, ACADEME, Sept.-Oct. 1991, at 8, 9, 11. Duke Professor Stanley Fish concurs that the neoconservatives have generalized "a few tired incidents" into an assertion of a crisis. The crisis is largely fabricated. Stanley Fish, THERE'S NO SUCH THING AS FREE SPEECH, AND IT'S A GOOD THING, TOO 11, 55 (1994). The American Council on Education surveyed 360 senior administrators during 1990–91, finding that "controversies over the political or cultural content of remarks made by invited speakers are reported by one in ten institutions and by 20 percent of the nation's doctoral universities." Complaints from faculty "about pressures to alter their course content" were reported at 5 percent of all institutions and 12 percent of the doctoral universities. "Significant controversy over the political or cultural content of information presented in the classroom" was reported at 4 percent of all institutions and 10 percent of the doctoral universities. American Council on Education, CAMPUS TRENDS 1991 at 17, 40. ACE's assistant director for public affairs interpreted these data to indicate that the PC controversy "has been overblown by the media." *Administrators Worried About Budgets, Not PC*, ACADEME, Sept.-Oct., 1991 at 6.

Data from senior administrators or even the majority of faculty about suppression of dissent should be viewed with caution. For example, during McCarthyism Schrecker found extensive denial that there was any problem of suppression. Lazarsfeld and Thielens found only a minority of faculty recognized a threat and were concerned and a much smaller minority was actually affected in their conduct. Both Lazarsfeld and Thielens, studying McCarthyism, and Ladd and Lipset, studying the 1960s, found that the political predisposition of faculty members substantially influenced their attitude toward coercive tactics. Thus, during McCarthyism, conservative professors were much less likely to see a problem of suppression than liberal professors. Since faculty members to the left of center dominate many departments in the humanities and social sciences today, particularly at the elite universities, there would be few dissenters in these faculties who would be subject to suppression from the fundamentalist academic left and the tendency of colleagues who were left of center would be to minimize any concern. The relevant group on whom to focus a survey concerning coercion is those faculty members publicly dissenting from any tenet of the current orthodoxy.

In light of these considerations and the fact that only a modest minority of campus and faculties were significantly affected by coercive tactics during both McCarthyism and the 1960s, the ACE data do show significantly more serious problems of coercion at the research universities. This was also true in the earlier two periods.

254. Anthony Flint, *Putting "PC" in its Place, Educator's Say "Political Correctness" Debate Obscures Diversity Discussion*, BOSTON GLOBE, July 8, 1991,

at National/Foreign p. 1; James Boyle, *The PC Harangue*, 45 STAN. L.REV.
1457, 1459 (1993). Stories of coercion are said to be isolated incidents. Bill
Marvel & Barbara Kessler, *A Culture War: Political Correctness Provokes Back-
lash*, DALLAS MORNING NEWS, April 24, 1994 at 1A.
255. Teachers for a Democratic Culture, *Statement of Principles*, in BEYOND P.C.:
TOWARD A POLITICS OF UNDERSTANDING 67–68 (Patricia Aufderheide,
ed. 1992).
256. See Joseph Salemi, *Behind the Curtains, TCD and UDI at Hunter College*, MEA-
SURE, May 1992, at 8. The liberal university conversion project claims that
giant corporations and wealthy families have set up conservative foundations to
funnel money to conservative groups to wage ideological war on campus. Their
agenda is to stifle democratic practices and maintain the power structure as it is.
Anthony Flint, *Anti-PC Activists Trade War Stories at Harvard*, BOSTON
GLOBE, April 12, 1994, at National/Foreign p. 22; Christopher Daly, *Group
Fights Political Correctness*, WASH. POST, April 23, 1994 at A8. Professor Ellen
Messer-Davidow argues that the Right, consisting of conservative foundations,
think tanks, training programs, grassroots organizations and legal centers, "will
continue to manufacture conservative victim stories." This is a strategy "to impose a right wing America." Ellen Messer-Davidow, *Manufacturing the Attack
on Liberalized Higher Education*, SOCIAL TEXT, Sept. 1993, at 51, 68, 70.
257. Nat Hentoff, *Whitewashing Political Correctness*, WASH. POST, Spet. 21, 1991,
at A23. This statement was issued publicly but not by a standing AAUP committee.
258. The National Council for Research on Women, TO RECLAIM A LEGACY OF
DIVERSITY v (1993).
259. Stephan Thernstrom, *McCarthyism: Then and Now*, ACAD. QUESTIONS, Winter 1990–91, at 14, 15.
260. See Woodward, *supra* note 66, at 37. During the weeks of sit-ins in her class by
the Black Student Alliance and investigations of students' charges, Iowa State
Professor Christie Pope felt isolated, except for her closest colleagues in the
history department. Christie Pope, *The Challenge Posed by Radical Afrocentrism*,
CHRON. HIGHER EDUC., March 30, 1994, at B2.
261. Berkeley, *supra* note 124. Ultimately the administration, the history department,
the faculty senate and the Assembly of the College of Arts and Sciences passed
resolutions supporting Professor Pope's academic freedom. Pope, *supra* note
200 at B3.
262. See William Simons, *Intimidation as Academic Debate*, ACAD. QUESTIONS,
Spring 1993, at 63, 65–69. The accusations against Professor Simons occurred
after one of Simons' colleagues, Professor Earnest Goodman made a public defense of the importance of selecting literature in education based on the quality of
the writing rather than the race or gender of the author. Eight faculty members
responded to Goodman in the student newspaper charging that they were being
intimidated by those on campus who shared Professor Goodman's views. This is a
guilt by association argument. While Professor Simons, an activist Democrat, did
have the benefit of a group of supporters, Professor Goodman, a conservative,
received no support in the face of personal attack. Letter to the Editor, Earnest
Goodman, ACAD. QUESTIONS, Fall, 1993, at 9–10. After the theft of 14,200
copies of the student newspaper in April, 1993 at the University of Pennsylvania,
sixteen law faculty signed a public letter urging the university president to condemn the minority students' action against the paper; *see also* Philip Gailey, *Preserve Diversity of Expression*, ST. PETERSBURG TIMES, July 31, 1993, at 20-A.
263. Kors, *supra* note 204, at 82. Exploring the reason for the adoption of speech
codes, University of Nebraska Professor Samuel Walker concludes that "[T]he

speech code movement was remarkably successful because campuses represented mini-republics where left-liberal coalitions dominated the political agenda." Another factor was the weakness of the many faculty who remained uninvolved. Samuel Walker, HATE SPEECH, THE HISTORY OF AN AMERICAN CONTROVERSY 134 (1994).

264. David J. Garrow, *Is There a Correct Way to Be Black?*, N.Y. TIMES, Sept. 1, 1991, at 3, 4 (reviewing Stephen L. Carter, REFLECTIONS OF AN AFFIRMATIVE ACTION BABY (1991)). Nat Hentoff reports that after a black student magazine at UCLA published an article claiming that the *Protocols of the Elders of Zion* was substantially true, black faculty members would not comment on the anti-Semitism of the article. One of the faculty said that black students already considered the black faculty to be insufficiently militant, and the professors didn't want to make the gap any wider. Nat Hentoff, FREE SPEECH FOR ME BUT NOT FOR THEE 161 (1992). After the Nation of Islam's Khalid Abdul Muhammed heaped scorn on Jews, gays and lesbians, Arabs, women, Catholics, and Whites in a speech at Kean College in New Jersey, black faculty members were silent. Nat Hentoff, *Equal Opportunity Bigot*, WASH. POST, Jan. 22, 1994, at A17.

265. In their interview study of individuals involved in Women's Studies Programs, Professors Daphne Patai and Noretta Koertge found that while dismayed by the coercion occurring in Women's Studies, many women and liberal male faculty members are hesitant to speak out for fear of being labeled reactionary or anti-feminist. Daphne Patai and Noretta Koertge, PROFESSING FEMINISM 208 (1994).

266. *See* Rauch, *supra* note 4, at 21-23, 26-27.

267. Christina Hoff Sommers, *Sister Soldiers*, NEW REPUBLIC, Oct. 5, 1992, at 29, 33. "This is certainly not the first time that fear of saying something wrong has stifled discussion in progressive movements. In the Communist party it was called 'correct lineism.' Unfortunately the tendency to use ideology as a weapon against others in the same movement has not been limited to communists or other Marxist-Leninists. Virtually every sector of the radical movement was overcome by this dynamic in the late sixties." Barbara Epstein, *Political Correctness and Identity Politics*, in BEYOND P.C.: TOWARD A POLITICS OF UNDERSTANDING 152 (Patricia Aufderheide ed. 1992).

268. *See The Nation: Faculty Attitudes and Activities, 1989-90*, CHRON. HIGHER EDUC., April 24, 1991, at 32; Robert Wyatt, FREE EXPRESSION AND THE AMERICAN PUBLIC 261 (1991).

269. Carnegie Foundation for the Advancement of Teaching, THE CONDITION OF THE PROFESSORIATE: ATTITUDES AND TRENDS, 1989 143 (1989).

270. *Id.*

271. Martin Anderson, IMPOSTORS IN THE TEMPLE 139-40 (1992). The *Delaware Spectator* at the University of Delaware investigated the party registration of members of Political Science and Sociology departments. The data is similar to the situation at the University of Colorado.

	University of Delaware	
	Political Science	Sociology Dept.
Democrats	14	13
Republicans	0	2
Independents	2	2
No Preference/minor party	2	3
Out of State	4	2
Not Registered	3	2

The Herd of Independent Thinkers, DELAWARE SPECTATOR, Oct. 6, 1993, at 1.

272. *See id.* at 140–41.

273. *See id.* at 7, 14–15. Ladd and Lipset found a tendency among faculty who were from nonscholarly cultures to respond favorably to students' coercive tactics and demands in the 1960s. Ladd and Lipset hypothesize that "the idea of the university," which the protesting students brought under attack, was one that nonscholarly professors—for different reasons—found appealing. They in a sense allied with students against a scholarly, research-directed conception of academic life. Everett Ladd, Jr. and Seymour Martin Lipset, THE DIVIDED ACADEMY 217–18 (1975). Less productive faculty members may also come to fear an academic left seeking to consolidate its hold on a faculty. For example, some fear that the program to prune deadwood proposed by University of Arizona humanities dean Annette Kolodny is motivated by the dean's desire for more strong feminists on the faculty. Is Dean Kolodny limiting "cutting edge" scholarship to mean strictly feminist literary interpretation? Bob Sipchen, *Sizing Up 1990: The Jury's Still Out*, LOS ANGELES TIMES, Dec. 20, 1990, at 10E.

274. George F. Will, *Curdled Politics on Campus*, NEWSWEEK, May 6, 1991, at 72. Administrators in Professor Pope's case first tried to make the controversy go away through concessions; they finally followed university rules and procedures. Pope, *supra* note 260, at B1, B2.

275. "World News Tonight with Peter Jennings," interview with Jeff Greenfield (ABC Television broadcast, May 18, 1993, at 63).

276. *See* Mandelstamm, *supra* note 78, at 17–18. After public accusations of racial insensitivity by students concerning class materials and discussion, Professor Stephan Thernstrom's main concern was lack of support from Harvard administration. He noted:

> I felt like a rape victim, and yet the silence of the administration seemed to give the benefit of the doubt to the students who attacked me. Maybe I was naive, but I expected the university to come to my defense. I mean, that's what academic freedom is about, isn't it? Instead I was left out there by myself, guilty without being proven guilty.

D'Souza, *supra* note 19, at 196. Harvard Professor Randall Kennedy notes that the Harvard administration took no investigatory or disciplinary action against Thernstrom. Randall Kennedy, *The Political Correctness Scare*, 37 LOYOLA L.REV. 231, 239 40 (1991). Thernstrom still is not certain whether the Harvard administration issued its "Open Letter on Racial Harassment" as a comment supporting the accusations against him, although he has heard it had been in the works for a long time before his incident. Jon Weiner, *What Happened at Harvard*, in BEYOND P.C. 97, 103–04 (Patricia Aufderheide ed. 1992) (Weiner concludes there were no free speech issues.)

277. Mandelstamm, *supra* note 78, at 16–17. President Sheldon Hackney of the University of Pennsylvania went beyond asking for a formal apology and suspended Professor Murray Dolfman for a semester to satisfy student protesters. *See supra* note 182.

278. George Will, *Politically Correct, But Wrong*, STAR TRIB., April 29, 1993, at A24.

279. *Freedom of Speech—Unless You Don't Like What's Said*, WASH. POST, June 12, 1993, at A21.

280. Christopher Shea, *Conflicts Involving Black Students Underscore Racial Divisions on 2 Campuses*, CHRON. HIGHER EDUC., April 28, 1993 at A32, A34.

281. Anthony Flint, *At Univ. Penn, A House of Mirrors*, BOSTON GLOBE, August 1, 1993, at A1; Christopher Shea, *Penn. Report Faults Campus Police For Response to Students' Taking Papers*, CHRON. HIGHER EDUC., August 4, 1993, at A27.
282. *Appeasing the Mob at Penn: No Punishment for the PC Set*, WASH. TIMES, Sept. 19, 1993, at B2; Jonathan Yardley, *Unfair Squeeze on the College Press*, WASH. POST, September 20, 1993, at B2.
283. Christopher Shea, *Penn. Won't Punish Black Students who Threw Away Campus Papers*, CHRON. HIGHER EDUC., September 22, 1993, at A35.
284. Greg Miller, *Bonfire of the Profanities: Campus Thefts Protest Press; Offended Activist Groups Are Taking, Even Torching, Stacks of Papers*, LOS ANGELES TIMES, July 28, 1993, at A5. In spring semester, 1992, protesters demanding more minority control of the *Collegian*, the student newspaper at the University of Massachusetts-Amhearst, twice invaded the paper's offices, destroyed property, and threatened and attacked staff members. The University's Chancellor Richard O'Brien responded that the whole situation was a struggle, "between the ins and the outs" and that he did not think the university should take sides. *Speech Codes and Censors*, WALL ST. J., June 10, 1992, at A14. O'Brien wrote a memorandum to the campus community, stating that "the administration has no wish to take sides in the issues between student protesters and the student newspaper.... (The situation) involves tension between three values that the institution holds dear: protecting free expression, including freedom of the press; creating a multicultureal community; and maintaining an environment free of harassment and intimidation. I am confident that our students can reach a resolution that embraces all three values." Richard O'Brien, Memorandum to the Campus Community, May 5, 1992.
285. *Levin v. Harleston*, 770 F. Supp. 895, 906 (S.D.N.Y. 1991), *aff'd in part & vacated in part*, 966 F.2d 85 (2d Cir. 1992).
286. Gary Crosby Brasor, *An Alumnus Learns How Might Makes Right at Bowdoin*, ACAD. QUESTIONS, Winter 1991–92, at 50, 53. The President of SUNY Binghamton was also unwilling to defend academic freedom by speaking out against and applying disciplinary action to repeated student occupations and disruptions to intimidate others. *See* Bernardo, *supra* note 68. Former University of Wisconsin Chancellor Donna Shalala reversed her earlier rejection of a speech code under threat of disruptive violence in October 1988. Barry Siegel, *Fighting Words*, L.A. TIMES, Magazine, March 28, 1993, at 14.
287. *GSU President Acts Hastily*, ATLANTA J. & CONST., November 11, 1992, at A14. In February, 1992, Khalid Abdul Muhammed delivered a speech at West Chester State University, near Philadelphia, that included anti-Semitic remarks. Muhammed agreed to field questions, but only from African-American students. When a white student protested that "I have a right to be called on too—my tuition dollars also paid for your talk," Muhammed demanded that, "If the authorities don't remove that student immediately, then we will remove him." Campus police dragged the student from the room; university administrators did nothing. Morton Klein, *Black Muslim Anti-Semitism: A Peril That Cannot Be Ignored*, ZOA REPORT, May-June 1994, at 2.
288. Christopher Shea, *Hispanic Students, Frustrated Over Pace of Reforms on Campuses, Raise the Ante*, CHRON. HIGHER EDUC., October 13, 1993, at A40. After 200 students seized Pomona College's administration building for two days in February, 1993, to demand more ethnic and gender diversity in faculty hiring and admissions, the administration conceded to many of the demands. Pomona College President Peter Stanley said the tactics used were "worrisome." Taking over a building "happened this time and we responded to it the way we did partly

because we thought their issues were legitimate ones. If there were reason to believe people were getting into the habit of taking over buildings, our reaction would be different." Mike Ward, *Students End Demonstration; College Vow Diverse Hiring*, LOS ANGELES TIMES, February 4, 1993, at J1.

289. Joseph Salemi, *Political Correctness at Dallas Baptist University: The Firing of David Ayers and John Jeffrey*, MEASURE, Aug.-Sept. 1992, at 1, 9.

290. *Berkeley Students, supra* note 193.

291. Felton, *supra* note 187.

292. Andrea Sachs, *Hiring Splits Harvard Law*, A.B.A. J., July 1992, at 30–31. Students at Pennsylvania State University, angered by a conservative student newspaper that publishes anti-feminist articles, stole 4,000 copies of the newspaper during spring semester, 1993. University police charged two women who had just graduated with theft, receiving stolen property and criminal conspiracy. The county attorney recommended the suspects' application for a first-offender program that would suspend the case and place them on probation. Christopher Shea, *Two Women at Penn State Charged in Theft of Right-Wing Newspaper*, CHRON. HIGHER EDUC., July 28, 1993, at A30. *Free Speech on Campus? It's a Matter of Debate*, N.Y. TIMES, September 24, 1993, at A26.

293. *See* D'Souza, *supra* note 19, at 102.

294. *See* Joseph A. Amato, VICTIMS AND VALUES: A HISTORY AND A THEORY OF SUFFERING at xix (1990).

295. *See id.* at 195–196; D'Souza, *supra* note 19, at 243. Richard Bernstein in *Dictatorship of Virtue* also observes that if the demands of multiculturalists are met, and any inequality in performance among status groups persists, that inequality must be blamed on the oppressiveness of the dominant culture. That culture must be changed even more. Paradoxically, in this construct, failure of multicultural ideology and practice can only lead to greater demands for reform. Richard Bernstein, DICTATORSHIP OF VIRTUE 251 (1994). The fundamentalist academic left's power within some faculties must also be denied to preserve the claim that they are carrying forward a tradition of protest on behalf of the meek and disenfranchised. *Id.* at 217–18, 229–231.

296. Calvin Trillin, *Harvard Law*, NEW YORKER, Mar. 26, 1984, at 53, 77.

3

Similarities in the Waves of Zealotry

A critical finding of this essay is that periods of zealotry have been frequent in higher education in the United States since the emergence of the modern university after the Civil War. Throughout the past 125 years, higher education in the United States has experienced seven waves of zealotry, occurring approximately every fifteen to twenty years. Zealotry in each wave enforced a strong ideology. These periods of zealotry have originated both from without and from within the university; they have occurred to enforce a variety of strong ideologies with religious, economic, political, social, or cultural roots.

At any given time, a variety of ideologies are competing for acceptance within a free society and its universities. If a particular ideology becomes dominant in the culture outside the universities, extreme proponents of the dominant ideology may attempt to impose the ideology on all forms of inquiry and expression within the university—in ideas, in speech, in action, in association. Examples are the religious fundamentalism of administrators and faculty in the nineteenth century, the unfettered capitalism of trustees and regents at the end of the nineteenth century, the patriotism of World War I, anticommunism prior to World War II, and McCarthyism of the late 1940s and early 1950s.

A strong ideology may also become dominant within the faculty or student body of the university itself and lead to populist intimidation from extreme proponents of the dominant ideology. They will seek to eliminate heresy—in ideas, in speech, in action, in association. While the five periods of zealotry up to the mid-1960s were first initiated by lay persons outside the student body and faculty, the last two waves were initiated within these two groups. Student activism in the 1960s was the first wave of zealotry since the Civil War in the United States involving a broad populist intimidation directed at academic speech initiated from inside the university by students. The fundamentalism of the radical academic left in the late 1980s and early 1990s has been the first period of zealotry in higher education in the United States involving a populist intimidation initiated principally by faculty.

During any particular period, it was difficult to predict the ideological direction from which the next wave of zealotry would come. For example, who could have predicted in 1954 that within thirteen years the activism of the late 1960s would come from the New Left and would be initiated by students?

In each period, zealots have labeled disagreement as heresy, demonstrating the moral turpitude of the heretic. Zealots then have employed a variety of coercive tactics to harass and eliminate heretical academic thought and speech. Termination of employment has been only one of many ways of intimidating a scholar. Among the other threats have been harassment and vilification through public accusations of moral turpitude, social ostracism, investigations, tribunals, adverse employment decisions for candidates for appointment, and untenured and tenured faculty short of termination, and disruption of classes. Adverse employment decisions short of termination have included threats to initial appointment, promotion, research funds, salary increases, reasonable teaching loads, and other professional opportunities outside the university.

Zealots have not been content to look for overt forms of heresy; they have sought also to penalize subtle traces of heresy in ideas. Any belief or association that raised doubts in their minds became evidence of heresy. Zealots also needed a supply of symbolic targets whom they could use to incite public passion and to create fear in others. As Hofstadter and Metzger observed almost forty years ago, "In a situation where the margin of safe divergence is obscure, the pale of orthodoxy undiscernible, the penalties of heresy unpredictable, the cautious man will blunder and the man of moderation will be martyred."[1]

Another critical finding of the research is that the faculty's response to zealotry has generally been to silently acquiesce in the coercive tactics and, thus, to condone them. Faculty members generally do not publicly defend academic freedom. The results are that the coercive tactics have silenced not only the target, but also the vastly greater number of potential speakers who steer wide of possible punishment. In each period zealots have distorted academic inquiry and speech by imposing significant restraints on the critique of accepted hypotheses and the presentation of new hypotheses.

Comparing just the patriotism of World War I with McCarthyism, Hofstadter and Metzger arrive at strikingly similar observations to those presented here. In both of those periods, suspicion frayed the social fabric; pathological types rose to prominence; the informer's repeated accusations of moral turpitude acquired the public's sanction; the bully's defamation became socially acceptable; and the investigator was allowed to make an inquisition without the customary judicial restraint. Finally, at both times the university community and the public, called upon to judge difficult issues of individual guilt or innocence, took refuge in the assumption that where there is smoke, there must be fire, and did not inform itself whether there may not in fact be simply a smoke screen.[2]

Similarly edifying is a comparison of the superpatriotism underlying the waves of zealotry during World War I, prior to World War II and McCarthyism.

Essentially this zealotry from outside the walls of the university and principally from the far right was the source of three separate waves of suppression within the university over forty years. Finally, during the late 1950s and 1960s, a widening consensus developed within the society that this superpatriotic zealotry was wrong, and had done great harm to the academy. Historian Arthur Schlesinger, Jr., observed in 1994 that "in the good old days, conservatives and hyperpatriots were the militant advocates of repression and censorship."[3] This history of three waves of zealotry over forty years motivated by superpatriotism, combined with the much earlier history of the long struggle against a zealotry motivated by religious fundamentalism, has conditioned the generations of academics developing from the 1960s to the present to perceive the far right and religious fundamentalism from outside the walls as the major threats to academic freedom.

Comparisons between and among the last three waves of zealotry, McCarthyism, student activism of the 1960s, and the current fundamentalism of the radical academic left, are similarly instructive. The fundamentalist academic left has borrowed tactics from both McCarthyism and the student activism of the 1960s. Should another wave of zealotry occur in the next twenty years, the coercive tactics employed would probably build on those successful in the last three waves.

Similarities between McCarthyism and the Current Fundamentalism

Extreme proponents of the ideology of anticommunism during the late 1940s and early 1950s and fundamentalism from the radical academic left today have employed similar tactics of public accusations of moral turpitude, ostracism, investigations or the threat of investigation, tribunals, and threats to employment to suppress competent opposing ideas and positions. During McCarthyism, accusations of moral turpitude were made based upon conjecture, hearsay, gossip, and innuendo not remotely akin to evidence. The accusation itself served as evidence. Similar manipulative persuasion has been used in the current wave. Once public accusations of moral turpitude against an academic are made during either period, the professor has been assumed guilty by a significant proportion of the academic community, and has carried the burden to prove a negative regarding his or her state of mind. Those accused must demonstrate that they have no covert disloyalty or bigotry through loyalty oaths or public apologies for unconscious bigotry. For some in the academic community, the accusation alone has been accepted as fact.

There is a wide spectrum of academic opinion on the degree to which the use of such tactics currently is similar to the use of such tactics during McCarthyism. For example, at one end of the spectrum is the claim that fears of coercive tactics are grossly exaggerated and based on the same few anecdotes endlessly recycled.[4] Close to this position, Georgetown law professor Mark Tushnet argues that while there may be efforts by liberals to enforce their views against conservatives, there is also a parallel phenomenon of "enforcement" of conservative ideology against liberals, feminists and others.[5] In any event, Professor Tushnet asserts that there is no similarity between McCarthyism and the current zealotry. Citing Ellen Schrecker's book, *No Ivory Tower: McCarthyism and the Universities,* he concludes that what made McCarthyism wrong was that behind Senator McCarthy's expressions lay the force of the government—or more broadly, official power. In contrast, discussions of political correctness, he argues, rarely provide examples of incidents in which, at the end of the day, official power was used to enforce political correctness.[6]

Tushnet's conclusion is a misreading of Schrecker's thesis and a substantial understatement of the coercive tactics employed by the fundamentalist academic left. It is also misguided to argue that coercive tactics enforcing conservative ideology offset those enforcing fundamentalist left ideology. Schrecker's major argument is that McCarthyism was played out in universities as a two-stage process. Government, usually by initiating an investigation, administered the first stage by identifying objectionable groups and individuals. The second stage of punishment was administered by the press, the public, the university trustees and administrators, and faculty colleagues. Schrecker points out that accusations of moral turpitude had a shattering effect on the lives and careers of the accused. They were ostracized. They could not obtain grants, promotions, or other professional opportunities. Many universities instituted separate investigations and tribunals. Ultimately approximately ninety to one hundred professors lost their jobs.

The critical point that Schrecker emphasizes is that the press, the public, university administrators and trustees, and faculty colleagues imposed punishment on the accused by public humiliation, ostracism, additional investigations, tribunals, diminished career opportunity, and in roughly ninety to one hundred cases, termination. Schrecker comments that "being fired, it turned out, did not always produce as much anxiety as the uncertainty [created by threats, accusations, investigations, and hearings] that preceded the actual, or possible, dismissal. This meant that many of the people who kept jobs may have suffered just as much emotionally as the people who lost theirs."[7] Writing on the topic of misperceptions concerning academic freedom, Professor Fritz Machlup concurs that there are many ways to intimidate a scholar other than termination of employment. Among these are threats to promotion, salary increases, research funds, reasonable teaching loads, and privacy. Intimidation also occurs through vilification and hostile investigations that drain money, time, and emotional and physical energy.[8]

Contrary to Tushnet's conclusion, a comparison of Schrecker's analysis of the tactics and results of McCarthyism and this essay's analysis of the tactics and results of the current fundamentalism shows significant similarities.

Tushnet's argument that efforts by conservatives to "enforce" their ideologies offset efforts by radical left fundamentalists is badly flawed. He offers no serious evidence of these conservative efforts, and if they do exist, such coercion is equally wrong.

Taking a position close to that of Tushnet, Harvard professor Randall Kennedy concedes that there is a subset of faculty who display an "unremitting hostility towards those who disagree with their 'line,'" but that, nonetheless, the evidence "fails even to come close to suggesting the systematic and wholesale repression that has come to be associated with the unscrupulous thuggery of Senator Joseph R. McCarthy."[9] During the "era of real McCarthyism," Kennedy points out that congressional committees investigated allegations of moral turpitude, some universities imposed loyalty oaths, candidates for faculty positions were excluded on the basis of political associations, and untenured and even tenured professors were terminated for political reasons at some institutions. "Fortunately, nothing like that exists on campuses nowadays."[10]

Professor Kennedy's assertion of "systematic and wholesale repression" during McCarthyism overgeneralizes and, thus, misrepresents what happened at that time. His assertion that "nothing like that exists on campus nowadays" substantially understates the repression of the current zealotry. Data from the Lazarsfeld and Thielens study of 2,451 social scientists in 1955 point out Professor Kennedy's overgeneralization with regard to McCarthyism. The data indicate that the majority of professors experienced no curtailment of their own academic freedom or that of colleagues. Roughly one-fifth of all respondents felt that their academic freedom was directly threatened. Conservative professors reported only one-half the level of concern or direct threat than did liberal professors. Since roughly 70 percent of the respondents voted Democratic in 1948 and 1952, this means that roughly 12 percent of the professors to the right of center felt threatened compared to 24 percent of those to the left of center. Approximately one-tenth of all 2,451 respondents adjusted their speech and conduct to reduce their exposure. Less than 2 percent of all respondents felt their career had been adversely affected. Professor Lionel Lewis's study indicates that the worst excess of McCarthyism where a professor's appointment was threatened for allegedly radical political beliefs, was limited to fifty-eight institutions of higher education out of 1900 existing at the time over the decade 1947–56. Of the sixty-nine terminations that Lewis discusses, thirty-one occurred in 1949–1950 at the University of California and the remaining thirty-eight occurred over the other nine years.

Professor Kennedy's assertion that "nothing" like McCarthyism exists on campuses nowadays substantially understates what is happening in the current zealotry. Public accusations of moral turpitude and ostracism to suppress competent academic inquiry and speech are occurring in some faculties. Investigations and the threat of investigation for one's ideas are occurring with some frequency. Subsequent to investigation, heretics may be subject to tribunals. Harassment and discrimination policies and speech codes provide an institutional structure rich in opportunities to threaten investigation of speech and a tribunal. The existence of institutional structures to carry out investigations and tribunals for heretical speech replicates the essence of McCarthyism. Threats to employment are also occurring. Mandatory sensitivity training for faculty and students that dictates a certain "line" is analogous to, although not as intrusive as, loyalty oaths. The current wave of zealotry is not yet over, and its full impact is yet to be assessed.

One of the investigators in the Lazarsfeld and Thielens study of the impact of McCarthyism on social scientists concurs that the differences between McCarthyism and the current fundamentalism are not as dramatic as Professor Kennedy suggests. In the 1950s, Harvard professor David Riesman participated in follow-up interviews to test the validity of the Lazarsfeld and Thielens survey. Riesman concluded that the earlier study had gotten it straight. Riesman observes now that current perceptions of McCarthyism are overstated. "McCarthyism is now seen as much more widespread than was really the case."[11] "The most intense intramural concerns aroused by McCarthyism were mainly experienced at the most eminent institutions, the more 'liberal' liberal-arts colleges and universities."[12] Reisman is "deeply concerned about the climate of higher education [now]. The issue that most concerns me is the freedom of conversation in the residential colleges and university centers, and how inhibited that is, out of fear of saying something sexist, racist, homophobic, or whatever. That, I think, has a profoundly chilling effect. Certain topics just can't be explored."[13]

Professor Kennedy's assertion that "nothing" like McCarthyism exists on campuses nowadays also assumes a political landscape today comparable to that existing during McCarthyism. During McCarthyism, the ideological zealotry came from the far right, and the most likely targets were to the left of center. Seventy percent of the respondents in the Lazarsfeld and Thielens study of 2,451 social scientists were voting to the left of center in the presidential elections in 1948 and 1952. During the current zealotry from the fundamentalist academic left, the most likely targets are to the right of center. However, many faculties in the humanities and social sciences are dominated by the left. There are virtually no faculty to the right of center on some of these faculties. Under these circumstances it is highly misleading to compare absolute numbers of faculty or proportions of total faculty who report either concern about academic freedom, actual threat to their own academic freedom, or actual adverse career effects. Given the political demographics of the professoriat in some fields and the direction from which the current ideological zealotry comes, the number of professors who report being threatened should be substantially lower now than occurred during McCarthyism. The relevant data base would be a survey of the impact of the current zealotry on professors in the humanities and social sciences who are publicly dissenting from some tenet at the current orthodoxy or whose views tend to be to the right of center.

At the other end of the spectrum of views comparing the relative degree of repression during McCarthyism with current fundamentalism are Professors David Bryden and Eugene Genovese and former Yale dean Donald Kagan. University of Minnesota professor David Bryden writes that academics today are nearly all left of center. Because of their "pervasive fear of being labeled racist, sexist, or homophobic, university debate today is far more stifled than it was in the 1950s by McCarthyism." A far broader array of topics are controversial and could lead to penalties.[14] University of Georgia professor Eugene Genovese agrees. "As one who saw his professors fired during the McCarthy era...I fear that our conservative colleagues are today facing a new McCarthyism in some ways more effective and vicious than the old."[15] Former Yale dean Donald Kagan sees a similar degree of coercion. "There is an imposed conformity of opinion. It takes real courage to oppose the orthodoxies. To tell you the truth, I was a student during the days of Joseph McCarthy, and there is less freedom now than there was then."[16]

These analyses at both ends of the spectrum suffer from overbreadth for several reasons. It is difficult to compare a populist intimidation initiated by faculty or students inside the university with an intimidation initiated from outside the faculty or student body. Both have different strengths and weaknesses in effectuating the goal of suppressing dissent. A zealotry effectuated by the trustees, regents, and administrators can more directly threaten employment. However, the faculty also has substantial power defining opportunity for employment, the conditions of employment for tenured and untenured professors, staff, and the learning environment and rewards and penalties for students. Public humiliation, ostracism, and harassment through investigations are powerful weapons of intimidation in the hands of peers.

It is more useful in assessing the impact of zealotry on universities to distinguish among the groups in the academic community: students, applicants for faculty appointment, the untenured professors, tenured professors, staff, and the administration. The more vulnerable the group, the lower the threshold where coercive tactics significantly stifle that group's academic inquiry and speech.

From this perspective, students, candidates for faculty employment, untenured professors, and staff are extremely vulnerable to accusations of moral turpitude, public humiliation, ostracism, and investigation. In many faculties the coercive tactics of zealots in the current fundamentalism have exceeded the threshold necessary to significantly suppress speech for these vulnerable groups. Whether the current coercion is as onerous as McCarthyism for these vulnerable groups does not seem very relevant. The results are substantially the same.

For deans and university presidents, the comparison between McCarthyism and the current fundamentalism is more problematic because few, if any, deans and presidents were accused during McCarthyism. In contrast the ideological construct of the fundamentalist academic left identifies deans and university presidents as the embodiment of the oppression endemic in society and the university. They are regularly a principal target of public accusations of bigotry, public humiliation, and adverse media attention. These accusations do threaten an administrator's opportunities for career advancement and mobility. Whether such accusations threaten current job security depends upon how much damage is inflicted on public perception and goodwill of the university, and the governing board's confidence that the administrator can continue to raise funds successfully. Deans and university presidents are probably subject to greater coercion in the current wave of zealotry than during McCarthyism.

Tenured professors are the only group for whom the current fundamentalism does not pose the same degree of threat to employment as McCarthyism did. There are no formal termination proceedings under a tenure code, although there are proceedings against tenured professors' academic speech under harassment and discrimination speech policies. The critical point is that the willingness of tenured professors to risk punishment in order to speak covers a spectrum. At one end is that subset of tenured professors dissenting from fundamentalist ideology who will speak freely as long as they do not suffer permanent loss of employment. These are few. At the other end of the spectrum is the subset of tenured professors whose speech is deterred by any threat of punishment.

Even for tenured professors, public accusations of bigotry, public humiliation, and ostracism impose both very substantial psychological costs and substantial damage to the possibility of grants, further academic advancement, mobility in the profession, and public service opportunities. For many tenured professors, these costs are sufficient to stifle competent dissent.

Investigation, the threat of investigation, and tribunals impose greater penalties and will stifle a further subset of tenured professors. There will remain a subset of tenured professors dissenting from fundamentalist ideology who cannot be intimidated except by more coercive measures directly threatening employment. While research found no formal tenure termination proceedings based purely on heretical ideas, extended internal and external investigations and possible sanctions under discrimination and harassment speech policies can achieve the same result. A professor can also be forced out if defense costs for external investigations are not indemnified by the university.[17]

These tactics have been successful in forcing out several tenured professors who could not withstand sustained vilification and investigation. A tenured professor under assault by investigations is unlikely to survive without an administration at least willing to indemnify defense costs. Some tenured professors have been sanctioned for academic speech allegedly violating discrimination or harassment speech policies. Sanctions have included suspension, probation, public reprimand, sensitivity training and therapy, and public apology. Schrecker has observed that many professors who kept their jobs during McCarthyism may have suffered just as much emotionally as those who lost theirs. This is true also in the current wave of zealotry.

Overall, the use of public accusations of moral turpitude, public humiliation, and ostracism is probably more widespread in this period of zealotry than in McCarthyism. The array of prohibited topics is wider and the zealots are themselves members of the academic community who can monitor daily activity of others. It is also important to remember that during McCarthyism the ideological zealotry came from the far right, and the most likely faculty targets were to the left of center. Roughly 70 percent of the respondents in the Lazarsfeld and Thielens study of social scientists voted Democratic in 1948 and 1952. The most likely faculty targets of the current zealotry will be to the right of center; however, many faculties in the social sciences and humanities have virtually no professors who are to the right of center. The isolation felt by those targeted in the current zealotry compounds the threat.

The use of investigations and the threat of investigation may be less widespread in this period than during McCarthyism, but investigations of competent academic inquiry and speech are occurring in some faculties. Data reporting how frequently complaints against speech and investigations of speech and tribunals are occurring on all campuses are not available. In any event, total body count will not be as important as a determination of the degree of threat to faculty members who are either publicly dissenting from some tenet of the current orthodoxy or who are to the right of center. It is clear that many hundreds of colleges and universities have speech codes, and the federal court cases striking down speech codes at the Universities of Michigan and Wisconsin indicate that investigations under speech codes occur with some frequency. In addition, many universities have adopted harassment and discrimination policies under which complaints against pure speech will trigger an investigation. Such investigations have been documented on a number of campuses. It is reasonable to assume that all students and faculty on these campuses are well aware of both the institutionalized apparatus for investigation of speech and instances where heretical speech has been investigated. They are also aware that the area of proscribed speech is not clearly defined. It may be defined entirely by the perception of the oppressed listener. Judgment about initiating an investigation lies in the hands of a bureaucracy often heavily influenced by fundamentalist ideology. This threat of investigation under vague standards by zealous prosecutors creates a vast penumbra of proscribed speech on major issues of the day.

This is the key point. The use of repeated unsupported accusations of moral turpitude, together with an institutionalized apparatus for investigations and tribunals to create the "big lie," were the most successful coercive strategies of McCarthyism, not the termination of employment. The zealots believed that the secretive nature of communist activities and conspiracies meant that communist subversive intentions would rarely be evident in overt speech or conduct, but rather must be inferred from patterns of association. In addition, accusation based on suspicion alone seemed justified in fighting secretive subversive intention and activity. An institutionalized apparatus of investigation and tribunal was also necessary to ferret out these secretive patterns of associations, intentions, and activities. Hofstadter and Metzger observed in 1955 that this apparatus of investigation "makes, or threatens to make, investigation—by trustees, by state legislative committees, by filiopietistic groups—a built-in characteristic of academic life, an organ of administration, interminable because it is non-specific, incalculable in effect because it rarely relates to professional behavior."[18]

This strategy of repeated unsupported accusations of moral turpitude with an institutionalized apparatus for investigations and tribunals is replicated in the current fundamentalism from the radical academic left. The mission of the fundamentalist here is to expose the hidden structures of oppression in the culture. It is a small and natural step for the fundamentalist to expose those with hidden motives of oppression and bigotry and the hidden conspiracies supporting the structures of oppression. Accusation based on feelings alone is justified in fighting the hidden oppressors. An institutionalized structure of zealous prosecutors is necessary to root out hidden motives of bigotry and conspiracy. Under vague standards, the prosecutors can investigate speech, conduct, and associations from which hidden motives and conspiracies of bigotry and oppression can be inferred. Thus, investigation is once again a built-in characteristic of academic life, inflicting incalculable harm because it rarely relates to professional competence.

Accusation, humiliation, and ostracism alone are sufficient threats to significantly suppress dissenting speech of the most vulnerable groups, students, candidates for employment, the untenured, staff, and some deans and presidents. They are also sufficient to suppress dissenting ideas of many tenured professors; if the threat of investigation and tribunal is apparent, a larger group of tenured professors will be silenced. The worst excess of McCarthyism, a formal termination proceeding, is occurring when a tenured professor's academic speech is subject to prosecution under harassment and discrimination speech policies. The most severe penalty imposed has been an indefinite suspension that the AAUP found was tantamount to a dismissal. Thus, among tenured professors whose ideas dissent from those of fundamentalist colleagues, the subset who will speak publicly is the group who can be suppressed only by a significant probability of actual employment termination. Even this subgroup's energy and capability for dissent will be vitiated by sustained tactics of vilification and investigation.

There are three other similarities between McCarthyism and the current fundamentalism. First, although the point is implicit in the preceding discussion, it bears emphasis that zealots in both McCarthyism and the current fundamentalism do not stop with targets who are clearly communists or bigots. The strategy is to go far beyond that limited circle and attack others for political advantage. Second, Lionel Lewis found that when the university specified formal charges during McCarthyism, the university rarely referred to political beliefs, relying instead on pretextual accusations of incompetence, dishonesty, or insubordination.[19] In the present zealotry, pretextual charges of discrimination and harassment serve the same purpose.

The last similarity between McCarthyism and the current fundamentalism is denial by the zealots that any suppression of academic inquiry and speech is occurring. Recall that during McCarthyism at no point did the vast majority of trustees, administration, or faculty who punished suspected communists admit that they were repressing dissent. On the contrary, they claimed that they were defending free speech and academic freedom. The same phenomenon is occurring today.

Similarities between Student Activism of the 1960s and the Current Fundamentalism

The student activism of the 1960s and the current fundamentalism of the radical academic left are the first widespread periods of zealotry involving a populist intimidation of academic speech initiated and sustained from within the faculty or student body themselves. Up to thirty years ago, institutions and faculties were able to rely principally on individual commitments to professional standards and individual self-discipline, guided and supported by academic traditions and collegial interaction, as the principal mechanisms inhibiting professional misconduct. However, as the 1973 joint Association of American Colleges and AAUP Commission on Academic Tenure found,

> the vast and rapid growth of the profession in recent years has surely weakened the force of professional tradition. And the reflection on campuses of broader social turmoil has presented acute problems of professional conduct, for which broad general professional standards and traditional reliance upon individual self-discipline have been inadequate.... [M]ost ominously, assaults upon academic freedom from within the institution by or with the toleration of members of faculties themselves have gone unpunished.[20]

This 1973 finding is again accurate twenty years later.

Student activism of the 1960s and the current fundamentalism share an ideological kinship. The ideology of the New Left in the 1960s and the ideology of the fundamentalist academic left in the late 1980s and early 1990s embrace the common theme that the current cultural, economic, political, and social structures in the United States have been created and are operated by a power elite to oppress the powerless. The structures are illegitimate and corrupt. This hidden hierarchy of power and privilege must be reversed, and the oppressed enfranchised. The university itself is controlled by a power elite to oppress the powerless. Standards of academic quality are themselves a mask for oppression.

Because the university itself is oppressive and corrupt, ideological zealots within the faculty and student body are free of attachments of institutional loyalty and community pride that, in other institutions like corporations or professional firms, normally moderate self-inflicted public disrepute.[21] In this ideological construct, creating disrespect for the university is a positive step in exposing its hidden corruption and illegitimacy.

Seeing the world metaphorically as consisting of oppressors and the oppressed, ideological zealots in these two waves are convinced, even while engaging in false charges of moral turpitude and disruption, that they are the innocent and oppressed victims of an organized but hidden social assault. They hold to a belief in the singular worth and exclusivity of the suffering of the adherents of the ideology. They assume a moral stance of blamelessness.

During both the 1960s student activism and the current fundamentalism, zealots employ tactics of confrontation and disruption to degrade and silence dissenting ideas. The tactics of confrontation include the use of ridicule, rudeness, inflammatory false accusations, and other forms of abusive language to degrade and silence others. These tactics are most effective against the most vulnerable groups, students, staff, and untenured professors. Harvard President Bok notes that "[i]n the past twenty-five years, we have all grown used to attacks on almost everything and everyone with any power, influence or visibility.... While much of this criticism is undoubtedly deserved, the temptations for exaggeration and excess are very strong."[22]

Community organizing techniques have been successful tactics in both periods. Focusing on a specific symbolic target around whom to incite and mobilize anger and passion and the media is a formidable threat. A small, well-organized group of zealots within the university can sometimes bring the university to its knees.

Zealots in both periods have disrupted or have threatened to disrupt speeches and classes to prevent unpopular dissenting views from being heard. Forced occupations of administrative buildings have been used to intimidate administrative decision making.

Clearly, incidents of disruption of speeches and classes and forced occupations during the current fundamentalism are more isolated, involve many fewer students, and are not so destructive as occurred during the student activism of the 1960s. However, many presidents and deans today remember the effectiveness of disruption in the 1960s in generating adverse media attention, damaging the university, and bringing down administrations. The threat of disruption today is sufficient to intimidate those administrators who are fearful of adverse media attention.

Appeasement of zealots through concessions has not been a very successful strategy for either 1960s student activism or the current fundamentalism. In both the 1960s and currently, the zealot's purpose is to force the university into confrontation and oppressive action to demonstrate the reality of oppression in the university. Thus, concessions are used to demonstrate an admission of guilt and to give rise to new demands that force the confrontation.

Faculty response to zealotry also has a similar underlying explanatory variable in both the 1960s and currently. During the student activism of the 1960s, Professors Ladd and Lipset discovered that the general ideological predisposition that faculty brought to political issues was a major determinant of the way they responded to the coercive tactics of the student radicals. They found both that there was a close association between left-of-center posture in politics and relatively high support for the student protests and that the politics of American academics was disproportionately to the left of center. They concluded further that the skew to the left was much more pronounced at the elite universities and that the degree of variation in political attitude by field was quite extraordinary. In some fields, like psychology, sociology, anthropology, political science, history, and philosophy, two-thirds or more of the professoriat characterized themselves as "liberal" or "left," while the average for all fields was 46 percent.[23] The politics of the professoriat currently is still disproportionately to the left of center, particularly in the elite universities and in some fields in the humanities and social sciences. There again seems to be an ideological solidarity that inhibits faculty members with left-of-center political views from defending the academic freedom of targets of the current zealotry from the fundamentalist academic left. Writing in 1969, Harvard professor Nathan Glazer observed that he never dreamed that a radical critique of American society could develop such enormous power that it became simply the new convention, and that a public defense of the liberal intellectual system against the radicals became in effect a conservative position held by a few.[24] This is again true in the 1990s.

Faculty response to the zealotry of the late 1960s and currently also shares another similar explanatory variable. After three waves of zealotry motivated by superpatriotism over a forty-year period, the professoriat and the general public finally came to see that this zealotry from the far right and outside the walls was wrong. The generations of scholars maturing since 1960 have been conditioned to believe that the major threat to academic freedom is both from outside the walls and from the far right. During the 1960s and currently, this conditioning leads to blindness among many faculty concerning threats to academic freedom from both the far left and inside the walls. If the pattern of these waves of zealotry from the far left is similar to that of the earlier three waves of zealotry from the superpatriots, there will be no wide consensus that coercion from the far left is equally wrong for another ten to fifteen years.

Similarities among McCarthyism, Student Activism of the 1960s, and the Current Fundamentalism

Proponents of any strong ideology may embrace zealotry to suppress freedom of academic thought and speech. However, the likelihood that an ideology will be combined with zealotry is highest when encouragement or permission for the coercion of others' speech is inherent in the ideology. For example, capitalism as an ideology does not explicitly endorse coercion of others' speech. In contrast the ideologies of McCarthyism, the student activism of the 1960s, and the fundamentalist academic left do support or condone correction or extirpation of heresy in others. The ideologies of the last three waves of zealotry are most similar to religious fundamentalism in terms of ideological encouragement or permission to eliminate heresy.

Zealots in the three most recent periods of zealotry also have employed similar advocacy tactics of manipulative persuasion. Accusations against individuals and institutions have been based on conjecture, gossip, hearsay, the twisting of any ambiguity, half-truth by omission, exaggeration, and misrepresentation. Innuendo is played out in forums like the media where there is no chance of due process in terms of adequate notice of the charges, a chance to tell the other side, and a neutral decision maker observing procedures that take pains with the facts and the rules applicable to the facts. Zealots in all three periods have searched for symbolic events and individuals against whom to incite passion and to mobilize the community.

In each of the three periods, a change came over the rules of academic discourse in the university. Advocacy tactics of manipulative persuasion displaced common academic standards of thoroughness and accuracy in the gathering of relevant evidence, careful and impartial consideration of the weight of the evidence, analytical reasoning, and balance and fairness in argument and controversy. The ideologies of both student activism of the 1960s and the fundamentalist academic left give ideological legitimacy to this displacement in arguing that the common standards of academic discourse are only instruments of oppression by an elite. Only the student activists of the 1960s openly acknowledged substituting advocacy tactics for the usual rules of academic discourse. They also made no bones about their willingness to use disruption and violence. During both McCarthyism and the current fundamentalism, zealots generally have denied the use of these tactics and have presented themselves to the public clothed with the credibility of scholars.

It is difficult to compare the relative coerciveness of the tactics employed in these last three waves of zealotry. The use of particular tactics was more severe and more widespread during the earlier two periods; for example, the use of investigations and threats to employment during McCarthyism and the use of disruption of speeches, classes, and administrative functions during the

1960s. However, the current fundamentalism combines the tactics successful in both earlier periods.

Faculty zealots responsible for the current fundamentalism are also far more entrenched in academia than the politicians of the 1950s or the students of the 1960s. The fundamentalists' tenacity in using this spectrum of tactics against dissenting inquiry or speech over an extended number of years may yet prove the most effective of all three periods in eliminating heresy.

The results of coercive tactics have been roughly the same in all three waves of zealotry. The universities were not overrun with zealots in any of these periods. The majority of professors and campuses were not directly affected. However, in each wave the zealotry had a major impact on targets at some campuses and within some faculties. Even if the most serious coercion has been concentrated in some universities or faculties, knowledge of the coercion is widespread, and the more vulnerable and cautious members of the broader academic community will steer clear of possibility of harm.

The usual faculty response in each of these three periods of zealotry has been not to counter the zealotry vigorously. Typically, few faculty give public support to the accused, or to the university. The ideological predisposition that faculty brought to political issues has been a major determinant of the way they have responded to the coercive tactics of zealots in all three waves. In general, faculty tend not to support academic freedom for dissenting ideas for which they have no sympathy. Administrators generally have been far more concerned with public relations than with freedom of academic inquiry and speech. Zealots thus discovered in each period that extreme tactics can be undertaken to assault the accused and the university without censure by the faculty. This public behavior of silent acquiescence and silent submission has been the ballast of ideological zealotry in all three waves. It repeatedly condones and rewards the tactics of zealotry.

Summary of the Similarities in the Seven Waves

The major purpose of this chapter is to review the historical record regarding freedom of academic inquiry and speech in American higher education since the emergence of the modern university 125 years ago. This review leads to the following findings:

1. Periods of zealotry in service of a variety of strong ideologies have been frequent in higher education, occurring approximately every fifteen to twenty years.
2. Waves of zealotry originated both from without and from within the faculty and the student body.
3. During any particular period, it was difficult to predict the ideological direction from which the next wave would come.

4. In each wave, zealots labelled disagreement as heresy, demonstrating the moral turpitude of the heretic, and justifying a variety of coercive tactics to harass and to eliminate heretical academic thought and speech. A favored tactic has been to subject alleged heretics to investigation and tribunal. These have been especially effective against vulnerable groups like students, candidates for appointment, and untenured faculty. In a number of these periods of zealotry, attacks on the academic freedom of competent dissent were disguised as pretextual accusations of other misconduct.

5. Once unleashed, zealotry did not stop with targets who were clearly heretics like communists or bigots; it attacked others for political advantage.

6. The usual faculty response of silent acquiescence in the face of coercive tactics has been the ballast of the ideological zealotry in each wave.

7. There were instances in each period where faculty or administration or both publicly defended academic freedom.

8. The major result in each wave was not just the silencing of the targets but also the silencing of a vastly greater number of potential speakers who would steer wide of possible punishment.

If these findings are correct, then both graduate students and established professors reading this book must give thought to the possibility of experiencing one or two waves of zealotry before the end of their academic careers. At this point, it is difficult to predict the ideological direction from which these future waves would come.

In light of these findings, self-interest dictates that every academic think through and act upon her or his responsibility to protect freedom of academic inquiry and speech. Reciprocal duties among faculty to speak publicly to protect competent dissenting academic inquiry and speech must be the principal line of defense against zealotry.

The next five chapters explore how the professoriat and the courts have attempted to protect freedom of academic inquiry and thought. They proceed by analyzing the meaning of academic freedom and related First Amendment doctrines in the order that they developed historically. Shortly after the turn of the century, the professoriat developed the concept of *professional academic freedom*, intending that academic professional organizations, faculties as collegial bodies, and the employment contract itself would protect the professional autonomy of individual professors engaged in professionally competent work from zealotry. Much later, in the last thirty-five years, the courts also developed a concept of *constitutional academic freedom*.

The next chapters define academic freedom in both of these meanings. Chapter 4 starts by examining how the concept of professional academic freedom developed in response to the historical absence of any protection for academic speech in the employment context.

Notes

1. Richard Hofstadter and Walter Metzger, THE DEVELOPMENT OF ACADEMIC FREEDOM IN THE UNITED STATES 327 (1955).
2. *Id.* at 505.
3. Arthur Schlesinger, Jr., *City University of New York Annual Doctoral Commencement*, May 26, 1994, at 3-4.
4. *See* discussion at notes 247-258 in chapter 2.
5. Mark Tushnet, *Political Correctness, the Law, and the Legal Academy*, 4 YALE J.L. & HUMAN. 127-29 (1992). In 1985, radical right activists formed an organization called Accuracy in Academia (AIA). In order to document and oppose efforts by the radical academic left to use the classroom for political indoctrination, AIA asked students to report Marxist and anti-American statements by professors. The press, the AAUP, administrators, and even the secretary of education, William Bennett, condemned these tactics. AIA dropped the tactic of reporting on professors and was ignored. *See* Julius Getman, IN THE COMPANY OF SCHOLARS 89-90 (1992); James Davison Hunter, CULTURE WARS: THE STRUGGLE TO DEFINE AMERICA 214-215 (1990). There have been incidents where conservative student newspapers unfairly or erroneously report accusations of moral turpitude against faculty members with whom the editors disagree. Tushnet, *supra*, at 156.
6. *Id.* at 152.
7. Ellen Schrecker, NO IVORY TOWER: MCCARTHYISM AND THE UNIVERSITIES 303 (1986). Professor Lionel Lewis observes that, "Perhaps the most salient characteristic of this crusade was widely publicized, indiscriminate, and largely unsubstantiated allegations of disloyalty to the country.... Indeed, this is what McCarthyism...has come to mean." Lionel S. Lewis, THE COLD WAR AND ACADEMIC GOVERNANCE 3 (1993).
8. Fritz Machlup, *Some Misconceptions Concerning Academic Freedom*, ACADEMIC FREEDOM AND TENURE 177, 184-85 (Louis Joughin ed., 1969).
9. *See* Randall Kennedy, *The Political Correctness Scare*, 37 LOY. L. REV. 231, 235-36 (1991).
10. *Id.* at 236-37.
11. David Reisman, *The State of American Higher Education: A Conversation with David Reisman (interview with Wilfred McClay)*, ACAD. QUESTIONS, Winter, 1994-95, at 29.
12. *Id.* at 16.
13. *Id.* at 29.
14. David Bryden, *It Ain't What They Teach, It's the Way They Teach It*, PUB. INT., Spring 1991, at 38, 46.
15. Eugene Genovese, *Heresy, Yes-Sensitivity, No*, NEW REPUBLIC, Apr. 15, 1991, at 30.
16. Dinesh D'Souza, *In the Name of Academic Freedom: Colleges Should Back Professors Against Students' Demands for "Correct" Views*, CHRON. HIGHER EDUC., Apr. 24, 1991, at B1, B3.
17. For example, in the author's situation described in the Preface, resignation from a tenured position would have been necessary if over $100,000 in legal defense fees for five external investigations had not been indemnified. Even with indemnification for defense costs for the five external investigations, defense of the five meritless internal investigations cost several thousand dollars in legal and expert fees, and all ten investigations took over 4,500 hours of the author's time and total energies for five and one-half years.

18. Hofstadter & Metzger, *supra* note 1, at 505-06.
19. Lionel Lewis, COLD WAR ON CAMPUS 97-100, 109 (1988).
20. Commission on Academic Tenure in Higher Education, FACULTY TENURE 42-43 (1973).
21. The willingness of ideological zealots to disparage their own institution and to bring it into public disrespect is extremely difficult for outsiders like alumni and trustees to comprehend. The attachments of institutional loyalty and community pride by which they live do not apply in a university setting for a particular ideological subset of professors and students.
22. Derek Bok, *What's Wrong With Our Universities?*, 14 HARV. J.L. & PUB. POL'Y 305, 308-309 (Spring 1991).
23. Everett Ladd, Jr., and Seymour Martin Lipset, THE DIVIDED ACADEMY: PROFESSORS AND POLITICS 368-69 (1975).
24. Nathan Glazer, REMEMBERING THE ANSWERS 280-81, 288-89, 293-94 (1970).

Part II

The Meaning of
Academic Freedom

4

Protection for Freedom of Expression for the Individual Scholar Employed in Higher Education—Professional Academic Freedom

For several hundred years after the founding of institutions of higher education in the United States, scholars labored under employment law doctrine holding that private and public employees had no right to object to conditions placed upon the terms of employment, including restrictions on free expression.[1] As the modern university developed in the late 1800s, and professors increasingly questioned and challenged the cherished beliefs of the time, the lack of employment or Constitutional law protection for academic speech became a critical problem. No clear standard for Constitutional protection of freedom of speech for professors as employees in the public universities developed until 1968. Except where employment contracts or statute provided otherwise, professors as employees in private universities remained subject to employer restrictions on employee speech in the workplace.[2]

Employer interference with professional speech at the turn of this century led academics in 1915 to organize a professional association, the American Association of University Professors (AAUP). The AAUP pressed university employers to grant professors rights of free inquiry and speech in scholarship and teaching without interference by lay boards of trustees and administrators.[3] "Lay" is used here to mean persons not belonging to the academic profession.

Out of these efforts has grown a unique tradition. The term *professional academic freedom* as used in this essay describes this American tradition that grants rights to professors to be free from employer interference in research, teaching, and intramural and extramural utterance. It also imposes on individual professors correlative duties of professional competence and ethical conduct. The faculty as a collegial body has correlative duties to defend academic freedom and to enforce the duties to be met by individual professors.[4] It is this tradition of faculty self-governance in peer review of professional competence and ethics that makes professional academic freedom unique, not the tenure system, which has many parallels in other settings. This tradition has been incorporated into employment contracts with individual professors. It is also protected by professional academic organizations like the AAUP and by accrediting authorities.[5]

This chapter explores the evolution of professional academic freedom over the last seventy-five years. The following chapter explores the evolution of Constitutional academic freedom. Over the past thirty-five years, the courts have developed a constitutional doctrine to protect the university and individual professors from interference and coercion by federal, state, or local government.

The story of the American tradition of professional academic freedom actually begins at least two centuries before the formation of the American Association of University Professors in 1915. Our tradition of professional academic freedom is rooted in the intellectual system that grew out of the Enlightenment's conviction that reason, if left free, could discover useful knowledge. This intellectual system is liberal in the sense that it favors individual freedom, openmindedness, and the use of reason to foster human progress.

The liberal intellectual system is understood as a social community with indefinite possibilities created by human intellectual diversity. The key insight on which the community is based is the recognition of the inherent fallibility of human thought. The bedrock idea is that "any and all of us might, at any time, be wrong."[6] Knowledge is always seen to be tentative and subject to correction. If no person is immune from error, it follows implicitly in the liberal intellectual system that no belief, no matter how strongly held, is above critical scrutiny for possible correction. No person can claim to be above being checked by others.[7]

Jonathan Rauch, in his recent book, *Kindly Inquisitors,* articulates two foundation stones for the liberal intellectual system. First is *the skeptical rule.* A person may "claim that a statement is established as knowledge only if it can be debunked, in principle, and only insofar as it withstands efforts to debunk it." Knowledge claims in this system must be capable of being checked and have withstood checking. Such claims are always provisional, standing only until proven false.[8] This is essentially what philosopher Karl Popper called the principle of falsifiability. For Popper, it is the possibility of "falsifying" every certainty in science or in the improvement of social life that is the mechanism of knowledge.[9] Second is *the empirical rule.* No person has personal authority over knowledge claims. A person may claim that "a statement has been established as knowledge only insofar as the method used to check it gives the same result regardless of the identity of the checker, and regardless of the source of the statement."[10]

In the liberal intellectual system, knowledge is the "rolling critical consensus of a decentralized community of checkers" who are applying these rules.[11] The system must protect freedom of speech in order for the decentralized community of checkers to produce knowledge, but it does not grant freedom to make knowledge claims. Only the consensus of critical checkers has the status of a knowledge claim. The liberal intellectual system, Rauch points out, "absolutely protects freedom of belief and speech, but it absolutely denies freedom of knowledge...there is positively no right to have one's opinions, however heartfelt, taken seriously as knowledge.... A liberal intellectual regime says that if you want to believe the moon is made of green cheese, fine. But if you want your belief recognized [and acted upon] as knowledge, there are things you must do. You must run your belief through the [system] for checking."[12]

This system is inherently antiauthoritarian. By imposing the obligation to check opinions and to cultivate rather than to curtail criticism, it deprives intellectual, social, religious, political, or ethnic authoritarians of all moral force.[13] In this system, the impulse to stamp out the offending or insensitive opinion is an impulse to destroy knowledge itself.[14]

The liberal intellectual system is not "nice." It denies the legitimacy of knowledge to some beliefs. The denial of that legitimacy causes anguish and pain to those whose cherished beliefs are attacked in the search for knowledge.[15] Since almost all current knowledge was once considered heretical and insensitive to existing beliefs of an earlier time, the anguish and pain caused in the pursuit of knowledge has been enormous. "In the pursuit of knowledge," Rauch observes, "many people...will be hurt, and...this is a reality which no amount of wishing or regulating can ever change. It is not good to offend people, but it is necessary. A no-offense society is a no-knowledge society."[16]

The university in a liberal intellectual system plays an important role as the one community whose mission is specifically the seeking, making, and disseminating of knowledge through public criticism.[17] The professoriat in the universities constitutes a significant proportion of the decentralized community of checkers on which knowledge production depends.

The major threat to the decentralized community of checkers in general, and the professoriat in particular, has been and will be from political, economic, ethnic, religious, or other groups who wish to prevent the anguish and pain that results when their beliefs are subjected to checking and criticism. This is the context in which the professoriat sought to gain autonomy to perform its role in the community of checkers.

The professoriat's demand for professional academic freedom developed naturally during the nineteenth century as higher education shifted its focus from essentially religious and moral training for the elite professions to a much broader intellectual inquiry based on the premise that trained reason, principally through the scientific method, could grasp the essentials of human activity and advance human welfare.[18] As Georgetown law professor Byrne notes, this endeavor presupposes

a progressive conception of knowledge. Understanding at any one moment is imperfect, and defects can be exposed by testing hypotheses against reality, through either adducing new data or experimentation. The process of hypothesis-experimentation-new hypothesis improves knowledge and brings us closer to a complete, more nearly objective truth about the world. Error is not dangerous so long as the process is continued, because acknowledged means will expose it; in fact, it [error] is actually beneficial (and inevitable) as part of progressive discovery.... The process of theory, dispute, and experiment, rather than producing anxiety about the continuity of the community, is celebrated as intrinsic to the pursuit of truth.[19]

This awareness of the possibility of error and fallibility does not mean that knowledge is unattainable, but that, to reach it, one must always be ready to reexamine and correct one's view and to tolerate those who contest established knowledge.

The professoriat saw a unique role for itself to contribute to the progress of knowledge as a community of checkers with specialized training, information, and skills. In virtue of a professor's special competence as a checker in some area of study, including knowledge of the existing scholarship and mastery of the techniques of investigation and validation in some academic discipline, the professoriat sought special rights of investigation and dissemination of knowledge.[20] It is this unique role that ultimately justified special employment protection for a professor's right to offend in the pursuit of knowledge. As Professor Byrne observes:

> Scholars work within a discipline, primarily addressing other scholars and students. Their audience understands and evaluates their speech within a tradition of knowledge, shared assumptions and arguments about methodology and criteria, and common objectives of exploration or discovery.... The ordinary criterion of success is whether, through mastery of the discipline's discourse, the scholar improves the account of some worthy subject that the discipline has previously accepted.[21]

The persons who may engage in this speech are rigorously controlled. The scholar must have completed the necessary undergraduate and graduate courses of study to be certified by her peers as competent to engage in the scholarly discourse of a discipline.[22] Within the constraints of the disciplinary discourse and the criteria for certification of professional competence, the scholar is "free to reach conclusions that contradict previous dogma, whether within the academy or throughout the larger society."[23] Professor Bryne defines the scholarship and teaching subject to the ethical and competency constraints of the discipline to be "academic speech."[24]

The essential requirement for this progressive conception of knowledge within a university setting is thus free discourse among academic professionals within the ethical and competency constraints of a discipline.[25] At the turn of the century the principal danger to the realization of free discourse among competent professionals was interference by the lay boards of trustees and regents who governed higher education in the United States. This interference took one of two forms. First, because of political, moral, or religious concerns, lay boards tended to distort intellectual inquiry by imposing constraints on the offering of new hypotheses or the criticizing of accepted ones.[26] Second, the free exchange envisioned was to occur among competent professionals. The exchange could tolerate error but not incompetence, and only academic professionals, not lay boards, could evaluate professional qualifications and performance.[27]

In the later nineteenth century and early twentieth century, American academics thus sought to wrest control over the evaluation of academic speech from "lay thinking" as represented by boards of trustees and regents. The principal motivation was the desire for conditions necessary to the search for knowledge. In order to contribute to the progress of knowledge as a community of checkers with specialized training, information, and skills, professors had to have special employment protection from their employer's interference for their right to offend in the pursuit of knowledge.[28] Professor Fritz Machlup saw this employment protection as the right of the people. "It is important that the few potential troublemakers are encouraged to voice their dissent, because on such dissent, however unpopular, the advancement of our knowledge and the development of our material, social, or spiritual improvements may depend."[29]

Emerging out of this conflict between professional academics and lay employers, professional academic freedom in the United States thus became a matter of conditions of professional employment advocated principally initially by the American Association of University Professors, a professional organization of academics, and in more recent years, by certifying authorities for colleges and universities. It has been incorporated into employment contracts. Essentially, university employers have agreed to grant exceptional vocational freedom to professors to inquire, to teach, and to publish without lay interference on the condition that professors meet certain correlative duties of professional integrity as individuals and as a collegial body. The principal responsibility to defend the academic freedom of competent academic speech rests with the faculty as a collegial body.

The most important document defining the American concept of professional academic freedom is the 1915 General Declaration of Principles by the American Association of University Professors (AAUP). It remains the foundation of the understanding of academic freedom within the academic world.[30] This document starts with the reality that "American institutions of learning are usually controlled by boards of trustees as the ultimate repositories of power."[31] Making no distinction between private or public universities, the 1915 statement takes the position that such boards are in a position of public trust to serve the public interest.[32] Universities serve the public interest by: (1) promoting inquiry and advancing the sum of human knowledge; (2) providing general instruction for the students; and (3) developing experts to advise government and the community on the solution of problems.[33] The function of the professional scholar in realizing these purposes is to deal at first hand, after prolonged and specialized technical training, with the sources of knowledge; and to impart the results of their own and their fellow-specialists' investigation and reflection, both to students and to the general public, without fear or favor. The proper discharge of this function requires...that the university teacher shall be exempt from any pecuniary motive or inducement to hold, or to express, any conclusion which is not the genuine and uncolored product of his own study or that of fellow specialists.[34]

Based on these arguments, the 1915 statement built a definition of professional academic freedom. Professional academic freedom must enable the individual scholar to perform the three functions of: (1) dealing with sources of knowledge and reflecting upon them toward some result; (2) imparting those results to students; and (3) imparting those results to the public. These three functions in turn relate closely to the university's three purposes of: (1) promoting inquiry and the advancement of human knowledge; (2) providing instruction to students; and (3) developing expert advisers for the community.

The 1915 statement defined the three elements of professional academic freedom necessary for scholars to perform their functions within the larger purposes of the university. These were: (1) freedom of inquiry and research; (2) freedom of teaching within the university; and (3) freedom of extramural utterance and action. In these three areas, trustees served the public trust by granting university teachers rights of freedom from lay interference so that neither intellectual inquiry and discourse nor decisions concerning professional competence to engage in the intellectual discourse would be distorted by lay bias.[35]

The 1915 statement recognized that the granting of these rights of freedom from lay interference rested upon the professor's meeting unique obligations. Each professor must observe personally and enforce through collegial action the ethical and competency constraints on scholarly inquiry and discourse. "Since there are no rights without corresponding duties, the considerations heretofore set down with respect to the freedom of the academic teacher entail certain correlative obligations."[36]

Correlative Duties of the Individual Faculty
Member in the 1915 Statement

Inherent in the concept of professional academic freedom in the United States are correlative duties for both individual university teachers and for the faculty as a collegial body. The principal correlative obligation of the *individual university teacher* is to comply with the ethical and competency constraints of professional scholarly inquiry and discourse.

The claim to *freedom of teaching* is made in the interest of the integrity and of the progress of scientific inquiry; it is, therefore, *only* those who carry on their work in the temper of the scientific inquirer who may justly assert this claim. The liberty of the scholar within the university to set forth his conclusions, be they what they may, is *conditioned* by their being conclusions gained by a scholar's method and held in a scholar's spirit; that is to say, they must be the fruits of competent and patient and sincere inquiry, and they should be set forth with dignity, courtesy, and temperateness of language. The university teacher, in giving instruction upon controversial matters, while he is under no obligation to hide his own opinion under a mountain of equivocal verbiage, should, *if he is fit for his position*, be a person of fair and judicial mind; he *should*, in dealing with such subjects, set forth justly, without suppression or innuendo, the divergent opinions of other investigators.[37]

Freedom of teaching and freedom of extramural utterance and action were seen to be closely related in the 1915 statement.[38] "The general principles which have to do with freedom of teaching in both of these senses seem to the committee to be in great part, though not wholly, the same."[39] The 1915 statement imposes higher correlative obligations on extramural utterances. "In their extramural utterances, it is obvious that academic teachers are under a *peculiar* obligation to avoid hasty or unverified or exaggerated statements, and to refrain from intemperate or sensational modes of expression."[40]

The 1915 statement does not clearly define "freedom of extramural utterance and action."[41] The principal question is whether this phrase may also include intramural speech outside of teaching and research. In the same paragraph as this freedom is first set forth, the 1915 statement defines extramural speech as "freedom of speech of university teachers *outside* their institutions" in contrast to "freedom of teaching *within* the university."[42] Of course, "extramural" means literally "outside of the walls of the university."

In a later paragraph however, the 1915 statement comments that "in their extramural utterances, it is obvious that academic teachers are under a peculiar obligation to avoid hasty or unverified or exaggerated statements, and to refrain from intemperate or sensational modes of expression. But subject to these restraints, it is not, in this committee's opinion, desirable that scholars *should be debarred from giving expression to their judgments upon controversial questions, or that their freedom of speech, outside the university,* should be limited to questions falling within their own specialties."[43] Two paragraphs later, "It is, it will be seen, in no sense the contention of this committee that academic freedom implies that individual teachers should be exempt from all restraints as to the matter or manner of their utterances, *either within or without the university*."[44]

These two references later in the 1915 statement give faint support to an argument that the meaning of "extramural utterances and actions" is not limited to speech outside the walls, but also includes speech inside the walls, other than teaching or research, that gives "expression to a judgment on controversial questions." The AAUP historical archives support the reading that "freedom of extramural utterance" meant not just freedom to speak beyond the walls, but freedom to speak outside of teaching and research within the walls without the warranty of a professional task or an acknowledged expertise.[45]

It is not necessary to stretch the meaning of "extramural utterance" in the 1915 statement to find academic freedom protection for intramural utterance other than teaching and research. The 1915 statement defines the teaching and research elements of professional academic freedom broadly in the context of the overall purpose each element was to serve. Professional academic freedom included "freedom of inquiry and research," so the university teacher could play a role in the university's larger purpose of "promoting inquiry and advancing the sum of human knowledge." Professional academic freedom also included "freedom of teaching," so the university teacher could play a role in the university's larger purpose of "providing instruction to students."

Thus, freedom of teaching includes intramural speech relating to the education of students, and freedom of inquiry and research includes intramural speech that involves critical inquiry. For example, intramural speech involving admissions, appointments, curriculum, tenure, or a lack of confidence in the administration because of decisions affecting the education of students is protected. Any intramural speech involving critical inquiry is protected.

Correlative Duties of the Faculty as a Collegial Body in the 1915 Statement

Within the American tradition of professional academic freedom, the principal correlative obligation of the *faculty as a collegial body* is to enforce in the first instance the ethical and competency constraints of the academic profession in the discipline when individual professors do not observe them. "[T]he power of determining when departures from the requirements of the scientific spirit and method have occurred, should be vested in bodies composed of members of the academic profession."[46] Only members of the profession have the competence to judge these requirements, and they "must be prepared to assume this responsibility for themselves...the responsibility cannot...be rightfully evaded."[47] If the profession "should prove itself unwilling to purge its ranks of the incompetent and the unworthy, or to prevent the freedom which it claims in the name of science from being used as a shelter for inefficiency, for superficiality, or for uncritical and intemperate partisanship, it is certain that the task will be performed by others."[48]

In championing the concept of peer review of professional competence and ethics, AAUP academic leaders took pains to argue that peer review would not shelter the incompetent or unethical professor. Before an audience of university presidents, John Dewey maintained that peer review would "facilitate the removal of incompetents by bringing into play the resources of highly critical connoisseurs." Many university presidents of the time disagreed, fearing that "professors were likely to protect professors and ignore the interests of students and the public."[49]

The 1915 statement conditions the rights of academic speakers on the performance of the correlative obligation to comply with the strictures of inquiry and discourse established by their discipline. Collegial responsibility to discipline departure from professional modes of inquiry and discourse is implicit in the statement's admonition that university teachers must have the capacity "for judicial severity when the occasion requires it."[50] However, the 1915 statement contended only competent professionals within the same discipline could determine which academic speech violated professional modes of inquiry and discourse.[51] The liberty granted to all professors is thus conditional upon the correlative obligation of the faculty as a whole to enforce the ethical and competency constraints of the discipline.

The 1940 AAUP Statement

The 1940 statement of principles adopted by the AAUP and the Association of American Colleges (AAC) incorporates in summary terms the rights and correlative obligations of professional academic freedom set forth in the 1915 statement. It sets up a framework of norms concerning rights and duties. This 1940 statement has been endorsed by almost all major educational certifying organizations in the United States,[52] and is commonly adopted by reference in academic employment contracts.[53]

Rights of Academic Freedom for Research and Teaching

In its introductory paragraphs, the 1940 statement reasons that universities are conducted for the common good, and the common good depends upon the free search for truth and its free exposition.

> Academic freedom is essential to these purposes and applies to both *teaching* and *research*. Freedom in research is fundamental to the advancement of truth. Academic freedom in its teaching aspect is fundamental for the protection of the rights of the teacher in teaching and of the student to freedom in learning. It carries with it *duties correlative with rights*.[54]

Immediately following the introductory paragraphs, under the heading "Academic Freedom," the 1940 statement sets forth three paragraphs that further define the concept. In paragraph (a), the statement provides that "teachers are entitled to full freedom in research and in the publication of the results, subject to the adequate performance of their other academic duties." In paragraph (b) the statement provides that "teachers are entitled to freedom in the classroom in discussing their subject, but they should be careful not to introduce into their teaching controversial matter which has no relation to their subject."[55]

*Rights of Academic Freedom for both Intramural Utterances Other
Than Teaching and Research and Extramural Utterance*

There is no specific reference in the 1940 statement to "freedom of extramural utterance and action," as there is in the 1915 statement. Paragraph (c) under
Academic Freedom provides that

> college and university teachers are citizens, members of a learned profession, and
> officers of an educational institution. When they speak or write as citizens, they
> should be free from institutional censorship or discipline, but their special position
> in the community imposes special obligations. As scholars and educational offic-
> ers, they should remember that the public may judge their profession and their
> institution by their utterances. Hence they should at all times be accurate, should
> exercise appropriate restraint, should show respect for the opinions of others, and
> should make every effort to indicate that they are not speaking for the institution.[56]

An interpretation adopted by both the AAUP and the AAC and issued contem-
poraneously with the 1940 statement refers to the "admonitions of paragraph
(c)" as applicable to the "*extramural* utterances of the teacher."[57]

The literal words of paragraph (c) of the 1940 statement clearly limit its
grant of academic freedom to extramural utterance in the sense of speech outside the walls of the university. The second sentence of paragraph (c) refers to
speaking or writing "as a citizen," recognizing that a teacher's special position "in the community" imposes special obligations. It is possible that "citizen" and "community" refer to citizenship in the university community inside
the walls as well as citizenship in the community outside of the walls. However, the third sentence of paragraph (c) urges teachers to remember that "the
public" may judge their profession and their institution by their utterances;
and the fourth sentence urges teachers to make every effort to indicate that
they are "not speaking for the institution." The contemporaneous interpretation comments that paragraph (c) deals with "extramural utterance." This evidence heavily favors reading paragraph (c) as granting academic freedom only
to speech outside the walls.[58]

The 1940 statement specifically grants rights of academic freedom to teaching and research, which are types of intramural utterance, but the statement
does not specifically address whether other types of intramural utterance may
not constitute teaching or research and thus have no academic freedom protection. However, the interpretation of "teaching" and "research" in the 1940
statement must be consistent with the policy rationale for academic freedom
developed in the 1915 statement and reflected in the 1940 statement. Thus,
"academic freedom in its teaching aspect" includes intramural utterance relating to the education of students, and academic freedom "in research" includes
intramural speech that involves critical inquiry.

There are differences of opinion about how broadly to construe these rights
of academic freedom for intramural speech other than teaching and research.

University of Illinois law professor Matthew Finkin fears that any restrictions on intramural speech will place a professor in the position of having to guess where his or her utterance lies on a spectrum from purely professional to purely aprofessional. This may harm the quest for knowledge within the university. He would protect practically all utterances of a professor within the walls.[59] University of Texas law school dean Mark Yudof believes that there must be a reasonable connection between a professor's speech and the linchpins of teaching or research, or the concept of professional academic freedom will become indistinguishable from the general demands for professional autonomy common in progressive labor management relations today. Thus, Yudof argues, inadequate salaries, uncomfortable offices, inadequate insurance, or lack of parking space may affect all university employees, and in the case of professors, may stifle creative impulses, but academic freedom must not be stretched too far to give special license to professors to comment on these matters.[60] While a close question, Yudof seems to have the better of this argument based on interpretation of the words used in the AAUP statements. The penumbra of protection for intramural speech should extend only to that speech linked reasonably closely to the true core focus of academic freedom: the education of students and critical inquiry.[61]

Correlative Duties of the Individual Faculty Member

The 1940 statement also sets up a framework of norms concerning duties.[62] It provides that academic freedom "carries with it duties correlative with rights." The general term "duties correlative with rights" is left open-ended in the 1940 statement. The statement lists several specific duties and mentions two more general duties, but there is no indication these are exhaustive of the concept of "duty."

The statement does define several specific duties. With respect to the right of academic freedom in research, the 1940 statement imposes a duty that "research for pecuniary return should be based upon an understanding with the authorities of the institution." With respect to the right of academic freedom in teaching of students, the 1940 statement imposes a specific duty that teachers "should be careful not to introduce into their teaching controversial matter which has no relation to their subject." With respect to the right of academic freedom for extramural utterances, the 1940 statement states a specific duty that when teachers "speak or write as citizens, they should be free from institutional censorship or discipline, but their special position in the community imposes special obligations. As scholars and educational officers, they should remember that the public may judge their profession and their institution by their utterances. Hence they should at all times be accurate, should exercise appropriate restraint, should show respect for the opinions of others, and should make every effort to indicate that they are not speaking for the institution."[63]

In the contemporaneous interpretation to the 1940 statement, administrators are given permission to file charges, if "the extramural utterances of the teacher have been such as to raise grave doubts concerning the teacher's fitness for his or her position."[64]

Describing more general correlative duties, the 1940 statement provides that tenured professors may be dismissed for "adequate cause," which may include "charges of incompetence" or reasons "involving moral turpitude."[65] These two general duties of professional competence and ethical conduct, referred to in passing in the text of the 1940 statement, are not further defined in the text of the 1940 statement or the contemporaneous interpretation. They also appear to define only partially the elements of the open-ended term "duties" correlative with rights used in the 1940 statement.

A number of other AAUP statements and comments help clarify the definition of "duties correlative with rights" in the 1940 statement. It is critical first to visualize clearly the framework of norms in the 1940 statement.

1. Rights of Academic Freedom
   a) Research
   b) Teaching
   c) Intramural Utterance Relating to the Education of Students or Involving Critical Inquiry
   d) Extramural Utterance

2. Correlative "Duties" of the Individual Faculty Member. The 1940 statement does not exhaustively define the open-ended term "duties." It lists several specific duties and mentions two general duties.
   a) Duties Relating to Research, Teaching, and Intramural Utterance
      i) Specific Duties
          1) Research for pecuniary gain should be based upon an understanding with the authorities of the institution.
          2) Teachers should be careful not to introduce into their teaching controversial material that has no relation to their subject.
      ii) General Duties
          1) Professional competence.
          2) Ethical conduct.
   b) Duties Relating to Extramural Utterance. Speech as a citizen is to be free of institutional censorship or discipline but subject to "special obligations." Teachers speaking as citizens should:
      i)   at all times be accurate;
      ii) exercise appropriate restraint;
      iii) show respect for the opinions of others; and
      iv) make every effort to indicate that they are not speaking for the institution.

The most important statement further clarifying the meaning of "duties correlative with rights" is an interpretive comment. In 1970, the AAUP adopted

Interpretive Comments For the 1940 Statement providing that "the Association of American Colleges and the American Association of University Professors have long recognized that membership in the academic profession carries with it *special responsibilities*. Both associations either separately or jointly have consistently affirmed these responsibilities in major policy statements, providing guidance to professors in their utterances as citizens, in their exercise of their responsibilities to the institution and to students, and in their conduct when resigning from the institution or when undertaking government-sponsored research. Of particular relevance is the Statement of Professional Ethics, adopted in 1966 as Association policy."[66]

The AAUP's 1970 Interpretive Comments for the 1940 statement recognize "special responsibilities" incumbent on members of the academic profession. These "special responsibilities" seem intended to further define the open-ended term "duties" in the 1940 statement. Special responsibilities themselves are defined in the AAUP's major policy statements, particularly the 1966 Statement of Professional Ethics.

Using this framework of norms as a guide, the essay explores next how other major policy statements develop further the 1940 statement's general duties of professional competence and ethical conduct in teaching, research, and intramural utterance. The essay then examines how other policy statements further define the duties of individual faculty members relating to extramural utterance.

This discussion is quite technical, but is necessary to define clearly the outer limits of professional academic freedom. Clarity is critical in a definition of the outer limits of faculty speech so that vagueness does not chill competent academic speech.

Further definition of the general duties of professional competence. The academic profession has struggled in the effort to define clear duties of professional competence. The 1940 statement refers to incompetence and moral turpitude in the discussion of termination for cause, but in a procedural context and without elaboration. In 1958, the joint AAC-AAUP Statement on Procedural Standards in Faculty Dismissal Proceedings acknowledged that "one persistent source of difficulty is the definition of adequate cause for the dismissal of a faculty member.... [C]onsiderable ambiguity and misunderstanding persist throughout higher education...concerning this matter. The present statement assumes that individual institutions will have formulated their own definitions of adequate cause for dismissal, bearing in mind the 1940 statement and standards which have developed in the experience of academic institutions."[67] Since the 1940 statement gives little guidance, it is the developed tradition of duties in higher education that provides the definition of professional competence.

The AAUP's 1966 Statement on Professional Ethics further defines the duty of *professional competence* to include the following general obligations:

1. to strive above all to be effective teachers and scholars;
2. to devote energies "to developing and improving...scholarly competence;"
3. in teaching, to "hold before students the best scholarly standard and ethical standards of [the] discipline;"
4. to practice "intellectual honesty;"
5. to acknowledge academic debt; and
6. "to exercise critical self-discipline and judgment in using, extending, and transmitting knowledge."[68]

The 1966 statement does not further define "effectiveness" as a scholar and teacher, "scholarly competence," "best scholarly standard," the exercise of "critical self-discipline and judgment in using, extending, and transmitting knowledge" or "intellectual honesty."

The 1915 statement, from which the 1940 statement's concept of a correlative duty of professional competence is drawn, lends some help. It provides that academic freedom for teaching may *only* be asserted by "those who carry on their work in the temper of the scientific inquirer." Academic freedom for a scholar's conclusions "is conditioned by their being conclusions gained by a scholar's method and held in a scholar's spirit." The 1915 statement further defines the phrases "temper of the scientific inquirer," "a scholar's method," and "a scholar's spirit" to mean that conclusions must: (1) be the fruit of "competent and patient and sincere inquiry;" and (2) especially on controversial matters, be the product of "fair" deliberation where the divergent opinions of other investigators are "set further justly, without suppression or innuendo."[69] Richard Hofstadter and Walter Metzger, examining the development of academic freedom in the United States, describe these traditions incorporated into the 1915 statement as "norms of neutrality and competence."[70]

In 1971, both the Association of American Colleges (AAC) and the AAUP established a Commission on Academic Tenure in Higher Education to evaluate the operation of the tenure system in higher education. The Commission reported its views (which were officially adopted by the AAC and the AAUP) in 1973.[71] The Commission found that a professor must demonstrate teaching effectiveness, scholarly competence and promise, and academic citizenship at a professional standard determined by the faculty.[72] Academic tradition should guide the faculty in defining these standards.[73] The Commission defined "adequate cause" for dismissal as: (1) demonstrated incompetence or dishonesty in teaching or research; (2) substantial and manifest neglect of duty; and (3) personal conduct that substantially impairs the individual's fulfillment of his or her institutional responsibilities.[74]

To summarize, the meaning of the 1940 statement's concept of a correlative duty of professional competence was slightly clarified in 1973 by the Commission on Academic Tenure in Higher Education. The implication of the definition of adequate cause for dismissal is that professional competence is satisfied if the professor is not demonstrably incompetent or dishonest in teaching or research, the professor does not substantially neglect assigned duties (in teaching, scholarship, and academic citizenship), and the professor does not engage in personal conduct that would substantially impair the professor's fulfillment of his or her institutional responsibilities. The concept is also developed to a greater degree by the 1966 statement's demand that academics strive to be effective teachers and scholars, to develop and improve scholarly competence, to hold before students the best scholarly standard, to practice intellectual honesty, and to acknowledge academic debt. A Statement on Plagiarism, adopted by the AAUP's annual meeting in 1990, reaffirms that "professors must also be rigorously honest in acknowledging their academic debts."[75] The 1915 statement, from which the 1940 statement's concept of a correlative duty of professional competence is drawn, helps to define the "exercise of self discipline and judgment" in the 1966 statement in terms of a scholar's method, which includes the correlative duties of "patient and sincere inquiry," and "fair" deliberation where the divergent opinions of other investigators are "set forth justly without suppression or innuendo."

This is still not a complete definition of professional competence for a faculty member. Some duties inherent in professional competence were so basic as to be assumed. The best example of an unstated but common understanding of professional competence is evident on the issue of falsification of evidence. Although the 1966 statement urges "intellectual honesty," and the 1915 statement emphasizes both the importance of painstaking and thorough inquiry and the prohibition against misrepresentation or distortion of others' work, the principal AAUP statements do not specifically prohibit falsification of evidence in teaching, research and intramural utterance.

Accuracy in the recording and use of evidence and nonfalsification are simply so fundamental as to be assumed in academic work.[76] The major canon of academic work has been honest and accurate investigation, and the cardinal sin has been falsification. With respect to extramural utterance, where this duty was not so fundamental and clear, the 1940 statement does state that teachers speaking as citizens shall "at all times be accurate." The standard of care for the duty of accuracy is high. The price of exceptional freedom to speak the truth as one sees it, Professor Rabban observes, is the "cost of exceptional care in the representation of that truth, a professional standard of care."[77]

There is, as former Harvard President Derek Bok has observed, a common definition of professional competence used to evaluate the academic work of faculty.[78] The common definition of professional competence can be pulled out from the AAUP statements and the unstated but long tradition of the academic profession. A faculty member cannot neglect any of the responsibilities assigned by the university employer: teaching, research, and academic citizenship. In satisfying these duties, the faculty member must meet a professional standard defined by faculty, which in turn is guided by academic tradition. In all her academic work, a faculty member must meet general duties of both practicing "intellectual honesty" and exercising "critical self-discipline and judgment in using extending, and transmitting knowledge." In teaching in particular, a professor is "to hold before students the best scholarly standards and ethical standards of the discipline." The traditions of the profession further define intellectual honesty, critical self-discipline and judgment, and best scholarly standards to include the following duties of inquiry and argument:

1. to gather the evidence relevant to the issue at hand through thorough and painstaking inquiry;
2. to record the evidence accurately;
3. to give careful and impartial consideration to the weight of the evidence;
4. to reason analytically from the evidence to the proposition;
5. to seek internal consistency;
6. to exercise courage when the evidence contradicts what the scholar and teacher had hoped to achieve;
7. to set forth justly without misrepresentation or distortion the divergent evidence and propositions of other investigators;
8. to present evidence and analysis clearly and persuasively; and
9. to be rigorously honest in acknowledging academic debt.

In research, the faculty member must develop and improve her scholarly competence. The tradition of the profession is that the faculty member is to use this competence to develop and improve the account of some area of knowledge.[79]

In the 1940 statement, the AAUP gained for professors exceptional vocational freedom to inquire, to teach, and to publish without lay interference. The principal price of this exceptional freedom is that professors must meet correlative duties of professional competence in their academic work.[80] The standard of care professors must meet in the satisfaction of these duties is higher for the untenured than for the tenured. The candidate for tenure carries the burden to demonstrate excellence in the satisfaction of these duties. The termination of tenure requires the institution essentially to demonstrate gross negligence in the performance of these duties.[81]

Further definition of the general duty of ethical conduct. In defining the open-ended term *duties* correlative with rights, the 1940 statement provides that tenured professors may be dismissed for "adequate cause," which may include charges "involving moral turpitude." The AAUP's 1970 Interpretive Comments for the 1940 Statement recognize special responsibilities incumbent on professors, particularly those in the AAUP's Statement on Professional Ethics. The 1966 Statement of Professional Ethics defines the general duty of ethical conduct to include the following obligations:

1. to demonstrate respect for students as individuals;

2. to make every reasonable effort to foster honest academic conduct and to assure that the professors' evaluations of students reflect each student's true merit;
3. to respect the confidential nature of the relationship between professor and student;
4. to avoid any exploitation, harassment, or discriminatory treatment of students;
5. not to discriminate against or to harass colleagues;
6. in the exchange of criticism and ideas to show due respect for the opinions of others;
7. to strive to be objective in professional judgment of colleagues;
8. to defend the academic freedom of students and colleagues;
9. to practice intellectual honesty, particularly not permitting outside interests to compromise freedom of inquiry; and
10. to avoid creating the impression of speaking or acting for the university.[82]

A 1970 statement by the AAUP's Council, Freedom and Responsibility, affirms several of these duties of ethical conduct. The 1970 statement provides that "membership in the academic community imposes on students, faculty members, administrators, and trustees an obligation" to do the following:

1. "to respect the dignity of others;"
2. "to acknowledge their right to express differing opinions;"
3. "to foster and defend intellectual honesty;"
4. *not* to express dissent or grievances in ways
   i) that disrupt classes or speeches or
   ii) that "significantly impede the functions of the institution;"
5. to provide an atmosphere "conducive to learning" with "even-handed treatment in all aspects of the teacher-student relationship;"
6. *not* to force students "by the authority inherent in the instructional role to make particular personal choices as to political action or their own part in society;"
7. *not* to intrude material that has no relation to the subject or to fail to present the subject matter of the course as announced to the students and as approved by the faculty;
8. to base evaluation of students and the award of credit on "academic performance professionally judged, and not on matters irrelevant to that performance, whether personality, race, religion, degree of political activism, or personal beliefs;" and
9. to foster and defend the academic freedom of students and colleagues.[83]

In three places, the 1970 statement emphasizes this last duty of individual faculty members to foster and defend the academic freedom of students and colleagues.[84]

These later statements further defining the general duty of ethical conduct articulated in the 1940 statement build on a tradition of intellectual and moral habits appropriate to scholarly conversation. At the peak of the scholarly enterprise are the conversational norms of civilization. Michael Oakeshott captures many of these norms in a quotation from an Eton schoolmaster:

> At school you are not engaged so much in acquiring knowledge as in making mental efforts under criticism.... A certain amount of knowledge you can indeed with average faculties acquire so as to retain; nor need you regret the hours you spend on much that is forgotten, for the shadow of lost knowledge at least protects you from many illusions. But you go to a great school not so much for knowledge as for arts and habits; for the habit of attention, for the art of expression, for the art of assuming at a moment's notice, a new intellectual position, for the art of entering quickly into another person's thoughts, for the habit of submitting to censure and refutation, for the art of indicating assent or dissent in graduated terms, for the habit of regarding minute points of accuracy, for the art of working out what is possible in a given time, for taste, discrimination, for mental courage and mental soberness. And above all you go to a great school for self-knowledge.[85]

Further definition of the general duties of individual faculty members relating to extramural utterance. The 1940 statement grants broad academic freedom for extramural utterance as a citizen subject to the "special obligations" of paragraph (c). Teachers speaking as a citizen should:

1. at all times be accurate;[86]
2. exercise appropriate restraint;[87]
3. show respect for the opinions of others; and
4. make every effort to indicate that they are not speaking for the institution.[88]

These special correlative duties relating to extramural utterance are subject to a lower standard of care than the general and specific correlative duties relating to teaching, research, and intramural utterance. The contemporaneous interpretation to the 1940 statement specifies that administrators may file charges if "the extramural utterances of the teacher have been such as to cause grave doubts concerning the teacher's fitness for his or her position."[89]

The 1964 Committee A Statement on Extramural Utterance basically restates paragraph (c) of the 1940 statement and the contemporaneous interpretation of the 1940 statement. It adds that the burden of proof on the administration to demonstrate that particular extramural utterance shows grave doubts concerning the teacher's fitness for her position is a heavy one. The administration carries the burden to make a clear demonstration with weighty evidence.[90]

The AAUP also occasionally publishes responses from the AAUP's Washington staff to letters of inquiry. The 1940 Statement's injunction for faculty members to exercise "appropriate restraint" is defined to refer "solely to choice of language and to other aspects of the manner in which a statement is made. It does not refer to the substance of a teacher's remarks. It does not refer to the time and place of his utterance."[91] The staff cites with approval Professor Ralph

Fuchs's statement that "a violation [of academic responsibility] may consist of serious intemperateness of expression, intentional falsehood offered as a statement of fact, incitement of misconduct, or conceivably some other impropriety of circumstance."[92]

Professor Finkin notes that the "special responsibilities" outlined in paragraph (c) of the 1940 statement subject extramural utterance to "a professional standard of care."[93] While true at a general level, this fails to recognize that the 1940 statement creates a different set of professional duties for extramural utterance than for teaching, research, and intramural utterance. The four correlative duties of academic freedom for extramural utterance are lower than the correlative duties of academic freedom for teaching, research, and intramural utterance describe earlier.[94] The four correlative duties applicable to extramural utterance were a compromise between the AAUP and the AAC. One of the most controversial issues addressed in the 1940 statement was the AAC's desire to subject the extramural utterances of academics to institutional discipline. The AAC insisted that faculty members reach a line of professional propriety long before they reached a boundary between legally protected speech and libelous, seditious, or obscene utterances.[95] The four correlative duties for extramural utterance in paragraph (c) of the 1940 statement were the result of prolonged negotiation over these issues.

The grant of rights of academic freedom to extramural utterance was a major achievement in 1940.[96] The Supreme Court did not articulate a clear test to protect freedom of speech of those academics who were government employees until 1968, and ultimately restricted such protection only to speech of public concern subject to a balancing test against the employer's interest. Academics in public higher education can claim protection for extramural speech under both the Constitution and professional academic freedom. Rights under the latter doctrine are subject to satisfaction of the four correlative duties. Academics in private higher education can assert only professional academic freedom.

It is critical to understand that breach of any of the four correlative duties attached to the right of professional academic freedom for extramural utterance can lead to discipline by the employer. For example, President John Silber of Boston University did not renew the contract of an untenured professor who "willingly and knowingly told a lie in order to make a rhetorical point" by asserting the existence of concentration camps in Massachusetts in a political speech. Silber found that this was a "gross betrayal of academic freedom through gross academic irresponsibility."[97] If the remark was an intentional falsehood offered as a statement of fact, it would not meet the duty to be "accurate." There would still be a question whether, in context, the falsehood causes grave doubts concerning the teacher's fitness for his position.

Correlative Duties of the Faculty as a Collegial Body

Professional academic freedom also imposes two correlative duties on the faculty as a collegial body: (1) the duty to determine when individual professors inadequately meet their responsibilities of professional competence and ethical conduct; and (2) the duty to foster and defend the academic freedom of colleagues. The 1940 statement briefly outlines the faculty's role in determining whether an individual professor has inadequately performed the correlative duties of academic freedom. The statement provides that "service [of tenured teachers] should be terminated only for adequate cause.... Termination for cause of a continuous appointment...should, if possible, be considered by both a faculty committee and the governing board of the institution."[98] The AAUP's 1970 Interpretive Comments for the 1940 statement adds that "a further specification of the academic due process to which the teacher...is entitled is contained in the Statement on Procedural Standards in Faculty Dismissal Proceedings."[99]

The 1915 statement on which the 1940 statement builds sets forth a clearer understanding of the correlative duty of the faculty, as a collegial body, to determine when individual professors inadequately meet their responsibilities. The faculty must acquire "the capacity for impersonal judgment in such cases, and for judicial severity when the occasion requires it."[100] The 1915 Statement exhorts the profession to be willing "to purge its ranks of the incompetent and the unworthy," and "to prevent...[academic] freedom...from being used as a shelter for inefficiency, for superficiality, or for uncritical and intemperate partisanship."[101]

The traditional conception in the 1915 statement gives faculty peers initial responsibility for enforcing the performance of academic duties. This suggests that further consideration by administration and boards is appropriate when faculty peers depart from professional standards of judgment. With respect to competency specifically, the AAUP's Committee A in 1946 reported:

> [T]he position of the Association [AAUP] is clear: far from protecting the incompetent, it welcomes and facilitates their elimination from the profession.... The Association...accepts the principle that institutions of higher education are conducted for the common good, and the common good demands competence. But in order that incompetents may be eliminated, and incompetents only, the Association insists upon two things: The first is that department heads, deans, and personnel committees shall be honest and courageous in their duty of detecting and eliminating the incompetent during the period of probation.... The second thing is that when an established teacher is accused of incompetence, he shall frankly be charged with it, given a hearing with due process, and retained or dismissed on the findings.[102]

Duke professor William Van Alstyne, former chair of the AAUP's Committee A on Academic Freedom and Tenure, emphasizes that professional academic freedom requires peers to be far more concerned than others in making certain of the ethical use of academic freedom.

> The price of an exceptional vocational freedom to speak the truth as one sees it, without penalty for its possible immediate impact upon the economic well-being of the employing institution, is the cost of exceptional care in the representation of that "truth," a professional standard of care. Indeed, a grave ethical failure in the integrity of a teacher's or a scholar's academic presentations, no matter of how little notice or coincidental concern it may happen to be to the particular institutional employer, is precisely the kind of offense to the contingent privilege of academic freedom that states a clearly adequate cause for a *faculty* recommendation of termination.[103]

Former Johns Hopkins professor Fritz Machlup also stresses that the faculty has a moral obligation to initiate action against professors who falsify evidence or distort the truth in the presentation of readily verifiable facts.[104]

In 1963, Committee A of the AAUP attempted to develop the meaning of paragraph (c) of the 1940 Statement on extramural utterance in terms of "academic responsibility." The Committee stated that academic freedom can endure only if it is matched by academic responsibility, but that academic responsibility is very difficult to define. While the primary source of a decent level of academic responsibility will always be the individual conscience, a faculty and administration have "a legitimate interest in the maintenance of proper standards of faculty responsibility on the part of all members of the academic community." For a judgment as to the line between expression of views and improper acts, "recourse should be had in the first instance to a committee of the faculty. Both traditionally and practically, it is the *duty* and within the particular competence of the faculty to make the distinction and to recommend any appropriate action."[105] "The policy of permitting disciplinary action to be initiated by the administration is not likely to result in impairment of free utterance by faculty members if under established academic traditions and procedures the initial and primary judgment of an accused individual's action rests with his colleagues."[106]

Similarly, the AAUP's 1966 Statement on Professional Ethics provides that the individual institution of higher education assures the integrity of members of the profession. "The individual institution...should normally handle questions concerning propriety of conduct within its own framework by reference to a faculty group."[107]

The 1966 statement also states a duty of ethical conduct to foster and defend the academic freedom of students and colleagues. The 1970 AAUP Council's Statement on Freedom and Responsibility also emphasizes in three places the faculty's duty as a collegial body to defend academic freedom and to uphold it by its own action. The Council urged faculties, during a period of zealotry,

> to assume a more positive role as guardian of academic values against unjustified assaults from its own members. The traditional faculty function in disciplinary

proceedings has been to ensure academic due process and meaningful faculty participation in the imposition of discipline by the administration. While this function should be maintained, faculties should recognize their stake in promoting adherence to norms essential to the academic enterprise.[108]

The 1973 report on faculty tenure by the joint AAC/AAUP Commission on Academic Tenure again emphasizes the theme of faculty responsibility to ensure that standards of competence and ethical conduct are met. "The faculty of the institution...must be the source for the definition and clarification of standards of professional conduct and must take the lead in ensuring that these standards are enforced."[109] The Commission noted that during the late 1960s assaults upon academic freedom from within the institution by or with the toleration of members of faculties themselves have gone unpunished. "In this situation there is a special urgency for faculties to accept their full corporate responsibility for the integrity of the profession. That responsibility cannot be avoided, it should not be assumed by others, and it must be fulfilled."[110]

While the AAUP during the last seventy-five years has developed a fairly clear definition of the rights and responsibilities of professional academic freedom, the courts have had a much more difficult time defining academic freedom in constitutional terms. The next chapter outlines the Supreme Court's efforts to define the extent to which the Constitution protects freedom of academic speech.

Notes

1. J. Peter Byrne, *Academic Freedom: A "Special Concern of the First Amendment,"* 99 YALE L.J. 251, 268-69 (1989).
2. *See* Mark T. Carroll, *Protecting Private Employees' Freedom of Political Speech,* 8 HARV. J. ON LEGIS. 35, 35-37 (1981). There are exceptions to the general principle. For example, the National Labor Relations Act protects the rights of workers to organize unions and to bargain collectively in the terms and conditions of employment. Many states protect employees' voting choices and other facets of employees' political speech from employer coercion. Speech raising issues of discrimination or sexual harassment is protected. Many states have made public policy exceptions to the at-will employment doctrine. *See id.* at 39–42.
3. *See generally* Byrne, *supra* note 1, at 269-70, 272. Professor Fuchs found that the prominent faculty members from the elite universities formed the AAUP because of both concern over the dismissals that had occurred and the belief that a national organization would increase professionalism similar to associations of lawyers and doctors. Ralph Fuchs, *Academic Freedom—Its Basic Philosophy, Function and History, reprinted in* ACADEMIC FREEDOM AND TENURE 253 (Louis Joughin ed., 1969).
4. *See* Byrne, *supra* note 1, at 298-300; Richard Hofstadter & Walter P. Metzger, THE DEVELOPMENT OF ACADEMIC FREEDOM IN THE UNITED STATES 413-60 (1955).
5. *See* Byrne, *supra* note 1, at 255.
6. Jonathan Rauch, KINDLY INQUISITORS 45 (1993).
7. *Id.* at 46.

8. *Id.* at 48–49.
9. Mario V. Llosa, *The Importance of Karl Popper*, ACAD. QUESTIONS, Winter 1991–92, at 16.
10. Rauch, *supra* note 6, at 49.
11. *Id.* at 116–17.
12. *Id.* at 116.
13. *Id.* at 77–78.
14. *Id.* at 79.
15. *Id.* at 12, 19.
16. *Id.* at 125–26.
17. *Id.* at 68–70.
18. Byrne, *supra* note 1, at 271–73.
19. *Id.* at 273–75 (quoting Robert M. MacIver, ACADEMIC FREEDOM IN OUR TIME 4–5 (1955)). "The modern university...is the true child of the Enlightenment. At its core stands the rational scientific pursuit of knowledge.... The value of cognitive rationality, as Talcott Parsons pointed out some time ago, provides the modern university with its autonomy." Brigget Berger, *The Idea of the University*, 58 PARTISAN REV. 315, 328 (1991).
20. John R. Searle, *Two Concepts of Academic Freedom*, in THE CONCEPT OF ACADEMIC FREEDOM 88 (ed. Edmund Pincoffs 1972).
21. Byrne, *supra* note 1, at 258. Eric Ashby defines the attitude of a research worker as the discipline of constructive dissent. Constructive dissent "fulfills one overriding condition: it must shift the state of opinion about the subject in such a way that other experts in the subject are prepared to concur. This is done either by producing acceptable new data or by reinterpreting old data in a convincing way. It is a very austere form of dissent and it is difficult to learn." Eric Ashby, *A Hippocratic Oath for the Academic Profession*, MINERVA, Autumn-Winter 1968–69, at 64.
22. Byrne, *supra* note 1 at 258–59.
23. *Id.* at 259.
24. *Id.* at 258.
25. *See id.* at 275.
26. *See id.* at 275.
27. J. Peter Byrne, *Racial Insults and Free Speech Within the University*, 79 GEORGETOWN L.J. 399, 417 (1991). *See* Byrne, *supra* note 1, at 276.
28. *See* Byrne, *supra* note 1, at 273. At another level, however, the struggle for professional autonomy was motivated by self-interest in employment security and improved salary. Laurence R. Veysey, THE EMERGENCE OF THE AMERICAN UNIVERSITY 386–92 (1965).
29. Fritz Machlup, *On Some Misconceptions Concerning Academic Freedom*, reprinted in ACADEMIC FREEDOM AND TENURE 177, 181–82 (1969).
30. Byrne, *supra* note 1, at 277; *see* David M. Rabban, *A Functional Analysis of "Individual" and "Institutional" Academic Freedom under the First Amendment*, 53 LAW & CONTEMP. PROBS. 227, 232 (1990) [hereinafter Rabban, *A Functional Analysis*].
31. American Association of University Professors (AAUP), *The 1915 General Declaration of Principles* 155, 158 (1915), *reprinted in* ACADEMIC FREEDOM AND TENURE app. A at 157–75 (Lewis Joughin ed., 1969) [hereinafter AAUP, *1915 Declaration*].
32. *See id.* at 160.
33. *Id.* at 163–64.
34. *Id.* at 162.

35. *See id.* at 162–63.
36. *Id.* at 168.
37. *Id.* at 168–69 (emphasis added).
38. *Id.* at 158.
39. *Id.*
40. *Id.* at 172 (emphasis added).
41. *Id.* at 158.
42. *Id.* (emphasis added).
43. *Id.* at 172 (emphasis added).
44. *Id.* at 173 (emphasis added).
45. *See* Walter P. Metzger, *Profession and Constitution: Two Definitions of Academic Freedom in America*, 66 TEX. L. REV. 1265, 1275 (1988).
46. AAUP, *1915 Declaration*, *supra* note 31, at 169.
47. *Id.* at 169–70.
48. *Id.* at 170.
49. Walter Metzger, *Academic Tenure in America—A Historical Essay*, *reprinted in* FACULTY TENURE 143–44 (1973).
50. *See* AAUP, *1915 Declaration*, *supra* note 31, at 170.
51. Byrne, *supra* note 1, at 278; *see* AAUP, *1915 Declaration*, *supra* note 31, at 173.
52. *See* American Association of University Professors (AAUP), *1940 Statement of Principles on Academic Freedom and Tenure*, *reprinted in* AAUP, POLICY DOCUMENTS & REPORTS 3 (1990) [hereinafter AAUP, *1940 Statement*].
53. Walter P. Metzger, *The 1940 Statement of Principles on Academic Freedom and Tenure*, 53 LAW & CONTEMP. PROBS. 3, 4 (1990).
54. AAUP, *1940 Statement*, *supra* note 52, at 3 (emphasis added).
55. *Id.*
56. *Id.* at 4.
57. *Id.* at 5 (emphasis added).
58. Some scholars argue that paragraph (c) does grant rights of academic freedom to intramural speech other than teaching and research. *See* Matthew W. Finkin, *"A Higher Order of Liberty in the Workplace": Academic Freedom and Tenure in the Vortex of Employment Practices and Law*, 53 LAW & CONTEMP. PROBS. 357, 366–67 (1990) (stating that the 1940 statement gives freedom of speech on any matter of intramural concern due an officer of the institution as a member of a learned profession) [hereinafter Finkin, *Higher Order*].
59. *Id.* at 377–78; *see* Matthew Finkin, *Intramural Speech, Academic Freedom, and the First Amendment*, 66 TEX. L. REV. 1323, 1337 (1988).
60. Mark Yudof, *Intramural Musings on Academic Freedom: A Reply to Professor Finkin*, 66 TEX. L. REV. 1351, 1355–56 (1988).
61. Focusing on the sentence in paragraph (c) of the 1940 statement reading, "[C]ollege or university teachers are citizens, members of a learned profession, and officers of an educational institution," a later AAUP statement asserts that the prerogative of a faculty member "to speak on general educational questions or about the administration and operations of his own institution is part of his right as a citizen and should not be abridged by the institution." *Joint Statement on Government of Colleges and Universities* (1966), *reprinted in* AAUP POLICY DOCUMENTS AND REPORTS 119, 122 at n.2 (1990). One author argues that this 1966 interpretation applies to intramural speech as well as to extramural. David Rabban, *Does Professional Education Constrain Academic Freedom?* 43 J. LEGAL EDUC., 358, 362 (1993). However, the weight of the evidence indicates that paragraph (c) of the 1940 statement applies only to extramural utterance.

62. Professor Metzger is uncertain whether the 1940 statement grants academic freedom on the condition that the duties included in the statement are to be obeyed. The negotiations between the AAUP and the AAC over the duties were prolonged, volatile and acrimonious. The parties saw the duties as obligatory. Metzger, *supra* note 53, at 3, 9, 47, 59.

63. AAUP, *1940 Statement, supra* note 52, at 4.

64. *Id.* at 5.

65. *Id.* at 4. "Moral turpitude" is used in the 1940 statement in the context that "[t]eachers on continuous appointment who are dismissed for reasons not involving moral turpitude should receive their salaries for at least a year from the date of notification." *See* AAUP, *1940 Statement, supra* note 52, at 4. It is clear that moral turpitude in this context is limited only to extreme violations of duties of ethical conduct. This is supported by the AAUP's 1970 Interpretive Comments for the 1940 statement, stating that the concept of "moral turpitude" applies to that kind of "behavior which goes beyond simply warranting discharge and is so utterly blameworthy as to make it inappropriate to require the offering of a year's teaching or pay." AAUP, *1940 Statement, supra* note 52, at 7. Thus, by implication, the duties of ethical conduct cover a spectrum from those duties whose violation is utterly blameworthy to those whose violation simply warrants discharge.

66. *Id.* at 5-6 (emphasis added).

67. AAUP, *Statement on Procedural Standards in Faculty Dismissal Proceedings, reprinted in* AAUP, POLICY DOCUMENTS & REPORTS 11, 12 (1990).

68. *See* AAUP, *Statement on Professional Ethics, reprinted in* AAUP, POLICY DOCUMENTS & REPORTS 75, 75-76 (1990) [hereinafter AAUP, *Professional Ethics*].

69. *See* AAUP, *1915 Declaration, supra* note 31, at 169.

70. Richard Hofstadter & Walter Metzger, THE DEVELOPMENT OF ACADEMIC FREEDOM IN THE UNITED STATES 410 (1955).

71. Commission on Academic Tenure in Higher Education, FACULTY TENURE at ix, xi (1973).

72. *Id.* at 34-41.

73. *Id.* at 41, 44.

74. *Id.* at 75.

75. AAUP, *Statement on Plagiarism, reprinted in* AAUP, POLICY DOCUMENTS & REPORTS 79, 79 (1990).

76. Fundamental to the academic profession is a belief in intellectual integrity. "As Clark noted, 'In the academic lexicon, knowledge must be handled honestly, for otherwise it misinforms and deceives, is no longer valuable in itself, and certainly of no use to society.'" William Tierney and Robert Rhoads, ENHANCING PROMOTION, TENURE AND BEYOND 12 (1993, Ashe-Eric Higher Education Report).

77. Rabban, *supra* note 30, at 242. Earlier Duke professor William Van Alstyne had commented that "the price of an exceptional vocational freedom to speak the truth as one sees it, and without penalty for its immediate impact upon the economic well-being of the employing institution, is the cost of exceptional care in the representation of that 'truth,' a professional standard of care." William Van Alstyne, *The Specific Theory of Academic Freedom and the General Issue of Civil Liberty in* THE CONCEPT OF ACADEMIC FREEDOM 76 (Edmund Pincoffs ed., 1972).

78. Derek Bok, *Universities: Their Temptations and Tensions*, 18 J.C. & U.L. 1, 2 (1991). A recent report by a panel of the National Academy of Sciences stresses

that scientists rely on an honor system based on tradition to safeguard the integrity of the research process. Panel on Scientific Responsibility and the Conduct of Research, National Academy of Sciences, RESPONSIBLE SCIENCE: ENSURING THE INTEGRITY OF THE RESEARCH PROCESS ix, 1 (1992). *See* text at note 21 *supra*.

79. *Id.* Clark Kerr, President Emeritus of the University of California, recently outlined the components of "the ethics of knowledge." The following actions are obligatory:

1. the careful collection and use of evidence, including the search for 'inconvenient facts,' as in the process of attempted 'falsification';
2. the careful use of the ideas and work of others;
3. the obligation to be skeptical of what is not fully proven;
4. an openness to alternative explanations;
5. civility in discourse, and reliance on persuasion rather than coercion;
6. open access to the results of research conducted within the university;
7. avoidance of drawing and advancing policy applications unless the full range of considerations entering into the policy making has been the subject of the study (scholars should not go beyond their knowledge);
8. separating personal evaluation, based on moral and political values, from the presentation of evidence and analysis; and as a corollary, making any personal evaluations explicit.

Clark Kerr, *Knowledge Ethics And The New Academic Culture*, CHANGE, Jan./Feb. 1994 at 13.

Berkeley sociology professor Martin Trow emphasizes the critical importance of the duty actively to search out and confront inconvenient facts and contrary opinion. "For example, a major function of quantification in the social sciences is that it embodies impersonal procedures that ensure the collection of negative as well as supporting evidence for whatever 'party opinion' we hold at the moment." Martin Trow, *Higher Education and Moral Development*, AAUP BULL., Spring 1976, at 20, 23.

In *The Academic Ethic*, Professor Edward Shils emphasizes that a university teacher who proceeds without respect for evidence and argument "is committing the ultimate treason against the university. Systematic disciplined investigation is its life-blood." Edward Shils, THE ACADEMIC ETHIC 102 (1983).

A panel of the National Academy of Sciences stresses that fabrication, falsification, or plagiarism are the cardinal sins of scientific misconduct. The integrity of the research process requires adherence "to honest and verifiable methods in proposing, performing, evaluating, and reporting research activities. The research process includes the construction of hypotheses; the development of experimental and theoretical paradigms; the collection, analysis and handling of data; the generation of new ideas, findings, and theories through experimentation and analysis; timely communication and publication; refinement of results through replication and extension of the original work; peer reviews; and the training and supervision of associates and students." RESPONSIBLE SCIENCE, *supra* note 78, at 5, 17–18. The panel stresses also care in reporting data and adverse evidence. *Id.* at 37, 47–48.

See generally on the characteristics of scholarship, Seymour Martin Lipset, REBELLION IN THE UNIVERSITY 203–04, 208 (1976); J. Peter Byrne, *Academic Freedom and Political Neutrality in Law Schools: An Essay on the Structure and Ideology in Professional Education*, 43 J. LEGAL EDUC. 315, 322 (1993). Professor Stephen Carter urges that:

A principal focus of modern scholarship...has been to assault the idea that one can evaluate anything without significant reference to one's own values that are defined by one's status and culture. This is a point well taken but does not answer the question of what one should try to do. The knowledge that perfectly unbiased observation is impossible should instill in all of us a healthy degree of caution on the certainty of our rightness, but scholars should *strive* for dispassion.

Stephen Carter, *Academic Tenure and "White Male" Standards: Some Lessons from the Patent Law*, 100 YALE L.J. 2065, 2071 (1991).

80. Rabban, *A Functional Analysis, supra* note 30, at 242; *see also* Matthew W. Finkin, *Intramural Speech, Academic Freedom and the First Amendment*, 66 TEX. L. REV. 1323, 1332 (1988); David M. Rabban, *Does Academic Freedom Limit Faculty Autonomy?*, 66 TEX. L. REV. 1405, 1409 (1988).

81. *See* William G. Hollingsworth, *Controlling Post-Tenure Scholarship: A Brave New World Beckons?*, 41 J. LEGAL EDUC. 141, 199–201, 205 (1991).

82. *See* AAUP, *Professional Ethics, supra* note 68, at 75–76.

83. *See* AAUP, *A Statement of the Association's Council: Freedom and Responsibility, reprinted in* AAUP, POLICY DOCUMENTS & REPORTS 77, 77–78 (1990) [hereinafter AAUP, *Freedom and Responsibility*].

84. *Id.*

85. Kenneth Minogue, *Can Scholarship Survive the Scholars*, ACADEMIC QUESTIONS, Fall 1991, at 62, 63. Professor McCloskey emphasizes the following conversational norms of scholarly conversation:

> The German philosopher Jurgen Habermas and his tradition call these Sprachetbik.... Don't lie; pay attention; don't sneer; cooperate; don't shout; let other people talk; be open-minded; explain yourself when asked; don't resort to violence or conspiracy in aid of your ideas.

Donald McCloskey, THE RHETORIC OF ECONOMICS 24–27 (1985).

86. The 1915 Statement provided that in extramural utterances, the university teacher was under a "peculiar obligation" to avoid hasty or exaggerated statements. *See* AAUP, *1915 Declaration, supra* note 31, at 172.

87. The 1915 Statement also directed teachers "to refrain from intemperate or sensational modes of expression." *Id.* at 172.

88. AAUP, *1940 Statement, supra* note 52, at 4.

89. *Id.* at 5.

90. AAUP, *Committee A Statement on Extramural Utterances, reprinted in* AAUP, POLICY DOCUMENTS & REPORTS 32 (1990).

91. *See* AAUP, *Advisory Letters from the Washington Office*, 49 AAUP BULL. 393, Winter 1963.

92. *Id.*

93. *See* Finkin, *Higher Order, supra* note 58, at 366–67.

94. *See* earlier discussion of correlative duties for teaching, research, and intramural utterance. By implication, if the correlative duties of academic freedom for extramural speech include the duties: (1) to be accurate at all times; (2) to exercise appropriate restraint; and (3) to show respect for the opinions of others, the correlative duties of professional competence and ethical conduct in teaching, research, and intramural utterance include these.

95. Metzger, *supra* note 53, at 51.

96. Professor William Van Alstyne has argued that the AAUP's extension of the protection of professional academic freedom to extramural utterance was a mistake.

One of his reasons is that attaching a claim for protection of academic freedom to extramural utterance implies a duty of accountability by "academic" standards for such speech. "The result...is that the individual so situated is rendered less free in respect to his nonprofessional pursuits than others." William Van Alstyne, *Reply to Comments*, in THE CONCEPT OF ACADEMIC FREEDOM 127 (Edmund Pincoffs ed., 1972). This argument misses the point. While it is true that all citizens can exercise their First Amendment rights without coercion by government, private employers can fire them for doing so unless the speech relates to whistleblowing, harassment or discrimination claims, or some other subset of speech protected by statute. Professional academic freedom protection for professors' extramural utterances protects faculty members at private universities from adverse employment consequences for speech that an employer does not like. As Van Alstyne has argued elsewhere, such exceptional vocational freedom to speak the truth as one sees it and without penalty for its immediate impact upon the economic well-being of the employing institution, is the cost of exceptional care in the representation of that "truth," a professional standard of care. William Van Alstyne, *The Specific Theory of Academic Freedom and the General Issue of Civil Liberty* in THE CONCEPT OF ACADEMIC FREEDOM 76 (Edmund Pincoffs ed., 1972). The tradeoff of rights and correlative duty for extramural speech seems reasonable.

97. *See* Finkin, *Higher Order, supra* note 58, at 367–68.
98. *See* AAUP, *1940 Statement, supra* note 52, at 3–7.
99. *See* AAUP, *1940 Statement, supra* note 52, at 8. The 1958 Statement on Procedural Standards in Faculty Dismissal Proceedings was approved by both the AAUP and the AAC.
100. *See* AAUP, *1915 Declaration, supra* note 31, at 169–70.
101. *Id.* at 170.
102. AAUP, *1946 Report of Committee A*, 31 AAUP BULL. 60–61 (1946).
103. William Van Alstyne, *The Specific Theory of Academic Freedom and the General Issue of Liberty* in THE CONCEPT OF ACADEMIC FREEDOM 76 (Edmund Pincoffs ed., 1972) (emphasis added).
104. Fritz Machlup, *On Some Misconceptions Concerning Academic Freedom* in ACADEMIC FREEDOM & TENURE 177, 189 (Louis Joughin ed. 1969).
105. AAUP, *"Academic Responsibility": Comments by Members of Committee A Incident to Consideration of the Koch Case*, 49 AAUP BULL. 40, 40 (1963) (emphasis added).
106. *Id.* at 41.
107. *See* AAUP, *Professional Ethics, supra* note 68, at 75.
108. *See* AAUP, *Freedom and Responsibility, supra* note 83, at 78.
109. Commission on Academic Tenure in Higher Education, FACULTY TENURE 42–43 (1973).
110. *Id.* at 43.

5

Protection for the Core Academic Affairs of Higher Education from Interference by the State—Constitutional Academic Freedom

Supreme Court cases mentioning "academic freedom" have been few and vague. As a consequence, lower court opinions dealing with the concept have been confused and contradictory.[1] Thus, the protection for academic freedom arising out of the First and Fourteenth Amendments (hereinafter constitutional academic freedom) remained poorly defined and developed until a 1990 decision of the Supreme Court, *University of Pennsylvania* v. *EEOC*,[2] significantly clarified its meaning.

A brief history of the earlier Supreme Court cases using the term "academic freedom" demonstrates the Court's lack of clarity concerning whether constitutional academic freedom referred to one or more of the following: (1) the corporate right of the university against outside content-based government interference; (2) the right of an individual faculty member against outside content-based government interference; or (3) the right of an individual faculty member at a public university against interference in scholarship, teaching, intramural, and extramural utterance by administrators and regents. The *University of Pennsylvania* decision clarifies that constitutional academic freedom protects only the first two of these rights; protection of the third is left to professional academic freedom, employment law, and the general free speech protection given to all public employees discussed in the next chapter.

The term *academic freedom* first appeared in Justice Douglas's dissenting opinion in *Adler* v. *Board of Education*,[3] a 1952 Supreme Court opinion responding to the government's efforts in the early 1950s to root out allegedly subversive government employees, including teachers. The petitioners in *Adler* challenged the constitutionality of the Feinberg Law that made ineligible for employment in the public schools members of any organization committed to the overthrow of the United States government by illegal means. Justice Douglas's dissenting opinion argued that the Feinberg Law violated the individual teacher's First Amendment right of freedom of expression and free inquiry. Justice Douglas noted that the Feinberg Law's "system of spying and surveillance...cannot go hand in hand with academic freedom."[4] Although this is the first appearance of the term *academic freedom* in a Supreme Court decision, Justice Douglas did not argue that academic freedom had separate First Amendment protection.

It was not until 1957 in *Sweezy* v. *New Hampshire*[5] that the Supreme Court ruled that the Constitution gave special protection to academic freedom. In *Sweezy*, a Marxist professor was summoned by the Attorney General of New Hampshire to testify about the content of his lectures.[6] At the time of *Sweezy* in 1957, New Hampshire law barred all subversive persons from employment by the state government. Thus, all state employees and candidates for elected offices were required to make sworn statements that they were not subversive persons.[7] The plurality, led by Chief Justice Warren, noted that the state's inquiry inflicted harm both on "the petitioner's liberties in the area of academic freedom," and on "freedom in the community of American universities."[8]

Justice Frankfurter, joined by Justice Harlan in a concurring opinion, argued that the interrogatories by the Attorney General concerning the content of a course not only interfered with the individual's exercise of constitutional rights, but also constituted an impermissible "government intrusion into the intellectual life of a university."[9] To give content to the university's right to be free from government intrusion, Justice Frankfurter quoted from a statement of South African scholars who defined "four essential freedoms of a university." These included the freedom "to determine for itself on academic grounds who may teach, what may be taught, how it shall be taught, and who may be admitted to study."[10]

The plurality and concurring opinions in *Sweezy* constituted the first decision where the Court suggested that academic freedom had special protection under the First Amendment. The Frankfurter concurring opinion is focused on the right of the university itself, rather than the right of individual faculty members, to be free from government interference, despite the fact that the Attorney General of New Hampshire on the actual facts of the case was enforcing speech restrictions on both an individual professor and the university as a whole.

The underlying policy rationale for constitutionalizing academic freedom is not well developed in *Sweezy* or in later cases. Professor Rabban points out that one paragraph of Chief Justice Warren's plurality opinion in the case contains the court's fullest discussion of the reasons for special First Amendment protection of academic freedom.[11]

> The essentiality of freedom in the community of American universities is almost self-evident. No one should underestimate the vital role in a democracy that is played by those who guide and train our youth. To impose any strait jacket upon the intellectual leaders in our colleges and universities would imperil the future of our Nation. No field of education is so thoroughly comprehended by man that new discoveries cannot yet be made. Particularly is that true in the social sciences, where few, if any, principles are accepted as absolutes. Scholarship cannot flourish in an

atmosphere of suspicion and distrust. Teachers and students must always remain free to inquire, to study and to evaluate, to gain new maturity and understanding; otherwise our civilization will stagnate and die.[12]

Frankfurter's concurring opinion in *Sweezy* also emphasized "the dependence of a free society on free universities," through their contribution to knowledge.[13]

Chief Justice Warren's rationale supporting academic freedom has several premises:

1. universities and professors play a vital role in a democratic society;
2. they train and guide students, the society's youth, to inquire, to study and to evaluate, to gain new maturity and understanding;
3. they make new discoveries to advance knowledge; and
4. these tasks require a high degree of freedom.

These rationales track closely the reasons for professional academic freedom articulated in the AAUP's 1915 and 1940 statements. The common good in a democracy depends upon the search for knowledge and its free exposition. The university is the principal cultural institution in a democracy dedicated to the search for knowledge. The basic function of professors is critical inquiry to advance knowledge, and the dissemination of the results of their inquiry through teaching and research. Professors require freedom from any constraints that inhibit the independence necessary to perform their function.[14]

Ten years after *Sweezy*, the Supreme Court in *Keyishian* v. *Board of Regents*[15] returned to the Feinberg Law loyalty oath upheld in *Adler* and found it unconstitutional. In *Keyishian*, several professors refused to comply with state laws that required public employees, including teachers at state universities, to sign a certificate stating both that they were not now communists, and that, in the event they had previously been communists, they had informed the president of the State University of New York of their membership.[16] The professors were warned that their refusal to sign the certificate would result in dismissal. Subsequently, the plaintiff, Keyishian, was notified that his one-year contract would not be renewed.[17]

In support of the professors' right to refuse to sign the loyalty oaths, the Supreme Court held that certain provisions of New York's Civil Service Law and Education Law were invalid to the extent that they required disclosing membership of the Communist party.[18] Justice Brennan found that, among other constitutional infractions, the Feinberg Law imperiled "academic freedom." In explaining the reasons for constitutional protection of academic freedom, he quoted Chief Justice Warren's paragraph from *Sweezy*, adding that

our nation is deeply committed to safeguarding *academic freedom*, which is of transcendent value to all of us and not merely to the teachers concerned. That freedom is therefore a special concern of the First Amendment, which does not tolerate *laws* that cast a pall of orthodoxy over the classroom.[19]

Brennan believed that the future "depends upon leaders trained through wide exposure to that robust exchange of ideas which discovers truth out of a multitude of tongues, [rather] than through any kind of authoritative selection."[20]

In the context of *Keyishian*, "academic freedom" was protection of the university and individual professors from "laws that cast a pall of orthodoxy over the classroom." The orthodoxy feared is not that of academics themselves, but of nonacademic government officials seeking to impose their views on the university and the persons within it.[21]

One decade later, the Supreme Court in 1978 handed down another decision defining a university's academic freedom rights. In *University of California Regents* v. *Bakke*,[22] the Court declared a university's special admissions program for minority applicants unconstitutional and ordered the university to admit Bakke, a white male student.[23] Bakke had been twice denied acceptance to the university's medical school. Minority students, however, with satisfactory credentials less than Bakke's were allowed admittance. In support of its special admissions program, the university argued that it was striving for a diverse student body.[24]

Justice Powell's plurality opinion agreed with the university that diversity, "clearly is a constitutionally permissible goal for an institution of higher education."[25] The opinion further recognized, as the Court did in *Sweezy*, that "academic freedom" is a "special concern of the First Amendment." Powell defined academic freedom as "the freedom of the university to make its own judgments as to education."[26] Powell, however, believed that ethnic diversity "is only one element in a range of factors a university properly may consider in attaining the goal of a heterogenous student body."[27] Thus, Powell rejected the university's argument and called it "flawed" in that the university believed that ethnic diversity was the *only* effective means of fostering diversity.[28] The Court still allowed the university to take race into consideration in its future decisions.

In *Widmar* v. *Vincent*,[29] Justice Powell again quoted with approval Frankfurter's "four freedoms" as a right of the university.[30] Justice Steven's concurrence stated that the majority's "public forum" analysis of the university facilities at issue in *Widmar* "may needlessly undermine the academic freedom of public universities."[31]

A 1985 decision concerning evaluation of student performance supports a university's right of academic freedom. In *Regents of the University of Michigan* v. *Ewing*,[32] the university defended itself from a charge that it had arbitrarily dismissed a student from its medical school in violation of the student's substantive due process rights. Writing for a unanimous court, Justice Stevens held that judges "should show great respect for the faculty's professional judgment" and "may not override it unless it is such a substantial departure from accepted academic norms as to demonstrate that the person or committee responsible did not actually exercise professional judgment."[33] By preserving its "reluctance to trench on the prerogatives of state and local educational institutions," the Court was fulfilling its "responsibility to safeguard their academic freedom, a special concern of the First Amendment."[34] By pointing to the academic freedom of educational institutions, Justice Stevens implies that universities have academic freedom rights, separate from the academic freedom of individual faculty members. Stevens further reinforced this view in a footnote, "Academic freedom thrives not only on the independent and uninhibited exchange of ideas among teachers and students...but also, and somewhat inconsistently, on autonomous decision-making by the academy itself."[35]

In 1990, the Supreme Court clarified the meaning of the First Amendment right of academic freedom. In *University of Pennsylvania v. EEOC*,[36] the university denied tenure to an associate professor, subsequent to which she filed a charge with the EEOC alleging that the denial of tenure was based on sexual discrimination. As part of its investigation of the charge, the EEOC requested information from the university, but the university refused to disclose certain materials, including a number of the professor's tenure file documents. In the subsequent suit brought by the EEOC to force the release of these materials, one of the university's arguments was that disclosure of confidential peer review evaluations would undermine the candid evaluations and discussion necessary to enable a university to make sound tenure decisions. The argument continued that requiring the disclosure of peer review evaluations on a finding of mere relevance thus constituted interference with the university's First Amendment right of academic freedom to "determine for itself on academic grounds who may teach."[37]

Justice Blackmun, writing for a unanimous court, rejected the university's argument for two reasons: (1) the "so-called academic freedom cases" involve government attempts "to control or direct the *content* of the speech engaged in by the university or those affiliated with it,"[38] but the university here does not allege any government attempt to influence the "content of university discourse toward or away from particular subjects or points of view"; and (2) the academic freedom cases involve *direct* government infringement on the asserted right of the university "to determine for itself on academic grounds who may teach."[39] In contrast, here the EEOC subpoena does not provide criteria that the university "*must* use in selecting teachers. Nor is it preventing the university from using any criteria it may wish to use, except those—including race, sex, and national origin—that are proscribed under Title VII."[40]

While the Court in *University of Pennsylvania* does not define "the precise contours of any academic-freedom right against governmental attempts to influence the content of academic speech through the selection of faculty or by other means,"[41] the decision does substantially clarify the focus of First Amendment protection for "academic freedom." Academic freedom under the First Amendment protects against *government* attempts to control or direct the university or those affiliated with it regarding either: (1) the content of their speech or discourse; or (2) the determination of who may teach.[42]

It is critical to understand also what the Court in *University of Pennsylvania* did not do. The Court defines constitutional academic freedom to grant both universities and faculty members freedom from direct governmental restrictions on either the content of speech or on the right of the university to determine who may teach. The *University of Pennsylvania* decision *does not* create an "institutional" academic freedom under which a university can claim "academic freedom" under the First Amendment as a bar to judicial review when the university itself is charged with restraining professors' academic speech rights created by contract, statute, or constitution. The decision recognizes only that judicial review of a university's decision should proceed under a prudential norm of academic abstention discussed in the next chapter.

Constitutionalizing academic freedom to preserve the autonomy of the university and those affiliated with it from government attempts to control or direct either the content of academic speech or discourse or the determination of who may teach preserves the intellectual independence of the modern university. Courts are to prevent direct political or democratic demands by government from undermining the premises upon which the university's vital contribution to democratic society rest.

This is an appropriate allocation of responsibility. When the university itself may be too weak to resist pressures from the state, the federal courts have the power to prevent the intrusion of the state on either the content of speech or faculty employment decisions. Federal courts are given no authority to interfere in the internal decisions of a university regarding faculty speech as a matter of academic freedom under the Constitution. It would be extremely inappropriate for courts to include "academic freedom" in its professional sense within the protection of the Constitution. This would require a federal court as a matter of constitutional law to determine whether a faculty member's speech met the competency and ethical constraints of professional inquiry and discourse. Judges as lay persons are among the class of persons whom professional academic freedom has historically sought to exclude from interference in academic affairs.[43] As lay persons, judges would tend to "protect points of view with which they were sympathetic or, more likely, protect all arguably respectable points of view, the judicial attitude most consistent with general First Amendment values."[44] The permissive standards of First Amendment jurisprudence appropriate to society at large severely undermine the correlative duties of professional academic freedom for academic inquiry and discourse, where new speech is met critically, worthy ideas are distinguished from dull, some speech is valued more highly, and those who fail to satisfy professional standards are excluded.[45]

Much of the confusion over the meaning of "academic freedom" has arisen because of a failure to distinguish constitutional academic freedom from professional academic freedom. The two doctrines address similar goals about the importance of free inquiry and speech in the university, but each has different legal roots, and each presents different opportunities and constraints to address the goals. Constitutional academic freedom is rooted in the First and Fourteenth Amendments and prohibits government attempts to control or direct the university or those affiliated with it regarding either: (1) the content of their speech or discourse; or (2) the determination of who may teach. Professional academic freedom is an employment law concept developed by the AAUP rooted in concern over lay interference by boards of trustees and administrators in professors' research, teaching, intramural, and extramural speech. It grants rights to professors to be free from lay interference by employers in research, teaching, and intramural and extramural utterance. It also imposes correlative duties of professional competence and ethical conduct on individual professors and of enforcement of these individual duties by the faculty as a collegial body.

The court has admonished state actors in the legislature and executive branches of government not to interfere directly with either the content of speech or the determination of who may teach at the university. However, when the court has been asked to take sides in disputes between the university and professors, "it found that it too, after all, was an arm of the prime state, and that it ought to apply its counsel of circumspection to itself." The court's reluctance to get deeply involved in academic decisions has become increasingly palpable as time has passed and is expressed as a prudential norm in the rhetoric of abstention.[46] We return to analyze the prudential doctrine of academic abstention in chapter 7.

Another source of confusion over the meaning of "academic freedom" arises because of a failure to distinguish professional academic freedom and constitutional academic freedom from the First Amendment cases providing Constitutional protection for freedom of speech in the public workplace. A subset of these public employee speech cases involves faculty speech in the public university context. Chapter 6 explores the additional free speech protection granted to professors at public universities.

Notes

1. *See* J. Peter Byrne, *Academic Freedom: A 'Special Concern of the First Amendment*, 99 YALE L. J. 251, 288 (1989).
2. *University of Pa. v. E.E.O.C.*, 493 U.S. 182 (1990).
3. *Adler v. Board of Education*, 342 U.S. 485, 509–10, (1952).
4. *Id.* at 510–11.
5. *Sweezy v. New Hampshire*, 354 U.S. 234 (1957).
6. *Id.* at 238.
7. *Id.* at 236.
8. *Id.* at 250.
9. *Id.* at 261.
10. *Id.* at 263.
11. *See* David M. Rabban, *A Functional Analysis of 'Individual' and 'Institutional' Academic Freedom under the First Amendment*, 53 LAW & CONTEMP. PROBS., 227, 239 (1991).

12. *Sweezy*, 354 U.S. at 250.
13. *Id.* at 262.
14. *See* American Association of University Professors (AAUP), *1915 Statement of Principles on Academic Freedom and Tenure, reprinted in* AAUP, POLICY DOCUMENTS & REPORTS 3 (Preamble) (1990), and the discussion of professional academic freedom in chap. 4; *see also* Rabban, *A Functional Analysis, supra* note 11, at 241.
15. *Keyishian v. Board of Regents of Univ. of State of N.Y.*, 385 U.S. 589 (1967).
16. *Id.* at 592.
17. *Id.*
18. *Id.* at 609–10.
19. *Id.* at 603 (emphasis added).
20. *Id.*
21. Byrne, *supra* note 1, at 298.
22. *Regents of Univ. of Cal. v. Bakke*, 438 U.S. 265 (1978).
23. *Id.* at 271.
24. *Id.* at 311.
25. *Id.* at 311–12.
26. *Id.* at 312.
27. *Id.* at 314.
28. *Id.* at 315.
29. *Widmar v. Vincent*, 454 U.S. 263 (1981).
30. *See id.* at 278–79.
31. *Id.* at 277–78.
32. 474 U.S. 214 (1990).
33. *Id.* at 225.
34. *Id.* at 226.
35. *Id.* at 226, n.12.
36. 493 U.S. 182 (1990).
37. *Id.* at 196.
38. *Id.* at 197 (emphasis added).
39. *Id.* at 198.
40. *Id.* (emphasis in original).
41. *Id.* at 198.
42. Professor David Rabban believes that the Court's endorsement of academic freedom to protect against government attempts to control or direct either the university or professors as to the content of speech or who may teach does not support the additional conclusion that the Court has rejected a constitutional right of individual professors to academic freedom against trustees and administrators. Rabban, *A Functional Analysis, supra* note 11, at 280–83.
43. Byrne, *supra* note 1, at 307.
44. *Id.* at 306.
45. *Id.*
46. Walter P. Metzger, *Profession and Constitution: Two Definitions of Academic Freedom in America*, 66 TEX. L. REV. 1265, 1315 (1988).

6

Protection for Freedom of Speech of Professors as Employees in the Public and Private Workplace

Since the founding of the country, courts in the United States have drawn distinctions between speech as an employee and speech as a citizen. Historically courts have granted speech as an employee almost no protection from employer coercion, but have granted speech as a citizen expansive protection from government coercion. In a typical finding, Justice Holmes, while still on the Massachusetts bench, noted in 1892 that

> there are few employments for hire in which the servant does not agree to suspend his constitutional rights of free speech as well as of idleness by the implied terms of his contract. The servant cannot complain, as he takes the employment on the terms which are offered him.[1]

Thus, while the courts had firmly established constitutional protection for freedom of speech of persons as citizens from the coercive power of government,[2] no constitutional protection was afforded for the speech of persons as employees in the workplace.

This hierarchial distinction where the constitutional right of free speech extended only to speech as a citizen, and not to speech as an employee, created critical problems of employer suppression of academic inquiry and speech during the early decades of the formation of the modern university in the United States. University employers could freely discipline heretical or dissenting speech. Given the absence of employment law or constitutional law, protection for employee speech that an employer might penalize, the professoriat, principally through the efforts of the American Association of University Professors (AAUP), developed the concept of professional academic freedom in the early part of this century. The development of professional academic freedom is described in chapter 4. Fifty years later, the courts finally moved in 1968 to provide some constitutional protection for freedom of speech, but only in the public workplace. This constitutional protection for professors in public universities is the subject of this chapter.

Post-1968 Exception: Some Constitutional Protection
for Freedom of Speech in the Public Workplace

The Pickering *and* Connick *Test For Defining*
What Employee Speech is Protected

For most of this century standard doctrine was that a public employee had no right to object to the conditions placed on employment, including those restricting speech. The Supreme Court did not articulate a clear test for protecting freedom of speech of persons as employees of public employers until 1968 in *Pickering* v. *Board of Education.*[3] In *Pickering,* Marvin Pickering, an Illinois public school teacher, sent a letter to a local newspaper in connection with a recently proposed tax increase criticizing both how the Board of Education and the district superintendent had allocated funds between athletics and education and how they had informed taxpayers.[4] The Board found the letter to be "detrimental to the efficient operation and administration of the schools of the district" and dismissed the teacher.[5] The Court held that teachers' exercise of their right to speak on issues of public importance may not be the basis for dismissal from public employment.[6] In upholding the teacher's First Amendment rights, the Court stated a new standard for determining when a public employee's freedom of speech receives First Amendment protection. The test developed by the Court allowed courts to "arrive at a balance between the interests of the teacher, as a citizen, in commenting upon matters of public concern and the interest of the State, as an employer, in promoting the efficiency of the public services it performs through its employees."[7]

Justice Marshall alluded to several factors as a basis to analyze the interests of both a public employer and its employees,[8] among them the interest of a public employer in allowing immediate supervisors to maintain discipline and the need for harmony among co-workers. Additionally, the employee's speech had to be of broad public concern. A false statement knowingly or recklessly made by the employee would not be protected.[9] In this particular factual context, Marshall noted favorably that since the teacher's statements were not directed toward any person with whom the teacher worked daily, the two considerations of maintaining harmony or discipline were not at issue.[10] Moreover, the teacher did not disclose any confidential information.

While the Supreme Court in *Pickering* required a balancing test for First Amendment protection for public employees, the test was only valid to the extent that the employee was speaking as a citizen. In *Connick* v. *Myers,*[11] a 1983 decision, the Court resolved the issue of whether the Constitution protects public employees when they speak, not as citizens, but as employees. Sheila Myers was an assistant district attorney in New Orleans who objected to a transfer directed by the District Attorney. To support her argument that the transfer was not sound administrative policy and was destructive of morale, Ms. Myers submitted a questionnaire to her co-workers asking questions about the fairness of office procedures, employee morale, the quality of leadership, and coercive pressures from management. She was dismissed summarily.[12]

In determining whether a public employee's comments about the conditions of the workplace received First Amendment protection, the Court stated a two-part analysis: the public employee's speech first must be shown to be of public concern; if so, then the employer's interest in "promoting the efficiency of the public service it performs" and the employee's interest in speaking out on public matters must be balanced.[13] If the public employee's statement is not of public concern, the employee's speech fails to receive First Amendment protection.

The first part of the *Connick* test that the matter is of public concern required the employee to show that the public is interested in the topic. The employee must demonstrate that the expression can "fairly be considered as relating to any matter of political, social or other concern to the community."[14] The Court assumed that the public is not generally interested in the individual personnel disputes that occur in the public workplace. Moreover, the Court made the "common sense realization that government offices could not function if every employment decision became a constitutional matter."[15]

Whether a public employee's speech addresses a matter of public concern or of personal interest, "must be determined by the content, form, and context of a given statement."[16] Considering the facts in *Connick,* the Court found that the questions posed by Myers to her co-workers were "mere extensions of Myers' dispute over her transfer to another section of the criminal court." In addition, "Myers did not seek to inform the public that the District Attorney's Office was not discharging its governmental responsibilities in the investigation and prosecution of criminal cases. Nor did Myers seek to bring to light actual or potential wrongdoing or breach of public trust."[17]

Although Ms. Meyers questioned the administration and morale of a public office, she developed the information in pursuit of a personal grievance, rather than in pursuit of *public disclosure* about the conduct of the district attorney's office. The Court noted:

> [T]he focus of Myers' questions is not to evaluate the performance of the office but rather to gather ammunition for yet another round of controversy with her superiors. These questions reflect one employee's dissatisfaction with a transfer and an attempt to turn that displeasure into a cause célèbre.[18]

"To presume that all matters which transpire within a government office are of public concern would mean that virtually every remark...would plant the seed of a constitutional case."[19] The prevention of constant constitutional litigation from hamstringing a government office's fulfillment of the responsibilities to the public was of particular importance. According to the Court, "the

First Amendment does not require a public office to be run as a roundtable for employee complaints over internal office affairs."[20]

The issue of coercive pressure from management to work in political campaigns on behalf of office-supported candidates was found to cross the "public concern" threshold. The Court noted that it had recently held such pressure to be "a coercion of belief in violation of fundamental constitutional rights.... In addition, there is a demonstrated interest in this country that government service should depend upon meritorious performance rather than political service."[21]

Essentially, the *Connick* analysis found that some of the employee's speech was not of public concern and some was of public concern. The "content, form, and context" of the employee's speech indicating part of the speech was not of public concern were: (1) the speech was a mere extension of the employee's personal dispute over an unwanted transfer; and (2) the employee did not seek to inform the public. The "content, form, and context" of the employee's speech indicating part of the speech was of public concern were that the speech was on a topic recently treated in both cases and public debate.

If the matter is of public concern, the second part of the *Connick* test required the employee to show that the employee's interests outweigh the government's interests. The public employee has an interest in participation in self-expression and participation in the public debate as a citizen. The critical variable in *Connick's* balancing step was "the government's interest in the effective and efficient fulfillment of its responsibilities to the public."[22]

The Court looked to a number of factors to determine whether a public employee's speech inhibited "the effective and efficient fulfillment" of the public employer's responsibilities.

1. "When close working relationships are essential to fulfilling public responsibilities, a wide degree of deference to the employer's judgment is appropriate."[23] The court found both that close working relationships between assistants and supervisors were important to the efficient and successful operation of the District Attorney's Office and that the questionnaire carried a clear potential of undermining office relationships.[24]

2. Manner, time, and place of the speech were relevant.[25] Here the fact that the questionnaire was distributed at the office, taking time away from employees' work, supported the fear of the employer that the functioning of the office was endangered.

3. Finally, the context in which the dispute arose was also significant.[26] "When employee speech concerning office policy arises from an employment dispute concerning the very application of that policy to the speaker, additional weight must be given to the supervisor's view that the employee has threatened the authority of the employer to run the office."[27] Myers's speech did arise from her own employment dispute over a transfer.

Connick's balancing step also requires a court to determine whether the threat to the government's interest in effective and efficient operations is actual or potential. The *Connick* court required a public employer to show a reasonable belief that the employee's action would disrupt or undermine effective operations.[28] This includes potential threats.[29] However, if the employee's speech "more substantially involved matters of public concern," then "a stronger showing [of potential disruption] may be necessary."[30] Thus, if the government employer seeks to penalize employee speech because of its potential threat to operations, the more substantial the degree of public concern of the employee's speech, the stronger the evidence must be of its potential threat to efficient operation.

Essentially, the Court's holding in *Pickering* replaced the long-held belief that public employees had no right to object to conditions in the workplace. Yet, as represented by *Connick,* if public employees are to comment about conditions in the public workplace, their expressions are protected by the First Amendment only to the extent first, that the comments are of public concern, and second, that the employer's interest in harmonious working relationships essential to fulfilling public responsibilities are outweighed by the employee's interest in speaking out on public matters. The Court's analysis in *Connick* remains the standard lower courts employ today for freedom of speech by persons as employees in the public workplace.[31]

The Connick *Test for Protected Speech in the Context of the* Mt. Healthy
Three-Step Analysis of Public Employee Retaliation Claims

The *Connick* test for protected speech fits into a broader analytical framework the courts consistently apply to public employee claims of employer retaliation for constitutionally protected activity. In *Mt. Healthy Bd. of Education* v. *Doyle,* the school board did not renew a teacher's contract after he disclosed to a radio station the contents of an internal memorandum mandating teachers' dress and appearance.[32] The Court established the analytical structure for public employee cases alleging constitutional violations and remanded the case. Initially, the employee has the burden of establishing that the conduct merits constitutional protection. In speech cases, the employee must therefore meet the two-part analysis of *Connick:* that the employees' speech is of public concern and that the employee's interest outweighs the public employer's interest in the effective and efficient fulfillment of its responsibilities to the public. Second, the employee must then carry the burden to show that this conduct was a "substantial" or "motivating" factor behind the dismissal. Third, if the employee sustains this burden, then the public employer has the burden of showing by the preponderance of the evidence that the same decision would have been made in the absence of the protected conduct.[33] The two-part *Connick* analysis is a question of law for the trial court to resolve. The second and third steps under *Mt. Healthy* are questions of fact ordinarily left to the jury.[34] This is the analytical framework used by lower courts in dealing with public employee allegations that adverse institutional action was prompted by exercise of constitutionally protected rights.[35]

Application of the *Connick* Test

The Connick *Test in the Lower Courts*

In applying the *Connick* test to the speech of public employees, lower courts have generally concluded that the employee speech was personal and not a matter of public concern.[36] Even where lower courts found that speech embraced a matter of public concern and proceeded to balance employer and employee interests, the holdings have often deferred to the public employer's fear of disruption of the workplace and found the employee speech unprotected.[37]

The first step of the *Connick* analysis, whether an issue is a matter of public concern, is to be determined as a question of law by the trial court based on "the content, form, and context of a given statement, as revealed by the whole record."[38] Speech critical of an employer's policy flowing from a particular dispute experienced by the speaker is a context that points toward a matter of personal, not public, concern.[39] The courts tend to regard such speech as an effort by the speaker to "gather ammunition for another round of controversy with her supervisors."[40]

Public employees who, before termination, resort to the media or who speak at meetings open to the public, are far more likely to prevail on a claim that the speech is of public concern than those who air their grievances only at work. As Professor Massaro points out, the courts "apparently regard these publication attempts as evidence of a desire to inform the public of the alleged misconduct in order to foster public debate. Moreover, statements to the media typically are not made on work premises. Thus, the courts may perceive the statements as posing a lesser threat to smooth office operation."[41] These decisions, ironically, seem to encourage employees to air their grievances in the media, thus exacerbating disruption of work, rather than encouraging the informal expression of work related problems among co-workers or to supervisors, where timely informal remedies may be pursued.[42]

When a lower court finds that an employee's speech embraces a matter of public concern, the court, again as a question of law, is to apply a balancing test where the employee must show that the employee's interest outweighs the government employer's interest. It is clear that once the balancing stage of the *Connick* test has been reached, the major focus has been on the interest of the government "in the effective and efficient fulfillment of its responsibilities to the public."[43] The greater the degree of disruption of the public workplace indicated by the facts, the greater the latitude of the public employer in disciplining employee speech.[44] A recent article lists five factors that the courts have recognized might affect the efficient fulfillment of the public employer's responsibilities to the public:

1. the extent to which the speech indicates the speaker's lack of fitness to perform his or her duties;
2. the extent to which the speech affects others in a way that limits the speaker's ability to perform his or her duties;
3. the effect of the speech on essential working relationships in the office;
4. the extent to which the speech disrupts routine, affects morale, and undermines discipline; and
5. the extent to which public confidence is affected.[45]

The Context of Higher Education

These general First Amendment principles applicable to citizens in public employment carry over to the decisions involving public higher education. The judicial tendency is to apply one set of rules to speech cases. Thus, for example, courts regularly fail to distinguish rules governing public employee speech generally from rules governing employee speech in public education. Moreover, even scholarly analysis of the public education cases has not generally distinguished between the cases originating in primary or secondary schools or in institutions of higher education.[46]

This approach ignores the *Connick* "context" requirement, both in the determination whether an issue is of public concern *and* in the balance between employer and employee interests. Public education at all levels is an area of great public debate; a broad range of topics would therefore be matters of public concern. For example, academic standards at all levels of public education would be a proper area of public concern. Thus, employee speech concerning educational policies on admission standards, curriculum, or grading would be in a context for employee speech that would generally satisfy the first step of the *Connick* analysis. This would still leave an unprotected area of private grievances by employees like protests over parking or office assignment for example.[47]

Similarly, a court in analyzing both stages of the *Connick* test should differentiate the "context" of primary and secondary education from that of higher education. The "context" of higher education is different from that of primary and secondary education because the mission is different. The mission of education at all levels is disseminating knowledge, but the mission of higher education includes also discovering and improving knowledge. As chapter 4 explored in detail, the central requirement for the improvement of knowledge within a university setting is free discourse among academic professionals within the ethical and competency constraints of a discipline. A professor's speech on a matter of public concern that meets professional standards of competence and ethical conduct should be protected regardless of its disruptive impact.[48]

Consider the first step in the *Connick* analysis, whether a professor's speech is of public concern. At one end of the spectrum are complaints about individual salary and perks; at the other end of the spectrum are a professor's writings and public statements on issues currently under public debate. The lower courts find these cases straightforward.

The lower courts generally hold consistently and correctly that individual salary and benefits, parking and office space, and assignment disputes in higher education do not involve matters of public concern. For example, the Fifth Circuit in *Dodds* v. *Childers* focused on the "primary intention" behind a professor's complaint about nepotism in the creation of a special training program for a relative of a trustee. For a matter to be of public concern, the speaker must have spoken predominantly as a citizen. A complaint that could have risen above the purely personal level but that was expressed only as an issue of employer favoritism was a personal grievance rather than an issue of public concern. The professor was concerned about her own job and working conditions, and did not suggest an improper allocation of funds or a general curricular problem. She also did not address her complaints to anyone outside the college.[49]

At the other end of the spectrum is disciplinary action based simply on the content of a professor's writings and public statements on an issue currently being publicly debated. A 1991 federal district court decision correctly emphasized the importance of protecting the freedom of inquiry of professors from the threat of investigation based simply on the content of writings and speeches on topics currently being publicly debated. In *Levin* v. *Harleston,* a tenured professor published research and made public statements about his views on the relationship between race and test scores and his objections to affirmative action.[50] The administration of the City University of New York: (1) created "shadow" sections into which Professor Levin's students, having been warned by the university that his views are "controversial," may voluntarily switch; (2) created an ad hoc committee of faculty to investigate Professor Levin's writings as conduct unbecoming a faculty member; and (3) tacitly approved the disruption of Professor Levin's classes by failing to identify and discipline persons who on numerous occasions disrupted and caused to be terminated philosophy classes being conducted by Professor Levin.

Applying *Mount Healthy City School District Bd. of Education* v. *Doyle* and *Pickering,* the court found in step one that the writings and statements of Professor Levin were "quintessentially issues of public importance," and were protected expression. There was no dispute as to the second step that Professor Levin's expression of controversial views was not merely a substantial or motivating factor, it was the only factor leading to employer actions. The burden then shifted to defendants to show that the complained of actions would have been undertaken in the absence of the protected conduct. The defendants did not make any such showing; they produced no evidence to indicate that students would suffer harm from Professor Levin's views expressed entirely

outside the classroom. The court enjoined the university from: (1) commenc-
ing or threatening to commence disciplinary proceedings based on Professor
Levin's expression of ideas; or (2) creating shadow sections. The trial court
also ordered the university to take reasonable steps to prevent disruption of
Professor Levin's classes.[51]

In 1993, the same federal district court judge reviewed another disciplinary action of the City University of New York based simply on the content of
a professor's public statements concerning a major current issue. In *Jeffries* v.
Harleston, Leonard Jeffries, the chairman of the Black Studies Department at
CCNY, gave a public off-campus speech in July, 1991, on the reform of the
educational system to reflect diverse, and particularly minority perspectives.
He spoke as an appointed consultant of the State Education Commissioner. In
the speech, Jeffries made strident attacks against individuals, and made de-
rogatory remarks about specific ethnic groups, including anti-Semitic remarks.[52] The remarks were racist and bigoted. The speech aroused an outcry
of protest. President Harleston condemned it as a clear statement of bigotry
and anti-Semitism. Three months later, the administration and governing board
limited Professor Jeffries' appointment as chair of the Black Studies Department to one year rather than the customary three-year term.[53] Jeffries brought
an action alleging denial of his rights under the first and fourteenth amendments. The jury found for Jeffries and awarded $400,000 punitive damages.

Applying *Mount Healthy City School District Bd. of Education* v. *Doyle* and
Connick, the court found that Jeffries' public off-campus speech was of substantial public concern.[54] The trial court found that there was sufficient evidence
for the jury to have reasonably inferred that Jeffries' July, 1991 speech was a
substantial and motivating factor in the decision of the governing board to deny
him a full three-year term as chair of the department. The burden then shifted to
the defendants to show either that the complained of action would have been
undertaken in the absence of the protected conduct or that the employee's conduct interfered with the university's "effective and efficient fulfillment of its
responsibilities to the public [citing *Connick*]."[55] The trial court found that the
university made no attempt to develop a systematic record that Jeffries' speech
had a disruptive impact on fundraising, on the functioning of classes, on stu-
dent-teacher relationships, on faculty relationships, or on the department's reputation.[56] The court upheld punitive damages of $370,000 and ordered Jeffries to
be reinstated as chair of the Black Studies Department.[57]

The cases considering professors' speech in the middle of the spectrum are
not clearly consistent. For example, in *Honore* v. *Douglas*, the Fifth Circuit
determined that a law professor's speech stating a lack of confidence in the
dean, and protesting against the school's admission policy, size of student
body, budget administration, and failure to timely certify students for the bar
examination created material issues of fact whether these were matters of a
public concern, and thus precluded summary judgment.[58] In contrast, in *Press-*

man v. *University of North Carolina,* a professor's complaint concerning the failure to recruit quality students and faculty, the failure to develop graduate programs, the general direction of the College, and policies on workload and grading was held to be a personal grievance.[59] A professor's statement opposing an affirmative action faculty appointment and threat to contact the candidate were held not to be of public concern in *Harris* v. *Arizona Board of Regents.*[60] In *Clark* v. *Holmes,* the Seventh Circuit held that a professor's public disputes with administrators, including discussions with students, over the professor's course content and excessive counseling of students were not matters of public concern.[61]

These "gray" cases in the middle of the spectrum would benefit from close analysis of the unique "context" of higher education to determine whether a matter is of public concern. The principal reason to narrowly define what is of public concern is to prevent constant constitutional litigation from hamstringing a government office's fulfillment of its responsibilities to the public. However, higher education is unique, clearly distinguishable from all other "contexts" including public secondary and elementary education. The university's unique responsibility to the public is to *improve* and disseminate knowledge. In this context the employer's responsibility to the public is best served by an environment of free debate constrained only by standards of professional competence and ethics. In the university "context," faculty speech relating to the core functions of teaching and scholarship in particular would be of "public concern" unless the speech did not meet professional standards. In this "context," only *Clark* v. *Holmes* of the gray-area cases appears to involve a matter not of public concern. A university administration can require that a professor comply with course content requirements and a failure to do so is professional misconduct.

Along the same vein, tone and manner of speech are part of "context," and a professor's failure to comply with professional standards thus influences a court's decision on whether a professor's speech is of public concern, especially in difficult cases in the middle of the spectrum. For example, the use of profanity influences a court to find the matter addressed is not of public concern.[62] Personal hostility, name calling, anger, and threats have the same effect.[63] Long-term infighting tends to indicate both that the matters addressed are not of public concern and that the employer's fears of disruption in the workplace are well-founded.[64]

In the second step of the *Connick* test, if the faculty member's speech is of public concern, the lower court is to balance the interests of the professor with those of the university. When close working relationships are essential to fulfilling the university's responsibility to the public, a degree of deference to the university's judgment is appropriate. Manner, time, and place of a professor's speech should be appropriate to the university's fulfilling its mission. Finally, the lower court should examine the context of a professor's speech to consider whether it might impair the university in meeting its responsibilities to the public.

Again, some lower court cases are not clearly consistent. In *Maples* v. *Martin,* several professors were reassigned to another department after they publicly criticized the department in which they worked. They did so both in oral comments and in a written report.[65] The Eleventh Circuit found of public concern those portions of the report critical of the curriculum, the facilities, faculty to student ratio, and poor student performance on the professional licensing exam. These were central to the professors' concern that the department's accreditation was in jeopardy. Accreditation is the type of subject usually of interest to the general public.[66] Applying the second balancing step of *Connick,* the court found that the report caused tension, distraction, poor communication, and disharmonious relationships in the department. The professors' speech was thus unprotected, and the reassignments were justified.[67]

In contrast, the Third Circuit in *Johnson* v. *Lincoln Univ. of the Com.,* distinguished broadly based criticisms of the university president and letters to the accrediting authorities from intensely personal controversies within the chemistry department.[68] The former took place "apart from any close working relationships" and were not likely to disrupt the workplace. With respect to the latter, even if there were some evidence of disruption caused by a professor's speech, such a finding was not controlling. Office disruption was a weight on the scale of the balancing test.[69]

Lower courts reaching the second step of the *Connick* test in cases involving faculty speech would again benefit from close analysis of the university's unique responsibility to the public of *improving* and disseminating knowledge. As chapter 4 explained, public higher education fulfills this responsibility largely through free debate among academic professionals constrained only by peer review of professional competence and ethical conduct. Such debate should be more robust than in any other workplace.

Thus, a professor's speech on a matter of public concern that meets professional standards should be protected regardless of the disruptive impact. This analysis would not protect unprofessional conduct like sustained disputes with and severe personal criticism of a professor's immediate supervisor. Such conduct seriously undermines close working relationships, and thus is unprotected speech.[70] The more hostile, rude, and unprofessional the speech, the less likely it is to be protected.[71] Knowingly false accusations and false statements made with reckless disregard for the truth against administrators and colleagues are not protected speech.[72] If the professors' speech met professional standards, a case like *Maples* v. *Martin* would be differently decided under this approach. There is at least one case where the First Amendment rights of a professor employed in a public university have been held to protect faculty speech that violates professional standards of competence or ethical conduct. In *Powell* v. *Gallentine,* the Tenth Circuit found that a professor's allegations of grade fraud by an adjunct professor under his supervision clearly involved a matter of public concern. The university then contended that the professor's interest in speaking could not outweigh the university's interest in the efficient operation of the university because the administration believed the professor's allegations were false. The Tenth Circuit held that whether the professor's allegations were false is irrelevant, "because even false allegations are entitled to First Amendment protection, unless they were knowingly or recklessly made."[73]

A professor's statement that is not knowingly false or that is not made with reckless disregard for the facts could still be far below the *affirmative* duties of inquiry and argument required by professional academic freedom. For example, the correlative duties of professional academic freedom require a professor affirmatively to gather all relevant evidence, to record it accurately, and to set forth justly the divergent evidence and propositions of other investigators. Clearly, advocacy tactics of manipulative persuasion that would satisfy the *Powell* v. *Gallentine* standard would fall far short of the standard of professional competence and ethical conduct required of a faculty member.

The analysis in the First Amendment cases relating to higher education should again focus on context. If peers determine that a professor's speech does not meet professional standards of competence or ethical conduct, a court could decide that the faculty member's speech does not involve a matter of public concern. In the university "context," faculty speech that is professionally incompetent or unethical does not serve the university's mission of improving knowledge. Even if a faculty member's speech found by peers to be unprofessional is a matter of public concern, the court may decide that the speech does not merit Constitutional protection because the professor's First Amendment rights do not outweigh the university's interest in the effective and efficient fulfillment of its responsibilities to the public. Faculty speech not meeting professional standards does not serve the university's mission of improving and disseminating knowledge. Judicial deference to peer judgment in these cases is strongly supported by the doctrine of academic abstention to which we turn in chapter 7.[74]

The *Connick* test as it is applied to protect a professor's speech in the unique context of public higher education is the third piece in the puzzle of understanding academic freedom. The fourth and final piece in the puzzle is the historic reluctance of courts themselves as state actors to interfere in the academic decisions of universities. This judicial circumspection is expressed as a prudential norm in the rhetoric of abstention.

Notes

1. *McAuliffe* v. *Mayor of New Bedford*, 29 N.E. 517 (1892).
2. *Grossjean* v. *American Press Co.*, 297 U.S. 233, 249–50 (1936).

3. 391 U.S. 563. Another possible source of protection for freedom of expressive conduct for public employees is the First Amendment's Petition Clause. The Supreme Court has not addressed the scope of the constitutional right to petition in the context of an alleged retaliatory discharge of a public employee. However, the Third Circuit recently held that the Petition Clause was implicated when a public university professor's conduct went beyond speech to include the filing of lawsuits and grievances under a collective bargaining agreement. *San Filippo v. Bongiovanni*, 30 F.3d 424, 442–43 (3d Cir. 1994).

4. *See id.* at 564. In 1961, the Board of Education presented a bond proposal to the voters to raise money to build two new schools. *Id.* at 565. The proposal was defeated, but a second proposal was approved later that year. *Id.* In 1964, the Board presented a tax increase proposal for educational expenses to the voters. Because the proposal was defeated, the Board also submitted a second proposal, which was expected to be defeated. *Id.* at 566.
   During the events surrounding the second proposal, plaintiff Pickering sent a letter to the local paper criticizing the Board's "handling of the 1961 bond issue proposals" and its allocation of funds between the schools' educational and athletic programs. *Id.* Pickering's letter also claimed that the superintendent of schools attempted to "prevent teachers in the district from opposing or criticizing the proposed bond issue." *Id.*

5. *Id.* at 564–65.

6. *See id.* at 568.

7. *Id.* at 568.

8. *Id.* at 569–70.

9. *See id.* at 579–82.

10. *See id. See generally* Matthew W. Finkin, *Intramural Speech, Academic Freedom and the First Amendment*, 66 TEX. L. REV. 1323, 1329–30 (1988). Finkin believes that Pickering is "[c]onsistent with modern precedent...[in that] public employees do not shed their free speech rights altogether once they enter government work." *Id.* at 1329. Yet, according to Finkin, the Court has "hedged" the exercise of public employees' free speech rights with certain limitations that "arise out of the employment relationship." *Id.* at 1329.

11. 461 U.S. 138.

12. *Id.* at 140–41.

13. *See id.* at 142–43; *see also* Finkin, *supra* note 10, at 1332.

14. *Connick*, 461 U.S. at 146–47.

15. *Id.* at 143, 147, 154.

16. *Id.* at 147–48.

17. *Id.* at 148.

18. *Id.*

19. *Id.* at 149.

20. *Id.* Because Myer's intraoffice questionnaire did not constitute speech on matters of public concern in the definition of *Pickering* and its progeny, the Court in *Connick* had no reason to "scrutinize" the reasons for her discharge. *See* id. at 148–49. According to the court, "[w]hen employee expression cannot be fairly considered as relating to any matter of political, social or other concern to the community, government officials should enjoy wide latitude in managing their offices, without intrusive oversight by the judiciary in the name of the First Amendment." *Id.* at 146. According to the Court,

> we hold only that when a public employee speaks not as a citizen upon matters of public concern, but instead as an employee upon matters only of per-

sonal interest, absent the most unusual circumstances, a federal court is not the appropriate forum in which to review the wisdom of a personnel decision taken by a public agency allegedly in reaction to the employee's behavior. *Id.* at 147.

21. *Id.* at 149.
22. *Id.* at 150.
23. *Id.* at 151–52.
24. *Id.* at 151–52.
25. *Id.* at 152.
26. *Id.* at 153.
27. *Id.*
28. *Id.* at 154. The Supreme Court in *Waters v. Churchill*, 62 LW 4397 (1994) considered whether the *Connick* test should be applied to what the government employer thought was said, or what the trial court ultimately determines to have been said. A four-justice plurality found that in determining whether a public employee was improperly disciplined for speech on a matter of public concern, a court should not decide what was said for itself, but rather should apply the *Connick* test to what the facts "as the government employer reasonably found them to be." *Id.* at 4402. The reasonableness of the employer's belief should be measured by the fact finding procedures it employed in resolving the matter. *Id.* Three concurring justices accused the plurality of creating a new requirement that public employers conduct an investigation before taking disciplinary action in cases involving employee speech. *Id.* at 4405.
29. *Connick*, 461 U.S. at 152.
30. *Id.* at 148–49. *See* Note, *Controversial Teacher Speech: Striking A Balance Between First Amendment Rights and Educational Interests*, 66 S. CAL. L.REV. 2533, 2558 (1993).
31. Two Supreme Court decisions illustrate this point. *See Rankin v. McPherson*, 483 U.S. 378 (1987); *Dun & Bradstreet, Inc. v. Greenmoss Builders, Inc.*, 472 U.S. 749 (1985). In *Dun & Bradstreet*, the petitioner credit reporting agency sent a report to five subscribers stating that respondent contractor had voluntarily filed a petition for bankruptcy. 472 U.S. at 751. The main issue in the case was a libel claim against Dun & Bradstreet; however, the Court evaluated the defendant's speech as to whether its expressions were of public concern, thus determining the extent, if any, of First Amendment protection the report would receive. *See id.* at 761–62. The court held that the reports were not a matter of public concern. *Id.* at 762.

    In *Rankin*, a clerical employee was discharged subsequent to her remark about an attempted assassination of the President of the United States. 483 U.S. at 379–80. Apparently after the report of the attempted killing, the employee said, "If they go for him again, I hope they get him." *Id.* at 380. Another employee overheard the remark and reported it to Rankin, who subsequently fired McPherson. *Id.* at 381–82. The Court held that based on the content, form, and context of the employee's speech the statement addressed the policies of the president and was not a threat on the president. The speech was of public concern. There was no showing of interference with the operation of the office by disturbing or interrupting others. *Id.* at 387.
32. *Mount Healthy Bd. of Educ. v. Doyle*, 429 U.S. 274, 282 (1977).
33. *Id* at 287. It seems possible that a professor's speech could satisfy the *Connick* standards but still be below professional standards of competence and ethics. A peer judgment of unprofessional conduct should help to satisfy the third step of *Mount Healthy*. In *Jeffries v. Harleston*, the court structured the analysis under

Mt. Healthy and *Connick* somewhat differently. The public employee must show first that the speech was on matters of public concern, and second, that the speech was a substantial or motivating factor in the discharge. If plaintiff establishes these elements, the burden shifts to the employer to show either: (1) that it would have made the same decision in the absence of the protected conduct; or (2) that the employee's conduct interfered with the employer's effective and efficient fulfillment of its responsibilities to the public [citing *Connick*]. *Jeffries v. Harleston*, 828 F.Supp. 1066, 1078-79 (S.D.N.Y. 1993), *aff'd in part & vacated in part* (as to punitive damages), 21 F.3d 1238 (2d Cir. 1994).

34. *Connick v. Myers*, 461 U.S. at 148, n.7 & 150 n.10; *Mt. Healthy Bd. of Educ. v. Doyle*, 429 U.S. at 287. On remand in *Mt. Healthy*, the federal district court held that the board of education had shown by preponderance of the evidence that it would have reached the same decision in failing to renew the contract of the untenured teacher even in the absence of protected speech by the teacher. The reasons included obscene gestures to correct students and an "s.o.b." name-calling incident. The Sixth Circuit affirmed. *Doyle v. Mt. Healthy Bd. of Educ.*, 670 F.2d 59 (6th Cir. 1982).

35. *See* Fernand N. Dutile, *Higher Education and the Courts: 1988 in Review*, 16 J.C. & U.L. 201, 213-15 (1989).

36. Toni M. Massaro, *Significant Silences: Freedom of Speech in the Public Sector Workplace*, 61 S. CAL. L. REV. 3, 20 (1987).

37. *Id.* at 21.

38. *Connick v. Myers*, 461 U.S. at 147-48.

39. *See id.*

40. *Id.* at 148; *see* Finkin, *supra* note 10, at 1332; *see also Kinsey v. Salado Indep. Sch. Dist.*, 916 F.2d 273 (5th Cir. 1990), *opinion vacated*, 950 F.2d 988 (5th Cir. 1992), *and cert. denied*, 112 S.Ct. 2275 (1992) (dispute over job performance is private speech and thus not protected); *Huang v. Board of Governors of Univ. of N.C.*, 902 F.2d 1134 (4th Cir. 1990) (public employee's expression of grievances concerning his own employment is not a matter of public concern and is thus not protected); *Lewis v. Blackburn*, 759 F.2d 1171 (4th Cir. 1985), *cert. denied*, 474 U.S. 902 (1985) (personal grievances about working conditions do not qualify as matters of public concern). In an Indiana case, professors complained that the University violated their free speech rights by denying them reappointment, promotion, and tenure in retaliation both for their criticism of the department's internal peer review committee and for their requests for external review. The court, finding the complaints did not address matters of public concern, distinguished classroom expression or general policy criticism from complaints made to protect complainants' personal interest. *Colburn v. Trustees of Ind. Univ.*, 739 F. Supp. 1268 (S.D. Ind. 1990), *aff'd*, 973 F.2d 581 (7th Cir. 1992).

41. Massaro, *supra* note 36, at 22-23. The mere fact that the forum is only internal is a factor to consider; it does not control the determination whether a matter is of public concern. First Amendment freedoms are not lost when a public employee arranges to communicate privately with his or her employer rather than to spread the views before the public. *See, e.g., Givhan v. Western Line Consol. Sch. Dist.*, 439 U.S. 410, 415-16 (1979) (stating that a teacher's criticism does not per se lose its protection merely because it was private expression directed at her superiors. The topic of racially discriminatory policies is inherently of public concern); *Kurtz v. Vickrey*, 855 F.2d 723, 729 (11th Cir. 1988) (noting that professors' criticism of university expenditures during a period of fiscal crisis was of public concern even though the professor took no steps to inform the public).

The question is whether the speech "can fairly be considered as relating to any matter of political, social, or other concern to the community." *Connick v. Meyers*, 461 U.S. at 146.

42. Massaro, *supra* note 36, at 22-23.
43. *Connick v. Myers*, 461 U.S. at 150.
44. Thomas W. Rynard, *The Public Employee and Free Speech in The Supreme Court: Self-Expression, Public Access to Information, and the Efficient Provision of Governmental Services*, 21 URB. LAW. 447, 463, 467 (1989).
45. *Id.* at 467-68.
46. Walter P. Metzger, *Profession and Constitution: Two Definitions of Academic Freedom in America*, 66 TEX. L. REV. 1265, 1298-1300 (1988).
47. Finkin, *supra* note 10, at 1347.
48. *See, e.g., Carey v. Board of Educ. of Adams-Arapahoe Sch. Dist.*, 598 F.2d 535, 539-43 (10th Cir. 1979); *Mabey v. Reagan*, 537 F.2d 1036, 1048 (9th Cir. 1976).
49. *Dodds v. Childers*, 933 F.2d 271, 273-74 (5th Cir. 1991); *see also Dorsett v. Board of Trustees for State Colleges and Universities*, 940 F.2d 121, 125 (5th Cir. 1991) (where a professor did not address his complaints about assignments of summer and overload classes to anyone outside the university, the private form and context indicate that the speech did not address a matter of public concern). In *Mahaffey v. Kansas Board of Regents*, a professor's formal grievance about salary, other perks, and position on the organizational chart was of personal, not public, concern. *Mahaffey v. Kansas Bd. of Regents*, 562 F. Supp. 887, 890 (D. Kan. 1983); *see Ferrara v. Mills*, 781 F.2d 1508, 1516 (11th Cir. 1986) (high school teacher's speech concerning class assignments held unprotected); *Cook v. Ashmore*, 579 F. Supp. 78, 84 (N.D. Ga. 1984) (speech regarding amount of advance notice due prior to termination of employment was personal and, therefore, unprotected by the First Amendment.); *Ballard v. Blount*, 581 F. Supp. 160, 163-64 (N.D. Ga. 1983), *aff'd*, 734 F.2d 1480 (11th Cir. 1983), *and cert. denied*, 469 U.S. 1086 (1984) (professor's criticism about denial of tenure to a colleague, low salary, and teaching assignment found unprotected); *Meyer v. University of Wash.*, 719 P.2d 98, 101 (Wash. 1986) (speech relating to salary issues with "only an attenuated relationship, if any, to public interest" did not impinge upon the protection afforded by the First Amendment.). In *Ghosh v. Ohio Univ.*, the Sixth Circuit found that a professor's grievance over teaching evaluations, salary, and nonrenewal of contract was a matter of private concern. "On the other hand, speech related to exposing waste, ineptitude, breach of public trust...and academic standards are matters of public concern." *Ghosh v. Ohio Univ.*, 861 F.2d 720 (6th Cir. 1988) (p. 5 of text in Westlaw), *cert. denied*, 490 U.S. 1006 (1989); *see also Ayoub v. Texas A & M Univ.*, 927 F.2d 834, 836 (5th Cir. 1991), *cert. denied*, 112 S.Ct. 72 (1991) (a professor's complaint about his individual salary, in contrast to a complaint about a general policy of discrimination against foreign born professors, was not of public concern).
50. *See Levin v. Harleston*, 770 F. Supp. 895, 889-903, 918-19 (S.D.N.Y. 1991), *aff'd in part & vacated in part*, 966 F.2d 85 (2d Cir. 1992).
51. *Levin v. Harleston*, 966 F.2d 85, 88-90 (2d Cir. 1992).
52. *Jeffries v. Harleston*, 828 F.Supp. 1066, 1073, 1075 (S.D.N.Y. 1993), *aff'd in part & vacated in part* (as to punitive damages), 21 F.3d 1238 (2d Cir. 1994). In November, 1994, the Supreme Court vacated and remanded for reconsideration in light of *Waters v. Churchill* discussed in note 28 *supra*, 63 LW 3381.
53. *Id.* at 1075.
54. *Id.* at 1084.

55. *Id.* at 1079.
56. *Id.* at 1080.
57. *Id.* at 1092–93.
58. *Honore v. Douglas*, 833 F.2d 565, 567, 569–70 (5th Cir. 1987). In *Johnson v. Lincoln Univ. of Com.*, the Third Circuit held that a faculty member's oral and written comments within the department and letter to the association of colleges regarding low academic standards both in general and specifically at one of the school's masters' programs raised matters of public concern. *Johnson v. Lincoln Univ.*, 776 F.2d 443, 451–52 (3d Cir. 1985). The court held that questions of academic standards are of apparent interest to the community upon which it is essential that public employees be able to speak out freely without fear of retaliatory dismissal. *See id.* at 452; See *Hamer v. Brown*, 831 F.2d 1398 (8th Cir. 1987). The court determined that a professor's speech to a state investigatory committee alleging inappropriate expenditures of public funds and poor management of a public program did relate to a matter of public concern. However, the professor "failed to establish a causal relationship between his protected speech and the termination of his...employment." *Id.* at 1403; *Trotman v. Board of Trustees of Lincoln Univ.*, 635 F.2d 216 (3d Cir. 1980), *cert. denied*, 451 U.S. 986 (1981). The court held that a faculty member's criticism of the university president's plan of retrenchment, including speeches, meetings, letters to the editor, telegrams to the governor, faculty resolutions, picketing and disruptions of classes related to a matter of public concern, and, except for the disruption of classes, were constitutionally protected conduct. The court remanded to the lower court to determine whether the president's actions created a chill prohibited by the First Amendment. *Id.* at 228–29.
59. *Pressman v. University of N.C. at Charlotte*, 337 S.E.2d 644, 646 (1985). In *Roseman v. University of Pennsylvania*, the court held that plaintiff's complaint to the dean and at a faculty meeting alleging that the acting dean had suppressed another professor's candidacy for the chair were essentially private communications which would undoubtedly have the effect of interfering with harmonious relationships with plaintiff's superior and co-workers. *Roseman v. Indiana Univ. University of Pa. at Ind.*, 520 F.2d 1364, 1368 (3d Cir. 1975), *cert. denied*, 424 U.S. 921 (1976). Similarly, the Seventh Circuit has held that even though "the public would be displeased to learn that faculty members were evaluating colleagues based on personal biases," a professor's letter to the dean requesting external review of the faculty's factionalism was more a matter of personal interest to the writers—because it affected their careers—than a matter of public concern. *Colburn v. Trustees of Ind. Univ.*, 973 F.2d 581, 586 (7th Cir. 1992).
60. *Harris v. Arizona Bd. of Regents*, 528 F. Supp. 987, 999 (D. Ariz. 1981).
61. *Clark v. Holmes*, 474 F.2d 928, 931 (7th Cir. 1972), *cert. denied*, 112 S.Ct. 3026 (1973). *Accord, Keen v. Penson*, 970 F.2d 252, 257 (7th Cir. 1992). In *Bishop v. Aronov*, 926 F.2d 1066, 1074 (11th Cir. 1991), the Eleventh Circuit also held that a university has authority to reasonably control the content of its curriculum, particularly that content imparted during class time. Professor Michael Olivas criticizes this holding as much broader than necessary to control the instructor's injection of religious beliefs into the classroom. Michael Olivas, *Reflections on Professorial Academic Freedom: Second Thoughts on the Third "Essential Freedom,"* 45 STANFORD L. REV. 1835, 1847 (1993).
62. *See Martin v. Parrish*, 805 F.2d 583, 584 (5th Cir. 1986) (where the professor made statements that the attitude of the class "sucks" or is "a bunch of bullshit," and that "if you don't like the way I teach this Goddamn course, there is the

door"); *Megill v. Board of Regents of State of Fla.*, 541 F.2d 1073, 1083 (5th Cir. 1976) (noting that the use of profane terms in an academic setting is not constitutionally protected).

63. *Russ v. White*, 541 F. Supp. 888, 896 (W.D. Ark. 1981), *aff'd*, 680 F.2d 47 (8th Cir. 1982).

64. See *Landrum v. Eastern Ky. Univ.*, 578 F. Supp. 241, 246–47 (E.D. Ky. 1984) (noting that a professor's verbal and written criticism of the curriculum and administration, including a letter distributed to faculty accusing both the Dean of being a "Hitler who frequently lied" and the department chair of "using informants to keep tabs on faculty members," were tangentially related to matters of public concern, but were unprotected forms of speech due to hostile tone and names. While the court recognized a necessity for allowing more divergent views in a university setting, the extensive period of time over which "verbal assaults" were leveled at the administration, and the "intense hostility" displayed toward the university administration counterbalanced this factor.); *Harden v. Adams*, 841 F.2d 1091, 1092 (11th Cir. 1988) (finding that professor's fights with faculty members who were administrative superiors and professor's attempts to involve students in the dispute tended to indicate disputes were not of public concern).

65. *Maples v. Martin*, 858 F.2d 1546, 1548–49 (11th Cir. 1988).

66. *Id.* at 1553.

67. *Id.* at 1554.

68. *Johnson v. Lincoln Univ.,*, 776 F.2d 443, 452–53 (3d Cir. 1985).

69. *Id.* at 454.

70. See *Cotton v. Board of Regents of Univ. System of Ga.*, 395 F. Supp. 388, 389, 394 (S.D. Ga. 1974), *aff'd*, 515 F.2d 1098 (5th Cir. 1975) (a professor's prolonged and severe public criticism of an immediate supervisor based on a personality conflict resulted in disruption of the pharmacology department. Because the hostility was directed toward a person with whom the speaker would normally be in daily contact and the speech raised questions concerning harmony among co-workers and discipline by immediate supervisors, the court held that the speech was not protected in consideration of the factors alluded to in *Pickering*.); *Chitwood v. Feaster*, 468 F.2d 359, 360–61 (4th Cir. 1972) (bickering and running disputes with administrators are not protected by the First Amendment. A college has a right to expect a teacher to work cooperatively and harmoniously with the head of the department. "If one cannot or does not...he does not immunize himself against loss of his position simply because his non-cooperation and aggressive conduct are verbalized.").

71. In *Boem v. Foster*, 670 F.2d 111 (9th Cir. 1982), an instructor in the Defense Language Institute sent a letter to his supervisor charging the supervisor with a "strong inclination and propensity to be a little self-styled dictator in miniature without competency," and further with "unprofessional conduct on the job...and...intimidation and harassment of fellow employees." *Id.* at 112. Applying *Pickering*, the court agreed with the arbitrator that the letter did not contain any constructive comment and reflected "a breakdown in the relationship between petitioner and his supervisor...[and] seriously undermined the effectiveness of the working relationship." *Id.* at 113. The tone of communication is not determinative of whether a matter is an issue of public concern, rather it is only a factor to be considered. Core speech protected by the First Amendment is not deprived of protection merely because it is "strident." *Trotman v. Board of Trustees of Lincoln Univ.*, 635 F.2d 216, 225 (3d Cir. 1980), *cert. denied*, 451 U.S. 986 (1981); *see also Harris v. Board of Trustees of State Colleges*, 542 N.E.2d 261, 267, n.10 (Mass. 1989).

Unprofessional conduct like the criticism of administration and colleagues in front of students, a captive audience dependent upon the instructor for grades and recommendations, is not protected because it is destructive of the internal functioning of the institution. *See Clark v. Holmes*, 474 F.2d 928, 931 (7th Cir. 1972), *cert. denied*, 411 U.S. 972 (1973). Unprofessional conduct like demeaning, insulting, and inappropriate comments to students is not protected. Keen v. Penson, 970 F.2d 252, 257–58 (7th Cir. 1992).

72. *Garrison v. Louisiana*, 379 U.S. 64, 75 (1964).
Justice Brennan noted:

> Calculated falsehood falls into that class of utterances which are no essential part of any exposition of ideas, and are of such slight social value as a step to truth that any benefit that may be derived from them is clearly outweighed by the social interest in order and morality...hence the knowingly false statement and the false statement made with reckless disregard of the truth, do not enjoy constitutional protection. *Id.*

See Fong v. Purdue Univ., 692 F. Supp. 930, 955–56 (N.D. Ind. 1988), *aff'd*, 976 F.2d 735 (7th Cir. 1992). In *Fong*, a professor engaged in false allegations directed at a wide array of administrators and colleagues. For example, he falsely alleged that a president of the university was guilty of "a heinous crime," and others were falsely accused of "serious criminal conduct." The court found that false accusations are not protected speech. *Id.*; *Megill v. Board of Regents of State of Fla.*, 541 F.2d 1073, 1083–85 (5th Cir. 1976). In *Megill*, a professor made a series of public accusations concerning the university president and events on campus that were not true. The court upheld that Board of Regent's decision not to grant the professor tenure because of a "lack of the attributes of professionalism and maturity needed for a tenured member of the academic community." The court stated, "The First Amendment protects the right to make a statement. It does not, however, clothe a person with immunity when his statements are shown to be false and inaccurate, when their truth could be easily ascertained." *Id.*

73. *Powell v. Gallentine*, 992 F.2d 1088, 1091 (10th Cir. 1993).

74. *Keen v. Penson*, 970 F.2d 252, 259 (7th Cir. 1992) (judicial review of academic decisions is rarely appropriate, particularly where orderly administrative procedures are followed," citing *Regents of Univ. of Mich. v. Ewing*, 474 U.S. 214, 230 (1985)).

7

The Prudential Doctrine of Academic Abstention in Judicial Review of Academic Decisions

The Supreme Court in *University of Pennsylvania* applies the traditional prudential norm of academic abstention broadly to all legitimate academic decision making.[1]

> In keeping with Title VII's preservation of employers' remaining freedom of choice, courts have stressed the importance of avoiding second-guessing of *legitimate* academic judgments. This court itself has cautioned that "judges... asked to review the substance of a genuinely academic decision...should show great respect for the *faculty's* professional judgment." [citing *Regents of University of Michigan v. Ewing*, 474 U.S. 214, 225 (1985).] Nothing we say today should be understood as a retreat from this principle of respect for *legitimate* academic decision making.[2]

The abstention principles articulated in *Ewing*, a student academic discipline case, are that judges, when reviewing the substance of a genuinely academic decision affecting students, should show great respect for the faculty's professional judgment.[3] Judges should overturn a "genuinely academic decision" only if "it is such a substantial departure from accepted academic norms as to demonstrate that the person or committee responsible did not actually exercise professional judgment."[4] In *University of Pennsylvania*, the court extends these abstention principles to all legitimate academic decision making.

Thus, although not raised to constitutional dimension as part of a constitutional definition of academic freedom, the principle of academic abstention is broadly affirmed in *University of Pennsylvania*. This means that lower courts should first determine if judicial review involves the substance of an academic decision. Second, the reviewing court must determine if the academic decision is made legitimately through the exercise of the professional judgment of faculty. If so, the court on judicial review should give great respect or deference to the decision.

The Rationale for the Doctrine of Academic Abstention

The statement of the conditions under which academic abstention doctrine is applicable is clearer than the reasons behind the doctrine. Many courts give very substantial deference to academic decisions at the university level without a clear, coherent rationale.[5] When judicial decisions or scholarship do articulate a rationale for a broad doctrine of academic abstention, they mention one or more of the following three reasons.

First, courts encounter difficulties in enforcing terms in academic employment contracts due to uncertainties about the precise meaning of the terms.[6] The typical employment contract between a university and faculty is embodied in the university's tenure policies. The AAUP 1940 Statement of Principles on Academic Freedom and Tenure is often incorporated by reference.[7]

The context of academic employment contracts is unfamiliar to courts. Normally the purpose of contractual limitations on the employer's ability to terminate at will is to provide job security for the employee as an end in itself. However, job security is a secondary purpose of the academic due process provided in the academic employment contract. The principal purpose of academic due process is to protect the right of academic freedom while providing the means to enforce its correlative duties. The rights and the correlative duties of academic freedom exist for reasons of the common good far beyond job security of the individual professor. Peer judgment plays the critical role both of preserving the rights of academic speech to be free from lay interference and enforcing the correlative duties of professional competence and ethical conduct. As Professor Byrne points out, academic custom does not establish standards of adequacy that are sufficiently accessible to provide a legal standard or test for a court.[8] Many courts recognize that contractual principles appropriate in other employment contexts are inappropriate here. They resolve uncertainties about academic contractual relationships by simply deferring to the university's judgment.[9]

Second, along a similar theme, the question of relative institutional competence to make the necessary judgments heavily influences judicial review of academic decision making.[10] For example, the Supreme Court sees the university as a separate realm, striving for values and models of continuing personal relationships between student and teacher and among faculty different from society as a whole.[11] In *Board of Curators* v. *Horowitz,* the Supreme Court held that a student may be dismissed for academic reasons without a hearing using a Fourteenth Amendment procedural due process analysis. The court found that the procedural tools of judicial or administrative decision making were poorly adapted to the expert evaluation of cumulative information required in academic dismissal cases. Moreover, the "educational process is not by nature adversary; instead it centers around a continuing relationship between faculty and students."[12]

Because universities act upon values and models of personal relationships different from the legal standards of society at large, judges feel themselves incompetent to evaluate the merits of academic decisions.[13] For example, the Second Circuit articulated five factors that make the tenure decision more difficult to review than other employment decisions:

1. The lifelong commitment by the university that tenure entails accentuates the importance of colleagueship among professors.
2. Tenure decisions are often noncompetitive. An award of tenure to one individual does not necessarily preclude the tenure of another, whereas in other areas of employment a decision to hire one person means a decision not to hire another.
3. Tenure decisions are usually decentralized, and there is greater deference given to the department's position than in most employment decision-making processes.
4. There are numerous factors that a school considers in tenure deliberations that are peculiar to the university setting.
5. Tenure decisions are often a source of unusually great disagreement, and because opinions of a candidate are solicited from students, faculty members, and outside persons, tenure files are frequently composed of irreconcilable evaluations.[14]

These comparative institutional competence factors are often conflated into a finding that courts should defer to a university's academic decision making because of the many and varied, inevitably subjective factors, going into an academic decision.[15]

The third rationale for a broad doctrine of academic abstention is the same as that underlying constitutional academic freedom. Citing constitutional academic freedom, courts historically have admonished government actors in the legislative and executive branches not to interfere directly in the university with either the content of speech or the determination of who may teach. Courts recognize that, as an arm of state, they too should exercise caution in order to preserve the autonomy of the university and its constituents from the coercive power of the state.[16] Judge Stephen Breyer notes that "courts have wisely recognized the importance of allowing universities to run their own affairs (and to make their own mistakes). To do otherwise threatens the diversity of thought, speech, teaching and research both within and among universities upon which free academic life depends."[17]

The Scope of Judicial Review as a Function of the Type of Issue Presented

The three general reasons for a broad doctrine of academic abstention developed in the previous section contribute to an understanding of the scope of review articulated in the *University of Pennsylvania* decision. The Supreme

Court held in that case that lower courts should determine first if judicial review involves the substance of an academic decision. Second, the reviewing court must determine if the academic decision is made legitimately through the exercise of the professional judgment of faculty. When these conditions are met, the lower court should give great respect or deference to the decision.

These terms and this overall construct of judicial review need further definition to guide judicial review in a practical sense. "Substance" is being used here in the sense of the merits of a decision, and clearly excludes the procedural aspects of the decision. The closest analogy in administrative law would be a regulatory agency's determination of facts, including the agency's reasoning in applying legal rules to the facts.

The meaning of "academic decision" is ambiguous. "Academic" literally means pertaining to education, especially higher education. This interpretation is overly broad given the three purposes of the doctrine. The AAUP's efforts to define academic freedom to protect academic speech from lay interference shed some light on the traditional meaning of an academic decision deserving of protection from lay interference. Academic freedom protects from lay interference a professor's teaching, research, intramural speech relating to the education of students or involving critical inquiry, and extramural speech. The duties of academic freedom correlative with these rights are enforced by peer review in the first instance. An "academic decision" in the context of this tradition would include a professor's decisions concerning teaching, research, intramural speech relating to the education of students or involving critical inquiry, extramural speech, and peer judgment assessing another professor's performance of the correlative duties of academic freedom.

This reading of "academic decision" is supported by the qualifying phrase from *Ewing* that courts should give great respect to academic decisions made "through the exercise of the professional judgment of faculty." Consistent with *Ewing*, "academic decision" is defined above to include only professional judgment of individual faculty or the peer group.

The *University of Pennsylvania* decision grants judicial deference only to "legitimate" academic decision making. "Legitimate" means in accordance with established rules, principles, and standards. Decisions made pretextually for unlawful reasons like discrimination are thus not "legitimate."

Traditional administrative law concepts of judicial review of agency action help explain what a lower court judge is to do when applying this prudential norm of academic abstention in judicial review of university or faculty decisions. The reviewing court is to take evidence *de novo,* including evidence indicating the record considered by the academic decision maker, who may be, depending upon the situation, either a professor individually or the faculty in peer review.

On questions of law, including substantive or procedural rights granted by constitution, statute, regulations, or contract, the court should exercise an independent scope of review.[18] An independent scope of judicial review on questions of law does not imply that the court is to ignore the university's construction on the question of law at issue. At public universities, for example, the legislature has delegated power to the Board of Regents as the state agency responsible for the governance of the university. The Board's construction of its own enabling legislation and its own regulations would be entitled to the same judicial deference administrative agencies traditionally have enjoyed on these issues.[19] In the construction of ambiguous terms in the academic employment contract like "adequate cause" or "correlative duties," a court has some guidance. A number of courts have interpreted such vague terms in the context of traditional standards of faculty conduct set forth in AAUP statements.[20]

On questions of fact, including an academic decision maker's reasoning in applying legal rules to the facts, the court should independently determine whether an "academic decision" is at issue. An "academic decision" includes a professor's decisions concerning teaching, research, intramural speech relating to the education of students or involving critical inquiry, and extramural speech, as well as peer judgment assessing another professor's performance of the correlative duties of academic freedom. If an "academic decision" is at issue, the court should also independently determine whether it is "legitimate," that is, made in accordance with established rules, principles, and standards. In particular, the court will independently determine whether the decision was made pretextually for unlawful reasons like discrimination that are not "legitimate."[21]

If the court is reviewing a "legitimate academic decision," the court is to give great deference to the academic decision maker on questions of fact, including the decision maker's reasoning in applying legal rules to the facts. This scope of review on issues of fact is similar to the arbitrary and capricious scope of review for an informal record proceeding in administrative law. A reviewing court is to examine the evidence and the academic decision maker's findings of fact and reasoning and determine whether the decision has a rational basis.

This interpretation of the scope of judicial review set forth in the *University of Pennsylvania* and *Ewing* decisions addresses the three general reasons for the prudential doctrine of academic abstention. It respects the relative institutional competence of the academic decision maker, in contrast to the court, to make factual determinations on academic decisions. On factual issues, it protects academic decision makers within the university from direct interference by courts regarding the content of speech or the determination who may teach. Insofar as terms of academic employment contracts are poorly defined, this scope of judicial review gives judicial deference to peer review that reasonably interprets ambiguous terms and applies them to the facts.

The scope of review just articulated assumes that the decision under review finds the faculty, administration, and governing board in agreement, but occasionally there is disagreement among these constituencies. What is the proper scope of judicial review under the doctrine of academic abstention when the administration or trustees reverse the academic judgment of a faculty committee? The academic employment contract may specify that in the event of disagreement with faculty judgment, the administration and governing board are to follow specified *procedures* including findings requirements and reconsideration by the faculty. The reviewing court should apply the same independent scope of review specified earlier to determine whether the procedural obligations of the contract are met.

Academic employment contracts may not address the issue of disagreement in detail. The 1940 statement does not do so, stating only that "termination for cause of a continuous appointment...should, if possible, be considered by both a faculty committee and the governing board of the institution."[22] A further specification of the academic due process to which a professor is entitled is contained in the Statement on Procedural Standards in Faculty Dismissal Proceedings and approved by both the AAUP and the Association of American Colleges (the original signatories to the 1940 statement) in 1958. The 1958 statement provides in its introductory comments that "the faculty must be willing to recommend the dismissal of a colleague when necessary. By the same token, presidents and governing boards must be willing to give full weight to a faculty judgment favorable to a colleague."[23] In the procedural recommendations, the 1958 statement provides that "the president should transmit to the governing body the full report of the hearing committee, stating its action. On the assumption that the governing board has accepted the principle of the faculty hearing committee, acceptance of the committee's decision would normally be expected.... The decision of the hearing committee should either be sustained or the proceeding be returned to the committee with objections specified.... Only after study of the committee's reconsideration should the governing body make a final decision overruling the committee."[24] In 1966, the AAUP adopted a Joint Statement on Government of Colleges and Universities together with the American Council on Education and the Association of Governing Boards of Colleges and Universities (but not the Association of American Colleges). This 1966 AAUP Statement places greater constraints on administration and governing board reversals of faculty judgments than the earlier joint statements.

> The faculty has primary responsibility for such fundamental areas as...faculty status.... On these matters the power of review or final decision lodged in the governing board or delegated by it to the president should be exercised adversely only in exceptional circumstances.

> Faculty status and related matters are primarily a faculty responsibility.... The primary responsibility of the faculty for such matters is based upon the fact that its judgment is central to general educational policy. Furthermore, scholars in a particular field or activity have the chief competence for judging the work of their colleagues.... The governing board and president should, on questions of faculty

status, as in other matters where the faculty has primary responsibility, concur with the faculty judgment except in rare instances and for compelling reasons which should be stated in detail."[25]

In faculty status cases where administration and governing board reverse a faculty judgment, the court may thus find itself reviewing an employment contract either with specific procedural and findings requirements or with no contractual provision for the situation but with a spectrum of procedural and findings requirements set forth in joint AAUP/AAC or AAUP statements. To the extent that procedural rights are specified, including hearing requirements and the opportunity for faculty reconsideration after a governing board reversal, the reviewing court can independently review as a question of law whether or not the employer has given the procedures specified.

In a reversal case, a reviewing court still must deal with scope of review of issues of fact, including the governing board's reasoning in applying legal rules to the facts. The academic employment contract may specify, for example, that reversal may occur only "for compelling reasons." "Compelling reasons" may be undefined in the contract. The 1966 AAUP Statement on Government of Colleges and Universities does not define the term.[26] How will a reviewing court determine if the reasons given by the governing board are "compelling?" Should a reviewing court give deference to the administrative and governing board finding that there is a "compelling" reason?

Even if there is no contractual language governing a reversal, the reviewing court must decide whether the governing board and administration in this situation deserve the same great deference on issues of fact called for by the doctrine of academic abstention. There are strong arguments cutting both ways.

The first rationale for academic abstention was that courts encounter difficulty in enforcing the terms of academic employment contracts because of uncertainties about the precise meaning of the terms. The principal purpose of tenure and academic due process is not job security as in other employment contexts. Rather, academic due process is to serve the public good by protecting the rights of academic speech to be free from lay interference by the employer while enforcing the correlative duties of professional competence and ethical conduct. Peer review plays the crucial role in both safeguarding these rights from lay interference and enforcing these duties. Judges must give strong effect to the contractual protections of peer review, or academic freedom from lay interference will be lost. Administrative and governing board reversals thus deserve no judicial deference on issues of fact.

On the other hand, what if peer review is not working to enforce the performance of the correlative duties of professional competence and ethical conduct? For example, a proceeding to detenure is rarely brought and not always successful.[27] Has the profession proved itself "unwilling to purge its ranks of the incompetent and the unworthy, or to prevent the freedom which it claims in the name of science from being used as a shelter for inefficiency, for super-ficiality, or for uncritical and intemperate partisanship?"[28] During a wave of zealotry, faculty zealots and their facilitators may vote on faculty personnel issues based on ideology rather than on the academic merits.[29] If peer review is not working, then the administration and governing board may be the only effective decision makers upholding standards of professional conduct and competence. Chapter 10 discusses this further.[30]

The historical assumption underlying the AAUP's statements has been that the administration is laity like the governing board and therefore not qualified to assess professional speech. This may have been true earlier in this century. However, at this stage in higher education, nearly all deans, provosts, and university presidents are academics, highly qualified to apply professional criteria in judging academic speech. They contribute a second professional opinion on issues of professional competence and ethical conduct less biased by friendship or political alliance.

While the first rationale for academic abstention supports no judicial def-erence on issues of fact for administrative and governing board reversals, the second and third rationales do support such judicial deference. The second rationale for a doctrine of academic abstention is that judges feel themselves incompetent to evaluate substantive decisions about the rights or correlative duties of academic freedom because the university pursues values and models of continuing personal relationships substantially different from the rest of society. For example, judges as lay persons will tend to protect points of view with which they are sympathetic or even more likely to protect all arguably respectable points of view. This would replace professional competence as a standard. The third rationale for academic abstention is that the court, as an arm of the state, should support constitutional academic freedom by itself exercising caution in preserving university autonomy from judicial coercion. Both the second and third rationales support extending judicial deference on factual issues to the findings of the administration and governing board in reversal cases.[31]

With good arguments on both sides of the issue, there is no easy answer to the question of judicial deference to administrative and governing board re-versals of faculty judgment in faculty status cases. Professor Byrne argues that reviewing courts are ill equipped to resolve disputes about the compe-tence of scholarship or teaching and should only ascertain if peers or adminis-trators can establish that they acted in good faith to reject a candidate on academic grounds.[32] Professor Rabban argues that administrative reversals are not entitled the same deference as are peer decisions unless administrators present plausible evidence that faculty committees have deviated from pro-fessional standards.[33] This puts an initial burden of coming forward with plau-sible (not compelling) evidence on the administration. If this burden is met, the reviewing court should apply the doctrine of academic abstention to the decision of the administration and governing board. If there is no such evidence, the reviewing court must consider both enforcing the contract to protect the faculty's academic judgment and granting no deference to the administrative decision. This is a reasonable accommodation of the competing interests.

A divided vote of the faculty on an issue of faculty status itself provides plausible evidence that there are debatable issues of professional standards in a particular faculty status controversy. In many such cases, the governing board and administration may be seeking to change institutional direction or improve faculty quality with the support of only a portion of the faculty. On the other hand, administrative rejection of unanimous faculty recommendations should be more fully justified.[34]

Lower Court Decisions

Many lower courts appear to have been more deferential to both faculty and university decisions and administrative reversals than the academic abstention scope of review called for in the 1990 *University of Pennsylvania* decision. Some courts apply an overall scope of review of "loose rationality" to faculty status decisions by universities and generally defer to the university[35]; they do not even distinguish judicial review of faculty status decisions where administrators and governing boards confirm peer judgments from cases where they reverse peer judgment. Procedural irregularities may also be ignored.[36] All are granted broad academic abstention. Professor Metzger observes that "federal courts tend on the whole to credit official accounts of the reasons for termination, absent a flagrant misstep that calls administrative candor into question...judges say that they lack the expertise to serve as superboards of education. No doubt this is one reason why judges shy away from putting personnel decisions made by real boards to an unsparing good faith test."[37] Some lower courts first look independently at whether the adverse personnel decision is actually a pretext for unlawful discrimination or infringement on protected speech. Absent a finding of an unlawful pretext, these courts then are extremely deferential, finding that, "universities must be given a free hand in making such tenure decisions."[38]

At the other extreme is Judge Harry Edwards's 1987 opinion in *McConnell v. Howard University*. In reversing a unanimous faculty committee decision, the Board of Trustees found that Professor McConnell should be dismissed for his refusal to teach a class unless a disruptive student apologized or the administration took remedial action against the student. The university argued that the reviewing court should give broad deference to the governing board's decision because of the special nature of the university. Judge Edwards, formerly a professor of law at Michigan, rejected this argument, stating that "we do not understand why university affairs are more deserving of judicial deference than the affairs of any other business or profession.... We find no reason not to do here what courts traditionally do in adjudicating breach of contract claims: interpret the terms of the contract and determine whether the contract has been breached."[39] The court rejects a deferential standard of judicial review on factual determinations. "To us, this means that a court must make a de novo determination of the facts and of the application of the facts to the terms of the contract."[40] Judge Edwards's elimination of the doctrine of academic abstention in contract cases ignores the rationales for the doctrine, and is contradicted by the *University of Pennsylvania* decision in 1990. In a 1989 decision, *Kyriakopoulos* v. *George Washington University*, a different panel of the D.C. Circuit did not extend *McConnell*'s scope to all aspects of a professor's promotion decision. "This case does not involve a judicial recalculation of the University's evaluation of a professor's scholarly merit. The fact finder's scrutiny need extend only far enough to ensure that the University perform its contractual duty...to dispose of a professor's promotion application on no basis other than scholarly merit."[41] In other words, the reviewing court is to ensure that the university considered only the factor of scholarly merit enumerated in the contract; the reviewing court should then give deference to the academic evaluation of scholarly merit. The *Kyriakopoulos* court's analysis is very close to that of the *University of Pennsylvania* analysis.

The doctrine of academic abstention is grounded in sound reasons. After *University of Pennsylvania*, lower courts should clearly avoid the extremes of excessive judicial deference or none at all. The interpretation of *University of Pennsylvania* proposed here satisfies the rationales for the doctrine while addressing the concern that excessive employer interference in violation of contractual rights of professional academic freedom will go unchecked because of too much judicial deference.

Notes

1. Academic abstention in its traditional meaning is the refusal of courts to extend common law rules of liability to a college where doing so would interfere with the administrative good faith performance of its duties. J. Peter Byrne, *Academic Freedom: A 'Special Concern of the First Amendment'*, 99 YALE L. J. 251, 323 (1989). It has become the most consistent value which courts bring to any given factual situation concerning higher education. *Id.* at 323 n.280. It is now applied in cases involving the common law, the Constitution, statutes, or regulations. *Id.* at 325–26. For purposes of this essay, academic abstention is used in this broader modern meaning.
2. *University of Pa. v. E.E.O.C.*, 493 U.S. 182, 199 (1990) (emphasis added).
3. *Regents of the Univ. of Mich. v. Ewing*, 474 U.S. 214, 225 (1985).
4. *Id.*
5. *See* Byrne, *supra* note 1, at 325; Kathryn D. Katz, *The First Amendment's Protection of Expressive Activity in the University Classroom: A Constitutional Myth*, 16 U.C. DAVIS L. REV. 857, 862 (1983). "If...the clash is between faculty member and institution, or student and institution on an academic matter, the

institution will almost always prevail.... Judicial deference to the expertise of academic decision makers, particularly at the university level, is widespread." *Id.*

6. Martin H. Malin & Robert Ladenson, *University Faculty Members' Right to Dissent: Toward a Unified Theory of Contractual and Constitutional Protection*, 16 U.C. DAVIS L. REV. 933, 937–38 (1983).

7. *Id.* at 938.

8. *See* Byrne, *supra* note 1, at 308–09; Walter P. Metzger, *Profession and Constitution: Two Definitions of Academic Freedom in America*, 66 TEX. L. REV. 1265, 1310 (1988).

9. Malin & Ledenson, *supra* note 6, at 937–39, 967.

10. Katz, *supra* note 5, at 919. Courts see themselves as lacking the appropriate qualifications to assess professional competence or ethical conduct. Malin & Ledenson, *supra* note 6, at 968.

11. Byrne, *supra* note 1, at 325.

12. *Board of Curators of Univ. of Mo. v. Horowitz*, 435 U.S. 78, 90 (1978).

13. Byrne, *supra* note 1, at 325.

14. *Zahorik v. Cornell Univ.*, 729 F.2d 85, 92–93 (2d Cir. 1984).

15. *Mayberry v. Dees*, 663 F.2d 502, 519 (4th Cir. 1981), *cert. denied*, 459 U.S. 830 (1982); *see* Timothy Lovain, *Grounds for Dismissing Tenured Postsecondary Faculty for Cause*, 10 J. COLLEGE & UNIV. L. 419, 432 (1983–84).

16. *Bishop v. Aronov*, 926 F.2d 1066, 1075 (11th Cir. 1991), *cert. denied*, 112 S. Ct. 3026 (1992) (citing *Ewing* for the proposition that "academic freedom thrives not only on the independent and uninhibited exchange of ideas among teachers and students, but also, and somewhat inconsistently, on autonomous decision making by the academy itself"); *Parate v. Isibor*, 868 F.2d 821, 827 (6th Cir. 1989); *see* Metzger, *supra* note 8, at 1310.

17. *Vargus-Figueroa v. Saldana*, 826 F.2d 160, 162–63 (1st Cir. 1987); *See Villanueva v. Wellesley College*, 930 F.2d 124, 129 (2st Cir. 1991).

18. Justice Stevens observed in *Bakke* that academic freedom is the freedom of the university to make its own judgment as to education. Even while emphasizing the university's academic freedom, Stevens still independently found the university's actions unconstitutional. *Widmar* is similar. *See* David M. Rabban, *A Functional Analysis, of 'Individual' and 'Institutional' Academic Freedom under the First Amendment*, 53 LAW & CONTEMP. PROBS. 227, 256 (1991). Courts exercise an independent scope of review on questions of constitutional or employment law. *See Brown v. Trustees of Boston Univ.*, 891 F.2d 337, 360 (1st Cir. 1989), *cert. denied*, 496 U.S. 937 (1990); *Powell v. Syracuse Univ.*, 580 F.2d 1150, 1154 (2d Cir. 1978)., *cert. denied*, 439 U.S. 984 (1978).

19. *See Adamian v. Jacobsen*, 523 F.2d 929, 932 (9th Cir. 1975), *cert. denied*, 446 U.S. 938 (1980).

20. *See id.* at 934–35; *McConnell v. Howard Univ.*, 818 F.2d 58, 64 (D.C. Cir. 1987). Professor Rabban notes that "many [lower] courts have guided decision making by the understanding of academic freedom within the university community, particularly when the universities incorporate language from AAUP policy statements." David Rabban, *Does Academic Freedom Limit Faculty Autonomy?*, 66 TEX. L. REV. 1405, 1428 (1988). *Accord Greene v. Howard Univ.*, 412 F.2d 1128, 1135 (D.C. Cir. 1969); *Linn v. Andova-Newton Theological Sch.*, 638 F.Supp. 1114 (D. Mass. 1986) (applying AAUP regulations as part of employment contract and citing four other cases that apply AAUP statements).

21. Professor Rabban points out that judges routinely look into the factual background of academic decisions to determine whether the academic reasons given

for an adverse personnel decision were actually a pretext for unlawful discrimination or infringement on protected speech. This judicial inquiry into evidence of pretext frequently involves issues such as the timing of a decision and objective quantitative data. In this context, courts review professional judgments to see whether the stated academic grounds are "implausible" or "poorly substantiated" in order to determine whether the stated academic judgment is pretextual. A unanimous faculty recommendation rejected by the administration prompts courts to be skeptical of the administration's stated academic grounds. See Rabban, *A Functional Analysis, supra* note 18, at 288–90.

22. *See* American Association of University Professors (AAUP), *1940 Statement of Principles on Academic Freedom and Tenure, reprinted in* AAUP, POLICY DOCUMENTS & REPORTS, 3, 4 (1990).

23. *See* AAUP, *1958 Statement on Procedural Standards in Faculty Dismissal Proceedings, reprinted in* AAUP, POLICY DOCUMENTS & REPORTS 11, 12 (1990).

24. *Id.* at 13–14.

25. *See* AAUP, *Joint Statement on Government of Colleges and Universities, reprinted in* AAUP, POLICY DOCUMENTS & REPORTS 119, 123 (1990).

26. The AAUP's Committee T on College and University Government recently considered what reasons should be described as "compelling." Committee members noted in their discussion that the compelling reasons standard calls for something much stronger than disagreement with a faculty judgment. On the other hand a compelling reason does not mean a reason that is irresistible or that virtually commands a decision. A compelling reason should be one which "plainly outweighs persuasive contrary reasons." *The Standard of "Compelling Reasons" in the Joint Statement on Government of Colleges and Universities,* ACADEME, Sept.-Oct., 1993, at 54.

27. There were approximately 212,000 full-time professors with tenure in 1992. *The Nation,* CHRON. HIGHER EDUC., August 25, 1993, at 5. There are approximately thirty to fifty formal detenuring hearings each year of which roughly 75 percent are decided in favor of the administration. Telephone Interview with Jonathan Knight, AAUP (June 25, 1992). In the author's experience, a significant number of tenured faculty are reluctant to vote against friends or to vote for higher standards of performance to which they themselves will be held.

28. *See* American Association of University Professors (AAUP), *The 1915 General Declaration of Principles* 155, 170 (1915), *reprinted in* ACADEMIC FREEDOM AND TENURE app. A at 157–75 (Lewis Joughin ed. 1969).

29. *See* Rabban, *A Functional Analysis, supra* note 18, at 293.

30. See discussion of the role of the governing board in chap. 10.

31. A counter argument is that the judiciary is more deliberative and less political than the executive and political branches. Rabban, *A Functional Analysis, supra* note 18, at 286–87.

32. Byrne, *supra* note 1, at 308.

33. Rabban, *A Functional Analysis, supra* note 18, at 293.

34. The 1915 statement provides that "lay governing boards are competent to judge concerning charges of habitual neglect of assigned duties…and concerning charges of grave moral delinquency. But in matters of opinion, and of the utterance of opinion, such boards cannot intervene." AAUP, *1915 Declaration, supra* note 28, at 173. Professor Rabban makes the same distinction. *See* Rabban, *supra* note 18, at 286, 293. The author disagrees. Many of the correlative duties of ethical conduct require professional judgment, and the faculty should therefore

decide in the first instance whether a breach of professional judgment has occurred.

35. *See* Matthew W. Finkin, *A Higher Order of Liberty in the Workplace: Academic Freedom and Tenure in the Vortex of Employment Practices and Law*, 53 LAW & CONTEMP. PROBS. 357, 364 (1990).

36. *See* Malin & Ladenson, *supra* note 6, at 937-38.

37. Metzger, *supra* note 8, at 1310.

38. *See Brown v. Trustees of Boston Univ.*, 891 F.2d 337, 346 (1st Cir. 1989), *cert. denied*, 496 U.S. 937 (1990).

39. *McConnell v. Howard Univ.*, 818 F.2d 58, 69-70 (D.C. Cir. 1987).

40. *Id.* at 70 n.14.

41. *Kyriakopoulos v. George Washington Univ.*, 866 F.2d 438, 447 (D.C. Cir. 1989).

8

Where the Theory of Professional
Academic Freedom Fails

The last four chapters have outlined and analyzed the theoretical framework for the protection of academic speech. Without employment law or First Amendment protection for academic speech during the late 1800s, when the modern university emerged and professors increasingly questioned the cherished beliefs of the time, the professoriat had to create its own safe harbor. Developed during the last seventy-five years, professional academic freedom grants to professors the right to be free from lay interference by employers in research, teaching, and intramural and extramural utterance. It also imposes on individual professors correlative duties of professional competence and ethical conduct. The faculty as a collegial body has correlative duties to defend academic freedom and enforce the individual duties. Constitutional academic freedom developed in the last thirty-five years to protect content-based academic decisions of the university and individual professors from coercion by the government. In the same period, the prudential doctrine of academic abstention developed to protect academic decisions from undue interference by the courts. After many decades where First Amendment protection did not extend into the public workplace, the Supreme Court in 1968 finally granted First Amendment protection to individuals in government employment, including professors employed in public universities.

This theoretical framework was to protect unpopular but competent academic speech from suppression. Has the framework worked over the course of this century to achieve that result? There are of course countless individual instances where a governing board and administration have violated academic freedom by suppressing a professor's unpopular speech. The AAUP currently receives approximately 1,000 complaints a year and investigates the more serious of them. The AAUP may be able to vindicate the professor if there has been a serious violation of academic due process. Beyond these individual cases, academic freedom is most severely threatened when a strong ideology is widely shared and zealotry is unleashed to stamp out heretical thought more broadly. Chapters 1, 2, and 3 focused on and examined this phenomenon. The first three chapters' review of the historical record of the past 125 years regarding freedom of academic inquiry and speech indicates that waves of zealotry enforcing strong ideologies have occurred roughly every fifteen to twenty years in higher education. In each period, zealots labelled disagreement as heresy, demonstrating the moral turpitude of the heretic, and justifying a variety of coercive tactics to harass and to eliminate heretical academic thought and speech.

A reasonable expectation would be that as professional academic freedom developed and gained wide acceptance during the past seventy-five years, faculties would act to meet the correlative duty to protect academic freedom with increasing effectiveness. The most effective protection should be apparent in the most recent waves of zealotry. This has not happened. The findings of the first three chapters indicate that in the most recent waves of zealotry, professional academic freedom has often not adequately protected freedom of academic inquiry and discourse.

Another reasonable expectation would be that as professional academic freedom developed and gained wide acceptance during the past seventy-five years, faculties would act to meet the correlative duty to require professional competence and ethical conduct of individual faculty members with increasing effectiveness. Peer review, early AAUP academic leaders argued, would not shelter the incompetent or unethical professors; rather, it "would facilitate the removal of incompetents by bringing into play the resources of highly critical connoisseurs."[1] The findings in chapter 10 indicate that the peer review central to professional academic freedom may often not be working to fulfill this duty.

There are several explanations why the theory of academic freedom fails. First, it may be that the rationale underlying the reciprocal rights and duties of professional academic freedom was flawed from the beginning. The model of peer review underlying professional academic freedom may be based on the false premise that a collegium will in fact supervise itself. A collegium may in reality have a strong tendency toward silent acquiescence in the face of professional misconduct by peers in order to leave each member of the collegium a maximum amount of autonomy in work performance and behavior. Chapter 10 explores faculty neglect of its correlative duty to require professional competence and ethical conduct of peers.

A second explanation why the theory of academic freedom falls short in practice focuses on the correlative duty of the faculty as individuals and as a collegial body to defend the freedom of academic inquiry and discourse. The historical record is that during each period of zealotry, the faculty as a collegial body and the administration generally failed both to address the zealotry and to protect academic freedom. As Schrecker observes, "The extraordinary facility with which the academic establishment accommodated itself to the demands of the state may well be the most significant aspect of the academy's response to McCarthyism.... The academy did not fight McCarthyism. It contributed to it."[2] The faculty's usual public response of silent acquiescence in coercive tactics has been the ballast of the ideological zealotry of each wave. It may be that the expectation that faculty members will defend academic freedom is premised on an overly optimistic view of the professoriat's virtues. Chapter 9 explores the reasons for faculty neglect of its correlative duty to protect academic freedom.

A third explanation why the theory of academic freedom fails is applicable only to the student activism of the 1960s and the current fundamentalism of the radical academic left. These two periods of zealotry are unique. These are the first waves involving a broad populist intimidation initiated and carried out by zealots either from the student body or from the faculty itself.

Because these are the first waves of zealotry springing from inside the walls, there has been confusion whether professional academic freedom protects a faculty member's coercive tactics to eliminate dissenting speech. Does professional academic freedom mean immunity from employment consequences for whatever a professor says or does, particularly in intramural and extramural speech, unconstrained by duties of professional competence or ethics? Does academic freedom grant student zealots the same immunity from any academic or disciplinary consequences for whatever they say or do to advance their cause? The considerable confusion among faculty, administrators, governing boards, and the wider community about whether academic freedom protects the coercive tactics of faculty or student zealots, further inhibits any effective response to protect the academic freedom of the target.

Whether academic freedom protects faculty zealots' coercive speech and conduct poses a difficult issue. On one hand, professors are entitled to rights of academic freedom to protect their academic inquiry and speech from lay interference. On the other, at some point coercive tactics ripen into conduct that does not meet professional standards of competence or ethics. Chapter 10 explores where this line should be drawn.

Any claim that professional academic freedom means immunity for whatever a professor says or does in intramural or extramural speech unconstrained by correlative duties perverts the original understanding of professional academic freedom. The liberty of intramural and extramural utterance was never unbridled. University employers granted freedom from lay interference on the condition that individual scholars and teachers would meet the correlative duties of professional competence and ethics. The faculty as a collegial body was to define and enforce these duties in the first instance. To the degree that faculty and student zealots are successful in divorcing the rights of academic freedom from their correlative duties and the faculty fails to meet its duties, the rationale underlying the doctrine of professional academic freedom fails under these circumstances, and university employers may rightfully claim more discretion on employment issues. Chapter 10 examines this issue in detail.

Notes

1. Walter Metzger, *Academic Tenure in America—A Historical Essay, reprinted in* FACULTY TENURE 143-44 (1973).
2. Ellen W. Schrecker, NO IVORY TOWER: MCCARTHYISM & THE UNIVERSITIES 340 (1986).

Part III

Buttressing the Defense of Academic Freedom

9

Faculty Neglect of the Correlative Duties of Professional Academic Freedom

Earlier, chapter 4 described the two principal correlative duties of academic freedom for the faculty as a collegial body. First, the employment rights of free speech granted to all university professors are conditioned upon the correlative obligation of the faculty as a whole to enforce the competency and ethical constraints of the discipline when individual professors do not meet them. Chapter 10 explores the boundary where coercive tactics of faculty zealots cross this line. Second, professional academic freedom calls upon the faculty as a collegial body publicly to defend the academic freedom of its members against zealotry. This chapter explores the frequent neglect of this collegial duty to defend academic freedom publicly.

Zealots, whether from the right, the left, religion, the government, the church, boards of trustees, administrators, students, or faculty colleagues will continue to assault heretical thought and speech. This seems inevitable. It is critical that the faculty foster and defend competent voices of dissent during a period of zealotry because it is upon such dissent, however unpopular, that the advancement of our knowledge depends.[1] "It is not sufficient," Paul Walters said, "to support the rights of those who share our political and social ideas. We must stand for openness and for the right of all honestly held opinions to be heard."[2] The culture of an institution is largely defined by the faculty. Where there is a faculty culture that honors the correlative duty to oppose coercive tactics, then attacks on thought and speech will be moderated, and academic freedom exists.

The findings of chapter 3 indicate that faculties often publicly defend academic freedom of alleged heretics poorly during a period of zealotry. During each wave of zealotry, most egregiously during the last three since the 1940 statement, the faculty as a collegial body and the administration of many universities frequently failed both to address the zealotry and to protect the academic freedom of alleged heretics. Few faculty members gave public support to the accused. The faculty's usual public response of silent acquiescence to coercive tactics has been the ballast of the ideological zealotry in each period.

By repeatedly condoning the coercion and intimidation, Schrecker writes, the professoriat lost its nerve and self-respect in the McCarthy era.[3] Many faculty members lost both nerve and self-respect again in the 1960s and again in the late 1980s and early 1990s. The failure of so many colleagues to provide expected public support has created sad and sometimes bitter memories for the targets of zealotry.[4]

Why is the Faculty's Public Defense of Professional Academic Freedom in the Face of Zealotry Frequently so Weak?

Despite a number of periods of zealotry and seventy-five years of development of the rights of professional academic freedom, the academy's public defense of academic freedom in the three most recent waves of zealotry has been weak. It is puzzling how a small number of zealots can often successfully coerce and intimidate others in a university setting, yet a strong tendency to accommodate and acquiesce has characterized many academics in every wave of zealotry. Why is there so little collegial public defense of freedom of academic thought?

There are a number of tentative possible explanations for this faculty accommodation and acquiescence in the face of zealotry.

Inadequate Preparation

Many professors have an extremely limited understanding of the tradition and meaning of academic freedom. A survey funded by the Carnegie Foundation confronted professors with the topic of academic freedom by stating that "Academic Freedom is important to the profession. What does it mean in your work?" The responses indicate a very limited and generalized understanding of the rights of academic freedom and no recognition of the correlative duties of academic freedom.[5] Many professors also grossly underestimate the strength of the human instinct to suppress and censor the "wrong" thoughts and speech of others. They seem both unaware that waves of zealotry have occurred often in American higher education and uninformed about the duty academic freedom imposes on the collegial body to defend publicly the academic freedom of individual professors.[6] When the ethos of academic freedom is not well established, both faculty and administration bend quickly to whatever political winds are blowing the strongest. Without awareness that waves of zealotry could occur during their career, and what tactics to expect, faculty members are unprepared for and easily overwhelmed by well-organized and highly vocal zealots. They do not know how to resist zealots' tactics of coercion.

The cognizance of zealotry's threat to academic freedom that exists at any given moment appears to be backward, not forward looking. The professoriat is on guard against zealotries that have become widely recognized as wrong. For example, it took three waves of zealotry over a forty-year period motivated by superpatriotism for a wide consensus to form in the society and among the professoriat that this suppression from the far right was wrong. Similarly, because of the long struggle against religious fundamentalism in the late 1800s, the professoriat has some sensitivity to coercion from religious zealotries. Thus, the generations of professors maturing from the 1960s to the present are conditioned to see the principal threats to academic freedom as the far right and religious fundamentalists outside the walls. Many are not prepared and not yet willing to recognize coercion from the fundamentalist left inside the walls.

Without information defining the rights and correlative duties of professional academic freedom, many faculty members believe academic freedom means a right of absolute immunity from employment consequences for whatever faculty zealots say or do; and many seem largely unaware that the concept imposes correlative duties on both individual professors and the faculty as a collegial body. This ignorance and confusion lead faculty members to do nothing in the face of coercive tactics. They pursue a strategy of avoidance and apathy.

This problem of ignorance and confusion about the correlative duties of professional academic freedom has become worse in recent decades as traditional understandings of the obligations of faculty citizenship have broken down. In his 1990–91 Annual Dean's Report, Harvard Dean Henry Rosovsky observes that the "faculty of arts and sciences has become a society largely without rules, or to put it slightly differently, the tenured members of the faculty—frequently as individuals—make their own rules...there is no strong consensus concerning duties and standards of behavior."[7]

The joint AAC and AAUP Commission on Academic Tenure in Higher Education observed in 1973 that historically, institutions were able "to rely on individual self-discipline and the informed correctives of collegial association" to ensure that general professional standards are enforced. However, the commission found that the campus turmoil in the late 1960s presented "acute problems of professional conduct, for which broad general professional standards and traditional reliance upon individual self-discipline" were inadequate. The Commission believed that "the vast and rapid growth of the profession in recent years has surely weakened the force of professional tradition."[8] The data bear out a dramatic expansion of the professoriat in the last fifty years (see table 9.1). From 1940–90, the professoriat increased its numbers 677,000 or five and one-half times, with the largest increase of 225,000 occurring in the 1970s.[9]

Many faculty members apparently believe that graduate students and inexperienced professors will learn professional values, ethical standards, and academic traditions through informal interaction with and informal instruction by senior faculty members during collaborative work. This education, it is

TABLE 9.1
Number of Faculty in Institutions of Higher Education

Year	Faculty (# in thousands)
1899–1900	24
1909–1910	36
1919–1920	49
1929–1930	82
1939–1940	147
1949–1950	247
1959–1960	381
1969–1970	450
1979–1980	675
1989–1990	824

Beginning in 1969–70 the data include only instructional faculty with the rank of instructor or above.

assumed, occurs through "osmosis-like diffusion."[10] Osmosis-like diffusion breaks down when the professoriat dramatically increases in number.

During the current wave of zealotry, faculty ignorance about the liberal intellectual system itself is undermining professional academic freedom. The idea has taken hold that the liberal intellectual system is a kind of anything-goes pluralism in which all ways of believing are created equal and the major rules are to be sensitive and to be nice.[11] While the system historically has recognized the importance of civility in discourse, it totally rejects the notion that civil discourse in the pursuit of knowledge should not hurt people's feelings. Indeed, the breakthrough of the liberal intellectual system is its recognition that the productive advancement of knowledge depends upon the possibility of "falsifying" every certainty to discover error. Knowledge claims must always be seen as tentative and subject to constant checking. This checking process is painful, offensive, and not nice to those whose truth is being questioned.[12] This will be true for religious, political, social, or oppressed groups holding strong ideologies. Their natural instinct will often be to prohibit the checking process and to suppress heretics. They will claim that their pain is more important than the productive advancement of knowledge. Faculty who understand the liberal intellectual system will expect this and will be prepared to defend the system.

Ambivalence About Publicly Defending Academic Freedom for Opposing Ideas

Many professors seem highly ambivalent about speaking publicly to protect the expression of viewpoints that oppose their own. In their 1975 study,

The Divided Academy, Professors Everett Ladd, Jr., and Seymour Martin Lipset found that "the political thinking of academics is exceptionally ideological" and that faculty members are particularly susceptible to ideological division.[13] These ideological dimensions appear across a range of intramural as well as national issues.[14] "The ideological character of professorial thinking," Ladd and Lipset concluded, is of particular importance to understanding "the bitterness expressed against those of differing orientations."[15] Former Yale dean and provost Georges May concurs that academic disputes tend to be heated because professors believe they are engaged in the search for truth, and those who claim to seek the truth are quick to find infidels. "The university is the daughter of the church," May concludes. "We have inherited from it the costumes, the vocabulary and the concern for truth, and when the truth is at stake you may regard someone who disagrees with you as a heretic."[16] When professors share passions, sentiments and viewpoints with the zealots, their self-interest is served by permitting zealots to harass and intimidate competent opposing views. This ideology of solidarity with the zealots is predictable. The lust to censor opposing views is very strong. Recognizing the existence of a countervailing duty to protect the academic freedom of opposing views, some academics employ a utilitarian analysis to rationalize their response of avoidance, appeasement, or facilitation of the zealots' coercive tactics. The rationalization is that such tactics are for a good cause, and the speaker will not publicly oppose them even though privately the speaker does not fully approve of the tactics. Thus, during McCarthyism, many professors were strongly opposed to communism, leading to silence about protecting the academic freedom of the alleged proponents of communism.[17] Analyzing extensive questionnaire and interview data about faculty opinions in the 1960s, Professors Everett Ladd, Jr. and Seymour Martin Lipset concluded that the general ideological predisposition that faculty brought to political issues was a major determinant of the way they responded to student radicals.[18] The more liberal to left a professor was on wider political and social issues, the more likely he or she was to give at least tacit, and sometimes active support to student radicals.[19] The association between a left-of-center posture in politics and relatively high support for the student protests of the 1960s was extremely close.[20] Chapter 2 explored a number of reasons why, during the current wave of zealotry, liberal faculty members share an ideology of solidarity with the fundamentalist academic left. It is not in their self-interest to protect the academic freedom of those voicing heretical views. They may adopt strategies of avoidance, appeasement or actual facilitation of the zealots' coercive tactics.

This ambivalence to protect the academic freedom of opposing ideas becomes an acute problem when a faculty is dominated by those sympathetic to the goals of the zealots. Because few people will defend vigorously the rights of others to speak thoughts for which the listener has no sympathy, monolithic thought and little diversity of opinion on a faculty is inherently dangerous for rights of professional academic freedom. A number of faculties in the humanities and social services in the contemporary university are places of deep conformity in terms of ideologies to the left of center.

Fear of Damage to Reputation and Career

Professors know that mere accusations of moral turpitude scar a reputation, limit career possibilities, impose substantial costs of time, energy, and money necessary for defense, and result in social ostracism. In the public's perception, teachers are guilty of such charges until proven innocent. Many professors also know that zealots operate within an advocate's morality in making such accusations. Guilt by association has been a tactic in the three recent waves of zealotry. Many professors thus fear possible adverse consequences to their reputations and careers if they speak out in defense of the academic freedom of those who express heretical views; they know that they may also be vilified in retaliation for their public support of the accused's academic freedom. Fear of these consequences suppresses public support.

The group of colleagues who see themselves as just trying to do a job and support a family has no active malice toward the heretic, but they are highly influenced by fear of personal harm and by peer pressure. They want first to escape unnoticed, but if pushed many seek to please those who seem to be dominating developments. Lazarsfeld and Thielens found that during McCarthyism, many professors reported a willingness to join a support movement, but very few were willing to lead one because of fear of being singled out for punishment.[21] They also found that for another group of faculty, association with accused colleagues was thought to bring stigmatization and danger.[22] This group will pursue avoidance or appeasement of the zealots. Some of them may repudiate the heretic for causing ideological unpleasantness.

The group of professors motivated principally by personal prestige and reputation will be even more paralyzed by fear of career damage. They are extremely unlikely to risk career opportunity to support a principle like professional academic freedom.

Some faculty members are highly concerned about the reputation of the faculty or university itself; this group strongly disapproves of heretics who are the cause of external criticism of the university. For example, when a small group of academics at the University of California-Berkeley refused during McCarthyism to subscribe to a loyalty oath because they regarded it as an infringement on academic freedom, they were bitterly castigated by some colleagues for "creating a fuss" and endangering the position of Berkeley in public opinion.[23]

For some professors held hostage by their desire for respectability and propriety, the possibility of not "seeming anticommunist" or not "seeming sensitive to diversity" is enough. The risk that others may think they condone unpopular views with which they personally disagree silences them.[24]

Reprisal Based on Personal Grudges

Professor Owen Lattimore's experience during McCarthyism was that some colleagues who failed to protect his academic freedom were nursing old grudges. "There is always the additional danger that people with old personal grudges will give aid and comfort to a witchhunt.... You are defenseless against the man who is trying to work off a grudge, because everything depends upon how mean-spirited he is and how far he is willing to go."[25] A colleague nursing substantial personal grudges would tend to facilitate the coercive tactics of the zealots.

Common Traits of Academics

Common traits of persons who choose the academic life also explain the lack of public support for the targets of zealotry. Many academics are extremely independent with a focus on intellectual creativity.[26] They value a secure and stable environment where they can do their work alone.[27] Personal autonomy is highly valued.[28] They focus on their specific, immediate responsibilities of teaching and scholarship. This group's general rationale is "we have our work to do and these issues don't affect us," or "let's live and let live and just do our work without getting involved in controversy." They shield themselves from an awareness of what is happening. They do not want to become involved and may hold it against a colleague who seeks their help. Lazarsfeld and Thielens found that during McCarthyism many respondents preferred to escape unnoticed and exercise caution.[29] The fact that perhaps only three or four of every thousand professors would ever have occasion to say or write things that would bring them into conflict with zealots explains to Professor Fritz Machlup "why it is sometimes difficult to rally all faculty members to the vigorous support of academic freedom. There are always a good many professors in 'safe' subjects or with 'safe' ideas who resent the activities of the 'troublemakers' on the faculty."[30]

Similarly, some academics, at least in law schools, opted out of the practice world because of an aversion to confrontation and conflict. More generally academia may draw many people who are theoretically brilliant and assertive but timid on the level of personal conflict. They are highly susceptible to be cowed by intimidators and bullies. This leads to a natural aversion to conflict with zealots and the adoption of accommodation and appeasement as a principle, even in the face of extremely abusive and coercive conduct. The appeasement argument will start with the conclusion that "we should come to terms with the zealots in order to bring peace." It then works backward to find a suitable premise. Of course those faculty members who want to get on with their own work also are drawn to accommodation and appeasement of zealots in the belief that this will resolve the immediate conflict and allow the campus to return to normal quickly.[31]

In an analogous vein, the "moderate" faculty member sometimes has a conviction that the solution to any problem always lies somewhere between two "extremes." The target of zealotry immediately becomes one "extreme." Lazarsfeld and Thielens found that during McCarthyism, one faculty group's reluctance to back accused colleagues was the product of an inclination to follow the "middle of the road" and to disapprove of unconventionality.[32]

This desire to accommodate, appease, and find middle ground leads some colleagues to blame the victim of zealotry for not accommodating the zealots. Victims who raise issues of principle and the collegial duty of defense of academic freedom become "extremists on the other side," whose intransigence is causing unpleasantness. There is a sense that those being targeted by zealots for unpopular thoughts are getting their just desserts.

Those advocating appeasement of zealots seem generally unaware that appeasement rarely works because the demands of zealots flow not from evidence and reasoned analysis but from considerations of power. Zealots want to control the university and to eliminate heretics. Ideological zealots from the New Left in the 1960s and from the fundamentalist academic left today also will continue to escalate demands to provoke confrontation. This will demonstrate the oppression of the university. Concessions flowing out of appeasement policy will be trumpeted to the media as admissions of guilt, and a reason to further expose the hidden structures of oppression. Adverse media attention further weakens the negotiating position of the appeasers.[33] During the current wave of zealotry, the power of the oppressed status groups rests to a significant degree on their ability to demonstrate victim status. These groups cannot acknowledge satisfaction of their demands and concede their status as victims; their principle recourse is to raise further demands that cannot be met.

The academic tendency to intellectualize problems is another trait leading to avoidance and apathy and inhibiting public support of the targets of zealotry. Academics are, relative to others, particularly adept at self-delusion through rationalization. This leads to inaction in the face of moral duty. Intellectuals are also prone to see the target's distress as an abstraction. Having compared those who protected Jewish persons in the Second World War with those who, given the opportunity, did not, Humboldt University professors Samuel and Pearl Oliner conclude that "the emphasis on autonomous thought as the only real basis for morality continues to enjoy widespread acceptance." It is the vision of the moral hero who arrives at conclusions of right and wrong after internal struggle, guided primarily by intellect and rationality, that underlies much of Western philosophy. Unfortunately, the Oliner study, and numerous others, find "that few individuals *behave* virtuously because of autonomous contemplation of abstract principles." Such individuals often do "not in fact extend themselves on behalf of people in danger or distress. Ideology, grand vision, or abstract principles may inure them to the suffering of real people."[34]

Some academics also may discount the harm imposed by coercive tactics out of a belief that people should develop fortitude for assaultive rhetoric. This has some merit in principle, but vulnerable groups of people—especially, for example, newer and untenured faculty or faculty from a group with protected status, or students—may not have developed an extremely thick hide. Are the vulnerable to be left without protection? The real issue for discourse within academia is whether the discourse is competent and professional, not whether the listener should develop an extremely thick skin against personal abuse.

For all of these reasons, generally only a handful of faculty will publicly defend academic freedom in the face of zealotry. Courage has been in short supply in the professoriat. University of Minnesota professor David Bryden observes that "in twenty-five years of teaching law, I have known at most two or three colleagues who took principled positions in the face of sharp disapproval from the law school community, and they all paid a price for doing so."[35]

Administrative Neglect of Professional Academic Freedom

Many university presidents and deans have inadequately protected professional academic freedom in the last three periods of zealotry. Since a great number of them served earlier in their careers as faculty members, their acquiescence in tactics of zealotry has the same underlying causes as those described earlier for faculty members.

In addition, many senior administrators see their own career advancement and the university's need for both students and public and private resources as dependent upon favorable public relations. The principal threat to good public relations would be for some crisis to blow up on their watch. Thus, they want to avoid crisis and negative publicity at all costs. This fear of negative publicity made many senior administrators extremely vulnerable to the coercive tactics of zealots in each of the past three waves.

Georgetown Associate Dean Mark Tushnet adds that many senior university administrators today "really do not have any idea about the educational aims of their university. They see themselves as politicians and managers who happen to work in an educational institution."[36] Thus, "lacking a vision of what a university should be," they "bend to whatever wind happens to be blowing the strongest."[37] Seeing themselves as politicians, they attempt to buy off and accommodate as many political pressures as they can, making inappropriate concessions to those political forces threatening the most harm.

AAUP Response in the Last Three Waves of Zealotry

The AAUP was formed principally in response to the wave of zealotry occurring at the turn of the century. Its 1915 statement remains the most important document defining professional academic freedom. Later statements further develop the rights and responsibilities inherent in the concept, including the right of academic due process before termination of a tenured professor. Academic due process sets forth the procedures for the exercise of collegial judgment on issues of professional competence and ethical conduct.

Many of the AAUP's definitions and procedures have been incorporated into faculty employment contracts and accrediting agency requirements. During normal times, they provide significant protection for academic freedom from lay interference by the employer. In addition, the AAUP's staff and Committee A investigate alleged violations and make determinations of fact with the possibility of AAUP censure in the more egregious cases where administrations do not observe academic due process.[38]

Despite many decades of both contribution to defining professional academic freedom and useful intervention in individual cases involving denial of academic due process, the AAUP as a national organization did not play a major role in addressing the zealotry and protecting the academic freedom of zealotry's targets in the three most recent waves of zealotry. During McCarthyism, from the late 1940s through the mid-1950s, the AAUP's central office was almost totally ineffective because of the management style and personal problems of its executive director.[39] The AAUP Council was unable to rectify the situation until June of 1955 when the executive director died.[40] The worst excesses of McCarthyism had already occurred without AAUP intervention. During the decade 1947–1956, the AAUP received only approximately fifty-five complaints where the complainant charged that institutional authorities were violating academic freedom because of political beliefs or activities.[41] Targets apparently did not generally see the AAUP as an effective ally. During the student activism of the mid to late 1960s, the AAUP's formal statements said almost nothing about the widespread and egregious violations of academic freedom. The Joint Statement on Rights and Freedoms of Students adopted in 1967 makes only general exhortations that "students should exercise their freedom with responsibility," and that students should be free "to support causes by orderly means which do not disrupt the regular and essential operation of the institution." [42]

Finally in October, 1970, after the wave of zealotry had almost run its course, the AAUP Council adopted a statement titled "Freedom and Responsibility" that directly acknowledged and addressed the zealotry of the previous five years. "Continuing attacks on the integrity of our universities and on the concept of academic freedom itself come from many quarters. These attacks, marked by tactics of intimidation and harassment and by political interference with the autonomy of colleges and universities, provoke harsh responses and counter-responses."[43] The 1970 Council Statement emphasized the correlative duties of individual faculty members and the faculty as a collegial body to defend academic freedom. It urged faculty to assume "a more positive role as guardian of academic values against unjustified assaults from its own members."[44]

Twenty-one years later, the AAUP again delayed making any formal statement until the current zealotry had already inflicted harm for a number of years. The AAUP's first public statement in July, 1991 was to join in public accusations of lack of candor and bigotry against the targets of the current zealotry. An AAUP committee stated that the targets of current zealotry who bring public attention to their grievances "have been less than candid" and are motivated by "an only partly concealed animosity toward equal opportunity and its first effects of modestly increasing the participation of women and racial and cultural minorities on campus."[45] This position is far more damaging to academic freedom than the AAUP's ineffectiveness during the McCarthy period or the 1960s. It marks the first time in the organization's history where a public statement adopted the coercive tactics of the zealots in a particular wave of zealotry. In this case the AAUP committee used the fundamentalist's tactic of attributing "partly concealed" or hidden motives of bigotry to the targets of the zealotry.

The current and five preceding chairs of the AAUP's Committee A on Academic Freedom and Tenure (Professors Gorman, Finkin, Davis, Byse, Brown, and Van Alstyne) sent a letter to the Association objecting that the text of the Statement on the "Political Correctness" Controversy "imputes to critics of 'political correctness' a lack of candor, and 'an only partly concealed animosity toward equal opportunity.' No foundation is established, no evidence is adduced for these serious charges. By suggesting that critics of 'political correctness' have taken on a coercive tone, it overlooks the fact that many have voiced their concerns in a sober and reflective manner, rooted in a deeply felt respect for full and fair academic discourse."[46]

The executive committee of the California Conference of AAUP passed a resolution that called the AAUP Statement on the "Political Correctness" Controversy "an ad hominem attack on the motivations of the participants in a legitimate national debate." The executive committee asked its standing committee on academic freedom to investigate recent attempts to impose political views.[47]

In the fall of 1991, a Committee A statement indicated concern that universities were not following academic due process in sexual harassment proceedings. "Committee A has been informed by the Association's staff of a disturbing number of recent cases in which a severe sanction has been imposed on a faculty member accused of sexual harassment with no opportunity having been afforded for a hearing before faculty peers." Committee A urged compliance with academic due process in such cases.[48]

By 1992, Committee A started to take clear positions to protect academic freedom from coercion. For example, after several years of study, "Committee A determined, in effect, that the legitimate and valued exercise of the right of academic freedom would be too often jeopardized by attempts to distinguish speech from conduct and to distinguish permissible from impermissible speech. The conclusion reached by Committee A was that speech, no matter how arguably offensive, should not be banned and punished on the campus, but should rather be addressed through counter-speech and through the educational process."[49] Committee A also took a position that universities should not refuse to allow faculty members to receive foundation funding for their research channeled through the university, on the grounds that the university disapproved of the views or attitudes of the funding agency.[50]

Also in 1992, Committee A, encouraged by the AAUP Council, explored "the variety of forms in which so-called political correctness is manifested on American campuses. In an ongoing review, the staff is presenting information to the committee about recent situations that fall within the political correctness-rubric."[51] There were oral reports from staff at the fall 1992 and spring 1993 Committee A meetings but nothing formal ensued.[52] Given the AAUP's 1991 Statement on the "Political Correctness" Controversy, targets during the current zealotry would have even less reason to report complaints to the AAUP than during McCarthyism, when over the ten years from 1947–56 the AAUP received only approximately fifty-five complaints charging that political beliefs or activities were relevant to adverse action of institutional authorities.[53]

In 1994, AAUP staff again publicly stated concerns about the lack of academic due process in some sexual harassment proceedings.[54] Committee A published a report on the subject, *Academic Freedom and Sexual Harassment,* in the fall of 1994.[55] The report cautions that "there are important differences between the ordinary 'workplace' and the academic enterprise such that part 3 of EEOC Guidelines, if unreflectively applied to the university's academic functions without regard to the special needs of teaching and scholarship, would very likely circumscribe the academic freedom that the Association has worked so long to protect."[56] "At its best, the academic working environment... consists in robust exchange of ideas. Ideas whose expression may be felt to be intimidating, hostile, or offensive cannot be prohibited on the sheer ground that they are felt to be so."[57] The committee recommends that the AAUP adopt a revised policy on sexual harassment in the academic context.[58]

The AAUP's Committee T on College and University Government also issued a report published in mid-1994 and adopted by the AAUP Council that addresses the relationship of faculty governance to academic freedom. The report cautions that "dysfunctions [within the faculty] that undermine academic freedom may still occur: subtle (or not subtle) bullying on the part of the faculty itself, a covertly enforced isolation, a disinclination to respect the views of the off-beat and cranky among its members. That is to say...such incivilities may not issue in clear-cut violations of academic freedom, but a faculty member's academic freedom may nevertheless be chilled."[59]

Since McCarthyism, the AAUP has responded most effectively when there are clear cases of termination by administrators without academic due process. For example, when Dallas Baptist University dismissed Professor Ayers and Dean Jeffrey in 1991–92 without reasons or a hearing, the AAUP responded promptly and vigorously to the complaint received.[60] Similarly, the AAUP's investigating committee found that the procedures attending sanctions on Professor Donald Silva at the University of New Hampshire "failed substantially to meet the basic requirements of academic due process.... Indeed the committee finds the failures to be so serious as to raise grave doubts regarding the adequacy of procedural safeguards for any faculty member at the University of New Hampshire who is charged with sexual harassment under the institution's existing policies."[61]

The current zealotry's tactics of public accusation of moral turpitude, ostracism, investigation and tribunal, and disruption are more difficult for the AAUP to address. This type of assault on academic freedom usually does not fit into the model of the administration not following academic due process.

The AAUP's record in protecting academic freedom during the last three periods of zealotry is mixed. The AAUP reacts slowly to zealotry. In the early 1950s and late 1960s, the organization reacted so slowly to protect academics during a wave of zealotry that the zealotry had already run its course. The current wave of zealotry dates approximately from early 1988 with the initial adoption of campus speech codes; Committee A took a public position against speech codes in the fall of 1992. Ideological zealotry abroad in the society generally, like anticommunism, will affect the AAUP. It is a large organization susceptible to blocking and delaying tactics that will move slowly and cautiously during a period of zealotry.

If the ideological zealotry infects the professoriat, then there is reason to fear that the AAUP itself may join in the coercion of dissent. The organization's initial public statement during the current wave had this effect. Later public statements do address issues of academic freedom during the current wave.[62]

The AAUP's principal contribution to the protection of academic freedom is not its responsiveness to any particular wave of zealotry, but its work both in defining and developing the concept of academic freedom and academic due process and in challenging administrative violations of academic due process during normal times. During a period of ideological zealotry the concept of academic freedom provides principled defense arguments to the targets of zealotry. The cumbersome and expensive procedures of academic due process inhibit employment terminations during a period of zealotry by adding substantially to the transaction costs of a termination. They also slow down the process of termination, so there is a higher possibility the wave of zealotry will run its course before final action is taken.

The Unique Threat to Academic Freedom from
the Fundamentalist Academic Left

Undermining Professional Academic Freedom

In all earlier periods, zealots ignored the rights of academic freedom, using coercive tactics to suppress heretical thought and speech, but they did not assault the principle of academic freedom itself. The current wave of zealotry from the fundamentalist academic left is the first both to ignore rights of academic freedom and to deny the legitimacy of the premises upon which professional academic freedom rests. Fundamentalist ideology seeks to give intellectual legitimacy to the politicization of the university. To the degree the ideology gains acceptance, academics will be left without a principled defense when university employers or other groups choose to exercise political and economic power to interfere with academics' professional autonomy.[63] Professional autonomy will exist under these circumstances only as long as the professoriat exercises more political or economic power than employers or other groups. Understanding this threat from the fundamentalist academic left requires a brief review of both the fundamental premises of professional academic freedom and the ideology of the extremists in postmodern schools.

Professional academic freedom articulated in the 1915 and 1940 AAUP statements is rooted in a liberal intellectual tradition that presupposes a progressive concept of knowledge. Human understanding at any one point is imperfect, but defects can be exposed by testing hypotheses against reality. The process of hypothesis-experimentation-new hypothesis improves knowledge. It is the possibility of falsifying every knowledge claim that is the mechanism of knowledge. Within the university, this progressive conception of knowledge is realized through a discourse subject to unique disciplinary constraints of certification, professional competence and ethical conduct. An academic's professional audience understands and evaluates her speech within a tradition of knowledge, methodology, and criteria. There is a common set of standards used to evaluate the academic work of faculty and students. A scholar and teacher must meet the following duties of professional competence in her academic work:

1. to gather the evidence relevant to the issue at hand through thorough and painstaking inquiry;
2. to record the evidence accurately;
3. to give careful and impartial consideration to the weight of the evidence;
4. to reason analytically from the evidence to the proposition;
5. to seek internal consistency;
6. to exercise courage when the evidence contradicts what the scholar and teacher had hoped to achieve;

7. to set forth justly without suppression or innuendo the divergent evidence and propositions of other investigators;
8. to present evidence and analysis clearly and persuasively;
9. to be rigorously honest in acknowledging academic debt; and
10. to improve the account of some area of knowledge.

Earlier in this century, the principal danger to this progressive conception of knowledge was lay interference by governing boards. This interference imposed constraints on the offering of new hypotheses or the criticizing of accepted ones. Lay interference also occurred when lay judgments were substituted for professional judgments regarding professional qualifications and professional competence.

The 1915 and 1940 statements articulate the employment conditions necessary to secure the benefits of this progressive conception of knowledge. Essentially, university employers have agreed to grant exceptional vocational freedom to professors to inquire, to teach, and to publish without lay interference on the condition that professors meet certain correlative duties as individuals and as a collegial body. Professional academic freedom grants rights to professors to be free from lay interference in research, teaching, and intramural and extramural utterance. It also imposes on individual professors correlative duties of professional competence and ethical conduct. The faculty as a collegial body has correlative duties to enforce the individual duties and to defend academic freedom.

In contrast, the central belief of extreme proponents in the postmodern schools is that accurate representation of the way the world is, impartiality, and approximation of objective knowledge are myths. Each picture of reality is the product of social or personal factors. The progressive concept of knowledge based on the idea of movement toward objective knowledge or value is impossible. The social, political, and economic arrangements of society are therefore not the product of any paradigm of systematic thought that is better than any other, but simply the result of differences in power among social classes and status groups.

Since movement toward objective knowledge is impossible, and only viewpoints or perceptions exist, no academic's account of phenomenon can, in any objective sense, be more true than that of any other person. No distinctions can be made based on competence. Rationality, objectivity, accuracy and standards of intellectual quality and merit are slogans or masks of oppression designed to convince the oppressed that subordination is justice.

Extreme proponents in the diversity movement agree that these traditional standards of professional competence have no better justification or intrinsic value than constructs held by oppressed persons from status groups. In the alternative, extreme proponents in the diversity movement may argue that social equality is a higher goal than the progressive conception of knowledge and the rights and duties of professional academic freedom. Extreme proponents from both of these ideologies agree that higher education must be politicized to give voice and power to the ideas of oppressed persons and groups.[64]

The argument that perfectly unbiased observation is impossible and that all evaluation has significant reference to an academic's own values is well taken and valuable. Presumably this argument still acknowledges that there is benefit in striving to meet the common standards used to evaluate academic work. The important question is to what degree the aspirational goals are achieved.

The extreme position of the fundamentalist academic left is to deny the possibility of accurate gathering and use of evidence, impartial consideration of the weight of the evidence, analytical reasoning from the evidence to the proposition, and a progressive concept of knowledge.[65] These concepts are simply hegemonic fraud, concealing the power and oppression of the dominant Eurocentric culture and people. Academic inquiry and discourse thus are not about the ideas that people express, but about the people who express the ideas.[66]

This position is fatal to professional academic freedom. Our tradition of professional academic freedom is premised upon a progressive concept of knowledge. If there is no knowledge, and no way to distinguish fact from perception or reason from rhetoric, then professional academic freedom has no principled defense.

University of Chicago professor Edward Shils sums up the consequences of this assault on academic freedom.

> If there are no criteria of validity or truthfulness, because no statement can ever be truer than any other statements, then it is useless to attempt to assess the validity of the achievements of scholars and scientists. It is useless to attempt to assess the scientific or scholarly achievements of candidates for appointment or to decide which students have done well or poorly in their dissertations and examinations. What is there for academic freedom to protect except the security of tenure and the prerogative of frivolity.[67]

A few postmodern scholars are straightforward in acknowledging both that their ideology is fatal to professional academic freedom, and that large segments of the professoriat do not believe in the theory of knowledge underlying the system which they operate. In her 1988 book, *Reconnection,* University of Georgia professor Betty Jean Craige concludes that when postmodern scholars "abandon a belief in objectivity, we must redefine the principle of 'academic freedom,' for the public and for ourselves, in terms of contextual value. The discipline—and the academic world generally—cannot use the notion of academic independence from politics to support academic-evaluation-by-academics after it has shown society's intellectual activity to be inseparable from its political activity."[68] Professor Craige's equating academic freedom with independence from politics confuses the meaning of academic freedom. Scholarly work that meets the correlative duties of competence may in fact greatly influence politics. The critical point Craige makes is that when postmodern scholars abandon objectivity and claims of knowledge, they abandon also the rationale upon which academic freedom rests. They then have no principled defense against government or employer interference in scholarship, teaching and intramural and extramural utterance.

English professor and *New Yorker* literary editor Louis Menand is more direct in a 1993 article published in *Academe,* the AAUP's magazine. He first describes the progressive conception of knowledge on which professional academic freedom rests for justification.

> [The progressive conception of knowledge] is the model of science: knowledge develops by the accumulation of research findings, brick piled onto brick, monograph onto monograph, until the arch of knowledge about a field stands clearly defined against the background of mere undisciplined information. All these professional requirements [academic credentials, scholarship and peer review] were established to encourage the production of more bricks, to squeeze more toothpaste from the tube of truth.

> In any event, it is fair to say that almost no one in my field, and certainly almost no one in my generation, any longer believes in the theory of knowledge production from which the institutional structure of the modern university derives. The conventional wisdom among English professors and graduate students is that "knowledge" is subjective, relative, contingent, culturally determined, political—in no sense brick like except in its potential to do harm.

> In this state of intellectual affairs, it becomes very difficult to argue that professors need the protections associated with the concept of academic freedom, since so many professors now assert that their work is not about reaching the truth about a field, but about intervening politically in a conversation—a "discourse"—that is always and already political anyway.... If you are a professor who believes that "truth" is simply a name for what a particular group of people finds it advantageous to regard as given or universal, if you consider "knowledge" to be an instrument of political control, if you think that universities are sites for social indoctrination, you can hardly have much use for a concept grounded in the idea that intellectual inquiry is a neutral and disinterested activity.[69]

Menand forthrightly acknowledges that the challenge of postmodern ideology to the ground on which both the university and professional academic freedom stand is fundamentally different than earlier scholarly disputes. In those disputes, all disputants agreed that they were trying to get to superior knowledge about their subject, they disagreed on who knew the way. In the contemporary quarrel, the fundamentalist academic left is burrowing away at the ground on which the rest of academia is trying to stand.[70]

If the fundamentalist academic left succeeds in its project and successfully undermines and dismantles professional academic freedom, the consequences will be severe. In the face of zealotry from outside or inside the walls, professional autonomy will then be a function purely of the political power of the professoriat. Even though currently the professoriat does have power in the university, the ebb and flow of history teaches that power will from time to time shift to other constituencies.

University employers in particular would have no principled reason to grant professors vocational freedom from lay interference if the account of any subject is simply a subjective preference based on the social status and politics of the speaker. There would be no reason that academic employers should not assert their own subjective political preferences to the degree permitted to other employers.

As corporations, foundations, governments, courts, other groups, and the public at large come to understand the politicization of teaching and research within the university, they will see no principled reason to grant universities or professors academic independence. The threat of fundamentalist groups based on ethnicity and religion to academic independence bears special mention. In earlier centuries, religious fundamentalists often posed the greatest threat of authoritarian oppression. The most powerful force of authoritarian oppression of heretics and dissenters this century has been ethnicity, most often from the right. In service of the goal of empowering the oppressed, the fundamentalist academic left encourages claims of power based on ethnicity. Forces of ethnicity, without any check from academic freedom, pose a substantial threat of intellectual authoritarianism.

Academics' public credibility, which rests on the public perception that academics strive to meet traditional standards of professional competence in their teaching, scholarship, and public service, will also be lost. For centuries, scholars and teachers have worked to persuade society that knowledge will grow, and the public good will be served, by granting academic independence to individual professors and to universities. Society's willingness to give support to academic freedom is one of the remarkable achievements of humankind.

An ideology held by a significant subset of the faculty itself that both assaults the premises on which professional academic freedom rests and encourages the politicization of the university is a serious threat. It will drain the reservoirs of confidence, trust, and tolerance on which academic independence for the university and its scholars and teachers depend. It will also cause the society to be more vulnerable to the epidemics of mass irrationality and paranoia that recur through history. Ironically, the fundamentalists are probable long-run victims of their ideology and strategy. The concept of an apolitical university, even if a myth, serves most to protect radical academics on the left from threat of pressure and coercion from the conservative forces in society. At the height of 1960s student activism, Professor Noam Chomsky cautioned that

> one legacy of classical liberalism that we must fight to uphold, in the universities and without, is the commitment to a free marketplace of ideas.... Once the principle is established that coercion is legitimate [in the university], it is rather clear against whom it will be used. And the principle of legitimacy of coercion would

destroy the university as a serious institution; it would destroy its value to a free society. This must be recognized even in the light of the undeniable fact that the freedom falls far short of the ideal.[71]

Effectiveness of the Fundamentalist Academic Left

Threats to freedom of academic thought and speech have come from a variety of sources, boards of trustees and administrators, government, and the lay public in wartime. Newer to the scene are students, and newer still are significant numbers of the faculty itself. The current wave of zealotry is the first involving populist intimidation led principally by faculty. "The most dangerous threat to academic freedom," observes former AAUP president Paul Walters, "is that which comes from within the professoriat itself."[72]

The fundamentalist academic left is effective in many faculties, particularly in the humanities and social sciences. Its support, centered in the professoriat, cuts across student, staff, and administrative lines. In contrast to the generally poor organization of campus groups, many members of the fundamentalist academic left have a mission of achieving power to reshape the university; they can be a well-organized constituency on the campus. In this period of zealotry, the fundamentalists are silencing dissent by combining tactics successful during McCarthyism and the 1960s. They are doing what other campus groups rarely do, making public accusations of moral turpitude, threatening employment, implementing media campaigns, organizing students to protest, demonstrating, occupying buildings and offices, and disrupting university functions.[73]

The fundamentalist academic left has the tenacity to subject the targets of zealotry to vilification for extended periods. Radicals know, for example, that in a university environment with many open meetings, classrooms, and lectures, it is easy to set up continuing struggle meeting formats where a few zealots can degrade the target in concert.[74] This strategy wears down even the strongest of spirits. If the vilification continues for an extended period, an increasing number of colleagues desire appeasement and blame the victim of zealotry for dissenting and causing the unpleasantness.

The fundamentalists recognized that transforming and controlling the universities was a very long-term project. "After the Vietnam War," observes Jay Parini, an English professor at Middlebury College, "a lot of us [radicals] didn't just crawl back into our library cubicles; we stepped into academic positions. With the war over, our visibility was lost, and it seemed for awhile— to the unobservant—that we had disappeared. Now we have tenure, and the hard work of reshaping the universities has begun in earnest."[75] This hard work includes having the tenacity to devote energy to the day-to-day governance of the university—for example, service on appointments or diversity committees—over an extended period of years. Most other faculty will give some time to governance matters, but soon focus again on their own scholar-ship and teaching.[76] The hard work includes screening out applicants for ap-pointment or untenured faculty who don't have the proper ideology. City University of New York professor Louis Menand observes that "it is now regarded as legitimate by some professors to argue that the absence of a politi-cal intention or a multicultural focus in another professor's work constitutes prima facie disqualification for professional advancement."[77] John Patrick Diggins, author of *The Rise and Fall of the American Left,* pointed out in late 1992 that when liberals like him controlled appointments two decades ago, they opened the doors to the radical left in the cause of intellectual diversity. But "you weren't like us, you have closed the door behind you."[78]

Describing the situation at Harvard Law School, journalist Peter Collier observes that the critical legal studies scholars were organized from the time of their first national conference in 1977. They had an agenda—"think glo-bally, act locally"—and focused on obtaining control at the law school by becoming active in the student selection process, pushing for bright students with activist backgrounds, and in the faculty hiring committee, pushing for more critical legal studies scholars. Professor Charles Fried, former solicitor general in the Reagan Administration, observed that the Crits had a tremen-dous advantage because "they always act strategically."[79]

Past waves of zealotry in this century have lasted from three to ten years. McCarthyism ended when radical politicians lost political power. The 1960s student activism ended as student radicals graduated. The tenured fundamen-talist academic left is far more entrenched than the politicians of the 1950s or the student radicals of the 1960s. Before his resignation in 1992, Yale Presi-dent Benno Schmidt cautioned, "I believe the pressures to subvert the essen-tial academic character of universities are much greater elsewhere, and will become much greater at Yale."[80] John Gray, a fellow at Oxford University, predicts that "academic leftism will become even more virulent as it becomes increasingly localized in...universities...making Western universities the Western institutions with the least freedom of speech and expression."[81] The entrenchment of the fundamentalist academic left in tenured positions, and their tenacity in using a wide spectrum of tactics against dissenting inquiry and speech over a protracted period of years, may prove more effective in eliminating dissent than any previous wave of zealotry.

The dominance of the left on many faculties in the humanities and the social sciences is a tribute to the effectiveness and tenacity of the fundamen-talist academic left. This dominance means that the debate on critical issues is skewed. For example, in Stanford professor Mark Kelman's experience, "Most law school centrists have been remarkably silent and remarkably marginal as debates swirl about them."[82] Potential dissenters know that a significant degree of monolithic thought from the left is inherently danger-ous for rights of academic freedom. The risk is high because few people will vigorously defend the rights of others to speak thoughts for which the listener has no sympathy.

Because this is the first period of zealotry involving populist intimidation led principally by faculty, the response to coercive tactics is even more confused than earlier periods. Professional academic freedom was designed originally to protect against zealotry from outside the walls. In the current wave, some faculty zealots granted professional academic freedom are abusing it. A collegium like a faculty has extreme difficulty dealing with colleagues who engage in professional misconduct. Many colleagues believe it to be better to swallow as many offenses as possible in order to avoid confrontation and its risks,[83] and also to preserve the maximum amount of professional independence and autonomy.[84] The strong tendency is for collegia like faculties to acquiesce in collegial misconduct.[85] This strong tendency to acquiesce in collegial misconduct means faculty zealots are virtually unchecked. This adds to their effectiveness in the current wave of zealotry. The next chapter explores the outer limits of professional academic freedom for the faculty zealot.

Meeting the Challenge of Zealotry

Professional academic freedom requires that the faculty foster and publicly defend the academic freedom of colleagues. At many institutions in past periods of zealotry, the faculty as a collegial body and the administration have repeatedly failed both to address the zealotry and to protect academic freedom. They fail to give public support to the targets of the zealotry. The faculty response of acquiescence in coercive tactics has been the ballast of the ideological zealotry in each wave. The extraordinary facility with which faculty accommodate the coercive tactics of zealots is the most significant finding of Shrecker's study of McCarthyism and this book.

The causes of this failure are not clear. This chapter explored several tentative explanatory hypotheses.

1. Inadequate preparation. Many professors seem unaware that waves of zealotry occur regularly in American higher education and that the coercive tactics used are predictable. They also seem uninformed about the rights and duties of professional academic freedom, particularly the faculty's duty to defend publicly the academic freedom of competent academic speech.
2. Ambivalence about publicly defending academic freedom for competent opposing ideas.
3. Fear that public support for the accused will damage reputation and career.
4. Reprisal based on personal grudges.
5. Common traits of academics that inhibit public support for the target of zealotry include:

a. desire for the quiet life of scholarship;
b. aversion to conflict;
c. rationalization of inaction in the face of duty; and
d. excessive tolerance of coercive tactics.

The duty to foster and defend the academic freedom of colleagues is a critical cornerstone on which the rights of professional academic freedom rest. There will continue to be zealots and waves of zealotry. The professoriat created professional academic freedom to address this reality. The doctrine fails in the face of zealotry because of the repeated failure of many faculty to address the zealotry of the time and to give public support to defend the academic freedom of zealotry's targets.

Faculties must both explore the causes for this repeated failure and take reasonable corrective steps to address the causes. Effective remedies seem practicable for only some of the causes proposed earlier.

Education may be the simplest and best corrective. All faculty members should have an understanding of the history of professional academic freedom, its rationale, its critical importance to the profession and to the university, its rights and its correlative duties, particularly the duty to defend academic freedom. They should also understand that there will always be strong ideologies and zealots, that waves of zealotry have occurred regularly but the direction from which the next zealotry would come was hard to predict, that zealots attacked targets far beyond the circle of clear heretics for political advantage, and that similar coercive tactics have been in each wave. Finally, they should understand that being a bystander while zealots suppress the academic freedom of a colleague is not harmless. It is an act that condones the suppression. In light of the specific correlative duty to defend academic freedom, indifference in these circumstances is complicity.

Presently, socialization of novitiates into the ethics and traditions of the academic profession occurs essentially without formal instruction. The professoriat assumes that academic tradition is passed by osmosis. At least novitiate lawyers and doctors must study and know their code of ethics. Student doctors also directly observe instructor-doctors in almost all aspects of practicing professional life, and are regularly critiqued on technical, judgment, and moral error. Graduate students normally observe their professors in a narrow range of professional activities, with limited feedback on the students' own performance in practice situations.[86] New professors have very limited or no understanding of the theory and practice of professional academic freedom. Without any education of novitiates to the profession, the remembered tradition grows weaker and weaker. This is especially true given the vast and rapid growth of the academic profession during the second half of this century.[87]

This education of the professoriat must occur at the faculty or department level with the encouragement and support of the university. The preamble to the 1966 Statement on Professional Ethics points out that "in the enforcement of ethical standards, the academic profession differs from those of law and medicine, whose associations act to assure the integrity of members engaged in private practice. In the academic profession the individual institution of higher learning provides this assurance."[88] In 1973, the joint AAC and AAUP Commission on Academic Tenure emphasized more specifically that "the faculty of the institution, therefore, must be the source for the definition and clarification of standards of professional conduct and must take the lead in ensuring that these standards are enforced."[89]

Therefore, the simplest corrective is to design an educational program on professional academic freedom for all professors within each faculty or department. Once all existing professors have participated, the program would continue each year for new professors. Each faculty or department should also discuss annually the state of academic freedom within the faculty. Chapter 12 presents a more detailed proposal for a faculty educational program.

The most important benefit of education about professional academic freedom is that faculty members will understand the fundamental importance of academic freedom to each professor and the university. If academic freedom is compromised and lost, teaching, scholarship, and the university itself are without legitimacy in a liberal intellectual system. Faculty members should realize that academic freedom is never finally won. It must be continually defended in each generation.

With an awareness both of the critical importance of professional academic freedom to legitimate teaching and scholarship and of the faculty's individual and collegial duty to defend academic freedom, more faculty members may be willing to give public support to the targets of zealotry regardless of disagreement. The thinking of faculty members, Ladd and Lipset found, is exceptionally ideological. The goal of an educational program on academic freedom within a faculty is to foster an ideological commitment to academic freedom that offsets professors' tendency not to defend publicly the right of others to speak views with which the listener has no sympathy. The educational program should note in particular the dangers to academic freedom implicit in good intentions. Justice Louis Brandeis cautioned over sixty-five years ago that experience should teach us to be most on guard to protect liberty when the reasons given to restrict it are beneficent. We are naturally alert to repel invasion of liberty by the evil minded. "The greatest dangers to liberty lurk in insidious encroachment by men of zeal, well-meaning but without understanding."[90] Veteran faculty members should ask themselves whether they have ever spoken up to defend the academic freedom of those holding competent opposing views. The more a faculty member's ideas are advantaged by the coercive tactics of zealots, the higher is this duty.

Armed with an understanding of professional academic freedom, targeted faculty members will know that the response to ideological zealotry cannot be to seek the supremacy of their own opposing ideology within the university. The defense must insist on the primacy of professional academic freedom over any political agenda.

Insisting on the primacy of professional academic freedom will focus debate on the professional competence of the opposing ideas. "We can learn to live with each another," University of Pennsylvania professor Alan Kors comments, "as long as we insist that our colleagues' work be reasoned and analytically rigorous.... What should make things illegitimate, in terms of the university, is the departure from the world of reasoned discourse, rigorous arguments, rigorous analysis, and the intelligent relationship of data to theory."[91]

Robert M. Hutchins, a former president of the University of Chicago, argued that the excesses of McCarthyism in the universities could have been avoided if administrators had relied on "the standard of competence." This would have protected the university against teachers who sought to indoctrinate students because such a teacher would have been incompetent, and a standard of competence would have protected a competent professor against the university regardless of the professor's ideology. Making merit incidental in the assessment of faculty erodes academic freedom, as the principle of competence is the first line of defense in the protection of academic freedom. Lionel Lewis points out that "the failure to use universalistic criteria in the decision-making process has long been associated with infringements of academic freedom."[92] When political criteria became the reason for retention or dismissal, then academic freedom must keep retreating to unprincipled positions which cannot be held under sustained attack.

Writing about McCarthyism, Ellen Schrecker observes that academics were no more courageous than others in standing up to zealotry.[93] Speaking about the current zealotry, former Harvard President Derek Bok concurs.[94] A case can be made that academics are in fact less courageous than others in a period of zealotry. In either case, a simple comparison of the response of academics and nonacademics to the tactics of zealotry fails to recognize that academics, in contrast to others, have a specific correlative duty as individuals and as a collegial body to defend academic freedom. A simple comparison also fails to consider that tenured academics have the considerable protection of academic due process, the purpose of which is to strengthen faculty resolve to speak up by reducing employment risk. If academics have no more courage than others under these conditions, it is a double disappointment. They are failing to meet a specific correlative duty under conditions of employment security far greater than that enjoyed by others in the society. If nothing else, education about professional academic freedom may lead to more faculty willingness to speak up in defense of academic freedom out of embarrassment over these failures.

Knowledge that the entire faculty has discussed the collegial duty to defend professional academic freedom may create a feeling that reciprocity will occur. Information that most periods of zealotry historically originated from outside the university, that waves have occurred roughly every fifteen to twenty years, that zealots attacked not only clear heretics, but also others for political advantage, and that during any period, it was not possible to predict the direction from which the next wave would come, may lead to a sense that faculty members should all hang together to defend academic freedom or they may all hang separately in different waves of zealotry.

Lazarsfeld and Thielens in their 1955 study of social scientists found that many faculty members preferred to be cautious and not to defend academic freedom if he or she believed they could escape unnoticed. However, if the peer culture supported academic freedom, the cautious professor had a greater tendency to give public support to academic freedom.

> Still, for those concerned with the integrity of the professoriate, ours is an important result. A professional group such as a college faculty is characterized by frequent and continuous face-to-face contact. If, in such a group, there is a tradition of freedom, this climate of opinion can hold in line many who would otherwise break down under attacks from the broader community. From a policy point of view, then, any strengthening of such local traditions of academic freedom may have disproportionate influence on individual attitudes.[95]

It is critical to create a tradition of peer pressure to support academic freedom.

Although during any period of zealotry the direction of the next wave has been difficult to predict, the coercive tactics employed were more predictable. Faculty understanding of the tactics of zealotry in the past will reduce surprise, bewilderment, confusion, and fear if a wave of zealotry occurs in the future. Information about the long history of efforts directed at appeasement of zealots and the disastrous results of those efforts should challenge the common assumption that placating zealots will secure peace.

During McCarthyism, President Borgmann of the University of Vermont was in the best position to protect the targets of zealotry at his university, but he did not oppose the popular sentiment and the political pressure. David Holmes writes that Borgmann

> was a well-intentioned, moral man caught in a situation that ultimately overwhelmed him. In hindsight, we see that Borgmann and his university colleagues were unprepared by experience and knowledge to act with greater philosophical clarity and moral courage.

> Never again do we want to hear a man of President Borgmann's fiber and goodwill lament, as he did to Novikoff a few years later, "I have lost more than you did."[96]

The lesson, Holmes concludes, is that each generation of political and educational leaders needs to absorb the lessons of the past if our universities are to flourish.[97]

An educational program on professional academic freedom achieves success if only a few administrators and faculty members decide to give active public support to targets of zealotry. A few colleagues giving dependable and consistent public support may be sufficient for the target to hang on until a wave of zealotry wanes. The public support of a dean or university president may make the difference alone. Allies of a target who is tenured can use the AAUP's academic due process rights for a termination proceeding to help bog down formal efforts to force the target out of the university. A central mission of those defending academic freedom during a wave of zealotry is to buy time until the period passes.

Those professors and administrators who choose to address zealotry publicly and to defend academic freedom should draw some strength from stories of courage in the past. For example, during McCarthyism, Lionel Lewis finds that academic authorities at Antioch College, Yale University, the University of Chicago, IIT, MIT, the University of Rochester, and the University of Connecticut stood firm on evaluating only competence and ethical conduct, not the ideology of those accused.[98] Such stories teach by example to help others to examine their capacity to affirm what they profess to hold dear.

A professor or administrator who decides to speak publicly to address zealotry and to defend academic freedom should carefully think through how to do so. Such speech may in all likelihood cause the speaker to become a target of the zealots. Chapter 11 explores effective responses by the target of zealotry. Much of that chapter is relevant also to anyone speaking publicly to defend academic freedom.

A few points bear special emphasis. First, any faculty member defending academic freedom should make the case publicly that a wave of zealotry is occurring and that it involves issues of major importance. The communities both inside and outside of the walls must come to understand the zealots' ideology and tactics, how the tactics affect academic freedom, and what the costs are to that community. Focus on professional competence, ethical conduct and academic values. Hold the zealots' ideas to the test of professional competence. Point out failures to meet the common standards used to evaluate academic work. Hold coercive tactics to the correlative duties of professional competence and ethical conduct. Be openly and repeatedly vocal about failures to meet these duties.

Second, carefully observe professional standards of competence and ethical conduct. Do not engage in coercive conduct. Zealots will look for opportunities to bring any possible accusation of professional misconduct. Many Eastern European dissidents adopted a stance of calm, matter-of-fact decency in the face of suppression. Over time, undeserved suffering is a powerful moral force that may trigger sympathetic support.

Third, help the target to respond quickly and publicly to all accusations. Silence in the face of accusations will be characterized as admission. Repeated silence in the face of accusations is disastrous. Repeated, unrebutted false accusations will influence students, alumni, staff, colleagues and the community; the target becomes increasingly isolated.

Fourth, build an internal resistance group to help the target. The group can share information, organize meetings around a common strategy, help the target develop a record of what is happening, buy time through delaying tactics, and provide emotional support to the target.

Fifth, take small steps to stretch the limits of your confidence and strength. It is possible to overcome fear of intimidators through practice over time. Sixth, persevere. Relentless every day effort will bear fruit eventually.

Finally, during a wave of zealotry, take pride in what is defended, not discouragement from lost opportunities of articles not written or teaching improvements not done. Normally academics draw energy from classes taught well, speeches given and scholarship written, but during a period of zealotry, energy must flow from an awareness of the fundamental importance of academic freedom, what is put at risk, and what is defended. The university and the principles of academic freedom on which the university rests are among the most remarkable achievements of humankind. Academic freedom must be defended for the university to have legitimacy. A defense of academic freedom deserves great honor.

Notes

1. Fritz Machlup, *On Some Misconceptions Concerning Academic Freedom*, reprinted in ACADEMIC FREEDOM AND TENURE 177, 181-182 (Lewis Joughin ed., 1969).
2. Paul H. L. Walters, *Academic Freedom—Seventy Years Later*, ACADEME, Sept.-Oct. 1986, at 1a, 5a.
3. Ellen W. Schrecker, NO IVORY TOWER: MCCARTHYISM & THE UNIVERSITIES 300 (1986).
4. *See id.* at 308-09.
5. J. Burton Clark, THE ACADEMIC LIFE: SMALL WORLDS, DIFFERENT WORLD 134-139 (1987).
6. Schrecker, *supra* note 3, at 12-13. Writing in 1969, Harvard professor Nathan Glazer observed that when confronted with coercion of academic speech, many professors who believed it to be wrong had simply forgotten the answers necessary to defend academic freedom. Glazer urged the professoriat to remember what was forgotten and to answer publicly in order to defend the university. Nathan Glazer, REMEMBERING THE ANSWERS 293-94, 306 (1987).
7. Henry Rosovsky, HARVARD UNIVERSITY FACULTY OF ARTS AND SCIENCE, DEAN'S REPORT 1990-91, at 12 (1990-91).
8. Commission on Academic Tenure in Higher Education, FACULTY TENURE 41-43 (1973).
9. United States Department of Education, National Center for Education Statistics, DIGEST OF EDUCATION STATISTICS 173 (table 167) (1993). Ladd and Lipset report in their book, *The Divided Academy*, that the number of faculty in 1970 was 551,000 rather than the 450,000 for the same year reported in the Digest of Education Statistics (1993). Everett C. Ladd, Jr. & Seymour Martin Lipset, THE DIVIDED ACADEMY: PROFESSORS AND POLITICS 2 (1975).
10. *See* Judith Swazey, Karen Louis, Melissa Anderson, *The Ethical Training of Graduate Students Requires Serious and Continuing Attention*, CHRON. HIGHER EDUC., March 9, 1994, at B1, B2.

11. Jonathan Rauch, KINDLY INQUISITORS 19–22 (1993).
12. *Id.*
13. Everett C. Ladd, Jr. & Seymour Martin Lipset, THE DIVIDED ACADEMY: PROFESSORS AND POLITICS 199 (1975).
14. *Id.* at 42–44.
15. *Id.* at 51.
16. William Honan, *Ode to Academic Nastiness*, EDUC. SUPP. TO THE N.Y. TIMES, August 7, 1994, at 38.
17. Schrecker, *supra* note 3, at 311–12. Those professors opposed to communism did not generally speak up to protect academic freedom. Conservative professors reported only one-half the level of concern about threats to academic freedom as did liberal professors. *See* Paul Lazarsfeld & Wagner Thielens, THE ACADEMIC MIND: SOCIAL SCIENTISTS IN A TIME OF CRISIS 154 (1958).
18. Ladd and Lipset, *supra* note 13, at 210.
19. Seymour Martin Lipset, REBELLION IN THE UNIVERSITY 201, 198 (1976).
20. Ladd and Lipset, *supra* note 13, at 43–44.
21. Paul Lazarsfeld & Wagner Thielens, Jr., THE ACADEMIC MIND: SOCIAL SCIENTISTS IN A TIME OF CRISIS 104, 233–34 (1958).
22. *Id.*
23. Edward Shils, *Do We Still Need Academic Freedom?*, AM. SCHOLAR, Spring 1993, at 187, 205.
24. *See* C. Vann Woodward, *The Seige*, N.Y. REV., Sept. 25, 1986, at 8 (reviewing Ellen W. Schrecker, NO IVORY TOWER: MCCARTHYISM & THE UNIVERSITIES 312 (1986)).
25. Owen Lattimore, ORDEAL BY SLANDER 207–08 (1950).
26. William R. Brown, ACADEMIC POLITICS 10–11 (1982).
27. *Id.* at 19.
28. Judith Swazey, Karen Louis, Melissa Anderson, *The Ethical Training of Graduate Students Requires Serious and Continuing Attention*, CHRON. HIGHER EDUC., March 9, 1994, at B2.
29. Lazarsfeld & Thielens, *supra* note 21, at 104.
30. Machlup, *supra* note 1, at 181.
31. Ladd and Lipset, *supra* note 9, at 205.
32. Lazarsfeld & Thielens, *supra* note 21, at 233–34, 104.
33. *See* Dinesh D'Souza, ILLIBERAL EDUCATION: THE POLITICS OF RACE AND SEX ON CAMPUS 102, 104, 140, 243 (1991).
34. Samuel Oliner & Pearl M. Oliner, THE ALTRUISTIC PERSONALITY 257 (1988).
35. David Bryden, *Scholarship About Scholarship*, 63 COLO. L. REV. 641, 648 (1992).
36. Mark Tushnet, *Political Correctness: The Law and the Legal Academy*, 4 YALE J.L. & HUMAN. 127, 153–54 (1992).
37. *Id.* at 128.
38. The principles of professional academic freedom articulated in these interpretations and statements are applied in individual cases. The AAUP normally acts only upon the request of a faculty member who claims that his or her rights have been infringed. Approximately 800–1,000 complaints are processed each year. Formal investigation is undertaken only on those complaints that the AAUP's general secretary believes involve a *prima facie* denial of academic freedom. In the event an investigation is made, ultimately an ad hoc investigating committee prepares a report that is submitted to the Association's Committee A. These reports do not comprise a coordinated and systematic body of principle compa-

rable to that of a judicial tribunal. Each report is an elaborate factual presentation by a different ad hoc committee, and there is no practice of citing prior cases as precedent. The AAUP's docket has been overwhelmingly dominated by extramural utterance cases. Cases involving "conflicts over personal pride and prejudices, and charges of hierarchic insubordination and co-worker friction have for outnumbered disputes involving the content of teaching or research." The principal grievance in nearly all of these extramural utterance cases is the failure of the administration or lay governing board to follow procedural due process in putting the decision to recommend appropriate action in the first instance to a committee of the faculty. *See* American Association of University Professors, *Report of Committee A*, ACADEME, Sept.-Oct. 1993, at 36, 41; Thomas I. Emerson & David Haber, *Academic Freedom of the Faculty Member as Citizen*, 28 Law & Contemp. Probs. 525, 535 (1963); American Association of University Professors, *1943 Report of Committee A*, 28 AAUP. Bull. 15–17 (1943); Walter Metzger, *Profession and Constitution: Two Definitions of Academic Freedom in America* 66 TEX. L. REV. 1265, 1276 (1988).

39. David Holmes, STALKING THE ACADEMIC COMMUNIST 166–67 (1989).
40. *See id.* at 230.
41. Lionel Lewis, COLD WAR ON CAMPUS 277 (1988).
42. AAUP, *Joint Statement on Rights and Freedoms of Students* (1967), *reprinted in* AAUP, POLICY DOCUMENTS & REPORTS 153, 153–155 (1990).
43. AAUP, *A Statement of the Association's Council: Freedom and Responsibility*, *reprinted in* AAUP, POLICY DOCUMENTS & REPORTS 77, 77 (1990).
44. *Id.* at 78.
45. AAUP, *Statement on the "Political Correctness" Controversy*, ACADEME, Sept.-Oct. 1991, at 48. This statement was released to the press on July 30, 1991, and was originally printed in the Fall 1991 AAUP FOOTNOTES as a statement of the association. Miro Todorovich, *Whom Does AAUP Represent Today?*, MEASURE, Mar. 1992, at 1. The statement was not issued by a standing committee.
46. *"P.C." Debate Shows No Signs of Passing*, ACADEME, Nov.-Dec. 1991, at 8.
47. Courtney Leatherman, *AAUP Statement on the 'Political Correctness' Debate Causes a Furor*, CHRON. HIGHER EDUC., Dec. 4, 1991, at A-23.
48. AAUP Committee A on Academic Freedom, *Due Process in Sexual Harassment Complaints*, ACADEME, Sept.-Oct. 1991, at 47.
49. AAUP Committee A on Academic Freedom, *Report of Committee A 1991–92*, ACADEME, Sept.-Oct. 1992, at 47–48.
50. *Id.* at 49.
51. *Id.*
52. Letter from Jordan Kurland, AAUP Associate General Secretary, to Neil Hamilton (August 2, 1994).
53. Lionel Lewis, COLD WAR ON CAMPUS 277 (1988).
54. *See* the discussion in chapter two on sexual harassment investigations.
55. AAUP Committee A on Academic Freedom, *Academic Freedom and Sexual Harassment*, ACADEME, Sept.-Oct. 1994, at 64.
56. *Id.* at 64.
57. *Id.* at 65.
58. *Id.* at 66.
59. AAUP Committee T on College and University Governance, *Report On the Relationship of Faculty Governance to Academic Freedom*, ACADEME, July-August 1994, at 49.
60. *See* Joseph Salemi, *Political Correctness at Dallas Baptist University: The Firing of David Ayers and John Jeffrey*, MEASURE, Aug.-Sept. 1992, at 1, 11.

61. *Academic Freedom and Tenure: The University of New Hampshire*, ACADEME, Nov.-Dec. 1994, at 78.

62. The AAUP's record concerning investigation into violations of academic freedom attributable to the current zealotry appears to be stronger by 1992 when it investigated the dismissal of Professor Ayers and Dean Jeffrey from Dallas Baptist University. Prior to 1992, it is not clear whether the AAUP was investigating violations of academic freedom attributable to the current zealotry's tactics. For example, one account is that when the AAUP became aware of the situation at the University of Texas in 1991, the AAUP president's concern was not the threat to Professor Alan Gribben's academic freedom but the involvement of people outside the English Department in supporting Gribben in the controversy. *See* Katherine Mangan, *U of Texas's Postponement of Controversial Writing Course Kindles Debate Over Role of Outsiders in Academic Policy*, CHRON. HIGHER EDUC., Feb. 20, 1991, at A15, A19; Richard Bernstein, DICTATORSHIP OF VIRTUE 337 (1994). The AAUP did not investigate Gribben's situation although Gribben asserts that Ernst Benjamin, the AAUP's general secretary, declared that he was familiar with Gribben's case and publicly and repeatedly dismissed the notion that Gribben had been targeted by campus radicals. Alan Gribben, *Letter to the Editor*, N.Y. REV., Nov. 17, 1994, at 61. The AAUP's *Statement on the "Political Correctness" Controversy*, issued in 1991 at the time of the controversies in Texas, accused the critics of political correctness of harboring "an only partly concealed animosity toward equal opportunity" for "women and racial minorities on campus." Bernstein, *supra* at 338. Another account is that the AAUP took no side in the Texas battle and bears no responsibility in the matter. Louis Menand, *The Culture Wars*, N.Y. REV., Oct. 6, 1994, at 20.

63. Of course the waves of zealotry explored in this essay indicate that the aspiration of professional academic freedom has frequently been far greater than the reality. The doctrine has not stopped the suppression of competent academic thought. However, the test of a principle and its supporting institutional structure should not be the existence of failed expectation, but the degree of failed expectation relative to other institutional structures. Even with its failures, professional academic freedom and its supporting institutional structure have given more protection to freedom of academic inquiry and speech in the United States than the protection available in other countries like those of the former Soviet Union, where pure political and economic power have determined the right to speak. The existence of professional academic freedom at least provides a principled moral argument to minimize lay interference in academic speech. Georgetown Law Professor Peter Byrne cautions "that university life often fails to resemble these ideals has not destroyed their power to shape expectations and moderate behavior. So long as people perceive them to express a core of truth and an enduring potential, we shall have academic freedom in its traditional form; should they be abandoned as shams, higher education will change rapidly in directions we cannot predict." J. Peter Byrne, *Academic Freedom and Political Neutrality in Law Schools*, 43 J. OF LEGAL EDUC. 315, 318 (1993).

64. For example, after the University of New Hampshire's chapter of the AAUP stated that the criteria for harassment were too broad and would chill speech, an associate professor of women's studies at UNH circulated a letter stating:

> The (professor's association), indeed academia itself, has traditionally been dominated by white heterosexual men and the First Amendment and Academic Freedom (I'll call them FAF) have traditionally protected the rights of white, heterosexual men. Most of us are silenced by existing social condi-

tions before we get the power to speak out in any way where FAF might protect us. So forgive us if we don't get all teary-eyed about FAF. Perhaps to you its as sacrosanct as the flag or the national anthem, to us, strict construction of the First Amendment is just another yoke around our necks.

Suzanne Fields, *Crying 'Harassment' Like Little Boy Who Cried 'Wolf' Obscures the Real Thing*, SUN-SENTINEL (Fort Lauderdale), Jan. 27, 1994, at 19A.

65. Gertrude Himmelfarb, ON LOOKING INTO THE ABYSS: UNTIMELY THOUGHTS ON CULTURE AND SOCIETY 158-59 (1994).

66. Stephen Carter, *Academic Tenure and "White Male" Standards: Some Lessons from the Patent Law*, 100 YALE L.J. 2065, 2067 (1991).

67. Shils, *supra* note 23, at 209.

68. Betty Jean Craige, RECONNECTION 123 (1988).

69. Louis Menand, *The Future of Academic Freedom*, ACADEME, May-June 1993, at 11, 15-16.

70. *Id.* at 16.

71. Noam Chomsky, *The Function of the University in a Time of Crisis*, in Robert M. Hutchins and Mortimer J. Adler, eds., THE GREAT ISSUES TODAY 59 (1969). *See also*, Seymour Martin Lipset, REBELLION IN THE UNIVERSITY 210 (1976) (the myth of the apolitical university serves to protect unpopular minorities, that is, radicals).

72. Paul H. L. Walters, Presidential Address to the 72nd Annual Meeting of the AAUP, *reprinted in* 72 ACADEME 1a (1986).

73. *See generally* Alan Kors, Interviewed by Carol Iannone, *Thought Reform and Education: A View from the University of Pennsylvania*, ACAD. QUESTIONS, Fall 1988, at 75, 83; Joseph Salemi, *Behind the Curtains: TDC and UDI at Hunter College*, MEASURE, May 1992, at 1, 2.

74. *See* Jeanne J. Kirkpatrick, *My Experience with Academic Intolerance*, ACAD. QUESTIONS, Fall 1989, at 21-23.

75. Jay Parini, *Academic Conservatives Who Decry 'Politicization' Show Staggering Naivete About Their Own Biases*, CHRON. HIGHER EDUC., Dec. 7, 1988, at B1-B2.

76. "The traditionalist faculty tend to shun committee work as a waste of time, but many of those pushing for radical changes in the university actually like to fill their days with meetings." Alan Wolfe, *The New Class Comes Home*, 60 PARTISAN REVIEW 729, 734 (1993).

77. Louis Menand, *What are Universities For? The Real Crisis on Campus is One of Identity*, HARPER'S, December 1991, at 47, 52.

78. Letter to editor, *PC's Oppressive Hold on American Studies*, CHRON. HIGHER EDUC., December 16, 1992, at B7, B8. For example, work on themes of race/class/gender has become a virtual prerequisite for nomination to the Council of the American Historical Association. Alonzo L. Hamby, *Muddled Posturing by the Historical Association*, CHRON. HIGHER EDUC., Feb. 16, 1994, at B1 (quoting Professor Jerry Muller). The fundamentalist academic left is building on a tendency already apparent twenty-five years ago. Ladd and Lipset discovered that the degree of field related differentiation in political attitude was "really quite extraordinary." Ladd and Lipset, *supra* note 13, at 56, 368-69. They concluded that discipline differentiates faculty to such a high degree that there is not a politics of academia, there is a politics of each discipline. *Id.* at 92. Ladd and Lipset attribute this discipline differentiation to several factors: (1) a given discipline selectively recruits people with views consistent with dominant political orientation; (2) activist students are attracted to disciplines dominated by the

left; and (3) discipline socialization causes those with conflicting views to leave voluntarily. *Id.* at 67-70, 106.

79. Peter Collier, *Blood on the Charles*, VANITY FAIR, Oct. 1992, at 144, 148.
80. Benno Schmidt Jr., Address at Yale Baccalaureate Exercises (May 26, 1991).
81. John Gray, *Utopian Academics and the Collapse of Communism*, ACAD. QUESTIONS, Winter 1991-92, at 66, 69.
82. Mark Kelman, *Emerging Centrist Liberalism*, 43 FLA. L. REV. 417, 444 (1991).
83. Eliot Freidson, DOCTORING TOGETHER: A STUDY OF PROFESSIONAL SOCIAL CONTROL 213-14 (1975).
84. *Id.* at 243.
85. *Id.* at 237-39.
86. Robert T. Blackburn, *The Professor and His Ethics*, 53 AAUP BULL. 416, 418 (1967).
87. *See* Commission on Academic Tenure in Higher Education, *supra* note 8.
88. AAUP, *Statement on Professional Ethics*, *reprinted in* AAUP, POLICY DOCUMENTS & REPORTS 75 (1990).
89. Commission on Academic Tenure in Higher Education, FACULTY TENURE 42 (1973).
90. Alan Dershowitz, CONTRARY TO POPULAR OPINION 88-89 (1992).
91. Alan Kors, Interviewed by Carol Iannone, *Thought Reform and Education: A View from the University of Pennsylvania*, ACAD. QUESTIONS, Fall 1988, at 75, 86.
92. Lionel Lewis, COLD WAR ON CAMPUS 274-75 (1988).
93. Schrecker, *supra* note 3, at 300.
94. Derek Bok, HARVARD PRESIDENT'S REPORT 12 (1991).
95. Lazarsfeld & Thielens, *supra* note 21, at 104-06.
96. David Holmes, STALKING THE ACADEMIC COMMUNIST 250 (1989).
97. *Id.*
98. Lewis, *supra* note 92, at 266.

10

The Outer Limits of Professional Academic Freedom for the Faculty Zealot

Faculty members, through their research and teaching or other life experience, may develop a strong ideology, defined earlier as a dogmatically held set of beliefs about the world and the moral principles that ought to guide it. While dogmatically held beliefs may limit a faculty member's ability to discover and disseminate knowledge, they do not necessarily result in the coercion of others' academic speech. The ideologue may simply advocate her or his ideas with great passion, intensity, and conviction.

Extreme proponents of an ideology may also choose to embrace zealotry in service of the ideology. Such zealotry utilizes tactics of harassment and intimidation, particularly the labeling of disagreement as an act of moral turpitude, to promote the ideology and to eliminate heretical thought and speech. Historically such zealotry often initially came from outside the walls to suppress professors' academic inquiry and speech. The professoriat developed professional academic freedom early in this century to address these threats.

The unique aspect of the current fundamentalism from the academic left is the phenomenon of a significant number of zealots within the professoriat itself. They are using a variety of coercive tactics successful in suppressing dissent during McCarthyism and the student activism of the 1960s. This creates confusion because a peer review system is very poorly equipped to deal with violations of professional academic freedom that arise from within the faculty rather than from administrators. The violation does not appear on its face to be like the conventional case involving violation of academic due process by an administration. In addition, a faculty committee would rarely conclude that other faculty members were improperly motivated.[1] This fundamental confusion is compounded when a faculty zealot claims that professional academic freedom protects his or her coercive conduct. The claim in its strongest form is that professional academic freedom means immunity from employment consequences for whatever a professor says or does, particularly in intramural or extramural speech, unconstrained by duties of professional competence and ethics. The confusion among faculty, administrators, and boards of trustees created by arguments of this type has, in this wave of zeal-otry, exacerbated the faculty's usual public response of silent acquiescence to coercive tactics. This chapter explores this confusion in the context of the rights and cor-relative duties of professional academic freedom. The chapter applies the correlative duties to coercive conduct by faculty zealots to determine the point where coercive tactics ripen into conduct that does not meet standards of pro-fessional competence or ethics. The chapter proposes both aspirational con-duct goals for all faculty members and mandatory principles of professional conduct, enforced by penalties, that address extreme coercion by faculty zeal-ots. The chapter finally considers the role of the governing board if the faculty fails to meet its correlative duty to require professional conduct.

Harassing and Abusive Conduct Beyond the Limits of Professional Academic Freedom

Borrowing from McCarthyism and 1960s Student Activism

Faculty zealots currently combine the successful coercive tactics of McCarthyism with those of the student activism of the 1960s. Similar to McCarthyism, the chief weapon against competent disagreement with the or-thodoxy of the fundamentalist academic left is public accusation of moral turpitude. Accusations may be based on conjecture, gossip, hearsay, the twist-ing of any ambiguity, half truths by omission, exaggeration, or even beyond the advocate's morality, misrepresentation. Misinformation may be constantly repeated to create adverse perceptions of the accused. Public accusations of bigotry are often followed by adverse media attention. Such accusations lead to hostility and ostracism from many faculty and students.

Also borrowing from McCarthyism, faculty zealots sometimes initiate in-ternal and external investigations of the accusations of bigotry. These investi-gations may lead to a tribunal. An investigation gives a greater appearance of validity to the accusations. It imposes severe costs of time, energy, financial resources, and psychological exhaustion on the accused. Without indemnity for counsel fees, the accused may be driven quickly to financial hardship. Accusations of moral turpitude and investigations diminish career opportu-nity in terms of initial appointment, promotion, grants, prestigious public ser-vice, and appointments at other faculties. They are particularly devastating to untenured faculty and students.

Student zealots from the fundamentalist academic left in addition borrow tactics from the student activism of the 1960s. They may suppress competent academic inquiry and speech with which they disagree by disruption of speeches or classes. They may also occupy administrative offices seeking to force the administration to accept their agenda.

Analyzing the coercive tactics of the fundamentalist academic left in the current period of zealotry, former Harvard President Derek Bok distinguishes suppression of competent academic inquiry and speech through public accusations of bigotry and social ostracism from suppression as a consequence of deliberate attempts to harass professors and to disrupt speech. With respect to public accusations of bigotry and social ostracism to suppress competent academic speech, Bok suggests that the university encourage faculty and students to recognize that learning will only prosper if they refrain from imposing their own ideas by coercion, ridicule, ostracism, or other forms of intimidation. Bok believes the university should take a much stronger position regarding deliberate harassment and disruption and prohibit and penalize them.[2]

President Bok's comments, while sound, do not articulate the specific duties of professional academic freedom that apply to these tactics. Bok also does not define clearly how compliance with the specific duties of professional academic freedom is to be enforced. The task is to define clearly both the correlative duties that apply to these tactics and the means by which such duties will be enforced.

Limiting Duties in the 1940 and 1966 AAUP
Statements and Academic Tradition

Some academics understand professional academic freedom to mean immunity for whatever a professor says or does, unconstrained by correlative duties. This perverts the original understanding of professional academic freedom. University employers granted rights of freedom from lay interference to academic speech on the condition that individual scholars and teachers would meet correlative duties of professional competence and ethics and that the collegial group would act to enforce those duties. The liberty of intramural and extramural utterance in particular was never unbridled. For example, the founders of the AAUP, Columbia professor Walter Metzger observes, held that professors reached the limiting line of impropriety long before they approached the boundary between legally protected speech and slanderous utterance.[3]

The 1940 statement provides that professional academic freedom "carries with it duties correlative with rights," but the definition of the general term "duties" is only partly developed in the 1940 statement itself. The definition of "duties" is developed further in other AAUP statements. The task here is to pull together all those components of the definition of "duties" that define the outer limits of coercive conduct by the faculty zealot.

With respect to the right of academic freedom for extramural utterance, the 1940 statement mandates specific correlative duties. The teacher shall: (1) at all times be accurate; (2) exercise appropriate restraint; and (3) show respect for the opinions of others.

With respect to the teaching, research, and intramural utterance, the 1940 statement imposes a specific duty that teachers "should be careful not to introduce into their teaching controversial matter which has no relation to their subject." It provides also that tenured professors may be dismissed for adequate cause which may include charges of incompetence or conduct involving moral turpitude. The AAUP's Interpretive Comments to the 1940 statement, adopted in 1970, provide that the "special responsibilities" of university faculty are defined further in other policy statements, particularly the 1966 Statement on Professional Ethics.

The 1966 statement defines the duty of professional competence in general terms. It includes the general obligations to be an effective teacher and scholar and to hold before students the best scholarly and ethical standards of the discipline. The statement specifically mandates that professors shall practice intellectual honesty. The traditions of the academic profession further define "intellectual honesty" and "the best scholarly...standards of the discipline."

1. The most fundamental component duty implicit in the broad definition of professional competence is honesty and accuracy in the gathering, recording, and use of evidence. The major canon of academic work has been accurate and honest investigation and reporting of evidence. The cardinal sin is falsification. The 1940 statement mandates accuracy for extramural utterance; accuracy was simply assumed for teaching, research, and intramural utterance.
2. A closely related duty is the gathering of evidence through thorough inquiry.
3. A third closely related duty is the presentation of opposing evidence and argument without misrepresentation or distortion.

The 1966 statement is more specific in further defining duties of ethical conduct. Those components of the duty of ethical conduct that define the outer limits of coercion by a faculty zealot include these obligations:

1. not to harass any student or colleague;
2. not to discriminate against any student or colleague;
3. to strive to be objective in professional judgment of students and colleagues;
4. in the exchange of criticism and ideas, to show due respect for opinions of others; and
5. to defend the academic freedom of students and colleagues.

The 1970 statement by the AAUP's Council, Freedom and Responsibility, emphasizes in addition the duties:

6. to respect the dignity of others and to acknowledge their right to express differing opinions;

7. not to express dissent or grievances in ways either that disrupt classes or speeches or that significantly impede the functions of the institution; and

8. not to force students by the authority inherent in the instructional role to make particular personal choices as to political action.

The 1940 and 1966 statements provide that the faculty, as a collegial body, has a duty to determine when individual professors fail to meet their responsibilities. The question is how the faculty should approach the task of defining and enforcing these duties so that the outer limits of coercive conduct will be clear to the faculty zealot.

Applying the Duties to Harassing and Abusive Conduct

President Bok's distinction between suppression of academic speech through public accusations of moral turpitude and social ostracism and suppression as a consequence of deliberate attempts to harass professors and to disrupt speech suggests a useful structure of analysis. The correlative duties of professional competence and ethical conduct applicable to the coercive tactics of faculty zealots discussed above must be reformulated to facilitate our analysis. Correlative with the rights of professional academic freedom are duties:

1. to respect the dignity of others and to acknowledge their right to express differing opinions;

2. in the exchange of criticism or ideas, to show due respect for the opinions of others;

3. not to harass students or colleagues (harass means to badger with ridicule, false accusations, ostracism or other forms of intimidation);

4. not to use the authority inherent in the instructional role either to introduce partisan matters having no relation to the subject or to impose political choices on students;

5. to gather evidence through thorough inquiry;

6. to be accurate and honest in the gathering, recording and use of evidence;

7. to present opposing evidence and argument without distortion or misrepresentation; and

8. not to disrupt speeches or classes or to significantly impede the functions of the university.

Enforcement of the first three duties using significant penalties is problematic because ambiguity in the meaning of the duties combined with significant penalty will chill some competent academic speech that professional academic freedom is intended to protect. There is less risk that reasonable enforcement of the last five duties will inhibit competent scholarly inquiry or discourse. This chapter examines the first three as a group and then analyzes the last five duties in subsequent sections.

Civility and respect for the rights and dignity of others. It is critical for an academic community to understand and to foster the basic virtue of civility, defined as a genuine respect for the rights and dignity of others that are conceived as equal to one's own. The history of the concept of civility underscores its importance today. Several centuries ago, classical liberalism faced a dilemma in pursuing the division of church and state. The objective was to create conditions amenable to diversity of thought and belief. However, as diversity rather than unity became more common in medieval political and social life, with it came perpetual discord. The people were not accustomed to disagreement on fundamental issues. Indeed, premodern Christians were nearly unanimous in holding that charity demanded coercion of others in matters of faith. A Christian was obliged to do as much as possible to propagate the true faith and to uproot false ones, by force if necessary. This included the proscription and punishment of false teaching and severe punishment of heretics.[4]

Against this background, Professor Clifford Orwin writes, "The concept of civility in the sense of genuine respect for the rights and dignity of others that are equal to one's own, emerged." Professor Orwin describes civility as non-Christian but post-Christian. Civility (or tolerance) was the means by which its inventors sought to reconcile the requirements of civil tranquility with the existence of rival Christian sects. Its inventors presented civility not as a rejection but as the perfection of Christianity.[5] "A modern Christian is precisely one who accepts the correctness of civility as an interpretation of charity. He [or she] agrees...that charity forbids coercion in matters of faith."[6] A core of Christian charity thus became liberal tolerance of rival Christian sects, and even of the presence of non-Christian sects, so long as these sects were themselves tolerant.[7]

Professional academic freedom is built on this classical liberal tradition of civility. During the nineteenth century, higher education in the United States shifted to focus from essentially religious and moral training to a much broader intellectual inquiry that presupposes a progressive conception of knowledge. Academics came to understand that it is the possibility of falsifying every certainty in science or in social life that is the mechanism of advancing knowledge. The essential requirement for this progressive conception of knowledge within the university itself is free discourse among competent academic professionals. Free discourse among competent academic professionals occurs in an environment without coercion and intimidation of competent ideas and speech. Coercion and intimidation will thwart the possibility of falsifying certainties and the improvement of knowledge. Thus, intellectual discourse in the university community also requires civility in the sense of genuine respect for the rights and dignity of others in the discourse that are equal to one's own, and a mutual willingness to defend these rights. Each participant is to accord others the dignity appropriate to a bearer of equal rights.

The university community will then be one where competent speakers can disagree, see the other point of view, reconsider, and honor disagreement.

Faculty and students must develop the skill of argument without rancor and disagreement without personal invective. They must be able to argue and stake out positions without having their morality and character impugned. If this is not the case, then critical discussion of certain issues will be forbidden or curtailed; and the university will fail in its mission of advancing and disseminating knowledge.

Civility in the sense of genuine respect for the rights and dignity of others in the conversation that are equal to one's own serves more than just the progressive conception of knowledge. It is also a critical virtue for a culture whose metaphor is a mosaic. Substantial equality in a pluralistic society with fundamental cultural, social, and political differences can only occur in a state of civility or mutual respect for the rights and dignity of others.

For example, an environment without civility will tend to favor men. Aggression will be more successful. No matter how aggression is measured or observed, as a group males score more highly than females.[8] Men and women tend to have different beliefs about aggression. Women report more guilt and anxiety as a consequence of aggression, more vigilance about the harm that aggression causes its victims, and more concern about the danger that their aggression might bring to themselves.[9] Carol Gilligan notes that combative verbal tactics tend to be a male strategy of harassment and intimidation.[10] An environment condoning anger and combative verbal tactics like personal insults, rudeness, and violence of rhetoric will be conducive to male domination. Students and other vulnerable groups will also be at risk in an environment without civility.[11]

We are currently in a period where differences of view exist that are every bit as fundamental as the differences apparent centuries ago. When there are acute differences of opinion, each group should assume that it is not going to convince the other in the short run, but seek common ground where all can stand and from which the groups can work together. This is the common ground of civility.

It is critical for a diverse academic community to honor academic freedom's correlative duties: (1) to respect the dignity of others and to acknowledge their right to express differing opinions; (2) to show due respect for the opinions of others in the exchange of criticism of ideas; and (3) not to harass any student or colleague. However, ambiguity in the meaning of these duties is reason for caution in their enforcement. The process of falsifying certainties and advancing knowledge inevitably will demonstrate flaws in some cherished ideas and certainties. The process will also inevitably show some academics' teaching, research, intramural and extramural utterance not to be professionally competent. The process of questioning the certainties of the time or the professional competence of a colleague inevitably does offend the sensitivity of those whose certainties or competence are questioned. They will feel that they have not been accorded due respect; they may feel harassed because their cherished belief or professional competence is assaulted; their dignity is affronted. During the current period of zealotry, if they are members of a status group, they may charge that any ideas or speech that victims perceive as insensitive should be prohibited and that assessment of professional competence of victims is itself a form of oppression and harassment.

Jonathan Rauch emphasizes that respect for the rights and dignity of others does not mean that their ideas are entitled to respectability. A liberal intellectual system only validates and grants the respectability of knowledge to ideas that have been thoroughly checked by public criticism. Ideally, critical checkers would focus criticism on ideas and not engage in ad hominem attack on individuals. Civility and professional courtesy would be the rule.

> We would all like to think that knowledge would be separated from hurt. We would like to think that painful but useful and thus "legitimate" criticism is objectively distinguishable from criticism which is merely ugly and hurtful.... But what we would like to think is not so: the only such distinction is in the eye of the beholder. The fact is that even the most "scientific" criticism can be horribly hurtful, devastatingly so.... In the pursuit of knowledge many people—probably most of us at one time or another—will be hurt, and this is a reality no amount of wishing or regulating can ever change."[12]

The AAUP's Committee A, responsible for the investigation of violations of professional academic freedom, recognizes these dangers:

> Experience demonstrates that, to be free, speech requires breathing space. Yet the difficulty of defining categories of prohibited speech without impinging on speech that should be free is notorious. The inevitable openness of the terms defining a prohibition invites complaints against speech expressing ideas regarded as repugnant. It permits overzealous students, faculty and administrators—moved either by personal conviction or by political need—to apply pressure that seeks to silence those who express such views.... In these circumstances, the *threat* of disciplinary proceedings inevitably exercises a chilling effect, inhibiting speech to which an academic community cannot legitimately be closed (emphasis added).[13]

It is extremely difficult to decide when particular academic speech is offensive enough to warrant a penalty or to weigh the degree of offensiveness against the potential value of the communication. The risk of significant penalty on speech for violation of ambiguous standards will lead to excessive caution that will chill some competent academic speech that professional academic freedom is intended to protect. Justice Brennan observed over twenty-five years ago that when we must guess what conduct or utterance will be investigated and sanctioned, "one necessarily will steer far wider of the unlawful zone...for the threat of sanctions may deter...almost as potently as the actual application of sanctions."[14]

The academic community must make it clear that professional academic freedom offers no shelter for personal vilification, coercion, or intimidation.

It must stand for common adherence to the correlative duties of professional academic freedom that outline minimum standards of civility. Reasoned discourse depends upon civility. However, as the AAUP's Committee A observes, "Prudential considerations counsel against any general attempt to proscribe [extreme personal abuse] by regulation. However important they may be to a regime of reasoned discourse, norms of civility are not ordinarily susceptible to enforcement by penal sanctions."[15]

Given these risks of strict enforcement of the correlative duties of academic freedom relating to civility through penal sanctions, the academic community should focus its efforts on education and persuasion of its members to honor the basic virtue of civility. This education should occur in and out of the classroom. AAUP's Committee A makes several recommendations.

> Faculty members are, for example, responsible for establishing and maintaining a classroom atmosphere conducive to the education of their students, a responsibility that encompasses both the obligation to respect norms of civility appropriate to an academic environment and the obligation to ensure that their students also respect those norms…faculty authority over the classroom offers a way of dealing with it [incivility] that is far more satisfactory than disciplinary proceedings are likely to be. A faculty member's authority in the classroom does not depend on sanctions, but on suasion. The potential chilling effect of disciplinary proceedings is, therefore, substantially reduced. Of at least equal importance, placing responsibility on the faculty enhances the prospect that the problem will be recognized and addressed as an educational one.[16]

Students can be led to consider all the factors bearing on incivility, including the harm caused and the possible justification.

Committee A believes the same approach is possible outside the classroom.

> Despite obvious differences between the classroom and other campus settings, a similar approach—one that relies on education rather than discipline—is both feasible and desirable when problems arise outside the classroom…a range of institutional mechanisms is available that will permit members of the faculty or others to play a similar role when problems arise in those settings.[17]

The critical objective is to foster discussion that will lead members of the academic community to consider the full range of issues posed by the use of incivility. The community must have means to express that speech that may not be proscribed, but may nonetheless be morally objectionable.

It is important to note that some intramural utterance may not be protected academic speech and could be directly proscribed, subject only to standard employment law limitations. The 1940 statement extends rights of academic freedom beyond teaching and research to intramural utterance insofar as intramural utterance relates to the education of students or involves critical inquiry. The 1940 statement does not grant professional academic freedom to faculty intramural utterance that either addresses personal grievances unrelated to the education of students or does not involve critical inquiry. This is not protected academic speech. Incivility on these topics could be penalized with less concern about harm to the core protected functions of teaching and research.

Other institutional mechanisms to address problems of incivility in nonclassroom settings are: (1) the education of faculty concerning both the rights and correlative duties of professional academic freedom and the skills of frank discussion of complex, emotionally difficult issues; (2) some means to raise issues of incivility within the faculty; and (3) an annual faculty meeting to assess the state of professional academic freedom within the faculty.

An educational program for all faculty on professional academic freedom would be helpful. Administrators and the governing board should also attend a program. As indicated earlier in the essay, all faculty members should have an understanding of the history of professional academic freedom, its rationale, its critical importance to the profession and to the university, its rights and its correlative duties. They should also understand that there will always be strong ideologies and zealots, that periods of zealotry have occurred regularly, that similar coercive tactics of incivility have been used in each period, and that professional academic freedom is never finally won, it must be continually defended.

The most fertile breeding ground for incivility within a faculty is personnel decisions: appointment, retention, promotion, and tenure. The rejected candidate and her or his supporters will often feel that a challenge to a candidate's competence hardly demonstrates due respect for the rights and dignity of others. They may turn to personal attacks and incivility in retaliation.

Educational programs on professional academic freedom will help everyone in the community understand the collegial duty to assess professional competence. It is a correlative duty of the collegial body to examine critically the competence of peers, and to screen out the incompetent. Collegial judgment separating good art from bad art includes difficult questions about both what scholarly work is worth doing in a discipline and whether the work was done competently. The collegial body discharges its duty in respect to these value judgments if it makes them in consequence of a serious, open-minded effort to make sure that it has done justice to all relevant considerations (specifically excluding the candidate's political views) and that its assessments are reasoned.[18]

Educational programs will remind faculty, administrators, and the governing board of their duty not only to set an outstanding example of civility, but also "to challenge boldly and condemn immediately serious breaches of civility."[19] As the Council of the AAUP reminded the academic community during the previous wave of zealotry in 1970, the faculty in particular must "assume a more positive role as guardian of academic values against unjustified assaults from its own members."[20] This is even more true during the current period of zealotry, where faculty zealots are playing a more significant role, than during the student activism of the 1960s.

The faculty must understand that the culture is largely defined by the faculty. Where the faculty permits intolerance, incivility, and coercion, then attacks on thought and speech will continue. The faculty's usual public response of acquiescence and silent submission to coercive tactics has been the ballast of the ideological zealotry of each wave of zealotry. In many respects, faculties during the two most recent periods of zealotry are like dysfunctional families. Some members are constantly rude, intolerant, and coercive, but the dysfunctional community enables the incivility by denying the problem, covering it up, and avoiding it. The history of the most recent periods of zealotry confirms that enabling behavior only makes the conduct worse.

Faculty members must speak publicly against incivility to prevent dysfunction, to support the target, and to protect their own professional academic freedom. This is the most effective educational response. The more responsibility the faculty takes, the more likely that problems of incivility will be addressed as educational ones without formal sanction by the employer.

Educational programs could also assist members of the academic community to learn the skills of civility. In a society and in academic communities where fundamental differences exist among members, each member should have the following skills:

1. Reflective critical thinking. Each community member should use analytical reasoning on his or her own views, tradition and biases.
2. Deliberative dialogue. Each community member should learn the skill of deliberative dialogue with others with fundamental differences, in the belief that understanding and an improvement in knowledge can result from free and open interaction on ideas without ad personem attack.
3. Imaginative empathy. In a community that honors the differences among its members, each member should strive to stimulate and develop imaginative empathy. This empathy includes:
    a. listening skills;
    b. the ability to imagine oneself in the position of a person whose starting point may be radically different; and
    c. the ability to recognize the bonds between oneself and others.
4. Openness. Each community member should be open to the revision of fundamental commitments that reflective critical thinking, deliberative dialogue, and imaginative empathy might suggest. This is not the same as an openness that is essentially moral vacuity.

Educational programs on these skills will reduce incivility and coercion. In particular, they should reduce the excessive and unsubstantiated attacks on motive that are the most serious obstacle to civil academic inquiry and speech. Criticism will not be reduced to insult. This would make possible frank discussion of complex and difficult issues like diversity or personnel decisions.

Some faculty members may feel that any duties of civility are misguided and inappropriate. One line of argument is that the university's fundamental mission is the advancement and dissemination of knowledge. It is the possibility of falsifying every certainty that is the mechanism for improving knowledge. Therefore, the university is the place to think the unthinkable, to challenge the unchallengeable, and to speak the unspeakable. This argument recognizes only the rights of professional academic freedom and not its correlative duties. It also conflates what is a right with what is ethical.[21] Of course, thinking the unthinkable, challenging the unchallengeable, and speaking the unspeakable are protected by professional academic freedom; but they must meet the correlative duties of professional competence and ethics.

Another line of argument is that members of the academic community should develop fortitude for assaultive rhetoric. Essentially, if an academic can't stand the heat, she or he should get out of the kitchen. There is no question that experienced scholars should develop a reasonably thick skin for public criticism. It is in the nature of their work that they upset other people. They should learn how to handle direct and fundamental disagreement with calm, matter of fact decency.

The argument that those who can't take heat should get out of the kitchen has some merit, but is overstated. Good kitchens need cooling and venting systems so that all competent cooks can learn and work there. Vulnerable groups of people, especially for example newer and untenured faculty or students, may not have developed an extremely thick hide. Are the vulnerable to be left without protection?

Disputes on substantive issues fundamental to the discipline between and among committed partisans are a sign of health in a faculty. Bumping in research and scholarly debate is necessary for knowledge to advance. Smashing, trashing, and bludgeoning thwart free discourse among competent academic professionals. Committee A observes that,

> so long as the disputes do not rise to the level at which the department's work is impaired—so long, that is, as they are constrained within the bounds of good sense and fair play—the research as well as the teaching of the department's members may be enlivened and invigorated.[22]

What is needed, in former Harvard President Bok's view, "is not an end to criticism but criticism that is less given to rhetorical excess, more careful with its criteria for judgment."[23]

Other institutional mechanisms to address problems of incivility in nonclassroom settings mentioned earlier in this section were: (2) some means to raise issues of incivility with the faculty; and (3) an annual faculty meeting to assess the state of professional academic freedom within the faculty. The persons who are targets of professional discourse that violates duties of civility should not be forced either to suffer in silence or to engage in memo wars.[24]

The faculty should encourage targets to bring these issues for discussion before the faculty to help faculty members consider the impact of incivility on the community and to help develop a community consensus on the ethical duties of civility. The faculty should also open the floor at least annually for discussion on the state of professional academic freedom within the faculty and university.

The objective within each faculty is to build a tradition of civility appropriate to scholarly conversation. Each member of the community must understand that academic speech can serve its function of advancing and disseminating knowledge only if faculty and students refrain from imposing their ideas by accusations of moral turpitude, advocacy tactics of manipulative persuasion, ridicule, ostracism and other forms of intimidation.

Mandatory principles of professional conduct. Enforcement of the remaining five correlative duties of professional academic freedom through the use of penalties presents a diminishing risk of chilling competent academic speech as we progress down the list:

4. not to use the authority inherent in the instructional role either to introduce partisan matters having no relation to the subject or to impose political choices on students;
5. to gather evidence through thorough inquiry;
6. to be accurate and honest in the gathering, recording and use of evidence;
7. to present opposing evidence and argument without distortion or misrepresentation; and
8. not to disrupt speeches or classes or to significantly impede the functions of the university.

The 1940 statement imposes a specific duty that teachers "should be careful not to introduce into their teaching controversial matter that has no relation to their subject." The 1970 AAUP Council statement, Freedom and Responsibility, provides that faculty members have an obligation not to force students "by the authority in the instructional role to make personal choices as to political action or their own part in society." If a faculty member is using the power of the instructional role to force students to cover political topics that have no relation to the subject, the professor is not competently teaching the curriculum. If a faculty member is using the power of the instructional role to coerce students to make choices as to political action, the conduct directly assaults the fundamental premise of professional academic freedom: discourse among competent academic professionals must be free of coercion. While there is some risk that complaints based on these duties could be used by overzealous students, colleagues or administrators to suppress competent scholarly inquiry or discourse, the definition of misconduct is clearer here than with ambiguous categories of prohibited speech discussed above. The university has power to control curriculum and conduct in a classroom setting, for example, prohibiting prayer or requiring coverage of specific topics, that it does not have in contexts like open forums.

There is evidence that in the current period of zealotry some professors from the fundamentalist academic left are politicizing the classroom. The Bahls study, for example, found that many law students fear reprisals if they disagree with professors' political views in class or on exams.[25] There are numerous anecdotes of politicization of the classroom. The author is unaware of any thorough study of instances of politicization of the classroom. There must be a means for students to raise concerns about politicization of the classroom, for the faculty to investigate such concerns, and for the university to prohibit conduct crossing the lines discussed above.

The use of penalties to enforce the next three correlative duties, to gather evidence through thorough inquiry, to be accurate and honest in the gathering, recording, and use of evidence, and to present opposing evidence and argument without distortion or misrepresentation, poses even less risk of chilling competent academic speech. These duties define the cornerstones of professional competence. Any form of deceptive conduct seriously undermines the mission of the university: advancing and disseminating knowledge. Knowledge cannot progress if faculty members fail to meet the highest standards of integrity with respect to evidence and argument. Distortion or misrepresentation of evidence is always unacceptable. Relevant opposing evidence and argument must be addressed.[26] The faculty, emphasizes former Johns Hopkins professor Fritz Machlup,

> has a moral obligation to remove a member who for personal gain...deliberately and dishonestly distorts the truth in the presentation of *verified* or *readily verifiable facts*. In other words, the faculty has a moral responsibility to initiate action against the scoundrel who fakes evidence in research experiments, forges records to support his alleged findings, deliberately gives false testimony as a paid expert witness in private litigation, fabricates reports and figures, or disseminates what he knows to be fabrications, for the purpose of deceiving. (emphasis added)[27]

Duke professor William Van Alstyne similarly urges professional peers to be far more concerned than the administration or the trustees to make certain that colleagues use academic freedom ethically. "Indeed a grave ethical failure in the integrity of a teacher's or a scholar's academic representations, no matter of how little notice or coincidental concern it may happen to be to the particular institutional employer, is precisely the kind of offense to the contingent privilege of academic freedom that states a clearly adequate cause for a faculty recommendation of termination."[28]

These correlative duties of integrity with respect to evidence and argument apply to teaching, research and intramural utterance relating to the education of students or involving critical inquiry. Intramural utterance not related to these functions is not protected academic speech; university employers can require adherence to these duties for such speech as a matter of general employment practice. Extramural utterance, is also subject to the more limited correlative duty of integrity specifically described in the 1940 statement: the teacher shall at all times be accurate.

Intramural or extramural utterance making false accusations of moral turpitude against others in the academic community is one of many forms of deceptive conduct subject to these correlative duties of integrity with respect to evidence and argument. Another related form of deceptive conduct subject to these duties is the bringing of false charges leading to internal or external investigations and proceedings. In both of these situations, a professor's intramural utterance must meet correlative duties of thoroughness, accuracy, and honesty in the gathering, recording, and use of evidence supporting an accusation of moral turpitude or a formal charge. A professor also has a duty to present opposing evidence and argument without distortion or misrepresentation in making such accusations or bringing formal charges. A professor's extramural utterance in these situations must meet the correlative duty of accuracy.

A professor's accusation or formal charge impugning the integrity of others based on mere suspicions, suppositions, intuition, or non-existent evidence is conduct that reflects a reckless disregard for the truth or falsity of the statements made and is a violation of these correlative duties of professional academic freedom. Intramural and extramural utterance must be accurate. This means that at a minimum, for both intramural and extramural utterance, faculty members have an affirmative duty of *reasonable investigation* to determine first if there are facts supporting accusations or formal charges of moral turpitude. This duty is higher in intramural utterance where a professor has a duty first to gather evidence through *thorough* inquiry.

Similarly, if after reasonable investigation, a professor's accusation or formal charge of moral turpitude consists simply of tantalizing innuendo, the twisting of any ambiguity, attenuated circumstantial evidence, half-truth by omission or exaggeration, this conduct would reflect a reckless disregard for accuracy and honesty in the gathering, recording, and use of evidence in both intramural and extramural utterance. If the professor distorts or misrepresents opposing evidence and argument, this is conduct that reflects a reckless disregard for accuracy in intramural or extramural utterance. These are violations of the correlative duties of professional academic freedom. A professor has an affirmative duty to be accurate and not to distort or misrepresent the evidence from the investigation or the opposing evidence and argument. In intramural utterance a professor has in addition the affirmative duty to present opposing argument and evidence.

The standard of care to be applied to these correlative duties must reflect the level of integrity with evidence and argument essential to a competent professor. The standard is an objective one dependent on what a reasonable and competent professor should do in the same or similar circumstances. The fact that the specific accuser's feelings were genuine is not a defense. The accuser's subjective good faith or feelings are irrelevant.

The correlative duties both of accuracy and honesty in the gathering, recording, and use of evidence and of the presentation of opposing evidence and argument without distortion or misrepresentation also prohibit a professor from using an advocate's tactics of manipulative persuasion unless the professor has clearly indicated that she is not communicating as an academic or the circumstances are such as to not allow for the reasonable inference that she is communicating as an academic. There is a sharp distinction between the academic's mission of advancing and disseminating knowledge with its correlative duties of integrity with respect to evidence and argument, and the advocate's mission of persuasion with its duties of partisanship and manipulation. The advocate presents argument and evidence favorable to a particular interest. Regarding facts, half-truth by omission is condoned. If the advocate is an attorney, in many cases half-truth by omission is mandated by duties not to reveal client's confidential information. The slanting and manipulation of evidence and argument that are the stuff of advocacy and politics are the opposite of the academic's duties of integrity with respect to evidence and argument.

Because of decades of research, teaching, and public service that aspired to meet these correlative duties of integrity, students and the public perceive expression by academics as "disinterested evidence and argument." They give such expression honor and influence in the marketplace of ideas; without a specific disclaimer, the academic speaker is assumed to have drawn conclusions based on respect for evidence and scholarly methodology.[29] Nondisclosure when an academic is operating as an advocate is a form of deceptive conduct that violates the correlative duties of professional academic freedom.

There are instances in the present period of zealotry where fundamentalists are violating the correlative duties of integrity with evidence and argument. The use of repeated unsupported accusations of moral turpitude, followed in some cases by investigations, to create the "big lie," has been the most successful coercive tactic of both McCarthyism and the current zealotry from the fundamentalist academic left. Such accusations are often based on conjecture, rumor, gossip, hearsay, the twisting of any ambiguity, half-truth by omission, exaggeration, and sometimes misrepresentation. Misinformation is constantly repeated to create adverse perceptions of the accused among students and the public. Faculty zealots may encourage students not to take classes from the accused. Innuendo is played out in forums like the media where there is no chance of due process procedures that would take pains in developing the facts. These advocacy strategies of manipulative persuasion have been effective in silencing dissent.

False public accusations also sometimes take the form of formal charges leading to internal and external investigations of the accused. Investigations are particularly devastating to the accused and to the freedom of academic discourse in the community. The accused must spend enormous amounts of time, energy, and resources to defend him or herself. This intimidates the accused and the entire academic community. Professor Ralph Fuchs observes that the McCarthy investigations, operated "in terrorem" and led to loss of reputation by those subject to inquiry.[30] Being fired, Professor Schrecker writes, does not always produce as much anxiety as the uncertainty created by threats, accusations, investigations, and hearings. Many people who kept their jobs during McCarthyism may have suffered just as much as the people who lost theirs.[31] The AAUP's Committee A recently found that "colleges and universities cannot remain centers for the uninhibited exploration of all ideas if, on some subjects, students and faculty must measure their words against the risk of disciplinary proceedings."[32] For example, the Second Circuit found that the threat of discipline implicit in the investigation into Professor Levin's conduct ordered by CCNY President Harleston was sufficient to chill Professor Levin's First Amendment right of free speech.[33]

These tactics violate:

1. the affirmative duty of reasonable investigation to determine if there are facts supporting accusations or formal charges of moral turpitude;
2. the affirmative duty to be accurate and not to distort or misrepresent either evidence gathered in the preliminary investigation or the opposing evidence and argument; and
3. the affirmative duty not to use an advocate's tactics of manipulative persuasion unless the professor makes a disclaimer that the professor is not communicating as an academic.

The remaining question is whether all of these violations should be enforced with penalties or whether penalties for this conduct pose too much danger of chilling competent academic speech. Former Harvard President Bok recommends prohibiting (and implicitly penalizing) deliberate, overt attempts to impose orthodoxy and suppress dissent. For Bok, prohibiting and penalizing "harassment," which may include false accusations of bigotry, posed too much danger to competent academic speech because "harassment" was too vague. However, enforcing affirmative duties of reasonable investigation and accuracy through penalties poses far less danger to competent academic speech since, by definition, competent academic speech is the product of care and accuracy in evidence and argument. The requirements of these affirmative duties also create a much clearer line than proscription of vague conduct like "harassment."

It is still a tough call whether false accusations of moral turpitude that do not trigger a formal investigation but that are made without investigation and without attention to accuracy should be penalized. Such accusations, for example, may occur in the heat of an argument. It is possible that some competent academic speech could be chilled by sanctions against false accusations not meeting these affirmative duties. Education still seems the best means to address this type of coercion, but repeated use of false accusations of moral turpitude seriously undermines the professional academic freedom of colleagues.

The case for requiring professors to meet these affirmative duties before bringing formal charges leading to external and internal investigations is stronger. The chilling impact of an investigation on the accused and the academic community is much greater than an accusation. Failure to meet the affirmative duties before bringing formal charges given these consequences is more clearly a deliberate attempt to impose orthodoxy and should be penalized.[34]

The use of penalties to enforce the correlative duty not to disrupt speeches or classes or to significantly impede the functions of the university poses no risk of chilling competent academic speech. The university must honor rights of peaceful demonstration that have been the perennial recourse to those lacking political power who seek to influence decisions. However, the mission of the university to advance and disseminate knowledge demands that discourse among competent academic professionals must be free of coercion. The university cannot permit peaceful demonstration to cross the line to disrupt the opportunity of others to speak. In July, 1992, the AAUP's Committee A urged institutions to "adopt and invoke a range of measures that penalize conduct and behavior, rather than speech—such as rules against defacing property, physical intimidation or harassment, or disruption of campus activities."[35]

Disruption of campus activities through the forced occupation of buildings or shouting down speakers was a common tactic of coercion during the 1960s and is again evident during the current wave of zealotry. These are violations of the correlative duties of professional academic freedom. The university must make clear rules and enforce them to prevent these violations of academic freedom.

Faculty statement on professional conduct. The faculty should take the lead in addressing these violations of professional academic freedom. The faculty as a collegial body has clear duties to protect professional academic freedom. It is also in each faculty member's personal interest to protect the rights of professional academic freedom and to enforce its correlative duties since periods of zealotry have occurred frequently in higher education, and it has not been possible to predict accurately the direction from which the next wave would come. The tactics of the last several waves have been similar and would in all likelihood be repeated in a future wave of zealotry. At the end of the last wave of zealotry in the late 1960s, the AAUP Council in 1970 made the following plea:

> [P]lans for insuring compliance with academic norms should be enlarged to emphasize preventive as well as disciplinary action. Toward this end the faculty should take the initiative, working with the administration and other components of the institution, to develop and maintain an atmosphere of freedom, commitment to academic inquiry, and respect for the academic right of others.

[T]here is a need for the faculty to assume a more positive role as guardian of academic values against unjustified assaults from its own members.... [F]aculties should recognize their stake in promoting adherence to norms essential to the academic enterprise.

Rules designed to meet these needs for faculty self-regulation and flexibility of sanctions should be adopted on each campus.[36]

The Commission on Academic Tenure in Higher Education created by the AAUP and college administrators in the early 1970s was even more specific. Reflecting on the assaults on academic freedom from within the university during the previous decade, the Commission recommended that, "The faculty of the institution...must be the source for the definition and clarification of standards of professional conduct and must take the lead in ensuring that these standards are enforced."[37]

The Commission further specified:

that faculties should be authorized and encouraged to develop codes of professional conduct for the guidance of their members and as a basis for sanctions against those whose conduct falls below professional norms. Such codes should reflect the broad precepts embodied in such existing formulations as the 1940 Statement of Principles and the 1966 Statement of Professional Ethics and should attempt to articulate the traditional sentiments of academic persons as to the demands of their calling.... The very effort to provide a statement of professional standards will serve to dramatize the faculty's own responsibility for its integrity and that of the institution.

The Commission recommends that the faculty of each institution assume responsibility for developing a code of faculty conduct and procedures and sanctions for faculty self-discipline, for recommending adoption of the code by the institution's governing board, and for making effective use of the code when it has been approved.[38]

The AAUP's Committee A commented in July, 1992, during the current zealotry that freedom of expression requires toleration of "ideas we hate." This underlying principle does not change because the demand for silencing an enemy comes from within the academy. "Free speech is not simply an aspect of the educational enterprise to be weighed against other desirable ends. It is the very precondition of the academic enterprise itself." Committee A urges faculty members to play a major role. "[T]heir actions may set examples for understanding, making clear to their students that civility and tolerance are hallmarks of educated men and women."[39]

The faculty should in addition give attention to preventive measures like education on academic freedom, open discussion of issues of academic freedom, and skills training in conflict resolution. Each faculty also should consider and discuss the adoption of a faculty statement on professional conduct. The following statement is proposed as a possible starting point for discussion.

Faculty Statement on Professional Conduct

Diverse ideas and free and open discussion are fundamental to faculty life. The sharing, the exchange, and even the clash of ideas is essential if we are to succeed in our roles as teachers, scholars, and co-governors of the university.

To preserve the university as a forum for robust debate about diverse ideas and to prevent breakdowns in civility which interfere with the university's mission, we resolve ourselves against conduct that poisons faculty relations. Faculty includes those faculty members serving terms in administrative roles at the university. Disagreements should not degenerate into vilification.

To promote our ability to discuss diverse ideas and to function together as a faculty:

We recognize that we will often disagree with each other—sometimes intensely and even passionately.

We commit ourselves to keeping our discussions and our disagreements civil. This includes keeping disagreements from degenerating into ad personem attacks, as well as making sure that we express ourselves in the manner least damaging to faculty relations.

We require of ourselves and of our faculty colleagues, that no one of us charges another with misconduct without first having made reasonable efforts to establish a factual basis for the charge (including a face-to-face discussion with the person charged) and without indeed having established a reasonable basis in fact to substantiate the allegations.

In our oral and written communication regarding charges of misconduct we commit ourselves to the impartiality, accuracy, and fairness of scholars, not the zealous advocacy of litigators. Relevant contrary arguments and evidence must be acknowledged without distortion and addressed. The use of half-truth by omission and innuendo must be avoided.

We require also that faculty members will not use the authority inherent in the instructional role either to introduce partisan matters having no relation to the subject or to impose political choices on students. Faculty members will not attempt or assist in any way to disrupt speeches or classes or to significantly impede the functions of the university.

A statement on professional conduct should be adopted on each campus after faculty debate. In addition to adopting a statement on professional conduct, the faculty should decide what conduct mentioned in the statement will be grounds for sanction, the specific sanctions to be applied, and the person(s) who can trigger a proceeding that may result in a sanction, and the procedures to be followed for each type of sanction.

The faculty must draw several lines. First, what penalties are proper if a faculty member makes false public accusations of misconduct against another colleague in violation of these duties, but files no formal charges leading to internal or external investigation of the target. The faculty should have the power to hear evidence whether the professor making accusations has satisfied the duties outlined in the faculty statement on professional conduct. The faculty could issue a private warning for violation of these duties. The faculty could issue a public reprimand for repeated violations of these duties. Graduated sanctions to distinguish the degree of the violation and to provide the opportunity for correction are more fair when previously ignored duties are first enforced.

If a professor fails to meet the duties outlined in the faculty statement on professional conduct before bringing formal charges leading to internal and external investigation of the accused, the impact on the target is greater and the case for serious penalties is stronger. In such cases the faculty should have the power, in addition to private warnings and public reprimands, to consider a fine, a reduction in salary, suspension, or termination of a professor's contract.

The faculty should give clear notice of what is prohibited and how violations will be punished. In all sanctioning efforts, faculty judgment should play the critical role in the context of clearly defined procedural protections.

The remaining question is who can trigger a proceeding that may result in sanctions for a professor who violates the faculty statement on professional conduct. Even without a faculty statement on conduct, the administration under the 1940 statement and the tenure contract can bring charges against faculty members who violate the correlative duties of professional competence and ethics. These general duties include the mandatory principles of conduct discussed in the preceding section, for example the affirmative duty of reasonable investigation to determine if there are facts supporting accusations or formal charges of misconduct. A faculty statement on professional conduct will further clarify and emphasize both those duties and penalties for the breach of those duties.

The target of false accusations can file a grievance with the administration stating that conduct by a colleague(s) is violating both the target's rights of professional academic freedom and the accuser's correlative duties of professional academic freedom. The administration must consider and respond to the grievance.

What should the target do if the administration does nothing or the administration itself is violating these duties? What if, for example, the administration itself is making adverse decisions relating to the course or committee assignment or the allocation of research or travel funds because a faculty member is alleged to be a heretic? What if the administration makes accusations of moral turpitude that do not meet the correlative duties of professional academic freedom? Of course the target can file a grievance against the university itself for failure to protect the target's professional academic freedom. An adverse finding is highly unlikely, but this strategy helps create a record for litigation against the university.

In addition, the faculty should adopt a separate procedure to address these possibilities. The following procedure is a possible solution. In the event of administrative inaction on a grievance or in the event the administration or governing board itself is either violating the target's rights of academic freedom or not meeting the correlative duties of professional academic freedom, any faculty person should be able to make a grievance to the chairperson of the tenure committee. In an effort to resolve the problem amicably, the chairperson should meet promptly with the complaining faculty member, any colleague who is the subject of the complaint, and the member of the administration or governing board claimed to have committed the violation. If the chairperson concludes that these efforts have been unsuccessful, she shall serve a written notice to that effect on the parties.

If the chairperson notifies the parties that efforts to resolve the problem have proven unsuccessful, the faculty member can appeal to the tenure committee. The faculty member should carry the burden of establishing that the action complained of was either substantially the product of an effort to chill her rights of academic freedom or a violation of the mandatory principles of professional conduct stated previously. The tenure committee should have the power to recommend the reversal of the administrative action and to recommend sanctions for professional misconduct as described earlier.

The initiation of an investigation. Investigations have been a highly successful coercive tactic in both McCarthyism and the current wave of zealotry. They operate *in terrorem* on the accused and the community, grinding up energy, time, and personal and institutional financial resources. Given the chilling effects of investigations on professional academic freedom, before initiating an investigation, a university administration should require both some significant threshold factual support indicating misconduct and a threshold finding that the accusations are based on something other than speech protected by academic freedom. Administrators, for example, must not order an investigation because of accusations based on rumor, gossip, hearsay, conjecture, or intuition. The administration can screen out frivolous complaints by requiring both a threshold showing of credible evidence, which establishes the elements of faculty misconduct, and a threshold finding that the misconduct alleged is not speech protected by academic freedom.[40] Dean John Jeffrey at Dallas Baptist University is an example of an administrator who recognized that investigation of a false charge of misconduct is improper and coercive. Dean Jeffrey courageously responded to the request of the vice-president of academic affairs to investigate the academic speech of Professor David Ayers. "I cannot investigate charges in which the actions of the faculty member are well within the parameters of the Faculty Handbook and the AAUP guidelines. For me to investigate charges in which there is no hint of impropriety would in itself constitute a violation of academic freedom and AAUP guidelines."[41]

If the administration initiates an investigation, the accused should have reasonably detailed notice of all charges and an opportunity to present evidence to the investigator. If the investigation leads to formal charges and an administrative recommendation of a sanction, the accused faculty member must have a right to a hearing. Because the accused is in the limbo of the praiseless and blameless dead during an investigation, administrators should complete investigations expeditiously.

These measures of fair notice and fair process are of critical importance when issues are politically and emotionally charged. This is the time when professional academic freedom is most at risk.[42] For example, the AAUP's associate secretary reported that "the organization has seen a 'disturbing' increase this year [in 1992] in the number of calls from professors who have been accused of harassment and believe they have not received due process." She thinks that because the issue of sexual harassment has become so emotionally charged, administrators overreact.[43]

The relationship between the university's harassment and discrimination policy and professional academic freedom must be specified. There is a significant risk that the harassment and discrimination policy may be used as a speech policy to suppress dissent. This is particularly true if discrimination and harassment policies and speech codes are administered by administrators insensitive to issues of academic freedom and predisposed to favor the ideology of the fundamentalist academic left. There is evidence that this is occurring in the present wave of zealotry. If a professor is charged under the harassment and discrimination policy for conduct that is pure speech, the professor must have the right to appeal first to the tenure committee to demonstrate that the speech was professionally competent. If the tenure committee finds the speech to be professionally competent, then the speech is protected by professional academic freedom even if some members of the community perceive the speech as insensitive or hostile to cherished beliefs. The AAUP's Committee A recently commented that "[f]ree speech is not simply an aspect of the educational enterprise to be weighed against other desirable ends. It is the very precondition of the academic enterprise itself."[44]

The university administration must also recognize the possibility that zealots may make public accusations of moral turpitude to intimidate the accused faculty member but that the zealots will not come forward with a formal complaint. A formal complaint runs the risk of vindicating the accused after the hearing. Public accusations of moral turpitude without an investigation and a final determination leave an unresolved cloud over the reputation of the accused. The AAUP's Committee A commented almost fifty years ago that the greatest enemy of an academic career is rumor and uncertainty.[45]

The administration should provide an opportunity for a faculty member to request an investigation when public accusations of moral turpitude are not accompanied by formal charges leading to an investigation and ultimate resolution. This provides a mechanism to clear the good name of the accused.

Other accusations of professional misconduct. This chapter focuses on applying the correlative duties of professional academic freedom to coercive conduct by faculty zealots in order to determine the point where coercive tactics ripen into conduct that does not meet standards of professional competence or ethics. The analysis is applicable more broadly to other accusations of professional misconduct. For example, a faculty member may be accused of plagiarism or scientific misconduct. The impact of this type of public accusation of moral turpitude on the accused will be similar to an allegation of bigotry.[46] Any accusation that a researcher may have compromised the scientific integrity of a project can be the death knell of a career.[47] This type of accusation presents many of the same concerns about the adequacy of protection for the interests of a faculty member who may be falsely accused but who may lack a means of vindication. This type of charge may be made out of improper motive. Barbara Mishkin, a lawyer specializing in the defense of scientists accused of research misconduct, believes that the number of such cases is growing and that flawed personal relationships have much to do with the increase. "I think we have lost the sense of civility in science. We are now finding scientists who have been collaborating with each other filing allegations of scientific misconduct against each other the way divorcing spouses find it very satisfying to charge that the other spouse is guilty of sexually abusing the kids."[48]

Many of the mandatory principles of professional conduct discussed earlier apply here as well. A professor making accusations of professional misconduct should first meet those affirmative duties. The faculty statement on professional conduct proposed earlier would specifically apply to these situations. Given the chilling effects of investigations on professional academic freedom, the administration should also require some significant threshold factual support indicating misconduct before initiating an investigation. In those instances where public accusations of plagiarism or scientific misconduct do not lead to an investigation and ultimate resolution, the administration should again provide a mechanism for the accused to request an investigation to clear his or her good name. For the target of a charge of scientific misconduct or plagiarism, the discussion of lines of defense in the next chapter will be relevant. Selection of counsel and indemnification of attorney's fees will be of particular importance.[49]

The Role of the Administration and Governing Board if the Faculty Fails to Require Professional Conduct

Earlier discussion applied the correlative duties required of individual faculty members to the coercive conduct of faculty zealots. That discussion articulated a line across which coercive tactics ripen into conduct that does not meet standards of professional conduct. This section considers the role of the administration and governing board if the faculty fails to meet its correlative duty to require professional conduct of faculty zealots. A brief review of the historical development of professional academic freedom frames this issue in the proper context.

The reader will recall that professional academic freedom in the United States emerged out of conflict between professional academics and university lay employers. In the second half of the nineteenth century and early in the twentieth, professional academics came widely to adopt a progressive conception of knowledge. The essential requirement for this progressive conception of knowledge was free discourse among academic professionals within the competency and ethical constraints of a discipline. For many decades up to 1915, the principal danger to the realization of free discourse among competent professionals was interference by the lay governing boards and lay administrators. This interference occurred because either lay boards would impose constraints on free intellectual inquiry based on political, social or moral concerns or lay boards simply were not qualified to monitor and prevent incompetence in professional discourse.

In 1915 the AAUP articulated the concept of professional academic freedom, the principal purpose of which was the creation of conditions necessary for the improvement and dissemination of knowledge in the university. To this end, university employers ultimately agreed to grant exceptional vocational freedom to professors in research, teaching, intramural utterance related to the education of students or critical inquiry, and extramural utterance on the condition that professors meet certain correlative duties as individuals and as a collegial body.

Professional academic freedom clearly requires the faculty as a collegial body to determine when an individual professor inadequately meets his or her duties of professional competence and ethical conduct. The 1915 AAUP statement provides that the faculty must acquire the capacity for impersonal judgment in cases where individual professors fail to meet their responsibilities and for judicial severity when the occasion requires it.[50] The 1958 joint statement outlining procedures for dismissal provides that the faculty must be willing to recommend the dismissal of a colleague when necessary.[51] After witnessing faculty involvement in assaults on academic freedom in the 1960s, the AAUP's Council stressed the special need for faculty to assume a more positive role as guardian of academic values against unjustified assaults from its own members.[52]

If the faculty as a collegial body should fail in its duty to require professional competence and ethical conduct of individual faculty members, the rationale underlying the reciprocal rights and duties of professional academic freedom also fails. The university lay employer may then rightfully claim the same discretion given other public or private employers on employee speech issues. If the professoriat, the 1915 statement warns, "should prove itself unwilling to purge its ranks of the incompetent and the unworthy, or to prevent the freedom which it claims in the name of science from being used as a shelter for inefficiency, for superficiality, or for uncritical and intemperate partisanship, it is certain the task will be performed by others."[53] University of

Texas Law professor Rebecca Eisenberg emphasizes that the authors of the 1915 statement did not argue for unqualified professional autonomy, to the contrary, the authors warned that the *only* way to preserve freedom from lay interference is through a system of accountability to professional peers.[54] University of Texas Law professor Rabban stresses the same point,

> Standards of scholarly inquiry and professional ethics define the extent to which academic freedom protects individual autonomy. The traditional conception makes faculty peers primarily responsible for applying these limiting standards. But it also advises administrators and governing boards to monitor the faculty peers and overrule their substantive decisions when there are compelling grounds for concluding that the peers themselves have departed from professional standards of judgment.[55]

There is evidence that some faculties do fail in their duty to require professional competence and ethical conduct of individual faculty members. A good litmus test of a faculty's willingness to enforce the correlative duties prohibiting professional misconduct is how it handles enforcing the cardinal duty of academic work: that it not be dishonest. Falsification of evidence and plagiarism would be examples of clear violations of this duty. Some faculties appear to be unwilling to enforce even this cardinal duty. For example, Dr. Judith Swazey finds that many cases in the 1980s show "the difficulties that physicians, other university faculty, and their institutions have in facing the fact that misconduct does occur, and in devising and using appropriate policies and procedures to deal with such deviations from proper professional conduct.... [I]n the words of Dr. Paul Friedman, a member of the Institute of Medicine's Committee on the Responsible Conduct of Research, the academic community has exhibited an 'indecisive response to 'well publicized cases of research fraud or serious misconduct.'"[56] A survey of members of the American Association for the Advancement of Science published in 1992 reports that 54 percent of the respondents believe that "universities are lax in their investigation of fraud and misconduct cases."[57] Notorious cases of intellectual fraud were sufficiently numerous that in 1989 the federal government created the Office of Scientific Integrity in the National Institutes of Health.[58] Estimates of the frequency of occurrence of misconduct in science differ widely. Confirmed instances of science misconduct are relatively rare, but the incidence of science misconduct may be substantially underreported because of fear of retaliation.[59] No one disputes that even a few well-publicized cases of research misconduct impose severe losses in public credibility and subsequent fruitless scientific research that relies on the earlier fraudulent data.[60] Plagiarism seems to be a serious problem in higher education. "[M]any scholars, whistle blowers, and institutions," Carolyn Mooney reports, "say the handling of academic plagiarism remains uneven and, in many cases, ineffective... some scholars say they are frustrated...because they think the academic community doesn't take seriously enough an offense that is the very antithesis of what scholars do."[61] Cheating among students also seems widespread. A 1990 survey of Rutgers University students revealed 45 percent cheated occasionally and another 33 percent cheated on an average of eight courses apiece during their college studies. Faculty members resist using disciplinary processes.[62]

A study published in the *American Scientist* in 1993 pulls together these themes. The Acadia Institute surveyed 2,000 doctoral candidates and 2,000 faculty members in chemistry, civil engineering, microbiology, and sociology concerning exposure to perceived misconduct.[63] The data indicate that incidents of what faculty members and graduate students

> perceive as scientific misconduct and questionable research practice are more widespread than many people have assumed. For example, 8 percent of the faculty members and 7 percent of the students surveyed report that they have observed or have other direct knowledge of plagiarism by faculty members in their own departments. Further, nearly one-third of the faculty members have firsthand knowledge of student plagiarism. Six percent of our faculty respondents and 9 percent of the students report instances of data fabrication by faculty members.
>
> Both groups report knowing about substantially more instances of ethically questionable research practices than instances of outright scientific misconduct. For example, 22 percent of the faculty respondents say they know of department members who have overlooked sloppy use of data; almost one-third report cases of inappropriate credit given for authorship of research papers.[64]

Faculty members also reported substantial differences between their espoused values and the actual practice in their departments. In principle, 74 percent of the faculty respondents believe they and their colleagues should exercise collective responsibility for the conduct of their graduate students to a great extent, "but only 27 percent judge that they and their departmental colleagues actually manifest to a great extent their shared responsibility for their students' professional-ethical conduct." Only 55 percent of the faculty respondents believe they should exercise responsibility for the conduct of their colleagues to a great extent, but "just 13 percent judge that faculty in their department exercise a great deal of shared responsibility for their colleagues' conduct, whereas 30 percent hold that there is very little or no manifestation of collegial responsibility."[65] The authors conclude that "our survey data, and statements by faculty and graduate students whom we have interviewed, challenge the idea that faculty actually practice an ethic of collective governance."[66]

Twenty-five years ago, University of Michigan professor Robert Blackburn observed the same thing. "[W]e police ourselves not at all. When brethren become impossible to manage and engage in intolerable behavior, from causes ranging from mental illness to Machiavellian desire, we quickly turn the problem over to 'the administration' (and then frequently carp at these people for their unethical and inhumane resolution of a deep human problem). As a group, however, we do not deprive him of a place to practice; we do not ostracize him."[67]

From a fifty-year perspective of defending professional academic freedom, Professor Sidney Hook observed that the systematic politicization of the university which began in the late sixties has diminished the faculty's willingness to enforce the academic ethic.

> But I have been saddened to observe a reluctance on the part of faculties to correct abuses of the academic ethic. Few can be found who are willing to take disciplinary measures against individuals who have clearly violated the responsibilities of honest teaching. There seems to be a complete indifference to the behavior of teachers who use their classes as a bully-pulpit for the propagation of political and other ideas that have no relation to the subject matter of their courses, or whose one sided, extremely partisan commitments to controversial issues are reflected in biased reading lists and unscholarly assignments.[68]

Reflecting on four decades of experience in higher education, former dean of the Harvard Faculty of Arts and Sciences Henry Rosovsky noted his firm belief in 1991 that "there has been a secular decline of professional civic virtue in FAS (Faculty of Arts and Sciences).... FAS has become a society largely without rules, or to put it slightly differently, the tenured members of the faculty—frequently as individuals—make their own rules."[69] Since the way a profession chooses to deal with wrongful conduct becomes its code of ethics, many faculties in the early 1990s have de facto no widely accepted and enforced code of ethics defining duties of professional conduct. When professional misconduct exacts no meaningful disincentive, and indeed enjoys the same currency in the profession as ethical behavior, we should not be surprised when by degrees, the former replaces the latter and become the de facto behavioral standards of the profession.

It may be that these results are predictable in any system where determinations of professional misconduct rest on peer review. The model of peer review underlying professional academic freedom may be based on the false premise that a collegium will in fact supervise itself. A collegium in reality may have a strong tendency to become a "delinquent community."

In *Doctoring Together: A Study of Professional Social Controls,* published in 1975, Eliot Friedson studied a large medical group to observe how the day-to-day work of doctoring was controlled by the physicians.[70] The doctors formed what Friedson calls a collegium, which insisted that self-government was solely its own legitimate function,[71] but which left "individuals free to work in their own ways within the very broad limits set by obvious unethicality or incompetence."[72] Friedson found that the collegium consistently abdicated the role of exercising organized sanctions, permitting all but gross and obvious deviance in performance, so long as intercollegial relations remained manageable.[73]

The collegium's rules of etiquette, in Friedson's view, took priority over standards of performance and accountability, and "discouraged critical attitudes toward colleagues, the communication of critical information to others about the performance of colleagues, the discussion of critical evaluations with colleagues, and the undertaking of collective social control."[74] Large numbers of offending actions remained unexamined and unacknowledged and often the offender remained unaware of the fact that his or her action was offensive to others.[75] Friedson notes the paradox that physicians in the group would complain of others' professional misconduct, but then find fault with and resist administrative efforts to address the issue.[76]

These rules of silent acquiescence in the face of professional misconduct were designed, in Friedson's analysis, to leave each member of the collegium a maximum amount of autonomy in work performance and behavior.[77] To describe this collegium, Friedson borrows the term "delinquent community" from sociological studies of French school children and personnel in French bureaucracies. In "delinquent communities," members show "a conspiracy of silence against superior authority...in an effort to create for each member a zone of autonomy.... Any change that is apt to...restrict the individual zones of autonomy in favor of a systematized and rational approach to the problem, will be resisted with all the strength the group can muster."[78]

The origin of the delinquent community of physicians, Friedson argues, lies in its position of vulnerable privilege. Over the past century physicians gained an effective occupational monopoly over practice, but the monopoly is vulnerable to possible imposition of external control. The collegium defends this privileged position by preventing the public from learning of its occupational excesses and imposing external control on the individual zones of autonomy.[79]

Faculties at many universities today are almost identical in structure to the medical group Friedson studied. Throughout the past fifty years, power has shifted from governing boards and administration to the faculties; and professors have gained almost complete control over the services offered, the standards of evaluation of the services, and the qualifications for membership in the profession. From their extensive study of faculty members in chemistry, civil engineering, microbiology and sociology, Swazey, Louis and Anderson find that the culture of the academic profession everywhere emphasizes personal autonomy.[80] They conclude that personal autonomy takes strong precedence over a norm of collegial self-governance.[81] Professor William Brown hypothesizes that the faculty collegium will not exercise sanctions because academics work independently with a focus on creativity. He or she requires stability for the exercise of creativity. It is better to ignore misconduct by a colleague than to impose sanctions that will threaten stability and harm creativity.[82] Professor John Braxton and Alan Bayer also find supporting empirical evidence that professional solidarity shapes attitudes toward research misconduct in general and toward taking action against wrongdoing in a particular case. Professional solidarity protects the academic profession from lay interference as well as allows each individual professor a maximum degree of autonomy.[83] At least for tenured faculty members, the faculty collegium seems largely to have abdicated its responsibilities in the face of professional misconduct.[84]

One obvious remedy is educating the faculty about academic freedom, particularly concerning the correlative duty of the faculty as a collegial body to enforce the competency and ethical constraints of the discipline when individual faculty do not meet them. The tendency of a faculty to become a delinquent community that does not supervise itself might be mitigated by knowledge of the fundamental importance of our legacy of academic freedom to each faculty member and to the university. Chapter 12 develops the elements of an effective faculty educational program on academic freedom.

In the absence of effective professional socialization in the correlative duties of academic freedom, this tendency of a faculty collegium to silently acquiesce in collegial professional misconduct is exacerbated during the current wave of zealotry. Earlier discussion established that many faculties have not been responding to protect academic freedom from collegial coercion and harassment in the late 1980s and early 1990s.

What does this mean for the administration and governing board attempting to address the coercive tactics of faculty zealots in the current period of zealotry? The first question to ask is whether the administration should be distinguished from the governing board in analyzing appropriate responses to faculty zealotry. Early in this century university presidents were often not professional academics so that members of the governing board and the chief administrator were both considered "laity" for purposes of establishing rights of academic freedom. Administrators were not chosen from or with the assent of the faculty, but were the deputies of the governing board that employed the faculty. As the century progressed, an increasing proportion of presidents and deans had service as distinguished faculty members earlier in their career, and faculties came to play a major role in their selection.

The president's formal powers in a private university are generally defined by nonprofit corporation statutes. The president is in charge in the same sense in which a chief executive officer directs a private company. He or she is responsible to a governing board of trustees that functions similar in power to a board of directors. The board has the ultimate legal authority to make decisions on behalf of the university.

Reality differs from the formal statutory model. Faculties now wield much of the power in universities and liberal arts colleges. One reason is that presidents and deans, coming from the faculty, look to the professors as peers with whom they consort professionally and socially.[85] Another is that tenured professors are all but invulnerable to discharge so that a president or dean has little power over the people who are the senior management of the institution. Given the substantial role that faculties play in the selection of presidents and deans, career opportunity is enhanced by avoiding controversy with tenured faculty. A third reason is that accrediting authorities insist that faculty play a major role in all academic decisions. For example, Stanford president Gerhard Casper observes that today "power comes from the bottom up. The most important decisions are those concerning admissions, curriculum, and faculty appointments, and there are the areas where the university president has almost no power."[86] These are all areas where accrediting authorities insist that faculty play the dominant role. A fourth reason for the shift in power to the faculty is that over time governance issues tend to be dominated by people with the strongest sense of direction and interest. When boards of trustees were dominated by those with religious fervor, the boards had a clear sense of direction and energy to carry it out. Through the course of this century, professors have come to have a much stronger interest in, and energy for university governance than the governing boards.[87]

At this particular time in the historical development of higher education in the United States, the governing board may be in the best position to address the coercive tactics of faculty zealots. The board has the legal authority to do so. The board has some distance from university life so that board members may both be able to see the situation more clearly and be less susceptible to coercive tactics. Paradoxically, given the last four decades of education of the board by accrediting authorities, the AAUP, and the popular press, board members may be the constituency most respectful of professional academic freedom. The focus here is therefore on suggestions for governing boards to address faculty zealotry, but the same suggestions are applicable also to university presidents and deans. The most important single step that a governing board can take to address the problem of faculty zealots is to educate its existing and new members on professional academic freedom. Board members must understand the university's mission of improving and disseminating knowledge, the fundamental importance of professional academic freedom to that mission, the rights and correlative duties of professional academic freedom, and the outer limit of professional academic freedom for the faculty zealot. They should also be aware of the history of waves of zealotry in higher education, the shift of power in the university over the past fifty years from governing boards and administrations to the faculty, the tendency of faculty collegia to acquiesce in and condone professional misconduct, and the faculty's resistance to any administrative efforts to control misconduct in order to preserve maximum individual autonomy. In any particular period of zealotry, the governing board should also educate itself regarding the ideology of the prevailing moralism and its tactics. In the current period, board members should be familiar with the ideology and tactics of the fundamentalist academic left.

Education on professional academic freedom will prepare the board to respect rights of professional academic freedom during normal times and to protect academic freedom during periods of zealotry. The board must recognize that through McCarthyism in the 1950s, boards themselves were the chief threat to professional academic freedom. The last two periods of zealotry are historically unusual populist intimidations from students and faculty. It seems highly probable that the boards themselves will again be a threat during a future wave of high moralism and zealotry. A board will then understand that any intervention to protect professional academic freedom in the current zealotry poses a particularly difficult and delicate task. Any board intervention in this wave of zealotry to combat the professional misconduct of faculty zealots must minimize the risk that precedent set now will weaken protection for rights of academic freedom when the zealotry is from the board itself in the future.

Education of the board regarding the ideology and tactics of the fundamentalist academic left in the current wave of zealotry will help the board recognize what is happening and overcome confusion and inertia. For example, governing boards may not understand clearly that the university is a major battleground for the fundamentalist academic left. The fundamentalists believe that the current rules and forms of American society, including the values and forms of the university itself, lack any legitimacy and are in place simply because of the oppressive power of class and status groups currently at the top of the hierarchy, principally Eurocentric white males. Concepts like impartiality, rationality, academic merit and the search for knowledge lack any inherent legitimacy and are simply masks for this oppression. The fundamentalist academic left's goal is to reveal this vast hidden structure of oppression, convince the oppressed to see the world as totally politicized, empower the oppressed to engage in politics, and end the oppression. An intermediate objective is to capture the meaning giving bodies in society, principally education, to promote this ideology.[88] The fundamentalists' politicization of the university itself is thus justifiable and necessary both as a reflection of the need to shift power to the oppressed in the university and as a means to the ultimate goal of transforming society through control of the meaning giving bodies.

Understanding the fundamentalist academic left's rejection of traditional academic values, its ultimate goal, and its intermediate goal of capturing the meaning giving bodies in society and politicizing the university in particular, will help the board avoid confusion and see its responsibility. The board must understand that the fundamentalists' politicization of the university poses a unique threat to rights of academic freedom. Professional academic freedom was not historically designed with zealotry from the faculty itself in mind. The original focus was to protect faculty from pressures by lay boards and administrations.

Boards may also be confused by the fundamentalists' tactics and the faculty's response to the tactics. For example, because the university itself is seen as oppressive and corrupt, zealots within the faculty and student body are free of the normal attachments of institutional loyalty and community pride that moderate self-inflicted public disrepute in other institutions like corporations, professional firms, or nonprofit organizations. Zealots want to bring the university to its knees and do not fear severe economic damage to the university. This may be the hardest point for outsiders like boards of trustees to comprehend:

the attachments of institutional loyalty and community pride by which they live do not apply in the university setting for one subset of employees. Board members may also be confused by the failure of concessions to buy peace with faculty and student zealots. The board must understand the zealot's purpose is to expose the realities of hidden oppressive structures by forcing the university into confrontation and oppressive actions. Thus, concessions by the governing board must be met with new demands that ultimately force the confrontation. Zealots also cannot be appeased or they lose their status as victims and their political power. The zealots' tenacity in pursuing these goals over years is also critical information for the board.

The faculty's acquiescence in and facilitation of the tactics of zealotry may also be confusing for the board. The general reasons for the faculty's abdication of its correlative duty to protect academic freedom were explored earlier. One reason bears particular emphasis in this wave of zealotry. On many humanities and social science faculties in the late 1980s and early 1990s, professors on the left of the political spectrum dominate. Thus, while the majority of faculty may be unpoliticized, their political, social and economic goals substantially resemble those of the zealots and lead them to be sympathetic with the zealots' goals. This tendency toward monolithic thought is inherently dangerous for rights of academic freedom. Few people, even in the university, will defend vigorously the right of others to speak thoughts for which the listener has no sympathy. The board may reflect a wider diversity of thought on many issues than the faculty and at least some board members should therefore have a greater interest in protecting the expression of diverse views.

The governing board must understand that paradoxically, on some campuses today the board itself will be more willing to protect professional academic freedom than many faculty. Over the past half of a century, the AAUP, accrediting agencies, and the professoriat have been extremely successful in educating governing boards regarding the rights of professional academic freedom. In the last three decades since the early 1960s, governing boards have granted academics unprecedented freedom to say and do things that earlier were subject to severe sanction.[89]

Finally, the education of the board must outline how the principles of the correlative duties inherent in professional academic freedom provide the means to address the professional misconduct of faculty zealots and to protect academic freedom. Again the board must understand the importance of moving carefully in using these principles. Overreaction now will expose rights of academic freedom to external attack in a future period of zealotry, when the board itself may be infected with an extreme moralism.

Beyond education of existing and new members on professional academic freedom, what should the governing board do during this wave of zealotry? The board must equip itself with an institutional means to receive different views from individual students and faculty members concerning academic freedom. In the short term, the governing board should undertake an assessment of the degree to which both the mission of the university to improve and disseminate knowledge and rights of professional academic freedom are threatened by the tactics of student and faculty zealots. Any assessment must take into account the reality that targets and potential targets of the zealots will fear vilification or worse if they come forward. The board must keep in mind that even in normal times, perhaps only three or four of every 1000 professors ever have occasion to say or write things that would bring them into conflict with zealots and who therefore need the protection of academic freedom. Given the tendency toward monolithic thought in some faculties, there may be even fewer dissenters. Clearly the issue is not how the majority of faculty perceive the problem of suppression of dissent. For example, during McCarthyism, Shrecker found extensive denial that there was any problem of suppression. Lazarsfeld and Thielens found that conservative professors were much less likely to see any problem during McCarthyism than liberal professors. The opposite will be true today. The focus of any inquiry today should be on the experience of professors who are publicly dissenting from any tenet of the current orthodoxy, or who would wish to do so (if a faculty has any). Professors to the right of center would be more likely targets than those to the left of center, although professors of any political persuasion who publicly advocate quality and standards may be a target. Many faculty may minimize the problem by characterizing it as merely factional infighting or "faculty politics." If specific targets are identified, the board can provide both public and private support and indemnification for a defense. In the long term the board could utilize an ombudsman on the issue of academic freedom.

If the board finds either specific targets or a general problem of unprofessional conduct or both, the board should give the faculty an opportunity to correct the problem. Specifically, the board should ask the faculty to educate itself on the rights and correlative duties of professional academic freedom. Many professors may be uninformed on the correlative duty that the faculty as a collegial body enforce the competency and ethical constraints of the discipline when individual professors do not meet them. Education about the correlative duties of academic freedom might combat the tendency of a collegium to emphasize collegial harmony and autonomy in condoning professional misconduct. Many professors also may be unaware of the correlative duty as individuals and as a collegial body to defend the academic freedom of others. The board can also encourage faculty discussion of issues of professional academic freedom and professional misconduct. The board should bear in mind that the solution is not more committees. This favors those faculty members who like committees. Finally, the board can appeal to senior faculty specifically as a group to intervene in correcting problems of professional misconduct.[90]

If these faculty efforts are given time to work but, after a reasonable time problems of professional misconduct and threats to professional academic freedom persist, the board could ask the administration to bring charges of professional misconduct against faculty zealots as appropriate. If charges are brought, but the faculty is unwilling to police its own ranks, the board should consider the seriousness of the threat to professional academic freedom and the mission of the university. If the threat is serious, and there is clear and convincing evidence that the faculty is failing to perform its correlative duty to hold individual faculty members accountable for professional misconduct, then the board can make a finding of compelling circumstances and intervene to overrule the faculty decision, impose penalties and protect academic freedom.

If the board makes a determination to intervene, it must minimize the risk that the intervention will do more harm than good to protect professional academic freedom in the long run. To minimize this risk, for example, the board could appoint a review committee consisting of distinguished academics from other institutions to consider cases of professional misconduct.

The governing board should give a full and honest explanation of its actions. Accountability is the willingness to explain decisions backed by evidence to students, faculty, alumni, and the public. This will also help these constituencies understand what is occurring in higher education.

The board should also keep in mind its own limitations. Board members are volunteers who serve usually out of a combination of motives: service to the community and (in some cases) their alma mater; prestige; and networking opportunities. While the board is removed from daily interaction with faculty and student zealots, zealots may be able to subject the board to the same tactics successful within the walls: false accusations of bigotry, other forms of harassment, demonstrations, litigation, and adverse media coverage. Some board members may be highly vulnerable to coercive tactics and for them, the costs of board membership will outweigh the benefits of a fairly low level of coercion. The board has to be prepared for this and decide if it has long term staying power.

The governing board can play a positive and critical role in preserving academic freedom in this period of zealotry. The next chapter explores a spectrum of responses by the target of zealotry to help the target survive in higher education.

Notes

1. Julius Getman, IN THE COMPANY OF SCHOLARS 89 (1992).
2. Derek Bok, HARVARD PRESIDENT'S REPORT 11, 12 (1991).
3. Walter P. Metzger, *Profession and Constitution: Two Definitions of Academic Freedom in America*, 66 TEX. L. REV. 1265, 1284, n.42 (1988).
4. Clifford Orwin, *Civility*, AM. SCHOLAR, Autumn 1991, at 553, 556.
5. *Id.* at 557.
6. *Id.* at 556.
7. *Id.* at 558.

8. Leonard Eron, *Prescription for Reduction of Aggression*, AM. PSYCHOLOGIST, Mar. 1980, at 244, 251.

9. Alice Eagly & Valerie Steffen, *Gender and Aggressive Behavior: A Meta-Analytic Review of the Social Psychological Literature*, 100 PSYCHOL. BULL. 309, 325 (1986).

10. Carol Gilligan, IN A DIFFERENT VOICE 5–8, 41 (1982).

11. For example, the American Association of Law Schools recommends that "law professors should treat colleagues and staff members with civility and respect. Senior law professors should be particularly sensitive to the terms of any debate involving their junior colleagues." 1992 HANDBOOK OF THE ASSOCIATION OF AMERICAN LAW SCHOOLS 59, 61 [hereinafter HANDBOOK].

12. Jonathan Rauch, KINDLY INQUISITORS 125–26 (1992).

13. AAUP Committee A, *Academic Freedom and Tenure: A Preliminary Report on Freedom of Expression and Campus Harassment Codes, reprinted in* ACADEME, May-June 1991, at 23, 25.

14. *See Keyishian v. Board of Regents*, 385 U.S. 589, 604 (1967).

15. AAUP Committee A, *supra* note 13, at 23–24.

16. *Id.* at 25.

17. *Id.*

18. AAUP Committee A, *Some Observations on Ideology, Competence and Faculty Selection, reprinted in* ACADEME, Jan.-Feb. 1986, at 1a, 2a.

19. AAUP Committee A, *On Freedom of Expression and Campus Speech Codes, reprinted in* ACADEME, July-Aug. 1992, at 30, 31.

20. AAUP, *A Statement of the Association's Council: Freedom and Responsibility, reprinted in* AAUP, POLICY DOCUMENTS & REPORTS 77, 78 (1990).

21. Legality and civility are separate questions. The fact that the law permits an action does not make it ethical in the individual case. The First Amendment, for example, protects from government sanction many forms of speech that assault the dignity of and deny respect to others in an unethical manner.

22. AAUP Committee A, *supra* note 18, at 2a.

23. Derek Bok, *What's Wrong With Our Universities?*, 14 HARV. J.L. & PUB. POL'Y 305, 333 (Spring 1991).

24. Academic protocol, as well as common courtesy, calls for seeing a colleague before making public accusations. The accused may have a satisfactory explanation. The accused colleague also then has an opportunity to prepare a response before public accusations occur.

25. Steven C. Bahls, *Political Correctness and the American Law School*, 69 WASH. U. L.Q. 1041, 1044 (1991).

26. HANDBOOK, *supra* note 11, at 61. "[D]istortion or misrepresentation is always unacceptable. Relevant evidence and arguments should be addressed.... The scholar's commitment to truth requires intellectual honesty and open-mindedness."

27. Fritz Machlup, *On Some Misconceptions Concerning Academic Freedom, in* ACADEMIC FREEDOM & TENURE 177, 189 (Louis Joughin ed., 1969).

28. William Van Alstyne, *The Specific Theory of Academic Freedom and the General Issue of Civil Liberty in* THE CONCEPT OF ACADEMIC FREEDOM 76 (Edmund Pincoff, ed. 1972).

29. *See* J. Peter Byrne, *Academic Freedom: A "Special Concern of the First Amendment,"* 99 YALE L.J. 251, 259 (1989). Professor Edward Shils emphasizes that academics enjoy the special attention and respect of the public because they are presumed by the audience to speak with the authority conferred by intensive and scrupulous study of the subjects involved. When an academic allows him or

herself to be identified by academic connection and rank, he or she is claiming "the authority which is acknowledged to inhere in methodically acquired expert knowledge, disinterestedness, and abstention from passionate partisanship." Edward Shils, THE ACADEMIC ETHIC 86 (1983).

30. Ralph F. Fuchs, *Academic Freedom—Its Basic Philosophy, Function, and History, in* ACADEMIC FREEDOM AND TENURE 242, 258 (Louis Joughin ed., 1969).

31. Ellen W. Schrecker, NO IVORY TOWER: MCCARTHYISM & THE UNIVERSITIES 303 (1986).

32. AAUP Committee A, *supra* note 13, at 25.

33. *Levin v. Harleston*, 966 F.2d 85, 89–90 (2d Cir. 1992).

34. The discussion at the end of chapter 6 is relevant in determining whether a professor's failure to meet affirmative duties of investigation and accuracy can be penalized. The First Amendment may protect a professor's speech at a public university as long as it is not knowingly false or made with reckless disregard for the truth.

35. AAUP Committee A, *supra* note 19, at 30–31. The Woodward Report at Yale also emphasized that disruption of speeches or classes should be penalized. "We believe that the positive obligation to protect and respect free expression shared by all members of the university should be enforced by appropriate formal sanctions, because obstruction of such expression threatens the central function of the university." *Report of the Committee on Freedom of Expression at Yale*, 4 HUMAN RIGHTS 357, 359 (1975).

36. AAUP Council, *A Statement of the Association's Council: Freedom and Responsibility*, 56 AAUP BULL. 375, 376 (Dec. 1970).

37. Commission on Academic Tenure in Higher Education, FACULTY TENURE 42 (1973).

38. *Id.* at 44–45.

39. AAUP Committee A, *supra* note 19, at 31.

40. *See* AAUP Council, *supra* note 36; Ralph Fuchs, *Academic Freedom—Its Basic Philosophy, Function, and History, reprinted in* ACADEMIC FREEDOM AND TENURE 258 (Louis Joughin ed. 1969). Professor Fuchs recommends that "specific justification for each inquiry must be shown," because of the coercive effect of investigations.

41. *See* Joseph Salemi, *Political Correctness at Dallas Baptist University: The Firing of David Ayers and John Jeffrey*, MEASURE, Aug.-Sept. 1992, at 1, 9.

42. The danger to academic freedom is dramatically increased in high profile cases. The chances that a decision to initiate an investigation will be made on the merits are substantially lower when the media is pressuring the institution to do something. In these circumstances, the tendency is to proceed if the case is at all doubtful.

43. Courtney Leatherman, *Legacy of a Bitter Sex Harassment Battle: Rising Complaints, Frustrations, Fears*, CHRON. HIGHER EDUC., Oct. 14, 1992, at A-17, A-18.

44. AAUP Committee A, *supra* note 19, at 30–31.

45. AAUP Committee A, *Report of Committee A*, 30 AAUP BULL. 13, 16 (1945).

46. An accusation of scientific misconduct considerably damages a professor's reputation and standing. Melany Stinson Newby, Vice-Chancellor at the University of Wisconsin-Madison, proposes that before a government agency is allowed to make and publicize a finding of misconduct, the public and the scientific community should be able to assume that sufficient evidence exists and has been tested against an appropriate burden of proof. Melany Stinson Newby, *Let's Pro-*

tect the Rights of Scientists Who Are Accused of Misconduct, CHRON. HIGHER EDUC., April 28, 1993, at B1, B2.

47. Victoria Slind Flor, *Scientific Fraud and The Law,* NAT. L. J., Oct. 25, 1993 at 1.
48. *Id.* at 44.
49. *Id.* at 45. Attorney's fees for the defense of scientific misconduct investigations (internal and external) and tribunals can be very high. They are in excess of $200,000 in one of Barbara Mishkin's current cases (at one-half the normal rates). Indemnity for defense costs from the university will be critical.
50. AAUP, *The 1915 General Declaration of Principles* (1915), *reprinted in* ACADEMIC FREEDOM & TENURE app. A at 155, 159-79 (Louis Joughin ed., 1969) [hereinafter AAUP, *1915 Declaration*].
51. AAUP, *Statement of Procedural Standards in Faculty Dismissal Proceedings, reprinted in* AAUP, POLICY DOCUMENTS & REPORTS 11, 12 (1990).
52. *See* AAUP, *A Statement of the Association's Council: Freedom and Responsibility, reprinted in* AAUP, POLICY DOCUMENTS AND REPORTS 77, 78 (1990).
53. AAUP, *1915 Declaration, supra* note 50, at 170.
54. Rebecca S. Eisenberg, *Academic Freedom and Academic Values in Sponsored Research,* 66 TEX. L. REV. 1363, 1366-67 (1988).
55. David M. Rabban, *Does Academic Freedom Limit Faculty Autonomy?,* 66 TEX. L. REV. 1405, 1407-08 (1988).
56. Judith P. Swazey, *Are Physicians a "Delinquent Community"?: Issues in Professional Competence, Conduct, and Self Regulation,* 10 J. BUS. ETHICS 581, 585 (1991).
57. AAAS MEMBER OPINION POLL: SCIENTIFIC ETHICS AND RESPONSIBILITY, March, 1992, at 5.
58. Martin Anderson, IMPOSTORS IN THE TEMPLE 133-34 (1992). The Office of Research Integrity hasn't won one misconduct case on appeal and has been heavily criticized. Stephen Burd, *Fraud Office in Trouble,* CHRON. HIGHER EDUC., Nov. 24, 1993, at A21, A26.
59. *See* Note, *Science Misconduct and Due Process: A Case of Process Due,* 45 HASTINGS L.REV. 309, 317-18, 323-24 (1994); Judith Swazey, Karen Louis, Melissa Anderson, *The Ethical Training of Graduate Students Requires Serious and Continuing Attention,* CHRON. HIGHER EDUC., March 9, 1994, at B2.
60. *See Science Misconduct, supra* note 58, at 323.
61. Carolyn J. Mooney, *Critics Question Higher Education's Commitment and Effectiveness in Dealing with Plagiarism,* CHRON. HIGHER EDUC., Feb. 12, 1992, at A-13. The American Historical Association's *Statement on Plagiarism* notes that "What is troubling...is the reluctance of many scholars to speak out about the possible offenses that come to their notice." American Historical Association, *Statement on Standards of Professional Conduct* 16 (1993).
62. Leslie Fishbein, *Curbing Cheating and Restoring Academic Integrity,* CHRON. HIGHER EDUC., Dec. 1, 1993, at A52.
63. Judith Swazey, Melissa Anderson, and Karen Lewis, *Ethical Problems in Academic Research,* AMERICAN SCIENTIST, Nov.-Dec. 1993, at 542, 545 (2,600 of the 4,000 students and faculty surveyed returned the questionnaire).
64. Judith Swazey, Karen Louis, and Melissa Anderson, *The Ethical Training of Graduate Students Requires Serious and Continuing Attention* CHRON. HIGHER EDUC., March 9, 1994 at B1.
65. *Ethical Problems in Academic Research, supra* note 63, at 549.
66. *Id.* at 550.
67. Robert T. Blackburn, *The Professor and His Ethics,* 53 AAUP BULL. 416, 422 (1967).

68. Sidney Hook, OUT OF STEP 505 (1987).
69. Henry Rosovsky, DEAN'S REPORT, HARVARD UNIV. FAC. OF ARTS & SCI-
    ENCES 1990-91 at 10-12.
70. Eliot Friedson, DOCTORING TOGETHER: A STUDY OF PROFESSIONAL
    SOCIAL CONTROL 14-15 (1975).
71. *Id.* at 239.
72. *Id.* at 237.
73. *Id.* at 237, 241.
74. *Id.* at 241-242.
75. *Id.* at 216.
76. *See id.* at 99, 213, 219, 237, 241.
77. *Id.* at 243.
78. *Id.*
79. *Id.* at 244-45.
80. *Ethical Problems in Academic Research, supra* note 63, at 550.
81. *The Ethical Training of Graduate Students,* supra note 64, at B2.
82. William Brown, ACADEMIC POLITICS 17-19, 62-64 (1982).
83. John Braxton and Alan Bayer, *Perceptions of Research Misconduct and an Analy-
    sis of Their Correlates,* 65 J. HIGHER EDUC., 351, 355, 364-66 (May/June 1994).
84. In 1992, the number of full-time faculty members with tenure totaled roughly
    212,000. *The Nation,* CHRON. HIGHER EDUC., August 25, 1993, at 5. There
    are approximately thirty to fifty formal detenuring proceedings each year, of
    which roughly 75 percent are won by the administration. Telephone Interview
    with Jonathan Knight, AAUP (June 25, 1992). The AAUP's associate general
    secretary, Jordan Kurland, recently estimated that about 50 tenured professors
    are dismissed each year for cause, and about one-half of these go through the
    formal dismissal procedures. Carolyn Mooney, *Dismissals 'For Cause,'* CHRON.
    HIGHER EDUC., Dec. 7, 1994, at A17, A19. Dismissing a tenured professor
    "for cause" is a lengthy and expensive process. Such cases call for an enormous
    amount of time from faculty members called upon to judge the matter. A recent
    case at Rutgers University where a faculty panel found against a colleague re-
    quired 46 days of hearings. *Id.* This means that the chances that a tenured profes-
    sor will lose his or her job are almost infinitesimal. *See* Jacob Neusner, *What It
    Takes For Professors To Get Themselves Fired,* CHRON. HIGHER EDUC., March
    17, 1993, at A52. Professor Neusner recounts his experience that a tenured pro-
    fessor who canceled a course because of anger at the administration received no
    penalty nor did a professor who refused to go to department meetings or to serve
    on committees. Some faculty members' usual responses to administrative initia-
    tives to address professional misconduct, in the author's experience, is to pre-
    serve maximum faculty autonomy in work performance and behavior by attacking
    the administration.
85. Paul Brest, *The Disorderly University: A Reply to Mark Tushnet,* 4 YALE J. L. &
    HUMAN., 381, 383 (1992).
86. Thomas Sowell, *Power Without Responsibility,* FORBES, Feb. 14, 1994, at 85.
87. Henry G. Manne, Comment on Peter Byrne's "Academic Freedom and Political
    Neutrality," 43 J. LEGAL EDUC. 340, 341-42 (1993).
88. Mark Kelman, *Emerging Centrist Liberalism,* 43 FLA. ST. U. L. REV. 417, 428,
    443 (1991).
89. Edward Shils, *Do We Still Need Academic Freedom,* AMERICAN SCHOLAR,
    Spring, 1993, at 187, 206.
90. A defender of academic freedom should be extremely reluctant to risk the au-
    tonomy of faculty peer review by resorting to either intervention by the govern-

ing board or outside legal procedure. Such actions damage the tradition of professional academic freedom, but the damage may be less than that inflicted by faculty zealots. Calling for board intervention is like calling for artillery fire on your own position because you have been overrun. There will be injury from friendly fire.

11

Effective Responses by the Target of Zealotry

In order to understand how to make an effective response, the professor targeted by zealotry must first understand what is happening. Targets may experience an extended period of confusion where they cannot believe, do not understand, and grossly underestimate what is happening.[1] This confusion may disable them from making an effective response until it is too late.

This chapter first outlines common coercive tactics in a wave of zealotry and the target's initial response of amazement and confusion. The discussion emphasizes the importance of self-education about past periods of zealotry, the ongoing zealotry, and professional academic freedom. The chapter then discusses eight lines of defense that a target should consider in any wave of zealotry. Finally, the chapter explores the unique problems of the target in the current period of zealotry from the fundamentalist academic left within the faculty itself.

The seven waves of zealotry in higher education during the past century and a quarter since the emergence of the modern university share common characteristics. Each has been rooted in a strong ideology and has embraced zealotry to enforce the ideology. Those who disagree are heretics, and zealots vilify any disagreement as an act of moral turpitude. Zealots then employ a variety of coercive tactics to harass and to eliminate heretical academic thought and speech.

The first two waves of zealotry were initiated by the governing boards and administrations. The next three, including McCarthyism, were initiated principally outside the university and motivated by a superpatriotism; the governing board and administration would often respond with investigations threatening the employment of the target. The coercive tactics of McCarthyism itself were the most sophisticated of these earlier waves. The use of repeated false accusations of moral turpitude followed by an investigation and a tribunal to create the "big lie" was the most successful tactic of McCarthyism. Hostility, ostracism, isolation, and adverse employment consequences followed.

During the student activism of the late 1960s, zealots employed tactics of confrontation and disruption to degrade and silence dissenting ideas. The tactics of confrontation included the use of ridicule, rudeness, obscenity, inflammatory false accusations, struggle meetings, and other forms of violent and abusive language. The tactics of disruption included both threatened and actual obstruction of speeches, classes, and administrative operations.

The current wave of zealotry from the fundamentalist academic left within the faculty itself borrows tactics from both McCarthyism and the student activism of the 1960s. Similar to McCarthyism, zealots in the current period employ tactics of false public accusation of moral turpitude, ostracism and hostility, investigations or the threat of investigation, and threats to employment. Similar to the student activism of the late 1960s, the fundamentalist academic left uses or threatens to use both the tactics of confrontation and the tactics of disruption.

Zealots in all of the last three waves have employed similar advocacy tactics of manipulative persuasion. Accusations of moral turpitude against individuals or institutions have been based on conjecture, gossip, hearsay, the twisting of any ambiguity, half truth by omission, exaggeration, and misrepresentation. Misinformation has been constantly repeated to create adverse perceptions of the accused. Advocacy tactics of manipulative persuasion have displaced traditional standards of academic discourse flowing from the correlative duties of professional academic freedom.

The extraordinary facility with which many academics accommodate themselves to the tactics of zealotry is the most significant aspect of all the waves of zealotry. It is particularly surprising in the last three periods which have occurred after the widespread acceptance of the 1940 statement and the concept of professional academic freedom. The typical response of silent acquiescence in the coercive tactics of zealotry is repeated in each wave.

Amazement and Confusion

How should the target respond to these tactics? The target may initially experience amazement and confusion in the face of zealots' coercive tactics. The situation feels like living in Ionesco's play, *Rhinoceros,* where even ordinary and normal people start snorting and rampaging about, oblivious to facts and reason. False public accusations of moral turpitude aim at a teacher's soul and spirit. Such accusations may be so antithetical to a teacher's aspirations that they fundamentally undermine the teacher's self-concept. It is like being swept off one's feet and tumbled by a large wave.

The principal initial questions to answer are, "What is happening?" and "Why me?" These are difficult questions early in a period of zealotry where the zealots' ideology and tactics are not yet clear. For example, few academics would have anticipated ten years ago that a professor's strong advocacy of academic quality in admissions, faculty appointments and tenure decisions would come to be characterized as a mask for oppression and bigotry in the late 1980s and early 1990s. Similarly, few academics in the early 1960s predicted the wave of student zealotry in the mid to late 1960s. Hofstadter and Metzger comment that one of the "consistent and significant features" of the earliest academic freedom cases after the Civil War was that "the participants were temperate evolutionists who, in the course of events, were trapped into conflict with authority and were surprised into suffering for the cause."[2] Early in a period of zealotry, targets may also be dumfounded by the substitution of tactics of manipulative persuasion for traditional standards of scholarly discourse. For example, in the early stages of McCarthyism, the use of respected false public accusations of moral turpitude followed by investigations and tribunals to create the "big lie" surprised Professor Owen Lattimore at Johns Hopkins. He was further amazed at how his life came to be taken over by investigations, hearings, litigation, lawyers, and the necessity of spending vast proportions of his time and energy defending himself. Lattimore was caught unaware when meetings, interviews and hearings became occasions for entrapment. Questions were not asked just to obtain information but rather to lay a trap where ambiguous words could be twisted or where an answer might be contradicted by other evidence on which zealots could base a perjury charge.

After being tumbled by the initial shock of being the target of the tactics of zealotry, the accused may wishfully believe that the zealotry is a passing phenomenon that, like a bad dream, will go away tomorrow. The tendency then would be to do nothing. The accused also may experience substantial astonishment and confusion over the absence of public and private collegial support. The lack of support may cause the accused to want to withdraw into isolation.

As quickly as possible, the target of zealotry must seek to overcome amazement and confusion, wishful thinking, and any tendency to withdraw. Once a professor realizes a wave of zealotry is underway and that she or he is a target or potential target, professional survival depends upon engagement, not withdrawal. The next two sections outline how the target should best engage in a defense.

Self-Education about Waves of Zealotry and Professional Academic Freedom

The first critical step is for the target to educate herself about waves of zealotry and professional academic freedom. This gives perspective, a sense of what tactics to expect, and an awareness of the tools available for defense. The knowledge both that waves of zealotry occur regularly in academic life and that if history repeats itself, an academic teaching for forty years could experience at least two waves helps to reduce the target's feelings that the situation is a unique and unprecedented unfairness. A healthier view is that zealotry has occurred regularly in academic life, and the mature academic must learn to deal with it. Understanding the coercive tactics commonly used in recent waves will help the target anticipate and prepare for what is to come.

There are still the questions, What is happening now? and Why me? The answer is partially found through study of the ideology underlying the zealotry of the moment. The target should know what is going on locally and nationally in the ongoing wave. Zealots will seek to eliminate first those academics whose public positions clearly threaten their ideology. However, heretics who clearly and publicly threaten the ideology have been only one subset of the targets in recent waves of zealotry. Targets must understand that once zealotry is unleashed, it may assault targets far beyond the limited circle of clear heretics, for example, actual communists or actual bigots. It could attack others simply for political advantage. For example, during McCarthyism, the zealots vented their accumulated resentments against liberal intellectuals, not just communists. Moreover, zealotry feeds on symbolic "incidents" or "demons" around which or whom community organizing builds to incite and influence passion. Symbolic "incidents" may be created totally by manipulative persuasion; facts indicating that the target is without fault are irrelevant to the zealots. For example, during McCarthyism, Professor Owen Lattimore carefully rebutted each accusation during his five and one-half-year inquisition. This did not faze Senator McCarthy and his supporters. They kept right on baying down other false trails. Zealots understand the decisive importance of symbolic "demons" and the power of compounded false accusations. A significant segment of the community will believe that where there is so much smoke, there must be fire. Lattimore also discovered that once he was identified as the symbolic "demon," compromise or a soft moderate approach on his part made no difference. "He was dead center in the sights of the inquisitors and no substitute victim could have replaced him."[3]

Self-education concerning waves of zealotry and professional academic freedom generally, and the ideology of the current zealotry specifically, will help targets and potential targets to fight the natural tendencies of most academics to focus on teaching and scholarship and hope the trouble goes away quickly. It won't. Accept what is and move on to what can be done about it. What are the tools available to the target for defense?

Eight Lines of Defense

Targets in a period of zealotry have several lines of defense: (1) forcing a continuous public debate with the zealots; (2) corresponding quickly and publicly to all false accusations of moral turpitude; (3) pressing colleagues to take a stand to defend professional academic freedom; (4) directly appealing for support from students, alumni, and the public; (5) securing counsel to respond to internal and external investigations; (6) filing formal grievances and complaints with the administration both documenting violations of professional academic freedom and requesting the university to protect contractual rights of professional academic freedom; (7) bringing litigation against the university employer to protect contractual rights of professional academic freedom; and (8) taking maximum advantage of the procedural protections surrounding tenure.

The first line of defense is forcing a continuous public debate with the zealots. Make the case publicly that a period of zealotry is occurring and that it involves issues of major importance. At a minimum, the zealots' coercive tactics involve important issues of rights and duties of professional academic freedom. To demonstrate what is happening, the target should tell personal stories about the coercive tactics and the impact of zealotry on the target's academic freedom. The target must educate the various communities inside and outside the walls about what is at stake if the zealots' ideology and tactics prevail.

The target must take every opportunity to openly question the zealots' ideology and tactics. Hold the ideas to the standards of professional competence. Point out failure to meet the common standards used to evaluate academic work. Hold coercive conduct to the correlative duties of professional competence and ethical conduct. For example, insist on professional treatment of evidence and a professional standard of reasoning and analysis. Be openly vocal about failures to meet these standards and duties. The ensuing public debate will clarify the zealots' ideology and tactics and help internal and external communities to understand the threat to professional academic freedom. The debate will mitigate the tendency of those outside the university to see disputes within academia as finger-pointing, petty office politics. Patience is a virtue in this public debate. Zealots tend to make grave mistakes of excess because their passion prevents them from exercising objectivity and good judgment. They are often blind to lines of propriety. Senator McCarthy and his supporters are good examples. The target must seize on these excesses when they occur and point them out publicly.

The defense must insist on the primacy of professional academic freedom over any political agenda. The response to ideological zealotry cannot be to seek the supremacy of an opposing ideology within the university.

The target must observe professional standards of competence and ethical conduct and above all refrain from coercive tactics. The target cannot play by the zealots' rules. Double standards work to the target's disadvantage. Violations of the correlative duties by the target that are far less serious than the violations of the zealots may be seized upon as further charges. The target must also exercise care in avoiding *unintended* symbolic incidents to be seized on by zealots. The target will be disadvantaged by the surprise in such incidents. For example, a target may be surprised by "struggle meeting" tactics or encirclement in informal situations where zealots in turn attack the target. Any unprofessional conduct by a surprised and unprepared target will be trumpeted as a further charge. Anticipation of and careful preparation for symbolic incidents can turn them to a target's advantage.

The target must learn the skill of handling direct and fundamental disagreement with calm, matter of fact decency. Former Yale president Schmidt observes that "a liberated mind will strive for the courage and composure to face ideas that are fraught with evil, and to answer them."[4] Many Eastern European and Soviet dissidents demonstrated this skill in the face of the most severe repression of ideas. Over time, undeserved suffering without retaliation is a powerful moral force that may trigger sympathetic support.

As with the Eastern European and Soviet dissidents, persevere in building skills of composure and self-control and in delivering a public message about the zealotry. All these skills take time to develop. Take small steps to stretch confidence and strength. Keep repeating the same themes and evidence over the years that the period of zealotry runs. Remember that a new idea that is unfamiliar to its audience becomes clear only through persistent, repeated contact.

The target must understand that during a wave of zealotry, conventional patterns of trust and loyalty and propriety among colleagues, students, the administration, and the university itself may have to be reformulated. Commitment to professional academic freedom and the university's mission of improving and disseminating knowledge may, during a period of zealotry, require action that in normal times would be viewed as disloyal or improper. For example, the target must have credible evidence to establish what is happening. During both McCarthyism and the present fundamentalism from the radical academic left, zealots and facilitating faculty and administration largely have denied the existence of coercion. The target must create written documentation of what is happening through memoranda, letters, and written minutes of all meetings (even when others are taking formal minutes). Memoranda and letters to the administration and governing board can set forth coercive tactics and the impact of the tactics on the target's rights to professional academic freedom. If possible the target should consider openly (not secretly) tape recording critical meetings.

While it is difficult for professors traditionally loyal to the institution to do so, targets should provide detailed factual accounts of what is happening in campus media and campus forums. In addition, the target may need to create new forums for discussion of the issues raised by zealots. Bring in outside speakers with points of view that are diverse from the prevailing orthodoxy. The target should not use her or his classroom for these purposes. This invites an accusation that the target is violating a correlative duty of professional academic freedom to keep politicized extraneous material out of the classroom.

A second line of defense is to respond quickly and publicly to all false accusations of moral turpitude. Silence in the face of such accusations will be characterized as an admission. Silence in the face of a series of repeated accusations is disastrous. Repeated unrebutted false accusations will influence students, alumni, staff, colleagues, and the community to ostracize the target. The target becomes increasingly isolated over time.

Fully disclosed facts tend to drive out the distortions of false allegations. The target should send memoranda to faculty and administration answering false accusations and dispelling rumors. The target needs good credible documentation of the facts to rebut the twisting of every ambiguity and innuendo. If the false accusations have spread more widely, the target should answer them publicly through means appropriate to each affected constituency. For example, if false accusations have been spread within the student body, the target should respond through the student newspaper.

If the zealots seek media coverage for their accusations of moral turpitude, the target must be prepared to speak to the media immediately. The story will get maximum coverage on the first day and the media may include an immediate response along with the allegations. A later response may get no coverage. Be prepared to explain to a reporter what is happening in clear, strong language and images understandable to the public. There is still no guarantee that even an immediate response will be covered. As Owen Lattimore found, "the man who is accused is at a disadvantage with his accuser when it comes to headlines and newspaper space. This commonplace observation becomes very poignant when you are the man accused, and a man like McCarthy ruthfully exploits his advantage by making the accusations so sensational that the revelation of the truth seems drab and dull by comparison."[5]

The target must make a similar decision with respect to public meetings and hearings called to discuss the accusations of moral turpitude. These may be events covered by the media. One strategy is not to attend. Zealots will seize on this as evidence of admission of the charges. Another is to make qualified, carefully guarded, and prepared statements which will reduce the risk of error or entrapment. A final strategy is to take such meeting or hearings head on and respond to the zealots directly as dictated by the opportunities and demands of the moment. Professor Lattimore chose this last course in responding to McCarthy and never regretted it.[6]

Once a false public accusation of moral turpitude occurs, the truth never catches up. A subset of people always believe it. The target has to accept this reality and fight publicly to minimize damage and isolation.

A third line of defense is pressing colleagues to take a stand to defend professional academic freedom against the coercive tactics of zealots. This is a relatively faint hope, but is worth trying. During waves of zealotry, faculty repeatedly have failed both to address the zealotry and to protect academic freedom. They generally have failed to give public support to alleged heretics. Chapter 9 offered several tentative explanations for this response. Most academics have no active malice toward the target but they are highly influenced by fear of coercive tactics. Those with an ideological kinship with the zealots may see the unjustly accused target as "an unfortunate casualty in the war against _____ (fill in the ideological goal of the zealotry)."

To the degree that inadequate knowledge and preparation are the cause of these repeated faculty failures, the target can educate her or his colleagues and hope for a stronger defense. The target can inform colleagues about both the history of waves of zealotry in higher education and the rights and correlative duties of professional academic freedom, particularly the correlative duty to defend professional academic freedom. Colleagues should know that the faculty response of silent acquiescence in coercive tactics has been the ballast of ideological zealotry in each wave. They should also know that efforts to appease zealots in past waves have not been successful. This may help them to resist academics' strong tendency to rationalize each concession.

Many colleagues may avoid knowing the devastating costs that the zealots' tactics impose on the target. It has been common this century for people to avoid responsibility for the destructive excesses of zealotry by claiming, "I did not know." The target should share the personal story of the impact of coercive tactics. The target should force colleagues to see both that they are making a choice by staying silent and that silence severely damages the target. In the face of an affirmative duty to defend academic freedom, an academic's indifference to the suppression of colleagues is complicity.

The target should also emphasize the risk that colleagues may come to grief once the zealots eliminate the initial targets. For example, McCarthyism did not stop with academics who were clearly communists, it built upon accumulated resentments to go far beyond the tiny circle of actual communists, attacking also liberals for political advantage. Looking at 126 cases of McCarthyism, Lionel Lewis found that only one third of the principals could objectively be characterized as being somewhere between mildly and very radical.[7]

The target should search for allies among those alienated, threatened, or attacked by zealots. A study of physicians found that those physicians who had been sued felt much more strongly than the nonsued physicians that the plaintiff's case was unjustified and that settling a suit was tantamount to an admission of guilt. Unsued physicians tended to believe that accusations are brought only against physicians who are guilty of negligence.[8] The same should be true with faculty. Those who are not under attack may tend to distance themselves from the accused. But over time some other colleague may be personally confronted with the possibility of being a target, and his or her attitude might change. The target should seek allies among the disaffected. Ladd and Lipset found that in the 1960s the initial reaction of many nonactivist professors and students was that the activists had a good point, and that the university ought to negotiate and compromise. Repressive tactics by the police often radicalized this nonactivist group. Subsequently a slow process of disillusionment with the activists occurred as concessions in the initial major confrontations did not bring peace or return the campus to normal but rather new demands and the escalation of protest.[9]

Reminding colleagues that there will always be zealots, that if history repeats itself, several waves of zealotry may occur during a career together, and that the direction of the next wave has been difficult to predict may also engender some sense of mutual self-interest to support one another. The target must also commit him or herself to defend others' academic freedom publicly. A target should be realistic in assessing the success of efforts to enlist colleagues and administrators to defend academic freedom publicly. History suggests strong public support is uncommon.

The target should build an internal resistance group among any colleagues giving dependable and consistent support. The group should assess and utilize the unique skills of each member to highest advantage. Each should share information in order to assess what is happening. It is critical, for example, to organize in order to have a common strategy at meetings and with the press. The group should consider a strategy of buying time through delaying tactics in the hope the wave of zealotry will wane.

If the accused is without public support from any colleague or the administration, the situation is grim. The target will be totally isolated within the community. It seems probable that the zealots' coercive tactics will eventually drive the accused out under these conditions. For many targets, the workplace may simply become too unpleasant to endure. The accused must still fight to minimize the damage to the accused's future employment and to professional academic freedom and the university.

A fourth line of defense is directly appealing for public support from academics at other institutions, academic organizations, accrediting authorities, students, alumni, and the public. Each of these steps bears careful study since each will take time, but may bear little fruit. Academics at other institutions may give private moral support but rarely seem to give public support because they are also fearful for the reasons discussed earlier. Accrediting agencies, professional groups, and the AAUP may be conflict averse, very slow to react to zealotry, or controlled by zealots. For example, history indicates that the AAUP has not responded in a timely manner to recent waves of zealotry. The AAUP's principal assistance to a target is the theoretical work that defines professional academic freedom and the procedural due process that protects tenure. The AAUP's investigations have historically focused on violations of academic due process by the administration and governing board, so to the degree possible, a grievance should be framed in this context.

Appeals through the media for public support from students, alumni, and the public may make sense as a strategy of desperation if everything else is failing. The target should have been trying to force a continuous public debate with the zealots. Assess the degree to which any of these constituencies have taken an interest in the debate. Are the students, for example, totally intimidated by the zealotry, or are there some students who are less inhibited than faculty colleagues in speaking out? If the campus and local media are controlled by persons slanted towards the zealots' ideology, this strategy may backfire. It is in any event a volatile strategy; it is difficult to predict the reaction of the media and the outside constituencies. It is better that the media and outside constituencies come to have an interest in the issues because of a lively public debate than because of personal appeals for help.

An appeal to the alumni or the public through the media will offend some colleagues' sense of propriety and institutional pride. For example, during McCarthyism, Shrecker reports that some academics tried to defend the accused through internal channels but believed that active open opposition through press releases violated the norms of the academic community.[10] A target's media strategy may result in some further alienation of middle of the road faculty.

A target has to assess the situation on a continuing basis and make predictions concerning the strategy of the zealots. The tactics of the last several waves of zealotry have been predictable and probably will be repeated again. The zealots' next step after false public accusations of moral turpitude, hostility and ostracism has frequently been to initiate internal and external investigations and tribunals.

If the zealots move to initiate internal and external investigations, the target's situation becomes substantially more complex and hazardous. Previously, the target was fighting false accusations of moral turpitude, hostility, and ostracism, both inside and outside the walls. Once an investigation is unleashed, the accused is fighting a war on more fronts, the most crucial of which is the investigation itself.

An investigation is a direct threat to employment. If the misconduct alleged is minor, an internal investigation may involve a very informal process of inquiry by the administration. However, any adverse finding placed in the target's employment file may set the stage for the next round of charges where zealots seek heavier sanctions because of the target's repeated transgressions. Employment itself will then be at risk. Any adverse finding in an investigation may also become a symbolic event around which zealots rally. Even a modest adverse finding may be trumpeted and have dramatic consequences far beyond a target's normal expectations. Accusations of more serious misconduct may lead to investigation followed by some type of internal tribunal. Internal and external investigations may also lead to litigation or professional licensing tribunals aimed at the target. This will be another front. Settlement of the litigation may be trumpeted as an admission of guilt. Once a target is a symbol, it may not even be possible to concede partially or completely and hope the zealots leave the target alone. The zealots may seek a greater symbolic victory against a weakened opponent. The idea is to destroy the target, so that everyone in the community will take note and be forewarned. It is wishful thinking to believe that there is a place to hide once a target becomes a symbol.

If the target makes an assessment that internal and external investigations and tribunals are probable, the target must move to the next line of defense. The next line of defense is securing counsel to prepare for and respond to internal and external investigations and possible tribunals and litigation. If the tea leaves clearly point toward investigation, the target should obtain counsel sooner rather than later, but in no event later than the receipt of notice of first investigation.

The selection of counsel is an important decision and requires investigation and thought. The target needs a highly competent lawyer with excellent judgment who is experienced in both litigation and more informal administrative proceedings. If possible, the lawyer should have some experience in or with higher education, because both the procedures and the politics of informal proceedings in higher education are unique.

Even with relevant experience, the lawyer will tend to focus on the litigation and external and internal investigations or administrative proceedings, not on the other coercive tactics of the zealots and the internal political battles that undermine the target's standing in the community, employment, and ability to defend the litigation or internal and external proceedings. For example, it is possible to win early battles in litigation, but lose the war because the situation internally within the faculty becomes politically untenable for the target. The case will never get to trial because the zealots will create enough political pressure to cause the university to settle, and the target will never get a chance to clear her name. Meanwhile, the settlement will be trumpeted as an admission of guilt calling for internal investigations and other career damage for the accused.

The target must educate counsel to understand that the war has many fronts, both internal and external, and that the situation internally within the university is much more politically charged than other employment litigation counsel may have tried. Counsel should understand the ideology of the zealots, common tactics of zealots, the power of the zealots within the university, and the rights and duties of professional academic freedom. For example, counsel inexperienced with higher education and waves of zealotry may not see the danger that zealots will seize upon concessions or settlement in litigation or administrative proceedings as an admission of guilt to be leveraged into increased political pressure against the target. The objective is to make the target a symbol of the moral turpitude that must be eliminated. Counsel may underestimate the tenacity of zealots and the serious danger in tactics of appeasement. Counsel may also not anticipate how tactics in the litigation or external proceeding, like, for example, an aggressive deposition of a person of oppressed status in the current zealotry, may be twisted into a symbolic event for internal and external political gain.

Educated, highly competent counsel can provide invaluable assistance to the target. For example, while a target may understand university politics, most professors are completely naive about internal and external investigations, tribunals and litigation. Targets generally may not realize that the record starts with issuance of a complaint, that anything the target does or says subsequently may be part of the record, that there is just one opportunity to make an internal record, and that this record is the basis on which any appeals to higher authority will rest. Targets do not generally know how to create a good paper record. They are naive about how difficult it is to prove facts without any documentation, and about the care that should go into the creation of written documentation. They need to develop the habit of carefully and deliberately documenting meetings and events in writing through contemporaneous notes, memoranda, and letters. The target may not realize the importance of unbiased witnesses to prove facts, or the danger of entrapment at meetings during the investigation. Targets must know how to deal with questions where the purpose is not to obtain information but rather to entrap the target for purposes of further charges of lying and perjury. Targets may also not be aware of procedural rights at tribunals, and how to use those procedures to create a strong record. Counsel can educate the target on these matters.

Counsel can also act as a detached adviser and source of moral support. Counsel can help the target avoid wishful thinking and precipitous and rash acts motivated by anger and the desire for revenge. Zealots may hope to provoke an unprofessional response that then becomes further ammunition against the target. A target needs someone to help make a detached assessment of the situation on a regular basis. In particular, the target needs a regular assessment of where to put the scarce resources available for defense to make the greatest difference. This includes an assessment of the capabilities and energies of the target and of counsel, the realities of the particular institution including the collegial and administrative support for the target, and what works best given the realities of the situation. Where should counsel focus his or her energies? Where should the target focus her or his scarce energies for best results? Good counsel is also there to serve as a confidant and unconditional ally.

The target must obtain counsel's assistance on the critical question of who pays for the attorney's fees. Without either indemnification for attorney's fees or the unique good fortune of a pro bono representation, the target may be driven from academia simply because the costs of defense are too high. For example, in Professor Owen Lattimore's case, Abe Fortas, Thurman Arnold, and the Arnold, Fortas, and Porter law firm contributed $250,000 in pro bono time in addition to a defense fund raised by friends of $38,000.[11]

Once an investigation is underway, counsel for the target should immediately seek indemnification from the employer. The law on indemnification will differ from state to state and between public and private universities. In Minnesota for example, indemnification of attorney's fees for employees of a nonprofit corporation like a private university is mandatory. The nonprofit corporation shall indemnify the attorney's fees and judgments and penalties of an employee made or threatened to be made a party to a proceeding by reason of the employment relation undertaken by the employee. A proceeding means "threatened, pending, or completed civil, criminal, administrative, arbitration, or investigative proceeding, including a proceeding by or in the right of the corporation."[12] The employee must have acted in good faith and have reasonably believed that the conduct was in the best interests of the corporation.[13] The indemnity policy for the University of Minnesota, a public university, is very similar but appears in a resolution of the Board of Regents rather than a statute.[14]

Under this type of statutory indemnity provision, a target will receive indemnity for attorney's fees only when the employee is made a party to a proceeding by reason of the employment relation undertaken by the employee. Clearly, if the investigation concerns whether a professor in teaching, research or governance activities violated a harassment or discrimination policy or a speech code prohibiting "insensitivity," the charges do relate to actions undertaken by reason of the professor's employment relation. Much more problematic would be an external investigation concerning a professor's membership in the Communist party or lying about membership in the Communist party. Neither of these charges at first glance relate to actions undertaken by reason of the professor's employment relation. On the other hand, at least indemnification should extend to an internal investigation where the issue would be the professor's fitness as a teacher in light of the accusations. Of course, a hostile administration or governing board may deny indemnification by asserting that the professor did not act in good faith or that no reasonable employee could believe that the conduct was in the best interests of the corporation. The university may also resist providing counsel for internal investigations of the target.[15] Under no circumstances should a target represent herself in these internal proceedings. The risks are too great. The target may have to bring litigation to force indemnification.

The retention of good counsel and indemnification of attorney's fees are critical steps to defend against investigations. However, indemnification will cover only attorney's fees incurred in defending a proceeding. Counsel's advice is extremely useful in helping the target decide whether to go on the offensive and initiate investigations and litigation against the zealots. Counsel is essential to initiate litigation. Since indemnification will not cover costs incurred in initiating investigations or bringing litigation, the target must consider the costs to be borne by the target, and the target's ability to bear those costs.

A good offense is sometimes the best defense. The sixth line of defense for a target is the filing of grievances and complaints with the university administration and governing board *both* documenting violations of the target's professional academic freedom and requesting the employer university to protect contractual rights of academic freedom.

There are several preliminary steps that a target should consider taking before making a formal grievance. These are consistent with the earlier theme that a target should force a continuous public debate with the zealots. Before making a formal grievance, a professor could request a faculty meeting agenda item to discuss the state of professional academic freedom within the faculty and to consider violations of the professor's rights of professional academic freedom. Public debate at a faculty meeting would inform colleagues of the situation, demonstrate a good faith effort to resolve matters through reasonable debate, possibly gain some support, and lead to a resolution without a formal complaint. Along a similar vein, the target could ask the governing board to make an assessment of the state of contractual rights of professional academic freedom within the faculty.

If these steps seem useless or prove unfruitful, the next step would be to file a formal grievance with the administration and governing board documenting violations of the target's contractual rights of professional academic freedom and requesting the university to protect those rights. During McCarthyism, for example, the target would have filed a grievance setting forth how the university itself was violating contractual rights of professional academic freedom by retaliation against ideas through adverse course or governance assignments, adverse salary action, university investigations, or other actions having a chilling affect on rights of academic freedom. At a public university, the target should make every effort to formulate the grievance so that the employer is retaliating for speech on a matter of public concern. Matters of public concern were defined in chapter 6.

Constituencies within the university other than the administration or governing board, like students and faculty, may violate duties of professional academic freedom and interfere with the target's rights of academic freedom. The target should first file a formal grievance against student or faculty zealots for violating the correlative duties. The students may be subject to discipline under the student conduct code. In faculties that have adopted the AAUP's 1940 statement, the dean has the implicit power to bring proceedings against faculty members who violate the correlative duties of professional competence and ethics. Tenure codes usually are drafted in the same general language, and give the dean explicit power to bring proceedings. These general duties of professional competence and ethics include the mandatory principles of conduct described earlier in chapter 10. If the university does nothing or responds inadequately, the target should file a grievance against the university for not fulfilling its contractual duties to protect the target's academic freedom. During the student activism of the 1960s for example, the target of classroom disruption could have filed a grievance against the students for violation of the student conduct code. If the university failed to respond to protect the target's contractual rights to academic freedom, then the target could file a grievance against the university itself.

During the current zealotry from the fundamentalist academic left, common tactics are false public accusations of moral turpitude, manipulative persuasion, ostracism, struggle meetings, misuse of the classroom for political purposes, baseless internal and external investigations, removal of the target from faculty governance or teaching responsibilities, dissuasion of student enrollment in the target's classes, and disruption of speeches, classes, and university functions. None of these tactics meet the correlative duties of professional academic freedom outlined earlier. The target should file grievances against students or faculty members using these tactics. The university has a contractual duty to enforce the student conduct code and the tenure code so that professors are not harassed in the performance of their employment. The university has a duty to protect the academic freedom of the target. If the university does nothing or itself directly violates rights of academic freedom for example, by initiating investigations without any threshold finding that accusations have some legitimate basis, the target should file a grievance against the university.

There is a small possibility that filing an internal grievance will prompt further reflection and remedial action by the administration or governing board to address the target's complaint. The probabilities are not high because administrators and governing boards historically have been either the source of zealotry, active facilitators of zealotry originating outside the walls, or cowed spectators.

The major purpose of internal grievances is to create a record that the university as an employer bound by contract to protect rights of professional academic freedom did not take action to do so. The target needs to create a clear paper record showing that the university is not meeting its contractual obligations. The record will be stronger if the university is shown to fail repeatedly to fulfill its obligations. On the basis of this record, the target can bring litigation to enforce contractual protections of professional academic freedom.

In bringing grievances, the target must exercise great care to meet all of the correlative duties mentioned in chapter 10. For example, the target must both conduct a reasonable investigation to determine if there are facts supporting the charge and be accurate in representing the evidence gathered and the opposing evidence and argument. Document everything. Failure to exercise care well above the minimum standard of care with respect to these duties invites counter charges and more trouble.

The target's seventh line of defense is to bring litigation against the university employer for breach of contract to force the employer to protect rights of professional academic freedom. At public universities, the target should consider also claims under the *Connick* and *Pickering* line of cases for violations of First Amendment rights in the public workplace. Where applicable, the target could consider claims for defamation, intentional infliction of emotional distress, reverse discrimination, or, if the target is a member of a protected class, harassment and discrimination. The complainant could seek either injunctive and declaratory relief or damages or both. Seeking injunctive and declaratory relief ordering the university employer to protect First Amendment rights or contractual rights of professional academic freedom should be somewhat less divisive than seeking a damage remedy. Where appropriate, the target may choose also to name board members, administrators, students or faculty members individually for any of these causes of actions or also for tortious interference with contractual rights. The complainant could seek damages from these individuals.

McConnell v. Howard University is an example of the contractual argument the target could make.[16] The university terminated a professor's appointment as a tenured professor for neglect of professional responsibilities. The professor refused to teach a class until the university took disciplinary action against a student who refused to refrain from talking in class and called the professor "a condescending, patronizing racist." The professor argued that by nature of the university setting and the existence of the student conduct code, the university had an implied contractual duty to protect a teacher's professional authority in the classroom. The professor filed a grievance requesting disciplinary action against the student, but the university did nothing. A faculty grievance committee heard the university's charges against the professor and agreed with the professor that "[a] teacher has the right to expect the University to protect the professional authority in teacher-student relationships."[17]

The court of appeals found that the professor should be allowed to demonstrate at trial that the university owed him a contractual duty to protect his professional authority in the classroom and that the university's actions constituted a breach of that duty.[18] The court noted its previous position in Greene v. Howard University that "contracts are written, and are to be read, by reference to the norms of conduct and expectations founded upon them. This is especially true of contracts in and among a community of scholars. Surely, among a community of scholars, one who is assigned to teach must have some semblance of control over the classroom."[19]

Levin v. Harleston is an example of constitutional claims which the target could make against public universities.[20] The court of appeals found that the university's creation of parallel or "shadow classes" and the university's encouragement of the continued erosion in the size of Professor Levin's class if he did not mend his extracurricular ways was the antithesis of freedom of expression for a public employee protected by the First Amendment.[21] The court enjoined the university from creating these sections predicated solely upon Professor Levin's protected expression of ideas. The Second Circuit also found that the threat of discipline implicit in an investigation of Professor Levin's conduct ordered by the university president was sufficient to chill Professor Levin's right of free speech. The court gave declaratory relief that disciplinary proceedings, or the threat thereof (through an investigation), predicated solely on Levin's continued expression of his views outside the classroom violated Levin's First Amendment rights.[22]

Bringing litigation against the university employer will chew up far more of the target's time and energy in the discovery process than the target may initially anticipate. It will substantially disrupt the target's life. It will also severely disrupt the community and is one of the last lines of defense. This type of litigation is similar to others in which there is a long-term personal relationship at issue like divorce and child custody cases. Such litigation tends to be extremely divisive and bitter. Litigation operates in the advocate's morality of manipulative persuasion, not the academic ethic of a scholar. The costs to the plaintiff of such litigation in terms of time, money and emotional well-being are high. Most of the academic plaintiffs who bring litigation against their university employer lose their cases. For example, the LaNoue and Lee study of employment discrimination cases in universities found that only about 20 percent of plaintiffs in academic discrimination cases won on the merits. The doctrine of academic abstention discussed earlier makes this low probability of success in litigation against a university very predictable. Even the winners usually changed jobs, and of those winners who stayed, many subsequently filed lawsuits for retaliation.[23] On the other hand, organizations like the Center for Individual Rights have provided very successful representation in a number of high profile cases defending academic freedom against universities.[24]

The LaNoue and Lee study also found that even colleagues who initially sided with the plaintiffs soon began avoiding them because the colleagues needed to maintain a good relationship with the institution.[25] As depositions and other discovery move forward, it is inevitable that colleagues will be drawn unwillingly into the dispute, and may hold grudges about the waste of resources and energy.

If the plaintiff names faculty colleagues individually as defendants in addition to the university, the level of divisiveness, disruption and animosity will be substantially higher. Individual faculty members will fight much harder because of their fears about reputational damage and diminished career opportunity. They will see that any finding against them, even a partial victory for the plaintiff, or any settlement, will be perceived as a cloud over their reputation and career. Settlement will be much harder if the plaintiff names individuals. If the plaintiff names only the university as a defendant, faculty members tend to see the administration as "them," not "us" and will be more willing to sacrifice "them" for the sake of peace.

If the zealots' tactics have created a situation where the target has little or nothing left to lose, litigation against the university employer is an option. The target should refrain from naming individuals unless the zealots have already brought litigation against the target. Then, naming individuals in counterclaims is an effective response. The target's focus in litigation against the university should be on procedural irregularities like the failure to address grievances or double standards in treatment, not on the university's substantive evaluations that will be covered by academic abstention.

The university is susceptible to adverse media publicity generated by the target in connection with the litigation. Adverse publicity hurts student and faculty recruitment, fundraising and legislative appropriations. The university will weigh settlement carefully as an option to avoid adverse publicity.

The eighth line of defense for tenured targets is taking advantage of the procedural protections surrounding tenure. One of the AAUP's principal contributions to professional academic freedom is its work defining academic due process. These procedural protections in turn have been incorporated into the contractual tenure code provisions of many universities. The cumbersome and costly procedures of a detenuring proceeding inhibit a university from terminating the target's employment by adding substantially to the transaction costs of a termination.

If the university brings a termination proceeding, the target should utilize every procedural device possible to slow down the proceeding. The longer it takes, the higher the possibility that the wave of zealotry will run its course before final action is taken. For example, if challenges for cause concerning the membership of the detenuring hearing committee are permitted, the target should use them. Ask for a factual hearing on each challenge. Within the bounds of the correlative duties and the law, the target should use every opportunity to create an environment where colleagues cannot sit on the fence. Adverse media attention will put pressure on the university. Keep in mind that the courts tend to give substantial deference to the university on substantive decisions under the doctrine of academic abstention but no deference for procedural errors. Serious procedural errors may also be a basis for an AAUP investigation.

There is a wide spectrum of stances from which the target will determine the appropriate use of each line of defense. For example, University of Georgia professor Eugene Genovese advocates an extremely aggressive stance. Recognizing that university administrators and faculty colleagues will respond to whatever wind seems to be blowing the strongest, Professor Genovese offers "[t]he Law of Liberation through Counterterror. In every such political struggle, honorable men and women can defeat terrorism only by unleashing counterterrorism against cowardly administrators and their complicit faculty."[26] "Let us," Genovese urges, "drive into their brains the terrifying recognition that counterterrorists will (figuratively) draw their blood for every concession made to terrorists...and that, despite every smart move known to God and man, they will find no place to hide from any war that the terrorists unleash.... By raising the price of sleaziness as high as the price of a staunch defense of their campuses, we shall liberate administrators to stand on their own professed principles, secure in the knowledge that they have nothing left to lose."[27]

Adopting Professor Genovese's proposal, the target will go after the administration and complicit faculty with hammer and tongs in an aggressive counter offensive. Such a stance may work for targets who are by nature street fighters; but many academics do not have a street fighter's feistiness or quickness in combat. They aren't good at it. For example, while a street fighter draws energy from initiating litigation, most faculty will find that initiating litigation will be an enormous drain, chewing up vast amounts of energy in discovery, and pulling the target even further away from teaching, research, and public service. One danger to a target pursuing this strategy is that he or she will catch the same type of extreme moralism, anger, and bitterness that infects the zealots. The zealotry will result then in a counter zealotry that also violates the correlative duties and undermines professional academic freedom. The situation spirals downward as justice stalks justice.

A somewhat more moderate stance is the simple *Tit for Tat* negotiating strategy proposed by Professor Robert Axelrod. Tit for Tat is merely the strategy of starting with cooperation, and thereafter doing what the other player did in the previous move. Obviously this is constrained for the target by the correlative duties of professional academic freedom. The target could inform the zealots, the administration and complicit faculty that this is the strategy. Tit for Tat is nice in that it is never betrays first. It is retaliatory in that infractions do not go unpunished, but not vengeful, in that it extracts an equal measure of punishment for each betrayal. It is forgiving in that it will forgive as soon as the other side ceases to betray. It is also simple and easy to understand. The problem is that Tit for Tat may not be forgiving enough since once the other player defects, Tit for Tat always responds with retaliation, resulting in an unending echo of retaliations.[28]

Tit for Tat could be constrained further by a commitment both to respond to betrayal using lines of defense as consistently as possible with the strengths of a scholar and teacher. The target would conduct herself in a manner considerably above the minimum required by the correlative duties of professional academic freedom. This would substantially restrain the target's responses when zealots engage in conduct violating those duties. This stance seeks to set an example of how to deal with fundamental disagreement.

A target could further modify Tit for Tat by being more forgiving, absorbing more of the zealots' coercive tactics without retaliation. As undeserved suffering without retaliation becomes increasingly obvious, it should become a powerful moral force that may trigger the sympathetic response of faculty bystanders. Absorbing and forgiving also attempt to lead the way out of a cycle of justice stalking justice. Unfortunately, the history of waves of zealotry in higher education suggests that a strategy of forgiving and absorbing is naive. Faculty colleagues often have not provided public support to a target under any circumstances. Zealots may interpret this strategy as a sign of weakness, not strength, and a reason for further attack.

Dealing with Sadness, Anger, and Emotional and Physical Exhaustion

As a wave of zealotry develops, a target may experience substantial confusion over the absence of public and private collegial support. The lack of support may weigh heavily on the accused. Collegial silence regarding the coercive tactics that totally dominate the life of the accused may lead to feelings of isolation and despair. For example, during McCarthyism, the failure of so many liberal colleagues to provide expected public support created sad and often bitter memories for the targets of the zealotry.

During a wave of zealotry, the target may also be ground down by the tenacity of zealots. The target may wishfully want to believe that the zealotry is a passing phenomenon and that, like a bad dream, it will go away tomorrow. This is a gross underestimation of the tenacity of zealots; recent periods of zealotry have lasted three to ten years.

If coercive tactics move beyond false accusations of moral turpitude, ostracism, and hostility to investigations, the accused may experience disabling insecurity and isolation for extended periods. During the period of investigation, the accused may feel she is running through the fields of limbo where dwelt what Dante called "the praiseless and blameless dead." The accused is under a cloud in the community. There is great uncertainty as to reputation, standing in the community, career and financial security. An extended investigation also causes exhaustion and numbness. If the government itself instigates the investigations, the target's problems are multiplied because of the far greater resources of the government to chew up the target's life. The accused's life may get taken over by investigations, tribunals and hearings, litigation, lawyers and the necessity of spending enormous portions of energy and time defending oneself. There is very little if any time for the scholarly and teaching activities that give energy.[29]

During a period of zealotry, the target should expect strong emotional responses of fear, grief, anger, sadness, and bitterness. The accused may greatly fear initially for the loss of both reputation and career opportunity. The accused may fear for loss of employment and ability to support a family. As false public accusations of moral turpitude are made, the target may grieve over the reality that once such false charges occur, the truth never catches up. There is a permanent loss of reputation among a subset of the community. There may also be feelings of anger directed against the zealots and the injustice of their coercive tactics, and of sadness and bitterness over the weakness of so many colleagues. There is the sadness also of coming to know more about the dark side and weakness in human nature than the accused ever wanted to know.

Dealing with these emotions and making a defense take both time and energy. A significant degree of exhaustion and numbness is inevitable. Despair and depression are serious risks. One of the most difficult tasks of the innocent person is to resist the immense pressure to trade a lifetime of ethical conduct and positive contribution for the cessation of an unjust prosecution. The target has to guard against emotional and physical deterioration.

The accused must have clear priorities to allocate the scarce emotional and physical resources available. The following priorities may help to allocate scarce resources once zealots initiate investigations: (1) Focus enough energy on teaching to be substantially above the adequate level. Good teaching will suffice for the duration of the zealotry. Waste as little energy as possible regretting or worrying about teaching excellence foregone. (2) Perform governance activity at a level that safely exceeds grounds for a charge of incompetence. (3) Cut back on other career activity that does not relate to defense, particularly scholarship and public service. Waste as little energy as possible lamenting scholarship or public service foregone; and (4) Put the remaining energy and time into defense, into family, friends, supporters, and advisers, and into personal time to restore energy. Focus especially on working with and empowering allies giving public support.

It is critical for a target to attend to her or his job so as to give the zealots no alternative grounds to bring charges of professional incompetence or unethical conduct. The target must exercise caution to observe the correlative duties of professional academic freedom. For example, do not be provoked into an unprofessional response to the zealots' tactics. Do not politicize the classroom. Do not refuse to conduct classes until the institution exercises appropriate disciplinary measures against student zealots. These will result in charges of moral turpitude, incompetence or neglect of duty. The fact that other professors may be violating the correlative duties may call for a grievance against them but is not a justification for the target to violate these duties.

It is also critical to work through fears about reputational loss, damage to career opportunity, and confrontation with intimidators. Take small steps to overcome these fears and to stretch the limits of confidence and strength. It is possible to overcome fear of intimidators, especially if the target can let go of the fears that intimidators play on. Many of the zealots' coercive tactics intimidate others because of fear of reputational damage. For example, many academics fear accusations of moral turpitude. Work at letting go of these fears. Accept that once accusations of moral turpitude are public, some members of the community will always think badly of the accused. One subset of the community will believe where there is smoke, there must be fire. Another subset will believe the worst because it is in their political interest to do so. The accused must fight false accusations but cannot control what these groups of people think. In a sense, once false accusations of moral turpitude are public, the target has nothing more to lose, and should be liberated from reputational fears. What is important is what the accused thinks of herself. Living true to that is the objective.

Normally academics only see value in, and draw energy from classes well taught, scholarship published, and public service rendered. From this perspective, if significant time goes into fighting zealotry rather than teaching and learning, the zealots have already won.

During a wave of zealotry, the target must see value in and draw energy from what is defended, not discouragement from lost opportunities of teaching improvements not made, articles not written, and career advancement no longer possible. This is why self-education concerning professional academic freedom and waves of zealotry is so important. The target must understand the fundamental importance of academic freedom to each faculty member, to the mission of the university, and to the achievement of human potential. The target must know that because periods of zealotry have occurred roughly every fifteen to twenty years, academic freedom is never finally won, it must be continually defended. From an awareness of both the fundamental importance of academic freedom and what zealotry puts at risk, the target can honor herself for the defense of academic freedom and draw energy from what is defended. The target must give herself credit for small victories, for staying power and perseverance, for integrity in staying true to personal values and ethics. One of the greatest contributions an academic can make is an honorable defense of the principles on which the university rests. The target should constantly empower supporters by reminding them of this cause.

The target is not trying to win in the sense of defending the university from capture, but rather to survive as a curator of values until a dark age passes. Waves of zealotry generally have lasted 3–10 years. The high moralism, passion and anger driving the zealotry tends to diminish over time both out of fatigue and as other people come to see fundamentalism for what it is. Perseverance and staying power are critically important for the target.

Finally, when the wave of zealotry has passed, the target must focus on recovering emotional health. The objective is to handle life's blows without bitterness. Knowledge that waves of zealotry occur with frequency, and that many others have also been targets helps in the process of forgiving life for its many injustices. In particular, the target should not overly personalize the betrayal of colleagues. It has happened many times before. The target has to let go of the past and move back to focusing on the positive aspects of teaching and research.

Unique Problems of the Target in the Current Wave of Zealotry from the Fundamentalist Academic Left

Because this is the first period of zealotry involving a populist intimidation led principally by faculty, the target's situation is even more confusing than in earlier waves. One source of confusion is the public's poor understanding of the oppression model ideology of the fundamentalist academic left and how false accusations of bigotry are being used to suppress alleged heretics. Another source of confusion is that faculty zealots deny that any problem of coercive tactics exist. This is similar to the denials of the governing boards and administration during McCarthyism. Third, lay persons who have never experienced first-hand the tactics of faculty and student zealots have difficulty believing the stories of the victims for two reasons. For one group of the public, the image of the university as a place for reasoned debate and civility is deeply imprinted, and the stories of coercion by faculty members seem unreal. For another group, the entire matter is denigrated as petty office politics without consequences; the problem is characterized as "academic."

Even if these issues are clarified, a fourth source of confusion is how professional academic freedom protects against coercion by faculty zealots. Professional academic freedom was not originally designed with zealotry from and the politicization of the faculty itself in mind. It was designed so that faculty members could protect professional academic speech from lay interference by the governing board and the administration. Indeed, faculty zealots may claim that professional academic freedom protects their coercive conduct from employer sanctions.

Because governing boards, administrations, alumni, students, the public and many faculty members don't know what to make of this unique situation, the confusion puts targets and potential targets at grave risk. A target must cut through the confusion quickly to control damage.

A potential target must first assess where her faculty and university are headed. The degree to which a university or a faculty within any particular university is experiencing coercive tactics from the fundamentalist academic left covers a wide spectrum. Some universities and some faculties seem untouched while others are experiencing substantial zealotry and coercion. If the target concludes that the trend of zealotry and coercion is increasing, it is critical to act sooner rather than later in mobilizing a response.

The first step is self-education about the ideology of the fundamentalist academic left and its tactics. The potential target must also understand that the correlative duties incorporated into professional academic freedom provide the means to address the professional misconduct of faculty zealots.

This self-education provides the basis for the first line of defense, creating a continuous public debate with faculty zealots. The target must constantly make a public case that an important educational debate is occurring in the university, but that the zealots are using tactics of coercion and intimidation to suppress heretics.

An educated community may take an interest in the oppression model of extremists in the postmodern schools and the diversity movement. The community should understand the implications of oppression model ideology on the following concepts: (1) the university's mission of advancing knowledge; (2) intellectual quality and achievement; (3) objectivity and disinterested inquiry; (4) advancement based on merit; and (5) professional academic freedom. Perhaps most important, an educated community will be able to distinguish the ideology of the fundamentalist academic left from traditional liberalism. The target also has to educate all constituencies both about how the zealots use false accusations of bigotry to assault heretics and about how the correlative duties of professional academic freedom provide the means to address this type of professional misconduct.

These will be new ideas, unfamiliar to many listeners. For example, the correlative duties have been largely neglected in recent decades out of faculty self-interest. Outsiders may be unaware that many faculties are delinquent communities with no tradition of observing and enforcing the correlative duties as a collegial body. The target must keep telling her stories of coercion and how coercion violates the correlative duties. An unfamiliar new idea becomes clear to its audience through persistent repeated contact.

The target's second line of defense, responding quickly and publicly to all false accusations of moral turpitude, is particularly critical in the current period of zealotry. The community needs explanation in order to understand how false accusations of bigotry serve the underlying oppression model ideology of the fundamentalist academic left. Faculty zealots in this wave often have substantial media and community organizing skills. They know that media plays a much larger role today than in the past, and that if they can make the target into a highly visible media symbol of bigotry, facts won't be significant. They know that universities are extremely vulnerable to adverse media attention that may harm fundraising and the recruitment of students and faculty. It is critical that the target pressure the media to include the target's response each time zealots make a false accusation. This will mitigate the possibility that constantly repeated false accusations about the accused will make the target into a public symbol of bigotry.

Most people are more vulnerable to the opinion of their coworkers than to the opinion of other groups. Professors are no different. They are more vulnerable to accusations of moral turpitude and other coercive tactics by colleagues than to similar tactics by any other constituency in the university. The target must quickly develop a thick skin to protect against collegial insult and vilification. The target must also learn how to cope with struggle meeting tactics where faculty zealots surround the target and in sequence attack the target. The zealots hope to provoke the target into mistakes like not attending meetings at all or making an unprofessional response at a meeting. The target must attend faculty and committee meetings to prevent both isolation and charges of neglect of duty. The target should avoid meetings where only zealots are present. Such struggle meetings, unwitnessed by neutral parties, are an invitation to misrepresentation and additional false accusation. The target must train herself to respond to personal attack with calm, matter of fact decency. Subject to "in your face" vilification, a mature academic can ask for a few more specifics.[30]

The third line of defense, pressing colleagues to take a stand to defend professional academic freedom, is unusually difficult in this period of zealotry. It is problematic since the zealotry is from the radical academic left and the substantial majority of university professors in many faculties, particularly in the humanities and social sciences, is left of center. This substantial liberal majority, University of Minnesota professor Bryden notes, does not resonate to partisan political polemic about the power of the fundamentalist academic left. However, Bryden observes that meritocratic sentiments often coexist with political liberalism. Many professors in the liberal majority favor academic quality and excellence. In the abstract, they also support the desirability of a politically neutral, nonpartisan university.[31] It is possible that the target could convince one or more members of this liberal majority to lend public support if they see the link between professional academic freedom and academic quality and excellence. Another argument appealing to liberals is to point out self-interest in preserving academic freedom. Once a zealotry is unleashed, it assaults targets for political advantage far beyond the limited circle of clear heretics. A liberal who advocates academic quality is at risk.

Although unusual, there are instances where significant numbers of faculty colleagues step forward to give public support to the target. At the State University of New York College at Oneonta, the fundamentalist academic left subjected Professional William Simons to a campaign of falsehood and character assassination and intimidation. Seven colleagues in the history department signed a letter correcting the factual record and supporting professional academic freedom. This ended the public accusations of bigotry.[32]

The target must consider the fourth line of defense: a direct appeal for public support from students, alumni and the wider public. It is difficult to predict the reaction of the media. In some cases, the strategy works. Eden Jacobowitz, the student charged with calling others "water buffaloes" at the University of Pennsylvania, believes that if it weren't for the spotlight of the press shining on his case, he might have been expelled. Going to the media was the only thing he could do.[33] The media will tend to see students as powerless and more deserving of sympathy and support. The media tend to be more confused by stories where false allegations of bigotry are used to attack faculty advocates of quality and merit in personnel decisions on admissions, appointments, promotion and tenure. These stories are factually complicated and may be ignored or misreported.

It is also important for potential targets in this wave of zealotry to move early to the fifth line of defense, and to secure counsel, at least for preliminary advice on how to handle employment issues. The critical battleground for ideological zealotry within the faculty itself is hiring, promotion, and tenure. Personnel decisions on appointments, promotion, and tenure, pose the greatest danger of investigations and litigation. The target's advocacy of academic quality in making these personnel decisions may be characterized as oppression and bigotry. The target must know how to document personnel decisions.

Counsel can also help targets learn that meetings with zealots are occasions for entrapment through questioning. For example, the target should approach "mediation" or "facilitation" meetings structured by zealots with eyes open. The format may resemble a struggle meeting or a deposition more than a mediation. Counsel can help the target question naive traditional assumptions about confidentiality and collegial loyalty in these settings.

Many academic targets have limited financial resources to secure counsel before any formal investigation or litigation occurs which might trigger indemnity of attorney's fees. If resources are insufficient to retain counsel, the target can contact attorneys who are representing targets in this wave of zealotry on a pro bono or reduced fee basis. For example, the ACLU, the Individual Rights Foundation or the Center for the Study of Popular Culture in Southern California and the Center for Individual Rights in Washington, D.C. provide such services.

Counsel can assist in developing the target's sixth and seventh lines of defense by filing grievances with the administration and if necessary bringing litigation against the university employer to protect contractual rights of professional academic freedom. Counsel can explain several principles unique to this wave of zealotry that are not obvious to most professors. First, even though the coercive conduct suppressing rights of academic freedom is by colleagues (and students), the focus of the legal strategy has to be forcing the university employer to take protective action. The ultimate legal responsibility for governing the institution and dealing with unprofessional conduct by faculty and students is placed on the governing board and by subdelegation the university president and faculty deans. If the governing board acquiesces in and perpetuates a persistent and continuing pattern of professional harassment, the governing board's action and inaction are fostering and tolerating a hostile work environment. This is a breach of the target's contractual rights. A second principle not obvious to most professors is that the correlative duties of professional academic freedom provide the means to combat the zealots' professional misconduct. For example, if colleagues use the classroom to politicize the students, file a grievance based on violation of correlative duties in the 1940 statement. A number of professors are bringing litigation against university employers alleging violation of the professors' rights of academic freedom. Professors Levin and Jeffries at City University of New York brought successful actions against the university. At least four professors have brought litigation against their universities, challenging the application of vague harassment and discrimination speech policies to a faculty member's academic speech.[34]

A target who understands and responds to the unique problems of this wave of zealotry, including the retention of counsel, does not guarantee professional survival, she only increases its probability. This probability decreases as the period of zealotry lengthens in duration. As a period of zealotry is extended, the cumulative emotional and physical toll of coercive tactics on the target and her supporters increases. Individuals have different thresholds of exhaustion that they can endure, but eventually all but the strongest spirits succumb. It is certain that if a wave of zealotry is protracted, support for the target will gradually diminish as each supporter reaches his or her threshold. A target may not have enough perseverance and staying power to hold on through a prolonged wave of zealotry.

The single greatest danger to targets in the current wave is its potential duration. While religious fundamentalism after the Civil War and unfettered capitalism of trustees at the turn of the century persisted for more than a decade, and McCarthyism continued for a decade (1947–56), other earlier waves of zealotry in this century have generally lasted three to six years. This wave dates approximately from early 1988 with the adoption of the initial speech codes. Generally, the high moralism and passion that drive zealotry tend to diminish over time both out of fatigue and as other people come to see zealotry for what it is. Sometimes also zealots are in positions with fixed terms that expire. For example, McCarthyism ended as radical politicians lost political power, and the 1960s student activism ended as student radicals graduated.

There are several factors indicating that the current wave of zealotry may have substantial longevity. First, this is the first wave of zealotry led principally by faculty. Many faculty zealots are entrenched in tenure which gives them unique job security and staying power.

Second, the zealots recognize that their project is a very long-term transformation of the culture, with a principal early objective of capturing the meaning giving institutions in the culture, particularly higher education, to promote fundamentalist ideology. The controversy over multiculturalism, author Paul Robeson, Jr. notes, "is at the heart of a profound ideological struggle over the values of American culture and the nature of U.S. civilization."[35] The power base of the left in America, adds philosopher Richard Rorty, is now in the universities.[36] Former Yale president Benno Schmidt noted in 1992 that the pressures to subvert the essential academic character of universities were strong elsewhere and would become much greater at Yale.[37]

A third factor suggesting the unique longevity of the current zealotry is that the skew to the left is substantial on many faculties, particularly in the humanities and social sciences. Academic freedom depends upon some multidimensional disagreement within a faculty. However, Ladd and Lipset observed in 1975 that the degree of field related variation in political attitude was quite extraordinary. A number of fields were dominated by faculty members to the left of center politically.[38] This domination has continued to the present. Ladd and Lipset point out that the faculty are more or less the permanent state of the university, and are less likely to reflect fluctuations in popular views and behavior. They predict that the turnover rate for the next two decades (1975–1995) will be very low. "Earlier moods, waves, and experiences should continue to inform academic orientations for a long time to come."[39]

Ladd and Lipset conclude that, "The ideological bent of a discipline subculture thus is not a casual thing. It possesses 'staying power.' The array of fields, in terms of the political outlook of their members, described here appears as a persisting feature of academic life."[40] On the other hand, Ladd and Lipset also find that older cohorts in academia became more "moderate" as they aged compared to their earlier positions closer to the liberal extreme.[41] As the large cohort of academics who entered the profession in the 1960s and 1970s ages, their politics may moderate to some degree.

Another factor indicating a protracted period of zealotry is that strong ideologies based on ethnicity and race have historically unleashed virulent and prolonged zealotries. Current destructive ethnic conflicts in the Middle East and Eastern Europe indicate the power and perseverance of these ideologies. The ideology of the fundamentalist academic left is that both culture and all human endeavors and relationships are simply expressions of power of the ethnic, racial, and gender groups currently at the top of the hierarchy. The redistribution of power based on ethnicity, race and gender will create a preferred egalitarian society.

A zealotry based on ethnic, racial and gender differences will have substantial staying power. Historically, a celebration of ethnicity has been most likely to unleash dangerous forces of brutal irrationalism and hatred, often from the extreme right. It is possible that the current wave of zealotry from the fundamentalist academic left could be followed closely by a wave initiated from outside the university by the extreme right.[42]

A fifth factor that may support a protracted period of zealotry is the Clinton Administration. For example, zealots from the fundamentalist academic left or facilitators of the zealots could use the power of government to suppress heretics in higher education. Both Donna Shalala, appointed as Secretary of Health and Human Services, and Sheldon Hackney, appointed as chairman of the National Endowment for the Humanities, have been facilitators of the fundamentalist academic left during their service as university presidents. Shalala, as President of the University of Wisconsin, initiated the drafting of one of the early speech codes and supported the code after it was adopted. The code, effective September 1, 1989, unleashed numerous investigations and nine instances of sanctions for speech that was perceived to be insensitive. Nonetheless, a high level administrator denied there was any punishment under the code. In October of 1991 a federal district court issued a declaratory judgment striking down the speech code as unconstitutional content based abridgment of free speech. The administrator of the speech code on the Madison campus, who initially supported the code, found after experience that the code did suppress academic speech and was unworkable.[43] In December, 1992, Shalala stated that "I was very clear that I was opposed to a speech code in the classroom, in artistic endeavors, in speakers on campus."[44] In a March, 1993 speech, Shalala commented that "the idea that anyone at the University of Wisconsin would ever shut up on any issue is hilarious to those of you who are gradu-ates."[45] These denials are contradicted by the record. Although President Clinton announced in August, 1993 that he would nominate Professor Luis Sequiera from the University of Wisconsin for the post of Assistant Secretary of Agri-culture for Science and Education, Professor Sequiera discovered that Health and Human Services Secretary Shalala had complained about him to the White House. Professor Sequiera was one of Shalala's primary campus critics on the issue of speech codes. Professor Sequiera's nomination was stalled, and he withdrew from consideration in November, 1993.[46]

Under Sheldon Hackney's leadership as President, the University of Penn-sylvania also adopted a speech code. In April, 1993, when University of Penn-sylvania black students, angry at the insensitivity of an editorial writer, seized 14,000 copies of the student newspaper, Hackney's first statement was that "two important university values, diversity and open expression, seem to be in conflict."[47] Of course strong moralisms always conflict with free speech. The cornerstone of academic freedom is to protect speech against strong moralisms. In 1991, Hackney wrote an opinion article for the Philadelphia newspaper titled "Campuses Aren't Besieged by Politically Correct Storm Troopers," in which he states that fears of suppression of speech are greatly exaggerated and characterizes the present wave of zealotry as simply two warring factions on the contemporary campus battlefield.[48] In contrast, during his senate confirmation hearings Hackney called political correctness "intel-lectually dishonest" and "very intolerant." He stated that the "water buffalo" case had led him to believe that Penn should abandon its "hate speech" code.[49] This was an honest public acknowledgment of the problem.[50]

Extrapolation from these two high-level appointments suggests that per-sons who have facilitated the coercive tactics of the fundamentalist aca-demic left may also fill lower level positions in the Clinton Administration. It is reasonable to assume that some will continue to facilitate coercive tac-tics with government power. For example, a plausible hypothesis is that during the next several years there will be an increase in government inves-tigations of heretical thought and speech. There will also be more govern-mental interference in professional discourse. For example, at the end of the Bush Administration, a committee investigated charges that federally spon-sored research searching for a biological basis for violence was insensitive and harmful to African Americans. The committee recommended that the Health and Human Services Department create a permanent advisory com-mittee, which would include many members of minority groups to monitor violence research. Franklyn Jenifer, the President of Howard University and the chairman of the investigating committee, said that laymen, not just sci-entists should sit on review committees. "Scientists assume that anything they want to do is socially acceptable, that the search for knowledge should always be ok."[51]

The Office for Civil Rights (OCR) in the Department of Education currently is substantially more aggressive than during the Bush Administration in citing college and universities for violating the civil rights laws. A comparison of 1992 with 1993 indicates an 87 percent increase in citations for discrimination based on disability (from 46 to 86); a 100 percent increase in citations for discrimination based on sex (from 22 to 44), and a 12 percent increase in citations for discrimination based on race (from 8 to 9).[52]

The Education Department's March 1994 investigative guidelines on racial harassment also indicate that the Clinton Administration will expand on these efforts to undermine professional academic freedom through investigation. The guidelines provide that a violation may be found "if a recipient has created or is responsible for a racially hostile environment—i.e., harassing conduct (e.g., physical, verbal, graphic, or written) that is sufficiently severe, pervasive or persistent so as to interfere with or limit the ability of an individual to participate in or benefit from the services, activities or privileges provided by a recipient." Harassment is to defined from the viewpoint of a reasonable person of the same age and race as the victim.[53] The general counsel for the American Council on Education points out that this broad definition of harassment "fails to distinguish between conduct that is primarily expressive, and thus entitled to First Amendment protection, and conduct whose expressive conduct is incidental."[54] "If followed, they [the guidelines] would cause most schools to violate the First Amendment."[55] The AAUP has urged review of the policy out of concern that the guidelines threaten academic freedom.[56] While the guidelines state that they do not explicitly endorse speech or conduct codes to the extent that they violate the First Amendment, some college officials think that the result will be that universities must adopt speech policies.[57]

A last factor supporting the possibility that this wave of zealotry will be prolonged is that the wave has already lasted seven to eight years, but shows few signs of waning. Coercive tactics like those at the University of Pennsylvania in the spring of 1993 continue to occur. At Harvard Law School for example, a group of female law students in 1993 threatened Professor Alan Dershowitz with formal charges of sexual harassment for creating an atmosphere hostile to women during two days of classroom work on the situation of men falsely accused of rape. Many professors avoid teaching classes where discussions of race, gender and sexual preference are most likely to arise, and will discuss the problem only behind closed doors, Dershowitz says. They don't want to be out front on the issues.[58] The rash of book burning conduct like newspaper theft and the frequently acquiescent administrative response is also a troubling trend.

It may be that this wave of zealotry has peaked and is receding somewhat. The Republican majorities in Congress may limit or check facilitation of zealots' coercive tactics by the Clinton Administration. Certainly the fundamentalist left's use of speech codes to suppress heretics has been significantly hobbled by the federal courts in the Wisconsin and Michigan cases. In *R.A.V. v. St. Paul,* a 1992 decision, the United States Supreme Court found unconstitutional a city criminal ordinance that prohibited actions known "to arouse anger, alarm or resentment in others on the basis of race, color, creed, religion or gender."[59] The majority interpreted the ordinance as content-based. While a blanket proscription of fighting words would have been constitutionally permissible, proscription of a narrow category of speech was not.[60] Hate speech laws may not single out racial, sexual or religious threats for prosecution. Hate speech codes at public universities seem highly suspect following the *R.A.V.* decision.[61] Relying on the *R.A.V.* decision, a Michigan federal district court permanently enjoined Central Michigan University from enforcing its "discriminatory harassment policy" because the policy was an unconstitutional infringement on the First Amendment.[62] In 1993 several universities, including the University of Pennsylvania, scrapped their speech code policies.[63] However, there are limits to lawsuits' effectiveness. Michael Grove, executive director of the Center for Individual Rights, observes that, "But you don't turn this sort of supertanker around with one or two lawsuits. The nation's colleges believe they are embarked on a crusade to do good and anyone who asks questions about their methods is necessarily bad. And we're running short of professors sufficiently secure to speak out against the gathering forces of compulsory group-think."[64] Boston University President John Silber believes that the high tide of this wave has been reached because people increasingly laugh at the heavy handed tactics of coercion.[65]

It also may be, as reporter Caroline Mooney recently wrote, "Any lull in the cultural war is temporary, say warriors on the left and the right alike—the result perhaps, of a new era of government and an inevitable dip in media interest. Both sides are using the lull to regroup, study the enemy, and look for better ways to make their case."[66] In the balance, the six factors discussed above make it probable that this wave of zealotry will extend significantly beyond seven years.

It may also be that this particular wave of zealotry will wane but that another wave of zealotry from the left will occur in the not too distant future if history repeats itself. Higher education experienced three waves of zealotry over a forty-year period motivated by superpatriotism. Finally, in the late 1950s and 1960s, a widening consensus developed in the society that this superpatriotic zealotry was wrong and had inflicted great harm on academic inquiry and speech. Academics maturing in the 1960s through the present have been socialized to see the principal danger to academic freedom from the far right and outside the walls. There is not yet a wide consensus within higher education that the coercion of the late 1960s and today from the fundamentalist academic left is wrong. Will it take forty years for a consensus to develop that a zealotry from the fundamentalist left and inside the walls is equally wrong? It so, there could be a third wave of zealotry from the left early in the next century.

A protracted period of zealotry poses a grave danger to targets. The bottom line is that a target must assess the situation in her faculty and university on a continuing basis. If the target concludes that the zealotry may extend another four years or more, the target must consider the effect of cumulative exhaustion on her supporters and herself. As coercive tactics grind heretics down over time, an increasing number of supporters may essentially abandon the target and an increasing number of avoiders on the faculty may become hostile, wanting to sacrifice the target to buy peace. The target must also analyze her own staying power. In Eastern Europe, only a relative handful of dissidents had the will and fortitude to resist zealotry for ten years or more. It may be that even without formal termination, a target cannot hold onto her position if this period of zealotry is prolonged.

Notes

1. This was the author's experience. Owen Lattimore, discussed in chapter 1, and Alan Gribben, discussed in chapter 2, describe similar reactions.
2. Richard Hofstadter and Walter Metzger, THE DEVELOPMENT OF ACADEMIC FREEDOM IN THE UNITED STATES 327 (1955).
3. Robert Newman, OWEN LATTIMORE AND THE LOSS OF CHINA 375 (1992).
4. Benno Schmidt, *Universities Must Defend Free Speech*, WALL ST. J., May 6, 1991, at A16. Former Hamline University Law Dean George Latimer commented that "you know that you are a mature lawyer when someone is screaming expletives in your face and you can ask for a few more specifics."
5. Owen Lattimore, ORDEAL BY SLANDER 210-211 (1952). Defense lawyer Robert Shapiro emphasizes that "there is no question that media coverage can and does affect the ultimate outcome of widely publicized cases." He outlines how to deal with wire services, newspapers, tabloids and television news. Robert Shapiro, *Harnessing the Power of the Press*, LEGAL TIMES, June 27, 1994, at 22-27. Professor Don Cardinal outlines how to deal with potentially hostile press interviews concerning controversial research. Don Cardinal, *Researchers and the Press: A Cautionary Tale*, CHRON. HIGHER EDUC., Oct. 12, 1994, at B3.
6. Newman, *supra* note 3, at 280.
7. Lionel Lewis, COLD WAR ON CAMPUS 100-101 (1988).
8. Sara Charles et al., *Sued and Non-Sued Physicians' Self Reported Reactions to Malpractice Litigation*, 142 AM. J. PSYCHIATRY 437, 440 (1985).
9. Everett C. Ladd, Jr., & Seymour Martin Lipset, THE DIVIDED ACADEMY: PROFESSORS AND POLITICS 207-09 (1975).
10. Ellen W. Schrecker, NO IVORY TOWER: MCCARTHYISM & THE UNIVERSITIES 313 (1986).
11. Robert P. Newman, OWEN LATTIMORE AND THE LOSS OF CHINA 425, 438-39 (1992). In the author's case, the college indemnified attorney's fees of more than $100,000 for the defense of three lawsuits and two external investigations. In defending Professor Donald Silva at the University of New Hampshire, the Center for Individual Rights provided $275,000 of pro bono legal services. Jerry Carroll, *Political Correctness Takes a Nosedive*, S.F. CHRON., Oct. 26, 1994, at E7.
12. Minn. Stat. Ann. Sec. 317A.521, Subd. 1(a) (1989).
13. *Id.* Sec. 317A.521, Subd. 2.

14. University of Minnesota Board of Regents' Policy on Indemnification and Defense of Employees, adopted March 8, 1985.
15. *See* Barry Gross, *Salem in Minnesota*, ACADEMIC QUESTIONS, Spring 1992, at 67, 72.
16. *McConnell v. Howard Univ.*, 818 F.2d. 58 (D.C. Cir. 1987).
17. *Id.* at 65.
18. *Id.*
19. *Id.* at 64, note 7; *see also Greene v. Howard Univ.*, 412 F.2d 1128, 1135 (D.C. Cir. 1969).
20. *Levin v. Harleston*, 966 F.2d 85 (2d. Cir. 1992).
21. *Id.* at 88–89.
22. *Id.* at 89–90. Another example of litigation against the university is Professor Cynthia Griffin Wolff's April, 1992 complaint against MIT seeking damages and declaratory relief for "actions and inactions" (1)" in breach of the Institute's Policies and Procedures constituting, in substantial part, the contractual relationship between the Institute and Professor Wolff, "(2)" in breach of the implied covenant of good faith and fair dealing inherent in that contractual relationship," and (3)" in violation of Professor Wolff's academic freedom and of her civil rights protected under Massachusetts General Laws, chapter 12, Section 11 I." MIT wrongfully acquiesced in and perpetuated "a persistent and continuing pattern of professional, political and sexual harassment towards Professor Wolff in the workplace". Professor Wolff alleged that her colleagues verbally abused her and excluded her from programs because she did not agree with their radical ideological views, that her colleagues retaliated against her for Professor Wolff's opposition on the promotions of certain professors by excluding her from teaching in the women's studies program, and that the MIT did not respond to her repeated grievances to remedy the malicious atmosphere. Specifically, Professor Wolff cited as a breach of contract MIT's failures: (1) to prevent retaliation against her for her responsible participation in the peer review process; (2) to take necessary action with respect to faculty members who had engaged in conduct incompatible with the responsibility of a faculty member, including but not limited to harassment and discrimination; and (3) to maintain an environment of respect and academic freedom within the MIT community. The complaint also cited MIT's knowing acquiescence in the personal and professional harassment of Professor Wolff which unreasonably interfered with her work and created a hostile work environment.

Professor Wolff also cited university inaction as a breach of MIT's implied covenant of good faith and fair dealing. She alleged that the university without legitimate justification: (1) systematically excluded Professor Wolff from the Institute's Women's Studies Program and the Institute of Cultural Studies; (2) wrongfully and without justification refused to provide Professor Wolff a joint appointment in the Literature Section and the Writing Program in order to alleviate the severe harassment of Professor Wolff within the Literature Section; (3) acquiesced in, and in effect ratified, retaliation by certain of her colleagues against Professor Wolff for her participation in the tenure/peer review process; and acquiesced in the continued verbal and sexual harassment against Professor Wolff within the Literature Section. Finally, the complaint alleged that MIT, by intimidation and coercion, both directly and vicariously, interfered with Professor Wolff's civil rights. Plaintiff's Complaint at 1-2, 5-18, 19-20, *Wolff v. Mass. Inst. of Technology* (Massachusetts Superior Trial Court Cir. 1992) (No. 92-2430).

MIT reached a settlement with Professor Wolff six months after she filed her lawsuit. The settlement has a confidentiality provision so the specific terms are unknown, but Professor Wolff indicates, "All I can say is I'm very happy about it." She is now a member of the Writing Program as she had requested earlier. Denise K. Magner, *MIT, Professor Reach Settlement in Lawsuit*, CHRON. HIGHER EDUC., Mar. 31, 1993, at A-16.

23. Jon Schultz, Book Review, 72 JUDICATURE 307, 308 (1989) (reviewing George La Noue & Barbara Lee, ACADEMICS IN COURT: THE CONSEQUENCES OF FACULTY DISCRIMINATION LITIGATION (1987)). Professor Terry Leap finds in his study of academic discrimination cases that faculty plaintiffs discover the financial, time and energy costs of litigation to be enormous. The case takes over the plaintiff's life. Terry Leap, TENURE, DISCRIMINATION AND THE COURTS 14–15 (1993).

24. *See* Michael P. MacDonald, *Defending Academic Freedom*, THE HERITAGE LECTURES No. 371, November 21, 1991, at 1–2.

25. Schultz, *supra* note 23; Leap, supra note 23 at 16–17. Professor Leap finds that litigation tends to split the faculty into factions with substantial animosity.

26. Eugene D. Genovese, *Heresy, Yes—Sensitivity, No: An Argument for Counterterrorism in the Academy*, NEW REPUBLIC, Apr. 15, 1991, at 30, 32.

27. *Id.*

28. Robert Axelrod, THE EVOLUTION OF COOPERATION at viii, 175–77 (1984).

29. For example, in September, 1993, George Mason Law Professor Michael Krauss offered an example in class discussion of racist speech that might constitute an assault. The example was a Ku Klux Klan demonstration on a street in a previously all-white neighborhood in front of a house into which a black family had just moved: the hooded Klansmen burned a cross and screamed "Kill the niggers." A faculty colleague brought a complaint and investigation internally. Students petitioned for an apology. Media coverage was substantial. A second complaint followed for retaliation in lowering the grade of a student affected by the earlier incident. A faculty committee investigated, the president appointed a second committee to investigate, the Department of Education investigated. Although all complaints were dismissed, Professor Krauss spent "hundreds of demoralizing hours" over 2 years defending himself. His children were interrogated by classmates at school about their father's conduct. Michael Krauss, *When You Face the PC Inquisition*, WASH. TIMES, Jan. 27, 1995, at A21; Michael Krauss, *The Day My Number Came Up in the "Politically Correct" Lottery*, NAS LAW SECTION NEWS, Fall 1994, at 7.

30. Zealots and faculty facilitators may call struggle meetings to discuss the accusations of moral turpitude. If the target does not attend, the target's silence may be portrayed as an admission of guilt. The target must keep in mind how the media will cover struggle meetings. While the struggle meeting format may not be a formal meeting of the faculty, the media will not make such fine distinctions. A minority of the faculty may attend such meetings but the media may report the viewpoints expressed and votes taken as those of the faculty. The target must try to mitigate this damage.

31. David P. Bryden, *It Ain't What They Teach, It's the Way That They Teach It*, 103 PUB. INTEREST 38, 47 (1991).

32. William Simons, *Intimidation as Academic Debate*, ACAD. QUESTIONS, Spring 1993, at 63, 68.

33. Christopher Shea, *Resolution of Racial Harassment Case at U. of Penn. Leaves Everyone Dissatisfied*, CHRON. HIGHER EDUC., June 2, 1993 at A24, A26.

34. Andrew Blum, *Profs Sue Schools on Suspension*, NAT'L L.J., June 6, 1994, at A6, A7; Courtney Leatherman, *Fighting Back*, CHRON. HIGHER EDUC., March 16, 1994 at A17, A18.

35. Paul Robeson Jr., PAUL ROBESON JR. SPEAKS TO AMERICA at I (1993).
36. Richard Rorty, *quoted in* HETERODOXY, November 1992, at 3.
37. Benno Schmidt Jr., Address at Yale Baccalaureate Exercises (May 26, 1991).
38. Ladd and Lipset, *supra* note 9, at 56–60.
39. *Id.* at 301–302.
40. *Id.* at 92.
41. *Id.* at 186–87, 197.
42. John M. Ellis, *The Origins of PC*, CHRON. HIGHER EDUC., Jan. 15, 1992, at B-1 to B-2. Todd Gitlin cautions that identity politics is a disturbing position for the left since adherents of these views walk head-on into the traditional nationalist trap—a trap that can lead to fascism, brutal irrationalism, and oppression of minorities. Todd Gitlin, *On the Virtues of a Loose Canon*, in BEYOND P.C.: TOWARD A POLITICS OF UNDERSTANDING 188 (Patricia Aufderheide ed. 1992). Historically, in Professor Hofstadter's observation, anti-intellectualism has been widespread in the United States but stays normally at a low to moderate level. Over time, the public tends to accumulate grievances against intellectuals, and anti-intellectualism grows. A wave of zealotry from outside the university builds on these accumulated resentments against intellectuals in general, and the public vents them somewhat indiscriminately. Richard Hofstadter, ANTI-INTELLECTUALISM IN AMERICAN LIFE 38–43 (1962).
43. Barry Siegel, *Fighting Words*, L.A. TIMES, Mar. 28, 1993, Magazine, at 14.
44. William Freivogel, Clinton Nominee Rejects Political Correctness Label, ST. LOUIS POST-DISPATCH, Dec. 20, 1992, at 7A.
45. *HHS Secretary Donna Shalala Address to U.S. Chamber of Commerce*, REUTER TRANSCRIPT REPORT, March 30, 1993.
46. Scott Jaschik, *Scientist Says Campus Stand May Have Cost Him U.S. Post*, CHRON. HIGHER EDUC., Nov. 10, 1993, at A26.
47. George F. Will, *Politically Correct, but Wrong*, STAR & TRIB., Apr. 29, 1993, at A24.
48. Stephen Burd, *Clinton Names U. of Pennsylvania Chief to Take Over Humanities Endowment*, CHRON. HIGHER EDUC., Apr. 21, 1993, at A-19, A-21.
49. Stephen Burd, *Hackney Clears Hurdle in Run for the NEH*, CHRON. HIGHER EDUC., July 7, 1993, at A26, A33.
50. In March, 1994, under Hackney's leadership, the National Endowment for the Humanities convened a balanced group of scholars to explore the nature of an American identity. Stephen Burd, *A National Conversation that Avoids 'Ideological' Warfare*, CHRON. HIGHER EDUC., March 16, 1994, at A26.
51. David L. Wheeler, *Federal Research Effort on Violence is Not Racist, Review Concludes*, CHRON. HIGHER EDUC., Mar. 24, 1993, at A-12.
52. Scott Jaschik, *New Focus on Civil Rights*, CHRON. HIGHER EDUC., June 22, 1994, at A27.
53. Dept. of Education, Racial Incidents and Harassment Against Students at Educational Institutions; Investigative Guidance; Notice 59 F.R. No. 47, March 10, 1994, at 11448, 11449.
54. Scott Jaschik, *First Amendment Implications of Harassment Rules to be Studied*, CHRON. HIGHER EDUC., April 27, 1994, at A24.
55. Mary Jordan, *Harassment Guidelines Questioned*, WASH. POST, May 1, 1994, at A19.
56. *AAUP Opposes OCR Guideline Proposals on Racial Discrimination*, FOOT-NOTES, Fall 1994, at 2.
57. *First Amendment Implications of Harassment Rules to be Studied*, *supra* note 54.

58. Charles A. Radin, *An Ivory Cower: Some Say "P.C. Cops" Making Professors Cringe*, BOSTON GLOBE, Jan. 20, 1993, National/Foreign, at 1.
59. *R.A.V. v. St. Paul*, 112 S. Ct. 2538, 2541 (1992).
60. *Id.* at 2548.
61. *See* Gregory Heiser and Lawrence Rossow, *Hate Speech or Free Speech: Can Broad Campus Speech Regulations Survive Current Judicial Reasoning?*, 22 J. LAW & EDUC. 139, 150–51 (1993); Ronald Rotunda, *A Brief Comment on Politically Incorrect Speech in the Wake of R.A.V.*, 47 S.M.U. L. REV. 9, 20 (1993); Scott Jaschik, *Campus 'Hate Speech' Codes in Doubt After High Court Rejects a City Ordinance*, CHRON. HIGHER EDUC., July 1, 1992, at A19, A22.
62. *Dambrot v. Central Michigan University*, 839 F.Supp. 477, 481–82 (E.D. Mich. 1993) (the policy went beyond suppressing offensive speech and suppressed also "negative connotations" that are "unintentional.")
63. *See* Christopher Shea, *Penn will Drop Its Policy on Racial Harassment*, CHRON. HIGHER EDUC., Nov. 24, 1993, at A20; Richard Ek, *College Drops Harassment Ban*, SAN FRAN. CHRON., Dec. 4, 1993, at A18 (Chico State drops its racial harassment policy); Jackie Fitzpatrick, *Education, Not Rules, Free Speech at U. Conn.*, N.Y. TIMES, May 23, 1993, Sec. 13CN, at 4 (University of Connecticut and Rutgers Univ. change disciplinary policy).
64. Jerry Carroll, *Political Correctness Takes a Nosedive*, S.F. CHRON., Oct. 26, 1994, at E7.
65. Radin, *supra* note 58.
66. Carolyn J. Mooney, *A Lull in the Campus Battles Over "Political Correctness,"* CHRON. HIGHER EDUC., Apr. 21, 1993, at A-14 to A-15.

12

The Wavering Flame of Academic Freedom

Academic freedom is not a strong beacon that illuminates the entire university. It is rather a wavering flame of recent historical development. It is an idea not widely shared outside the academic world, and often misunderstood, unappreciated, and undefended within academia. Academic freedom is denied in theory and in practice by much of the world most of the time.[1] Beginning as a spark at the turn of this century, academic freedom in the United States even after seventy-five years is a flame that flickers in the winds of strong ideology and zealotry. The idea of academic freedom has been repeatedly threatened since the modern university emerged 125 years ago as waves of ideological zealotry in higher education ebb and flow. Zealots in each wave share both a common passion to censor opposing views and common tactics of vilification, investigation, tribunal, and disruption. The common result is to silence not only those punished, but also a vastly greater number of potential speakers, especially the vulnerable groups in the university community, who will steer clear of possible punishment.

This suppression of the wrong thought and speech of others assaults the university's essential purpose in a liberal intellectual system. The university is the one community in the liberal intellectual system whose specific mission is the seeking, making, and disseminating of knowledge through unrestrained public criticism. The professoriat in the universities constitutes a significant proportion of the decentralized communities of checkers on which knowledge production in a liberal intellectual system depends. The essential requirement of progress in the production of knowledge within a university setting is free discourse among academic professionals within the ethical and competency constraints of a discipline. If this free discourse is compromised, teaching, scholarship, and the university itself are without legitimacy in a liberal intellectual system.

Over the course of this century, the professoriat developed a tradition of academic freedom to protect this free discourse. Out of sustained efforts by the professoriat grew an American tradition of professional academic freedom that grants rights to professors to be free from employer interference in research, teaching, and intramural and extramural utterance. With these rights came reciprocal duties. As Professor Van Alstyne observed over twenty years ago, "The price of an exceptional vocational freedom to speak the truth as one sees it, without penalty for its possible immediate impact upon the economic well being of the employing institution, is the cost of exceptional care in the representation of that truth, a professional standard of care."[2] The tradition thus imposes correlative duties of professional competence and ethical conduct on individual professors. The faculty as a collegial body has correlative duties to defend academic freedom and to enforce the duties to be met by individual professors. The tradition of faculty self-governance in peer review of professional conduct makes professional academic freedom uniquely different from tenure systems in other employment settings.

Many faculty members have not had any significant grounding regarding the tradition of academic freedom in the United States. As a result they poorly understand the concept, particularly the correlative duties of academic freedom. At the same time, many faculty members realize that education concerning these matters is important. For example, the Swazey, Lewis, and Anderson survey of research misconduct published in 1994 found that 88 percent of the faculty respondents and 82 percent of the graduate students surveyed believed that "ethical preparedness" training should be an important part of their academic departments and universities.[3] Paradoxically, the survey also found that "only a minuscule proportion (4 percent of faculty members and 3 percent of students) think that their departments actually take a very active role in this area."[4] Organized educational programs on professional values, ethical standards and academic traditions seem to be rare.

There exists an enormous divergence between the perceived importance of "ethical preparedness" training and the implementation of formal educational programs to meet the need. Many faculty members apparently believe that graduate students will learn professional values, ethical standards, and academic traditions through informal interaction with and informal instruction by faculty members during collaborative work. Faculty assume that this education occurs through "an osmosis-like diffusion" from a faculty member who plays an important role in a graduate student's professional socialization.[5] The same assumption presumably exists regarding the professional socialization of new faculty members by senior faculty mentors.

Reality contradicts these assumptions. Swazey, Louis, and Anderson report that substantially less than half of the graduate students in their survey had a mentor who was significantly attending to the transmission of professional values and ethical standards.[6] Faculty advisers for graduate students are not generally acting as true mentors on these issues. These findings challenge the conventional wisdom of relying on the osmosis strategy for the professional socialization of graduate students and new faculty.[7]

In an earlier day when the academic profession was much smaller it may have been possible to maintain the remembered tradition of academic free-

TABLE 12.1
Number of Faculty in Institutions of Higher Education*

Year	Faculty (number in thousands)
1899–1900	24
1909–10	36
1919–20	49
1929–30	82
1939–40	147
1949–50	247
1959–60	381
1969–70	450
1979–80	675
1989–90	824

*Beginning in 1969–70, the data include only instructional faculty with the rank of instructor or above.

dom through the efforts of mentors. University of California President Emeritus Clark Kerr remembers that "there was a generally understood academic ethic that was part of the orientation of the...professoriat, and this ethic was reinforced by advice and personal pressure when it was not voluntarily followed."[8] However, by 1973 the AAUP Commission on Academic Tenure in Higher Education observed that "the vast and rapid growth of the profession in recent years has weakened the force of professional tradition."[9] The data bear out a dramatic expansion of the professoriat in the last fifty years.

Table 12.1 indicates that from 1940–1990, the professoriat increased its numbers 677,000 or five and one-half times, with the largest increase of 225,000 occurring in the 1970s.[10] These enormous increases in the number of faculty members in higher education make "osmosis-like diffusion" of professional values, standards and traditions very problematic. The increasing diversity of the professoriat also may inhibit osmosis-like diffusion. President Emeritus Kerr adds further that the new academic culture is different. "It involves less commitment to the local academic community and to citizenship obligations within it. Faculty members have more attachments to economic opportunities off campus and to off-campus political concerns on campus. The campus is more of a means to non-academic ends. In this new situation, implicit contracts governing behavior and informal means of enforcement are less effective. They may need, increasingly, to be reinforced by more formal codes of behavior."[11]

There is a great need for serious and continuing attention to the transmission of professional values, ethical standards and academic traditions. There should be explicit instruction for novitiates and continuing regular educational engagement for veteran faculty on these issues. What would effective instruction on these issues look like in specific terms? The following suggestions may stimulate faculty debate on this question.

1. Basic educational programs, one for faculty development and one for graduate students, should lay a foundation in terms of our heritage of academic freedom in a liberal intellectual system. A grounding in our tradition of academic freedom requires knowledge of several fundamentals:

- the history of waves of zealotry in the United States;
- the history of the development of professional and constitutional academic freedom, First Amendment protection for professors at public universities, and academic abstention;
- the specific rights of academic freedom and the rationale supporting these rights;
- the specific correlative duties of academic freedom and the rationale supporting these duties;
- the importance of the legacy of both the rights of academic freedom as well as the professoriat's individual and collegial responsibilities to honor and enforce the correlative duties of academic freedom to the legitimacy of the professoriat's work in a liberal intellectual system; and
- the probability that, if history repeats itself, a wave of zealotry will occur roughly each generation in higher education. The critical question in each period of zealotry is whether the faculty's response of silent submission to coercive tactics will again be the ballast of the zealotry, or whether the faculty will be more effective in limiting the damage of the zealotry.

2. Building on this foundation, more advanced programs would emphasize small group peer discussion of dilemmas based on realistic problems involving both the defense of academic freedom and the enforcement of the ethical and competency constraints of the discipline when individual professors do not meet them.[12] An annual program to cover new developments and to apply the correlative duties to current problems would be useful. Faculty members should discuss the state of academic freedom within the faculty at least annually.

3. Once a knowledge base concerning the rights and correlative duties of academic freedom is established, another useful step would be for the faculty to define further the correlative duties as they apply to a particular discipline and in a particular faculty. The AAUP statements and the academic traditions on which they rest are necessarily general in describing the correlative duties. Ambiguity in the application of these general principles to a specific discipline or in a particular faculty may lead to problems of lack of notice and unfairness in individual cases.

Over twenty years ago, the Commission on Academic Tenure in Higher Education created by the AAUP and college administrators urged faculties to consider and discuss the adoption of a faculty statement on professional conduct. The Commission recommended that, "The faculty of the institution...

must be the source for the definition and clarification of standards of professional conduct and must take the lead in ensuring that these standards are enforced."[13]

The Commission further specified:

> The Commission believes that faculties should be authorized and encouraged to develop codes of professional conduct for the guidance of their members and as a basis for sanctions against those whose conduct falls below professional norms. Such codes should reflect the broad precepts embodied in such existing formulations as the 1940 Statement of Principles and the 1966 Statement of Professional Ethics and should attempt to articulate the traditional sentiments of academic persons as to the demands of their calling.... The very effort to provide a statement of professional standards will serve to dramatize the faculty's own responsibility for its integrity and that of the institution.

> The Commission recommends that the faculty of each institution assume responsibility for developing a code of faculty conduct and procedures and sanctions for faculty self discipline, for recommending adoption of the code by the institution's governing board, and for making effective use of the code when it has been approved.[14]

Both President Emeritus Kerr, and earlier Professor Eric Ashby, urge faculties to adopt a "declared professional code of practice" to address the problem of a disintegrating profession.[15] A professional code of practice should include what conduct mentioned in the code would be grounds for sanction, the specific sanctions to be applied, and the procedures to be followed for each type of sanction. The faculty should give clear notice of what is prohibited and how violations will be punished. In all sanctioning efforts, faculty judgment should play the critical role in the context of clearly defined procedural protections.[16]

The faculty's consideration of a code of professional conduct is itself educational. The debate that occurs during the drafting and adoption of standards will help individual professors and the collegial group understand the correlative duties of academic freedom. The faculty could revisit the statement annually to consider its effectiveness and possible amendment.

In drafting a code of professional conduct, the faculty may be able to build on the work of others. Chapter 10 earlier recommended a faculty statement on professional conduct to consider. Professional societies or government agencies may have already drafted guidelines that further define the correlative duties in particular contexts. For example, in 1985 the editors of nearly twenty journals published by the American Chemical Society published "Ethical Guidelines to Publication of Chemical Research." The guidelines outline the ethical obligations of authors, manuscript reviewers, and journal editors.[17] Professional academic societies should strongly consider assisting in developing this type of guideline.

4. Educational programs and statements on professional conduct should be undertaken within departments or faculties by discipline, not across faculties

within the university. Over the past 50 years, common knowledge among the various disciplines has thinned, and the fields have become more self-contained. Socialization of graduate students and new professors occurs primarily within a field, and in particular the local incarnation of the field of study, the academic department.[18] The AAUP and the professional associations in each discipline could be of great service in developing materials for educational programs, but in the final analysis it is the individual departments within the university that must provide the faculty development programs to strengthen the tradition of academic freedom.

The results of educational programs on academic freedom are difficult to predict. On the positive side, a solid understanding of the fundamentals should help faculty members to resist attempts to impose orthodoxy and suppress dissent. For example, education will inform the professoriat that in past periods of zealotry, investigations and the empanelment of tribunals to identify and penalize dangerous speech have consistently been among the most powerful tools of suppression. Armed with this knowledge, faculty members may be more willing to resist the creation of any institutionalized apparatus for the investigation of speech. Faculty members may also understand that being a bystander while zealots suppress the academic freedom of a colleague is not harmless. It is an act that condones suppression. In the face of affirmative duties to defend academic freedom, a faculty member's indifference to the suppression of colleagues is complicity. Faculty members will also know that zealotry does not stop with suppression of clear heretics, others will also be at risk if zealots see political advantage. In addition, an increased awareness of the importance of academic freedom to the legitimacy of teaching, scholarship, and the university itself may increase faculty members' willingness to give public support to a target regardless of disagreement. Education on the tradition of academic freedom may also lead faculty members to see that academic freedom depends upon some multidimensional disagreement within a faculty. Monolithic though or little diversity of opinion on a faculty are inherently dangerous for rights of professional academic freedom. Few people will defend the rights of others to speak thoughts for which the listener has no sympathy.

Peer discussion concerning issues of academic freedom may create a climate of reciprocity and peer pressure to support professional academic freedom. If there is a tradition of academic freedom within a faculty, the climate of opinion may empower some faculty members who would otherwise remain silent out of fear of zealots.

Ladd and Lipset found that academics are distinguished by the intensely ideological character of their thinking on both intramural and extramural issues.[19] Faculty members holding strong ideological positions may be bitter towards those of different orientation.[20] If their ideological predisposition is the same as that of the zealots, faculty members tend to support coercive tactics.[21] Educational programs on academic freedom may help create an ideological commitment to academic freedom that offsets professors' tendency not to defend publicly the right of others to express views for which the listener has no sympathy.

The same argument applies to the tendency of the faculty collegium to abdicate its responsibilities in the face of professional misconduct by a colleague. Many professors may be misinformed on the correlative duty that the faculty as a collegial body enforce the ethical and competency constraints of the discipline when individual professors do not meet them. Education about this correlative duty and its importance in maintaining academic freedom and the legitimacy of scholarly work may help create an ideological commitment that combats the tendency of the collegium to become a delinquent community that emphasizes collegial harmony and individual autonomy in condoning professional misconduct. A study of research misconduct published in 1994 suggests that training may not have a significant impact on misconduct. Expectations should be modest.[22]

Clearly a strategy of faculty development programs to strengthen the remembered tradition of academic freedom within the professoriat itself is a very long-run strategy. This type of long-run educational strategy enjoyed some success with the governing boards over the past seventy-five years. Academics today have the freedom to say and do things that seventy-five years ago were the object of severe sanctions by governing boards and administrators. In the last forty years since McCarthyism, governing boards generally have not been infected with zealotry; this may be due in part to awareness of the extensive scholarly criticism of the governing boards' role undermining academic freedom during McCarthyism. The same long-term educational strategy may work with the professoriat.

A strategy of educational programs to strengthen the tradition of academic freedom within the professoriat will most clearly help professors who become targets in a future wave of zealotry. Targets will take strength from the discovery that periods of zealotry have occurred frequently in higher education and that the target shares much in common with people who lived and worked, acted and suffered many years in the past. For a thinking person, a conversation with the past, Yale professor David Bromwich notes, creates many strong feelings of solidarity. "To believe on reasonable grounds that in a given cause, though one may have few living allies, and perhaps no visible ones, somebody in a similar predicament once felt the same intuition, can be a sustaining knowledge and the beginning of a persuasive self-trust."[23]

In an ideal world, faculty development programs would dramatically improve the remembered tradition of academic freedom within the professoriat. A faculty with a strong tradition of academic freedom would ideally work to create an atmosphere without coercion in which all professors and students, no matter how timid or unwilling to sacrifice, would feel free to express an unpopular dissenting view.

In the light of historical experience, these ideal results seem highly unlikely. A large part of the world, including, in the final analysis, many in academia itself, strongly resist the central premise of a liberal intellectual system that all knowledge claims are revisable. The lust to censor in the name of other higher moralities is extremely strong. Academics occupy a salient particularly exposed to this lust. Historical experience suggests that the construct of academic freedom to protect free discourse in the university from this strong lust to censor was flawed from the beginning. The construct assumed that the human nature of faculty members would be better than it has proven to be. Hofstadter and Metzger noted this problem almost forty years ago.

> No one can follow the history of academic freedom in this country without wondering at the fact that any society, interested in the immediate goals of solidarity and self-preservation, should possess the vision to subsidize free criticism and inquiry, and without feeling that the academic freedom we still possess is one of the remarkable achievements of man. At the same time, one cannot but be appalled at the slender thread by which it hangs, at the wide discrepancies that exist among institutions with respect to its honoring and preservation; and one cannot but be disheartened by the cowardice and self-deception that frail men use who want to be both safe and free. With such conflicting evidence, perhaps individual temperament alone tips the balance toward confidence or despair.[24]

The principal flawed assumption about human nature underlying the construct of academic freedom is the presumed willingness of faculty members to defend academic freedom and to give public support to colleagues targeted by zealotry. The historical record indicates that many faculty will not defend academic freedom publicly against the ideological zealotry of the day. Many are born bystanders whose indifference grows lethal in a period of zealotry when the target is left without allies. The second flawed assumption about human nature underlying the construct of academic freedom is the presumed ability of faculty members to fulfill their duties of peer review of colleagues responsibly. The historical record indicates a strong tendency for the faculty collegium to become a delinquent community that abdicates the performance of its correlative duty to monitor and enforce the duties of competence and ethical conduct to be met by individual professors. If the construct of academic freedom is flawed in its assumptions about human nature, why not admit that the emperor has no clothes and discard the doctrine of academic freedom?

The fact that human self-interest and weakness cause a principle and its supporting institutional structure to fall short of the ideal is disappointing but not determinative. The test of academic freedom should be the benefit it provides to the university's mission relative to its costs. Are the benefits of the professoriat's holding out and trying to live up to the ideals of academic freedom greater than the costs? If so, does academic freedom achieve these results better than alternative principles and institutional arrangements?

As an aspirational matter, the principle of free inquiry and speech is critical to the university's mission of seeking, making and disseminating knowledge. Without free discourse, teaching, scholarship, and the university itself are without legitimacy in a liberal intellectual system. The conditions necessary for a faculty member to feel free to engage in academic speech vary widely. A few heroic academics with courage like Galileo's will speak freely without any protection from zealots. At the other end of the spectrum, the timid faculty member unwilling to sacrifice will not speak if there exists any risk of punishment. While academic freedom and the supporting institutional structure of peer review have not been able to create an atmosphere where the timid will feel protected from the winds of zealotry, they have created enough protection so that some of those with moderate but not heroic courage will also speak. There have been instances in each wave of zealotry where courageous faculty members, or the administration, or both have fought the rising tide of zealotry and defended the academic freedom of the heretic. The institutionalized framework of peer review can shelter islands of dissent in recurring floods of zealotry. Its greatest strength is that within a system of peer review, a small number of people of high principle and courage can step forward and do a great deal to protect targets from the worst excesses of zealotry. A peer review system provides sufficient protection so that the courageous can speak publicly and, with few colleagues defending academic freedom, have a reasonable chance of weathering the zealotry.

Because of the tendency of collegia to abdicate responsibility for effective peer review, an institutional structure to protect academic freedom that relies upon peer review imposes substantial costs of excessive protection for those whose conduct is incompetent or unethical but not grossly so. These costs of excessive protection for unprofessional conduct might be mitigated by faculty educational programs emphasizing the forgotten correlative duties of academic freedom. Are these costs greater than the benefits? Given the vital importance of free discourse to the mission of the university, the benefits outweigh the costs. Could an alternative institutional structure looking to other means to protect free discourse achieve higher net benefits? The principal alternative institutional players to perform this role of protecting free discourse are the governing boards or the courts. Both pose severe problems. The governing boards historically were the agent of zealotry. They will be once again. The courts, as discussed earlier in the analysis of the doctrine of academic abstention, are not well equipped to pass judgment on issues of academic competence and ethics. The reliance on peer review in the current institutional structure of academic freedom provides the most protection. Even when the professoriat itself is infected with zealotry, peer review provides the means through which a small number of courageous colleagues can do much to protect heretics. For academic freedom to have meaning and for the university to have legitimacy, there must be some academics who will enter the fray publicly and sacrifice to protect academic freedom for the sake of the university. This book is dedicated to one of them. There have been, there are now, and there will be others. The university serving its mission of seeking, discovering, and disseminating knowledge is one of humankind's most remarkable achievements. One of the greatest contributions an academic can make is an honorable defense of the principles on which the university rests.

Notes

1. *See Report of the Committee on Freedom of Expression at Yale*, 4 HUMAN RIGHTS 357, 358 (1975).
2. William Van Alstyne, *The Specific Theory of Academic Freedom and the General Issue of Civil Liberty*, THE CONCEPT OF ACADEMIC FREEDOM 59, 76 (ed. Edmund Pincoffs 1972).
3. Judith Swazey, Karen Lewis, Melissa Anderson, *The Ethical Training of Graduate Students Requires Serious and Continuing Attention*, CHRON. HIGHER EDUC., March 9, 1994, at B1, B2.
4. *Id.* at B2. A panel of the National Academy of Sciences issued a report in 1992 that summarized the factors in the research environment that may contribute to misconduct. These included inadequate training in the methods and traditions of science, and the increasing scale and complexity of the research environment, leading to the erosion of peer review, mentorship, and educational processes in science. Panel on Scientific Responsibility and the Conduct of Research, Committee on Science, Engineering, and Public Policy, National Academy of Sciences, National Academy of Engineering, Institute of Medicine, RESPONSIBLE SCIENCE: ENSURING THE INTEGRITY OF THE RESEARCH PROCESS 30–31 (1992).
5. *Id.*
6. *Id.*
7. *See id.* In his book, *The Ideal of the University*, Robert Paul Wolff also notes that doctoral candidates frequently do not have any mentor relationship with a veteran researcher. Robert Paul Wolff, THE IDEAL OF THE UNIVERSITY 22 (1992).
8. Clark Kerr, *Knowledge Ethics and the New Academic Culture*, CHANGE, Jan./Feb. 1994 at 9–10.
9. Commission on Academic Tenure in Higher Education, FACULTY TENURE 41–43 (1973).
10. United States Department of Education, National Center for Education Statistics, DIGEST OF EDUCATION STATISTICS 173 (table 167) (1993). Ladd and Lipset report in their book, *The Divided Academy*, that the number of faculty in 1970 was 551,000 rather than the 450,000 for the same year reported in the *Digest of Education Statistics* (1993). Everett C. Ladd Jr. & Seymour Martin Lipset, THE DIVIDED ACADEMY: PROFESSORS AND POLITICS 2 (1975).
11. Clark Kerr, *supra* note 8, at 9–10.
12. A panel of the National Academy of Sciences recommended early education of young investigators to train them in the traditions and methods of science and to instill research ethics. RESPONSIBLE SCIENCE, *supra* note 4, at 30, 64, 130, 145. The panel recommends three alternative approaches to ethics education. *Id.* ta 130–33.

13. Commission on Academic Tenure in Higher Education, FACULTY TENURE 42 (1973).
14. *Id*. at 44-45.
15. Clark Kerr, *supra* note 8 at 12; Eric Ashby, *A Hippocratic Oath For the Academic Profession*, MINERVA, Autumn/Winter 1968-69 at 64-66. A panel of the National Academy of Sciences recommends that research institutions should urge faculty to develop formal guidelines for the conduct of research. RESPONSIBLE SCIENCE, *supra* note 4, at 13. The process of formulating guidelines itself may be extremely valuable for those who participate. *Id*. at 137.
16. *See id*. at 102, 105-107.
17. Joseph Bunnett, *Scientists' Responsibility in Handling Misconduct*, CHRON. HIGHER EDUC., March 23, 1994 at B6; Publication Division of the American Chemical Society, ETHICAL GUIDELINES TO PUBLICATION OF CHEMICAL RESEARCH (1985). These guidelines were reaffirmed in 1989.
18. Melissa S. Anderson, Karen S. Lewis, Jason Earle, *Disciplinary and Department Effects on Observations of Faculty and Graduate Student Misconduct*, 65 J. OF HIGHER EDUC., 331, 332 (1994); Ladd and Lipset, *supra* note 10, at 56-57.
19. Ladd and Lipset, *supra* note 10, at 42-44, 46.
20. *Id*. at 51.
21. *Id*. at 43-44.
22. *See* Anderson, Lewis, and Earle, *supra* note 8 at 342-43. However, the authors still support educational programs on ethics. The findings "suggest that between exposure to misconduct and the absence of opportunities to discuss these issues openly future researchers are being socialized in an environment that may create ambivalence about basic values of the academy, namely, the obligation of the scholarly community to uphold the highest standards of research behavior and to enforce the values of the broader society regarding the behavior of professional employees. Misconduct cannot, in all likelihood, be prevented but recent calls for increased opportunities for students and faculty to talk about scientific values...seem a minimal response." Id at 343.
23. David Bromwich, *The Future of Tradition*, DISSENT, Fall 1989, at 556.
24. Richard Hofstadter & Walter Metzger, THE DEVELOPMENT OF ACADEMIC FREEDOM IN THE UNITED STATES 506 (1955).

Appendix A[*]
The 1915 Declaration of Principles

Editor's Note[1]: Throughout its history the American Association of University Professors has sought the formulation, the recognition, and the observance of principles and procedures conducive to freedom of thought, of inquiry, and of expression in colleges and universities. At the organizational meeting of the Association on January 1 and 2, 1915 it was voted that the Association form a Committee on Academic Freedom and Academic Tenure, which should include members of a joint Committee on Academic Freedom and Tenure of the American Economic Association, the American Political Science Association, and the American Sociological Society, which had been constituted in 1913 to study and report on problems of academic freedom and tenure in teaching and research in economics, political science, and sociology. Pursuant to this action Dr. John Dewey, the Association's first President, appointed a Committee of fifteen members as follows: Edwin R.A. Seligman (Economics), Columbia University, Chairman; Charles E. Bennett (Latin), Cornell University; James Q. Dealty (Political Science), Brown University; Edward C. Elliott (Education), University of Wisconsin; Richard T. Ely (Economics), University of Wisconsin; Henry W. Farnam (Political Science), Yale University; Frank A. Fetter (Economics), Princeton University; Guy Stanton Ford (History), University of Minnesota; Charles A. Kofoid (Zoology), University of California; James P. Lichtenberger (Sociology), University of Pennsylvania; Arthur O. Lovejoy (Philosophy), The Johns Hopkins University; Frederick W. Padelford (English), University of Washington; Roscoe Pound (Law), Harvard University; Howard C. Warren (Psychology), Princeton University; Ulysses G. Weatherly (Sociology), Indiana University.[2]

The Association's first Committee on Academic Freedom and Academic Tenure was established primarily to formulate principles and procedures, the observance of which would insure intellectual freedom in colleges and universities. It was not anticipated that the Committee would be called upon to engage in extensive investigatory work. In this connection it is pertinent to note Dr. Dewey's statement as Chairman of the organizational meeting of the Association in reference to the Association's interest in academic freedom.

*Reprinted from, American Ass'n of Univ. Professors, *Academic Freedom and Tenure* 155–176 (Louis Joughin ed., 1969).

> *The defense of academic freedom and tenure being already a concern of the existing learned societies will not, I am confident, be more than an incident in the activities of the Association developing professional standards.*

The Committee had scarcely been formed, however, when a number of alleged infringements of academic freedom were brought to its attention. Eleven such cases were considered during 1915. These cases were diverse in character, viz., dismissal of individual professors, resignation of professors in protest of dismissals of colleagues, dismissal of a university president, and a complaint of a university president against the institution's governing board. Apropos of these unanticipated demands that were made on the Association during 1915, Dr. Dewey spoke as follows in his Presidential Address to the Annual Meeting of that year:

> *In concluding I wish to say a word about the large place occupied in this year's program by the question of academic freedom in its relation to academic tenure. I have heard rumors of some criticism on this point. Some have expressed to me fear lest attention to individual grievances might crowd out attention to those general and "constructive" matters which are the Association's reason for existence. Let me say for the reassurance of any such that none of the officers of the Association, least of all those who have been overwhelmed by the duties incident to these investigations, regard this year's work as typical or even as wholly normal.... The investigations of particular cases were literally thrust upon us. To have failed to meet the demands would have been cowardly; it would have tended to destroy all confidence in the Association as anything more than a talking body. The question primarily involved was not whether the Council should authorize the investigation of this or that case, but whether the Association was to have legs and arms and be a working body. In short, as conditions shape themselves for us, I personally feel that the work done on particular cases this year turned out to be of the most constructive sort which could have been undertaken.... The amount and quality of energy and the time spent upon these matters by our secretary and by the chairman of our committee of fifteen are such as to beggar thanks. These gentlemen and the others who have labored with them must find their reward not only in the increased prosperity of this Association in the future, but, above all, in the enhanced security and dignity of the scholar's calling throughout our country.*

Despite the unexpected volume of work incident to the investigation of individual cases during its first year, the Committee was able to complete a comprehensive report concerning academic freedom, which was approved by the Annual Meeting of the Association held in Washington, D.C., December 31, 1915 and January 1, 1916. In presenting this report to the meeting the Committee said:

> *The safeguarding of a proper measure of academic freedom in American universities requires both a clear understanding of the principles which bear upon the matter, and the adoption by the universities of such arrangements and regulations as may effectually prevent any infringement of that freedom and deprive of plausibility all charges of such infringement. This report is therefore divided into two*

*parts, the first constituting a general declaration of principles relating to aca-
demic freedom, the second presenting a group of practical proposals, the adoption
of which is deemed necessary in order to place the rules and procedure of the
American universities, in relation to these matters, upon a satisfactory footing.*

*Largely as a result of the interest in the principles enunciated in the 1915
Declaration of Principles, the American Council on Education in 1925 called a
conference for the purpose of discussing the principles of academic freedom
and tenure, with a view to formulating a succinct statement of these principles.
Participating in this conference were representatives of a number of organizations of higher education. At this conference there was formulated a statement
of principles known to the profession as the 1925 Conference Statement on Academic Freedom and Tenure. In the formulation of this statement, the participants were not seeking to formulate new principles, but rather to restate good
academic custom and usage as these had been developed in practice over a
long period of time in institutions whose administrations were aware of the
nature of the academic calling and the function of academic institutions. [In
both] the 1925 Conference Statement and the subsequent adaptation of the principles set forth therein—the 1940 Statement of Principles, ... the principles set
forth in the Declaration of 1915 are adhered to, adapted, and strengthened....*

A. General Declaration of Principles

The term "academic freedom" has traditionally had two applications—to
the freedom of the teacher and to that of the student, *Lehrfreiheit* and
Lernfreiheit. It need scarcely be pointed out that the freedom which is the
subject of this report is that of the teacher. Academic freedom in this sense
comprises three elements: freedom of inquiry and research; freedom of teaching within the university or college; and freedom of extra-mural utterance and
action. The first of these is almost everywhere so safeguarded that the dangers
of its infringement are slight. It may therefore be disregarded in this report.
The second and third phases of academic freedom are closely related, and are
often not distinguished. The third, however, has an importance of its own,
since of late it has perhaps more frequently been the occasion of difficulties
and controversies than has the question of freedom of intra-academic teaching. All five of the cases which have recently been investigated by committees
of this Association have involved, at least as one factor, the right of university
teachers to express their opinions freely outside the university or to engage in
political activities in their capacity as citizens. The general principles which
have to do with freedom of teaching in both these senses seem to the committee to be in great part, thought not wholly, the same. In this report, therefore,
we shall consider the matter primarily with reference to freedom of teaching
within the university, and shall assume that what is said thereon is also applicable to the freedom of speech of university teachers outside their institutions,

subject to certain qualifications and supplementary considerations which will be pointed out in the course of the report.

An adequate discussion of academic freedom must necessarily consider three matters: (1) the scope and basis of the power exercised by those bodies having ultimate legal authority in academic affairs; (2) the nature of the academic calling; (3) the function of the academic institution or university.

Basis of Academic Authority

American institutions of learning are usually controlled by boards of trustees as the ultimate repositories of power. Upon them finally it devolves to determine the measure of academic freedom which is to be realized in the several institutions. It therefore becomes necessary to inquire into the nature of the trust reposed in these boards, and to ascertain to whom the trustees are to be considered accountable.

The simplest case is that of the proprietary school or college designed for the propagation of specific doctrines prescribed by those who have furnished its endowment. It is evident that in such cases the trustees are bound by the deed of gift, and, whatever be their own views, are obligated to carry out the terms of the trust. If a church or religious denomination establishes a college to be governed by a board of trustees, with the express understanding that the college will be used as an instrument of propaganda in the interests of the religious faith professed by the church or denomination creating it, the trustees have a right to demand that everything be subordinated to that end. If, again, as has happened in this country, a wealthy manufacturer establishes a special school in a university in order to teach, among other things, the advantages of a protective tariff, or if, as is also the case, an institution has been endowed for the purpose of propagating the doctrines of socialism, the situation is analogous. All of these are essentially proprietary institutions, in the moral sense. They do not, at least as regards one particular subject, accept the principles of freedom of inquiry, of opinion, and of teaching; and their purpose is not to advance knowledge by the unrestricted research and unfettered discussion of impartial investigators, but rather to subsidize the promotion of the opinions held by the persons, usually not of the scholar's calling, who provide the funds for their maintenance. Concerning the desirability of the existence of such institutions, the committee does not desire to express any opinion. But it is manifestly important that they should not be permitted to sail under false colors. Genuine boldness and thoroughness of inquiry, and freedom of speech, are scarcely reconcilable with the prescribed inculcation of a particular opinion upon a controverted question.

Such institutions are rare, however, and are becoming ever more rare. We still have, indeed, colleges under denominational auspices; but very few of them impose upon their trustees responsibility for the spread of specific doctrines. They are more and more coming to occupy, with respect to the freedom enjoyed by the members of their teaching bodies, the position of untrammeled institutions of learning, and are differentiated only by the natural influence of their respective historic antecedents and traditions.

Leaving aside, then, the small number of institutions of the proprietary type, what is the nature of the trust reposed in the governing boards of the ordinary institutions of learning? Can colleges and universities that are not strictly bound by their founders to a propagandist duty ever be included in the class of institutions that we have just described as being in a moral sense proprietary? The answer is clear. If the former class of institutions constitute a private or proprietary trust, the latter constitute a public trust. The trustees are trustees for the public. In the case of our state universities this is self-evident. In the case of most of our privately endowed institutions, the situation is really not different. They cannot be permitted to assume the proprietary attitude and privilege, if they are appealing to the general public for support. Trustees of such universities or colleges have no moral right to bind the reason or the conscience of any professor. All claim to such right is waived by the appeal to the general public for contributions and for moral support in the maintenance, not of a propaganda, but of a nonpartisan institution of learning. It follows that any university which lays restrictions upon the intellectual freedom of its professors proclaims itself a proprietary institution, and should be so described whenever it makes a general appeal for funds; and the public should be advised that the institution has no claim whatever to general support or regard.

This elementary distinction between a private and a public trust is not yet so universally accepted as it should be in our American institutions. While in many universities and colleges the situation has come to be entirely satisfactory, there are others in which the relation of trustees to professors is apparently still conceived to be analogous to that of a private employer to his employees; in which, therefore, trustees are not regarded as debarred by any moral restrictions, beyond their own sense of expediency, from imposing their personal opinions upon the teaching of the institution, or even from employing the power of dismissal to gratify their private antipathies or resentments. An eminent university president thus described the situation not many years since:

> In the institutions of higher education the board of trustees is the body on whose discretion, good feeling, and experience the securing of academic freedom now depends. There are boards which leave nothing to be desired in these respects; but there are also numerous bodies that have everything to learn with regard to academic freedom. These barbarous boards exercise an arbitrary power of dismissal. They exclude from the teachings of the university unpopular or dangerous subjects. In some states they even treat professor's positions as common political spoils; and all too frequently, both in state and endowed institutions, they fail to treat the members of the teaching staff with that high consideration to which their functions entitle them.[3]

It is, then, a prerequisite to a realization of the proper measure of academic freedom in American institutions of learning, that all boards of trustees should understand—as many already do—the full implications of the distinction between private proprietorship and a public trust.

The Nature of the Academic Calling

The above-mentioned conception of a university as an ordinary business venture, and of academic teaching as a purely private employment, manifests also a radical failure to apprehend the nature of the social function discharged by the professional scholar. While we should be reluctant to believe that any large number of educated persons suffer from such a misapprehension, it seems desirable at this time to restate clearly the chief reasons, lying in the nature of the university teaching profession, why it is to the public interest that the professional office should be one both of dignity and of independence.

If education is the cornerstone of the structure of society and if progress in scientific knowledge is essential to civilization, few things can be more important than to enhance the dignity of the scholar's profession, with a view to attracting into its ranks men of the highest ability, of sound learning, and of strong and independent character. This is the more essential because the pecuniary emoluments of the profession are not, and doubtless never will be, equal to those open to the more successful members of other professions. It is not, in our opinion, desirable that men should be drawn into this profession by the magnitude of the economic rewards which it offers; but it is for this reason the more needful that men of high gifts and character should be drawn into it by the assurance of an honorable and secure position, and of freedom to perform honestly and according to their own consciences the distinctive and important function which the nature of the profession lays upon them.

That function is to deal at first hand, after prolonged and specialized technical training, with the sources of knowledge; and to impart the results of their own and of their fellow-specialists' investigation and reflection, both to students and to the general public, without fear or favor. The proper discharge of this function requires (among other things) that the university teacher shall be exempt from any pecuniary motive or inducement to hold, or to express, any conclusion which is not the genuine and uncolored product of his own study or that of fellow-specialists. Indeed, the proper fulfillment of the work of the professoriat requires that our universities shall be so free that no fair-minded person shall find any excuse for even a suspicion that the utterances of university teachers are shaped or restricted by the judgment, not of professional scholars, but of inexpert and possibly not wholly disinterested persons outside of their ranks. The lay public is under no compulsion to accept or to act upon the opinions of the scientific experts whom, through the universities, it employs. But it is highly needful, in the interest of society at large, that what purport to be conclusions of men trained for, and dedicated to, the quest for truth, shall in fact be the conclusions of such men, and not echoes of the opinions of the lay public, or of the individuals who endow or manage universities. To the degree that professional scholars, in the formation and promulgation of their opinions, are, or by the character of their tenure appear to be, subject to any motive other than their own scientific conscience and a desire for the respect of their fellow-experts, to that degree the university teaching profession is corrupted; its proper influence upon public opinion is diminished and vitiated; and society at large fails to get from its scholars, in an unadulterated form, the peculiar and necessary service which it is the office of the professional scholar to furnish.

These considerations make still more clear the nature of the relationship between university trustees and members of university faculties. The latter are the appointees, but not in any proper sense the employees, of the former. For, once appointed, the scholar has professional functions to perform in which the appointing authorities have neither competency nor moral right to intervene. The responsibility of the university teacher is primarily to the public itself, and to the judgment of his own profession; and while, with respect to certain external conditions of his vocation, he accepts a responsibility to the authorities of the institution in which he serves, in the essentials of his professional activity his duty is to the wider public to which the institution itself is morally amenable. So far as the university teacher's independence of thought and utterance is concerned—though not in other regards—the relationship of professor to trustees may be compared to that between judges of the Federal courts and the Executive who appoints them. University teachers should be understood to be, with respect to the conclusions reached and expressed by them, no more subject to the control of the trustees than are judges subject to the control of the President with respect to their decisions; while of course, for the same reason, trustees are no more to be held responsible for, or to be presumed to agree with, the opinions or utterances of professors than the President can be assumed to approve of all the legal reasonings of the courts. A university is a great and indispensable organ of the higher life of a civilized community, in the work of which the trustees hold an essential and highly honorable place, but in which the faculties hold an independent place, with quite equal responsibilities—and in relation to purely scientific and educational questions, the primary responsibility. Misconception or obscurity in this matter has undoubtedly been a source of occasional difficulty in the past, and even in several instances during the current year, however much, in the main, a long tradition of kindly and courteous intercourse between trustees and members of university faculties has kept the question in the background.

The Function of the Academic Institution

The importance of academic freedom in most clearly perceived in the light of the purposes for which universities exist. These are three in number.

A. To promote inquiry and advance the sum of human knowledge.

B. To provide general instruction to the students.

C. To develop experts for various branches of the public service.

Let us consider each of these. In the earlier stages of a nation's intellectual development, the chief concern of education institutions is to train the growing generation and to diffuse the already accepted knowledge. It is only slowly that there comes to be provided in the highest institutions of learning the opportunity for the gradual wresting from nature of her intimate secrets. The modern university is becoming more and more the home of scientific research. There are three fields of human inquiry in which the race is only at the beginning: natural science, social science, and philosophy and religion, dealing with the relations of man to outer nature, to his fellowmen, and to ultimate realities and values. In natural science all that we have learned but serves to make us realize more deeply how much more remains to be discovered. In social science in its largest sense, which is concerned with the relations of men in society and with the conditions of social order and well-being, we have learned only an adumbration of the laws which govern these vastly complex phenomena. Finally, in the spiritual life, and in the interpretation of the general meaning and ends of human existence and its relation to the universe, we are still far from a comprehension of the final truths, and from a universal agreement among all sincere and earnest men. In all of these domains of knowledge, the first condition of progress is complete and unlimited freedom to pursue inquiry and publish its results. Such freedom is the breath in the nostrils of all scientific activity.

The second function- which for a long time was the only function- of the American college or university is to provide instruction for students. It is scarcely open to question that freedom of utterance is as important to the teacher as it is to the investigator. No man can be a successful teacher unless he enjoys the respect of his students, and their confidence in his intellectual integrity. It is clear, however, that this confidence will be impaired if there is suspicion on the part of the student that the teacher is not expressing himself fully or frankly, or that college and university teachers in general are a repressed and intimidated class who dare not speak with that candor and courage which youth always demands in those whom it is to esteem. The average student is a discerning observer, who soon takes the measure of his instructor. It is not only the character of the instruction but also the character of the instructor that counts; and if the student has reason to believe that the instructor is not true to himself, the virtue of the instruction as an educative force is incalculably diminished. There must be in the mind of the teacher no mental reservation. He must give the student the best of what he has and what he is.

The third function of the modern university is to develop experts for the use of the community. If there is one thing that distinguishes the more recent developments of democracy, it is the recognition by legislators of the inherent complexities of economic, social, and political life, and the difficulty of solving problems of technical adjustment without technical knowledge. The recognition of this fact has led to continually greater demand for the aid of experts in these subjects, to advise both legislators and administrators. The training of such experts has, accordingly, in recent years, become an important part of work of the universities; and in almost every one of our higher institutions of learning the professors of the economic, social, and political sciences have been drafted to an increasing extent into more or less unofficial participation in the public service. It is obvious that here again the scholar must be absolutely free not only to pursue his investigations but to declare the results of his researches, no matter where they may lead him or to what extent they may come into conflict with accepted opinion. To be of use to the legislator or the administrator, he must enjoy their complete confidence in the disinterestedness of his conclusions.

It is clear, then, that the university cannot perform its threefold function without accepting and enforcing to the fullest extent the principle of academic freedom. The responsibility of the university as a whole is to the community at large, and any restriction upon the freedom of the instructor is bound to react injuriously upon the efficiency and the *morale* of the institution, and therefore ultimately upon the interests of the community.

The attempted infringements of academic freedom at present are probably not only of less frequency than, but of a different character from, those to be found in former times. In the early period of university development in America the chief menace to academic freedom was ecclesiastical, and the disciplines chiefly affected were philosophy and the natural sciences. In more recent times the danger zone has been shifted to the political and social sciences- though we still have sporadic examples of the former class of cases in some of our smaller institutions. But it is precisely in these provinces of knowledge in which academic freedom is now most likely to be threatened, that the need for it is at the same time most evident. No person of intelligence believes that all of our political problems have been solved, or that the final stage of social evolution has been reached. Grave issues in the adjustment of men's social and economic relations are certain to call for settlement in the years that are to come; and for the right settlement of them mankind will need all the wisdom, all the good will, all the soberness of mind, and all the knowledge drawn from experience, that it can command. Toward this settlement the university has potentially its own very great contribution to make; for if the adjustment reached is to be a wise one, it must take due account of economic science, and be guided by that breadth of historic vision which it should be one of the functions of a university to cultivate. But if the universities are to render any such service toward the right solution of the social problems of the future, it is the first essential that the scholars who carry on the work of universities shall not be in a position of dependence upon the favor of any social class or group, that the disinterestedness and impartiality of their inquiries and their conclusions shall be, so far as is humanly possible, beyond the reach of suspicion.

The special dangers to freedom of teaching in the domain of the social sciences are evidently two. The one which is the more likely to affect the privately endowed colleges and universities is the danger of restrictions upon the expression of opinions which point toward extensive social innovations, or call in question the moral legitimacy or social expediency of economic conditions or commercial practices in which large vested interests are involved. In the political. social, and economic field almost every question, no matter how large and general it at first appears, is more or less affected with private or class interests; and, as the governing body of a university is naturally made up of men who through their standing and ability are personally interested in great private enterprises, the points of possible conflict are numberless. When to this is added the consideration that benefactors, as well as most of the parents who send their children to privately endowed institutions, themselves belong to the more prosperous and therefore usually to the more conservative classes, it is apparent that, so long as effectual safeguards for academic freedom are not established, there is a real danger that pressure from vested interests may, sometimes deliberately and sometimes unconsciously, sometimes openly and sometimes subtly and in obscure ways, be brought to bear upon academic authorities.

On the other hand, in our state universities the danger may be the reverse. Where the university is dependent for funds upon legislative favor, it has sometimes happened that the conduct of the institution has been affected by political considerations; and where there is a definite governmental policy or a strong public feeling on economic, social, or political questions, the menace to academic freedom may consist in the repression of opinions that in the particular political situation are deemed ultra-conservative rather than ultra-radical. The essential point, however, is not so much that the opinion is one or another shade, as that it differs from the views entertained by the authorities. The question resolves itself into one of departure from accepted standards; whether the departure is in the one direction or the other is immaterial.

This brings us to the most serious difficulty of this problem; namely, the dangers connected with the existence in a democracy of an overwhelming and concentrated public opinion. The tendency of an overwhelming and concentrated public opinion. The tendency of modern democracy is for men to think alike, to feel alike, and to speak alike. Any departure from the conventional standards is apt to be regarded with suspicion. Public opinion is at once the chief safeguard of a democracy, and the chief menace to the real liberty of the individual. It almost seems as if the danger of despotism cannot be wholly averted under any form of government. In a political autocracy there is no effective public opinion, and all are subject to the tyranny of the ruler; in a democracy there is political freedom, but there is likely to be a tyranny of public opinion.

An inviolable refuge from such tyranny should be found in the university. It should be an intellectual experiment station, where new ideas may germinate and where their fruit, though still distasteful to the community as a whole, may be allowed to ripen until finally, perchance, it may become a part of the accepted intellectual food of the nation or of the world. Not less is it a distinctive duty of the university to be the conservator of all genuine elements of value in the past thought and life of mankind which are not in the fashion of the moment. Though it need not be the "home of beaten causes," the university is, indeed, likely always to exercise a certain form of conservative influence. For by it nature it is committed to the principle that knowledge should precede action, to the caution (by no means synonymous with intellectual timidity) which is an essential part of the scientific method, to a sense of the complexity of social problems, to the practice of taking long views into the future, and to a reasonable regard for the teachings of experience. One of its most characteristic functions in a democratic society is to help make public opinion more self-critical and more circumspect, to check the more hasty and unconsidered impulses of popular feeling, to train the democracy to the habit of looking before and after. It is precisely this function of the university which is most injured by any restriction upon academic freedom; and it is precisely those who most value this aspect of the university's work who should most earnestly protect against any such restriction. For the public may respect, and be influenced by, the counsels of prudence and of moderation which are given by men of science, if it believes those counsels to be the disinterested expression of the scientific temper and of unbiased inquiry. It is little likely to respect or heed them if it has reason to believe that they are the expression of the interests, or the timidities, of the limited portion of the community which is in a position to endow institutions of learning, or is most likely to be represented upon their boards of trustees. And a plausible reason for this belief is given the public so long as our universities are not organized in such a way as to make impossible any exercise of pressure upon professorial opinions and utterances by governing boards of laymen.

Since there are no rights without corresponding duties, the considerations heretofore set down with respect to the freedom of the academic teacher entail certain correlative obligations. The claim to freedom of teaching is made in the interest of the integrity and of the progress of scientific inquiry; it is, therefore, only those who carry on their work in the temper of the scientific inquirer who may justly assert this claim. The liberty of the scholar within the university to set forth his conclusions, be they what they may, is conditional by their being conclusions gained by a scholar's method and held in a scholar's spirit; that is to say, they must be the fruits of competent and patient and sincere inquiry, and they should be set forth with dignity, courtesy, and temperateness of language. The university teacher, in giving instruction upon controversial matters, while he is under no obligation to hide his own opinion under a mountain of equivocal verbiage, should, if he is fit for his position, be a person of a fair and judicial mind; he should, in dealing with such subjects, set forth justly, without suppression or innuendo, the divergent opinions of other investigators; he should cause his students to become familiar with the best published expressions of the great historic types of doctrine upon the questions at issue; and he should, above all, remember that his business is not to provide his students with ready-made conclusions, but to train them to think for themselves, and to provide them access to those materials which they need if they are to think intelligently.

It is, however, for reasons which have already been made evident, inadmissible that the power of determining when departures from the requirements of the scientific spirit and method have occurred, should be vested in bodies not composed of members of the academic profession. Such bodies necessarily lack full competency to judge of those requirements; their intervention can never be exempt from the suspicion that it is dictated by other motives than zeal for the integrity of science; and it is, in any case, unsuitable to the dignity of a great profession that the initial responsibility for the maintenance of its professional standards should not be in the hands of its own members. It follows that university teachers must be prepared to assume this responsibility for themselves. They have hitherto seldom had the opportunity, or perhaps the disposition, to do so. The obligation will doubtless, therefore, seem to many an unwelcome and burdensome one; and for its proper discharge members of the profession will perhaps need to acquire, in a greater measure than they at present possess it, the capacity for impersonal judgment in such cases, and for judicial severity when the occasion requires it. But the responsibility cannot, in this committee's opinion, be rightfully evaded. If this profession should prove itself unwilling to purge its ranks of the incompetent and the unworthy, or to prevent the freedom which it claims in the name of science from being used as a shelter for inefficiency, for superficiality, or for uncritical and intemperate partisanship, it is certain that the task will be performed by others—by others who lack certain essential qualifications for performing it, and whose action is sure to breed suspicions and recurrent controversies deeply injurious to the internal order and the public standing of universities. Your committee has, therefore, in the appended "Practical Proposals" attempted to suggest means by which judicial action by representatives of the profession, with respect to the matters here referred to, may be secured.

There is one case in which the academic teacher is under an obligation to observe certain special restraints—namely, the instruction of immature students. In many of our American colleges, and especially in the first two years of the course, the student's character is not yet fully formed, his mind is still relatively immature. In these circumstances it may reasonably be expected that the instructor will present scientific truth with discretion, that he will introduce the student to new conceptions gradually, with some consideration for the student's preconceptions and traditions, and with due regard to character-building. The teacher ought also to be especially on his guard against taking unfair advantage of the students' immaturity by indoctrinating him with the teacher's own opinions before the student has had an opportunity fairly to examine other opinions upon the matters of question, and before he has sufficient knowledge and ripeness in judgment to be entitled to form any definitive opinion of his own. It is not the least service which a college or university may render to those under its instruction, to habituate them to looking not only patiently but methodically on both sides, before adopting any conclusion upon controverted issues. By these suggestions, however, it need scarcely be said that the committee does not intend to imply that it is not the duty of an academic instructor to give to any students old enough to be in college a genuine intellectual awakening and to arouse in them a keen desire to reach personally verified conclusions upon all questions of general concernment to mankind, or of special significance for their own time. There is much truth in some remarks recently made in this connection by a college president:

> Certain professors have been refused re-election lately, apparently because they set their students to thinking in ways objectionable to the trustees. It would be well if more teachers were dismissed because they fail to stimulate thinking of any kind. We can afford to forgive a college professor what we regard as the occasional error of his doctrine, especially as we may be wrong, provided he is a contagious center of intellectual enthusiasm. It is better for students to think about heresies than not to think at all; better for them to climb new trails, and stumble over error if need be, than to ride forever in upholstered ease in the overcrowded highway. It is a primary duty of a teacher to make a student take an honest account of his stock of ideas, throw out the dead matter, place revised price marks on what is left, and try to fill his empty shelves with new goods.[4]

It is, however, possible and necessary that such intellectual awakening be brought about with patience, considerateness, and pedagogical wisdom.

There is one further consideration with regard to the classroom utterances of college and university teachers to which the committee thinks it important to call the attention of members of the profession, and of administrative authorities. Such utterances ought always to be considered privileged communications. Discussions in the classroom ought not to be supposed to be utterances for the public at large. They are often designed to provoke opposition or arouse debate. It has, unfortunately, sometimes happened in this country that sensational newspapers have quoted and garbled such remarks. As a matter of common law, it is clear that the utterances of an academic instructor are privileged, and may not be published, in whole or part, without his authorization.[5] But our practice, unfortunately, still differs from that of foreign countries, and no effective check has in this country been put upon such unauthorized and often misleading publication. It is much to be desired that test cases should be made of any infractions of the rule.

In their extramural utterances, it is obvious that academic teachers are under a peculiar obligation to avoid hasty or unverified or exaggerated statements, and to refrain from intemperate or sensational modes of expression. But subject to these restraints, it is not, in this committee's opinion, desirable that scholars should be debarred from giving expression to their judgments upon controversial questions, or that their freedom of speech, outside the university, should be limited to questions falling within their own specialties. It is clearly not proper that they should be prohibited from lending their active support to organized movements which they believe to be in the public interest. And, speaking broadly, it may be said in the words of a nonacademic body already once quoted in a publication of the Association, that "it is neither possible nor desirable to deprive a college professor of the political rights vouchsafed to every citizen."[6]

It is, however, a question deserving of consideration by members of this Association, and by university officials, how far academic teachers, at least those dealing with political, economic, and social subjects, should be prominent in the management of our great party organizations, or should be candidates for state or national offices of a distinctly political character. It is manifestly desirable that such teachers have minds untrammeled by party loyalties, unexcited by party enthusiasms, and unbiased by personal political ambitions; and that universities should remain uninvolved in party antagonisms. On the other hand, it is equally manifest that the material available for the service of the State would be restricted in a highly undesirable way, if it were understood that no member of the academic profession should ever be called upon to assume the responsibilities of public office. This question may, in the committee's opinion, suitably be made a topic for special discussion at some future meeting of this Association, in order that a practical policy, which shall do justice to the two partially conflicting considerations that bear upon the matter, may be agreed upon.

It is, it will be seen, in no sense the contention of this committee that academic freedom implies that individual teachers should be exempt from all restraints as to the matter or manner of their utterances, either within or without the university. Such restraints as are necessary should in the main, your committee holds, be self-imposed, or enforced by the public opinion of the profession. But there may, undoubtedly, arise occasional cases in which the aberrations of individuals may require to be checked by definite disciplinary action. What this report chiefly maintains is that such action cannot with safety be taken by bodies not composed of members of the academic profession. Lay governing boards are competent to judge concerning charges of habitual neglect of assigned duties, on the part of individual teachers, and concerning charges of grave moral delinquency. But in matters of opinion, and of the utterance of opinion, such boards cannot intervene without destroying, to the extent of their intervention, the essential nature of a university—without converting it from a place dedicated to openness of mind, in which the conclusions expressed are the tested conclusions of trained scholars, into a place barred against the access of new light, and precommitted to the opinions or prejudices of men who have not been set apart or expressly trained for the scholar's duties. It is, in short, not the absolute freedom of utterance of the individual scholar, but the absolute freedom of thought, of inquiry, of discussion, and of teaching, of the academic profession, that is asserted by this declaration of principles. It is conceivable that our profession may prove unworthy of its high calling, and unfit to exercise the responsibilities that belong to it. But it will scarcely be said as yet to have given evidence of such unfitness. And the existence of this Association, as it seems to your committee, must be construed as a pledge, not only that the profession will earnestly guard those liberties without which it cannot rightly render its distinctive and indispensable service to society, but also that it will with equal earnestness seek to maintain such standards of professional character, and of scientific integrity and competency, as shall make it a fit instrument for that service.

B. Practical Proposals

As the foregoing declaration implies, the ends to be accomplished are chiefly three:

1. To safeguard freedom of inquiry and of teaching against both covert and overt attacks, by providing suitable judicial bodies, composed of members of the academic profession, which may be called into action before university teachers are dismissed or disciplined, and may determine in what cases the question of academic freedom is actually involved.

2. By the same means, to protect college executives and governing boards against unjust charges of infringement of academic freedom, or of arbitrary and dictatorial conduct—charges which, when they gain wide currency and belief, are highly detrimental to the good repute and the influence of universities.

3. To render the profession more attractive to men of high ability and strong personality by insuring the dignity, the independence, and the reasonable security of tenure, of the professional office.

The measures which it is believed to be necessary for our universities to adopt to realize these ends—measures which have already been adopted impart by some institutions—are four:

Action by faculty committees on reappointments. Official action relating to reappointments and refusals of reappointment should be taken only with the advice and consent of some board or committee representative of the faculty. Your committee does not desire to make at this time any suggestion as to the manner of selection of such boards.

Definition of tenure of office. In every institution there should be an unequivocal understanding as to the term of each appointment; and the tenure of professorships and associate professorships, and of all positions above the grade of instructor after ten years of service, should be permanent (subject to the provisions hereinafter given for removal upon charges). In those state universities which are legally incapable of making contracts for more than a limited period, the governing boards should announce their policy with respect to the presumption of reappointment in the several classes of position, and such announcements, though not legally enforceable, should be regarded as morally binding. No university teacher of any rank should, except in cases of grave moral delinquency, receive notice of dismissal or of refusal of reappointment, later than three months before the close of any academic year, and in the case of teachers above the grade of instructor, one year's notice should be given.

Formulation of grounds for dismissal. In every institution the grounds which will be regarded as justifying the dismissal of members of the faculty should be formulated with reasonable definiteness; and in the case of institutions which impose upon their faculties doctrinal standards of a sectarian or partisan character, these standards should be clearly defined and the body or individual having authority to interpret them, in case of controversy, should be designated. Your committee does not think it best at this time to attempt to enumerate the legitimate grounds for dismissal, believing it to be preferable that individual institutions should take the initiative in this.

Judicial hearings before dismissal. Every university or college teacher should be entitled, before dismissal or demotion, to have the charges against him stated in writing in specific terms and to have a fair trial on those charges before a special or permanent judicial committee chosen by the faculty senate or council, or by the faculty at large. At such trial the teacher accused should have full opportunity to present evidence, and if the charge is one of professional incompetency, a formal report upon his work should be first made in writing by the teachers of his own department and of cognate departments in the university, and, if the teacher concerned so desires, by a committee of his fellow-specialists from other institutions, appointed by some competent authority.

The above declaration of principles and practical proposals are respectfully submitted by your committee to the approval of the Association, with the suggestion that, if approved, they be recommended to the consideration of the faculties, administrative officers, and governing boards of the American universities and colleges.

EDWIN R. A. SELIGMAN (Economics), Columbia University, *Chairman*
CHARLES E. BENNETT (Latin), Cornell University

JAMES Q. DEALEY (Political Science), Brown University
RICHARD T. ELY (Economics), University of Wisconsin
HENRY W. FARNAM (Political Science), Yale University
FRANK A. FETTER (Economics), Princeton University
FRANKLIN H. GIDDINGS (Sociology), Columbia University
CHARLES A. KOFOID (Zoology), University of California
ARTHUR O. LOVEJOY (Philosophy), The Johns Hopkins University
FREDERICK W. PADELFORD (English), University of Washington
ROSCOE POUND (Law), Harvard University
HOWARD C. WARREN (Psychology), Princeton University
ULYSSES G. WEATHERLY (Sociology), Indiana University

Notes

1. The "Editor's Note," here printed with minor omissions, was written for a 1954 reproduction of the Declaration of Principles (AAUP Bulletin, 40:89–112, Spring, 1954).
2. In view of the necessity of investigating an incident at the University of Pennsylvania, Professor Lichtengerger resigned in August, 1915, and was replaced by Professor Franklin H. Giddings (Sociology), Columbia University. Professor Elliott, having been elected Chancellor of the University of Montana, resigned in October. Professor Ford resigned in December, on account of inability to attend the meetings of the committee.
3. From "Academic Freedom," an address delivered before the New York Chapter of the Phi Beta Kappa Society at Cornell University, May 29, 1907, by Charles William Eliot, President of Harvard University.
4. William T. Foster, President of Reed College, in The Nation, November 11, 1915.
5. The leading case is Abernathy vs. Hutchinson, 3 L.J., Ch. 209. In this case, where damages were awarded, the court held as follows: "That persons who are admitted as pupils or otherwise to hear these lectures, although they are orally delivered and the parties might go to the extent, if they were able to do so, of putting down the whole by means of shorthand, yet they can do that only for the purpose of their own information and could not publish, for profit, that which they had not obtained the right of selling."
6. Report of the Wisconsin State Board of Public Affairs, December 1914.

Appendix B*
The 1940 Statement of Principles on Academic Freedom and Tenure with 1970 Interpretive Comments

In 1940, following a series of joint conferences begun in 1934, representatives of the American Association of University Professors and of the Association of American Colleges agreed upon a restatement of principles set forth in the 1925 Conference Statement on Academic Freedom and Tenure. This restatement is known to the profession as the 1940 Statement of Principles on Academic Freedom and Tenure.

The 1940 Statement is printed below, followed by Interpretive Comments as developed by representatives of the American Association of University Professors and the Association of American Colleges during 1969. The governing bodies of the associations, meeting respectively in November 1989 and January 1990, adopted several changes in language in order to remove gender-specific references from the original text.

The purpose of this statement is to promote public understanding and support of academic freedom and tenure and agreement upon procedures to assure them in colleges and universities. Institutions of higher education are conducted for the common good and not to further the interest of either the individual teacher[1] or the institution as a whole. The common good depends upon the free search for truth and its free exposition.

Academic freedom is essential to these purposes and applies to both teaching and research. Freedom in research is fundamental to the advancement of truth. Academic freedom in its teaching aspect is fundamental for the protection of the rights of the teacher in teaching and of the student to freedom in learning. It carries with it duties correlative with rights.[1][2]

Tenure is a means to certain ends; specifically: (1) freedom of teaching and research and of extramural activities, and (2) a sufficient degree of economic security to make the profession attractive to men and women of ability. Free-

---

*Reprinted from, American Ass'n of Univ. Professors, Policy Documents & Reports 3–10 (7th ed. 1990).

dom and economic security, hence, tenure, are indispensable to the success of an institution in fulfilling its obligations to its students and to society.

Academic Freedom

(a)   Teachers are entitled to full freedom in research and in the publication of the results, subject to the adequate performance of their other academic duties; but research for pecuniary return should be based upon an understanding with the authorities of the institution.
(b)   Teachers are entitled to freedom in the classroom in discussing their subject, but they should be careful not to introduce into their teaching controversial matter which has no relation to their subject.[2] Limitations of academic freedom because of religious or other aims of the institution should be clearly stated in writing at the time of the appointment.[3]
(c)   College and university teachers are citizens, members of a learned profession, and officers of an educational institution. When they speak or write as citizens, they should be free from institutional censorship or discipline, but their special position in the community imposes special obligations. As scholars and educational officers, they should remember that the public may judge their profession and their institution by their utterances. Hence they should at all times be accurate, should exercise appropriate restraint, should show respect for the opinions of others, and should make every effort to indicate that they are not speaking for the institution.[4]

Academic Tenure

After the expiration of a probationary period, teachers or investigators should have permanent or continuous tenure, and their service should be terminated only for adequate cause, except in the case of retirement for age, or under extraordinary circumstances because of financial exigencies.

In the interpretation of this principle it is understood that the following represents acceptable academic practice:

1.   The precise terms and conditions of every appointment should be stated in writing and be in the possession of both institution and teacher before the appointment is consummated.
2.   Beginning with appointment to the rank of full-time instructor or a higher rank,[5] the probationary period should not exceed seven years, including within this period full-time service in all institutions of higher education; but subject to the proviso that when, after a term of probationary service of more than three years, in one or more institutions, a teacher is called to another institution it may be agreed in writing that the new appointment is for a probationary period not more than four years, even though thereby the person's total probationary period in the academic profession is extended beyond the normal maximum of seven years.[6]

Notice should be given at least one year prior to the expiration of the probationary period if the teacher is not to be continued in service after the expiration of that period.[7]

3. During the probationary period a teacher should have the academic freedom that all other members of the faculty have.[8]

4. Termination for cause of a continuous appointment, or the dismissal for cause of a teacher previous to the expiration of a term appointment, should, if possible, be considered by both a faculty committee and the governing board of the institution. In all cases where the facts are in dispute, the accused teacher should be informed before the hearing in writing of the charges and should have the opportunity to be heard in his or her own defense by all bodies that pass judgment upon the case. The teacher should be permitted to be accompanied by an advisor of his or her own choosing who may act as counsel. There should be a full stenographic record of the hearing available to the parties concerned. In the hearing of charges of incompetence the testimony should include that of teachers and other scholars, either from the teacher's own or from other institutions. Teachers on continuous appointment who are dismissed for reasons not involving moral turpitude should receive their salaries for at least a year from the date of notification of dismissal whether or not they are continued in their duties at the institution.[9]

5. Termination of a continuous appointment because of financial exigency should be demonstrably *bona fide*.

1940 Interpretations

At the conference of representatives of the American Association of University Professors and of the Association of American Colleges on November 7–8, 1940, the following interpretations of the 1940 *Statement of Principles on Academic Freedom and Tenure* were agreed upon:

1. That its operation should not be retroactive.

2. That all tenure claims of teachers appointed prior to the endorsement should be determined in accordance with the principles set forth in the 1925 Conference Statement on Academic Freedom and Tenure.

3. If the administration of a college or university feels that a teacher has not observed the admonitions of paragraph (c) of the section on Academic Freedom and believes that the extramural utterances of the teacher have been such as to raise grave doubts concerning the teacher's fitness for his or her position, it may proceed to file charges under paragraph (a)(4) of the section on Academic Tenure. In pressing such charges the administration should remember that teachers are citizens and should be accorded the freedom of citizens. In such cases the administration must assume full responsibility, and the American Association of University Professors and the Association of American Colleges are free to make an investigation.

1970 Interpretive Comments

Following extensive discussions on the 1940 Statement of Principles on Academic Freedom and Tenure with leading educational associations and with individual faculty members and administrators, a joint committee of the AAUP and the Association of American Colleges met during 1969 to reevaluate this key policy statement. On the basis of the comments received, and the discussions that ensued, the joint committee felt the preferable approach was to formulate interpretations of the Statement in terms of the experience gained in implementing and applying the Statement for over thirty years and of adapting it to current needs.

The committee submitted to the two associations for their consideration the following "Interpretive Comments." These interpretations were adopted by the Council of the American Association of University Professors in April 1970 and endorsed by the Fifty-sixth Annual Meeting as Association policy.

In the thirty years since their promulgation, the principles of the *1940 Statement of Principles on Academic Freedom and Tenure* have undergone a substantial amount of refinement. This has evolved through a variety of processes, including customary acceptance, understandings mutually arrived at between institutions and professors or their representatives, investigations and reports by the American Association of University Professors, and formulations of statements by that association either alone or in conjunction with the Association of American Colleges. These comments represent the attempt of the two associations, as the original sponsors of the *1940 Statement*, to formulate the most important of these refinements. Their incorporation here as Interpretive Comments is based upon the premise that the *1940 Statement* is not a static code but a fundamental document designed to set a framework of norms to guide adaptations to changing times and circumstances.

Also, there have been relevant developments in the law itself reflecting a growing insistence by the courts on due process within the academic community which parallels the essential concepts of the *1940 Statement*; particularly relevant is the identification by the Supreme Court of academic freedom as a right protected by the First Amendment. As the Supreme Court said in *Keyishian v. Board of Regents*, 385 U.S. 589 (1967), "Our Nation is deeply committed to safeguarding academic freedom, which is of transcendent value to all of us and not merely to the teachers concerned. That freedom is therefore a special concern of the First Amendment, which does not tolerate laws that cast a pall of orthodoxy over the classroom."

The numbers refer to the designated portion of the *1940 Statement* on which interpretive comment is made.

1. The Association of American Colleges and the American Association of University Professors have long recognized that membership in the academic

profession carries with it special responsibilities. Both associations either separately or jointly have consistently affirmed these responsibilities in major policy statements, providing guidance to professors in their utterances as citizens, in the exercise of their responsibilities to the institution and to students, and in their conduct when resigning from their institution or when undertaking government-sponsored research. Of particular relevance is the *Statement on Professional Ethics*, adopted in 1966 as Association policy. (A revision, adopted in 1987, was published in *Academe: Bulletin of the AAUP* 73 [July-August 1987]): 49.)

2. The intent of this statement is not to discourage what is "controversial." Controversy is at the heart of the free academic inquiry which the entire statement is designed to foster. The passage serves to underscore the need for teachers to avoid persistently intruding material which has no relation to their subject.

3. Most church-related institutions no longer need or desire the departure from the principle of academic freedom implied in the *1940 Statement*, and we do not now endorse such a departure.

4. This paragraph is the subject of an interpretation adopted by the sponsors of the *1940 Statement* immediately following its endorsement which reads as follows:

> If the administration of a college or university feels that a teacher has not observed the admonitions of paragraph (c) of the section on Academic Freedom and believes that the extramural utterances of the teacher have been such as to raise grave doubts concerning the teacher's fitness for his or her position, it may proceed to file charges under paragraph (a)(4) of the section on Academic Tenure. In pressing such charges the administration should remember that teachers are citizens and should be accorded the freedom of citizens. In such cases the administration must assume full responsibility, and the American Association of University Professors and the Association of American Colleges are free to make an investigation.

Paragraph (c) of the *1940 Statement* should also be interpreted in keeping with the 1964 "Committee A Statement on Extramural Utterances" (*AAUP Bulletin* 51 [1965]:29), which states *inter alia*: "The controlling principle is that a faculty member's expression of opinion as a citizen cannot constitute grounds for dismissal unless it clearly demonstrates the faculty member's unfitness for his or her position. Extramural utterances rarely bear upon the faculty member's fitness for the position. Moreover, a final decision should take into account the faculty member's entire record as a teacher and scholar."

Paragraph V of the *Statement on Professional Ethics* also deals with the nature of the "special obligations" of the teacher. The paragraph reads as follows.

> As members of their community, professors have the rights and obligations of other citizens. Professors measure the urgency of other obligations in the light of their responsibilities to their subject, to their students, to their profession, and to their institution. When they speak or act as private persons they avoid creating the im-

pression of speaking or acting for their college or university. As citizens engaged in a profession that depends upon freedom for its health and integrity, professors have a particular obligation to promote conditions of free inquiry and to further public understanding of academic freedom.

Both the protection of academic freedom and the requirements of academic responsibility apply not only to the full-time probationary as well as to the tenured teacher, but also to all others, such as part-time faculty and teaching assistants, who exercise teaching responsibilities.

5. The concept of "rank of full-time instructor or a higher rank" is intended to include any person who teaches a full-time load regardless of the teacher's specific title.*

6. In calling for an agreement "in writing" on the amount of credit for a faculty member's prior service at other institutions, the *Statement* furthers the general policy of full understanding by the professor of the terms and conditions of the appointment. It does not necessarily follow that a professor's tenure rights have been violated because of the absence of a written agreement on this matter. Nonetheless, especially because of the variation in permissible institutional practices, a written understanding concerning these matters at the time of appointment is particularly appropriate and advantageous to both the individual and the institution.**

7. The effect of this subparagraph is that a decision on tenure, favorable or unfavorable, must be made at least twelve months prior to the completion of the probationary period. If the decision is negative, the appointment for the following year becomes a terminal one. If the decision is affirmative, the provisions in the *1940 Statement* with respect to the termination of services of teachers or investigators after the expiration of a probationary period should apply from the date when the favorable decision is made.

The general principle of notice contained in this paragraph is developed with greater specificity in the *Standards for Notice of Nonreappointment*, endorsed by the Fiftieth Annual Meeting of the American Association of University Professors (1964). These standards are:

Notice of nonreappointment, or of intention not to recommend reappointment to the governing board, should be given in writing in accordance with the following standards:

(1) *Not later than March 1 of the first academic year of service*, if the appointment expires at the end of that year; or, if a one-year appointment terminates during an academic year, at least three months in advance of its termination.

---

*For a discussion of this question, see the "Report of the Special Committee on Academic Personnel Ineligible for Tenure," *AAUP Bulletin* 52 (1966): 280–82.
**For a more detailed statement on this question, see "On Crediting Prior Service Elsewhere as Part of the Probationary Period," *AAUP Bulletin* 64 (1978): 274–75.

(2) *Not later than December 15 of the second academic year of service*, if the appointment expires at the end of that year; or, if an initial two-year appointment terminates during an academic year, at least six months in advance of its termination.

(3) At least twelve months before the expiration of an appointment after two or more years in the institution.

Other obligations, both of institutions and of individuals, are described in the *Statement on Recruitment and Resignation of Faculty Members*, as endorsed by the Association of American Colleges and the American Association of University Professors in 1961.

8. The freedom of probationary teachers is enhanced by the establishment of a regular procedure for the periodic evaluation and assessment of the teacher's academic performance during probationary status. Provision should be made for regularized procedures for the consideration of complaints by probationary teachers that their academic freedom has been violated. One suggested procedure to serve these purposes is contained in the *Recommended Institutional Regulations on Academic Freedom and Tenure*, prepared by the American Association of University Professors.

9. A further specification of the academic due process to which the teacher is entitled under this paragraph is contained in the *Statement on Procedural Standards in Faculty Dismissal Proceedings*, jointly approved by the American Association of University Professors and the Association of American Colleges in 1958. This interpretive document deals with the issue of suspension, about which the *1940 Statement* is silent.

The *1958 Statement* provides: "Suspension of the faculty member during the proceedings is justified only if immediate harm to the faculty member or others is threatened by the faculty member's continuance. Unless legal considerations forbid, any such suspension should be with pay." A suspension which is not followed by either reinstatement or the opportunity for a hearing is in effect a summary dismissal in violation of academic due process.

The concept of "moral turpitude" identifies the exceptional case in which the professor may be denied a year's teaching or pay in whole or in part. The statement applies to that kind of behavior which goes beyond simply warranting discharge and is so utterly blameworthy as to make it inappropriate to require the offering of a year's teaching or pay. The standard is not that the moral sensibilities of persons in the particular community have been affronted. The standard is behavior that would evoke condemnation by the academic community generally.

Endorsers

Association of American Colleges, 1941
American Association of University Professors, 1941
American Library Association (adapted for librarians), 1946

Association of American Law Schools, 1946
American Political Science Association, 1947
American Association of Colleges for Teacher Education, 1950
American Association for Higher Education, 1950
Eastern Psychological Association, 1950
Southern Society for Philosophy and Psychology, 1953
American Psychological Association, 1961
American Historical Association, 1961
Modern Language Association of America, 1962
American Economic Association, 1962
American Agricultural Economics Association, 1962
Midwest Sociological Society, 1963
Organization of American Historians, 1963
American Philological Association, 1963
American Council of Learned Societies, 1963
Speech Communication Association, 1963
American Sociological Association, 1963
Southern Historical Association, 1963
American Studies Association, 1963
Association of American Geographers, 1963
Southern Economic Association, 1963
Classical Association of the Middle West and South, 1964
Southwestern Social Science Association, 1964
Archaeological Institute of America, 1964
Southern Management Association, 1964
American Theatre Association, 1964
South Central Modern Language Association, 1964
Southwestern Philosophical Society, 1964
Council of Independent Colleges, 1965
Mathematical Association of America, 1965
Arizona-Nevada Academy of Science, 1965
American Risk and Insurance Association, 1965
Academy of Management, 1965
American Catholic Historical Association, 1966
American Catholic Philosophical Association, 1966
Association of Education in Journalism, 1966
Western History Association, 1966
Mountain-Plains Philosophical Conference, 1966
Society of American Archivists, 1966
Southeastern Psychological Association, 1966
Southern Speech Communication Association, 1966
American Association for the Advancement of Slavic Studies, 1967
American Mathematical Society, 1967

College Theology Society, 1967
Council on Social Work Education, 1967
American Association of Colleges of Pharmacy, 1967
American Academy of Religion, 1967
Association for the Sociology of Religion, 1967
American Society of Journalism School Administrators, 1967
John Dewey Society, 1967
South Atlantic Modern Language Association, 1967
American Finance Association, 1967
Association for Social Economics, 1967
United Chapters of Phi Beta Kappa, 1968
American Society of Christian Ethics, 1968
American Association of Teachers of French, 1968
Eastern Finance Association, 1968
American Association for Chinese Studies, 1968
American Society of Plant Physiologists, 1968
University Film and Video Association, 1968
American Dialect Society, 1968
American Speech-Language-Hearing Association, 1968
Association of Social and Behavioral Scientists, 1968
College English Association, 1968
National College Physical Education Association for Men, 1969
American Real Estate and Urban Economics Association, 1969
History of Education Society, 1969
Council for Philosophical Studies, 1969
American Musicological Society, 1969
American Association of Teachers of Spanish and Portuguese, 1969
Texas Junior College Teachers Association, 1970
College Art Association of America, 1970
Society of Professors of Education, 1970
American Anthropological Association, 1970
Association of Theological Schools, 1970
American Association of Schools and Departments of Journalism, 1971
American Business Law Association, 1971
American Council for the Arts, 1972
New York State Mathematics Association of Two-Year Colleges, 1972
College Language Association, 1973
Pennsylvania Historical Association, 1973
Massachusetts Regional Community College Faculty Association, 1973
American Philosophical Association,* 1974

---

*Endorsed by the Association's Western Division in 1952, Eastern Division in 1953, and Pacific Division in 1962.

American Classical League, 1974
American Comparative Literature Association, 1974
Rocky Mountain Modern Language Association, 1974
Society of Architectural Historians, 1975
American Statistical Association, 1975
American Folklore Society, 1975
Association for Asian Studies, 1975
Linguistic Society of America, 1975
African Studies Association, 1975
American Institute of Biological Sciences, 1975
North American Conference on British Studies, 1975
Sixteenth-Century Studies Conference, 1975
Texas Association of College Teachers, 1976
Society for Spanish and Portuguese Historical Studies, 1976
Association for Jewish Studies, 1976
Western Speech Communication Association, 1976
Texas Association of Colleges for Teacher Education, 1977
Metaphysical Society of America, 1977
American Chemical Society, 1977
Texas Library Association, 1977
American Society for Legal History, 1977
Iowa Higher Education Association, 1977
American Physical Therapy Association, 1979
North Central Sociological Association, 1980
Dante Society of America, 1980
Association for Communication Administration, 1981
American Association of Physics Teachers, 1982
Middle East Studies Association, 1982
National Education Association, 1985
American Institute of Chemists, 1985
American Association of Teachers of German, 1985
American Association of Teachers of Italian, 1985
American Association for Applied Linguistics, 1986
American Association of Teachers of Slavic and East European Languages, 1986
American Association for Cancer Education, 1986
American Society of Church History, 1986
2Oral History Association, 1987
Society for French Historical Studies, 1987
History of Science Society, 1987
American Association of Pharmaceutical Scientists, 1988
American Association for Clinical Chemistry, 1988
Council for Chemical Research, 1988
Association for the Study of Higher Education, 1988

American Psychological Society, 1989
University and College Labor Education Association, 1989
Society for Neuroscience, 1989
Renaissance Society of America, 1989
Society of Biblical Literature, 1989
National Science Teachers Association, 1989
Medieval Academy of America, 1990
American Society of Agronomy, 1990
Crop Science Society of America, 1990
Soil Science Society of America, 1990
Society of Protozoologists, 1990
Society for Ethnomusicology, 1990
American Association of Physicists in Medicine, 1990
Animal Behavior Society, 1990

Notes

1. The word "teacher" as used in this document is understood to include the investigator who is attached to an academic institution without teaching duties.
2. Bold-face numbers in brackets refer to Interpretive Comments which follow.

Appendix C*
Statement on Professional Ethics

The statement which follows, a revision of a statement originally adopted in 1966, was approved by the Committee B on Professional Ethics, adopted by the Council, and endorsed by the Seventy-third Annual Meeting in June 1987.

Introduction

From its inception, the American Association of University Professors has recognized that membership in the academic profession carries with it special responsibilities. The Association has consistently affirmed these responsibilities in major policy statements, providing guidance to professors in such matters as their utterances as citizens, the exercise of their responsibilities to students and colleagues, and their conduct when resigning from an institution or when undertaking sponsored research.[1] *The Statement on Professional Ethics* that follows sets forth those general standards that serve as a reminder of the variety of responsibilities assumed by all members of the profession.

In the enforcement of ethical standards, the academic profession differs from those of law and medicine, whose associations act to ensure the integrity of members engaged in private practice. In the academic profession the individual institution of higher learning provides this assurance and so should normally handle questions concerning propriety of conduct within its own framework by reference to a faculty group. The Association supports such local action and stands ready, through the general secretary and Committee B, to counsel with members of the academic community concerning questions of professional ethics and to inquire into complaints when local consideration is impossible or inappropriate. If the alleged offense is deemed sufficiently serious to raise the possibility of adverse action, the procedures should be in accordance with the *1940 Statement of Principles on Academic Freedom and Tenure*, the *1958 Statement on Procedural Standards in Faculty Dismissal Proceedings*, or the applicable provisions of the Association's *Recommended Institutional Regulations on Academic Freedom and Tenure*.

---

*Reprinted from, American Ass'n of Univ. Professors, Policy Documents & Reports 75–76 (7th ed. 1990).

The Statement

I. Professors, guided by a deep conviction of the worth and dignity of the advancement of knowledge, recognize the special responsibilities placed upon them. Their primary responsibility to their subject is to seek and to state the truth as they see it. To this end professors devote their energies to developing and improving their scholarly competence. They accept the obligation to exercise critical self-discipline and judgment in using, extending, and transmitting knowledge. They practice intellectual honesty. Although professors may follow subsidiary interests, these interests must never seriously hamper or compromise their freedom of inquiry.

II. As teachers, professors encourage the free pursuit of learning in their students. They hold before them the best scholarly and ethical standards of their discipline. Professors demonstrate respect for students as individuals and adhere to their proper roles as intellectual guides and counselors. Professors make every reasonable effort to foster honest academic conduct and to ensure that their evaluations of students reflect each student's true merit. They respect the confidential nature of the relationship between professor and student. They avoid any exploitation, harassment, or discriminatory treatment of students. They acknowledge significant academic or scholarly assistance from them. They protect their academic freedom.

III. As colleagues, professors have obligations that derive from common membership in the community of scholars. Professors do not discriminate against or harass colleagues. They respect and defend the free inquiry of associates. In the exchange of criticism and ideas professors show due respect for the opinions of others. Professors acknowledge academic debt and strive to be objective in their professional judgment of colleagues. Professors accept their share of faculty responsibilities for the governance of their institution.

IV. As members of an academic institution, professors seek above all to be effective teachers and scholars. Although professors observe the stated regulations of the institution, provided the regulations do not contravene academic freedom, they maintain their right to criticize and seek revision. Professors give due regard to their paramount responsibilities within their institution in determining the amount and character of work done outside it. When considering the interruption or termination of their service, professors recognize the effect of their decision upon the program of the institution and give due notice of their intentions.

V. As members of their community, professors have the rights and obligations of other citizens. Professors measure the urgency of these obligations in the light of their responsibilities to their subject, to their students, to their profession, and to their institution. When they speak or act as private persons they avoid creating the impression of speaking or acting for their college or university. As citizens engaged in a profession that depends upon freedom for its health and integrity, professors have a particular obligation to promote conditions of free inquiry and to further public understanding of academic freedom.

Notes

1. 1961   *Statement on Recruitment and Resignation of Faculty Members*
   1964   *Committee A Statement on Extramural Utterances (Clarification of sec. lc of the 1940 Statement of Principles on Academic Freedom and Tenure)*
   1965   *On Preventing Conflicts of Interest in Government-Sponsored Research at Universities*
   1966   *Statement on Government of Colleges and Universities*
   1967   *Joint Statement on Rights and Freedoms of Students*
   1970   *Council Statement on Freedom and Responsibility*
   1976   *On Discrimination*
   1984   *Sexual Harassment: Suggested Policy and Procedures for Handling Complaints.*

Appendix D*
A Statement of the Association's Council:
Freedom and Responsibility

*The following statement was adopted by the Council of the American Associa-
tion of University Professors in October 1970. In April 1990, the Council
adopted several changes in language that had been approved by Committee B
on Professional Ethics in order to remove gender-specific references from the
original text.*

For more than half a century the American Association of University Professors has acted upon two principles: that colleges and universities serve the
common good through learning, teaching, research, and scholarship; and that
the fulfillment of this function necessarily rests upon the preservation of the
intellectual freedoms of teaching, expression, research, and debate. All components of the academic community have a responsibility to exemplify and
support these freedoms in the interests of reasoned inquiry.

The *1940 Statement of Principles on Academic Freedom and Tenure* asserts the primacy of this responsibility. The *Statement on Professional Ethics*
underscores its pertinency to individual faculty members and calls attention
to their responsibility, by their own actions, to uphold their colleagues' and
their students' freedom of inquiry and to promote public understanding of
academic freedom. The *Joint Statement on Rights and Freedoms of Students*
emphasizes the shared responsibility of all members of the academic community for the preservation of these freedoms.

Continuing attacks on the integrity of our universities and on the concept
of academic freedom itself come from many quarters. These attacks, marked
by tactics of intimidation and harassment and by political interference with
the autonomy of colleges and universities, provoke harsh responses and
counter-responses. Especially in a repressive atmosphere, the faculty's responsibility to defend its freedoms cannot be separated from its responsibility to
uphold those freedoms by its own actions.

---

*Reprinted from, American Ass'n of Univ. Professors, Policy Documents & Reports
77–78 (7th ed. 1990).

I.

Membership in the academic community imposes on students, faculty members, administrators, and trustees an obligation to respect the dignity of others, to acknowledge their right to express differing opinions, and to foster and defend intellectual honesty, freedom of inquiry and instruction, and free expression on and off the campus. The expression of dissent and the attempt to produce change, therefore, may not be carried out in ways which injure individuals or damage institutional facilities or disrupt the classes of one's teachers or colleagues. Speakers on campus must not only be protected from violence, but also be given an opportunity to be heard. Those who seek to call attention to grievances must not do so in ways that significantly impede the functions of the institution.

Students are entitled to an atmosphere conducive to learning and to even-handed treatment in all aspects of the teacher-student relationship. Faculty members may not refuse to enroll or teach students on the grounds of their beliefs or the possible uses to which they may put the knowledge to be gained in a course. Students should not be forced by the authority inherent in the instructional role to make particular personal choices as to political action or their own part in society. Evaluation of students and the award of credit must be based on academic performance professionally judged and not on matters irrelevant to that performance, whether personality, race, religion, degree of political activism, or personal beliefs.

It is the mastery teachers have of their subjects and their own scholarship that entitles them to their classrooms and to freedom in the presentation of their subjects. Thus, it is improper for an instructor persistently to intrude material that has no relation to the subject, or to fail to present the subject matter of the course as announced to the students and as approved by the faculty in their collective responsibility for the curriculum.

Because academic freedom has traditionally included the instructor's full freedom as a citizen, most faculty members face no insoluble conflicts between the claims of politics, social action, and conscience, on the one hand, and the claims and expectations of their students, colleagues, and institutions, on the other. If such conflicts become acute, and attention to obligations as a citizen and moral agent precludes an instructor from fulfilling substantial academic obligations, the instructor cannot escape the responsibility of that choice, but should either request a leave of absence or resign his or her academic position.

II.

The Association's concern for sound principles and procedures in the imposition of discipline is reflected in the *1940 Statement of Principles on Aca-*

demic Freedom and Tenure, the *1958 Statement on Procedural Standards in Faculty Dismissal Proceedings*, the *Recommended Institutional Regulations on Academic Freedom and Tenure*, and the many investigations conducted by the Association into disciplinary actions by colleges and universities.

The question arises whether these customary procedures are sufficient in the current context. We believe that by and large they serve their purposes well, but that consideration should be given to supplementing them in several respects:

First, plans for ensuring compliance with academic norms should be enlarged to emphasize preventive as well as disciplinary action. Toward this end the faculty should take the initiative, working with the administration and other components of the institution, to develop and maintain an atmosphere of freedom, commitment to academic inquiry, and respect for the academic rights of others. The faculty should also join with other members of the academic community in the development of procedures to be used in the event of serious disruption, or the threat of disruption, and should ensure its consultation in major decisions, particularly those related to the calling of external security forces to the campus.

Second, systematic attention should be given to questions related to sanctions other than dismissal, such as warnings and reprimands, in order to provide a more versatile body of academic sanctions.

Third, there is need for the faculty to assume a more positive role as guardian of academic values against unjustified assaults from its own members. The traditional faculty function in disciplinary proceedings has been to ensure academic due process and meaningful faculty participation in the imposition of discipline by the administration. While this function should be maintained, faculties should recognize their stake in promoting adherence to norms essential to the academic enterprise.

Rules designed to meet these needs for faculty self-regulation and flexibility of sanctions should be adopted on each campus in response to local circumstances and to continued experimentation. In all sanctioning efforts, however, it is vital that proceedings be conducted with fairness to the individual, that faculty judgments play a crucial role, and that adverse judgments be founded on demonstrated violations of appropriate norms. The Association will encourage and assist local faculty groups seeking to articulate the substantive principles here outlined or to make improvements in their disciplinary machinery to meet the needs here described. The Association will also consult and work with any responsible group, within or outside the academic community, that seeks to promote understanding of and adherence to basic norms of professional responsibility so long as such efforts are consistent with principles of academic freedom.

Index

AAUP. *See* American Association of University Professors

Academic abstention, 215-24

Academic left, fundamentalist: dissent, hostility to, 56; ideology of, 56-59, 106n.8, 248, 250; media, use of, 70-71; results of, 88-93; similarities to other waves of zealotry, 141-54; tactics of, 63-88, 147, 150-54, 242, 247. *See also* Faculty, Zealotry

Academic speech and inquiry, 89, 149, 154, 162

Academics, common traits of, 241-43

Acadia Institute, 293

Accuracy in Academia, 155n.5

Adams, Henry Carter, 12

Adler, Felix, 11

Adler v. Board of Education, 187-89

Administrators: academic freedom, failure to defend, 137n.284, 137n.286, 137n.287, 243; academic left zealotry, response to, 103-05; McCarthyism, response to, 28-29; as religious fundamentalists 9-11; student activism (1960s), response to, 39-40; as targets of zealotry, 146. *See also* Duty to defend academic freedom

Altbach, Philip, 132n.248

American Association for the Advancement of Science, 292

American Association of University Professors: *1915 statement, General declaration of principles of academic freedom*, 14, 163-67, 172, 178, 244, 248-49, 355-71 *text*; *1940 statement, Statement of principles on academic freedom and tenure*, 3, 167-80, 220, 244, 248-49, 269-85, 373-83 *text*; *1970 Interpretive comments*, 171, 174, 178, 270; academic freedom violations, investigations of, 3, 229, 262n.38, 264n.62; Committee A on Academic Freedom and Tenure, 17, 179, 244-47, 274-75, 278, 283-85, 345-47; Committee T on College and University Government, 226n.26, 246-47; creation of, 13-14; ineffectiveness of, 244; *Joint statement on government of colleges and universities*, 220-21; *Joint statement on rights and freedoms of students*, 244; *Report on academic freedom and sexual harassment*, 246; sexual harassment, 76, 83, 109n.64, 245-46; *Statement of principles on academic freedom and tenure*, 216; *Statement on extramural utterance*, 176, 179; *Statement on freedom and responsibility*, 175, 179-80, 244-45, 270-71, 279, 284-85, 389-91 *text*; *Statement on plagiarism*, 173; *Statement on political correctness*, 96, 245-46; *Statement on procedural standards in faculty dismissal proceedings*, 171-72, 178, 220; *Statement on professional ethics*, 171-75, 179, 257, 385-87 *text*; wartime limitations on academic freedom, 16-17; zealotry, response to, 244-47; zealotry tactics, use of, 245

American Bar Association. Section of General Practice, 69

American Council on Education: *Joint statement on government of colleges and universities*, 220-21; Special Committee on Campus Tensions, 36-37; survey of administrators, 133n.253

American Economic Association, 13

American Historical Association, 77

393

Robeson, Paul, Jr., 333
Rochester University. *See* University of
Rochester
Rorty, Richard, 60, 108n.38, 333
Roseman v. University of Pennsylvania,
211n.59
Rosovsky, Henry, 237, 294
Ross, Edward, 13
Rutgers University, 293
Ruud, Mark, 32

SDS. *See* Students for a Democratic
Society
SNCC. *See* Student Nonviolent Coordi-
nating Committee
San Francisco State University, 80
Sanderson, Stephen, 120n.143
Santa Rosa Junior College, 116n.124
Sarich, Vincent, 73, 96, 126n.190
Scalia, Antonin, 114n.117
Schafer, William, 15–16
Schappes, Morris, 18
Schlesinger, Arthur, Jr., 63–64, 66, 141
Schmidt, Benno: on academic leader-
ship, 102; on free speech, 63, 75, 91,
93; on the results of zealotry, 39; on
universities, 93, 254, 333
Schrecker, Ellen W.: academic institu-
tions contributions to McCarthyism,
230–31, 236, 255, 258; McCarthyism
as a two-stage process, 142;
McCarthyism's effect on the aca-
demic community, 283; support for
the accused, 30
Self-censorship, 91, 113n.102, 131n.222,
131n.228, 135n.267, 144. *See also*
Speech, Speech codes
Seligman, E.R.A., 14
Sequiera, Luis, 335
Sexual discrimination, 191
Sexual harassment, 74–77, 109n.64,
114n.123, 117n.127, 117n.137,
119n.143, 120n.143, 245–46
Shalala, Donna, 334–35
Shils, Edward, 184n.79, 250
Shockley, John, 116n.124
Silber, John, 177, 337
Silva, Donald, 82–83, 130n.219, 247
Simons, William, 96, 111n.76, 134n.262
Skeptical rule, 160

Smith College, 121n.158
Smith, James Allen, 12
Smith, Robert C., 80
Snyder, Graydon, 121–22n.160
Speech: civility, 272–79; extramural,
165–70, 176–77, 231, 246, 269; in-
tramural, 165–70, 231, 246, 270–81;
political constraints on, 89; sanctions
on, 146–47, 274; via anonymous note
in classrooms, 91–92. *See also* Hate
speech, Self-censorship
Speech codes, 74–77, 94–96, 117n.131,
117n.137, 118n.141, 118n.142,
134–35n.263, 144, 147, 289, 334–37
Spiegel, Frederick, 83
Spinred, Phoebe, 66
Stanford, Jane Lathrop, 13
Stanford University, 13, 86, 122–23n.163,
131n.231
State University of New York at
Binghamton, 85, 125n.188, 127n.193,
137n.286
State University of New York at
Oneonta, 96, 111n.76
Stevens, John Paul, 190–91
Stone, Geoffrey, 65–66
Strossen, Nadine, 86, 91
Struggle meetings, 38, 70, 111–12n.78,
124n.182, 125n.188, 126n.189,
126n.190, 253, 340n.30
Student activism (1960s): ideology of,
31–34; similarities to other waves of
zealotry, 149–54; tactics of, 35–38,
150–54
Student Nonviolent Coordinating Com-
mittee, 31. *See also* Student activism
(1960s)
Students for a Democratic Society,
31–36. *See also* Student activism
(1960s)
Sullivan, Louis, 126n.189
Suppression of academic speech and
inquiry. *See* Academic speech and
inquiry
Supreme Court and academic freedom,
177, 187–93, 196, 216–18
Suspension of academic freedom during World War I. *See* Columbia
University
Swazey, Judith, 292, 295, 344